THE BODY

ELECTRIC

THE BODY

ELECTRIC

America's Best Poetry

from The American Poetry Review

With an introduction by **HAROLD D. BLOOM**

Edited by **STEPHEN BERG**

DAVID BONANNO

and **ARTHUR VOGELSANG**

W · W · NORTON & COMPANY

New York   London

The text of this book is composed in Caledonia,
with display type set in Rockwell
Composition by Allentown Digital Services
Division of R.R. Donnelley & Sons Company
Manufacturing by Haddon Craftsmen

Library of Congress Cataloging-in-Publication Data

The body electric : America's best poetry from the American poetry review /
edited by Stephen Berg, David Bonanno, and Arthur Vogelsang ; with an introduction
by Harold D. Bloom.
    p.   cm.
Includes index.
ISBN 0-393-04826-8
    1. American poetry—20th century.   I. Berg, Stephen.   II. Bonanno, David.
III. Vogelsang, Arthur.

PS586 .B54 2000
811'.5048—dc21   99-055513

W. W. Norton & Company, Inc., 500 Fifth Avenue, New York, N. Y. 10110
www.wwnorton.com

W. W. Norton & Company Ltd., 10 Coptic Street, London WC1A 1PU

1 2 3 4 5 6 7 8 9 0

. . . in them the divine mystery / . . . the same old beautiful mystery

—Walt Whitman, "I Sing the Body Electric,"
1855

Contents

(dates in parentheses denote year of *The American Poetry Review* publication)

Preface

We chose poems for *The Body Electric* from the first 161 issues of *The American Poetry Review*—from November/December 1972 through September/October 1999. For this single volume we selected from over eight thousand poems that we had judged worthy of publication in the magazine. Sometimes we chose from forty or fifty poems that a poet had published with us over this twenty-seven-year period. Space limitations, even in a book as large as this, meant that many excellent poets could not be included, nor could many long poems. Some poets are represented by only one or two poems because only a few of their poems appeared in *APR*.

No anthology can be all that its editors, poets, and readers would like it to be. We have tried to create a gathering of as much of the best poetry we published as possible, and of the various aesthetic, philosophical, and social concerns of the poets.

Most of the poems appear in *The Body Electric* as they were originally published in *The American Poetry Review*, even though they may have been revised later for book publication. We are extremely grateful for the cooperation of the poets in this anthology and to their editors and publishers for their generosity.

Stephen Berg
David Bonanno
Arthur Vogelsang

Introduction

HAROLD D. BLOOM

1

This anthology takes its title from Walt Whitman, who shares with Emily Dickinson an aesthetic eminence not quite achieved by even the strongest American poets of the century just ending: Wallace Stevens, Hart Crane, T. S. Eliot, Robert Frost, and, as many would add, Marianne Moore, Ezra Pound, William Carlos Williams, and others. There are admirable poems in this anthology—by Robert Penn Warren, John Ashbery, A. R. Ammons, Anne Carson, Douglas Crase, Amy Gerstler, Louise Glück, Jorie Graham, Donald Hall, John Hollander, Claudia Keelan, Charles Simic, and many more—but I am not one of the editors of this book, and so need neither puff nor degrade it. Nor do I wish again, in my oncoming old age, to engage in any polemics against those who substitute concerns of gender, class, race, ethnic origin, or sexual orientation for the authentic questions of poetry, which must involve cognitive and aesthetic values. "I am tired of cursing the Bishop," sang Yeats's Crazy Jane, and I am now of her party. As a teacher and critic of American poetry, I am not altogether persuaded that our twentieth-century achievement is equal to European glories in the same period: Valéry, Trakl, Montale, Lorca, Rilke, Cernuda, Hardy, D. H. Lawrence, Yeats, Mandelstam, Ungaretti, Celan, Akhmatova, a baker's dozen somewhat beyond North American sublimities. That of course invokes five languages, but Europe is hovering on the verge of becoming a single nation, and may complete this process within another generation. Poetry belongs to a language rather than a nation, but Western tradition (still, I assume, a coherent notion) increasingly will become a rivalry between Europe and the United States: economic, and so necessarily cultural. There is no new Yeats, Lorca, or Montale on any European horizon that I can perceive, nor do I detect, as yet, with any certainty a Wallace Stevens or Hart Crane commencing a poetic career among us. But a true critic, as I conceive it, lives in hope.

I intend therefore to devote part of this Introduction to aspects of the history and the idea of American poetry, in that long phase that proceeds from Emerson through to our contemporaries Ashbery and Ammons, thus foregrounding a number of the younger poets in this anthology. The reader can find copious defenders of the ongoing thing elsewhere; my own function is a little different. And since I have limped off too many canonical battlefields, like Falstaff conspicuously keeping alive at Shrewsbury, I want to declare my warfare over. What is useful (or not) is now my primary concern, and controversy interests me no more. This should then be a mild and amiable Introduction, founded upon the fiction that the "cultural" ideologies of the last thirty years never were, and the related fiction that we still have universities in the English-speaking world. I will add a third fiction:

We continue to have rational standards of taste and judgment in literary matters.

Emerson, who was at any one moment too diverse to be characterized, was not specifically a literary critic. You can think of him as an essayist, as a lecturer, and as an endless ruminator in his marvelous Notebooks. And yet he must be accounted the best practical literary critic his nation has produced, because of his immediate response (dated 21 July 1855) to Whitman's gift, through the United States Postal Service, of the first edition of *Leaves of Grass.* How would you or I have reacted, one hundred and forty-four years ago, at being confronted by that amazing volume, hand-printed, personally designed; its style and substance bursting out of any possible context to sing the Body Electric?

When we read Milton's *Paradise Lost* these days (I assume a few eccentric handfuls do, outside the universities, and two or three diehards within), the poem is mediated for us by more than three hundred years of criticism, some of it quite good and helpful. How extraordinary it must have seemed to its first seventeenth-century readers! Nearly a hundred and fifty years after the first *Leaves of Grass,* we have virtually no good Whitman criticism, and the going stuff in the universities is worse than helpless. What calls itself "Queer Criticism" is risible, and I rather doubt that a school of "Onanistic Criticism," much closer to the actualities of Whitman's work, will soon take its rightful place in our fallen academies.

Emerson had no one and nothing to mediate Whitman's originality for him. He read for himself, and sent his response to Whitman:

> I am not blind to the worth of the wonderful gift of *Leaves of Grass.* I find it the most extraordinary piece of wit and wisdom that America has yet contributed. I am very happy in reading it, as great power makes us happy. It meets the demand I am always making of what seemed the sterile and stingy nature, as if too much handiwork, or too much lymph in the temperament, were making our Western wits fat and mean.
>
> I give you joy of your free and brave thought. I have great joy in it. I find incomparable things said incomparably well, as they must be. I find the courage of treatment which so delights us, and which large perception only can inspire.
>
> I greet you at the beginning of a great career, which yet must have had a long foreground somewhere, for such a start. I rubbed my eyes a little, to see if this sunbeam were no illusion; but the solid sense of the book is a sober certainty. It has the best, namely, of fortifying and encouraging . . .

"Wit and wisdom" were and are exactly right, and as we drift into the year 2000, *Leaves of Grass* remains our "most extraordinary piece" of imaginative literature, surpassing in sublime sprawl its possible rivals: Dickinson's poetry, *Moby-Dick, Huckleberry Finn,* Henry James (considered as a totality), Faulkner (the same), and the major poets of the dying century (Frost, Stevens, Eliot, Hart Crane). Emerson's phrases remain exactly right, beyond "wit and wisdom": "great power," "free and brave thought," "large perception," "solid sense," "fortifying and encouraging." Later, in 1863, Emerson interestingly linked Whitman with the Mormon Moses, Brigham Young, who had turned a vast desert into a habitable garden. "And we must thank Walt Whitman for service to American literature in the Appalachian enlargement of his outline and treatment."

Whitman, professed follower of Emerson, has provided the paradigm for most of our best poetry since. I do *not* mean our Howlers and allied inchoate rhapsodes, but poets whose form and rhetoric initially seem anything but Whitmanian: Stevens, Eliot, Hart Crane, Ashbery, Ammons. The most poignant and memorable of overt invocations of "our father, Walt Whitman" (James Wright) is by Stevens:

> In the far South the sun of autumn is passing
> Like Walt Whitman walking along a ruddy shore,
> He is singing and chanting the things that are part of him,
> The worlds that were and will be, death and day.
> Nothing is final, he chants. No man shall see the end.
> His beard is of fire and his staff is a leaping flame.

Stevens sometimes insisted that he did not greatly care about Whitman, particularly his "tramp poet" persona, but that was mere anxiety of influence (to appropriate a common phrase). Walt here is at once Yahweh, Moses, and Aaron, but most of all he is Whitman, walking the shore in the great *Sea-Drift* poems. Read Stevens deeply enough and a submerged form, like Whitman's drowned swimmer in "The Sleepers," will rise up and break surface. Who wrote these lines, Whitman or Stevens?

> Sigh for me, night wind, in the noisy leaves of the oak.
> I am tired. Sleep for me, heaven over the hill.
> Shout for me, loudly and loudly, joyful sun, when you rise.

Read Eliot's *The Waste Land* against its submerged precursor-poem, "When Lilacs Last in the Dooryard Bloom'd." The lilacs, the song of the hermit-thrush, the murmur of maternal lamentation, the three walking down a road together—these belong to both poems, amidst much else in common. It is not so much that Whitman broke the new wood, as Pound acknowledged; I think Emerson already had done that. Rather, the difficult nuances of the American poetic stance, the divisions within the self of the seeker for Self-Reliance, are Whitman's great invention, a psychic cartography with which we are yet not wholly familiar. American poets of the century now dying were Whitmanian (Hispanic poets as well as those writing in English) in exactly the way nineteenth-century poets, English and American through Emerson, were Wordsworthian. Our idea of the poem was Whitmanian, even in the masquerade of the Pound-Eliot Axis. Wordsworth, as William Hazlitt observed, began new on a *tabula rasa* of poetry, despite his debts to Milton and Shakespeare. Whitman, whether in Biblical forms or in Emersonian stances, did not start out that new, but the nuances of the poetic ego were altogether his own, and can baffle us still. Neither the classical associationist psychology, with its reliance upon rhetoric, or the Freudian psychic cartography, beginning to be formulated just after Whitman's death, provide a good fit for his intricate evasions. We cannot say that, in Whitman, *ethos* is character, *pathos* is personality, and *logos* is the mediating principle between the two. Nor is it coherent to identify the Whitmanian "soul" with the superego, "self" with ego, and "real me" or "me myself" with the id. The Whitmanian psychic triad defies analysis, and yet is central to "Song of Myself," the *Sea-Drift* elegies, the "Lilacs" lament for Lincoln, "Crossing Brooklyn Ferry" and "The Sleepers," and those are Whitman's six major poems. With Dickinson's fifty or so best lyrics, they are the glory of American poetic achievement.

Both of Whitman's selves, and his soul, and his body, were all characterized by him as electric, probably meaning the *élan vital,* which animates his ego in rare moments of fused unison, where he believes in, and sustains the illusion, that he speaks with the force of all things flowing. D. H. Lawrence, whose last, best poems owed everything to Whitman, nevertheless protested these outrageous synecdoches in which the Whitmanian ego and every possible entity merged together. Himself troubled by divisions in the self, tormented both by World War I and hideous ambivalence toward the mother, Lawrence indicted Whitman for lying to himself and to us. But "this awful Whitman" was also: "Whitman, the one man breaking a way ahead." Lawrence, a great reader when he calmed down, made out of Whitman the great death-poems: "Bavarian Gentians," "Ship of Death," and the heartbreaking "Shadows." They fall into the most contaminating of Whitman's visions, which identifies night, death, the mother, and the sea. Stevens, Eliot, Hart Crane came at last to that identification, which Whitman made into the American mythology, whose inevitable poetic genre is the shore-ode, commencing most powerfully with "As I Ebb'd with the Ocean of Life," and proceeding through "The Idea of Order at Key West," "The Dry Salvages," and "Voyages" on to Elizabeth Bishop's "At the Fishhouses" and "The End of March," and A. R. Ammons's "Corson's Inlet" and "Saliences."

Whitman's self or persona: "Walt Whitman, one of the roughs, an American" is accessible enough, and so his more persuasive "real me" or "me myself," which is both in and out of the game and watching and wondering at it, prophesying the John Ashbery of "Soonest Mended." But what is the Whitmanian soul? Whitman said that his soul and his real me could only have master-slave abasements to one another, which may mean that the "rough" persona of *Song of Myself* is only a mediating entity, whose work is to keep the soul and the true self from getting at one another. That seems to me a more suggestive account of the divided egos that crowd this anthology than anything their therapists could give them. Approaching Millennium, American poets write not to integrate their egos (most would argue otherwise) but to keep going by keeping the warring soul and real self apart. William Empson, in a conversation we once had about Hart Crane, repeated his conviction that poetry was now "a mug's game," and that Crane impressed him as paradigmatic because either "The Broken Tower" would get written or else Crane would die. In that instance both happened.

The last time I wrote an Introduction for an anthology of contemporary poetry, I received a torrent of published abuse, particularly for my insistence that cognitive and aesthetic difficulty was now more than ever essential if poets were to give us something more than "consciousness-raising" (call it cheerleading, really). Though I am elderly and battered-out, too weak to go on responding to a politicized rabblement, I am also archaic enough to remember a fair amount of poetic history. Most of it is an ocean of Period Pieces, and plucking Lady Mary Chudleigh or Mrs. Felicia Hemans out of that maelstrom would be a bad joke, except that what is taught in our universities are now mostly bad jokes. One colleague reproached me for not having introduced her to Elizabeth Barrett Browning's "The Cry of the Children," when I had taught a Victorian poetry graduate seminar almost forty years ago. I told her to sit alone, indoors or out, and chant the poem (to call it that) aloud to herself, listening as carefully as she could. She stalked off with some intensity, and I rather doubt my advice was taken. But I urge readers of this Introduction to undergo the experience, because its educational value is immense.

No critic dare stand forth and shout: "No more Period Pieces!" The critic probably is one himself, and even a rock-like ego can sustain the doubt: "What if, fifty years hence, Wallace Stevens's *The Auroras of Autumn,* which sings daily in and to my heart, is universally regarded as one more Period Piece?" If every shred of the aesthetic is purged at last, from the academies and the media, who will know anymore that *The Auroras of Autumn* is Whitman's legacy at its strongest? If imaginative literature is no longer an agon, but rather a communal quilting-bee, then no one ever will know again a Period Piece when first they see it. Doubtless everyone will be happier for this.

2

Though a few poets represented in this volume belong to the Brave New World of communal uplift, most do not. Rather than particularize, which seems to me invidious when I had nothing to do with selecting for this book, I will discuss poems or parts of poems as they move me and do what I think a critic should perform: *the work of appreciation.* Where there are so many poets, and so many good poems, my procedure may be even more haphazard than subjective, and perhaps I will reread this volume, after it is published, and discover that I have omitted the best achievements in it. Confronted by such an abundance, I am compelled to be impressionistic, and can only hope that I will not prove wholly unjust. My sequence will be alphabetical, thus following the book's design.

I commence with A. R. Ammons, whose poems, for a third of a century now, have enlarged my existence. "An Improvisation for the Stately Dwelling" I find unbearably poignant, even as I, like my friend Archie, move into the shadow of our common mortality:

> This fall morning is pretty much
> like a fall morning
> > the bottoms of poplars
> and tops of beeches
> leafless
> > a wind NNW
> > has re-lifted the geese

>   and sent them southerly
>   I know a man whose cancer has
>   got him just to the point
>   he looks changed by a flight of stairs
>   people pass him and speak
>   extra-brightly
>   he asks nothing else
>   he is like a rock
>   reversed, that is, the rock has a solid
>   body and shakes only
>   reflected in the water but he shakes
>   in body only,
>   his spirit a boulder of light
>   nature
>   includes too much
>   and art can't include enough
>   the sky is soft this morning
>   all gray,
>   regioned here and there with ivory
>   light
>   the flames of climbing vines are
>   shedding out, falling back,
>   stringing fire
>   the brook almost blisters with
>   cool equations among fallen colors
>   what is to become of us we know
>   how are we to be taken by it or take it

I quote all of this, because it is so nuanced that it cannot be taken apart without doing it violence. How I wish I *could* say that my own spirit is "a boulder of light," as I go on shaking "in body only." Ammons so gently touches the universal that we have to listen very hard to hear ourselves inevitably in what calls itself "an improvisation." "The art itself is nature," a grand Shakespearean formula, is evoked by "nature / includes too much / and art can't include enough." What is "too much" in one, and beyond exclusion for the other, is death our death:

>   what is to become of us we know
>   how are we to be taken by it or take it

I turn to another contemporary and old acquaintance, John Ashbery, the poet of our climate. The dozen poems by Ashbery included in this volume could serve as a wonderful brief anthology of what is best in him: eloquence, comedy, pathos, vision, and most of all the uncanny sense that *this* extraordinary voicing catches the Spirit of the Age:

> The song makes no mention of directions.
> At most it twists the longitude lines overhead
> Like twigs to form a crude shelter. (The ship
> Hasn't arrived, it was only a dream. It's somewhere near
> Cape Horn, despite all the efforts of Boreas to puff out

Those dropping sails.) The idea of great distance
Is permitted, even implicit in the slow dripping
Of a lute. How to get out?
This giant will never let us out unless we blind him.

This giant, like the ogre who isn't there in Browning's "Childe Roland to
the Dark Tower Came," is close enough to poetic tradition to make us in-
terestingly uncomfortable. Ashbery is always saying it to keep it from hap-
pening, though it always happens anyway:

The event combined with
Beams leading up to it for the look of force adapted to the wiser
Usage of age, but it's both there
And not there, like washing or sawdust in the sunlight,
At the end of the mind, where we live now.

The allusion to Stevens's death-poem, "The Palm at the End of the
Mind," is palpable, and part of Ashbery's value to all of us is that he exem-
plifies the traditional sublimity of poetic tradition, precisely as he swerves
to get away from it. The apotropaic function of great poetry, its attempt to
perform a warding-off of death, is more subtly enacted by Ashbery than in
any poet since Hart Crane.

Great wit is rare in modern poetry; there is so much of it in Anne Carson
that one wishes she could give transfusions to other poets. Her "The Truth
About God" derives from the early Kabbalah of Isaac the Blind, yet turns
Kabbalah into an irony I never could have expected:

I have a friend who is red hot with pain.
He feels the lights like hard rain through his pores.
Together we went to ask Isaac.

Isaac said I will tell you the story told to me.
It was from Adam
issued the lights.

From the lights of his forehead were formed all the names of the world.
From the lights of his ears, nose and throat
came a function no one has ever defined.

From the lights of his eyes—but wait—
Isaac waits.
In theory

the lights of the eye should have issued from Adam's navel.
But within the lights themselves occurred
an intake of breath

and they changed their path.
And they were separated.
And they were caught in the head.

And from these separated lights came
what pains you
on its errands (here my friend began to weep) through the world.

For he assured it is not only you who mourn.
Isaac lashed his tail.
Every rank of world

was caused to descend
(at least one rank)
by the terrible pressure of the light.

Nothing remained in place.
Nothing was not captured except
among the shards and roots and matter

some lights
from Adam's eyes
nourished there somehow.

Isaac stopped his roaring.
And my friend by now drowsy as a snake subsided
behind a heap of blueblack syllables.

This also requires being quoted in all its ironic completeness. But why does she title it "Flexion of God"? When you contract a flexor, a limb or joint in your body is bent. God's flexion is not so much muscular as it is a creation-by-catastrophe. The Adam Kadmon, scarcely distinguishable from God, suffers within his primal lights "an intake of breath," *mezamzem,* which is God's holding in of his breath. This is the *zimzum* that instructs us by the disaster of the breaking lights, teaching us what Carson ends by calling "a heap of blueblack syllables." I recall once writing somewhere: "God had breathing trouble, and the trouble created the world." Carson goes that several better: we all of us are her friend "red hot with pain" who "feels the light like hard rain through his pores."

Carson is a great original; so, oddly, is Douglas Crase, even though he writes in the idiom of Ashbery. Always the revisionist, he performs a kind of *askesis* in relation to Ashbery, wonderfully exemplified by his "There Is No Real Peace in the World," with its not wholly reassuring close: "The cows / Are freshening off schedule again. There is nothing to fear." A parallel revisionism is at work in the refreshingly comic Amy Gerstler, whose "A Fan Letter" is one of the few recent poems that render me grateful with laughter. Any writer, the "Dear Literary Hero," who received this "Fan Letter," would be well advised to take ship immediately, since the poem is as terrifying as it is funny. I forebear quoting from it, as it too could only be read entire.

With Louise Glück and Jorie Graham, two utterly different writers, I have been slow to apprehend their achievement, but now begin to see what their many admirers long since have found: the high seriousness of profoundly reflective consciousnesses. Glück's "Unwritten Law" is an authentically difficult poem:

> Interesting how we fall in love:
> in my case, absolutely. Absolutely, and, alas, often—
> so it was in my youth.
> And always with rather boyish men—
> unformed, sullen, or shyly kicking the dead leaves:
> in the manner of Balanchine.
> Nor did I see them as versions of the same thing.
> I, with my inflexible Platonism,
> my fierce seeing of only one thing at a time:
> I ruled against the indefinite article.
> And yet, the mistakes of my youth
> made me hopeless, because they repeated themselves,
> as is commonly true.
> But in you I felt something beyond the archetype—
> a true expansiveness, a buoyance and love of the earth
> utterly alien to my nature. To my credit,
> I blessed my good fortune in you.
> Blessed it absolutely, in the manner of those years.
> And you in your wisdom and cruelty
> gradually taught me the meaninglessness of that term.

We go from the dry, forlorn gesture of "interesting" to the undoing of the twice-repeated "blessed." I take it that the "unwritten law" is erotic repetition, the overdetermined pattern by which most of us fall in love. "Inflexible Platonism" is also Freud's shrewd myth of our questings beyond the Pleasure Principle. What is subtly difficult here is tone or stance. The doublet, "wisdom and cruelty," verges upon a fusion of those qualities, and the placement of "gradually," to commence the final line, is both wise and cruel. I hear no regret in "Unwritten Law": only the wry self-acceptance of: "To my credit." It is a poem that can sustain many rereadings. So can Jorie Graham's "For One Must Want / To Shut the Other's Gaze," which demands a very active reader, since it is a scenario for a drama either already completed or still to be composed. This is a poem of the Era of Beckett, and is truly praiseworthy for setting the mind in motion. Five times we are given the admonition: "Explain," but if: "The real plot was invisible," then explanation is unlikely. If provocation is essential to poetry, and I think it is, then this is a permanently troubling poem.

One of the first really good poems to be written by an American was William Cullen Bryant's "To a Waterfowl," which is presumably why Donald Hall employs the same title for his absolutely unsettling initial poem in this volume (the other one is also unsettling). One goes on admiring Hall's gusto, hoping one is not joining "the approbation of feathers." Weathered into toughness, his poems know more than enough, and touch a limit that I suspect cannot be transgressed, if they still are to be poems.

John Hollander's thirteen thirteeners, "Some Walks With You," part of *Powers of Thirteen*, his strongest work, offer a different kind of toughness: elegance, fierce nostalgia, formal splendor, qualities to be found here also in the single poems of Richard Howard and Donald Justice.

Claudia Keelan, new to me, is very welcome, particularly for the enigma, "Blue Diamond," but judging by the other two poems here, she is endlessly enigmatic, again almost always what one hopes for in poems.

I pass over many others, who are old friends and distinguished poets, including Philip Levine and William Merwin, and omit also Frank O'Hara, James Schuyler, and David Shapiro, all well represented here, in order to pause at Charles Simic's "Pain," which upsets me, because of its eloquently universal application. Perhaps, as I begin slowly to apprehend, what moves me about this collection, *The Body Electric,* is how many of its poems are capable of wounding me afresh, or of reopening old wounds. These poems include Gary Snyder's prophetic "Out of the soil and rock" and the late May Swenson's marvelous excursion into her earlier life, "Something Goes By." I would feel guilt in thus rushing by, except that I want to conclude this Introduction with a tribute to Robert Penn Warren, a great poet and good friend of many years, whose wise conversation I go on missing. There are a dozen splendid poems by Warren in this anthology, but I choose "Death of Time" to brood upon a little more thoroughly than I have been able to do for any other poem in *The Body Electric:*

> Over meadows of Brittany, the lark
> Flames sunward, divulging, in tinselled fragments from
> That height, song. Song is lost
> In the blue depth of sky, but
> We know it is there at an altitude where only
> God's ear may hear.
>
> Dividing fields, the hedges, in white
> Bloom powdered, gently slope to
> Blue of sea that glitters in joy of its being.
>
> Yes—who was the man who on the midnight street-corner,
> Alone, once stood, while sea fog
> Put out last lights, electric or heavenly?
> Who knows that history is the other name for death?
> Who, from the sweated pillow, wakes to know
> How truth can lie? Who knows the jealousy,
> Like a cinch-bug, under the greenest turf, thrives?
> Who learned that kindness can be the last cruelty?
>
> I have shut my eyes and seen the lark flame upward.
> All was as real as when my eyes were open.
> I have felt earth breathe beneath my shoulder blades.
> I have strained to hear, sun-high, that Platonic song.
>
> It may be that some men dying, have heard it.

Warren though he never, as a critic, abandoned the School of T. S. Eliot, nevertheless had a fondness for Shelley's "To a Skylark." We tended to quarrel, amiably enough, at long lunches after his retirement, when he would come in to use the Yale Library, and I was on campus, between classes. But though we fought over Emerson, whom he loathed, and Wallace Stevens, who did not move him, he forgave Shelley because of "To a Skylark." I remember remarking to him that people tended to dislike the poem's notorious opening stanza, because they misread it thinking that Shelley was staring at the lark as he intoned: "Bird thou never wert." But Shelley meant that the lark flew so high that its song seemed disembodied, as Warren agreed, and told me later that thinking about "To a Skylark" had helped prompt "Death of Time."

Hawks and eagles are more frequent in Warren's poetry than are larks, and Warren's face, in my memory, tends to have a hawk-like aspect. "Death of Time" is very different from his images of sudden descent, as in his superb poems about hawks, or his "Eagle Descending," a kind of elegy for Allen Tate. Here we are given first a flaming image of ascent, until the lark's song is lost to an altitude beyond human hearing.

The following image—of fields, hedges, sea glittering "in joy of its being"—is an epiphany answering the joy of the lark's song, overt in Shelley, implicit in Warren. But then, as so often in late Warren, we are in the harsh realm of memory, where "history is the other name for death." A powerful secular moralist, rather awesome in the pained clarity of his judgments, Warren enumerates here what hurt him most, whether in himself or others: truth that is a pragmatic lie, hidden jealousy, misplaced kindness. In a vision of the lark's upward flame, lying prone on the earth, he has strained to hear what cannot be heard, the Platonic Idea of the lark's song.

Shelley, in "To a Skylark," had suggested that the lark knew "things more true and deep" of death, than we could know, as though the unseen bird was, like Hamlet, death's ambassador to us. Warren ends "Death of Time" with a parallel surmise, but one that centers upon the act of dying, rather than the state of death. It may be that some poets anyway, like Warren, have heard that inaudible music as they died.

THE BODY

ELECTRIC

The Deserter

Through the hole in the hut's wall,
I watch the old woman who put me up,
leaning against a wooden tub, elbow deep in wash water.
At my feet, the red coat,
stained from the burning of the last village,
red-black like smoked leather,
rubbed with spices and pieces of charred wood.

I go to her, feeling an itch somewhere inside my mouth,
knowing I've got to leave everything of myself here.
I raise the rifle, as she presses a white shawl
far down in the water, and fire.
She dies quietly; even her heart spits blood
through clenched teeth.

I take bread, onions, radishes and set out,
leaving my rifle behind, while the wind is down
and stillness, with its knives of powdered lead,
slashes the coarse, brown hair from my arms
as I hold them, empty, at my sides.

The Anniversary

You raise the axe,
the block of wood screams in half,
while I lift the sack of flour
and carry it into the house.
I'm not afraid of the blade
you've just pointed at my head.
If I were dead, you could take the boy,
hunt, kiss gnats, instead of my moist lips.
Take it easy, squabs are roasting,
corn, still in its husks, crackles,
as the boy dances around the table:
old guest at a wedding party for two sad-faced clowns,
who together, never won a round of anything but hard times.
Come in, sheets are clean,
fall down on me for one more year
and we can blast another hole in ourselves without a sound.

New Crops for a Free Man

I drop the torch of rags in a bucket of water,
then watch the field burn.

Behind me, another fire, my woman,
under sheets wrinkled and stiff from heat and sweat,
throws them back and rises.
She cracks her knuckles, leans from the window and yells,
but I keep my head turned toward the thing I understand.
She's hot from a match I never lit
and strokes her breasts, cone-shaped candles,
whose wicks, her nipples, aflame, burn holes in her hands, in me.

Go back to sleep, I don't need you now.
I just want the dirt under my fingernails to become mountains,
to listen to my heartbeat inside the rocks
and scream as my own death slides into bed
with her ass bloody and sweet when I lick it,
one stalk of wheat no man
can pull from the ground and live to eat.

Everything: Eloy, Arizona 1956

Tin shack, where my baby sleeps on his back
the way the hound taught him;
highway, black zebra, with one white stripe;
nickle in my pocket for chewing gum;
you think you're all I've got.
But when the 2 ton rolls to a stop
and the driver gets out,
I sit down in the shade and wave each finger,
saving my whole hand till the last.

He's keys, tires, a fire lit in his belly
in the diner up the road.
I'm red toenails, tight blue halter, black slip.
He's mine tonight. I don't know him.
He can only hurt me a piece at a time.

Wallpaper

He said in his mother's house, growing up
he remembered roses, and his friend said
his mother could not abide print on her walls,
whether determined children swinging their swing ropes taut,
or tidy cottages, their chimney-smoke trained upwards.
She wanted no pretense of happiness,
the rooms gift-wrapped with trotting horses or teakettles pouring.
She could not abide them and tore off, sanded, painted blank
the little dogs barking, ladies with umbrella and muff.
His companion remembered his mother on a stepladder
rolling out roses, hundreds of roses, thousands
since she papered not just the halls and the living room
but the kitchen alcove where he and she sat
eating meal after meal after his father left
and she relied solely on him for company,
for belief in *something* in her fury and grief.
Still she insisted they live in this perpetual celebration
of rose petals, which grew vague with repetition,
vague with his vivid daydreams of running away.
We were standing all three at a party,
and since I could not tell yet whether these two men
were paired or paired only in their interest of me,
I was listening, carefully, leaning back against the wall
like Vuillard's sister in the painting of his mother and sister,
the print of her dress the same pattern as the wallpaper,
so that she is disappearing into the wall, as I was,
the better to listen for who these men might be
by what they were saying of their mothers.

Redwing Sonnets

He's carrying on with a distracting song
this early morning while I'm revising
a poem I've tried for years to make as strong
as I'm able. I think it's a redwing
blackbird—but I'm not sure—not having learned
the little lore that comes from staying put
long enough in a place to hear birdsong
or to know what that whatchamacallit
with a hanging thingamajig is called.
I tell you, I think half the fun (or more)

of being alive in the world is learning
the names of things so there are no *things* at all
left in the world, so that dying you know
exactly what you are leaving behind.

Which is why I've stuck with this old poem
I mentioned that treats an awful period
in my life when I fell for the wrong men,
had a score of phobias that ran riot
over my common sense and a closet
I could barely close for all the skeletons
I didn't want to name or talk about.
Now that I'm happy I should sink those bones
deep in a repressed memory, but some
perverseness keeps me going back to name
those sadnesses as if my tongue
could cure by catalogue, as if a song
were all that was needed against the pain
of having been so lost—the redwing's gone—

taking his song along. Now all that's left
is that awful silence which as a girl
I was taught to fill up with pretty talk
so as to make everyone comfortable;
the kind of talk that is equivalent
to vacuum cleaner noise, sucks everything
interesting out of talk and isn't meant
to ease a three-o'clock in the morning
terror, say. Against such talk I write
or try to anyway—that other kind
of talk that is as awful as silence
if it hits the mark, when just the right
string of words will make your life fall in line
and shine with an eloquent radiance.

Just the other night at a reception
I was politely working my way out
after fulfilling the obligation
that had brought me there. Oh dreary night!
I was ready for stars, a heady rain
or cool breeze tangling my skirt in my legs—
when a Fred or a Tom, a nametag name,
came up to me. I'm not sure what he said
but with a few questions he'd taken us
deep into the spell of the night going on
outside those closed windows. I could have wept
for finding at long last this oasis
of real talk. The breeze blew in. The stars came on
inside that room. I thanked him when I left.

I was driving somewhere far with a friend,
some talk was going on: she said, I said—
the kind of conversation rightly penned
dialogue in the handbooks. Then instead
of her next cue, she asked me what I thought
of her, *really* thought. Oh Jesus, I thought,
we still have a long ways to go and what
do I know what she means to do with what
I tell her. Use it to sue me?! Call it
a risk I took or say that small Tercel
drove me to higher ground. I told the truth
mostly, as Huck says, then asked what she thought
of me. I could've stopped the car right there
as this was where we'd wanted to get to.

I bought a record of common birdsongs
so as to learn to tell the birds apart,
but I gave up trying to follow along.
I'd have one bird down, say, a meadowlark,
chee-up-trill. But right on its tailfeathers
came the peewee with its *pee-ah-wee,*
sounding just like the *zee-zee* of the warbler
or the *drink your tea* (so it sounded to me)
of the towhee. Finally, to top it all,
the mockingbird mimicking everyone.
It was bird-Babel worse than biblical
to human ears, which should humble us some
to think our poems no more than mating trills
for the birds: *whan-that-aprill, whan-that-aprill.*

I had this friend—we were always talking.
She'd come over or I'd go to her place
and as she let me in we'd start talking
up the stairs to her flat. I was amazed
we ever got sat down with coffee cups
in our hands or ever stopped our talking
long enough to drink what was in those cups.
We'd take a walk and suddenly look up
lost, but finish our points before trying
to discuss our way back. Were we crazy
binge-talkers or sensing the imminence
of what became our lives' parting, maybe
we were preparing then for this silence?

I've heard said that among the eskimos
there are over a hundred words for snow:
the soft kind, the hard driving kind, the roll
a snowball kind: snow being such a force
in their lives, it needs a blizzard of words.

In my own D.R. we have many rains:
the sprinkle, the shower, the hurricane,
the tears, the many tears for our many dead.
I've asked around and find that in all tongues
there are at least a dozen words for talk:
the heart-to-heart, the chat, the confession,
the juicy gossip, the quip, the harangue—
no matter where we're from we need to talk
about snow, rain, about being human.

Only a few times has talk failed me,
times when I realized nothing that I said
or heard would help, when I felt I could be
talking outside my species, times the dead
would have made more involved listeners, times
I could tell by the narrowed eyes, cocked head
that all I said was being ground down fine,
then mixed with shards of mistrust to be fed
right back to me, while the same marinade
was stewing inside me. I don't know how
to turn a talk around once it goes bad.
Sometimes I think of writing as a way
of going back to those failures and somehow
saying exactly what I wish I'd said.

He's back—perched on the line—not just a song
from some distracting whatchamacallit,
but obvious in his glossy uniform—
which might explain why he's my favorite,
recalling with his gorgeous epaulettes
my childhood in a dictatorship
when real talk was punishable by death,
though some—like him—refused such censorship.
As now he belts his song, breaking the hold
of that past as his *compañeros* come,
a regiment on the line, all going strong,
affirming that the saying of the world
is what we're meant to do with chirps or words.
So you take it from here, redwing blackbirds!

An Improvisation for the Stately Dwelling

This fall morning is pretty much
like a fall morning
     the bottoms of poplars
and tops of beeches
leafless
    a wind NNW
    has re-lifted the geese
    and sent them southerly
    I know a man whose cancer has
    got him just to the point
    he looks changed by a flight of stairs
people pass him and speak
extra-brightly
he asks nothing else
he is like a rock
reversed, that is, the rock has a solid
body and shakes only
reflected in the water but he shakes
in body only,
his spirit a boulder of light
    nature
    includes too much
and art can't include enough
the sky is soft this morning
all gray,
regioned here and there with ivory
light
the flames of climbing vines are
shedding out, falling back,
stringing fire
the brook almost blisters with
cool equations among the fallen colors
what is to become of us we know
how are we to be taken by it or take it

An Improvisation for Jerald Bullis

It's not much of a fall with
hemlocks

the new green already
advanced,

needles inwardly hidden
turn brown
and make not much of shedding

catch the right
windy day to catch
the right show

one day in a high wind,
every ready needle already
gone, nothing
will fall
though the billows of boughs
    heave and slosh
    but another day after a
    calm
    the needles wait in a small wind
    for the windtwist to reap them,
    a bunch, salience, weave, or warp
    of them coming down
    spinning or
striking boughs and, whooshed up,
spinning again
till
on the ground
a fairly unnoticeable, diffuse
browning
comes over things,
particular needles subsumed and
nothing outlined

so many falls all summer and
even earlier in earliest spring and
later falls than fall, wild carrot
seeds held in ribbed cups
sprinkling out over ice

the speaker, delivered out of himself,
places his "I"
anywhere
in rose or rat
and feels the speech he has deserved to
say,
himself so much given over, unfolded, that he
is mostly without interest

light fills volumes
shade clears

the big garden spider sits in air between
the two hedge headlands and doesn't move
enough to close down for dusk

Above the Fray Is Only Thin Air

How do you account for things: take night
before last, a dry night, still, leaves from

the maple by the driveway worked a solid
semicircle on the driveway, really pretty but

thick: I raked it up in the afternoon: but
last night around midnight a drizzle that

turned slowly into a quiet rain started and
kept up till day and after day: but not more

than a few leaves fell, and plenty are still on
the tree: except right at the tip of some

branches, now stick sprays, where, by the way,
the hornets' nest rides right out in the open,

stiller than a balloon: but, I mean, why
didn't the weighted wet leaves come down, even

in bigger droves than on the dry night: my theory
founded on guesswork is that the dry night got

so dry it got crisp, and crisp cracked off the
stems from the branches: and so the leaves

just fell off: they didn't need any breeze or
rain: is that wonderful: do you suppose it's

so: who knows: maybe the night of the crisp
fall was really no more than a bear climbing

up there and shivering the tree, shaking them
down: I would just as soon know the answer to

some things as how a galaxy turns. . . .

Widespread Implications

How sweetly now like a boy I dawdle by ditches,
broken rocky brooks that clear streams through

the golden leaves: the light so bright from
the leaves still up, scarlet screaming vines

lining old growths high or rounding domes of
sumac: how like a sail set out from harbor

hitting the winds I flounder this way and that
for the steady dealing in the variable time:

old boys are young boys again, peeing arcs
the pleasantest use of their innocence, up

against trees or into boles, rock hollows or
into already running water! returned from

the differentiation of manhood almost back to
the woman: attached but hinge-loose, flappy,

uncalled for and uncalled, the careless way
off into nothingness: where, though, but in

nothingness can the brilliance more brightly
abide, the ripple in a brook-warp as gorgeously

blank as a galaxy: I dropped the mouse,
elegantly supersmall, from the trap out by the

back sage bush, and all day his precious little
tooth shone white, his nose barely dipped in

blood: he lay belly up snow white in the
golden October morn, but this morning, the

next, whatever prowls the night has taken him
away, a dear morsel that meant to winter

here with us

Spit

thinking I'd better be prepared when I went
out to meet the ocean, I blew myself up but

burst in time: so the next morning,
actually nearly before light, I converted

myself into a ghost crab, peeked out of my hole
over the sand, and there it was, the whole

wide thing, gray as the morning and on no
business but its own: when it washed over me

I waited, sealed off, underground until it
washed away: then I came out and the

ocean had become itself again: even so, the
sight burst my horizon: women's preferences

evolve the form of man, I'm told, a pretty
lousy trail of taste, the women apparently

wanting strength but not too much, independence
but heavily nurtured, paunches, wheezes, and

some broken-down feet: men, though, choose
women, too, but hardly a shriveled-up old

shrew or shrunken prune hasn't been fucked
over, over and over: the results lie and limp

in the streets: run-over heels and busted
belts decorate open air fashion: what went

wrong, you may ask: or is it right: why doth
perfection here and there in the wildest

statistic only appear: c'est la vie: yep:
something is more cockeyed than broad shouldered:

desire is the supreme beautician: she (or he)
deodorizes and/or fertilizes most any patch: he

(or she) rushes forward in her own perfection
till a port in some exigency (storm, I mean)

releases her to a free moment of disgust.

Breaking the Rock Down

Now that we've finally arrived here
you won't let me hold you.
And were you stopped along the way by a reason to believe
you've escaped with it and made thinkable
that web of incomplete darkness, crawling with
rumors on a far side of evening.

So the menus are left unopened.
Business as usual. I heard nothing, nothing
about *you*, though this time some shard of
ricocheting gossip will have an effect—
it will hurt somebody. Will you avoid that too?

If we could just get back here
we'd hardly notice the music and
voices that slip in from the bar, the ground fog
rising to the height of the city.
And for all the vicious man-made shoving
we are angry spectators craving admirers
when we bet the farm on selfish confusion, as if time were
an accident, dragging it all down to rock
and breaking the rock down.

It's okay to feel afraid. It must be.
But what seeks your measure in the eyes of
other survivors? You're seized again,
and again fighting back, again fighting unfairly,
expecting each pool of resilience to contain you
and to judge you. When someone reacts
you think you are winning, that winners possess more.
And the truth, the truth stays with the resemblance
but honesty, forgive me, grows tired
and it takes what I know about myself
and leaves the way I came—alone.
And now you are telling me how much you need me,
need my friendship, but what about
who it is you are?

Evolving Similarities

I know there are pigeons smaller than we are
roaming the parks and alleys.
I have seen us go down lightly
and sideways
and get back home again one day at a time.
For people like us
there are pigeons everywhere.

I know moss-covered brick
and the short walk back to the studio.
I'm familiar with reclining nudes
and the orange goldfish.
In the dankest of circumstances
I too have dialed the number
and thought twice and tested each one of them

as if anybody stands a chance around here
and no one carries our messages.
If there's something you still need
believe me
they will pick up the phone.

Because the body's *not* stupid.
Because the flesh remembers
and taking care comes first.
A young mother cradles an infant to her breast
and it feels like love.
Like we can do something.

Because you would save every last one of them
you are already forgiven.
It doesn't matter now
that nothing in this world is direct.
Our life is layered.
First we weep
and then we listen and eat something
and weep again

and listen.
And eat again.
And it doesn't matter anymore
at the bottom of your story

at the very-most bottom of recovery.
And confession.

And then popped for it.
Even the one who's picked up unconscious
is resisting arrest.

And it just happens to be perfectly okay
to feel like you're understood.
They'll follow you anywhere.
They will peck at your shoes in the plaza.
A cluster of violets on the floor of the rain forest
pumping water

making food.

I know that dread is wrapped up in knowing.
I know the way dread tends to consume itself.
And I apologize
for just barely listening.
But if I cry tonight
tell me
who is there among us who will call your bluff?

Veils of Prayer

When the sky darkens
and turns white, and the green
and blue leaves deepen—
showers of mist, bamboo, the lemons shine.
A light was left on, white azalea, I had left a light on for you.
Do not come back, not now. Though still here
I too can't return.

Only the edges
go on like this, long into dusk, the soul
drains us in seconds.
And the nothing that's left, and the no more
hope, and what I wouldn't
kill off or trade away, fuck over, dismiss, make a joke of, this
failure of solitude, my own dark
standing alone in the dark hand that feeds me.

Into this night . . . and drunker.
The drone of the crickets. Voices without mouths, without glare,
the fence just fading away, everything
and my own exhausted space,
to privacy.
          Into this night,
I swear it, years disappear without a voice of your own,

a middle ground, all those
reasons for giving in, for holding on, leaving
again and again,
to poison—all those islands of blame.
                              And ain't nobody lives there.
Trees high on the ridge. The laconic wires.
Lit windows and shutting down.
A sigh in the shrubs, on the porches, and shutting down.
When the sky darkens . . .
When the dark finds the needle . . .

Please. Not ever.
I'm still failing. Unforgiven. Alone.
That you can be right if you want to.
I won't recognize you.
That we may never be resolved.
That I may be at peace.
That I may heal into the husk of my heart.

The Nothing That Is

That there was later on
among the tables and the tents of swirling light
the most exotic chill of laughter,
wrists, and touchable,
the need to touch and hear the distance,
umbrella damp, the last few
ugly words come back to pain
already lifted.

Not answering.
Not answering and, therefore,
not alone, double-fisted, this public
alley, this private wooden desk and room,
the cards and letters
I'm afraid of.

That there was later still,
but briefer, another cover, another
leap of faith and most of us, the untouched
sand and ether. Not you,
but blankly. Not her,
the looping swallows, the muffled eaves.
In the liquid light of traffic,
jasmine, cough and shatter. The hand
pressed close.
The mere sensation.

Twilight

That he might just snap again was part of it, blind himself, and, well, you're there.
You'd climb the wooden stairs again, lock the bathroom door behind you, will
   yourself away.
                         Maybe get it right this time, I don't know, the card I
thought to send, a thousand crows on a Chinese screen, a light from down below
   somewhere, everything.

Among schools of flashing fish, a shadow and its camera, we've all been there
   before.
Among the fruit and praying figures, his latest medication, his threatening, stupid
   call, each dangerous time.
You talk to him, put aside a little money for somebody else, pen messages and
   stay. Move again.
                         And it's a better story there,

it must be. The beginning of a street, a slant of houses. Glint and shimmerings,
   porches, and leaves. And now the twilight,
instantaneous. The tables, and the chairs. How the unseen break bread together,
   carefully.

L. S. ASEKOFF ■ ▪ ▪ ▪ ■ ▪ ■ ■ ■ ▪ ■ ■ ■ ▪ ■

Invisible Hand

Perhaps there has never before been such an open sea,
the malady of death & the long affair
in the absence of history.
Because we love the things we lose,
we are tempted by the cynic's dogma—
a lantern in a briar bush,
the monstrous fish with a human face.
& there are close calls.
As the ferryboat slides from the slip,
the unborn whisper to the dead.
"*La viá del tren subterráneo es peligrosa.*"
"I was held on Angel Island waiting for my witnesses to appear."
"The women's umbrellas protect us from strange suns."
Let the Evangel open the Book of Numbers,
the poor man count his sheep,
sequela . . . septentrion . . . phalaros . . . ,
the delirious plowing of this sea leads us to
"the merchant who sailed to Constantinople,"
"the woman who sold three pearls,"

the pursuit of the eversame in the name of the new,
the sins of the fathers outliving their sons.
& what furrows our wake? Mere wind & spray?
A seahorse exploding into a star?
The pale cataclysm with fins?
The trapdoor springs to the lucid nightmare.

Entering the city, we give up the sky.
Here is the dawn of the bearded men,
waterdrinkers in smoky cafés,
where slender fingers twist wire & crepe for funerals of spring
& the lamplighter is an underworld informant.
"My brothers,
in the ruined palace where poison is a sacrament,
the great ones spent thirty years in chains
dreaming of the sun,
while we are blackmailed by the theatre of white telephones
& jailed for a song of small flowers.
Now the red radio brings news of the dead.
Give us back our names! they cry.
Must we sail forever under this dark sky?
What was our crime?
A taste for chocolate?
The bittersweet oranges of Palestine?"
As the cave billows with shadows & smoke,
we see the children, heads on fire,
a deaf alphabet signing away—hostages to futurity.

North Star

You are facing the harbor & the open sea.
Behind you, smoldering ruins, the iron city.
Across fragrant waters, the country of forgotten names.
You are travelling light, carrying nothing with you
but what you have lost. Tomorrow, you have been told to bring
only herbs & spices—almond, vanilla, sage, rosemary, rue.
I guess you could say you are doing as well
as can be expected. Cell by cell,
your hands are beginning to forget the feel of her flesh—
her neck, her breasts, her thighs. You are cured,
almost cured. Day by day, the language you speak has become
a barbarous mockery of your mother tongue.
Only this morning you woke to the familiar smell
of a tiny blue flower you no longer know the name of.
Still, you are fearful of calling too early
& hearing it ring & ring & ring . . . & thinking . . . & then
beginning to think . . . Just yesterday, you walked into the gloom

& lit a candle in her name & made a wish,
a wish for her. What kind of wish you will not say.

So, you are in the belly of the beast. Stormy
weather. You have reefed your sails
& are riding it out, scooping water with a net.
As wave after wave sweeps over you,
the old nausea returns—an underground cloud,
black wing. Overhead, amber waters close,
darkly gold as a toad's eyelid. When you stare at your hands,
how distant they seem from you. Look in the mirror,
what do you see? Your oldest friend,
truest enemy. *To slay the monster,*
a voice says, *you must first find him.*
After death, comes forgiveness. (In moonsilver darkness
she slides from room to room, silent & voluptuous
as a wolf.) *Where there is lawful terror,* you cry,
the stars are claws! Then you pull the red thread,
& everything unravels in your hands . . .
                                        Shuddering,
you wake to the throb & thrum of water & screw.
Churning like an oiled swan,
the *North Star* turns from the harbor
& breasting the waves, steams for the open sea.
In the thrilling clarity of a new freedom
you see everything as though for the first time—
the red axe bolted to the wall, lifeboats lashed to the deck,
the captain astride the bridge, wild-eyed & drunk on vodka,
steering into the stinging salt spray.
The strong current swiftly unfolds bolts of luminous blue.
Pearly grey clouds float overhead—light tenders in a sea of oil.
Beside you, she stirs—all white & gold.
With a free hand you stroke her long, lovely neck.
Smiling under the sun's blade she whispers,
Darling, you will be my avenger!

Crowdoll

for Douglas Culhane

To take the darkness in,
make friends with it,
lift up & out into the night
this limp broken wing
nailed to a melting shadow,
poor forked plaything

in blackface vanishing,
as though to say,
"After every why
a why-not." Risen
from fiery leaves,
the crowdoll's thin
smokesignals ask
forgiveness of
the keeper of stars
when a tree falls,
& you,
dark, anarchic, restless,
beholden only
to your own mind's
echoing, shapeless
shapeshifting *of* of "of" . . .

Starwork

If we are lucky
there will be time to imagine
how the dead might admire
this halo of cities but for now
we must follow the directions
one hand leaves for the other.
As in conversation sparks fly upward
so allegory takes wing against wreckage of night,
the swan song of a sun in its solitude.
In whose interest do they labor, we wonder,
these silhouettes of desire
cast back at us by the orphaned event?
& when no man remembers his mother or father
what can measure our loss—*techné*
as *telos?* At the vanishing point
where the mullah who fed his master's gold bird
gives way to the Sand Reckoner
sifting grains of light
lip service is paid to the names
once strange to us—problems of navigation
that leave us all in the dark.

JOHN ASHBERY ■ ■ ■ ■ ■ ■ ■ ■ ■ ■ ■ ■ ■ ■ ■

Business Personals

The disquieting muses again: what are "leftovers"?
Perhaps they have names for it all, who come bearing
Worn signs of privilege whose authority
Speaks out of the accumulation of age and faded colors
To the center of today. Floating heart, why
Wander on senselessly? The tall guardians
Of yesterday are steep as cliff shadows;
Whatever path you take abounds in their sense.
All presently lead downward, to the harbor view.

Therefore do your knees need to be made strong, by running.
We have places for the training and a special on equipment:
Knee-pads, balancing poles and the rest. It works
In the sense of aging: you come out always a little ahead
And not so far as to lose a sense of the crowd
Of disciples. That were tyranny,
Outrage, hubris. Meanwhile this tent is silence
Itself. Its walls are opaque, so as not to see
The road; a pleasant, half-heard melody climbs to its ceiling—
Not peace, but rest the doctor ordered. Tomorrow . . .
And songs climb out of the flames of the near campfires,
Pale, pastel things exquisite in their frailness
With a note or two to indicate it isn't lost,
On them at least. The songs decorate our notion of the world
And mark its limits, like a frieze of soap-bubbles.

What caused us to start caring?
In the beginning was only sedge, a field of water
Wrinkled by the wind. Slowly
The trees increased the novelty of always being alone,
The rest began to be sketched in, and then . . . silence,
Or blankness, for a number of years. Could one return
To the idea of nature summed up in these pastoral images?
Yet the present has done its work of building
A rampart against the past, not a rampart,
A barbed-wire fence. So now we know
What occupations to stick to (scrimshaw, spinning tall tales)
By the way the songs deepen the color of the shadow
Impregnating your hobby as you bend over it,
Squinting. I could make a list
Of each one of my possessions and the direction it
Pointed in, how much each thing cost, how much for wood, string, colored ink,
    etc.

The song makes no mention of directions.
At most it twists the longitude lines overhead
Like twigs to form a crude shelter. (The ship
Hasn't arrived, it was only a dream. It's somewhere near
Cape Horn, despite all the efforts of Boreas to puff out
Those drooping sails.) The idea of great distance
Is permitted, even implicit in the slow dripping
Of a lute. How to get out?
This giant will never let us out unless we blind him.

And that's how, one day, I got home.
Don't be shocked that the old walls
Hang in rags now, that the rainbow has hardened
Into a permanent late afternoon that elicits too-long
Shadows and indiscretions from the bottom
Of the soul. Such simple things,
And we make of them something so complex it defeats us,
Almost. Why can't everything be simple again,
Like the first words of the first song as they occurred
To one who, rapt, wrote them down and later sang them:
"Only danger deflects
The arrow from the center of the persimmon disc,
Its final resting place. And should you be addressing yourself
To danger? When it takes the form of bleachers
Sparsely occupied by an audience which has
Already witnessed the events of which you write,
Tellingly, in your log? Properly acknowledged
It will dissipate like the pale pink and blue handkerchiefs
That vanished centuries ago into the blue dome
That surrounds us, but which are, some maintain, still here."

The Couple in the Next Room

She liked the blue drapes. They made a star
At the angle. A boy in leather moved in.
Later they found names from the turn of the century
Coming home one evening. The whole of being
Unknown absorbed into the stalk. A free
Bride on the rails warning to notice other
Hers and the great graves that outwore them
Like faces on a building, the lightning rod
Of a name calibrated all their musing differences.

Another day. Deliberations are recessed
In an iron-blue chamber of that afternoon
On which we wore things and looked well at
A slab of business rising behind the stars.

Variant

Sometimes a word will start it, like
Hands and feet, sun and gloves. The way
Is fraught with danger, you say, and I
Notice the word "fraught" as you are telling
Me about huge secret valleys some distance from
The mired fighting—"but always, lightly wooded
As they are, more deeply involved with the outcome
That will someday paste a black, bleeding label
In the sky, but until then
The echo, flowing freely in corridors, alleys,
And tame, surprised places far from anywhere,
Will be automatically locked out—*vox
Clamans*—do you see? End of tomorrow.
Don't try to start the car or look deeper
Into the eternal wimpling of the sky: luster
On luster, transparency floated onto the topmost layer
Until the whole thing overflows like a silver
Wedding cake or Christmas tree, in a cascade of tears."

Saying It to Keep It from Happening

Some departure from the norm
Will occur as time grows more open about it.
The consensus gradually changed; nobody
Lies about it any more. Rust dark pouring
Over the body, changing it without decay—
People with too many things on their minds, but we live
In the interstices, between a vacant stare and the ceiling,
Our lives remind us. Finally this is consciousness
And the other livers of it get off at the same stop.
How careless. Yet in the end each of us
Is seen to have traveled the same distance—it's time
That counts, and how deeply you have invested in it,
Crossing the street of an event, as though coming out of it were
The same as making it happen. You're not sorry
Of course, especially if this was the way it had to happen,
Yet would like an exacter share, something about time
That only a clock can tell you: how it feels, not what it means.
It is a long field, and we know only the far end of it,
Not the part we presumably had to go through to get there.
If it isn't enough, take the idea
Inherent in the day, armloads of wheat and flowers
Lying around flat on handtrucks, if maybe it means more
In pertaining to you, yet what is is what happens in the end
As though you carcd. The event combined with

Beams leading up to it for the look of force adapted to the wiser
Usages of age, but it's both there
And not there, like washing or sawdust in the sunlight,
At the end of the mind, where we live now.

Lost and Found and Lost Again

Like an object whose loss has begun to be felt
Though not yet noticed, your pulsar signals
To the present death. *"It must be cold out on the river
Today."* "You could make sweet ones on earth."

They tell him nothing. And the neon Bodoni
Presses its invitation to inspect the figures
Of this evening seeping from a far and fatal corridor
Of relaxed vigilance: these colors and this speech only.

The Archipelago

Well, folks, and how
about a run for the sister islands?
You can see them from where you stand—
will you barter vision for the sinking feeling
of lumps of clay?
           The daffodils
were out in force, as were, improbably, the nasturtiums,
which come along much later, as a rule. But so help me,
there they were.
           She said, may I offer you some?
His tangling so guttered him,
all he said was "Boats along the way."

Really, there are so many kinds of everything
it halts you when you think about it,
which is all the time, really—oh, not *consciously,*
that would be a waste, but in sly corners,
like a rabbit sitting up straight, waiting for what?
We can study drawing and arithmetic, and the signs
are still far away, like a painted sign
fading on the side of a building. Oh, there is so much to know.
If only we weren't old-fashioned, and could swallow
one word like a pill, and it would branch out prettily
to all the other words, like the sun following behind the cloud shadow
on a hummock, and our basket would be full,
too ripe for the undoing, yet too spare for sleep,
and the temperature would be exactly right.

Miserere! Instead I am browsed on by endless students,
clumps of them, receding to this horizon and the next one—
all the islands have felt it

have had their rest disturbed by the knocking knees of foals,
by kites' shrieking. And to think I could have had it
for the undoing of it,
                    snug in the tree-house, my plans
open to the world's casual inspection, like an unzipped fly—
but tell us, you must have had more experiences than that?

Oh the cross-hatched rain, fanning out from my crow's feet,
the angry sea that always calms down,
the argument that ended in a smile.
These are tracks that lovers' feet fit.
But in the end they flag you down.

My Philosophy of Life

Just when I thought there wasn't room enough
for another thought in my head, I had this great idea—
call it a philosophy of life, if you will. Briefly,
it involved living the way philosophers live,
according to a set of principles. OK, but which ones?

That was the hardest part, I admit, but I had a
kind of dark foreknowledge of what it would be like.
Everything, from eating watermelon or going to the bathroom
or just standing on a subway platform, lost in thought
for a few minutes, or worrying about rain forests,
would be affected, or more precisely, inflected
by my new attitude. I wouldn't be preachy,
or worry about children and old people, except
in the general way prescribed by our clockwork universe.
Instead I'd sort of let things be what they are
while injecting them with the serum of the new moral climate
I thought I'd stumbled into, as a stranger
accidentally presses against a panel and a bookcase slides back,
revealing a winding staircase with a greenish light
somewhere down below, and he automatically steps inside
and the bookcase slides shut, as is customary on such occasions.
At once a fragrance overwhelms him—not saffron, not lavender,
but something in between. He thinks of cushions, like the one
his uncle's Boston bull terrier used to lie on watching him
quizzically, pointed ear-tips folded over. And then the great rush
is on. Not a single idea emerges from it. It's enough
to disgust you with thought. But then you remember something William James
wrote in some book of his you never read—it was fine, it had the fineness,

the powder of life dusted over it, by chance, of course, yet still looking
for evidence of fingerprints. Someone had handled it
even before he formulated it, though the thought was his and his alone.

It's fine, in summer, to visit the seashore
There are lots of little trips to be made.
A grove of fledgling aspens welcomes the traveler. Near by
are the public toilets where weary pilgrims have carved
their names and addresses, and perhaps messages as well,
messages to the world, as they sat
and thought about what they'd do after using the toilet
and washing their hands at the sink, prior to stepping out
into the open again. Had they been coaxed in by principles,
and were their words philosophy, of however crude a sort?
I confess I can move no farther along this train of thought—
something's blocking it, as so often happens. Something I'm
not big enough to see over. Or maybe I'm frankly scared.
What was the matter with how I acted before?
But maybe I can come up with a compromise—I'll let
things be what they are, sort of. In the autumn I'll put up jellies
and preserves, against the winter cold and futility,
and that will be a human thing, and intelligent as well.
I won't be embarrassed by my friends' dumb remarks,
or even my own, though admittedly that's the hardest part,
as when you are in a crowded theater and something you say
riles the spectator in front of you, who doesn't even like the idea
of two people near him talking together. Well he's
got to be flushed out so the hunters can have a crack at him—
this thing works both ways, you know. You can't always
be worrying about others and keeping track of yourself
at the same time. That would be abusive, and about as much fun
as attending the wedding of two people you don't know.
Still, there's a lot of fun to be had in the gaps between ideas.
That's what they're made for! Now I want you to go out there
and enjoy yourself, and yes, enjoy your philosophy of life, too.
They don't come along every day. Look out! There's a big one . . .

Operators Are Standing By

In some of the stores they sell a cheese rinse
for disturbed or depressed hair. You add whiskey
to it at the last moment. Now that
it's nearly Christmas, we could buy
such things, you and I, and take them with us,
though it seems like
only yesterday I hit that halloween homerun.
It backed up and kind of flowed back

into my side I think, creating a "strawberry
jar" effect. There was nothing Olin
or I could do about it.

Determining everyone is a bigshot
is sometimes all he cares about.
I've slept on the ground with him,
and deep in a birchbark canoe.
Once there was two of him.
At school no one could tell us apart
until we smiled, or his big laugh came unbuttoned.
Fatally, venery has taken its toll
of him these last years. I can't
get near him without being reminded of Venus,
or the hunt. I come in six different packages,
from the "jewel case" to Wrigley's spearmint.
In the time of friendly moose
droppings I followed them to the Shedd Aquarium.
No one was selling tickets that day.
I wandered in and out of the fish tanks,
stopping occasionally to leave a hand print
on the plate glass for the benefit of some fish or other.

Chapter II, Book 35

He was a soldier or a Shaker. At least he was doing *something*,
going somewhere. Often, in the evenings, he'd rant about Mark Twain,
how that wasn't his real name, and was he hiding something?
If so, then why call himself a humorist?
We began to tire of his ravings, but (as so often happens)
it was just at that point that a salient character trait
revealed itself, or rather, manifested itself within him.
It was one of those goofy days in August
when all men (and some women) dream of chocolate sodas.
He confessed he'd had one for lunch,
then took us out to the street to show us the whir and dazzle
of living in some other city, where so much that is different goes on.
I guess he was inspired by Lahore. Said it came to him
in his dreams every night. And little by little
we felt ourselves being transported there. Not that we wanted
to be there, far from that. But we were either too timid
or unaware to urge him otherwise. Then he mentioned Timbuktu.
Said he'd actually been there, that the sidewalks were pink
and the huts made of mother-of-pearl, not mud, as is commonly
supposed. Said he'd had the best venison and apple tart
in his life there.
        Well, we were accompanying him in the daze
that usually surrounded him, when we began to think about ourselves:

When *was* the last time we had done so? And the stranger shifted shape
again (he was now wearing a zouave's culottes), and asked us
would we want to *live* in Djibouti, or Providence, or Lyon, now that
we'd seen them, and we chorused (like frogs), Oh no, we
want to live in New York, not that the other places aren't as splendid
and interesting as you say. It's just that New York
feels more like home to us. It's ugly, it's dirty, the people are rude
(kind and rude), and every surface has a fine film of filth
on it that behooves slobs like us, and will in time turn to diamonds,
just like the mother-of-pearl shacks in Timbuktu. And he said,
You know I was wrong about Mark Twain. It was his real name,
and he was a humorist, a genuine American humorist for the ages.

My Name Is Dimitri

I am going to be your host tonight.
Do you wish the fiddle or the fish?
The hen with ivory sauce is very fine, very light.
An experience unlike any other pushes you

toward what holy extremities? To a margin of uncertainty
where not just drinks are muddled and an old frump
of a past straddles you. Uncertainty polishes the china
to a mirror-like daze.

A World War I soldier wants to say Thank you,
fuck you, from all the trenches his heart is bleeding
from, from the aghast question and the problem of novelty
to the tip of sores that ends this peninsula
back where it began, where the pilgrims trod.

There is so much in Warsaw—
too many restaurants, too few connections
that would otherwise make things interesting.
We have nothing to cling to, only torn memories

of a station between stations that wasn't
the one that was supposed to be there. An altar of roses
climbed halfway up the stadium, which was full of misfits
with no store to come home to. Still, there was the bus,

a place beyond all others, curdled in the neat sky.
An insane child wishes the grass whipped less
at the bends where the posts are. The merger of innocents
matters less than the hum of interim authority and the screech of descants

that take you by surprise as they tide you over.
Goodnight. The dashboard is heavy with imagery

in entranced colors like the plumes of a canary
or lyre-bird. Keep the rats out of that granary

and all will be well for a century, but if the mailman
leaves me no mail it will be a vast appointed mistake,
vast as a throne room in an old castle by the sea,
as Thuringia. The moss grew for me, and there
the matter rested, in salt-pits and other geographical refuse.
Besides, they were coming over the ridge,
would save us, and then we'd see what we would see—
despondent daughters of the Hellespont, fickle as creation
and the lives that extend it down to this trough.

The Walkways

To know how to walk in the night, to have
a goal, to reach it in the darkness, the shadows.
                                                    —JOUBERT

The man behind you spoke to the tracery
as it killed him. The witches' envoy
brought a ball to the guest of honor.
It was covered with vapid inscriptions about not
exhuming the past until the day
when smoke rises from a hole in the ground
alarming no tots, but then a journey like a cipher
elaborates its undoing. To have knitted scarlet
hairnets in the epistolary novel of my Russian phrase-book
and cloned them to a besmirched integrity
was my plan all along. There was no need to get your
balls in an uproar. Now, during one of the violinist's durable
encores the horse is teed off again, galloping toward the horizon
with the frail buggy and its precious cargo (two terrified
jeunes filles) in tow; the violet ribbon comes undone
and precious antique letters pepper the landscape
of early spring with plangent, mourning-dove complaints.

Why did you never write me? I bled for centuries
from that tiny puncture wound. One day I woke up whole
and it was all unreal, though I could hear the music
of your fingertips sliding over vellum, the scenery.
Meanwhile I had been getting stronger every day
without anyone's suspecting it, myself least of all.
When I finally stood up my head towered above the hills
and brass gates, terrorizing the little folk
beneath, who raced like ants in all directions.
Now I was past caring. Those feverish gifts

from many Christmases ago ceased to implore
or annoy. I eyed them wanly. Only a picture of a barefoot girl
sitting on a fence rang a distant bell, and that sullenly,
too deeply buried in today's growth
to answer my clear call.

I understand by this that you are taking over.
Wait—here is the key. Now that Lord Chesterfield has joined us
you'll need it to unlock conversations, great ones,
as a great wind is great. I am lucky to have come so far, only so far,
though the pantheon receives us all. Such is its way.
To be roofed and slavish, and then unstitched by apes,
is all a fellow needs, these modern days, unkempt, mourning
beside a gate, forever undecided,
like a partially opened umbrella.

Limited Liability

And one wants to know everything about everything.
Such is my decision, though I will abide by others,
that goes without saying. Still, I fell off the sandbar
walking back towards shore, and that was a time of sorrow,
even of great sorrow, for myself and many others.
No, make that a few others. Whatever I was
trying to do automatically broke the hearts
of those in the seats on either side of mine.
It was wild like weather, yet you couldn't just live in it,
you had to drool, your facial muscles had to twitch,
at least some of them. About the time the thought
of living in England occurs, and one succeeds in eating a
little asparagus and custard, the old guard revives its dug-in
positions. You knew about these. They were like lace and spring,
they went away but they never really did. They require a context
of mourning, and public relations. If a cock is being sucked
at a certain moment, it will not jiggle the seismograph, provoke regret
from one who is esteemed and dry, but rather break out disjunctedly
in another hemisphere, and people will start reasoning
from there on. The kid was only a gas-station attendant;
he couldn't have been more than seventeen or eighteen, yet the evening
wind begins promptly to blow, the morbid goddesses sing
that a brooch came undone and pricked one's finger, all silently:
so much for revanchisme. "But of course." And like it says here,
cooperation is part of the school of things, only don't get too close
to overboard, and be burned by the musing that sets in then.
Is that why cows live in clusters, why the foxglove
covers for the hay, and all gets done in a day like it was
supposed to, only there are no more feet to bathe?

I confess I was leery
the first time she told her story
but having heard it enough I can never get enough of what it was determined
should never be shielded from the rain or its attendant wetness;
by the same token they are always with us. Once I started
to count the ways I was indebted to the elk and its house
of night, some old saw had me battling again, kicking up moss
and letting it settle, along with other debris. No
one saw me when I came here; I swear it. You can have a handle
on me now, only don't abuse it
too much or yet. The sky popped out of the oven
like a tin of blueberry muffins, and there's so much to say.
Only I don't feel I'm dry enough. Yet. Take ten,
there's a good caddy. Go do someone's bidding,
then meet me under the larch when the storm explodes. I'll tell you then.

ROBIN BECKER ▪ ▪ ▪ ▪ ▪ ▪ ▪ ▪ ▪ ▪ ▪ ▪ ▪ ▪ ▪ ▪ ▪

A History of Sexual Preference

We are walking our very public attraction
through eighteenth-century Philadelphia.
I am simultaneously butch girlfriend
and suburban child on a school trip,
Independence Hall, 1775, home
to the Second Continental Congress.
Although she is wearing her leather jacket,
although we have made love for the first time
in a hotel room on Rittenhouse Square,
I am preparing my teenage escape from Philadelphia,
from Elfreth's Alley, the oldest continuously occupied
residential street in the nation,
from Carpenters' Hall, from Congress Hall,
from Graff House where the young Thomas
Jefferson lived, summer of 1776. In my starched shirt
and waistcoat, in my leggings and buckled shoes,
in postmodern drag, as a young eighteenth-century statesman,
I am seventeen and tired of fighting for freedom
and the rights of men. I am already dreaming of Boston—
city of women, demonstrations, and revolution
on a grand and personal scale.
               Then the maitre d'
is pulling out our chairs for brunch, we have the
surprised look of people who have been kissing
and now find themselves dressed and dining

in a Locust Street townhouse turned café,
who do not know one another very well, who continue
with optimism to pursue relationship. *Eternity*
may simply be our mortal default mechanism
set on *hope* despite all evidence. In this mood
I roll up my shirtsleeves and she touches my elbow.
I refuse the seedy view from the hotel window.
I picture instead their silver inkstands,
the hoopskirt factory on Arch Street,
the Wireworks, their eighteenth-century herb gardens,
their nineteenth-century row houses restored
with period door knockers.
Step outside.
We have been deeded the largest landscaped space
within a city anywhere in the world. In Fairmount Park,
on horseback, among the ancient ginkos, oaks, persimmons
and magnolias, we are seventeen and imperishable, cutting classes
May of our senior year. And I am happy as the young Tom Jefferson,
unbuttoning my collar, imagining his power,
considering my healthy body, how I might use it in the service
of the country of my pleasure.

Sad Sestina

for Susanna Keysen

Today's sadness is different from yesterday's:
more green in it, some light rain, premonition of departures
and the unpacking of books and papers. *It's not a bad thing
to be sad,* my friend Susanna says. *Go with it.* I'm going by foot
into this sadness, the way we go as children into the awful
schoolday and the hours of cruelty and misunderstanding,

the way we go into family, into the savagery of standing
up for ourselves among siblings and parents, in yesterday's
living room, where secrecy turns to habit and we learn the awful,
unthinkable fact: time twists our days into a series of departures.
When he was mad, my father used to say *Someone's got to foot
the bills,* and I think of him now, this man who knew one thing

for sure: you had to pay your own way, since nothing
came for free in this life. A young dyke, grandstanding
before the relatives, I held my sadness close, one foot
already out the door. Who could believe in yesterday's
homilies while women cruised me, seventeen and hot for departure?
Today's sadness unfurls without drama, without the awful

punishments or reprisals of that house. In its place, the awful,
simple, mystery of human melancholy. Most days, I'd trade anything
to be rid of the blues, accustomed to flight and departure,
strategies that saved my life. Today I'm befriending it, standing
beside my sadness, like a pal down on her luck, who knows yesterday
isn't always a good predictor for tomorrow. A rabbit's foot

won't help; when the time comes, it's a question of putting my foot
in the stirrup and riding the sad horse of my body to the awful
little stable at the edge of town. And there to wait while yesterday
has its way with time. Susanna said, *To be sad is not a bad thing*,
and I believe her, as I pull the heavy saddle from the standing
horse and hang the bridle away. Sadness readies for my departure,

and I for hers. In a most unlikely departure
from the ordinary, even the tough butch on a bike will be a tenderfoot
when it comes to goodbyes. We carry on, notwithstanding
all the good times gone and December's awful
cheerfulness. Susanna, if I ever discern something
useful about sadness, I'll wish I'd known it yesterday.

I've put distracting things aside and discovered, underfoot,
no wisdom absent yesterday. Still, a saint would find this awful:
a standing date with change, a season of departures.

Why We Fear the Amish

Because they are secretly Jewish and eat matzoh on Saturday.
Because they smell us in fellowship with the dead works
of darkness and technology. Because we doubt ourselves.
We find their clothing remorseless; we find their beards unsanitary.
Who among us is not ashamed, speeding, to come upon a poor
horse pulling a cart uphill, everyone dressed the same?
We believe in the state and they believe in the button.

With their fellow Pennsylvanians, the Quakers, they hold noisy pep rallies.
They know the quilting bee, the honey bee and the husking bee
are the only proper activities for women.
Even their horses are thrifty and willing to starve for Christ.
In the Poconos, the men vacation with Hasidim and try on
each other's coats. Back home, no tractors with pneumatic tires.
Pity the child who wants a radio and must settle for a thermos.

When the world shifts to Daylight Savings Time, there's no time
like slow time, to stay out of step. In Standard Time
their horses trot faster than ours, for the Amish

set their clocks ahead. In January, they slaughter the animals.
In March, they go to the sales. In April, they plant potatoes.
In June, they cut alfalfa. In August, they cut alfalfa again.
In October they dig potatoes. In December they butcher and marry.

They modify the milk machine to suit the church, they change
the church to fit the chassis, amending their lives with hook-and-eyes.
Their dress is a leisurely protest against chairmindedness.
We know their frugality in our corpulence. We know their sacrifice
for the group in our love for the individual. Our gods are
cross-dressers, nerds, beach-bums, and poets. They know it.
By their pure walk and practice do they eye us from their carts.

Sonnet to the Imagination

In early March, I watch you sleep, your mouth
open, as if surprised to find yourself
a few hours of rest. I imagine you, a little girl
in New Haven, learning your Hebrew, squirming
under the floodlight of your parents' gaze
the way an only child absorbs the family
depression and rage. You were already
falling in love with revolution, her language
and arguments; her women and children, her Algerias,
her Santiagos. The decades of politics and travel
and lovers became us. Now, I want your mouth
on my mouth and wonder where this wanting will lead
if we let it wander, darling, as I wonder who
you will be after my imagination has ravished you.

Midlife

Everyone here wears a full head of dark hair. Mornings,
they casually allude to parties, getting to sleep at three or four.
As usual, there are a few great beauties;
most still eat eggs.
They treat me like an older sister, hip but no
all-nighters. What happened to my competitive spirit?
My rakish scarf? Like an old man, I miss my
basset hound.

Back home, my Mountain Laurel creates curb appeal,
my mailbox salutes, a sturdy citizen on the road.
Last month I felt great communion with my neighbors

as we all cursed and mowed. Then we hauled
our recycling bins to the street in unison, we made
the collective squeal of our village.

Still, I like these young people,
some of whom still read poetry
and smoke cigarettes.
We share a taste for the linen suits I found
along the Avenue, when I lived in a studio
in Cambridge, city of brick and rescued greyhounds.
Restless, I didn't even know that wanting
was already a kind of having.

Today over lunch I will have an argument with myself
and enjoy it thoroughly, taking both sides,
gesturing and furrowing my brow. Though secure
employment is a sure sign of age, it's so still
in this glade of light and leaves that I might mistake
myself for a bear, a deer.

Life Forms

When a whale rolls ashore
the villagers know a drowned person
is coming home
who may have started life
as a halibut, shucked tail and fins
for a musher's lot.
If she's going to die soon,
a woman may hear the owl call her name.
A screech owl is a person
punished for speaking out of turn.
I didn't know the canoe
in the museum
had been a two-headed sea serpent
the Kwakiutl fed with seals.
I didn't know that raven's wings
could open to reveal
a human head.
A woman washing in a stream refused
to come when her husband called.
Her leather apron slapped the shore,
became a tail. She grew thick fur
and slipped from her marriage
disguised as a beaver.
We stopped at Nenana to place our bets

on the exact minute of the ice breakup.
I wanted to see the clock that stops
when the ice goes out.
I wanted to see the salmon-man
who pumps gas at the filling station,
forced into the human world
after leaping upriver.

MARVIN BELL ▪ ▪ ▪ ▪ ▪ ▪ ▪ ▪ ▪ ▪ ▪ ▪ ▪ ▪ ▪ ▪

The Self and the Mulberry

I wanted to see the self, so I looked at the mulberry.
It had no trouble accepting its limits,
yet defining and redefining a small area
so that any shape was possible, any movement.
It stayed put, but was part of all the air.
I wanted to learn to be there and not there
like the continually changing, slightly moving
mulberry, wild cherry and particularly the willow.
Like the willow, I tried to weep without tears.
Like the cherry tree, I tried to be sturdy and productive.
Like the mulberry, I tried to keep moving.
I couldn't cry right, couldn't stay or go.
I kept losing parts of myself like a soft maple.
I fell ill like the elm. That was the end
of looking in nature to find a natural self.
Let nature think itself not manly enough!
Let nature wonder at the mystery of laughter.
Let nature hypothesize man's indifference to it.
Let nature take a turn at saying what love is!

Someone Is Probably Dead

1

I already knew the secrets of light
before the snow.
It's the little light snowflakes—the dust,
not the pancakes—that make me crazy.
It's the little ones that make a blanket
of my coat and shut

out the stars and a chance to think.
Sometimes, there can be a blizzard where I stand
and nowhere else.
It's the same when a bright sun
in a hard sky
makes the plants in the window fuller.
I take it personally.
And even now, hiding from the snow,
just ten P.M., a Tuesday,
I sit under a green bursting indoors plant
with this feeling. The plant, surviving
nights I forgot to give it heat,
waterless weeks and a rough way
of doing business with it, all the time in its own way
picking off the red hairs of sunlight
and turning out succulent leaves that look like
skin on thick thumbs
or something worse—guts, maybe—manages. Doesn't
pilfer or make everyone around it miserable
against the day it will be picked up by one limp wing
and thrown down into the fly-infested trash.

2

Sometimes, I'll have been sick for three years,
but not with fever and thrashing
and the sheets torn round so that any doctor
would see at once a tight damp picture of illness.
No, sick with calm,
the catatonia of still beauty, the pretty prison
of memory, sometimes
just a face, just a name. It's a wonder
we're alive, we so much prefer the dead.

3

So once I took a ride in Chicago.
The cabbie's name was Purchase Slaughter.
He was all business. Not a star.
But a name that goes from here to there.
So I'm going to put him right here in front of you
and explain to you that when you drive
a taxi in the city for ten hours a day forever
you end up sitting perfectly still
and the city goes by you, turns right and left,
stops and starts up and you immobile
in your thoughts. Mr. Slaughter,
the anti-hero of these lines,
probably stands tonight in the snow off Lake Michigan

and curses the weather
which robs him of his income
and makes him live another life—or nothing.

4

It's stupid to pretend we can be someone else,
when someone else is dead.

A True Story

One afternoon in my room,
in Rome,
I found, wedged
next to the wheel of a wardrobe,
so far under
no maid's broom could touch it,
a pouch made from a sock.
Inside were diamonds
in several sizes. Spread on the carpet,
they caught in my throat.
I knew that, from that moment on,
I would never answer the door.
All of my holiday
would be a preparation
for leaving. First,
I would have to leave the hotel,
probably the city.
I knew someone I could trust
and another with nerve.
She would carry home
half of them, perhaps in her underwear,
if it was not of the kind
customs officers like to touch.
I would carry the others
by way of Zurich,
stopping to purchase
eucalyptus cigarettes, chocolates
and a modest music box.
with its insides exposed.
After that, who knows?
Keep them for years?
Lug them into the shade and sell cheap?
A trip to a third country?
A middleman?
So long as I didn't look up,
there with the stones before me

in the old room in the old city—
where embellishment of every fixture
and centuries of detail
took precedence
over every consideration
of light, air or space—
so long as I did not look up
to my suspicion,
I held the endless light of a fortune
and the course of a lifetime.

In retrospect, it was entirely appropriate
that my diamonds
were the ordinary pieces
of a chandelier, one string of which
had been pulled down
by a previous tenant of room three,
perhaps in a fit of ecstacy.
For I found, also—a diamond-
shaped third of its cover
hanging down from behind the wardrobe,
face to the wall—
the current issue of one of those men's
monthlies in which half-
nude women, glossy with wealth,
ooze to escape
from their lingerie.
And in the single page in its center,
someone had held his favorite
long enough to make love.
The pages were stuck together elsewhere also,
in no pattern,
and the articles on clothing and manners
left untouched.

So this was no ordinary hotel room,
or the most ordinary of all!
Men had come here many times no doubt
to make love by themselves.
But now
it was also a place of hidden treasure.
The rush of wealth and dark promise
I took from that room
I also put back. And so too everyone
who, when in Rome,
will do what the Romans do.

How I Got the Words

I was in Hawaii, but the letter
had come from Alaska. I hadn't read it
when a breeze lifted it out the open louvres
of what I called "my office"
and there it proceeded like a kite or light
hat rocking to one side and then the other
looking both ways for a landing
before swooping one way only for earth.
It was gone. I stood on the ground
and tried to guess. Vacancies everywhere.
So I let a second paper go
through the slot and into the hand of the wind
which here comes a thousand miles
and takes away the sucking part of the heat—
which now I see again carries your letter,
written on two sides, with more compassion
than any poor bodied brain with heart
can hope to heaven for,
and *cradles* it down and down to where
such gentleness will not protect it longer,
and then gives it an alley of air
such as the sleekest aircraft might require
to down itself down the very arc of the earth.
I followed to your letter the blank page
which landed exactly next to it
by every physical and mental measure
only as you had filled your page to me
by putting words next to silence,
and the sound of hundreds of lungs
to bear it away, if one has friends.

To Be

How could I wake from childhood
when everywhere I went there was breathing
like a mother's breath at the ear of her child
before words; when in all places
there was touch and people who defied
the magazines, who did not look perfect and dead;
when my bodyguard was luck
and my texts were songs and the humming of the planets.

It was necessary that I hear a sizzle
in the lungs, and a hum on the wires. Fate decreed
that the magazines should multiply,

the child in me gradually decipher the air,
and the planets die. Fate, which is Kingdom Come,
called me out of the crowd
where I was shopping or doing some busywork,
and told me to stop singing and just be.

But I had an idea. Didn't the sun make it impossible
to look at the sun? Wasn't the night
known only by nuance, the darkness unstudied?
If I contained the earth and all of its flowers
but did not once look at them, would anyone know?
Thus, in my neighborhood, passion—even rapture!—
survived in secret, and still a child appears
in the guise of a grownup at dusk and story-time.

Street Fair: The Quartet

The morning spent itself
into exhaustion moving the clouds,
and the Olympic mountains labored
to bring forth sunlight, and the sun itself!
Then there was sustained applause
for the big woman who sang the blues,
for the frail, anxious woman
singing jazz that leaped among the furniture,
for the beautiful one,
and for the one with the false hand
planted at the cuff of her blouse
like a cutout of a glove.
And two were white and two were black.

New clouds came,
and some were white and some were black.
The songs of the four women rose into the sky.
And the tune of a speck of sand
was amplified in the center of a seashell
until it was expanded like the bread
inside a slaughtered holiday turkey.
America, a great eagle,
heaped air inside its chest and was proud,
and underneath the concrete on which there stood
the harmonies of four women,
two white and two black,
was the webbing on which the city also stood.

How much was in the great snow-topped mountain
hunkered down below the horizon

behind the singers and their songs
to threaten and survive us! Here, the music
shrouds us with the absolute sincerity of a dream
and the true wordless evidence of touch
that renders the entire body a heart,
a heart bearing the drawn out pulse of a pearl in an oyster,
so that some dance slowly to the notes and keep low,
and some rise higher like hands unfolding.
It was the best of illusions, worthy of life!
That everyone within the sound of a song
can dance at the same time on the wire of a spider.

Marco Polo

1.

He was heroic, fugitive, in love with the machinery
of the sea, and every song he sang was of the sea.

His smile was golden, and a skeleton's grimace
in the earth, for every smile ends up in a grimace.

In his famous hands, a chisel could whistle,
and in hands such as his, an insect might sing.

He whose chances rode the foaming oceans
toward ivory-hued dresses of a new substance.

Thus, among ashes, a scrawny angel may sing,
from a naked belly, of a delicate emptiness.

2.

When Marco Polo set his compass for gold
and ivory, and his dictionary for Chinese,

when Marco Polo set his chisel for a smooth bow
(to stir the waves to foam) and a stern like ice,

when Marco Polo fixed his stare on silky dresses
and the porcelain look of China, and when he had

sailed his scrawny machine to a fugitive corner
of the globe, and the faces of his crew were ashen,

and even the rigging grimaced like a skeleton, why
then Marco Polo landed, and the caged insects sang!

3.

With a chisel, he found his gold. And ivory, and ashes.
With a borrowed dictionary, he talked and he sang.

With machinery, foam. With machinery, the fugitive.
With machinery, a grimace. With machinery, insects.

With machinery, a skeleton. With scrawny rigging,
a belly of ashes in a fugitive skeleton. With a chisel,

the gold for machines to carry the burnished dresses
to England, though he himself sang mainly of the gold.

He was the Marco Polo of tea and gunpowder,
devoured by the Oriental machinery of the silkworm.

CHARLES BERNSTEIN ▪ ▪ ▪ ▪ ▪ ▪ ▪ ▪ ▪ ▪ ▪ ▪ ▪ ▪

The Age of Correggio and the Carracci

Thanks for your of already some
weeks ago. Things
very much back to having returned
to a life that
(regrettably) has very little in
common with, a
totally bright few
or something like
it. Was
delighted to get
a most remarkable & am assuming
all continues, well
thereabouts. Fastens
the way of which spirals
fortuitously by leaps
& potions, countering thingamajig
whoseits. Contending, that is, as
fly-by-night succumbs to
dizzied day. Bright
spot, stewed
proclivity, over carousels of
indistinguishable sub-
limation. Say, grab
the crack, secure the

figs: monumentality rings
only once, then pisses
its excess into the subverbal
omnipotence of a clogged
throat (smote). Haze knows
a different diffidence
which dares not
expire
like the Generals who know something
we won't cotton
to, but swing on the trees
just the same: an ant's blood
crazy for canasta (my aunt
with the cherry-blossomed chemise
& cockamamy schemes, praying for
Zoroaster).

Freud's Butcher

Many folks are in a snit
They say the new poetry's not a kick
They pout and pester from academic writing posts
About emotions turned into ghosts of ghosts

Hejinian, Silliman—the tide is over
Andrews, McCaffery—abandon your mowers
You're before your time then out of date
It's not market forces nor fate

A friend of mine named Edith Jarolim
Told me a story from before meats were frozen
Seems her mother's uncle kept the beef supplied
To the distinguished family of Sig Freud's bride

Frau Freud kept kosher, so Sigi too
The mind might wander but the diet laws must do
Art and religion don't always agree
The one's by the rule, the other sometimes free

Memories

1. Grandfathers

The farm never seemed the same after gramps died
Grace kept saying, "Every life has its tide"

But to have his testicles cut that way
Even if he had done what, whatever they say

The corn grew high as a boy in britches
I loved the smell of the bulls and bitches
Motorcars and kikes seemed a world away
We thought we would always lounge in the hay

The first time I was in Kansas City
All the boys and girls looked so damn pretty
I said to my great friend, hey Joe, I said
How come gramps said we'd be better off dead

Than drinkin' the sweet liquor and tasting the fruits—
The muscles and turnips and duckling soups
Such that we never ever none did had
When, oh when, we were tiny lads

2. Heritage

Don't you steal that flag, my Mama had qualms
But a boy gotta have something to boast on
Crack that rock, slit that toad
Nature's a hoot if you shoot your load

Flies in the oven
Flies in the head
I'll kill that fly
Till I kill it dead
And no more will that fly
Bother me
As I roam and I ramble
In the tumbleweed

3. Tough Love

My Dad and I were very close
I like to say, int'mately gruff:
We hunted bear, skinned slithy toes
You know, played ball and all that stuff.
Daddy had his pride and maybe was aloof
But when he hit me, that was proof—
Proof that he cared
More than he could ever share.
How I hated those men who took him away!
Pop was a passionate man
Just like me
And I'll teach my son, Clem
To love just like we men.

4. Sisters

William Kennedy Smith
He is an honorable man
And Mike Tyson's
A giant in my clan.
The liberals and the fem'nists
Hate men and vivisectionists.
But when they want the garbage out
Who do they ask, we guys no doubt.

TED BERRIGAN ▪ ▪ ▪ ▪ ▪ ▪ ▪ ▪ ▪ ▪ ▪ ▪ ▪ ▪ ▪ ▪ ▪

Six Sonnets

XIV

We remove a hand . . .
In a roomful of smoky man names burnished dull black
And labelled "blue" the din drifted in . . .
Someone said "Blake-blues" and someone else "pill-head"
Meaning bloodhounds. Someone shovelled in some
Cotton-field money brave free beer and finally "Negroes!"
They talked . . .
He thought of overshoes looked like mother
Made him
Combed his hair
Put away your hair. Books shall speak of us
When we are gone, like soft, dark scarves in gay April.
Let them discard loves in the Spring search! We
Await a grass hand.

XXII

Go fly a kite he writes
Who cannot escape his own blue hair
who storms to the big earth and is not absent-minded
& Who dumbly begs a key   & who cannot pay his way
Racing down the blue lugubrious rainway
day brakes and night is a quick pick-me-up
Rain is a wet high harried face
To walk is wet hurried high safe and game
Tiny bugs flit from pool to field and light on every bulb
Whose backs hide doors down round wind-tunnels
He is an umbrella. . . .

Many things are current
Simple night houses rain
Standing pat in the breathless blue air.

XXV

Mud on the first day (night, rather
I was thinking of Bernard Shaw, of sweet May Morris
Do you want me to take off my dress?
Some Poems!
the aeroplane waiting to take you on your first
getting used to using each other
Cowboys!   and banging on my sorrow, with books
The Asiatics
Believed in tree spirits, a tall oak, swans gone in the rain,
a postcard of Juan Gris   not a word
Fell on the floor   how strange   to be gone in a minute
I came to you by bus   to be special for us
The Bellboy   letters   a key   then to hear from an old
stranger
The Gift: they will reside in Houston following the Grand
Canyon.

XXVIII

to gentle, pleasant strains
just homely enough
to be beautiful
in the dark neighborhoods of my own sad youth
i fall in love.   once
seven thousand feet over one green schoolboy summer
i dug two hundred graves,
laughing, "Put away your books! Who shall speak of us
when we are gone? Let them wear scarves
in the once a day snow, crying in the kitchen
of my heart!" O my love, I will weep a less bitter truth,
till other times, making a minor repair,
a breath of cool rain in those streets
clinging together with slightly detached air.

XXIX

Now she guards her chalice in a temple of fear
Calm before a storm. Yet your brooding eyes
Or acquiescence soon cease to be answers.
And your soft, dark hair, a means of speaking
Becomes too much to bear. Sometimes,
In a rare, unconscious moment,
Alone this sudden darkness in a toybox

Christine's classic beauty, Okinawa
To Laugh (Autumn gone, and Spring a long way
Off)   is loving you
When need exceeds means,
I read the Evening World / tho oporto,
The funnies, the vital statistics, the news:

XXXIII

Où sont les neiges des neiges?
The most elegant present I could get.
The older children weep among the flowers.
They believe this. Their laughter feeds the need
Like a juggler. Ten weeks pregnant. Who
Believes this? It is your love
Must feed the dancing snow, Mary
Shelley "created" Frankenstein. It doesn't
matter, though. The shortage of available materials
Shatters my zest with festivity, one
Trembling afternoon—night—the dark trance
Up rainy cobblestones   bottle half empty
Full throttle   mired
In the petty frustrations of off-white sheets

JOHN BERRYMAN ▪ ▪ ▪ ▪ ▪ ▪ ▪ ▪ ▪ ▪ ▪ ▪ ▪

The Alcoholic in the 3rd Week of the 3rd Treatment

He has taught the Universe to realize itself,
and that must have been: very simple.
Surely he has a recovery for me
and that must be, after all my complex struggles: *very* simple.

I do, despite my self-doubts, day by day
grow more & more but a little confident
that I will never down a whiskey again
or gin or rum or vodka, brandy or ale.

It is, after all, very very difficult to despair
while the wonder of the sun occurs this morning
as yesterday & probably tomorrow.
It all is, after all, very simple.

You just never drink again all each damned day.

[O all the problems other people face]

O all the problems other people face
we have intensified & could not face
until at last we feel completely alone
thick in a quart of company a day.

I knew I had a problem with that stuff
& problems with my wife & child & work;
but all what help I found left me intact
safe with a quart of feral help a day.

DT's, convulsions. Hospitals galore.
Projectile vomiting hours, intravenous,
back in the nearest bar the seventh day.
God made a suggestion. I went home

and I am in the 4th week of a third treatment
& I am *hurting*, daily, & when I jerk
a few scales seem to fall away from my eyes
until with perfect clarity enough

seems to be visible to keep me sane
& sober toward the bed where I will die.
I pray that You may grant me a yielding will.

          I pray that my will may be attuned to
             Your will for & with me.

4th Weekend

Recovering Henry levelled & confronted;
helpt Mary Lou, was helpt by Mary Lou;
accepted incest, etc.
Major his insights into other burns,
grand his endeavours on their sick behalf,
on the trip into sick himself

he stuck. He did perceive a wilderness,
a need to penetrate & civilize it,
was well aware of courage
up to the effort; open to suggestion;
praying without cease; busy with his pals,
joyous in their recovery.

And that is where he stands, beloved friends.
He's opened up the roads: ended at torrents.

Toss him a hurtful clue.
He has four ah excruciated letters
(he sees) to send off. Maybe grinding them out
will bridge me back not only to those injured souls
but toward my own awful center,
finding there welcome.

The Recognition

A scrotal burning, night, all day, night two.
Mal-diagnosis 'infection', ineffective treatment.
A specialist: 2nd degree burn, from friction: a cortisone derivative.

Twenty-four hours later, not so bad!

I read[1] her desolation, then her (worse?)
'He wants to *hurt* me too, the man I love
& have been tender & forgiving to'
and then her terrible fear before my terrible rage.

Last night on the telephone she was remote
& short, and I wondered if some awful thing
she'd had from me had come back on her
and if today she'd say 'I can't go back to it,

you'll have to leave.' Times all afternoon
this frightful verdict flickered in & out
when she came warm & worried about a *pupil*,
a little, black—Fantastic! she still loves me!

5th Tuesday

We are all 44 at a fine point in this place
from 8 A.M. when Mini-group begins
until the last one the Snack Room leaves to face
another night alone where his Past grins
        saying 'This is *my* round.'

But eight of us, called the Repeaters Group,
dance on a needle of almost despair
of which the truth today is: we could hope
while we were nine, before one had to fare
        out to the whiskey world.

1. 'Read' (1.5) is present tense.

Jack went it was, on Friday, against the word
of the staff & our word . . . violent relief
when Sunday night he & his son, absurd
in ties & jackets, for a visit brief
      looked back in, looking *good*.

We hadn't had for Jack, specially Jack
who back in treatment after just two weeks
out dry, had not budged one inch, much hope; stack
eight loving *wills* together, though, and speaks
      loudly The Group to save him.

Ticklish but trust increasing as all day
Monday no news, relaxing into *our*
violence of the possibility of recovery . . .
this morning, just before Group, looking sour
      Jack weaving from the elevator.

Phase Four

I will begin by mentioning the word
'Surrender'—that's the 4th & final phase.
The word. What is the thing, well, must be known
in Heaven. 'Acceptance' is the phase before;

if after finite struggle, infinite aid,
ever you come there, friend,
remember backward me lost in defiance,
as I remember those admitting & complying.

We cannot tell the truth, it's not in us.
That truth comes hard. O I am fighting it,
my Weapon One: I know I cannot win,
and half the war is lost, that's to say won.

The rest is for the blessed. The rest is bells
at sundown off across a dozen lawns,
a lake, two stands of laurel, where they come
out of phase three mild toward the sacristy.

Group

A feeling Jon is far more anxious for her
sobriety than he says, and more resents
her menace ('If you make me angry, I'll
drink') than he smiles & says.

A feeling they are both resigned to all
that's ill between them & has been & will
for sorry years to come, a 'happy' pair.
'Where's the Serenity Prayer?'

Where sober as you sit here, intimate
in one supreme refraining, full even of love
your privates twitch with theirs under ordeal:
ah Wednesday night is hell.

Each hopeless fear slowly around the circle
gnaws into view, or blurts. Each long-dry throat
still, still with horror & passion runs
immortal alcohols.

Dry Eleven Months

O yes. I've had to give up somewhat here,
illusion on illusion, big books long laboured, a power
of working wellness to some, of securing this house,
the cocktail hour,—
but I am not without a companion: there's left Fear.

I've tried my self, found guilty on each charge
my self diseased. That jury poll was easy;
so was the recommendation, on solid showing
the assassin had been crazy.
But so too were judge & jurors. Now I see sitting large

and sane and near an altogether new
& well advised tribunal. When my ticker stops,
as thrice this fitful year it has done, & re-starts—
each while poor spirit drops
a notch—well, when it quits for good, I'm afraid of you.

16 December 1971

ROBERT BLY ▪ ▪ ▪ ▪ ▪ ▪ ▪ ▪ ▪ ▪ ▪ ▪ ▪ ▪ ▪ ▪ ▪

Snowbanks North of the House

Those great sweeps of snow that stop suddenly six feet from the house,
thoughts that go so far,
boys get out of high school and read no more books,
the son stops calling home,
the mother sets down her rolling pin and makes no more bread . . .
the wife looks at her husband one night at a party and loves him no more,
the energy leaves the wine, and the minister falls leaving the church,
it will not come closer,
the one inside moves back, the hands touch nothing, and are safe.

The father grieves for his son, and will not leave the room where the coffin
    stands,
he will not eat, he turns away from his wife, and she sleeps alone.

The sea lifts and falls all night, the moon goes on through the unattached
    heavens alone,
the toe of the shoe pivots in the dust,
the man in the black coat turns and goes back down the hill, no one sees him
    again, nor knows why he came or why he turned away and did not climb the
    hill.

The Exhausted Bug

for my father

   Here is a tiny, hard-shelled thing. He is the length of a child's tooth,
and clearly the fire of life is flickering out there. Its upper shell, the shape
of a long seashell, wears its overlapping sidings, eight of them, all delicate
brown, shaded as if it were some great cloth made for delicate wrists. The
two antennae look bent and discouraged. When I turn it over with the tip
of my Pilot ballpoint pen, the white legs move appealingly, even though
my first response is confusion, as when we see the messy underside of
any too-well-protected thing. It has twelve legs, six on each side, pale as
tapioca. There are two pincers that come out to protect the head from
hostile knights; or perhaps the pincers are meant to take hold of food.
What else could they be?
   I guess that it has exhausted itself, perhaps over weeks, trying to escape
from this cloisonné dish on my desk. This dish is too little to hold a
breakfast roll, and yet it is a walled Sahara to this creature, some
courtyard in which the portcullis is always closed, and the knights, their
ladies, their horse-drangers always, mysteriously, gone.

The sharp lamplight lit up the dish; it is odd that I did not see him
before. I will take him outdoors in the still chill spring air and let him
drink the melted snow of late afternoon on this day when I have written
of my father stretched out in his coffin.

Two Ramages for Old Masters

1

Silent in the moonlight, no beginning or end.
Alone, and not alone. A man and a woman lie
On open ground, under an antelope robe.
They sleep under animal skin. Can a modern man
And woman live so? How many years?
The robe thrown over them, rough
Where they sleep. Outside, the moon, the plains
Silent in the moonlight, no beginning or end.

2

Whitman, how many hours I have loved your vowels!
It's a stair of sound, and a barefooted dancer coming down.
My master, my lover, my teacher! You call to death,
But death does not hear its clammy name.
The master sings like a dark rabbi
Among ocean herbs on the shore: "Press close,
Bare-bosomed night." Be blessed, teacher,
By the Torah and the Bible inside the naked seed.

A Dream of William Carlos Williams

You were dead, but how sleek and darkly calm you were!
"There is some change," I said. Your wife said,
"There is a big change!" A third person was with us—
We all laughed about form, how sweet it is, *what*
It is! While you laughed, your rocker broke. "You fell

Out of it!" I shouted, but you were startled
To think of leaving form. As we walked out
The back door and down the wooden stoop,
You asked about form in my poems. I found myself
Lying, saying I cared nothing about form. . . .

On the Oregon Coast

for William Stafford

The waves come—the large fourth wave
Looming up, thinking, crashing down—all
Roll in so prominently I become small
And write this in a cramped script, hard to read.

Well, all this fury, prominent or not
Is also hard to read, and the ducks don't help,
Settling down in furry water, shaking
Themselves, and then forgetting within a minute.

Remembering the fury, it is up to us, even
Though we feel small compared to the loose
Ocean, to keep sailing and *not* land,
And figure out what to say to our children.

The Gaiety of Form

1

How sweet to weight the line with all these vowels!
Body, Thomas, the codfish's psalm. The gaiety
Of form lies in the labor of its playfulness.
The chosen vowel reappears like the evening star
Daily in the solemn return the astronomers love.
When "ahm" returns three times, then it becomes
A note; then the whole stanza turns to music.
It comforts us, says: "I am here, be calm."

2

"In the sad heat of noon the pheasant chicks
Spread their new wings in the moon dust."
When we choose so, the vowel has its own husband
And children, its nooks and garden and kitchens.
The smoking table gives plebian sweets
Never equalled by the chocolates French diners
Eat at evening, and gives us pleasures abundant
As Turkish pears picked in the garden in August.

My Father's Neck

Your chest, hospital gown
Awry, looks
Girlish today,
It is your bluish
Reptile neck
That has known weather.
I said to you: "Are
You ready to die?"
"I am," you said,
"It's too boring around
Here." He has in mind
Some other place
Less boring. "He's not ready
To go," the doctor said.
There must have been
A fire that nearly
Blew out, or a large
Soul, inadequately
Feathered, that became
Cold and angered.
Some four-year-old boy
In you, chilled by
Your mother, misprized
By your father, said,
"I will defy, I will
Win anyway, I
Will show *them.* "
When Alice's well-
Off sister offered
To take your two
Boys in the Depression,
You said it again.
Now you speak similar
Defiant words to death.
This four-year-old-
Old man in you does
As he likes: he likes
To stay alive.
Through him you
Get revenge,
Persist, endure,
Overlive, overwhelm,
Get on top.
You gave me
This, and I do
Not refuse it.
It is
In me.

EAVAN BOLAND ·············

Anna Liffey

Life, the story goes,
Was the daughter of Cannan,
And came to the plain of Kildare.
She loved the flat-lands and the ditches
And the unreachable horizon.
She asked that it be named for her.
The river took its name from the land.
The land took its name from a woman.

A woman in the doorway of a house.
A river in the city of her birth.

There, in the hills above my house,
The river Liffey rises, is a source.
It rises in rush and ling heather and
Black peat and bracken and strengthens
To claim the city it narrated.
Swans. Steep falls. Small towns.
The smudged air and bridges of Dublin.

Dusk is coming.
Rain is moving east from the hills.

If I could see myself
I would see
A woman in a doorway
Wearing the colors that go with red hair.
Although my hair is no longer red.

I praise
The gifts of the river.
Its shiftless and glittering
Re-telling of a city,
Its clarity as it flows,
In the company of runt flowers and herons,
Around a bend at Islandbridge
And under thirteen bridges to the sea.
Its patience at twilight—
Swans nesting by it,
Neon wincing into it.

Maker of
Places, remembrances,
Narrate such fragments for me:

One body. One spirit,
One place. One name.
The city where I was born.
The river that runs through it.
The nation which eludes me.

Fractions of a life
It has taken me a lifetime
To claim.

I came here in a cold winter.

I had no children. No country.
I did not know the name for my own life.

My country took hold of me.
My children were born.

I walked out in a summer dusk
To call them in.

One name. Then the other one.
The beautiful vowels sounding out home.

Make of a nation what you will
Make of the past
What you can—

There is now
A woman in a doorway.

It has taken me
All my strength to do this.

Becoming a figure in a poem.

Usurping a name and a theme.

A river is not a woman.
    Although the names it finds
        The history it makes
And suffers—
    The Viking blades beside it,

The muskets of the Redcoats,
    the flames of the Four Courts
Blazing into it
  Are a sign.
    Any more than
A woman is a river,
  Although the course it takes,
    Through swans courting and distraught willows,
Its patience
  Which is also its powerlessness,
    From Callary to Islandbridge,
      And from source to mouth,
Is another one.
      And in my late forties
Past believing
  Love will heal
    What language fails to know
And needs to say—
  What the body means—
    I take this sign
And I make this mark:
    A woman in the doorway of her house.
    A river in the city of her birth.
The truth of a suffered life.
  The mouth of it.

The seabirds come in from the coast.
The city wisdom is they bring rain.
I watch them from my doorway.
I see them as arguments of origin—
Leaving a harsh force on the horizon
Only to find it
Slanting and falling elsewhere.

Which water—
The one they leave or the one they pronounce—
Remembers the other?

I am sure
The body of an aging woman
Is a memory
And to find a language for it
Is as hard
As weeping and requiring
These birds to cry out as if they could
Recognize their element
Remembered and diminished in
A single tear.

An aging woman
Finds no shelter in language.
She finds instead
Single words she once loved
Such as "summer" and "yellow"
And "sexual" and "ready"
Have suddenly become dwellings
For someone else—
Rooms and a roof under which someone else
Is welcome, not her. Tell me,
Anna Liffey,
Spirit of water,
Spirit of place,
How is it on this
Rainy Autumn night
As the Irish sea takes
The names you made, the names
You bestowed, and gives you back
only wordlessness?

Autumn rain is
Scattering and dripping
From car-ports
And clipped hedges.
The gutters are full.

When I came here
I had neither
Children nor country.
The trees were arms.
The hills were dreams.

I was free
to imagine a spirit
in the blues and greens,
the hills and fogs
of a small city.

My children were born.
My country took hold of me.
A vision in a brick house.
Is it only love
that makes a place?

I feel it change.
My children are
growing up, getting older.
My country holds on
to its own pain.

I turn off
the harsh yellow
porch light and
stand in the hall.
Where is home now?

Follow the rain
out to the Dublin hills.
Let it become the river.
Let the spirit of place be
a lost soul again.

In the end
It will not matter
That I was a woman. I am sure of it.
The body is a source. Nothing more.
There is a time for it. There is a certainty
About the way it seeks its own dissolution.
Consider rivers.
They are always en route to
Their own nothingness. From the first moment
They are going home. And so
when language cannot do it for us,
cannot make us know love will not diminish us,
there are these phrases
of the ocean
to console us.
Particular and unafraid of their completion.
In the end
everything that burdened and distinguished me
will be lost in this:
I was a voice.

PHILIP BOOTH ▪ ▪ ▪ ▪ ▪ ▪ ▪ ▪ ▪ ▪ ▪ ▪ ▪ ▪ ▪

Sixty-Six

Waking himself,

after an after-

hour before the

reached for the

without any alarm,

lunch nap not a half-

burial service, he

motel note-pad beside

the head of his

words, the six

sure, getting

interment, he

written down.

sense, sense he

loss, now that

beyond whatever

they came to him

And had now

gone out of the

of his head. No,

his blue button-

his tie in the

those words, all

each other, were,

at home in his

due time, if he

of him, keep his

Rechecking his

again how he

the car, backed

his key to the

to the graveside.

bed to find the six

profound words he was

up for this afternoon's

had, going to sleep,

The words had made beautiful

now sensed as terrible

both he and the words were

it was they meant when

from wherever they'd come.

gone back to; or altogether

world in having gone out

that wasn't true. Buttoning up

down, hoisting his pants, tying

mirror, and combing, he knew that

six, though far from him and

in one form or another, surely

old Unabridged. From which, in

refound two, and could, for the life

mind open, all might come back.

fly, he straightened up, checked

looked, took his flightbag out to

to drop off on the TV top

wordless motel, and drove straight

Fog-Talk

Walking the heaved cement sidewalk down Main Street,
I end up where the town bottoms out: a parking lot
thick with sea-fog. There's Wister, my boyhood friend,

parked on the passenger side of his old Dodge pick-up.
He's waiting for Lucia, the girl who drives him around
and feeds him, the one who takes care of him at home.

Wister got married late. Like me. Wifeless now, no kids,
we're near sixty-eight, watching the ebb, looking out into
the fog. Fog so thick that if you got shingling your roof

you'd shingle three or four courses out onto
the fog before you fell off or sun came. Wister knows
that old joke. Not much else, not any more. His mind drifts

every whichway. When I start over to his old pick-up,
he waves to my wave coming toward him, his window half up,
half down. He forgets how to work it. I put my head

up close. *Wister,* I say, *you got your compass with you
to steer her home through this fog?* Wister smiles at me with
all sorts of joy, nodding yes. He says *I don't know.*

HENRY BRAUN ■ ■ ■ ■ ■ ■ ■ ■ ■ ■ ■ ■ ■ ■ ■ ■

To Fat Boy, The Bomb

*The treaty was signed this morning
in the East Room*

We burn cities.
With your permission,
the only animal that runs toward fire
to save, to gawk, to liven up the night,
cancels with fire the quick network of borders.
I celebrate, with your permission, the borders
of human beings, the profiles lifting and turning
in drivers' seats, the parallels that bend
and meet at the tear ducts of the eye.
No longer frightened of fontanels,
I touch the soft craters of the mind cap
and root my nose gratefully in whorls
of babies' ears. I celebrate the skin,

the curves of women, the straight hips of men,
my hand with its own life
and tiny Pavlovian memories
of cusps in the arms of chairs and handkerchiefs
drawn like cold brooks through the fingers.
I sing the damaged hands of Les Eyzies,
and Friday's footprint,
triangles in tempera of the holy.
As over the hump of windowsill more evening
crawls, I contemplate full moons
of countdown, after nine of which we come
with hanks of cord trailing from our bellies.
I celebrate, with your permission, the bellies,
the treasure kegs of ageing males,
big bodies coming out of showers,
and the taut ramparts of little girls.
The approaching sine curve of an elbow
gazed at and touched by a pregnant woman,
I gaze at, and also touch, then sing
the double string between the eyes of lovers.
Faces, known and unknown, delineate
like the moon suddenly in breaks of cloud.
I celebrate and sing
all the beloved faces, all, Fat Boy,
and tickle the cittern for the cloud as well.
I wave as if positioned for goodbye
and, at the same time, for hello
in the borderless shadow of the lingam.

OLGA BROUMAS ▪ ▪ ▪ ▪ ▪ ▪ ▪ ▪ ▪ ▪ ▪ ▪ ▪ ▪ ▪

After *The Little Mariner*

I woke up in the dark
of a moon steamed against glass
black as if glazed with ebony
or soft lead handled in the blind
of another's dream and he
the crossroader
the atmospheric horseman
the marksman who can calm the deep
by taking a teenager

down from his constellation and instructing
him to walk across the surf then kneel
inside the pelago a broadcast

charging the elements
with Rilke's terror and my soul
rang in the air above
the bedclothes rustled through my limbs
on the bed were paralyzed
transparent

I could see
a ribbon song begin
from the lungs of his penis
inside my body like a swallow
of ice-cold milk in August
gleaming and slow like mercury
upstream and through my lips
and then my soul
fell into or my body rose.

On Earth

When we drove up to the curb the woman
in the dun colored house stained by the rain of days
when this was a village beyond the city
came to the gate to shrilly
claim the parking space.
She argued with my mother, unpacified
by the steady line of the wall
and the small rear entrance
we needed to reach
across the street but my mother
mildened by it said "half an hour, half
an hour" and we crossed.
My uncle was there. I held my sister
and then her husband wheeled
his motorbike along the lane, helmet in hand.
We waited for the man
whose job it was to see the bones were ready.
Sometimes the flesh is slow.
Sometimes a daughter buries a mother
twice in the reddish earth as mother had.
All the allowable extensions
having passed we waited
holding a bottle of wine. The priest
came to take it saying
it was good, the bones
were dry. Uncle and I
followed him to the washing house:
a dun marble sink through the limed
doorway; by its step

two ossuaries stop our feet. The priest
directed my attention gently
from the smaller bones
I instantly chose as father, dapper, petite, lithe
dancer in uniform at Easter leading his
circle of men, to the raw and bold
armful stained deeply
already by the wine. Earth, blood, vine.
We said a benediction. The widow
of the small-boned man held up his picture
and his ring. He had been bald and portly.
Through the heat,
the moisture rising from the sprinkled earth,
the crickets and the flies and bees, the distant
scrape of digging, the thin
voice of my sister rose
and rounded the chapel to meet me.
I held it so it too could see.
Good bones. Thick bones. Bones drinking deep.
I carried them
with the woman whose job it is
further behind the chapel
for their day in the sun and vaulted night
and wrote a number on the box in magic marker
I gave back to the woman with a tip.
My uncle was telling a detailed story
about his alarm clock and how it broke
and he returned it to the store and got a new one
thirteen months later with a new
warranty. My mother, his sister,
listened to him. We walked to the front
gate to sign the papers
and back past the famous Sleeper
that drove its sculptor mad by never waking
to our car and the quiet
landswoman eating the noonday meal
with her husband, his truck pulled to the yard.

Next to the *Café Chaos*

the lambent cobblestones refract the blue
and yellow of *L'Afreak Electronique*
into a frazzled dayglow
batting the piss-crossed wall that jogs
the curved canal from *Milky Way*
to ambient *Paradiso*
regulars spiking the street.

Under that blinking sign,
the neon-pale geraniums rappelling
on burgher curtains drilled with light
at night and night
tobacco-stained by day, we lunge
made slow by the urge to love
untrammeled by the sirens'
aggrandizing thrust. A gaseous flame

leapt from the greengold filth of the canal,
the squatters' barricades lit up and their annointed faces
appeared in the journalistic probe
outlined in kohl like convict masks.
Unhinged from the mirage

and refuged on a park bench by the swans
imperial sashay we splay
a fist across each other's back
and loaded with fact like methedrine
by the unvanquished halo from the *Terra
Incognita*'s strobe we hug.

The Pealing

As in a parable the truant father
arrives. The birth
attendent there and I
mistrust him but our panting

friend accepts him and we three begin
with her the three days broken
in portions of seven
agonizing breaths

and the uncounted minute
and a half we sleep
between them like a heart
rests calculable

lengths of lifetime
between beats.
Each third and fourth
breath brings her eyes to panic

so fierce her head tilts
on the axis
her eyes locked into mine
and once again I am

inside the camp
the peaked cap
and eyes implacable
and blue with pleasure.

Souls rose with the smoke
and settled over Europe
as now the random hot
spots of Chernobyl.

Some say the hippies
now the Greens
are these souls born.
I recognized the Jewish toes

of Esther, the scholarship
girl from Athens in the pool
at the American consulate
cocktail party honoring the brain

drain we were part of
and bent to kiss them in the stupor
of that event before her
eyes held mine and we both

stopped. I live
since then with Jews.
I leave the room
where my Armenian

friend exhales
and sleeps for ninety seconds
and rouses and breathes and screams and sleeps
her third night

before dawn
to weep. So many
born. Such
natural pain

and still the clubs the whips
barbed wire cattle prods napalm
Klansmen and Afrikaners.
On break a midwife

talks me down. On Demerol
at last my friend is sleeping
deeper between pains.
I cross the hospital

to see another friend
and help him shift position
and suction his mouth and hold
his gaze. "White cars," he rasps,

"bridge sky." Twelve hours
to his death. It's Solstice.
Yellow flowers
lunge in the heated air

petals omnivorous, pistils
throbbing. I make it back
by noon to tell him it's
a boy. The head spilled

blue, cyanic, ocean blue
in flat dawn light, pale blue
and sudden in six breaths and Beth
stopped a long moment

as in strobe
elbow to knee
inscribed dark totem with two heads
one fierce, one blue.

The obstetrician slipped the cord
loose from his neck
they howled
he flopped

rubbery and engorged.
Plum testicles:
waxy, veined, seamed
still to the tree.

STEPHANIE BROWN ■ ■ ■ ■ ■ ■ ■ ■ ■ ■ ■ ■ ■ ■

Interview with an Alchemist in the New Age

Someone, if you pay the price, can hypnotize you
and you can speak, from memory, oh so long ago imbedded into your soul,
about the past, and history, and your place in it, how you struggled
in the heat and the dust near the Great Pyramid of Giza,
how you gazed into the mirror of your beloved,

how you took a bow with your fellow thespians, in Greece,
how a sycophant betrayed you in the Hall of Mirrors at Versailles,
how he kissed you before the duel when he was murdered for you
—in the country somewhere, in the South—
and you were forced to marry the victor. Or
how you didn't starve during the famine that killed your child,
that's the source of the nagging pain in your side,
and you can feel—it's still very real—the leeches placed on your chest
though of course with these primitive mechanisms of medicine,
you bled to death. Is this why
you fear the scalpel so?
Were you cauterized in a tribal-rite clitorectomy?
Were you a castrato?
When your teeth rotted in Spain in the 17th century,
what had you done that was remiss?
Where does it now fit?
Was, perhaps, the Armada involved?

Because it's yours, it's your Karma, buddy, it's *your problem*
It's *your* history, and history is your problem.
It's your responsibility, now,
to change the tire on your neighbor's car
because you once beheaded him because he once beat you at a game of chess
when you were the King of France, when you were ruthless.
And now you're not ruthless: see, there's a kind of symmetry involved.
Just think,
Albert Einstein may already have come back,
maybe he's a kid,
maybe he's in the womb and is about to be born.
Maybe he'll arrive by space-ship.
These are extraordinary times, of course—that's why.

Have we ever felt the tenor of the spiritual with such force before?
Is this not the end of time?
Oh, I don't know. It's weird, all right, and it's kind of neat
to bear the children while wearing a costume from the Middle Ages,
to wait for the Pony Express to ride into town,
to be the shaman for the Eskimos,
to be the butler for Henry Ford!
George Washington's dentist—where is he now!
History, after all, doesn't belong to Cinderella, or to Henry VIII,
or to Jesus—perhaps you wiped his forehead before the Crucifixion—
Who knows?
Well, wouldn't it be fun to think about?
And it might help you work out the problem you're having with your father
or with the guy at the 7-11 who constantly berates you,
who once even hurled a doughnut at you—
(You rowed together in a ship just like in "Ben-Hur")

Anyhow, who does it harm
(since you were once Mozart, send in the harpsichord music now)
if you pay to be hypnotized and to find out
how karmic or unkarmic you are?
Oh, no, it's not just kidding around, really—
You'll never know for sure if you were really a monk once,
but if you were—well, wow.

Chapter One

We librarians went to Baja last weekend and sat in the sun
Ho! Ho! It's funny, isn't it? Though not really Henry Jamesian
It's not so simple that we're prim and went to the exotic
Though perhaps that's what the story really is.
We librarians went to Baja last weekend and sat in the sun
and walked on the beach and played tennis at the Head Clerk's club
Though we were vacationing without hierarchy.
In this way I love my job, bureaucrat that I am, I love
to rank, to answer, to box; I love the boolean in logic.
So perhaps that's why we went: Baja Mexico, if you've never been,
is about rusted cars growing into grass
on the side of the highway and shacks,
and roadside stands for olives and honey,
and Americans driving fast to the beach-and-tennis clubs they've built,
and the surfers in the ocean, waiting, rocking;
You see men standing in the no-man's land of the border,
waiting to cross: The border patrol jeeps with their rifles
ride by in the dust
Dirt roads and beer advertising everywhere
you look when you drive through Ensenada. We librarians
went to Baja last weekend and sat in the sun and we got a joke running:
what's the next fad in publishing after Co-Dependency?
It was a category of men who don't want to be success objects, we decided.
Self-help books for men who are eaten alive by women-mad-for-money.
You make them take a quiz, and everyone fits the category.
But my ex-boss, sitting there, and I are both in love with alcoholics,
She's married to hers and I've decided not to marry mine.
So maybe since we're prim and bookish we need the wild type—
I've thought about it. We laugh about these books
but just, just maybe. My ex-boss, now an administrator,
is the daughter of blacklisted Hollywood screenwriters.
She said they used to vacation right where we were when she was a kid.
They would dig for clams
in the bay that's going to be dredged into a marina for Americans.
Her family lived in exile, in Mexico.
She told me one day her husband doesn't believe those things
Really happened in America.

It's hard, though, to vacation without hierarchy.
Someone is the best tennis player, the best storyteller, the best
gossip, has the best body, gets along best. And you remember
where you stand as an employee. You remember
you're an American in a foreign country.
We librarians went to Baja and sat in the sun:
A day in the life, a *fête gallante*—
There was a house I wanted to run away from. Could I?

No, No Nostalgia!

I thought I'd end up a Hippie American Gothic
Those people who nod their heads and listen carefully
And hug one another from arms inside of overalls
Round eyes in round glasses
But I never liked the kitchens they had
Overrun with jars full of saved things
And bins full of grains gotten from bins full of grains
which were gotten on all-day-long shopping-expedition-type shopping trips.
The car, the van rode very slow. . . .
But I liked the long-haired women who kneaded bread
and calmly carried their bodies to the beach where they stripped
their clothes off unselfconsciously, and swam.
You know, bearded men and Vietnam and all that. . . .
But they were very stern with me when I didn't understand
soldiers and helicopters and the *meaning* of long hair and of
mind expansion.
This was the world of my older siblings
They were my parent-surrogates, said I
after a few months of my Jungian-oriented therapy.
Three hippie sisters who were mothers.
(Aha.) The other parents were mostly on a fabulous vacation to France
So I had to hate it, and I had to like it later and I had to hate it.
I had to throw up at the sight of sprouts,
and the elixirs measured out in eye-droppers,
and the sea salt and the paperbacks about cancer as a Tri-Lateral plot
and the water distiller which ran all night long.
(If my brother-in-law lay on the couch all day and smoked pot,
wasn't he merely lazy?)
Grant Wood got it right: those faces
American toughness and humorless virtue are all right
It's the judgmental part I can do without
The way they raise the kids: everyone greeted with
a vision of wholesomeness, with suspicious mouths.

Schadenfreude

If this were a movie
the sound of sizzling would foretell disaster
because you're walking out of the room leaving something cooking
because you have too many burners going
There should be the sound of trumpets, thin and mournful
You're going to walk into your murder.
It begins to smoke.
All the same I'm humming.
The attacker hides behind the door.
I'm whistling a happy face.
Minutes before you start shrieking, again and again
before the plaster falls down around you
before the strangulation begins
folding up clothes and putting them into drawers—your back
turned—
while the skillet, in close-up, keeps sizzling.
Minutes before the shrieking and choking.
The cupboards become lit.
Watch the doll's mouth melt.
This audience won't pity you
like big round workers who don't get pity
when they step on the bus steps in the morning and make the bus
sag momentarily. Like wizened up bodies
holding canes, heads bowed under golf hats
on their ways downtown—
This audience will laugh—
the way your eyes bulge out and your tongue is unhinged
how you return to find a kitchen filled with smoke
when we all know it's your gluttony that's caused it.
(It's the way you locked your lies up in the closet
that's led me to hate you.)
So when your doom comes—
a knife thuds into your back, let's say,
or an arrow is shot into your ribs
or a razor is pulled across your face
or you trip on a roller skate near the open cellar stairs
or you walk into a sliding glass door
or you are hung from the shower curtain rod in a plastic white shower
or you are stabbed with pinking shears
or demoralized with an axe handle
or beaten down the spine with a rake
or forced to swallow some golf balls
or sliced at the waist and the wounds salted
or if you merely carpet burned your arm on the carpet
It will feel great to watch
you get it

or at least to see you experience
some slight, future, discomfort,
chagrin,
embarrassment.

Feminine Intuition

I. Little Red Riding Hood

Astrid comes from upstate New York.
She comes from distress.
She's enthusiastic about it.
She doesn't belong, but she tries hard.
Her husband hurts her, but they have a drug-free life.
They roller skate and take up fads enthusiastically,
Neon clothing and the like.
He's an air traffic controller, so they move constantly.
This time it's California. After the picnic
I said, "She reminds me of Little Red Riding Hood."
My husband said, "Yeah."
We were doing the dishes.
I can't say some other things, so I say this.

II. Plastic Surgery, Skipped Dessert

That simple woman thought I was simple, but I was not.
I was never simple.
Not trees, stars, plot.
She smoked her fingers down to the yellow.
She had the harsh hearty laughter
Of the women who believe the men will leave them.
All the mothers I knew went nuts.
Hair the color of a screwdriver.
It's a cliché, but it's an altar.
Cotton candy spun into a knot.
Especially rich women, with art.
Kimono, muumuu.
Ice cubes.

But I was never simple. I was never simple.
The way I was raised, the men never leave a woman.
She was a woman: I could not trust her.

III. A Woman Clothed with the Sun

Imagine, all over America, women are losing bone mass.

Brittle old ladies: we create them.
Coiffured movie sirens lounging around the pool transmogrify
into brittle old sea hags.
(They don't know anything: they just nag.)
Let's let them swim out to sea.
Let's give them a spiny seahorse to ride on.
"Goodbye brittle old ladies, beautiful ones—
Ride out against the horizon and the orange sun!"

I Was a Phony Baloney!

I was a real phony baloney.
I was not a, never was a, member of the Republican party
But I was a real phony baloney.
I pretended to be meek but I was not
I pretended to be silent but I was seething
I thought I was confessional but I was teething
On my gristly, phony baloney.
I cared about my shoes (I was chattering) not really
As much as you might have thought:
Oh, sure I was (fill in the blank) and I was (fill in this spot)
But I was a real phony baloney.
I was thinking of how to overthrow the power plot
While I pretended to tend to my petty thoughts
My eyes were narrowing into harmful harmless slots
I took it out on (Blank) and (Her name I forgot)
I was a real phony baloney.
I pretended to be meek but I was not
I pretended to be weak but I was a block
of solid phony baloney.

Envoi:
I pretended to be sighing but I was enjoying my lot:
I was a sorry, sorry. (Baloney.)

Marriage

One day my husband came home with a jar of generic peanut butter.
He used it for the mousetraps.
One, two, three, they were dead.
One squealed as his fur was pulled off into the glue.

He threw him into the sewer only half-dead.
The day before he had been running.
Hopping out of the trash can onto my foot.
Running along the edge of the closet.
Another: four.   Another: five.   Another: six.

I said I would make peanut butter cookies.
He said, are you going to use that generic peanut butter? Gross.
He did not want the cookies.
He said, I don't even like peanut butter cookies.
I said, you told me you liked them.
He said, I don't remember.

Not remembering!
As it went on, I actually stomped my foot.
Not remembering what he says!
He was taking off his tie. He was hanging up his shirt.
He says, you need to be more strong.
He doesn't know that this will never make sense to me.
I'm not interested in being strong, as he is not interested in remembering.

CHRISTOPHER BUCKLEY ▪ ▪ ▪ ▪ ▪ ▪ ▪ ▪ ▪ ▪

The Presocratic, Surfing, Breathing Cosmology Blues . . .

> When the great waters went everywhere, holding the germ, and generating light,
> Then there arose from them the breath of the gods.
>> "Hymn to the Unknown God"
>> —from the *Rig Veda*

> Let's get real gone.
>> —Elvis Presley

The idea of an infinite number of stars brought Newton to his knees, for that would turn
the sky into a blazing haze—flame rises naturally—and so reasoned Empedocles
Homer, and Anaxagoras who filled the farthest reaches with fiery light. . . .

The back pages of cosmic history blow open, a bright litter of particles swimming in
the blue backwash of quasars, kernels back at the beginning smoldering
finally through to us now, telescopes probing not just into space
but into time. . . .

So galaxies in the Coma Cluster appear to us as they looked seven hundred million years
ago, about the time the first jellyfish—its own roseate nucleus of cells and
spinning arms—was developing on earth,

where, some years later, I would turn up at 9, walking tip toe along Miramar Beach,
  avoiding the pink and scattered nebulae washed up for a mile around—
    a sting like hot coals, a cold quivering mass of burning stars.

Or where I sit now, admiring a sugar maple, flag of impending flame, angelic breathing
  we attribute to trees as we bivouac at the perimeter of nothing as instrumental
    as beauty, and are mainly recursive, among other elemental things.

What wouldn't it be worth to have time again to worry about incursions of fog over
  the blacktop, the starry orange groves dissolving on the drive to school,
    to worry about the spelling of grey or gray, or Mississippi, the mysterious
      lives of Saints, a laundry line of levitating miracles commemorated
        along the church's tomb-dark walls

where beeswax candles, placed cross-wise on my throat, would save me from choking
  on the bones of fish, and holy water sprinkled along the air keep a sea-wide
    iniquity from seeping under the closed door of the soul so I might be
      admitted to the beatific company of clouds, the clear apertures
        in an updraft of wind.

And I in fact sometimes pondered the unsubstantiated Soul—invisible, but *something*
  just the same—like a glass of water filled to different levels during music class,
    sounding a high or low note as a finger orbited the transparent rim.

Or in back bookcases, *The World Book Encyclopedia,* all the blank space edging dark
  columns of letters proclaiming the Hittites' fierce knowledge of iron, the Code
    of Hammurabi, The Lighthouse at Pharos, and the first space capsule
      burning like a thimble of coal in the stratosphere.

Yet, when we think about it, our youth lasts all our lives, trailing us like a comet tail of ice
  and dust, or the way angels, like knots in a rope of light, are still let down
    to us from the dark in Caravaggio's first "St. Matthew," the one sent up
      in flames in the bombing of Berlin

whose atoms are still associated in the grey haze that constantly resettles that sky, re-
  claiming its dust in the thin half-light of loss, in the past riding that freight
    of light out to a universe where all things are contingent upon each other,
      upon, as Anaximander had it, "The Indefinite."

There's much that matters in that dark where my hands are full of the brilliant dross
  off the recent edge of discovery, data no one in school had the least idea existed
    when I took my D in General Science.

Now I'm writing it all down—Vacuum Genesis, Lookback Time—thinking I'm getting
  somewhere, only to realize I need another course in Italian Cinema just to
    make the metaphors make sense!

Was it Luchino Visconti's *Death in Venice* or Vitorio De Sica's *Brief Vacation?* Dirk
  Bogarde on the Lido coughing out the dark matter of his lungs for some

blond boy in a bathing suit as Mahler's symphony moved like a cloud
of melting glass over the sea,

or that beaten angel of a housewife escaping her truck driving, mule-headed husband
in Torino with black stars on her X-rays, a silt of light slowing in her veins
which took her up to the state sanitarium in the snowy Alps, a comet-quick
brush with a younger man reconstituting the rose-colored clouds
of her lungs, but sending her finally back?

And I remember holding my breath, the universe expanding inside my lungs as I was
tumbled like a rag in the spin-cycle of a ten foot surf a quarter mile off shore,
riding the point break at Rincon and plunged into the white salt-roar
of froth, my chest burning as I shot up to that heaven

of air above the surface—and while heaven could, in theory, have been anywhere, it
was there that minute as I swallowed the air's cool light, mindless of every
molecule and the constant state of flux all things are in.

And regardless of the frenzy of atoms and the sub-atomic voids, I'd have sold my soul
for my dinged-up plank, anything to hold to and fill my flattened pipes
before the next wave with its five feet of churning soup rolled in,
beneath which I'd have to dive, count ten, and come up again
gasping toward a low tide of rocks.

In college, staring out past the spires of Italian cypress, wind bending the invisible
blue beyond the second story classroom windows, the thick glass sinking,
soaked with old light, the Presocratics were proclaiming the single source
to everything. Half conscious, at swim in the 60s, I was reaching
for the first idea that would keep my head above dark waters.

And, like Einstein, whom I hadn't read, I didn't bother about the details and showing
my work—all the math and elegant equations—I just wanted to know what was
on God's mind when he shook up this boule de niege and let time-space
float out and gather here with our little neighborhood of
respiration and recourse to nothing but light?

But, at 19, I had recourse to little beyond beer and the bylaws of poker? Was it or wasn't it
Air? Aneximines proclaimed everything was—just rarefied and condensed—
while Thales assured us all things were water, and I'd seen plenty of that.

They both fared better than Heraclitus who favored fire—for, the obvious consideration
of our weight aside, as air, we were almost spirits already, and shouldn't we
shine then at last among the aethers? Yet sinking in the specific gravity
of over 40 years, the best I come up with most nights is moonlight
through the trees, its mist lifting almost imperceptibly
through the leaves . . .

It turns out the Ionians were not far off track; cosmic radiation—the original red hot
atomic spin and background hum—can be tuned-in from any cold rock

in a universe 90% back-filled with a dark and missing theoretical matter—
that bang and microwave broadcast even the deaf still hear . . .

And so, I have little more on hand than air and a forecast of air where it is unlikely
I'll find myself free of the old aptitude of starlight to break our hearts—though
I look into the infinite, the nothingness, the nowhere, and the dark
as if I recognized the light in its last disguise.

CHARLES BUKOWSKI ■ ■ ■ ■ ■ ■ ■ ■ ■ ■ ■ ■

b

the wisdom of the
bumblebee crawling
the handle of the
water pitcher is
enormous as the
sun comes through
the kitchen win-
dow I think again
of the murder of
Caesar and down in
the sink are three
dirty water glasses

the doorbell rings
and I stand deter-
mined not to answ-
er.

Drooling Madness at St. Liz

Sherri told me they had been
lovers in there
but she had gotten off course
waylaid a few weeks or so
and she showed me the place
in the Cantos where he wrote
about it:
Ez was grabbing the bars
looking at the moon and
asking,
where is she tonight?

one would think a wise man
would see past that but the
fact is that some wise men
become that because
of their feelings.

anyhow, so you see
the old boy got hooked on
the trivialities of the flesh
just like the rest of us.

I kept wanting to ask her
about the new lover she had been
with but since she didn't tell
me I figured it was about
usual. which doesn't mean it
isn't all right. wasn't.

actually, though, at times
like that I think mostly of
yellow lampshades & also of
toilets flushing. especially
when it happens to me. Ezra,
though, I think was more
beautiful and kind.

not much singing

I have it, looking to my left, the cars of this
night coming down the freeway toward
me, they never stop, it's a consistency
which is rather miraculous, and now a
night bird unseen in a tree outside
sings to me, he's up late and I am too.
my mother, poor thing, used to say,
"Henry, you're a night owl!"
little did she know, poor poor thing,
that I would close 3,000 bars . . .
"LAST CALL!"
now I drink alone on a second floor,
watching freeway car headlights,
listening to crazy night birds.
I get lucky after midnight, the gods
talk to me then.
they don't say very much but they
do say enough to take some of the
edge off of the day.

the mail has been bad, dozens of
letters, most of them stating,
"I know you won't answer this but . . ."
they're right: the answers for myself
must come first
I have suffered and still suffer many
of the things they complain
of.
there's only one cure for life.
now the night bird sings no more.
but I still have my freeway
headlights
and these hands
these same hands
receiving thoughts from my alcohol-
damaged brain.

the pleasure of unseen
company
climbs these walls,
this night of gentle quiet and
a not very good poem
about it.

MICHAEL BURKARD ▪ ▪ ▪ ▪ ▪ ▪ ▪ ▪ ▪ ▪ ▪ ▪

The Personal Histories ("More Darkness")

Gogol (his namesake)
used to make the telephone calls
during the name day parties.
There were plural waters
upon his brain
and a lunar landscape
of darkness and craters
in the back of his head.

"Hello, Althea? I hate it here.
No one cares for me.
Well, no, I haven't helped matters any."

When the landlord told him
to close the drapes during winter days
(the sun would make the apartment
that hot)

he regretably did not understand
this meant "more darkness."
Gogol's not in need of "more darkness."

One day in this curtain drawn darkness
he wrote: "Dear Althea,
I hate it here. I offer you my breath
and my vague depression. I offer you
my white box where I used to keep my beach stones.
I wanted to repeat the word "smoke"
to you, so often repeated
you would worry if solace wasn't offered.
The repetition went something like this:

I've given you the forgotten smoke . . ."

Gogol couldn't carry it out.

That winter his curtains always
remained drawn,
and no one came to him.
By nightfall on almost any night
he had taken to rearranging his beach stones
in various places in the apartment.

Gogol told me he did sometimes go for evening
strolls by himself, and sometimes felt
good enough to glide to some private windows
and watch the personal histories which
were being accounted for. He likened the strolls
to a stone without wind, fog without wind,
and the histories there
like his footfalls in the grass.

Foolish Thing

I tried repeating, which feels now
like a foolish thing. The night is
snowless, warm, oddly bright: bright
lapping like identity of water, simple

simple water. I heard a woman say
'the desire to destroy myself
was lifted from me; from that moment
on I desired life.' Gradually: she
began to embrace the difficult, it

was in this where desire breathed
from a different mouth, and the nose
was snowless, or the snow was calm,
calm enough for a life to breathe.

Often I feel like I am still insane.
But I breathe now, and the hours aren't lead,
aren't eaten, the old images slowly shed
their skin, my skin. I live in a house
which isn't mine: the sea's across the street,

stars are out, the tide is high, hide.
Hide my breath the foolish thing says,
there is no breath in repetition. I am
still, I am still.

My Aunt and the Sun

When I was farthest away from my children
I was the most childish.
And I could hear the bells say so.
I could hear the selfish range
of their composition.

My aunt brutalized me on Sundays:
silence, enforced silence, only the stones
dropping from the black leaf of her carriage.
Upon my head, upon my head.
She walked and she walked to the white river,
so-called because it was private to a child,
and she was a child.

The sun is always a child which no one
ever dreams. Nothing sustained in the dream
or the sun. It is the thought of the sun
and the nothing sustaining which forced the man
to ask, "Did you ever dream of the sun?"
    Sun: the sun is redundant desire.

I was the most childish redundancy you've ever seen.
My aunt composes the formula for a bell.
The fish are bruised by nets which catch them.
The leaf is on the water, the river flows.

The Dogs on the Cliffs

They are there
after having long departed
from their memory, and whether there is any memory
of a master is hard to say, for they were
born into an island
which was poor, could not support the birth of dogs
except with the whiteness of the tourists'
faces, a whiteness like the wallets
and purses, the loose change of the lives
which brought them and their own memories to this island,
summer after summer,
injury after jury.

The jury on the island says this:
the dogs may roam each summer
til it is obvious they are a menace,
chickens attacked, an occasional tourist
attacked, lingering now in small
pathetic packs. And thus they are herded
to the sea from the cliffs above,
enticed perhaps by some ice memory
(surely the local islanders don't entice them fully
with a little meat, are they that hungry?)

—an ice memory of the dogs of the year before,
and the fall before that, in the month of September,
upon an island which despises animals anyway—

and the dogs are brought to the cliffs and herded off.
To the sea. To the rocks and the sea below.
It is a long drop, even for a dog.

•

I did not so much live upon this island
as hear this story, more vividly told, with a particular
dog which followed a particular man—the dog even did a double
take one summer—when the man reappeared on Eos after departing
for a month to Athens—and the dog followed the double take—
just seeing the face twice—with following.

So the story is not mine, but I feared the man would never tell it—
though versions of stories like this must abound.

I can hear the stories on the cliffs,
I can hear the lamps wailing sometime
much later in the winter, in winter

when the animals are dead, all of them, all
the past times down below
near the rocks off Eos.

Now the ice memory wakes: the jury reports
in a different dream
that the town and the villas are sold out
already for still another summer,
another history for history,
another past
for past.

Today, after only
glancing
at the morning paper

I thought of that phrase
history repeating itself,

thought if history repeats itself
it is still the same history,
more repetition, no
history

because it's the same history
the same hysteria
which could include even me
again.

[I have a silence in the rain]

I have a silence in the rain
and I have my horses.
I have my shoes and I have my name,

the beginning of the street
and the street downtown, between the canyons,
and the trees which shine my shoes.

I have a silence and an end,
an end which is not critical,
not the weight. The houses bloom

and they've never been mine,
but there were beings in the rooms,
there were souls to each of the houses,

each of the rooms,
and this extended to the prison of the city
and the prison of the sea, the towns

there, by that sea, at that end
which was narrow
and itself. It was so much itself—

that end—
that I was uneasy there, a facade
it seemed, I had a reputation

for going nowhere.
I was always elsewhere
and that was why. I extended my weight

to my shoes and the few trees
and the horses—and the old closed motel
on the thing I called the bluff, the motel

closed for years, staring in the terribly pink sunset
with its pink vases
and pink doors. And the silence which stared.

The horses were below.
The horses were weight, in the evening
they shined too.

2 Poems on the Same Theme

Unlike my friend John I like the painting entitled
Biography: it is a little one-sided with primitivism
but I forgive it that. Still, I've always been
haunted by John's silence about this one, an absolute
silence. A student says the painting was stolen
from his own idea: and I am wondering if mentioning
this could be construed as another steal: the snow
is falling—stolen: the song the parakeet is
chirping is for all I know stolen, stolen among
numerous songs which have passed cage to cage,
gene to gene, without anyone calling thief.
Bags of stone are beside the railroad bridge, the
train is standing still waiting for the workers
to clear from the bridge: a light snow is falling
in the painting: the workers have dots for eyes:
near another bag of stone the woman still walks
along, offended years later still by the death on

her way to her wedding. The husband-to-be and the
parents of the long-awaiting-bride stolen from her
in a foreign country, Germany I think. Or so the
story goes. She goes, the painting goes, the weak
like me forget it and drive into the country.
John is dreaming we've boarded the train again,
dreaming who will get off first, and where, when.

○

My friend John has
never said a peep about
my poem Biography. A
student of mine says
I stole it from her.
I received a registered
piece of me guaranteeing
I hear her opening argument
and another letter later.
I did not answer this
latter letter. I thought
I tried stealing a tone
from Montale, or how I
heard him. The biography
the student says was
Modigliani, the subject
of mine is female. This
is beginning to sound like
a hollow offense. John's
silence feels like a key
to a refrain of silence:
so I am looking at a
reproduction of Grandma
Moses' In the Park, the
obvious silence of the couple
about to cross the covered
bridge on foot, and the eternal
silence of the river and
the house above the couple
and the river. I wish I
were dreaming of John and
I boarding a train again,
who would get off first,
where, when. And I am
wondering this Christmas
morning in 1985 what the
walker in Clinton New York
is doing: the story goes
her husband-to-be and

her parents disembarked
for death the day of
her wedding in a foreign
country, Germany I think.
I tried writing about her
twice, a poem called
Moonlike Leaf and another
called Out There. Neither
addressed her fully.

Breathless Storm

10:30. A long and thin
railway building's
been converted into an
antique shop. Snow's

predicted. There are 7
chimneys she can count
from looking southwest
from the hotel window,

only 2 if she sits to
look southeast. No one
is coming. There is a
"Beware of the Dog"

sign on a shed and
she thinks, unfairly,
of herself when she
reads this and stares

upon it. Life is not
so much reflection
she reflects as a
study in insistence,

yours, mine, and the
random scope of all
the other lives out
there which also,

it seems, find their
way home to studies
in insistence too.
The screams, the fortunes,

the meanderings of the
life in its ordinary
branches, tributaries
that someone else

conveniently pees upon.
Oh well. I am
excited by the prospect
of traveling alone

to Nova Scotia
Canada, home of
my mother's birth,
for I have never

seen it in winter.
But I will not go
there feeling like this,
no, I will not knock

upon my sister's door
upon the way there
nor my mother's sister's
door on Crescent Ave.

I will see them instead
in another life, where
the moon wanes there
as well and the sun

waxes hot in summer
and the solstice and
equinox are demarcations
even in a land called heaven.

Meditation Brought About by George Bogin's Translation of Jules Supervielle's Poem "The Sea"

Something in the letter found in the box, and something just out there in the winter white, and something in the sky, something less than discontent: sheer light blue through one window, at least for now—something in the way you got out of her, I mean got out of the relationship, something in the way you got out of the relationship truly neglected the vision of the nova you then brought to George (the nova in the sky, not the car. And not the "no cars in the sky" which the kindergarten teacher actually warned her class about before the little ones began drawing. Not the nova car I wrecked and was lucky to have not placed in the sky along with myself. Appropriate white man constellation: el nova in el sky). And something in my endless awkwardness when George would tell me I had more feeling than any of the others, I was ashes with feeling . . . and my awkwardness with this was not unlike the awkward and incomplete version I or I-and-Lisa brought to George about the sky nova flash, incredible distance / closeness / vastness / vanishing witnessed by us the night before

—something in the torn pieces of blue paper the little girl has typed upon, a letter to her friend she calls it, but also angry at the friend she says for not wearing a dress the two of them as later the letter tries to explain had planned . . . ashes with feeling . . .

Something, something, but you can't put your finger on it. The old postcard? The postcard which you referred to as "pre-car." The postcard you felt this dis-ease looking at but kept anyway in an isolated place where you were bound to see it again, by itself, and yet not quite see anything or anything you could be sure of because of this dis-ease. Ashes with feeling? Another version of it? As a writer with more feeling than the others, isn't there a pressure upon you to know what you are talking about, or at least to not know in some manner which would reveal itself as acceptance, not pretended but felt? Is this the feeling, to be a few moments from it, and still feel it?

What about George's feelings? Doesn't it take a feeler to recognize another feeler? What about Lisa's feelings? What about another George, who walked into the recovery meeting like he was a friend of Al Capone's, appropriately oblivious. Maybe there's a planet named Capone? Lisa?

Remember Bob looking at a card you also had, and unlike this village-corner-card of dis-ease this other card is a corner you like, ashes with feeling again, but Bob looks at the card for just a moment and sees a person/figure walking on the street and you had never for these years and all this looking seen this figure. The figure is all but gone, erased, erased ashes, but Bob sees it, Bob with his magic eye . . . a retina with more feeling than the others . . . an iris with more feeling than the others . . . Is that it? Is that him? Who is he?

George Bogin translated many poems by Jules Supervielle. Today I am looking at a copy of wonderful old IRONWOOD #23, Michael Cuddihy's magazine, incredible Michael Cuddihy with incredible retina and iris and ashes. I am saying to myself let's look at some of the poems in this issue because since I had a few in there myself I probably never really took a close look at anyone else's—and some of this feels true—or it could be my bad memory for poems which has never improved despite anyone's feelings or retina—or it is a sideways memory which remembers a life just to the side of everyone's poems, not unlike (again) ashes, or the retina dashing off to another place it accounts for, sometimes truly, sometimes counterfeit. I start to read a poem by Carruth, I read a part of it, a favorite reading habit of mine, just parts, especially with favorite poets . . . you wouldn't think this was true, but it is, if I am reading you line by line all the time I am probably feeling trapped, and with more feeling than the others this is a major turnoff, not unlike turning off not only the road but the wrong road at the wrong time . . .

I start to read a poem by Carruth, I read part of it, and then I see George's translations are in there, and I look at two and feel this slight turning going on. Something in me knows this feeling.

—But is there a wrong time? Is there a wrong road? Is there a wrong sea? A wrong sea . . .

In a few moments or a minute or two I am moving small boxes, cigar boxes. The house I am living in is being torn up upstairs, and I am moving small boxes, still another box. And knowing it is letters I decide to look inside and pretty quickly among about one hundred or more pieces of paper I come across accidentally a letter from Ruth Bogin written just after George's death. And now I am wanting to drive somewhere, this feeling of slight turning is turning into trapped, and I don't care if it's a wrong road or a wrong road to a wrong sea at anytime: I want to come up with an excuse to get moving, to get away from something, with me more feeling than the others, me with more ashes in my retina than the others. Me with endless vacations at wrong seas.

But a part of me like a part of someone's poem is saying just stay still and sit with these poems/translations of George's and Jules's—and there is one translation entitled "The Sea" and I don't read the whole thing but the first half or so is very unlike any poem or drawing about the sea I have ever heard—the poem is on to something, and as I say that now I also have this sense that the poem "about" the sea has also put me on to myself, and George, and a recollection of many things, and people I have not met, and people I would deeply like to see again, people when I got to know George a little bit, and Lisa, and whatever that was in the sky.

And I have some vague memory of a telephone call to George when I received from him a book of his own poems, making the call from the Waters' house, from the warm climate, and I have this continual sense that his book-title included the word "wave." The sense is now a word which is a continuum, a wave. And George's face merges with Arthur's, as it has before, and I see George's wife, Ruth, and his daughter, Nina, neither of whom I have ever seen.

Weather

to Jo and Ed

When I used to stay at my brother's
I would turn once a visit inside a
book called *Weather* and look for the
green and dark green and whitish and
little yellow little drawing of what
was intended to be a parent and a child
walking in the rain under an umbrella.
It was a place from the place nobody
minded and the rain could remind me
that I would be back at my brother's
again, even if it was a world I resisted
or wanted to resist. Because I would
have to sleep on the couch even after
all these years, and it was the same
couch even after all these years, and
notes and objects and formulae from
the past and the family past would always
give me a tinge of suffocation, if only
just at first. Until the second night,
when so tired from teaching and everyone
else's agendae during a day I would be
glad I only had to drive nine miles before
driving another two hundred and seventy
"home." And my brother would not be
asking for much if anything at all, and
I would be on the couch knowing I had
a slight feel for why blood is thicker
than water. And I ended this unexpectedly
even for myself, and was sort of stunned
for years for having given up this job.
Probably because I had something off
or wrong somewhere about my mother or
my brother or my blood or my teaching.

HAYDEN CARRUTH   ▪ ▪ ▪ ▪ ▪ ▪ ▪ ▪ ▪ ▪ ▪ ▪ ▪ ▪ ▪

The Cows at Night

The moon was like a full cup tonight,
too heavy, and sank in the mist
soon after dark, leaving for light

faint stars and the silver leaves
of milkweed beside the road,
gleaming before my car.

Yet I like driving at night
in summer and in Vermont:
the brown road through the mist

of mountain-dark, among farms
so quiet, and the roadside willows
opening out where I saw

the cows. Always a shock
to remember them there, those
great breathings close in the dark.

I stopped, taking my flashlight
to the pasture fence. They turned
to me where they lay, said

and beautiful faces in the dark,
and I counted them—forty
near and far in the pasture,

turning to me, sad and beautiful
like girls very long ago
who were innocent, and sad

because they were innocent
and beautiful because they were
sad. I switched off my light.

But I did not want to go,
not yet, nor knew what to do
if I should stay, for how

in that great darkness could I explain
anything, anything at all.
I stood by the fence. And then
very gently it began to rain.

Paragraph 23

In filthy Puerto Rico there lives a bird with no
legs and transparent wings, a somewhat small
bird whose flight is awkward and slow
yet it spends its whole

existence in flying. Luckily it knows how
to ride high currents above the eagles, hawks, crows
and all the preying host that seeks
its life continually. As long as it keeps
above them, soaring between them and the sun,
it cannot be seen, partly
because the predators are blinded by the exceeding shine
of brightness, partly because the heart
of the bird is the only thing that shows, a speck
in its transparency. High it flies, flies, flies, hungry and hurt,
until at last it falls forever on filthy Puerto Rico. And the name of this bird is
    blank.

Paragraph 36

So I was past caring   so many, too many men,
so many children /   body broken, slack
as the spirit   skin & bone
like a burlap sack
with a litre of rice in the bottom.
                                No one
wants lugging that around,
                            let the others run,
I said, and sat right down, there
where I was, and looked up into the air
to see it coming /
                    and when it came (that spout
of flaming jelly)   I cursed
and quickly made a great sound: no shriek, no shout,
more like an enormous croak—the worst
I had ever heard.
                    For once then   *once*   I knew
what I had done was the most
                            and maybe the first
human thing I had ever been permitted to do.

Essay on Death

1. The prisoner ran forward. First his head
was lopped off by one sergeant swinging
        a scimitar, and secondly his neck-
            stump was seared

by another sergeant with a glowing iron plate.
Then the next prisoner ran. And the next. How far

can a man run after he has been
decapitated? The Emir

and the Sultan had a wager and were pleased to see
one prisoner run almost to the courtyard gate,
to freedom. Then the Potentates
lost interest and the

wager lapsed. But now think of those runners! Did
their bodies really strive for freedom without
their heads? Did the severed heads
cry out in shame?

Our horror takes us only to the instant
when they ran in front of the first of the two
sergeants. Then ignorance begins.
And yet I see that

courtyard, I see those bodies running atilt
with neck-stumps spraying blood (in spite
of cauterization), I see the twitching
corpses. Here in this

apartment complex in Syracuse where I live
I look out on our courtyard where the Christmas
lights are shining in every window
and strung in the little

trees, lighting the snow. Might this be another
carnage? Are the two courtyards connected
by anything more than their pro-
pinquity in

my mind? I have offered one candle, which I
believe is enough for an old man. But truly these
gleamings here are peaceful, they
are quiet, they

are no violence. Beyond the corruptions of faith
and of every kind of faith, which makes us still
eager for the bright impossible rationality
which the people of the caves

thought they had glimpsed when they knew that they
had minds, are all these lights of love. The stars
have come down to earth. When I walked out
to the mailbox, carrying

a letter for my daughter, who lives three thousand
miles away in a country of dessicated, smoldering
grass, though Christmas lights are shining
in her town too,

I walked with my stick on the crusted snow, and I
looked back up at my window, my one candle
in this extraordinary festival
of renewing light,

and I was touched by it. Through a narrow
passage between these buildings, up the shallow
flagged steps, out by the swimming
pool I walked,

and saw there in the mulberry tree a spray
of little lights as if flung from Saint Lucy's
little hand, lights set there
however

by the management, whose revenues will not
thereby increase one penny. And so various
they were!—all these glitterings,
these scintillations,

like stars, or like minerals rather, risen from earth,
ruby, emerald, diamond, sapphire, gold, and silver,
a splendor in the shabby suburban
winter, created

by us all for the sake of beauty and to praise
our knowledge of the turning season. Then this
is what we know? Not what those cut-off
grimacing heads

were thinking, nor how those Potentates in easy evil
could command those men to run the murderous
gauntlet; but rather that I walked
through lights of love

to send my loving father-message to a woman
far away. And what we do not know is precisely
death. In the heart of the light
is darkness and Christmas

is a mystery. Trudging back down the shallow
steps, down through the shimmering lights, I feel
an "irresistible gravitation,"
as Proust called it,

drawing me downward always, down the steps,
down into the ground, so that my feet become shadowy
    in earth, downward through loam and grit
        as if I were wading

in earth-flesh. My tread becomes slow and urgent,
and my window, as I approach, shining its small light
    in the multitude, seems to reveal
        behind my candle

shapes I do not recognize that remind me
of things I cannot remember, things that occur
    and withdraw in the windowframe as if
        at the edge of knowledge.

2. Once my friend Ray the Carver spoke of the
"relentless logic" of waiting, waiting. Is time then
    logical? At all events it resists
        refutation. When

the terrorist exploded his bomb by the ticket counter
in the air terminal, who was terrorized? Those broken
    and wistful corposes lying there
        in death and dismantlement,

or all of us who are looking at them? Carl Jung
told us that the first time he died he went zooming
    off into space where he saw a castle
        floating, warmly

lighted and full of comfort, which he presumed
to be his destination. Romantic boy! Let him
    look at the airport on Christmas
        Eve. Beyond that,

could enough castles exist for all the dead,
even in space? In fact the brain cells of the
    severed heads do continue
        to dream a little.

And the grimaces (that Mme. Defarge noted with such
satisfaction)? They may be only those of the violinist,
    Allen Tate, whose mouth uncontrollably
        twists in sensual

concentration. In the graduate student's story
an adolescent buried a kitten up to its neck
    in the ground and ran over it with a
        lawnmower.

When? In 1930 a boy shot his BB gun
from an attic window at a chickadee in the maple,
    not thinking he could hit it, and the bird
        closed its eyes

and leaned forward slowly and fell to the ground.
The boy ran down two flights of stairs and took
    the bird in his hands, but it was dead,
        which was enough

death in his life, he decided. And in 1944
Polish farmers stood in their pastures watching
    the trainloads of Jews go by, and they
        shook their fists

and made the throat-slitting gesture and laughed.
They laughed. And long ago Alexander, who was also
    blond, ordered the city of Susia
        "put to the sword"—

and how did they do it? Did the Macedonian
soldiers post themselves on each streetcorner
    and line up the citizens and stick them
        in their bellies

with dull bronze sabers? The shrieking, the blood,
the long agonies. Why did the soldiers and boys and
    Polish farmers do these things?
        What did they think

about death? What of their own deaths to come?
Why do people gather at the site of an accident,
    looking down at the victim who oozes
        on the pavement? Are they

fascinated merely by the mystery? Are they
envious, recognizing the one who has passed beyond
    death, who no longer must face it?
        It's true, a joy

is in it, joy in the power of killing, even
on television. But nothing is known. Killer
    and killed whirl in a stupid vortex of
        ignorance. No

story any more, no tale, no adventure. The three
bears have gone to work for Disneyland,
    and Goldilocks committed suicide
        in 1962.

Brains, bones, blood, synapses, little electrical
currents—but where do the souls go? Yes,
      when you say you love me, the tension
          and rapid heartbeat

and waves of my mind are measurable on the graph.
"Well, I'm a mighty tight woman," the night nurse
      sang, "oh, I'm a real tight woman." And also
          in a dark abandoned

house I hear the intimations nearby, the rustlings,
the ghost-ideas. Basta! Only the blues remain.
      "I dreamed I was standing on 18th and Vine,
          yes, I dreamed

I was standing, baby, on 18th and Vine,
and I shook hands with Piney Brown and I
      could hardly keep from cryin'." That's
          the way it is.

Overhead now I hear the police helicopter—
arrumpt, arrumpt—and its powerful spotlight
      sweeps across our courtyard, obliterating
          our Christmas lights

in a greenish brilliance like an exploding nebula
whose relentless logic reaches us eventually,
      eventually. The terrorized are all
          who wait, everywhere.

3. Age, the romanticists say, is vision and simpli-
city and brightened consciousness, but I say, Fraud
      fraud, blinded by the light. Even
          the trees are reeling.

4. Inside again, I switched on my lamp, and found
only my Japanese wind-carp and my Hindu
      cow-bells and the other strangely assorted
          objects I have

gathered over the years, which I know well.
No evil. And yet they are mysterious to me.
      I go to my chair. How often I have sat
          here in this cage

of light, reading, pretending to read, laboring
to read—sometimes to write, to make lines
      of language, glyphs on a page—but death
          has occupied me.

I imagine a pair of pudgy hands, like my little
grandson's hands but spotted with age, pushing
        against a huge gray leathery limp
                bag of nothing

that fills the room. Pushing. Sometimes in the last
year giddiness has taken me, but not giddiness,
        nothing known or named, a moment
                of being alive so

altered, so abrupt in unexpectedness, that I have
moaned and fallen, the light has sunk down to
        dimness, and in a bewilderment of pain
                and humiliation and

despair, I have seen a stunned iguana sprawling
from my chair onto the carpet, vomiting black
        blood there. Even so I have read
                thousands of books,

a passionate searching, but have found nothing
not a part of knowledge. The iguana is dumb.
        So many pages of marvelous dying,
                but only gibberish

of death. And now from my neighbor's door
across the hall I hear music faintly, voices
        of women singing above deep tones
                of an organ-like wind

over the sea, not commonplace, a moment of great
beauty, and from the shopping plaza half a block
        away comes faintly the cry of a
                siren. Not

commonplace. My light blips. Someone has turned on
a television or perhaps the great grid of energy,
        civilization itself, has faltered far
                away. And my candle

grows a tall flame that flutters and dies and
leaves a rancid smell. In the courtyard
        lights still gleam, the headlights
                of a passing car

make tilting shadows that run along the opposite
wall, running away, and the Christmas lights
        are bright. But not as bright as they were
                a moment ago.

Crucifixion

You understand the colors on the hillside have faded,
      we have the gray and brown and lavender of late autumn,
the apple and pear trees have lost their leaves, the mist
      of November is often with us, especially in the afternoon
and toward evening, as it was today when I sat gazing
      up into the orchard for a long time the way I do now,
thinking of how I died last winter and was revived.
      And I tell you I saw there a cross with a man nailed
to it, silvery in the mist, and I said to him: "Are you
      the Christ?" And he must have heard me, for in his
agony, twisted as he was, he nodded his head affirmatively,
      up and down, once and twice. And a little way off
I saw another cross with another man nailed to it,
      twisting and nodding, and then another and another,
ranks and divisions of crosses straggling like exhausted
      legions upward among the misty trees, each cross
with a silvery, writhing, twisting, nodding, naked
      figure nailed to it, and some of them were women.
The hill was filled with crucifixion. Should I not be
      telling you this? Is it excessive? But I know something
about death now, I know how silent it is, silent, even
      when the pain is shrieking and screaming. And tonight
is very silent and very dark. When I looked I saw
      nothing out there, only my own reflected head nodding
a little in the window glass. It was as if the Christ
      had nodded to me, all those writhing silvery images
on the hillside, and after a while I nodded back to him.

Quality of Wine

This wine is really awful
I've been drinking for a year now, my
retirement, Rossi Chablis in a jug
from Oneida Liquors, the best
I can afford. Awful. But at least
I can afford it, I don't need to go out and beg
on the street like the guys
on South Warren in Syracuse, eyes
burning in their sockets like acid.
And my sweetheart rubs my back when I'm
knotted in arthritis and swollen
muscles. The five stages of death
are fear, anger, resentment, renunciation,
and—? Apparently the book doesn't say
what the fifth stage is. And neither

does the wine. Is it happiness? That's
what I think anyway, and I know I've been
through fear and anger and resentment and at least
part way through renunciation too, maybe
almost the whole way. A slow procedure,
like calling the Medicare office, on hold
for hours and then the recorded voice says, "Hang up
and dial again." Yet the days
hasten, they
go by fast enough. They fucking fly like the wind. Oh,
Sweetheart, Mrs. Manitou of the Stockbridge Valley,
my Red Head, my Absecon Lakshmi of the Marshlights,
my beautiful, beautiful Baby Doll,
let the dying be long.

ANNE CARSON ▪ ▪ ▪ ▪ ▪ ▪ ▪ ▪ ▪ ▪ ▪ ▪ ▪ ▪

8 Poems from "The Truth About God"

My Religion

My religion makes no sense
and does not help me
therefore I pursue it.

When we see
how simple it would have been
we will thrash ourselves.

I had a vision
of all the people in the world
who are searching for God

massed in a room
on one side
of a partition

that looks
from the other side
(God's side)

transparent
but we are blind.
Our gestures are blind.

Our blind gestures continue
for some time until finally
from somewhere

on the other side of the partition there we are
looking back at them.
it is far too late.

We see how brokenly
how warily
how ill

our blind gestures
parodied
what God really wanted

(some simple thing).
The thought of it
(this simple thing)

is like a creature
let loose in a room
and battering

to get out.
It batters my soul
with its rifle butt.

The God Fit

Sometimes God will drop a fit on you.
Leave you on your bed howling.
Don't take it meanly.

Because the outer walls of God are glass.
I see a million souls clambering up the walls on the inside
to escape God who is burning,
untended.

The God Coup

God is a grand heart cut.
On the road where man surges along He may,
as the prophet says,
tarry.

God's Work

Moonlight in the kitchen is a sign of God.
The kind of grief that is a black suction pipe extracting you
from your own navel and which the Buddhists call

"no mindcover" is a sign of God.
The blind alleys that run alongside human conversation
like lashes is a sign of God.

God's own calmness is a sign of God.
The surprisingly cold smell of potatoes or money.
Solid pieces of silence.

From these diverse signs you can see
how much work remains to do.
Put away your grief, it is a mantle of work.

God's Handiwork

The best way to insult God
is to damage your uniqueness,
which God has worked on.

By God

Sometimes by night I don't know why
I awake thinking of prepositions.
Perhaps they are clues.

"Since by Man came Death."
I am puzzled to hear that Man is the agent of Death.
Perhaps it means

Man was standing at the curb
and Death came by.
Once I had a dog

would go with anyone
Perhaps listening for
little by little the first union.

Flexion of God

I have a friend who is red hot with pain.
He feels the lights like hard rain through his pores.
Together we went to ask Isaac.

Isaac said I will tell you the story told to me.
It was from Adam
issued the lights.

From the lights of his forehead were formed all the names of the world.
From the lights of his ears, nose and throat
came a function no one has ever defined.

From the lights of his eyes—but wait—
Isaac waits.
In theory

the lights of the eye should have issued from Adam's navel.
But within the lights themselves occurred
an intake of breath

and they changed their path.
And they were separated.
And they were caught in the head.

And from these separated lights came
what pains you
on its errands (here my friend began to weep) through the world.

For be assured it is not only you who mourn.
Isaac lashed his tail.
Every rank of world

was caused to descend
(at least one rank)
by the terrible pressure of the light.

Nothing remained in place.
Nothing was not captured except
among the shards and roots and matter

some lights
from Adam's eyes
nourished there somehow.

Isaac stopped his roaring.
And my friend by now drowsy as a snake subsided
behind a heap of blueblack syllables.

God's Name

God had no name.
Isaac had two names.
Isaac was also called The Blind.

Inside the dark sky of his mind
Isaac could hear God
moving down a country road bordered by trees.

By the way the trees reflected off God
Isaac knew which ones were straight and tall
or when they carried their branches

as a body does its head
or why some crouched low to the ground in thickets.
To hear how God was moving through the universe

gave Isaac his question.
I could tell you his answer
but it wouldn't help.

The name is not a noun.
It is an adverb.
Like the little black notebooks that Beethoven carried

in his coatpocket
for the use of those who wished to converse with him,
the God adverb

is a one-way street that goes everywhere you are.
No use telling you what it is.
Just chew it and rub it on.

RICHARD CECIL ▪ ▪ ▪ ▪ ▪ ▪ ▪ ▪ ▪ ▪ ▪ ▪ ▪ ▪ ▪ ▪

Apology

The war is fought by soldiers in machines
manufactured by their wives: steel skin,
for example, impervious to a caress.
But I am single. I line up with conscripts.
I'm issued sleep confiscated from a civilian
in a safe country. I'm handed a photograph
of his lover to tape inside my locker.
I'm marched to a bed too narrow for her
and me and him together, though he lies
inside me, though she's very slender.
How heavy this green blanket
lies against my neck! How cold this rifle!
I'm told the dream which he surrendered,

half in one ear, half in the other,
about Alaska. But it twists inside me.
Which of us is wolf? Which caribou?
Which the tundra? Nobody volunteers his throat,
his appetite, or his cold white isolation
for the sake of peace to anybody else tonight.
We circle on the snow, but the snow drifts over.

I wake beside you thousands of mornings later
when the sergeant shakes my shoulder
to ask if I want a kiss. If it seems too rough,
too desperate for one night's separation
with only sleep between us, excuse me,
there was a war lost and almost a soldier
with it, not in the jungle with the rest,
but solitary, hunted, on the ice.

Threnody for Sunrise

Please, when you ask me in this dream
distracting you from the tapping sound of rain
against your opened screen, why we dress
so lightly for your dream's cold wind, listen
carefully to my answer. It will be scrambled,
half-drowned by the rattling of your pane.
You'll have to lean completely off your balance
toward my face, grasping my thin lapels.

I think, at the altitude that we'll meet,
my suit of customary black, your blanket,
will be less cold and strange and useless
than the formal greatcoats made of clouds
we wore in dreamless sleeps. They dragged behind,
erasing footprints with their swallow tails.
How often you brushed against me in the dark
looking for sleep's exit! You'd wake, forget

that the clear divisions of day from night
cage you in two adjoining soundproof cells.
If one seems better furnished and better lit,
think how spacious, how possible to hide in,
how few the regulations enforced in sleep.
I've watched you lounging in the vestibule
waiting for the gate to open or to shut
and thought—what if the lock sticks?

Wouldn't you prefer the dream, the wings?
I wish I could have asked before tonight

or that the rain would change to snow, reseal
your window's cracks to block the gray dawn
that's just about to drag across your face.
Please don't press a mirror to your mouth
before I draw the sheet over it—
just hold the light, the heat, the breath.

Threnody for Sunset

It's five o'clock. Someone's taped my name out
above my timecard's slot. I search the rack,
touching hands that reach around me deftly
punching in or out—dayshift, nightshift,
a card between each steady thumb and finger.
My hand trembles because there's nothing in it.
I squeeze the cold iron handle of my lunchbox
to stop the rattle in its empty thermos.

Tonight, there seem to be a hundred Chevys
parked where I always park my Chevy.
I choose the one my key fits. It starts,
coughs, and stops, and will not start again,
its gauges stuck on empty, on cold, on zero
in the faint green dashboard lights that flicker,
overload their fuses, and go out.
Didn't I fill my gas tank just this morning?

I walk reluctantly to the locked gate,
whose attendant seems to be asleep.
He doesn't stop me, he doesn't wave me through.
I wait. It's almost dark. Red clouds reflect
against the eastern window of the plant.
Through it, when I squint and stare obliquely,
I see the outline of my black machine
against the blacker shadow of the skyline.

I see a light that might be the first star
or the bedroom lamp from my distant high apartment—
my wife undressing for her bath, singing—
appear inside the dimming clouds' reflection.
I walk toward it, but when I press my face
against the chilly pane, it disappears,
just as she drops her nightgown. I see, instead,
a fading smudge of breath against the glass,

which blocks, for half a second, the constellation
that fills the window of my night replacement.

Wild Provoke of the Endurance Sky

Be uncovered!
Hoe with look life! Sun rises.
Rice of suffering. Dawn
          in mud,
this is roof   my friend
O country   o cotton   drag
of the wild provoke,
there's a thousand years   How are
you growing?
No better to in a stranger.
Shack, village,
              brother,
wild provoke of the endurance sky!

Caught in the Swamp

High is the dark clouds
and the harbor and
the egg as the antelope
frightens us through the
swampy harbor. We burn
our food, and the egg
has a seal of abandon
              in its blueness.
Which are we humming at last?
It is the running of the shiny antelope
we smell, not love.
Is it the bed?

White Fish in Reeds

Hold me
till only,   these are my
              clothes   I sit.
Give them   more songs than
the flower
These are my clothes to a
boat   Streets
have no feeling
Clouds move

Are people woman?
Who calls you
on a sun shirt sleeves down his ecstasy
The hair you are
becoming? Mmmm

That this temperate is where
I feed   The sheep sorrel flower is
And I want to
be
among all things
that bloom
Although I do not
love flowers

Grow

I fight and fight.
I wake up.
The oasis is now dark.
I cannot hear anything.

The wind is felt
and the stars and the sand
so that no one
will be taken by pain.

I sit next to the bushes,
Hercules couldn't move me,
and sleep and dream.

The sand, the stars are solid
in this sleeping oasis,
alone with the desert and
the metaphysical cigarette.

Data

To indicate is to
turn off   in a world
away from ease.
Rotating in a mean format of oxygen.
First make and then
made all alone until
the end of a blank.
The smoke opens up and out

comes a word
in a new storage of love.
Turning off or
turning on the calcareous bases
we find our selves in
are set there by IT.
Divine and more
divine each day, no control,
but in another world.

TOM CLARK ▪ ▪ ▪ ▪ ▪ ▪ ▪ ▪ ▪ ▪ ▪ ▪ ▪ ▪ ▪ ▪

As the Human Village Prepares for Its Fate

While everything external
dies away in the far off
echo of the soul
    still there's a mill wheel turning
it is like a good
kind of tiredness in
the moment before sleep
    by some distant stream
a note of peace
in a life which
will never be peaceful
    as the daylight fades
the dream disintegrates
but the shadow holds
no power
    over what's about to happen

[Before dawn there you lie]

Before dawn there you lie
sleepwalking circles in
your particularly nil
corner of eternity where

each routine circuit of
the mind plants another
iron pillar of thought around
which the next circuit's routed;

no change, no relief appears;
then, with kick from ancient
energy of sun coming
up somewhere, sleep—sent to release

the hapless circuit traveler
from his pains—bears the
next instant into dream
fields of freedom; and life

happens to you all over again
in a way that, outside the moon cavern,
cannot be spoken of,
or thought, or named.

Time

2500 years Before Proust
Xerxes overthrew the stalwart
Lacedaemonians at Thermopylae.
He built a bridge of boats, allowed
His anima her autonomy and
His prow to be cut through by her armada,
Carving out a dark continent of desire
To identify with the object's body
That lasted 2500 years.
Through her nothingness there flowed
An invisible current. He sacrificed
Himself before her in an effort to
Recapture all the points of space she had
Ever occupied. It was vain—and when he took to
Thrashing the sea of events with rods
In an absurd attempt to punish
The engulfing of his treasure
Fate lost patience with his act,
His fleet was destroyed at Salamis
The same year he pillaged Athens.

On the Beach

The storm has ended and death steps back
Into the waters once more. All our troubles
Are behind us once and for all.
The moon looks down in single glory.
The apocalyptic view of the world

Supposes things do not repeat themselves.
But they do. And they do. And they do.
The sky clouds up. A new storm comes on.
Apocalyptic thinking presumes
All this has never happened before
And will never happen again. I know,
As the moon beams down on the photo-plankton,
All this will never happen again, too.
Wisdom is cold and to that extent stupid.

LUCILLE CLIFTON ∎ ∎ ∎ ∎ ∎ ∎ ∎ ∎ ∎ ∎ ∎ ∎ ∎

shapeshifter poems

1

the legend is whispered
in the women's tent
how the moon when she rises
full
follows some men into themselves
and changes them there
the season is short
but dreadful   shapeshifters
they wear strange hands
they walk through the houses
at night   their daughters
do not know them

2

who is there to protect her
from the hands of the father
not the windows which see and
say nothing   not the moon
that awful eye   not the woman
she will become with her
scarred tongue   who   who   who   the owl
laments into the evening   who
will protect her   this   prettylittlegirl

3

if the little girl lies
still enough
shut enough

hard enough
shapeshifter may not
walk tonight
the full moon may not
find him here
the hair on him
bristling
rising
up

4

the poem at the end of the world
is the poem the little girl breathes
into her pillow   the one
she cannot tell   the one
there is no one to hear   this poem
is a political poem   is a war poem   is a
universal poem but is not about
these things   this poem
is about one human heart   this poem
is the poem at the end of the world

[here is another bone to pick with you]

here is another bone to pick with you
o mother whose bones i worry for scraps,
nobody warned me about daughters;
how they bewitch you into believing
you have thrown off a pot that is yourself
then one night you creep into their rooms and
their faces have hardened into odd flowers
their voices are choosing in foreign elections and
their legs are open to strange unwieldy men.

[cruelty. don't talk to me about cruelty]

cruelty. don't talk to me about cruelty
or what i am capable of.

when i wanted the roaches dead i wanted them dead
and i killed them. i took a broom to their country

and smashed and sliced without warning
without stopping and i smiled all the time i was doing it.

it was a holocaust of roaches, bodies,
parts of bodies, red all over the ground.

i didn't ask their names.
they had no names worth knowing.

now i watch myself whenever i enter a room.
i never know what i might do.

the lost women

i need to know their names
those women i would have walked with
jauntily the way men go in groups
swinging their arms, and the ones
those sweating women whom i would have joined
after a hard game to chew the fat
what would we have called each other laughing
joking into our beer? where are my gangs,
my teams, my mislaid sisters?
all the women who could have known me,
where in the world are their names?

sorrow song

for the eyes of the children,
the last to melt,
the last to vaporize,
for the lingering
eyes of the children, staring,
the eyes of the children of
buchenwald,
of viet nam and johannesburg,
for the eyes of the children
of nagasaki,
for the eyes of the children
of middle passage,
for cherokee eyes, ethiopian eyes,
russian eyes, american eyes,
for all that remains of the children,
their eyes,
staring at us,   amazed to see
the extraordinary evil in
ordinary men.

january 1991

they have sent our boy
to muffle himself
in the sand. our son
who has worshipped skin,
pale and visible as heaven,
all his life,
who has practiced the actual
name of God,
who knows himself to be
the very photograph of Adam.
yes, our best boy is there
with his bright-eyed sister,
both of them waiting in dunes
distant as Mars
to shutter the dark veiled lids
of not our kind.
they, who are not us, they have
no life we recognize,
no heaven we can care about,
no word for God we can pronounce.
we do not know them,
do not want to know them,
do not want this lying at night
all over the bare stone county
dreaming of desert for the first time
and of death and our boy and his sister
and them and us.

[won't you celebrate with me]

won't you celebrate with me
what i have shaped into
a kind of life? i had no model.
born in babylon
both nonwhite and woman
what did i see to be except myself?
i made it up
here on this bridge between
starshine and clay,
my one hand holding tight
my other hand; come celebrate
with me that everyday
something has tried to kill me
and has failed.

night vision

the girl fits her body in
to the space between the bed
and the wall. she is a stalk,
exhausted. she will do some
thing with this. she will
surround these bones with flesh.
she will cultivate night vision.
she will train her tongue
to lie still in her mouth and listen.
the girl slips into sleep.
her dream is red and raging.
she will remember
to build something human with it.

GILLIAN CONOLEY ▪ ▪ ▪ ▪ ▪ ▪ ▪ ▪ ▪ ▪ ▪ ▪ ▪ ▪

Beckon

Dead cold spots in the air,
others bright and richly colored as opera,

my old dress is worn out,
torn up, dumped,

another thing the mad made.
Saddles laid out to dry,

vowels left up in the air as if something is better
left unsaid as if I could have.

And truth is music's mute half,
a sentence broken into,

the half tone of a husband
waiting alone in a car,

so that only the sun warrants a red mane.
A figure passes quickly

in the ever-unquiet breath
of you, you, you and sometimes me.

The future nude, an absolute night
troubled by how we will live up

to the day's sequence of images in full sail,
as wind folds other things,

and ink branches and conceives.
Last night was floral,

a satin comforter fell
into violence, old

strangely beautiful voices
in the thin thread of my dreams

in the thin thread of my speech.
I was embarrassed because I wanted lines in the face

and the laughter that spills over
to bring me luck's child.

I had a dream like seconal, sleepy rule of birth,
odor of seduction. I had only prayer, prayer

and science. On a street young girls gathered,
loud with nothing to say, as in an attempt to explain a local fire.

Beauty and the Beast

That the transactions would end.

That the rose would open
            (her appearance in a Cyrillic blouse),

leaving the sense
that one had reached for it—

dust gray blue green manifold red and torn,
            his studied performance of a romantic mood.

He is still eating other small beasts.

She is sleeping alone
coiffed in the pleated moments,

only rising to bathe before the mirror
with its grand so what.

But we who have held the book with both hands
and let the syntax shape us

we are not evermore
as mirror or sleep.

In our modern cloven space
events dissolve to the sexual instant,

each of us holding the hairy hand
with thrilling lucidity.

So we never find what we mean
but it flakes off on our hands,

so the pleasures we most desire
go unexpressed,

people of the future will also have

light, fragile conversation
and a hidden cottage with shutters carved,

where each summer we return
with no misgivings, no spectacle—

Nothing to be afraid of.

Only the 16th century air,
making it impossible to breathe more purely.

And she is femaling him.
And he is maling her.

And someone says, the end.
And someone says,

no, this is my body.

The Masters

The photographs were yellow where death is a bidden slow form splitting cells
   though the day
is tremor, open, a red tanager

seen on the way to the hospital like in the foreign thriller
the Burmese monk (the spirit? the unaccountable? what doesn't "fit in?")

draped in scarlet and seen
once, twice, before slipping back into the forest—

I walk inside my body's healthy maze, all my heroines spent and exhausted,
all your masters assholes by now,

between existence and non
the humiliation of a hospital gown, the same wide shoulders

as when we first met and I could hold you and not be defined
by the whole question of I, angry and afraid, a thin, tired radiance—

The ghosts of erotica wanting to know could they still
get a rise out of us,

but we were just a space some others had their eyes on,
our breath, our fumes—

A part of me was putting personal belongings in a plastic bag,
a part of me was pressing against space,

the Fates in the corner hiking their skirts
as I helped you from the bed, a faint, colorless laugh.

The World

It was just a gas station. It was not spectacular carnage.
A woman in the parking lot, red I Love Lucy kerchief, dousing his shirts with
    lighter fluid,
a great love and a paranormal morning.
In the far fields   the aliens arriving, switching off the ignition,
new crisp list of abductees   though the closest we get is the radio.
Cool gray summer morning the first heat making an aura.
Let light. She lights each panel. Fires twisting.
Whatever must seek out its partner and annihilate with it. A great love.
The expansion today is just a gas station. It is not spectacular carnage.
So one has a set of events from which one finds one can't escape   to reach a
    distant observor.
And a star is born.

Red giant, super giant, white dwarf.
We observe a large number of these white dwarf stars.
Giant Sirius, the brightest in the night sky,
dog star. What we could have been had not the star
been present, too much presence emanating
away from us—red the I Love Lucy kerchief draped over the lamp.
A she-ness to the table. Pearls on the bread plate, make-up on the napkin,
a couple of burned-out butts.
(Alien intake valves?)

And come night: a supper club.
High risk behavior in cinemascopic rain.
The heat released in this reaction,
which is like, a controlled hydrogen bomb explosion,
which is like, what makes stars shine.
Boy Pegasus   Boy Mercury   Sister Venus
the stars so compulsively readable   the sun eight light minutes away,
Birth mark. At the red end of the spectrum. Three gold-jacketed overly friendly
    men smiling,
poling before the nymph of a red river   burning in the presence of the floor
    plans.
For the world is one world now   not that you may own your own home.
Sinter me, sister. Threescore skullduggery, endless cradle holding a space open.
Rufous skylark,   tell us off the skiff,
sun up, the next day,   we're looking into a box.
Let's see the world.   Are you coming with me.   What's for dinner.

GREGORY CORSO ■ ■ ■ ■ ■ ■ ■ ■ ■ ■ ■ ■ ■ ■

30th Year Dream

                I dreamed a man unknown to me in a city no
        where on earth   I am the architect of that elsewhere world for sure
            he was tall and a long black beard,   and he stood in a tall hairy
                coat and Polish Rabbi hat he told me 'Christ wants to
                    see you' handing me a piece
            of white paper with an address thereon   I refused it
            happily (or was it smart-alecky) refused it telling him 'Like
                I know where He/he lives,   And away I
        skipped down a winding street I don't remember getting the asphalt
            for and when could I have steam-rollered it?   still
                I am the architect of elsewhere world
                and the way the Lord built this here world
            is the way I, in dreams build . . . I think therefore it is
        or I dream therefore I build (?) Anyway away I skipped into
        an earthless yet familiar direction (where a place is familiar
            to me yet not of earth must mean that I possess recall of all
                these people and streets and buildings created by my
                dream's mind) but soon found myself looking for His
                name on the directories of huge buildings all looking
                        alike deadend lost   O   how   I
        trembled to see the look on my face when I ran back to the tall
            man no more there   that look of a smart-alec struck dumb

with blix-eyed surprise   the agony of self-contempt
woke me up cursing me hitting me spitting on my legs 'Damn
impulsive goon-faced proletariat-Shelley greaseball dopey fuck!
And cried, 'denied . . . denied . . . denied'

DOUGLAS CRASE ▪ ▪ ▪ ▪ ▪ ▪ ▪ ▪ ▪ ▪ ▪ ▪ ▪ ▪ ▪ ▪

There Is No Real Peace in the World

The fact of life is it's no life-or-death matter,
Which is supposed to make it easier to choose. People die,
For sure, and that's a personal apocalypse for them
And a revision of heaven and earth for those "left
To follow after" (as your great-grandfather's obituary would say)
So that a few are always being rearranged on maps
Redrawn by family accident or folly, like separate Europes
After their awful wars. War isn't the easiest metaphor
To go by though, nor, here's the point, is it reliable
Since all the individual hells added up remain exactly
Individual, and whether they blaze like Berlin or not
Are kept in those unassailable bunkers, Born and Died,
Passed in and out of this world, the whole world minus one,
Which never felt the flames nor ever knew. No,
No sooner has one perished than the rest survive,
Which ought to be proof that yes-or-no options aren't final
As they seem to be, except for the problem that the survivor
In our time includes memories out of all proportion to
The experience ahead of him and is intent on living up to them,
On Germany where there's only Idaho. It's inescapable
How history has targeted the tiniest, safest life
With the knowledge that chance and power, unmitigated,
Are always impending out of the godless distance toward it
The way there is always a comet impending toward the earth
And it's only a question now of how close and when,
A recombinant message which has breached the world
And altered the code so thoroughly that issues graceful once
As travel or turning the calendar beget features of flight,
Contortion and alarm instead. If it's in the inheritance
It's in the life, and why should it be disregarded
Because the evidence, the rock-hard impact,
Is still to occur? By then it would be too late
For the genius of worry is to duck the Gotterdammerungs
That might establish its validity, to live close enough

To the border to get away and know where to do it
(Minnesota, Montana, never Niagara Falls), to have
Plenty of birth certificates on hand, a respectable lawyer
And a self-sufficient farm tucked into an unknown corner
Of that same Idaho. But the truth is, as I said, to date
It's only Idaho, a kind of demilitarized zone at most
Where life is interchangeable with the regrets expressed
When it is over, nothing to touch off the silos for.
There's grain in the hopper and wives sweet with biphenyls
Under the skin, or else fatigue—who knows for sure? The cows
Are freshening off schedule again. There is nothing to fear.

CAROLYN CREEDON ▪ ▪ ▪ ▪ ▪ ▪ ▪ ▪ ▪ ▪ ▪ ▪ ▪

litany

Tom, will you let me love you in your restaurant?
i will let you make me a sandwich of your invention and i will eat it and call
it a carolyn sandwich. then you will kiss my lips and taste the mayonnaise and
that is how you shall love me in my restaurant

Tom, will you come to my empty beige apartment and help me set up my
     daybed?
yes, and i will put the screws in loosely so that when we move on it, later,
it will rock like a cradle and then you will know you are my baby

Tom, I am sitting on my dirt bike on the deck. Will you come out from the
     kitchen
and watch the people with me?
yes, and then we will race to your bedroom. i will win and we will tangle up
on your comforter while the sweat rains from our stomachs and foreheads

Tom, the stars are sitting in tonight like gumball gems in a little girl's
jewelry box. Later can we walk to the duck pond?
yes, and we can even go the long way past the jungle gym. i will push you on
the swing, but promise me you'll hold tight. if you fall i might disappear

Tom, can we make a baby together? I want to be a big pregnant woman with a
loved face and give you a squalling red daughter.
no, but i will come inside you and you will be my daughter

Tom, will you stay the night with me and sleep so close that we are one
     person?
no, but i will lay down on your sheets and taste you. there will be feathers
of you on my tongue and then i will never forget you

Tom, when we are in line at the convenience store can I put my hands in your
back pockets and my lips and nose in your baseball shirt and feel the crook
of your shoulder blade?
no, but later you can lay against me and almost touch me and when i go i will
leave my shirt for you to sleep in so that always at night you will be pressed
up against the thought of me

Tom, if I weep and want to wait until you need me will you promise that
    someday
you will need me?
no, but i will sit in silence while you rage. you can knock the chairs down
any mountain. i will always be the same and you will always wait

Tom, will you climb on top of the dumpster and steal the sun for me? It's just
hanging there and I want it.
no, it will burn my fingers. no one can have the sun: its on loan from god.
but i will draw a picture of it and send it to you from richmond and then you
can smooth out the paper and you will have a piece of me as well as the sun

Tom, it's so hot here, and I think I'm being born. Will you come back from
Richmond and baptise me with sex and cool water?
i will come back from richmond. i will smooth the damp spiky hairs from the
back of your wet neck and then i will lick the salt off it. then i will leave

Tom, Richmond is so far away. How will I know how you love me?
i have left you. that is how you will know

ROBERT CREELEY ▪ ▪ ▪ ▪ ▪ ▪ ▪ ▪ ▪ ▪ ▪ ▪ ▪

Buffalo Evening

Steady, the evening fades
up the street into sunset
over the lake. Winter sits

quiet here, snow piled
by the road, the walks stamped
down or shovelled. The kids

in the time before dinner are
playing, sliding on the old ice.
The dogs are out, walking,

and it's soon inside again,
with the light gone. Time
to eat, to think of it all.

Be of Good Cheer

Go down obscurely,
seem to falter

as if walking into water
slowly. Be of good cheer

and go as if indifferent,
even if not.

There are those before you
they have told you.

This House

Such familiar space
out there, the window
frame's locating

focus I could
walk holding
on to

through air from
here to there,
see it where

now fog's close
denseness floats
the hedgerow up

off apparent ground,
the crouched, faint
trees lifting up

from it, and more
close down
there in front

by roof's slope, down,
the stonewall's conjoining,
lax boulders sit,

years' comfortable pace
unreturned, placed
by deliberation and

limit make their
sprawled edge. Here
again inside

the world one thought of,
placed in this aged box
moved here from

family site
lost as us, time's
spinning confusions

are what
one holds on to.
Hold on, dear house,

'gainst the long hours
of emptiness, against
the wind's tearing force.

You are my mind
made particular,
my heart in its place.

The Place

Afternoon it changes
and lifts, the heavy
fog's gone and the wind

rides the field, the flowers,
to the far edge
beyond what's seen.

It's a dream
of something or
somewhere I'd been

or would be, a place
I had made
with you, marked out

with string
years ago. Hannah
and Will are

no longer those
children
simply defined.

Is it weather
like wind blows, and all
to the restless sea?

Parade

Measure's inherent
in the weight,
the substance itself
the person.

How far, how
long, how high,
what's there
now and why.

Cries in the dark,
screams out,
silence,
throat's stuck.

Fist's a weak grip,
ears blotted with echoes,
mind fails focus
and's lost.

Feet first,
feet last,
what difference,
down or up.

You were the shape
I took in the dark.
You the me
apprehended.

Wonders!
Simple fools,
rulers, all of us
die too.

On the way
much happiness
of a day,
no looking back.

Echo

Brutish recall
seems useless now
to us all.

But my teeth you said
were yellow
have stayed nonetheless.

It was your handsomeness
went sour, your
girlish insouciance,

one said.
Was being afraid
neurotic?

Did you talk of it.
Was the high cliff jumpable.
Enough enough?

Fifty years
have passed.
I look back,

while you stand here,
see you there, still
see you there.

The Road

Whatever was else or less
or more or even
the sinister prospect
of nothing left,

not this was anticipated,
that there would be no one
even to speak of it.
Because all had passed over

to wherever they go.
Into the fiery furnace
to be burned to ash.
Into the ground,

into mouldering skin and bone
with mind the transient guest,
with the physical again dominant
in the dead flesh under the stones.

Was this the loved hand, the
mortal "hand still capable of grasping . . ."
Who could speak
to make death listen?

One grows older,
gets closer.
It's a long way home,
this last walking.

Time

How long for the small yellow flowers
ride up from the grasses' bed,
seem patient in that place—

What's seen of all I see
for all I think of it—
but cannot wait, no, *cannot* wait.

The afternoon, a time, floats
round my head, a boat I float on,
sit on, sat on, still rehearse.

I seem the faded register, the misplaced camera,
the stuck, forgotten box, the unread book,
the rained on paper or the cat went out for good.

Nowhere I find it now or even
stable within the givens, thus comfortable to reason,
this sitting on a case, this fact sans face.

SILVIA CURBELO

If You Need a Reason

for Adrian

The way things move sometimes,
light or air,
the distance between
two points, or a map unfolding
on a table, or wind,
never mind sadness.
The difference between sky and room,
between geometry and breath,
the sound we hear
when two opposites finally collide,
smashed bottle, country song,
a bell, any bridge, a connection.
The way some stories end in the middle
of a word,
the words themselves,
galaxies, statuaries, perspectives,
the stone over stone that is life,
never mind hunger.
The way things move, road,
mirror, blind luck. The way
nothing moves sometimes,
a kiss, a glance,
never mind true north.
The difference between history
and desire, between biology
and prayer, any light
to read by, any voice at the bottom
of the stairs, or the sound
of your own name softly, a tiny bone
breaking near the heart.

Tourism in the Late 20th Century

Blue boat of morning and already
the window is besieged
by sky. Grace takes no prisoners
in a town like this. Think of the girl
sipping white burgundy
in the local café, her straw hat

with its pale flower, indigenous
and small as the white roll
she's buttering one philosophical
corner at a time. Even the rain
that falls some afternoons here
is more conceptual, more a tribute
to rain than actual rain falling
on the tulips, a rumor
the wind carries all the way
down the beach.
And would you ask the sea
to explain itself? wrote Kerouac once
in a book about a woman
that was already a metaphor,
rose fading in its glass bowl.
He always knew the world is sentimental,
waving its lacy rags over the face
of the familiar, an architecture
of piano notes and hope.
And what about the girl,
her hat gone, her bread
finished, holding an armful
of tulips in the rain?
She knows each road leads
to other roads, to small towns
with solid names like *Crestview*
and *Niceville,* where even dust has
a genealogy and an address,
as if there's more forever there.
The tulips long to be metaphysical,
closed-mouthed, more faithful
than the rose. Let the windows
take over. Lean out the small
square of the day, past
the rain, past the idea
of rain, to where the sky
is snapshot blue, the sea
blue by association.

JAMES DICKEY ■ ■ ■ ■ ■ ■ ■ ■ ■ ■ ■ ■ ■ ■ ■ ■ ■

Eagles

If I told you I used to know the circular truth
Of the void,
            that I have been all over it building

My height
           receiving overlook

And that my feathers were not
Of feather-make, but broke from a desire to drink
The rain before it falls
           or as it is falling:

If I were to tell you that the rise of any free bird
   Is better

        the larger the bird is,

And that I found myself one of these
Without surprise, you would understand

That this makes of air a thing that would be liberty
Enough for any world but this one,
And could see how I should have gone

     Up and out of all

         all of it

    On feathers glinting

Multitudinously as rain, as silica-sparks around
One form with wings, as it is hammered loose
From rock, at dead
Of classic light: that is, at dead

    Of light.

       Believe, too,
While you're at it, that the flight of eagles has
For use, long muscles steeped only
In escape,
        and moves through
Clouds that will open to nothing

But it, where the bird leaves behind
All sympathy: leaves

The man who, for twenty lines
Of a new poem, thought he would not be shut
From those wings: believed

He could be going. I speak to you from where
I was shook off: I say again, shook
Like this, the words I had
When I could not spread:

When that bird rose

Without my shoulders: Leave my unstretched weight,
My sympathy grovelling
In weeds and nothing, and go
up from the human down-
beat in my hand. Go up without anything

Of me in your wings, but remember me in your feet

As you fold them. The higher rock is
The more it lives. Where you take hold, I will take

That stand in my mind, rock bird alive with the spirit-
life of height,
on my down-thousands
Of fathoms, classic

Claw-stone, everything under.

Weeds

Stars and grass
Have between them a connection I'd like to make
More of—find some way to bring them

To one level any way I can,
And put many weeds in amongst. O woman, now that I'm thinking,
Be in there somewhere! Until now, of the things I made up
Only the weeds are any good: Between them,

Nondescript and tough, I peer,
The backs of my hands

At the sides of my face, parting the stringy stalks.
Tangible, distant woman, here the earth waits for you
With what it does not need
To guess: with what it truly has
In its hands. Through pigweed and sawgrass

Move; move sharply; move in
Through anything,
and hurt, if you have to. Don't come down;

Come forward. A man loves you.

The One

No barometer but yellow
Forecast of wide fields, that they give out
Themselves, giving out they stand
In total freedom,

And will stand and day is down all of it

On an ear of corn. One. The color One:
One, nearly transparent
With existence. The tree at the fence must be kept

Outside, between winds; let it wait. Its movement,

Any movement, is not

In the distillation. Block it there. Let everything bring it
To an all-time stop just short of new
Wind   just short
Of its leaves;
                              its other leaves.

One.

Inside.

Yellow.

All others not.

One.

One.

The Three

I alone, solemn land

                              clear, clean land,

        See your change, just as you give up part
Of your reality:

                    a scythe-sighing flight of low birds
        Now being gone:
                    I, oversouling for an instant

With them,
          I alone
See you as more than you would have

    Be seen, yourself:
               grassland,
    Dark grassland, with three birds higher
    Than those that have left.
                They are up there
With great power:
           so high they take this evening for good
    Into their force-lines. I alone move

    Where the other birds were, the low ones,
    Still swaying in the unreal direction
    Flocking with them. They are gone

And will always be gone; even where they believe
    They were, is disappearing. But these three
    Have the height to power-line all

Land: land this clear. Any three birds hanging high enough
    From you, trace the same paths
  As strong horses circling
            for a man alone, born level-eyed

    As a pasture, but like the land

Tilting, looking up.

        This may be it, too.

Basics

I
Level

Who has told you what discoveries
There are, along the stressed blank
Of a median line? From it, nothing

Can finally fall. Like a spell-binder's pass
A tense placid principle continues

Over it, and when you follow you have the drift,

The balance of many compass needles
Verging to the pole. *Bring down your arms, voyager,*

And the soul goes out
Surrounding, humming
                    standing by means

        Of the match-up in long arm-bones

    Dropped:
                    held out and drawn back   back in
        Out of the open
                        compass-quivering and verging
            At your sides, as median movement

    Lays itself bare: a closed vein of bisected marble, where

            Along the hairline stem
        Of the continuum, you progress, trembling
With the plumb-bob quiver of mid-earth,
                                with others in joy

            Moving also, in line,

                Equalling, armlessing.

II
Simplex

    Comes a single thread
                    monofilament coming

        Strengthening   engrossing and slitting
            Into the fine-spun life

            To come, foretold in whatever
    Ecstasy there's been, but never suspected, never included
        In what was believed. The balance of the spiral
            Had been waiting, and could take

        What was given it: the single upthrust through
        The hanging acid, the helix spun and spellbound

    By the God-set of chemistry, the twine much deeper
            Than any two bodies imagined
            They could die for: insinuate, woven
                Single strand, third serpent
        Of the medical wood, circling the staff of life

Into the very body

Of the future, deadly
But family, having known from the beginning

Of the sun, what will take it on.

STEPHEN DOBYNS ▪ ▪ ▪ ▪ ▪ ▪ ▪ ▪ ▪ ▪ ▪ ▪ ▪ ▪ ▪ ▪

Frenchie

In memory of Francis "Frenchie" Phillips, 1929–1999

I was eating a chicken sandwich with mayonnaise
and reading about Russia when Frenchie stumbled
into the restaurant for a free cup of coffee.
He was drunk, but not too drunk to speak. Around me
blue-haired ladies nibbled Sunday dinners along with
other respectable types: bank clerk and plumber.
When he saw me, Frenchie asked how I was doing,
even though he has disliked me ever since I
kept him from hitting an old man with his crutch.
Frenchie needs a crutch because of the night he
dared the cop in the cruiser to drive over his foot.

Frenchie stood swaying at the front of the restaurant,
glaring at the blue-haired ladies who tried not to notice.
His face looks like a track team once sprinted across it.
In my book, the wife of the Russian poet was saying:
What will our grandchildren make of it if we all
leave the scene in silence. It was then Frenchie
decided to throw his cup to the floor and announce
he was going to die. Fragments of cup scattered around
my seat. Frenchie shouted: I'm sick and going to die and
no one cares. We all ate very quietly, as if listening
to the pop-pop of our taste buds self-destructing.

The waitress touched his arm. Oh, Frenchie, she said;
as if he wouldn't die; as if we would, but he wouldn't.
Don't give me that, he said. He was crying now. We each
pretended not to listen and I stared hard at my book,
but I thought we all had begun to imagine our own last
moments, as if Frenchie had put us in little theaters and
there on a stage the curtains were being noisily raised
and the elderly ladies, bank clerk, plumber, waitress

and myself—we all saw our funerals enacted before us: one
with a son come from Dallas, another with a sad Irish setter;
heaps of flowers, buckets of tears and an organ playing Bach.

But it's not so funny, because here we were on a Sunday
afternoon and I was concentrating on my chicken sandwich
and book where the woman was saying: What we wouldn't
have given for ordinary heartbreaks. And all of us
were trying to consume our small pleasures or at least
diversions, and I bet some of these ladies think too much
about death anyway, and here's Frenchie shouting I'm going
to die which takes the joy out of the meatloaf and mashed
potatoes. As for Frenchie, he's pure spite. I've seen him
hit little kids and he stands outside of bars making faces
at people through the glass and giving them the finger;

and just because the waitress was nice enough to give him
a cup of coffee he decided to remind us of the death
lurking in our future. So when he shouted that he's going
to die, I want to say: Sure, Frenchie, and can you do it
in the next few minutes? Let me help you find a truck,
walk you out to the end of the dock. Hey, I know a man
who's got a rabid dog. But maybe I was supposed to be
kind to him, take him home to meet my wife and kid,
let my wife cook him up some beans and franks, let him
fool around with my kid, wear my shirts and sweaters,
let him pat the cat. Hell, he'd probably eat the cat.

So none of that took place. Instead he stood there
shouting and his clothes were torn and he had vomit
on his shirt, and sure he would have liked someone
to give him ten bucks or a new life, but what he mostly
wanted was to grab us by our stomachs, our Sunday
dinners, yank us from our self-complacency and turn us
into witnesses, even though I had no wish to be a witness.
He wanted to make us sit up and say: Yes, you're
going to die, we're all going to die and that's too bad
and that's what sticks us in the same lousy boat
and no book or chicken sandwich will make it go away.

Maybe we should have stood up, confessed our mortality,
then crossed the street to the hardware that's open each
Sunday afternoon or wandered up to Barbara's Lunch or
the McDonald's out on the state highway. Maybe we ought
to have told everyone we met we were going to die and they
were going to die, until half the town is wandering around
tapping the other half on the shoulder, saying: Hey,
guess what? Then shake their hands and kiss them goodbye.
Maybe that would have been best, because in the restaurant

we all played dumb and nobody did a damn thing except
the waitress who said: Come on, Frenchie, you better go now.

As for me, I finished my sandwich, closed my book, pushed
past Frenchie and left, hoping to miss the tantrums,
the cops, the broken glass. But in the next few months,
I kept noticing Frenchie around town and he still
hadn't died, although twice I saw him being tossed
into the back of a cop car. Then this morning I see him
again as I'm driving through town, and it's a bright
blue morning at the beginning of March, and Frenchie
and a buddy are sunning themselves out in front of
the U-Ota-Bowl Alleys, and they're passing a bottle,
slapping their knees and having a high old time.

From this I guess Frenchie has forgotten he is
going to die, and I want to hang a U-turn, pull up
in front with my brand-new unpaid for Volkswagen,
get out wearing my fashionable corduroys, down jacket
and expensive boots. Then I want to grab Frenchie
by the ears, kiss him smack on his vomit mouth,
sit down, drink a little Old Duke red, tell a few
spiteful jokes, slap my knee and remind him that I'm
his witness, because even though he has forgotten
he's going to die, I haven't and what's more I'm
going to die too, as is his buddy, but what the hell.

In fact, maybe I should give him the car and down jacket,
not from guilt or that I've had better luck, but because
we're both going down the same slide. But who am I kidding?
I neither stopped the car nor waved, but drove straight to
my office with its books, papers and other shields against
the darkness, and after wasting time and making coffee and
staring out the window, I at last saw no hope for it and I
wrote down these words not because I saw myself in his eyes,
but from nothing more complicated than embarrassment.
The only way out of this life is to take him with me:
the left hand can't pretend it doesn't know the right.

The Great Doubters of History

The woman who kicked out the back window
of the police cruiser sits chain smoking and
drinking at a table by the dance floor.
Watching from a bar stool, you doubt she
weighs over a hundred pounds. She is gaunt,
bony and resembles a fierce pygmy
warrior. One time she ripped off her clothes

in the parking lot, defied police to touch her.
Another time she pursued a patrolman
down the street, then kicked him in the balls.
Maybe she's twenty. Here in the bar she
seems jittery, can't hold her liquor people
tell you, which is probably true but you also
respect someone who knows she has nothing
to lose. You too have nothing to lose but spend
much of your time telling yourself you do.
In fact, it seems the point of society is to
make people think they have something to lose
until a man goes through life as nervously
as if he were carrying a teetery
stack of plates up a dark flight of stairs.

Tomatoes

A woman travels to Brazil for plastic
surgery and a face lift. She is sixty
and has the usual desire to stay pretty.
Once she is healed, she takes her new face
out on the streets of Rio. A young man
with a gun wants her money. Bang, she's dead.
The body is shipped back to New York,
but in the morgue there is a mix-up. The son
is sent for. He is told that his mother
is one of these ten different women.
Each has been shot. Such is modern life.
He studies them all but can't find her.
With her new face, she has become a stranger.
Maybe it's this one, maybe it's that one.
He looks at their breasts. Which ones nursed him?
He presses their hands to his cheek.
Which ones consoled him? He even tries
climbing into their laps to see which
feels most familiar but the coroner stops him.
Well, says the coroner, which is your mother?
They all are, says the young man, let me
take them as a package. The coroner hesitates,
then agrees. Actually, it solved a lot of problems.
The young man has the ten women shipped home,
then cremates them altogether. You've seen
how some people have a little urn on the mantel?
This man has a huge silver garbage can.
In the spring, he drags the garbage can
out to the garden and begins working the teeth,
the ash, the bits of bone into the soil.
Then he plants tomatoes. His mother loved tomatoes.

They grow straight from seed, so fast and big
that the young man is amazed. He takes the first
ten into the kitchen. In their roundness,
he sees his mother's breasts. In their smoothness,
he finds the consoling touch of her hands.
Mother, mother, he cries, and he flings himself
on the tomatoes. Forget about the knife, the fork,
the pinch of salt. Try to imagine the filial
starvation, think of the ravenous kisses.

Allegorical Matters

Let's say you are a man (some of you are)
and susceptible to the charms of women
(some of you must be) and you are sitting
on a park bench. (It is a sunny afternoon
in early May and the peonies are in flower.)
A beautiful woman approaches. (Clearly,
we each have his or her own idea of beauty
but let's say she is beautiful to all.) She smiles,
then removes her halter top, baring her breasts
which you find yourself comparing to ripe fruit.
(Let's say you are an admirer of bare breasts.)
Gently she presses her breasts against your eyes
and forehead, moving them across your face.
You can't get over your good fortune. Eagerly,
you embrace her but then you learn the horror
because while her front is young and vital,
her back is rotting flesh which breaks away
in your fingers with a smell of decay. Here
we pause and invite in a trio of experts.
The first says, This is clearly a projection
of the author's sexual anxieties. The second says,
Such fantasies derive from the empowerment
of women and the author's fear of emasculation.
The third says, The author is manipulating sexual
stereotypes to achieve imaginative dominance
over the reader—basically, he must be a bully.
The author sits in front of the trio of experts.
He leans forward with his elbows on his knees.
He scratches his neck and looks at the floor
where a fat ant is dragging a crumb. He begins
to step on the ant but then he thinks: Better not.
The cool stares of the experts make him uneasy
and he would like to be elsewhere, perhaps home
with a book or taking a walk. My idea, he says,
concerned the seductive qualities of my country,
how it encourages us to engage in all fantasies,

how it lets us imagine we are lucky to be here,
how it creates the illusion of an eternal present.
But don't we become blind to the world around us?
Isn't what we see as progress just a delusion?
Isn't our country death and what it touches death?
The trio of experts begin to clear their throats.
They recross their legs and their chairs creak.
The author feels the weight of their disapproval.
But never mind, he says, Perhaps I'm mistaken;
let's forget I spoke. The author lowers his head.
He scratches under his arm and suppresses a belch.
He considers the difficulties of communication
and the ruthless necessities of art. Once again
he looks for the ant but it's gone. Lucky ant.
Next time he wouldn't let it escape so easily.

Nouns of Assemblage

Two scenes lie before us. In the first
is a huge glass case in which a buffalo
from the Old West sedately crops grass,
actually Astroturf. Despite our different
museum exposure, we all have observed this.

Two feet in front a prairie dog sits up
on its hind legs. The buffalo is at rest.
Few cares weigh upon its soul. Its head
is huge, the size of an armchair and one
might think the brain inside to be almost

as big but that would be mistaken. The brain
is the size of a pea and the rest is simply
padding to keep the brain from getting lost.
Our second scene takes us to the historic
plains of Nebraska. Here the buffalo extend

farther than the eye can see. A quick footed
acrobat might travel fifty miles jumping
from back to back. These beasts also lower
their heads as they calmly nibble the grass:
dusty but good. If any has a thought, it is

"Food source, food source," but articulated
very slowly—a thought like a tiny cloud
in an otherwise blue sky. Suddenly, one
buffalo topples to the ground. The others
mosey a little over to the left or right

thinking, if they could think, More grass
for us. Then another falls and another.
The Sharps buffalo rifle could knock one
of those bruisers off his pins from several
miles away, but what could be heard over

all that munching? Whenever one of the great
beasts feels a twinge of anxiety, it lifts
its mammoth head and looks across the fifty miles
of its brothers and sisters. Don't be silly,
it might say to itself as it moves to make use

of the grass patch of the newly deceased. This
returns us to our first scene with the buffalo
in a glass case. The quality of thought between
the dead and living buffalo is very slight—
the difference between a stagnant pool and one

that is barely moving. Was that the problem?
The prairie dog, if it could talk, would say not.
Look at the ancient Greeks and Egyptians,
the Romans and Persians. Pick your favorite
group. Aztecs or Hottentots. When one fell

and the others took notice, didn't they stifle
their fears with the thought, We are too numerous
to kill? The prairie dog watches the visitors
approach—differences in hair style and speech,
differences in dress. Do you see how he appears

to stare at each? Quizzical—that's how he looks:
twinkling eyes and perky ears. Perhaps he asks, Hey,
what's for dinner? Or, even better, To what peculiar
(pick your preferred noun of assemblage: gang,
horde, clamor, litter, swarm) do you belong?

RITA DOVE   ▪ ▪ ▪ ▪ ▪ ▪ ▪ ▪ ▪ ▪ ▪ ▪ ▪ ▪ ▪ ▪ ▪ ▪

Demeter, Waiting

No. Who can bear it. Only someone
who hates herself, who believes
to pull a hand back from a daughter's cheek
is to put love into her pocket—

like one of those ashen Christian
philosophers, or a war-bound soldier.

She is gone again and I will not bear
it, I will drag my grief through a winter
of my own making, refuse
any meadow that recycles itself into
hope. Shit on the cicadas, dry meteor
flash, finicky butterflies. I will wail and thrash
until the whole goddamned golden panorama freezes
over. Then I will sit down to wait for her. Yes.

Wiederkehr

He only wanted me for happiness,
to walk in air
and not think so much,
to watch the smile
begun in his eyes
end on the lips
his eyes caressed.

He merely hoped, in darkness, to smell
rain; and though he saw how still
I sat to hold the rain untouched
inside me, he never asked
if I would stay. Which is why,
when the choice appeared,
I reached for it.

NORMAN DUBIE ▪ ▪ ▪ ▪ ▪ ▪ ▪ ▪ ▪ ▪ ▪ ▪ ▪ ▪ ▪

An Annual of the Dark Physics

The Baltic Sea froze in 1307. Birds flew north
From the Mediterranean in early January.
There were meteor storms throughout Europe.

On the first day of Lent
Two children took their own lives:
Their bodies
Were sewn into goats' skins

And were dragged by the hangman's horse
The three miles down to the sea.
They were given a simple grave in the sand.

The following Sunday, Meister Eckhart
Shouted that a secret word
Had been spoken to him. He preached

That Mary Magdalene
Sought a dead man in the tomb
But, in her confusion, found
Only two angels laughing . . .

This was a consequence of her purity

And her all too human grief.
The Baltic Sea
Also froze in 1303—

      nothing happened that was worthy of poetry.

Hummingbirds

They will be without arms like God.

By the millions their dried skins will be sought
In the New World.
Their young will be like wet slugs.
They will obsess the moon
Over a field of night-flowering phlox.
Their nests will be a delicate cup of moss.

In pairs
They will feast on a tarantula in thin air.

They have made a new statement
About our world—a clerk in Memphis
Has confessed to laying out feeders
Filled with sulphuric acid. She says

God asked for these deaths . . .   like God
They are insignificant, and have visited us

Who are wretched.

Danse Macabre

The broken oarshaft was stuck in the hill
In the middle of chicory,
Puke-flowers the farmers called them, sturdy
Little evangels that the white deer drift through . . .

Nobody on the hill before
Had heard of a horse
Breaking its leg in a rowboat. But the mare
Leapt the fence, passed
The tar-paper henhouse,
And then crumpled at the shore.

It was April and bees were floating
In the cold evening barn; from the loft
We heard them shoot the poor horse.
We tasted gunpowder and looked
While your cousin, the sick
Little bastard, giggled and got
So excited he started to dance
Like the slow sweeping passes
Of a drawing compass—

Its cruel nail to its true pencil.

Sanctuary

My sister got me the script. I couldn't
Believe it. To work for Charles Barzon.
He was doing a film of *Thérèse Raquin.*
Zola's novel. The wife is in love
With her sickly husband's best friend;
They are on an outing—an accident is staged
On the river. They drown
The husband. The river takes him.
Then begin
The visits to the Paris morgue:
Each day from a balcony
They look down at a flat, turning wheel;
Eight naked corpses, unclaimed,
Revolving on a copper and oak bed.
A fine mist
Freshening the bodies. I was
To be one of them. I almost said no.

But Barzon's a genius. He took us aside,
One at a time. He gave us

Secret lives, even though we were the dead.
I was Pauline,
A sculptor's model of the period.
I would have to shave my groin,
Armpits, and legs.
Hairless, Pauline was a strange euphemism.
What is the scripture,
The putting on of nakedness?

"You'll be like marble," Barzon said.

I felt a little sick
With the slow revolutions and lights.
The cold mist raised my nipples.
My hair was ratted and too tight.
Between takes, we shared from boredom
Our secret lives:
To my right was a ploughman, kicked
In the chest by a horse. He staggered,
Barzon had told him, out of the field
Into the millrace.
To my left, a thief who had been knifed
In a Paris street. We were spread-eagled,
Cold and hungry. I looked over to the thief
Who was, to my surprise, uncircumcised . . .
I said, "Verily, this day you will be
With me in Paradise." For a moment the dead
In their places writhed—
Barzon was so upset saliva flew from his lips.

The dream occured that night. And every
Night since.
Three weeks now, the same dream:
One of the carpenters from the set
Is on a high beam way above us.
I don't know how I see him past the lights.
But there he is, his pants unzipped.
I scream. Barzon looks up from a camera
And says, "Get that son-of-a-bitch."
The workman slips
Just as a floodlight touches him.
Before he hits the floor, I'm awake.
The first thing I realize
Is that I'm not a corpse, not dead,
Then, in horror,
I see I am still naked and Thérèse Raquin's
Drowned husband
                    is sitting accusingly at the foot of my bed.

The Peace of Lodi

> The South had to lose the war;
> Lincoln had to be martyred if
> healing was to occur.
> —RUTH ANN HASTINGS

One night, after a storm, the sort of storm
That is preceded by a sulphur calm—
Birds suddenly silent, people with lamps
Climbing down into cellars—one night,
After such a storm, driving the old Ford
Through the Iowa countryside, we stopped suddenly
Before the incandescent light of a tree
That had been shattered
By lightning—black and lavender
Amish surrounding a smouldering linden: they were
Just sitting in their buggies
Speaking to their horses in low voices
While an Elder, who had soaked his sleeves in water,
Lifted up out of the great charred circumference
Of the tree, a pail filled with boiling honey.
It was one of those infinite distances,
Yet finite as that thickness of glass
Between us and the assassin who stood behind Lincoln
In that wax museum across from the whorehouse
In Phoenix.

Trakl

for Paul

In reality the barn wasn't clean, ninety men
Charged to you:
The burns, missing teeth, and dark jawbone
Of gnawed corn, gangrene from ear to elbow—
Even the dying
Returned to consciousness by the ammonia of cows.

You ran out looking beyond your hands
To the ground, above you a wind
In the leaves: looking up you found
Hanged partisans convulsing in all the trees.

Down the road in the garrison hospital,
In a cell for the insane, you were given
Green tea and cocaine . . .

With the blue snow of four o'clock
Came peace and that evening of memory
With Grete, her touch—in yellow spatterdock
She tied a black ribbon
Around the cock of a sleeping horse.
It was her *vivacious littles* as an admirer
Once put it. *Sister, trough.* . . .

How men talk. I read you first
In an overly heated room
Sitting in an open window. I left
For a walk in woods. Coming out
Into a familiar sinkhole, meadow
Now snow, deer ran over the crust—
Hundreds of them. I thought of my two uncles,

Their war, the youngest dead at Luzon,
The other, in shock,
At his barracks in California: Christmas evening
He looked up from the parade grounds and saw
An old Japanese prisoner
With arms raised, from the hands came
A pigeon. The bird climbed, climbed
Slowly and then dissolved

Like smoke from some lonely howitzer
Blossoming out over the bubbling bone pits of lye, over
The large sunken eyes of horticulture. . . .

Poem

A mule kicked out in the trees. An early
Snow was falling,
The girl walked across the field
With a hairless doll, she dragged
It by the green corduroy of its sleeve
And with her hands
Buried it beside the firepond.

The doll was large enough to displace earth
Making a mound
Which she patted down a dozen times.
Then she walked back alone.
The weak, winter sun
Sat on the horizon like a lacquered mustard seed.

She never noticed me
Beside the road drinking tea from a thermos.

The car cooling.
Did you ever want to give someone

All your money? We drove past midnight, ate,
And drove some more—unable to sleep in Missouri.

Anagram Born of Madness at Czernowitz, 12 November 1920

> There are still songs to sing
> On the other side of mankind.
> —PAUL CELAN

They were the strong nudes of a forgotten
Desert outpost, crossing through snow
Through the steam of a hot springs
Where they bathed twice daily against delirium.

It was during the conflict between the Americans
And North Koreans. We realized
They would use atomic weapons.
Our eyes were alive and you could read them.

How out on the glaciers
Angels were burning the large brooms of sunflowers,
A back growth without smoke. Each flower's head,
An alchemist's sewer plate of gold.

They were coming down in winter
And whatever they were, Mr. Ancel's ghost
Would meet them,
Saying, "You may go this far and no farther."

Like fountains in winter the heart-jet.
Is bundled in shocks of straw. Now, it's cold soldiers
In a swamp cooking a skull.
The harsh glazings in my room.

Grandmother ate a sandwich while dusting
A bone cudgel
In a beam of light
In the green cellar of the museum.

When the lard factory across the street
Began burning, soap-tubs collapsing with the floor,
She said, quietly,
"There, see, we must have imagined the whole thing . . .

I don't hear the bells. Do you children?
If there's an explosion, it will come as a wind
Peppered with things—
Hold onto me and we'll sing."

JOSEPH DUEMER ■ ■ ■ ■ ■ ■ ■ ■ ■ ■ ■ ■ ■ ■ ■

Theory of Tragedy

> How can we believe in anything again?
> —ECHECRATES, IN *THE PHAEDO*

Why didn't the first philosopher want to go on living
among the sun-warmed stones of his native city?
Wasn't the music, microtonal as sunlight on paving stones,
worthy of him? Didn't he have friends
whose particular talk he loved more than the cool beauty
of ideas? There was as yet no definition of tragedy.

His students say the old man believed deeply
In the clarifying power of disputation, urging them
that argument leads always toward truth, though
it never arrive There. He loved to form definitions, believing
them like music, for which, apparently, he had no ear.
There was as yet no definition of tragedy,

though everyone knew what he or she meant by the word—
a certain feeling in the bowel
as you filed from the theater after something by Sophocles,
a bristling of hairs on the small of the neck, evidence
of poison working out toward the skin,
the body politic purging itself of doubt, bending

its confident demotic beneath the weight of music
and dance. But out in the streets Socrates heard the passion
of speech slide into Rhetoric, which was invented, some say,
in order to contain the passions roused
in the populace by the music of speech.
There was, as yet, no definition of tragedy.

Was Socrates so sold on himself he couldn't *imagine*
(the whisper of god in his hairy old ear)
the fine words of those citizens talking among themselves
on the marble steps of the King Archon's palace?
He thought they were dangerous, tugged this way and that
like a tide destroying the walls of the city.

The rationalist philosopher Sherlock Holmes loved
to play music when not testing blood
stains on a carpet—scratching away like crazy at his violin—
a fine old instrument better than his skill—making music
the more terrible for its awful Victorian sentiment.
The problem of tragedy is how close it always must come

to sentiment. Both these philosophers hated democracy—
the dirty feet of the mob, the bumbling stupidity
of the man in the street, who loves the fat that sticks to his own bones
and therefore is no fit audience for tragedy. Tonight
as I read, the faint odor of skunk drifts through the window.
I imagine the dogs of Athens raising their noses

into an ancient breeze off the Aegean carrying the sour smell
of the philosopher's corpse after it accepted poison
from the jury of citizens. Would the private eye, so adept
at uncovering what others called *tragedy,* have been able to determine
the cause of death by examining the famous scene in the prison?
And had the first detective sniffed out the hemlock,

would he have deduced the fibers of the soul floating loose
in the damp air of the cell? What would he have thought
of the crooked smile on the round gray face?
And what analysis could have made the tears smearing the faces
of those wealthy and self-sufficient men gathered there
in the prison yield useful knowledge?

The outer stones of the prison, already warmed
by morning sun, and the city's air vibrant with music rising
from its streets, the shopkeepers sold fish, copper, fresh bread,
and red figure pottery common to that place and time, often
depicting Clytemnestra's bloody betrayal of Agamemnon
or famous episodes in Odysseus's long journey back

to his wife—both impossible fictions! The dogs might have
made some music with those old bones, even lacking
a theory of tragedy, which is really a theory of knowledge.
Tonight, odor of skunk hanging like a philosopher's soul
in the air, I sit beneath a xerox copy of a photograph—one of those
Greek vases called a *lekythos,* this one showing a daughter of Memory,

loosely draped, feet bare, sexy, her right hand indicating
a songbird on a branch sketched near her knees.
Without a definition of tragedy, we cannot understand
the dance our words and grammar pattern intersecting
the facts of the palpable world—a maple tree's black
branches against the amber/blue stripes of sunset,

perfume of skunk and wood smoke hanging in the air.
The old man always said his wisdom was nothing but ignorance,

and at the end of his life he couldn't prove the soul
survives the body. Perhaps it was nothing but a feeling,
like tragedy, which is only the awkward singing
of a small bird on a flimsy branch pointing toward memory.

ALAN DUGAN ■ ■ ■ ■ ■ ■ ■ ■ ■ ■ ■ ■ ■ ■ ■ ■

Swing Shift Blues

What is better than leaving a bar
in the middle of the afternoon
besides staying in it or else not
having gone into it in the first place
because you had a decent woman to be with?
The air smells particularly fresh
after the stale beer and piss smells.
You can stare up at the whole sky:
it's blue and white and does not
stare back at you like the bar mirror,
and there's What's-'is-name coming out
right behind you saying, "I don't
believe it. I don't believe it: there
he is, staring up at the fucking sky
with his mouth open. Don't
you realize, you stupid son of a bitch,
that it is a quarter to four
and we have to clock in in
fifteen minutes to go to work?"
So we go to work and do no work
and can even breathe in the Bull's face
because he's been into the other bar
that we don't go to when he's there.

Nomenclature

My mother never heard of Freud
and she decided as a little girl
that she would call her husband Dick
no matter what his first name was
and did. He called her Ditty. They
called me Bud, and our generic names
amused my analyst. That must, she said,
explain the crazy times I had in bed
and quoted Freud: "Life is pain."
"What do women want?" and "My
prosthesis does not speak French."

Poem for Elliot Carter on His 90th Birthday

I was walking behind Elliot Carter
up Eighth Avenue and saw that he
was waving his arms, and people looked at him
as if he was crazy, and he was
crazy: he was conducting the Juilliard
Chamber Orchestra soundlessly as it was
moving before him backwards seated
invisibly in formal black dress
as it performed his latest uncomposed piece
which he was composing slowly because
he writes slowly very slowly his wife
Helen always says and I say that he writes
for the performers not the audience
so that his music will go on
up the avenue for years and years
performed by the performers who
perhaps alone will hear it. So,
listen or don't listen, it will go on
playing anyway, invisibly unheard.

Barefoot Homiletics, After Wittgenstein and Boswell

Dew in the morning, dust at noon,
soreness in the evening, rest in brine.
Vertical soles all night, sideways
in colloquy, toes down in sex or up,
depending on the gender, depending on the case.
"The universe is everything that is the case."
Stubbed toes mean found rocks,
so all is detour to the tenderfoot
but traversible to callus. Calluses
are unshod graces, but a
bootless courage has its own
temerity. To strike a foot
with mighty force against a stone
is footless practice, and to say
"the universe is merely ideal"
is shoe philosophy, but
to watch your step is day
advice to the benighted since
feet have their feelings too.
So let the grass grow underfoot:
it tickles on the way to ground,
grass on the one side, roots on the other,
the balance of depths between.
That surface is falsely named

the surface. It is the case,
bare to the foot at the sole:
it is the top of the world
and the bottom of the sky to walk on.
So, seek water. Avoid the shod.

American Variation on How Rilke Loved a Princess and Got to Stay in Her Castle

She said that underneath the surface
of her beautiful skin and happiness
there was something she was scared of, it
could break out any time like hives, a
sense of loss, poverty, humiliation, or death.
Her beauty, children and three husbands
couldn't help her, and this is why
she married the Governor, the billionaire,
not because he was the governor but because
he had money and she needed money
to stop the terror, although the power helped,
and that I shouldn't hate her for this,
but understand her and love her,
so I did, and her husband gave me a grant,
not because I loved her or because
he was dyslexic but because
I was a good American poet.

Drunken Memories of Anne Sexton

The first and last time I met
my ex-lover Anne Sexton was at
a protest poetry reading against
some anti-constitutional war in Asia
when some academic son of a bitch,
to test her reputation as a drunk,
gave her a beer glass full of wine
after our reading. She drank
it all down while staring me
full in the face and then said
"I don't care what you think,
you know," as if I was
her ex-what, husband, lover,
what? and just as I
was just about to say I

loved her, I was, what,
was, interrupted by my beautiful enemy
Galway Kinnell, who said to her
"Just as I was told, your eyes,
you have one blue, one green"
and there they were, the two
beautiful poets, staring at
each others' beautiful eyes
as I drank the lees of her wine.

STEPHEN DUNN ▪ ▪ ▪ ▪ ▪ ▪ ▪ ▪ ▪ ▪ ▪ ▪ ▪ ▪ ▪ ▪ ▪

What They Wanted

They wanted me to tell the truth,
so I said I'd lived among them
for years, a spy,
but all that I wanted was love.
They said they couldn't love a spy.
Couldn't I tell them other truths?
I said I was emotionally bankrupt,
would turn any of them in for a kiss.
I told them how a kiss feels
when it's especially undeserved;
I thought they'd understand.
They wanted me to say I was sorry,
so I told them I was sorry.
They didn't like it that I laughed.
They asked what I'd seen them do,
and what I do with what I know.
I told them: find out who you are
before you die.
Tell us, they insisted, what you saw.
I saw the hawk kill a smaller bird.
I said life is one long leavetaking.
They wanted me to speak
like a journalist. I'll try, I said.
I told them I could depict the end
of the world, and my hand wouldn't tremble.
I said nothing's serious except destruction.
They wanted to help me then.
They wanted me to share with them,
that was the word they used, share.
I said it's bad taste
to want to agree with many people.

I told them I've tried to give
as often as I've betrayed.
They wanted to know my superiors,
to whom did I report?
I told them I accounted to no one,
that each of us is his own punishment.
If I love you, one of them cried out,
what would you give up?
There were others before you,
I wanted to say, and you'd be the one
before someone else. Everything, I said.

Because You Mentioned the Spiritual Life

A lone tern turns in the blowsy wind,
and there's the ocean and its timbrous repetitions,
and what a small pleasure it is
that the shade, halfway down,
poorly conceals the lovers next door.
    Fishing boats and sea air,
the moon now on the other side of our world
influencing happiness and crime.
The spiritual life, I'm thinking, is worthless
unless it's another way of having a good time.
      To you I'll say it's some quiet gaiety
after a passage through what's difficult,
perhaps dangerous. I'd like to please you.
So many travelers going to such a small state—
I can see the ferry, triple-tiered and white,
on its way to Delaware.
      I'm peeling and sectioning
an orange. I'm slipping a section into my mouth.
What a perfect thing an orange is
to think about.
      I should say to you
the spiritual life is what cannot be had
through obeisance, but we'll get nowhere
with talk like this.
A darning needle just zoomed by.
The dune grass is leaning west.
      Come join me on the deck,
the gulls are squawking, and an airplane
pulling a banner telling us where to eat
is flying low over the sand castles
and body sculptures the children have built.
The tide will have them soon. Moments
are what we have.

GERALD EARLY ▪ ▪ ▪ ▪ ▪ ▪ ▪ ▪ ▪ ▪ ▪ ▪ ▪ ▪

Amagideon; or When Lee Andrews and the Hearts Sang Only for Me

I. "All that pass by . . ."

In the lunar year of Tet,
The white and gold mummers strut past my street,
Hardeyed as Endicott, gorgeous as the daughter of Jerusalem,
On their way to glory and the house of glory;
Cold in the iron arrow of wind they were and coldly, coldly
They played the hot music of sin as no one listens
But everyone stares and thinks
About some dear old southland of the mind:
A large meadow where peasants sing hauntingly,
A square where girls wear kerchieves and dance by themselves,
A deep well where tired men drink clear water.
The mummers do not smile at anyone;
They are simply passing through on their way to another country;
They are visitors who, in passing, know the way out.
No one smiles at them in plumed splendor,
So much like the clergy of a Reformed Church at holiday,
So much like Calvinists gone to carnality,
So much like the dazzling armored conquerors of a strange land
It is, alas, just another pillaged dream,
A fantasy of serene and easy plunder
As a train of sleepwalkers in morning raiment,
Caught still in the opulent fury of the winter sun
In a forgotten place where people do not
Like the hot songs of innocence
Played in the iron arrow of cold wind, unmoved and unmoving.

II. ". . . clap their hands at thee."

On this plain, where the carnage
Is denied its feast of bells and prayer,
And when the eye is full of
The landscape of scandal and chances;

On this plain, where there
Are no trees, no sky, no billowing swell,
No grazing animals, no book
That reminds one of the myth of experience.

On this streetcorner as broad
As a broad, equivocal sea

And as hard and blank
As a wall built to hold back that sea;

There appear the ghosts of five black boys
Who have just walked and strolled,
As coolroot and coolloving in
Florsheim soft, soft shoes
Down and down the pavement project stairwell,
Sequined, hair dewed and done and damply cocked,
Zootthroated shirts and gold teeth aflame,
Gonads aflame like a cosmos;

They sing in Chaldee,
High-pitched as Vishnu the disobedient god,
As if there were no misery but the mere lilting sadness
Of homesickness and homelessness
And the final hope of a more final wisdom;
Singing as sad as Curtis Mayfield or Smokey Robinson,
Clyde McPhatter or Johnny Ace or some other
Drowning sentimental men, eyes thickly filmed
Over and over by requests to battered women to forgive them,
                by requests for one great song sung in glory,
And always knowing that nothing in this world is requited
But the very things that one does not want
Or the things that one does not deserve to have.

In the world of pederasty, cops with smoking batons,
Magical agonies of lust and dust, mojos, dead fucks,
Babies sailing into night, Coke and lye concoctions
For unfaithful lovers and lying friends,
Only paunchy hustlers with wounded prostates,
Only raunchy old girls with bad teeth
Remember when Sonny Til and Billy Stewart sang
On the corner the cool songs of experience
And remember that it was a time of moving and being moved.

There, on the streetcorner called
Diamond, Tioga, Grays Ferry, Dauphin,
Where pigeons swoop like mad darts,
Where hieroglyphic walls decay
In the opulent fury of the summersun,
Five black boys sing a solo song around
The campfire in gathering evening,
A vast song that can be heard across the widest prairie:
The old sweet song of the range.

Innocency or Not Song X

for jazz pianist Bud Powell

> There's a moon out tonight
> Let's go strolling . . .
> —THE CAPRIS

> Remember, I pray thee, who ever perished, being innocent?
> —JOB 4:7

It was not warm,
    not what he thought, not warm
But cool, dirty, dirty
    and cool, this very small space
Under the car, there,
    under, where he thought it would be warm.
A space, before he
    went under, down under, thought to be a yonder
That was yearning for
    him, for which he yearned himself, a calling.
To be under the car,
    the grit, the oil, the dark, cool metal mazed,
A sort of breathing
    thing, not breathing, as if one were buried,
Buried in the belly,
    of a calm machine, under and away, sheltered:
The high white moon which
    he could remember sometime ago, a shape of light;
Sometime ago, in his cell,
    amply detained as mad, he could remember, through
The mesh wiring, through
    it, the high white moon, there, circular, oracular,
A center of something
    not held, staring blankly, calmly back, as if
It were the expression
    of some impossibly contained oneness of fellowship
Like being alone in
    the church upon the hill called home, sweet home of the lord.
He could see it even
    when lying on the floor, straining up, staring,
His face sopping wet from
    the water they threw on him, icy water on a bitter night,
The bucket of dirty icy water
    to awaken him from the dreaming of the oddest thing:
In the cell, in the light
    of the moon, stood mocking the light, stood before him,
A huge rooster, almost monstrous,
    nearly three feet high, white and black and red, spangled,

An erect thing that did not,
    absolutely did not move and that did not seem as if it could;
But which loudly, loudly
    crew enough to shake the walls, out against the white moon;
And so he thought himself
    the powerful cock, bedazzled, chanting erectly not song x.
He lay beneath the car
    his face sopping with blood, escaping the police;
Absolutely not wanting
    to face the high white moon anymore ever;
Only wishing forever to
    stay mad and safe and small and hidden and down.
The face of his one
    last friend peered down, soft, white, a moon of sorts;
Please, he said, as if
    it were a prayer to a boyishly sweet, starry god.
Please, he said, bending down,
    and the other looked up, crumpled, as if a child,
So small from beneath the
    car, as if it were that heavy thing that, shielding light,
Stopped a thing so light
    so utterly untouched from being a kind of serial wonder;
His shoe touched the
    puddled gutter, his sleeve dragged the grease;
His face, beneath, under,
    could not be seen, only the buried voice, soft, grave,
With so much quivering
    that his friend could not imagine, even signifying yore,
That from that prostrate
    figure, that prostrate state, could come a humming utterance,
So dazed, fallen, so innocent,
    that, at its saddest, it could not possibly be any song at all.

Country or Western Music

for tenor saxophonist John Coltrane

> What I say is, for Christ's sake, you don't have to *kill*
> yourself to swing.
>   —COUNT BASIE

He could not imagine himself a hero at all
Of anything, remotely, standing there
Playing a long solo on the saxophone.
He could not imagine his playing heroic;
He could not see himself drawn in an epic;

He could only see all that dark blue darkness
And the playing was not the light but merely
The request, in nakedness next to nothing,
For some small light or some less darkness.

He thought of his saxophone as a confidence man,
Coiled and golden, like a serpent or a surprise,
Who offers him a choice between a glass vase
And any seven words ever uttered in the language.

The vase, for instance, is sitting on a table,
A glass vase, thick, pure, and clean, with
A body that suggests circles which are not circles
But the roundness of the something of a circle
Or an ellipsis or a parabola or a coin.
So, a glass vase sits, fat as a viol, upon the table.

It could be one thing or another to the eye,
Broken or whole, containing white flowers or black marbles,
Sitting on the edge of something or the center,
Gilded or bare, trembling or still, water or air or earth within.

But how words, up and out, lead to heaven.
The seven words shimmer, a dazzling throttling up
Of possibilities or the consumption of artifacts.
How we ache for voracious discourse, the princely imagination
Of fire at the end, desire, the metaphor as the ghost in the belly.

But it was not that he wanted, not to beguile;
Not to be beguiled by vases within or words up.
He did not want a human sound, a human meaning;
He did not want a human song, only warmth and movement,
An idyll burnished like metal by the inhuman guttural gold of himself.
It is not the great solo, not the song of songs,
But merely the cry of indifference, the quaver of solitude,
The eyes of the forsaken casted up, the arms dangling down.
It is the only and the last love he knows that we can ever know.

And so of course his solos are unfinished, incomplete, beginnings
Because the only way to con the confidence man is to keep him
Waiting for the ending he expects until he, like you,
Expects no ending at all.

RICHARD EBERHART ▪ ▪ ▪ ▪ ▪ ▪ ▪ ▪ ▪ ▪ ▪ ▪ ▪ ▪

Chart Indent

Ile Au Haut is way down there in the distance,
Given a particular kind of day, and if
You are not afraid of the ocean, have daring,
A stout boat and a stout heart

You might sail from here due South,
Pass Eagle Island Light, go into open
Ocean and make for Stonington, if plucky
Continue south to the high island.

Long before getting to Roaring Bull Ledge
Facing the open Atlantic, this
Open enough, you might find a small opening in
The chart and map of the watery world

And there find safe harbor, secure your vessel,
Cast anchor in a safe place, be warned by a native
Not to come far in, the out tide will strand you,
The sea is even treacherous in here, be careful.

You count on the treachery of the sea as endless,
You will haunt her, but you know that every year
She claims lives indifferently, you to be sagacious
And always try to outwit her. Duck in to Duck Harbor,

Sleep snug in sleek harbor, and when dawn comes
Awake to be going out into the ocean
As ancestors have done since time began
And hope you will make safe landfall.

The Immortal Picture

I want that picture, the perfect view
Of vessels outside our house riding easy,
Great ocean eventuated by islands,
A spectacle of order, harmony, and control

When we know everything is changeful and mortal,
We know the immortal picture is false,
The perfect view will not last,

Change comes on, good turns to bad,
Evil lurks in every picture of man,
Even though we have a good view for Christmas.

The beautiful body decays, the
Beautiful mind is destroyed, the
Great and powerful go to death,

The times change, the poem ends,
The poem ends because heartbreak
Overcomes human beings
Because they cannot control the world.
After twelfth night
We threw the Christmas tree over the cliff.

The Blunting

To survive things have to be blunted,
Raw experience is too fierce to endure.
The mind blots out much of experience
To make good sense of the rest.

The immediate is our hold on reality.
Even the past is always changing,
We see with clarity what we see,
But in no sense in total degree.

Things are best this way. We get on
Because we do not dare the whole view
Which, if we could comprehend it,
We would wonder whether it is true.

There must be a God's view of the universe
Which we are intelligent enough to imagine
But we are fated to a human condition
Which has, perforce, its own perdition.

If you are too wary it is too painful,
A blaze in the eyes is partially blinding,
The mysteries the Greeks knew as too deep
Are secrets the sybils are willing to keep.

LYNN EMANUEL ▪ ▪ ▪ ▪ ▪ ▪ ▪ ▪ ▪ ▪ ▪ ▪ ▪ ▪ ▪

The Technology of Spring

Today, Braddock Avenue's a parade
moving hood to bumper into the gloom.
The cold front is here from Canada.
All the maples shoulder the snow but
still the storm comes down gothic
and furious while that boy across
the street is coming to sell me
chances for a trip to Miami Beach—
water sports, and the sudden coming home
of recognition: I am in love with his
wayward interest in my livingroom.
I believe you should go for it
he says and, yes, the stuck door
of imagination opens to the pure

blue gameboard of a swimming pool,
streets cooled by the wash water
and brooms of Cuban women who
are so beautiful they loosen
the long laces of his breath.
And I, too, full of divorce and bluster,
and coming up from a beach wearing
the slick cool silver of my naked self
and composing two stanzas of such
luminous uncertainty they make
eternity's stopped clock run
and hope is poking her green nose
into everything and I am speechless
with rebirth.

She

The body has its own story   she said   Oh, yes?   I said.

The body   she insisted   has its own   no I said I suppose not   it doesn't

beginning middle end   its plot is not what you think she said   it doesn't matter   that it

matter that you hate   the end middle beginning   or that the body does   it says—

doesn't fit the theory   flesh, too, has a voice   and is quite articulate   the street

yes I say   I know what it says   it says the end is the end   no matter how you slice it

precisely   she said   she was herself quite eloquent   we were sitting in the café

disappearing behind the rainy plate glass window   behind us hovered the waiter and the good smell

of coffee   she was beautiful   bookish   I loved her serious glasses   she was

trying to explain about the body   and I did not want to hear it   but   she persisted   your

stories   Yes?   utilize the latest methods and theories   she said   they rearrange everything

strike out in new directions   nothing is certain   death to tradition!   why thank you I said

at her back the city wept with rain   and to the dominant paradigm I said

death to the dominant paradigm   of the beginning   the middle   all that sad etcetera

ahh   said she triumphantly   the politics of narrative   it interests you?   passionately

I replied   of course the body   she continued severely   I looked at her   her hair was long and as dark

as the earth and I said   the body is   of course   what my text struggles against   it struggles against

the beginning middle end   which is the narrative of the flesh   no matter how you slice it   and so

the body and I are like two people   arguing in a café about the way the story would go   I argue my position

vis-à-vis   the end middle beginning   and the body argues hers   yes   she said but   let's face it

no matter what you say   the body wins.

Homage to Sharon Stone

It's early morning and across the street
the windows of a hotel room are filled
with the tropical performances of a
woman undressing, inside *The Eatery,*
a child, blued by neon, is sitting at a table,
and my neighbors hitch themselves to
the roles of the unhappily married and
trundle their three mastiffs down the street.
I am writing this book of poems. My name
is Lynn Emanuel. I am wearing a bathrobe
and curlers; from my lips a Marlboro drips ash
on the text. It is the third of September 19°°,
I think, but sometimes I lose track.
And as I am writing this in my trifocals
and slippers, across the street, Sharon Stone,
her head swollen with curlers, her mouth
red and narrow as a dancing slipper,
is rushed into a black limo. And because
these limos snake up and down my street,
this book will be full of sleek cars nosing
through a shadowy ocean of words.
Every morning, Sharon Stone, her head
in a helmet of hairdo, wearing a visor
of sunglasses, is engulfed by a limo
the size of a Pullman, and whole fleets
of these wind their way up and down
the street, day after day, giving to the street
(Liberty Avenue in Pittsburgh, PA)
and the book I am writing, an aspect
that is both glamorous and funereal.
My name is Lynn Emanuel, and in this
book I play the part of someone writing
a book, and I take the role seriously
just as Sharon Stone takes seriously
the role of the starlet. I watch the dark
cars disappear her and in my poem
another Pontiac comes to doze
like a big animal at the cool troughs
of shady curbs. So, when you see
this black car, do not think it is a
Symbol For Something. It is just
Sharon Stone driving past the house
of someone who is, at the time,
trying to write a book of poems.

Or you could think of the black car as
Lynn Emanuel, because, really, as an author,

I have always wanted to be a car, even
though most of the time I have to be
the "I," or the woman hanging wash;
I am a woman, one minute, then I am a man,
I am a carnival of Lynn Emanuels:
Lynn in the red dress, Lynn sulking
behind the big nose of my erection,
then I am the train pulling into the station
when what I would really love to be is
Gertrude Stein spying on Sharon Stone
at six in the morning. But enough about
that, back to the interior decorating:
On the page, the town looks bald
and dim so I turn up the amps on
the radioactive glances of bad boys.
In a kitchen, I stack pans sleek with
grease, and on a counter there is a roast
beef red as a face in a tantrum. Amid all this
bland strangeness, is Sharon Stone who,
like an engraved invitation, is asking me,
Won't you, too, play a role? I choose
the black limo, and down the street the golden
moons of my limo headlights roll bringing
with them the sun, the moon, and Sharon Stone
who is staring out at the distant lit window
of a house where, all this time, someone
has been gravely labeling with her name, this poem.

Elsewhere

This isn't Italy where even
the dust is sexual, and I am not
eighteen clothed in elaborate
nonchalance. Onions's *Etymologies*
says memory is related to mourning.
I'm always remembering myself
out of some plain place in the middle
West, some every-small-town-I-have-ever-hated
and grieved my way out of in poetry, chipping
the distance open with a train, awling
open with the train's hooting
a silence which is stolidly American, sturdy, woodsy,
well, no, perhaps these woods are Dante's;
it's dark in here. I'm nearly fifty
rummaging through the ruined beauty
of a girl at twenty who couldn't interrogate
her heart for more than five minutes.

—Just listen

even in Corsica where the repeated call of the
lighthouse throbbed like a piston, and the thin whine
of an engine garroted the quiet, and I stood good
as a flower in my pastel shirtwaist, poked and
nuzzled by my date, and listened to the mixing,
like a cocktail, of the water and earth, the cool
gargle, the slushy breathing of the surf, and
wished I were somewhere else

to her describing, even then, a longing
to escape. And, like me, she only does it on the page
heaping up the elaborate scenery so
she can disappear into it. Nearly fifty.

On that flat EKG of horizon the silos are blips
repeating and repeating. There is a storm,
a thick, dark, hard knot of cloud, but it's stuck
in the chimney of my throat.

The fire is out, the cabin's dark
and beyond, the woods are a platoon
of black trees. It's so quiet
I can hear my heart like the blows
of an ax, each blow blurred by an echo,

I can hear my heart inside my chest
trudging onward across the bleak tundra.
What was I thinking?

I look again at her poems flowing with
images, a restlessness, a terrible sense of
what's coming: She's writing me,
the woman she becomes, who could not
or would not save her.

EDWARD FIELD ■ ■ ■ ■ ■ ■ ■ ■ ■ ■ ■ ■ ■ ■ ■ ■

Whatever Became Of: Freud?

Has the age of psychology really passed?
Aren't people interested anymore
in how their toilet training shaped them?
Nowadays, nobody talks of their "analysis," or even

the less respectable therapies that came into fashion
about the time we gave up on the couch—
encounter groups, group gropes, group games, and finally
just lying on the floor, screaming out the pain.
Or even, on the lowest level
(which we all descended to in desperation),
self-help books: How to overcome depression,
get more confidence, be popular

But usually, we were safely in the hands of Freud,
whose theories, a whole generation beyond Marx swore,
would rescue mankind from its lot,
and even, in the views of Reich, end war
when we liberated our sexuality
by working through the body's armouring
to release our soft and loving primal selves—
war and love supposedly being incompatible—
also by sitting for hours in the orgone box to absorb
the sexual energy of the universe.

Those were the years when we were all convinced
we were "neurotic," discussed our neuroses passionately,
analyzed our dreams with friends over coffee
and endless cigarettes—we were fiendish smokers—
talked of breakthroughs, insights, and sometimes with awe
of "graduation," when the "neurosis"
would finally be "cured," which meant
you had worked through your blocks, your inhibitions,
and you were no longer Acting Out Negative,
but had found your niche in society—
meaning, marriage, a career, and forgiving your parents.
We argued whether this meant the end of "creativity."

The air is clearer since "phallic symbol"
has gone the way of "penis envy" and "Freudian slip."
Nobody nowadays blames their failures on their neuroses,
and if you say "transferences," everyone assumes
you're talking about your bank accounts.
It's no longer news the discovery
(and Freud deserved the Nobel Prize for it)
that people's minds are always on sex.

But with the same obsession we had with Freud,
and the same narcissism (how we beat each other
with that faded cry), people nowadays are able to simply
turn away from "problems" and wallow in their pleasures,
making a cult of health, and devote themselves
just to working on their bodies. Did I say "just"?
Even Freud was always looking for the roots

of neurosis in the body. And as Claudette Colbert said
on observing Marilyn Monroe's buns,
"I would have had to start at thirteen."

Sadly, true. For us old devotees of the therapies,
the cornerstone of our faith, Talk
and you can change your history,
proved to be bad Freud, and even worse, a fraud—
far more expensive than the gym and stylish joggers.
Years of talking, and nothing got solved.
Except the language of it
seemed to define the losses of a generation,
and for all its radiant promises, that was all.

Callas

The voice that came out of her
seems to have chosen her as its earthly vehicle,
for reasons only the gods can know.

She spoke of it as separate from her, a wild creature
she had to struggle to master.

It floats like a slightly unwieldy bird with a small head,
whose wings can't quite control the over-large body
soaring dangerously low above jagged peaks,
wobbling in the updrafts.

Like an Egyptian sculpture of a priestess in profile,
she held up her large, arresting hands,
invoking the authority of the ancients—
hawks, serpents, bulls and suns surrounded her as she sang,
cut into stone.

She had that specialized genius for song
birds have, an intelligence of too high a vibration
for the practical matters of life.
But she was unfaithful to her gift—
even if for the perfectly human and understandable reasons
of being fashionable and getting a man—
otherwise she would never have dieted down,
but would have stayed fat for those spectacular tones,
living only for art.

It was almost too operatic that the man she suffered over
was, fatally, one of the great rats
who dismissed the most magnificent voice in the world
as just a whistle in her throat.

But after her sexless marriage, this was probably
the first man with a hard on she got together with,
and duck-like, fixated on, as is so common with us ordinary slobs.
With some men, whatever they are besides, the cock
is the best part of them, even if they themselves are monsters
and, like him, supremely selfish in their lives.
And perhaps his selfishness is what ravished her,
for it was sexuality in the raw, the one thing
singing wasn't.

Like Norma, the Druid nun, who broke her vows
for the love of a mere mortal—though not a Greek but a Roman—
she, too, was cast aside, not for any high priestess, but a more
earthly rival, famous widow, jet set icon,
who didn't need his powerful cock, just his power,
and a big allowance.

She threw away her magic voice for a man who threw her away
thunderclap in the heavens, an accusing dagger of lightning
and her crystal brain—
whose single-minded command like a bird's
was to soar, to sing—
shattered, and she fell.

Oh, the Gingkos

In this city where it's perfectly ordinary
to pass by people collapsed on the sidewalks,
or living under plastic on park benches like gypsy camps,
or on flattened cardboard cartons in doorways,
and the gorgeous shirtless Puerto Ricans
are muttering if not raving as they brandish knives,
and high-speed bicycles, free to ignore traffic rules,
whiz by in all directions,
what, I ask you, is there to be grateful for

except the trees along the streets?
And for them we have to thank John V. Lindsay,
who was universally belittled as mayor. But now,
let me set the record straight—attention, Historians:
It was he and he alone who got those trees planted,
the only thing the eyes can bear to look at these days
in a city rotten and stinking in the summer heat
like a garbage dump.

It is hard to imagine these streets anymore
without their trees. But the way I remember it,
after Lindsay was elected, the city was paralyzed by strikes—

teachers, subway and buses, garbagemen, all out,
until he was forced to play along
and made the banks happy by borrowing.
What the hell, he must have said,
what's a hundred thousand more for trees?

Oh, the gingkos he planted,
forests worth of ginkos, which only stink later
in the crisp days of fall.
Oh, the locusts, the sycamores,
oh, the stand of oak battling the fumes in Jackson Square,
oh, the green shade of the linden trees
of Abingdon Square in the Village, now alas,
taken over by a colony of the homeless,
but that's not Lindsay's fault.

I want to say it again and again—
in a country where the government
let's its people rot on the streets,
it was Mayor Lindsay who planted the trees—and oh yes,
put this also on his tombstone, may he live a thousand years:
He stopped the police from raiding gay bars.

CAROLYN FORCHÉ ■ ■ ■ ■ ■ ■ ■ ■ ■ ■ ■ ■ ■ ■

Return

for Josephine Crum

Upon my return to America, Josephine:
the iced drinks & paper umbrellas, clean
toilets & Los Angeles palm trees moving
like lean women, I was afraid more than
I had been, so much so and even of motels
that for months every tire blow-out
was final, every strange car near the house
kept watch & I strained even to remember
things impossible to forget. You took
my stories apart for hours, sitting
on your sofa with your legs under you
& fifty years in your face. So you know
now, you said, what kind of money
is involved & that *campesinos* knife
one another & you know you can't trust
anyone & so you find a few people you can

trust. You know the mix of machetes
with whiskey, the slip of the tongue
& that it costs hundreds of deaths.
You've seen the pits where men and women
are kept the few days it takes without
food & water. You've heard the cocktail
conversation on which depends their release.
So you've come to understand that men & women
of goodwill read torture reports with fascination.
And such things as water pumps & co-op gardens
are of little importance & take years.
It is not Che Guevara, this struggle.
Camillo Torres is dead. Victor Jara
was rounded up with the others & Jose
Marti is a landing strip for planes
from Miami to Cuba. Go try on
Americans your long & dull story
of corruption, but better to give
them what they want: Lil Milagro Ramirez,
who after years of confinement did not
know what year it was, how she walked
with help & was forced to shit in public.
Tell them about the razor, the live wire,
dry ice & concrete, grey rats and above all
who fucked her, how many times and when.
Tell them about retaliation: Jose lying
on the flatbed truck, waving his stumps
in your face, his hands cut off by his
captors & thrown to the many *hectares*
of cotton, lost, still & holding
the last few lumps of leeched earth.
Tell them Jose in his last few hours
& later how, many months later, a labor
leader was cut to pieces & buried.
Tell them how his friends found
the soldiers & made them dig him up
& ask forgiveness of the corpse, once
it was assembled again on the ground
like a man. As for the cars, of course
they watch you & for this don't flatter
yourself. We are all watched. We are
all assembled. Josephine, I tell you
I have not slept, not since I drove
those streets with a gun in my lap,
not since all manner of speaking
has failed & the remnant of my life
continues onward. I go mad, for example,
in the Safeway, at the many heads
of lettuce, papayas & sugar, pineapples

& coffee, especially the coffee.
And I cannot speak with American men.
It is some absence of recognition:
their constant scotch & fine white
hands, many hours of business, penises
hardened to motor inns & a faint
resemblance to their wives. I cannot
keep going. I remember the ambassador
from America to that country: his tanks
of fish, his clicking pen, his rapt
devotion to reports. His wife wrote
his reports. She said as much as she
gathered him each day from the embassy
compound, that she was tired of covering
up, sick of his drink & the failure
of his last promotion. She was a woman
who flew her own plane, stalling out
after four martinis to taxi on an empty
field in the *campo* and to those men
& women announce she was there to help.
She flew where she pleased in that country
with her drunken kindness, while Marines
in white gloves were assigned to protect
her husband. It was difficult work, what
with the suspicion on the rise in smaller
countries that *gringos* die like other men.
I cannot, Josephine, talk to them.
And so you say, you've learned a little
about starvation: a child like a supper scrap
filling with worms, many children strung
together, as if they were cut from paper
& all in a delicate chain. And that people
who rescue physicists, lawyers & poets
lie in their beds at night with reports
of mice introduced into women, of men
whose testicles are crushed like *cojones*
like eggs. That they cup their own parts
with their bedsheets and move themselves
slowly, imagining bracelets affixing
their wrists to a wall where the naked
are pinned, where the naked are tied open
and left to the hands of those who erase
what they touch. We are all erased
by them. We no longer resemble decent
men. We no longer have the hearts,
the strength, the lives of women.
We do not hold this struggle in our hands
in the darkness but ourselves & what little
comes to the surface between our legs.

Your problem is not your life as it is
in America, not that your hands, as you
tell me, are tied to do something. It is
that you were born to an island of greed & grace
where you have this sense of yourself
as apart from others. It is not your right
to feel powerless. Better people than you
were powerless. You have not returned
to your country, but to a life you never left.

Ourselves or Nothing

for Terrence Des Pres

After seven years and as the wine
leaves and black trunks of maples wait
beyond the window, I think of you
north, in the few lighted rooms
of that ruined house, a candle in each
open pane of breath, the absence of anyone,
snow in a hurry to earth, my fingernails
pressing half moons into the sill
as I watched you pouring three
then four fingers of Scotch over ice,
the chill in your throat like a small
blue bone, those years of your work
on the Holocaust. You had to walk
off the darkness, miles of winter
riverfront, windows the eyes in skulls
along the river, gratings in the streets
over jewelled human sewage, your breath
hanging about your face like tobacco.
I was with you even then, your face
the face of a clock as you swept
through the memoirs of men and women
who would not give up. In the short light
of Decembers, you took suppers of whole
white hens and pans of broth
in a city of liquor bottles and light.
Go after that which is lost
and all the mass graves of the century's dead
will open into your early waking hours:
Belsen, Dachau, Saigon, Phnom Penh
and the one meaning Bridge of Ravens,
Sao Paulo, Armagh, Calcutta, Salvador,
although these are not the same.
You wrote too of Theresienstadt,

that word that ran screaming into
my girlhood, lifting its grey wool dress:
the smoke in its violent plumes and feathers,
the dark wormy heart of the human desire to die.
In Prague, Anna told me, there was bread,
stubborn potatoes and fish, armies and the women
who lie down with them, eggs perhaps but never
meat, never meat but the dying.
In Theresienstadt she said there was only the dying.
Never bread, potatoes, fish or women.
They were all as yet girls then.
Vast numbers of men and women died, you wrote
*because they did not have time, the blessing
of sheer time, to recover.* Your ration of time
was smaller then, a tin spoon of winter,
piano notes one at a time from the roof
to the gutter. I am only imagining this,
as I had not yet entered your life
like the dark fact of a gun on your pillow,
or Anna Akhmatova's "Requiem"
and its final *I can* when the faceless woman
before her asked *can you describe this?*
I was not yet in your life when you turned
the bullet toward the empty hole in yourself
and whispered: finish this or die.
But you lived and what you wrote became
The Survivor, that act of contrition for despair:
*They turned to face the worst
straight-on, without sentiment or hope,
simply to keep watch over life.* Now,
as you sleep face down on your papers,
the book pages turning of themselves
in your invisible breath, I climb
the stairs of that house, fragile
with age and the dry fear of burning
and I touch the needle to music to wake you,
the snow long past falling, something
by Vivaldi or Brahms.
I have come from our cacophonous
ordinary lives where I stood at the sink
last summer scrubbing mud from potatoes
and listening to the supper plaice fish
in the skillet, my eyes on the narrowed
streets of rain through the window
as I thought of the long war,
that misted country turned to the moon's surface,
grey and ring-wormed with ridges of light,
the women in their silk *ao dais* along
the river, those flowers under fire, rolled

at night in the desperate arms of American men.
Once I walked your rooms with my
night-dress open, a cigarette from my lips
to the darkness and back as you worked
at times through to the morning.
That is the moment of waking, of return;
and this as I write enacts the same resolution,
the same kind of turn, away
from the monstrous inhumanity, away
from the despair and nihilism they authorize,
back to the small strands of life and decency
which constitute, however faint and scattered,
a fabric of discernible goodness amid that evil.
Always on my waking you were gone,
the blue holes of your path through snow
to the road, your face still haggard
in the white mirror, the pained note
where ten times you had written
the word *recalcitrance* and once:
you *will die and live*
under the name of someone
who has actually died.
I think of that night in a tropic hotel,
the man who danced with a tray over his head
and offered us free because we were *socialistas,*
not only that, he sang, but young and pretty.
Later as I lay on a cot in the heat naked
my friend was able to reach for the guns
and load them clicking in the moonlight
with only the barest of sounds;
he had heard them before me moving among the palms.
We were going to die there.
I remember the moon notching its way
past the leaves and the calm sense that came
for me at the end of my life. In that moment
the woman beside me became my sister,
her hand cupping her mouth, the blood
that would later spill from her face
if what we believed were the truth.
Her blood would crawl black and belly down
onto a balcony of hands and flashlights,
cameras, flowers, propaganda.
Her name was Rene and without knowing
her you wrote: *all things human take time,*
time which the damned never have, time for life
to repair at least the worst of its wounds;
it took time to wake, time for horror
to incite revolt, time for the recovery
of lucidity and will.

In the late afternoons you returned,
the long teeth shining from the eaves,
a clink in the wood half-burnt
and as you touched it alive:
ici repose un déporté inconnu.
In the mass graves, a woman's hand
caged in the ribs of her child,
a single stone in Spain beneath olives,
in Germany the silent windy fields,
in the Soviet Union where the snow
is scarred with wire, in Salvador
where the blood will never soak
into the ground, everywhere and always
go after that which is lost.
There is a cyclone fence between
ourselves and the slaughter and behind it
we hover in a calm protected world like
netted fish, exactly like netted fish.
It is either the beginning or the end
of the world, and the choice is ourselves
or nothing.

TESS GALLAGHER ■ ■ ■ ■ ■ ■ ■ ■ ■ ■ ■ ■ ■ ■ ■

The Hug

A woman is reading a poem on the street
and another woman stops to listen.
We stop too, with our arms around each other.
The poem is being read and listened to
out here in the open. Behind us
no one is entering or leaving the houses.

Suddenly a hug comes over me and I'm
giving it to you, like a variable star shooting light off
to make itself comfortable, then
subsiding. I finish but keep on holding you.
A man walks up to us and we know he hasn't come out of
nowhere, but if he could, he
would have. He looks homeless because of how he needs.
"Can I have one of those?" he asks you, and I feel you
nod. I'm surprised, surprised you don't tell him
how it is—that I'm yours, only
yours, etc., exclusive as a nose to
its face. Love—that's what they call it, love

that nabs you with "for me
only" and holds on.

So I walk over to him and put my arms
around him and try to
hug him like I mean it. He's got an overcoat on
so thick I can't feel him
past it. I'm starting the hug and thinking, "How big
a hug is this supposed to be? How long
shall I hold this hug?" Already
we could be eternal, his arms falling over my
shoulders, my hands not
meeting behind his back, he is so big!

I put my head into his chest and snuggle in.
I lean into him. I lean my blood
and my wishes into him. He stands for it. This
is his and he's starting to give it back so well
I know he's getting it. This hug. So truly,
so tenderly we stop having arms and I don't know
if my lover has walked away or what, or
if the woman is still reading the poem, or the houses—
what about them? the houses.

Clearly, a little permission is a dangerous thing.
But when you hug someone you want it
to be a masterpiece of connection,
the way the button on his coat
will leave the imprint of a planet in my cheek
when I walk away. When I try to find some place
to go back to.

Monologue at the Chinook Bar and Grill

A man who lost both legs, never-
mind how, was, Deano said, the most
courageous man he knew for a-
while. A man, he said, with a sense
of humor, opening up a shoe
repair shop there in Poughkeepsie on
the rugged south side where shoes need all
the attention they can get. He
was a man who loved feet, never-
mind whose. If your bedroom slip-
pers had the soles off, he
would hammer-tap them together again—good
as new. 'I got two hands, don't I?' he
kept saying and then he'd laugh

and it was true he was a man you liked seeing
in spite of the fact he wasn't all
there. Once he fell off his stool while
Deano was waiting at the counter for
a pair of loafers. The guy reached too far
for the phone and just like in a puppet show
he was snatched be-
low with a thud. That's how
Deano got a look at his stumps. The guy
hadn't bothered to get himself fixed
up with artificial limbs or else he
didn't have the benefits. Anyhow there

they were, these stumps all puckered together
and angry-looking. Red like
a monkey's ass, Deano said. Deano, being a
matter of fact guy, goes around and
lifts the man, well this half-a-man anyway,
back into the show. He said to Deano, could he
grab those socks over there while he
was at it, and put them onto the stumps, only
he didn't call them that—'my flippers,'
he said, like he was a seal; or, that humor,
the reflex of covering up for the public,
had made him into a comment on the seriousness
of human affairs. Deano pulled the socks

onto the flippers and crossed his legs as he
leaned back, telling me this in full comfort
where we sat, having a smoke between tries
at heaving a couch up a stairwell toward
my sister's livingroom. But the guy was a
slob, Deano said. All these candy wrappers
ankle-deep behind the counter and old pizza
crusts, you name it! Who would have
thought it, the face he put
on things. Then he'd heard from another
fellow, more-or-less friend, that the man
had fallen off his stool for him
too. He was telling Deano how he'd
scooped the old guy up again, bragging

like he was a better man than you guessed.
Deano asked him about the socks and
the flippers. The guy said he never. But
he was lying, Deano said. He didn't want to
admit he'd cozied up to those stumps
when the old guy asked him
to. And what was so shameful anyway,

Deano said, to do what the guy needed, just
like a friend, or if he had a wife, which
he didn't. Helping was what it was, and
if he got anyone at hand to do it, even
with a trick, like falling off on
purpose, so what? It was little enough.
And anyway, like the guy says, you
got two hands, right? And even

some things you can do for yourself, you'd
rather not. That's where the courage
came in, Deano said, how he got to think-
ing if it was him having to climb on-
to that stool every morning and put
a shoe, a stranger's shoe, onto his hand
and go to work on it. How did he
get up there anyhow without tip-
ping the damned thing over? Then he stood
up, and I said it was probably nailed
down. Deano just looked at me like
a trap door in his mind had
opened so I could drop through. What he

remembered most, Deano said—and now he was
pacing in the little hallway near the
stairs—was the sweet wild smell
of polish and the black smudges on his
shoulders where the guy's hands had hung on
while he lifted him. He didn't see it
until he got home and took his jacket
off to hang up. But who
could take such a guy serious? Deano said—a
man who'd set himself up in business like
a joke you had to laugh at, or cry.

AMY GERSTLER ▪ ▪ ▪ ▪ ▪ ▪ ▪ ▪ ▪ ▪ ▪ ▪ ▪ ▪ ▪

A Sinking Feeling

One feels like an animal
pacing its filthy cave.
Bits of bone litter the floor.
The rusty smell of turning meat
festoons the stagnant air.

One begins to think all action
leads to grief. Joints stiffen.
Arthritis prefigures rigor mortis.
The light is silver this late
in the year, razorlike, expedient,
on the verge of turning,
like that meat mentioned earlier.
Animals are happy on days like today.
Blessings meltdown upon post-modern
heads, copious as flocks
of white-winged religious tracts
fluttering south for the winter,
illustrated with watercolors
of adults, children and dogs greeting
dead friends in the afterlife.
How could anybody be glum
in this superlative weather? Well,
I'll tell you. The day is a young
bubble, with a tiny fire at its core.
My four brothers and I were accidentally
shrunk to the size of ants this afternoon
by our bumbling garage-inventor daddy.
Now we're trapped inside the bubble
as its rises, weaving, on dad's breaths
and mischievous breezes, floating towards
that open window. Bye.

A Fan Letter

Dear Literary Hero,

Now that you've gently
slit open my envelope,
you see naked before you
on this plain drugstore stationery
watermarked with my tears,
the shaky handwriting of one
who has been given a second chance
and desires to use it wisely.
Allow me to tell you a little
about myself. Before I was wiped
clean as the gilt-edged mirror
in my favorite gas station
lavatory—in other words,
prior to being remade
into a reflective, immaculate being
by ingesting physician-approved

chemicals resplendent
as the ingredients of lemon-scented
furniture polish, I felt compelled
to sleep with a grim local widower's
limp twin sons. Then I digressed
to the widower. Still unsatisfied,
I found myself eyeing
his shaggy Scottish deerhounds,
at which point I thought it best
to leave town quietly, by midnight bus,
and take up residence where
I wouldn't continue to shame
my prominent family, dashing
their political ambitions.
Brimming with remorse,
I legally changed my name
and that same night tried
to end my life in bungalow 444
of a cheap roadside motel
called The Log Cabin,
by consuming fool's parsley,
a fungus containing
several toxic compounds.
I didn't even get high.
Dread left a taste in my mouth
like old-fashioned cough syrup
flavored with horehound.
One of my cheeks
went perpetually red.
The other remained deathly pale.
I began to hang around
with old beer drinkers, to want
to lie down all the time.
I noticed a bubbling sensation
around my navel, which emitted
a squeaky hiss, as though
I were a punctured tire
leaking air. It became apparent
my poor tongue, which looked
like a dried orange peel,
was suddenly eight or nine inches
too long, an infirmity
which interfered with wound-licking
and wallpaper tasting.
Yours truly was in a bad way!
I craved meals of charcoal
and discarded tea bags, but consoled
myself with the contents
of coffee shop ashtrays. Doors

became my nemesis—I had to
unhinge them or become unhinged
myself. Then, in the hospital,
one of the meanest ward nurses
had your recent book sticking out
of her huge, shabby purse.
I filched it, just to get
under her skin. Was I surprised,
upon opening your tome and perusing
the first paragraph, to realize
my dark days were almost over.
These pages contained my salvation.
I read and recovered. Your sentences
gave me the kick in the teeth I
sorely needed. The voice of your thoughts
woke me like a rooster announcing
the end of the world, or maybe
a raven who'd grown teeth and learnt
to warble bawdy songs. Your seething words
cured me—reading each was like swallowing
leaf after leaf of a blessed, healing salad
made from ambrosia and ragweed.
I think we should meet. Every night
I stare at the photo of you
on your book's back flap, sitting
in a brocade overstuffed armchair,
smoking your pipe that resembles
a boar's tusk. I close my eyes
and perceive myself curled up
so cozily in your lap, and after that
I see the bright mayhem
of millions of fireworks,
lighting up the dark sky
of our like minds.

REGINALD GIBBONS ▪ ▪ ▪ ▪ ▪ ▪ ▪ ▪ ▪ ▪ ▪ ▪

Breath

I remember coming up,
pushing off from the bottom
through dull ringing silence
toward the undersurface of the water

where light sparkled—or patterns
fanned across the roof-fabric:
that deep comfort, long ago, of
being carried to the house
in the dark, half-asleep, only
half-interrupting the dreams
that had made the car a craft
among stars. But the air—
and the house—held
depths too, where someone else,
someone larger, locked the doors, did
late-night chores and turned out
the lights, too tired now
to stop the inevitable
fight, rising to it . . .

Underwater, you hear bodies
burble over you, smashing the sunlight—
and voices in other rooms begin
to swell, drawers shutting, bags
slammed down from closet shelves,
footsteps . . . Till a child's fear,
held under, shudders free, floating up
to explode with a gasp, and splashes
out of sleep, and sucks air,
and discovers that nothing
consoles, there is no air,
there is no waking, not anywhere.

We Say

We say a heart breaks—like
a stick, maybe, or a bottle
or a wave. But it seems
more like the field clump
that crackles upward from a match
and collapses, grass filaments
sparking in the ash-dust,
then going out. Today
I take myself down by steps,
one at a time, into the sadness
I admit I can't always reach.
There should be a room
at the bottom of the black stairway,
my friends sitting with strangers,
waiting, but there's no one,

only the memory, when
the pale air flickers as if
it were an invisible flame,
of my aunt in her hospital bed
and beside her, about to be left
alone—the last sister, and so soon—
my mother, bent over
the purse in her lap, eyes closed.
I can see the patent leather gloss
and the shiny clasp that until
just now she had been
snapping open and shut, till—
just now—it broke. That breaking—
like a voice that cracks, cursing
or crying, or the song that falls,
out of thinking too far ahead,
into a smouldering loneliness—
was that the sound of the heart?

The Ruined Motel

Give the mourning doves any sun
at all and they will begin to grieve.
Their song, riding the steam that poured up
from the snow on the window-ledge,
came in to us as we scanned
the damp wreck of a sea-side room,
all the things no one inherited:
the sour pink and beige paint,
a throng of water-stain shapes
on the walls—splotchy heads
and moldy animal herds—and behind us
brown vines leaning in at the door
to greet the webs and frost-burnt
mushrooms in the closet.

We sheltered there while our car
held alone the whole weedy expanse
of asphalt fronting the ocean,
and we listened to the cold wind
spill through the sea-grove and splash
against the line of downed carports
and the crowd of pines in the pool.
Looming ahead of us
at the end of the empty road, the shell
of the place had made us think

that it must have been ugly
even when new. Maybe ruined
it suits the small outpost of worshippers
nearby at Immanuel Baptist Church
(Fundamental and Independent)
who grasp their tradition with such force
they tear it apart, their fierce
conviction shredding the creeds
while doves coo and with a useless hiss
the sea bites into the beach-snow
and falls back across the crescent sands.

I was thinking. This was where we had brought
the nation, to neighboring new tries
either abandoned or shuddering inward with extremes—
till you said to me, The ghosts in this place
are unhappy. Then I too could hear them—
couples revenging the hours they had
together under ceilings
that never fell on them, the too-loud talk
at dinner and the hedging, hopeful
postcards in the morning.
We stepped away from them, from the boards
and slats of their collapsed beds,
from their fatigue, from musty air and dead wires,
and we went back into the salt wind,
the noisy swaying pines, out
of that heap of winter-storm
tide-wrack. We didn't want to make
any mistakes but those we could say were ours.

But in that time we stayed there
we took the loss into ourselves,
obsessed with it—not stones
but rotting beaverboard and cold snake-nests,
not columns but dark hallways half-floored with sand.
And if the light that fell on us
as we walked toward the water,
that warmed our bones and stirred the doves,
made the scene seem a lesson-book—
the angles of human space, the path
upward—what did we read?
Under light-shafts from broken clouds,
an immense illumination
of breached walls, frail trees,
a narrow road, snow on the dunes,
dry weed-wisps and bright bits of plastic . . .
and rolling in the waves
like heads that strove

against their own deformity
the great whelks
dashed and battered till hope
was the hollowness in their cold clean skulls.

JACK GILBERT ▪ ▪ ▪ ▪ ▪ ▪ ▪ ▪ ▪ ▪ ▪ ▪ ▪ ▪ ▪ ▪ ▪

Elephant Hunt in Guadalajara

El Serape's floorshow finished at one. The lights
went off and strong girls came like tin moths
to dance carefully with us for eight cents.
Now at last the old tenor has begun the deadly
three o'clock show with its granite Mexican music.
The girls are asleep in the side booths.
Where is it? Where in the name of Christ is it?

Pewter

Thrushes flying under the lake. Nightingales singing underground.
Yes, my King. Paris hungry and leisurely just after the war. Yes.
America falling into history. Yes. Those silent winter afternoons
along the Seine when I was always alone. Yes, my King. Rain
everywhere in the forests of Pennsylvania as the king's coach
lumbered and was caught and all stood gathered close
while the black trees went on and on. Ah, my King,
it was the sweet time of our lives: the rain shining on their faces,
the loud sound of rain around. Like the nights we waited
knowing she was probably warm and moaning under someone else.
That cold mansard looked out over the huge hospital of the poor
and far down on Paris grey and beautiful under the February rain.
Between that and this. That yes and this yes. Between, my King,
that forgotten girl, forgotten pain, and the consequence.
Those lovely, long-ago night bells which I did not notice grow
more and more apparent in me. Like pewter expanding as it cools.
Yes, like a king halted in the great forest of Pennsylvania.
Like me singing these prison songs to praise the grey,
to praise her, to tell of me, yes, and of you, my King.

Getting Ready

What if the heart does not pale as the body wanes,
but is like the sun that blazes hotter each day
on these immense, perishing fields? What then?
(Desire is not the problem. This far south,
we are careful not to mistake seizures for love.)
He sits there bewildered in a clamp of light.
In the stillness, the sun grinds him clean.

The Revolution

Robinson Crusoe breaks a plate on his way out,
and hesitates over the pieces. The ship begins
to sink as he sweeps them up. Sets the table
and stands looking at history for the last time.
Knowing precision will leak from him
however well he learns the weather or vegetation,
and despite the cunning of his hands.
His mind can survive only among the furniture.
Amid the primary colors of the island, he will
become a fine thing, perhaps, but a different one.

Prospero Listens to the Night

The intricately vast process has produced
a singularity which lies in darkness hearing
the whine of small owls, a donkey snorting
in the barley field, and frogs down near the cove
reciting Aristophanes. But what he listens to
is the dogs not barking. They are at each farm
in the valley and tell him what is out there.
The silence means no lover is abroad nor any
poor vagrant looking for where to sleep.
Evidently there was a lovely blonde woman
picking apples every cold morning last year
in Massachusetts until the snow came. The American
who laughed here in the summer at the mention
of Andy Kirk has gone back to Brussels.
"And His Clouds Of Joy," he'd answered and they sat
grinning. He can hear himself not hearing Verdi.
The dogs do not know of the spirits and hearts
of the eight bodies and five loves he listens to.
They do not bark at the vagrant lying quiet

among the heavy grapes under the titanic business
of the fiery rest of Heaven. They are ignorant
of the gentle women who go on standing behind
the dark windows of the farmhouses all night anyhow.
Who can be sure of what else they do not bark at?

To See if Something Comes Next

There is nothing there at the top of the valley.
Sky and morning, silence and the dry smell
of heavy sunlight on the stone everywhere.
Goats occasionally and the sound of roosters
in the bright heat where he lives with the dead
woman and purity. Trying to see if something
comes next. Wondering whether he has stalled.
Maybe, he thinks, it is like the Noh: Whenever
the script says *dances*, whatever the actor does next
is a dance. If he stands still, he is dancing.

The White Heart of God

The snow falling around the man in the naked woods
is like the ash of heaven, ash from the cool fire
of God's mother-of-pearl, moon-stately heart.
Sympathetic but not merciful. His strictness
parsing us is the discomfort of living this way
without birds. The maples without leaves make
death and the world visible. Not the harshness,
but the way this world can be known by pushing
against it. And feeling something pushing back.
The whiteness of the winter married to this river
makes the water look black. The water actually
is the color of giant mirrors set along the marble
corridors of the spirit, the mirrors empty
of everything. The man is doing the year's accounts.
Finding the balance, trying to estimate how he has
been translated. For it does translate him,
well or poorly. As the woods are translated
by the seasons. He is searching for a baseline
of the Lord. He searches like the blind man
going forward with a hand stretched out in front.
As the truck driver ice-fishing on the big pond
tries to learn from his line what is down there.
The man attends to any signal that might announce

Jesus. He hopes for even the faintest evidence,
the presence of His least abundance. He measures
with tenderness, afraid to find a heart more classical
than ripe. Hoping for honey, for love's alembic.

ALLEN GINSBERG ▪ ▪ ▪ ▪ ▪ ▪ ▪ ▪ ▪ ▪ ▪ ▪ ▪ ▪

No Way Back to the Past

On the Ferris Wheel rising to the full moon
by the canal, looking down on Ocean Grove
over a red-bulb-rooft green-lit carousel, silver Chariot of Muse with her Lyre,
 revolving all too fast
through years from 1937 with cousin Claire in Asbury Park
wandering Sunday morning from Belmar with a few pennies dimes for tickets in
 Playland—
the wire-mesh railed cage swinging under a canvas-flowered awning toward the
 full moon forty years later,
a bent Hunchback at the Gate pulling his iron-rod handle to bring the iron-
 spoked circle hung with pleasure cars to rest.
Whacky shack's painted toy-wizard witch-monster window
Machinery's laughing screaming lifting wooden eyelids
at fair skinned blond boys rubber-bumping electric cars along a sheet-tin floor,
with trolleypole antennae sliding and sparking across the silvery ceiling.
I used to ride the skooter with my cousins Claire and Joel Gaidemack or brother
 Gene,
cars shocking lightly on the happy floor, wheeling the toy Dodgem in a circle
turning round the curve, I looked up in the mirror
and saw a bald white bearded man in a white shirt staring in my eyes—
and entered in the giant wood Barrel-form slippery rolling underfoot reflecting
 mirrored through its other end *Time Tunnel,*

II

Time in the car with stepmother Edith at the wheel returning from the shore,
 the panic of Eternal space Unchanging
through which our phantom bodies pass now highway grandeur'd under blue sky.
And poor little Claire's gone, a ghost in my mind—
walking the big sandy beach, jumping granite boulders sharp edged on the jetty
 with
all us who played Jungle Camp in the Belmar weed-grown empty lot's leafy
 bower
before going to Asbury, the Mayfair Theater Sunday see Paul Muni's movie Dr.
 Pasteur.

One family house, sat on the porch at night and beat away the mosquitos
near the tiny Playland where Eugene worked, by a 20 foot ferris wheel &
      carousel with tiny horses going round
merrily on 16th Avenue across from Ocean's wide beach—
Old ladies with rolls of fat round their waists and silk stockings
on boardwalk benches faced the blue water spread's sunny waves—
Ocean side infancy, pails in brown salt puddles of sandcastles
A thrill at the heart, hearing German Attack Poland radio, I biked to tell Esther
      Cohen
or Claire Mann niece of movie mogul Louis B. Mayer of Metro
      Goldwin Mayer owned Mayfair Theater—
Riding under the full moon on the Ferris Wheel last night 40 years ago,
grabbing the brass ring from the horse riding up and down whirling slowly
      ecstatically to carousel toot tune
repeated, the floating balance and calm of marijuana Meditation
Now Mindy her second daughter's alive young vegetarian eyes
by the ocean at Long Beach, in the run down section cleaned white in late May
      shine—
So return through the past to this moment on Route 36 Sandy Hook to Perth
      Amboy
past Exxon whose gas our car burns the Rockefellers—David
they say wants to be loved liked respected—as long as he's loved and
      pharmacied—
I was car sick on the bus to Morristown, Naomi in Greystone that war year? she
      too afraid of Hitler—
my first mother a victim of persecution a Jewess crazed by Earth Electric
Meanwhile I went to the shore every year from 1935 till World War II
when I went to High School and campaigned for Irving Abramson for Congress
& lost to Congressman Gordon Canfield Republican Isolationist
I wrote Newsletters to Paterson Papers, thirteen years old saved vast clipping pix
      of Hitler and Hindenberg blow up
Claire whirling away at dances with her boyfriends, a normal Jewish crowd
that went to Showers and Proms. When I think of the bodies chill graves Coffins
      & Absence—
Then Claire grew up and got married to Jerry Gorlin and moved to the ocean
      library in Rumsen, NJ—
Cornell Hospital later rosey on the bed, hair cut for cancer therapy, I gave her a
      Buddhabook—
Sudden hearted Death, old Claire young cousin Claire
Louis Rose and Claire Names returning from Belmar through Perth Amboy and
      the Raritan River Bridge, outlooking Raritan Bay
—distant towers of World Trade Center, passing White Gas tanks flat on the
      marshes of Linden
Watercastles and barber-striped Transmission Towers electric-armed with wires
& smokestacks smelling industrial not far from Louis graveyard
Cracker stacks and flues & ironstairwayed metal tubes smoking at Elizabeth's
      border
& the big brown gas tanks sinking into earth on their skeleton struts—

Newark airport, Insurance buildings at left hand New York's skein of towers
 resting on the right horizon
Railroad *Southern* red Cars under Jersey City's red-brick church, green-copper
 spiked under blue sky
Look how bright Manhattan! towery below the hill, car graveyard by the
 Turnpike,
Higher than Empire State
Mayor Hague's Hospital, scandals not run properly my Grandmother didn't like
 the way she was treated.
Past the Exxon sign thru Holland Tunnel's bathroom-polished tile Good old N.Y.
 cobblestoned and sunny

May 20, 1978

Grim Skeleton

Grim skeleton come back & put me out of Action
looking thru the rainy window at the Church wall
yellow vapor lamped, 9pm Cars hissing in street water
—woken dizzy from neurotic sleep—papers piled on my desk
myself lost in manila files of yellow faded newspaper Clippings
at last after twenty five years tapes wound thru my brain
Library of my own deeds of music tongue & oratoric yell
Is it my heart, a cold & phlegm in my skull or radiator
Comfort cowardice that I slumber awake wrapped in Mexican
Blanket, wallet & keys on the white chair by my head.
Is it the guru of music or guru of meditation whose harsh force
I bear, makes my eyelid heavy mid afternoons, is't Death
stealing in my breast makes me nauseous waking, work undone
on a typewriter set like a green skull by the window
When I wake mornings unwilling to rise & take the Narcotic Times
above a soft Boiled egg and toasted English muffin daily noon?
Beauty, Truth, Revolution, what skeleton in my closet silent
makes me listen dumb to my own skull thoughts lethargic, in dark tonight
Gossip of Poets silenced by drunken Mussolinis every Country on Earth?
My own empty yatter of meditation, while I work and scream in frenzy
at my wooden shelf help up by iron filedrawers stuffed w/press paper
&   prophetic fake manuscripts, my ears itching & scabbed w/anger
at ghost Rockefeller Brothers pay off of CIA, am I myself the CIA
bought with acid meat & alcohol in Washington, silenced in meditation
on my own duplicity, stuck in anger at the puerto rican wounded
beerdrunk fathers walking East 12th street and their thieving kids
violent screaming under my window at 4AM. Some Fantasy of Fame
I dreamt in adolescence Came true last week over Television,
Now homunculus I made's out there in streets all over America
talking with my voice, accounted ledgered opinionated

interviewed & Codified in Poems, books & manuscripts, whole library
shelves stacked with ambitious egohood's thousand pages imagined
forth smart selft over half a lifetime! Who'm I now, Frankenstein
hypocrite of good Cheer whose sick stomached Discretion's grown
fifty years overweight—while others I hate practice sainthood in Himalayas
or run the petrochemical atomic lamplight machines, by whose power
I slumber cook my meat & write these verses captive of N.Y.C.
What's my sickness, flue virus or selfhood infected & swollen sore
confronting the loathed work of poetic flattery: Gurus, Rock stars
Penthoused millionaires, White House alrightnicks crowding my brain
with their orders & formulae, insults & smalltalk, threats & dollars
Whose sucker am I, the media run by rich whitemen like myself, jew
intellectuals afraid of poverty bust screaming beaten uncontrolled behind bars
or the black hole of Narcotics Cops & brutal mafiosi, thick men in dark hats,
hells angels in blue military garb or wall street cashmere drag
hiding iron muscles of money, so the street is full of potholes, I'm afraid
to go out at night around the block to look at the moon in the Lower East Side
with stricken junkies victimized, necks broken in damp hallways of
abandoned buildings gutted & blackwindowed from old fires. I'm afraid
to write my thoughts down lest I libel Nelson Rockefeller, Fidel
Castro, Chögyam Trungpa, W.S. Merwin, or Ed Sanders, Peter O.
yea Henry Kissinger & Richard Helms, faded ghosts of Power & Poesy
that people my brain with their paranoia, my best friend shall be Nameless.
Whose public speech is this I write? What stupid vast Complaint!
For what impotent Professor's ears, for which Newsman's brain wave?
Is this Immortal history to tell tales of 20th Century to striplings
naked centuries hence in my mind? To get laid by some brutal queen
Who'll beat my hairy buttocks punishment in a College Dorm? To show my ass
to god? To grovel in my own magic tinsel & glitter on stinking powdered pillows?
Agh! Who'll I read this to like a fool! Who'll applaud these lies

December 16, 1977

The Charnel Ground

". . . rugged and raw situations, and having accepted them as part of your home ground,
then some spark of sympathy or compassion could take place. You are not in a hurry to
leave such a place immediately. You would like to face the facts, realities of that particular
world . . ."
—FROM A COMMENTARY ON *THE SADHANA OF MAHAMUDRA*, CHÖGYAM TRUNGPA, RINPOCHE

Upstairs Jenny crashed her car & became a living corpse, Jake sold grass, the
    white bearded pot belly leprechaun silent climbed their staircase
Ex-janitor John from Poland averted his eyes, cheeks flushed with vodka, wine
    who knew what
as he left his groundfloor flat, refusing to speak to the inhabitant of Apt 24
Who'd put his boyfriend in Bellevue, calling police, while the artistic Buddhist
    composer

on sixth floor lay spaced out feet swollen with water, dying slowly of AIDS over a
  year—
The Chinese teacher cleaned & cooked in Apt 23 for the homosexual poet who
  pined for his gymnast
thighs & buttocks—Downstairs th' old hippy flower girl fell drunk over the
  banister, smashed her jaw—
her son despite moderate fame cheated of rocknroll money, twenty thousand
  people in stadiums
cheering his tattooed skinhead murderous Hare Krishna vegetarian drum
  lyrics—
Mary born in the building rested on her cane heavy legged with heart failure on
  the second landing, no more able
to vacation in Caracas & Dublin—The Russian landlady's husband from
  Concentration Camp disappeared again—nobody mentioned he'd died—
tenants took over her building for hot water, she couldn't add rent & pay taxes,
  wore a long coat hot days
alone & thin on the street carrying groceries to her crooked apartment silent—
One poet highschool teacher fell dead mysterious heart disrythmia, konked over
  in his mother's Brooklyn apartment, his first baby girl a year old, wife stoical a
  few days—
their growling noisy little dog had to go, the baby cried—
Meanwhile the upstairs apartment meth head shot cocaine & yowled up and
  down
East 12th Street, kicked out of Christine's Eatery till police cornered him, top a
  hot iron steamhole
near Stuyvesant Town Avenue A telephone booth calling his deaf mother—sirens
  speed the way to Bellevue—
past whispering grass crack salesman jittering in circles on East 10th Street's
southwest corner where art yuppies come out of the overpriced Japanese Sushi
  Bar—& they poured salt into potato soup heart failure vats at KK's Polish
  restaurant
—Garbage piled up, nonbiodegradable plastic bags emptied by diabetic sidewalk
  homeless
looking for returnable bottles recycled dolls radios half eaten hamburgers—
  thrown away Danish—
On 13th Street the notary public sat in his dingy storefront, drivers lessons & tax
  returns prepared on old metal desks—
Sunnysides crisped in butter, fries & sugary donuts passed over the luncheonette
  counter next door—
The Hispanic lady yelled at the rude African-American behind the Post Office
  window
"I waited all week my welfare check you sent me notice I was here yesterday
I want to see the supervisor bitch dont insult me refusing to look in—"
Closed eyes of Puerto Rican wino lips cracked skin red stretched out
on the pavement, naptha backdoor open for the Korean family Dry Cleaners at
  the 14th Street corner
Con Ed workmen drilled all year to bust electric pipes 6 feet deep in brown dirt
so cars bottlenecked wait minutes to pass the M14 bus stopped mid-road, heavy
  dressed senior citizens step down in red rubble

with Reduced Fare Program cards got from grey city Aging Department officers
   downtown up the second flight by elevators don't work—
News comes on the radio, they bombed Baghdad and the Garden of Eden again?
A million starve in Sudan, mountains of eats stacked on docks, local gangs &
   U.N.'s trembling bureaucrat officers sweat near the equator arguing over
Wheat piles shoved by bulldozers—Swedish doctors ran out of medicine—The
   Pakistan taxi driver
says Salman Rushdie must die, insulting the prophet in fictions
"No that wasn't my opinion, just a character talking like in a poem no judgment"
"Not till the sun rejects you do I," so give you a quarter by the Catholic Church
   14th St you stand half drunk
waving a plastic glass, flush faced, live with your mother a wounded look on your
   lips, eyes squinting,
receding lower jaw sometimes you dry out in Bellevue, most days cadging dollars
   for sweet wine
by the corner where Plump Blindman shifts from foot to foot showing his white
   cane, rattling coins in a white paper cup some weeks
where girding the subway entrance construction saw-horses painted orange
guard steps underground—And across the street the NYCE bank machine
   cubicle door sign reads
Not in Operation as taxis bump on potholes asphalt mounded at the crossroad
   when red lights change green
& I'm on my way uptown to get a cat scan liver biopsy, visit the cardiologist,
account for high blood pressure, kidneystones, diabetes, misty eyes &
   dysesthesia—
feeling lack in feet soles, inside ankles, small of back, phallus head, anus—
Old age sickness death again come round in the wink of an eye—
High school youth the inside skin of my thighs was silken smooth tho nobody
   touched me there back then—
Across town the velvet poet takes Darvon N, valium nightly, sleeps all day kicking
   methadone
between brick walls sixth floor in a room cluttered with collages & gold dot paper
   scraps covered
with words: "The whole point seems to be the idea of giving away the giver."

                                        August 19, 1992

Who Eats Who?

A crow sits on the prayerflagpole,
her mate blackwinged walks the wet green grass, worms?
Yesterday seagulls skimmed the choppy waves,
    feet touching foamed breakers
             looking for salmon? halibut? sole?
Bacteria eat paramecium or vice versa
Viruses enter cells, white cell count low—

Tooth & claw on TV, lions strike down antelopes—
Whales sift transparent krill thru bearded teeth.
Every cannibal niche fulfilled, Amazon
    headhunters eat testicles—
            Enemy's powers & energy become mine!

           Gampo Abbey, Nova Scotia 8/13/92

Not Dead Yet

Huffing puffing upstairs downstairs telephone
    office mail checks secretary revolt—
The Soviet Legislative Communist bloc
    inspired Gorbachev's wife and Yeltsin
to shut up in terror or stand on a tank
    in front of White House denouncing Putschists—
September breezes sway branches & leaves in
    a calm schoolyard under humid grey sky,
Drink your decaf Ginsberg old communist New
    York Times addict, be glad you're not Trotsky.

           9/16/91

Yiddishe Kopf

I'm Jewish because love my family Matzoh ball soup
I'm Jewish because my fathers mothers uncles grandmothers said "Jewish," all
    the way back to Vitebsk & Kaminetz-Podolska via Lvov.
Jewish because reading Dostoyevsky at 13 I write poems at restaurant tables
    Lower East Side, perfect delicatessen intellectual.
Jewish because violent Zionists make my blood boil, Progressive indignation.
Jewish because Buddhist, my anger's transparent hot air, I shrug my shoulders.
Jewish because monotheist Jews Catholics Moslems're intolerable intolerant—
Blake sd. "6000 years of sleep" since antique Nobodaddy Adonai's mind trap—
    OY! such Meshuggeneh absolutes—
Senior Citizen Jewish paid my dues got half-fare card buses subways, discount
    movies—
Can't imagine how these young people make a life, make a living.
How can they stand it, going out in the world with only $10 and a hydrogen
    bomb?

           October 1991

A Thief Stole This Poem

These days steal everything
People steal your wallet, your watch
Break into your car steal your radio suitcase
Break in your house, your SONY Hi 8 your CD VCR Olympus OM 2S
People steal your life, catch you on the street & steal your head off
Steal your shoes in the toilet
Steal your love, mug your boyfriend rape your grandmother on the subway
Junkies steal your heart for medicine, they steal your credibility gap over the
    radio
Cokeheads & blackmen steal your comfort, peace of mind walking Avenue A
    hands on your laundry they
steal your spirit, you gotta worry
Puerto Ricans steal white skin from your face
Wasps steal your planet for Junk bonds, Jews steal your Nobodaddy and leave
    their dirty God in your bed
Arabs steal your pecker & you steal their oil
Everybody's stealing from everyone else, time, sex, wristwatch
Steal your sleep 6 AM Garbage Trucks boomboxes sirens loud arguments
    hydrogen bombs
steal your universe.

                                                              12/19/91, 8:15

Homeless Compleynt

          Pardon me buddy, I didn't mean to bug you
                    but I came from Vietnam
          where I killed a lot of Vietnamese gentlemen
                              a few ladies too
          and I couldn't stand the pain
                         and got a habit out of fear
          & I've gone through rehab and I'm clean
                    but I got no place to sleep
                              and I don't know what to do
                                   with myself right now
          I'm sorry buddy, I didn't mean to bug you
                    but it's cold in the alley
                              & my heart's sick alone
          and I'm clean, but my life's a mess
                    Third Avenue
                         and E. Houston Street
               on the corner traffic island under a red light
                    wiping your windshield with a dirty rag

                                                       December 24, 1996

LOUISE GLÜCK ▪ ▪ ▪ ▪ ▪ ▪ ▪ ▪ ▪ ▪ ▪ ▪ ▪ ▪ ▪

Aubade

The world was very large. Then
the world was small. O
very small, small enough
to fit in a brain.

It had no color, it was all
interior space: nothing
got in or out. But time
seeped in anyway, that
was the tragic dimension.

I took time very seriously in those years,
if I remember accurately.

A room with a chair, a window.
A small window, filled with the patterns light makes.
In its emptiness the world

was whole always, not
a chip of something, with
the self at the center.

And at the center of the self,
grief I thought I couldn't survive.

A room with a bed, a table. Flashes
of light on the naked surfaces.

I had two desires: desire
to be safe and desire to feel. As though

the world were making
a decision against white
because it disdained potential
and wanted in its place substance:

panels
of gold where the light struck.
In the window, reddish
leaves of the copper beech tree.

Out of the stasis, facts, objects
blurred or knitted together: somewhere

time stirring, time
crying to be touched, to be
palpable,

the polished wood
shimmering with distinctions—

and then I was once more
a child in the presence of riches
and I didn't know what the riches were made of.

The New Life

I slept the sleep of the just,
later the sleep of the unborn
who come into the world
guilty of many crimes.
And what these crimes are
nobody knows at the beginning.
Only after many years does one know.
Only after long life is one prepared
to read the equation.

I begin now to perceive
the nature of my soul, the soul
I inhabit as punishment.
Inflexible, even in hunger.

I have been in my other lives
too hasty, too eager,
my haste a source of pain in the world.
Swaggering as a tyrant swaggers;
for all my amorousness,
cold at heart, in the manner of the superficial.

I slept the sleep of the just;
I lived the life of a criminal
slowly repaying an impossible debt.
And I died having answered for
one species of ruthlessness.

Unwritten Law

Interesting how we fall in love:
in my case, absolutely. Absolutely, and, alas, often—
so it was in my youth.
And always with rather boyish men—

unformed, sullen, or shyly kicking the dead leaves:
in the manner of Balanchine.
Nor did I see them as versions of the same thing.
I, with my inflexible Platonism,
my fierce seeing of only one thing at a time:
I ruled against the indefinite article.
And yet, the mistakes of my youth
made me hopeless, because they repeated themselves,
as is commonly true.
But in you I felt something beyond the archetype—
a true expansiveness, a buoyance and love of the earth
utterly alien to my nature. To my credit,
I blessed my good fortune in you.
Blessed it absolutely, in the manner of those years.
And you in your wisdom and cruelty
gradually taught me the meaninglessness of that term.

Roman Study

He felt at first
he should have been born
to Aphrodite, not Venus,
that too little was left to do,
to accomplish, after the Greeks.

And he resented light,
to which Greece has
the greatest claim.

He cursed his mother
(privately, discreetly),
she who could have arranged all of this.

And then it occurred to him
to examine these responses
in which, finally, he recognized
a new species of thought entirely,
more worldly, more ambitious
and politic, in what we now call
human terms.

And the longer he thought,
the more he experienced
faint contempt for the Greeks,
for their austerity, the eerie
balance of even the great tragedies—
thrilling at first, then
faintly predictable, routine.

And the longer he thought
the more plain to him how much
still remained to be experienced,
and written down, a material world heretofore
hardly dignified.

And he recognized in exactly this reasoning
the scope and trajectory of his own
watchful nature.

Condo

I lived in a tree. The dream specified
pine, as though it thought I needed
prompting to keep mourning. I hate
when your own dreams treat you as stupid.

Inside, it was
my apartment in Plainfield, twenty years ago,
except I'd added a commercial stove.
Deep-rooted

passion for the second floor! Just because
the past is longer than the future
doesn't mean there is no future.

The dream confused them, mistaking
one for the other: repeated

scenes of the gutted house—Vera was there,
talking about the light.
And certainly there was a lot of light, since
there were no walls.

I thought: this is where the bed would be,
where it was in Plainfield.
And deep serenity flooded through me,
such as you feel when the world can't touch you.
Beyond the invisible bed, light
of late summer in the little street,
between flickering ash trees.

Which the dream changed, adding, you could say,
a dimension of hope. It was
a beautiful dream, my life was small and sweet, the world
broadly visible because remote.

The dream showed me how to have it again
by being safe from it. It showed me
sleeping in my old bed, first stars
shining through bare ash trees.

I have been lifted and carried far away
into a luminous city. Is this what having means,
to look down on? Or is this dreaming still?
I was right, wasn't I, choosing
against the ground?

The Winged Horse

Here is my horse Abstraction,
silver white, color of the page,
of the unwritten.

Come, Abstraction,
by Will out of Demonic Ambition:
carry me lightly into the regions of the immortal.

I am weary of my other mount,
by Instinct out of Reality,
color of dust, of disappointment,
notwithstanding
the saddle that went with him
and the bronze spurs, the bit
of indestructible metal.

I am weary of the world's gifts, the world's
stipulated limits.

And I am weary of being opposed
and weary of being constantly contradicted by the material, as by
a massive wall where all I say can be
checked up on.

Then come, Abstraction,
take me where you have taken so many others,
far from here, to the void, the star pasture.

Bear me quickly,
Dream out of Blind Hope.

Mutable Earth

Are you healed or do you only think you're healed?

I told myself
from nothing
nothing could be taken away.

But can you love anyone yet?

When I feel safe, I can love.

But will you touch anyone?

I told myself
if I had nothing
the world couldn't touch me.

In the bathtub, I examine my body.
We're supposed to do that.

And your face too?
Your face in the mirror?

I was vigilant: when I touched myself
I didn't feel anything.

Were you safe then?

I was never safe, even when I was most hidden.
Even then I was waiting.

So you couldn't protect yourself?

The absolute
erodes; the boundary, the wall
around the self erodes.
If I was waiting I had been
invaded by time.

But do you think you're free?

I think I recognize the patterns of my nature.

But do you think you're free?

I had nothing
and I was still changed.
Like a costume, my numbness
was taken away. Then
hunger was added.

Eurydice

Eurydice went back to hell.
What was difficult
was the travel, which,
on arrival, is forgotten.

Transition
is difficult.
And moving between two worlds
especially so;
the tension is very great.

A passage
filled with regret, with longing,
to which we have, in the world,
some slight access or memory.

Only for a moment
when the dark of the underworld
settled around her again
(gentle, respectful),
only for a moment could
an image of earth's beauty
reach her again, beauty
for which she grieved.

But to live with human faithlessness
is another matter.

PAUL GOODMAN ▪ ▪ ▪ ▪ ▪ ▪ ▪ ▪ ▪ ▪ ▪ ▪ ▪ ▪ ▪

In the Jury Room, in Pain

Waiting to whimper or for Messiah
it doesn't matter much
if I wait in the jury room
of the Criminal Courts Building
until the prosecutor
challenges me again
because I don't believe
in *their* penal system

or if like yesterday I hover
eight miles high until
the iron roc descends

it doesn't matter where.
In between is better
than whence I came or where I go
to be with my headache
alone in purgatory.

Here watchfully I wend
and wander through the wonderful
landscape of Pains
where unexpectedly
the ache-trees in the grove
blossom into flowers
and small birds murmuring
hop from twinge to twinge.

Oh the days have vanished quickly by
during which I made a library
of useful thoughts for the Americans
and became a famous man;
but the one empty night of torment
in which I do not fall asleep
is when I write the poem
that says how my life was.

Birthday Cake

Now isn't it time
when the candles on the icing
are one two too many
too many to blow out
too many to count too many
isn't it time to give up this ritual?

although the fiery crown
fluttering on the chocolate
and through the darkened room advancing
is still the most loveliest sight
among our savage folk
that have few festivals.

But the thicket is too hot and thick
and isn't it time, isn't it time
when the fires are too many
to eat the fire and not the cake
and drip the fires from my teeth
as once I had my hot hot youth.

Sentences After *Defence of Poetry*

A man who fixed his eyes
with longing on the sun
might see the sun stand still
while he himself was carried
east on the turning earth
swept blinded into night:
so did I love some one
once, like Copernicus.

Stars are sweeping past me
—I can fix my attention
only on my sick body
and that is not still either,
I am upside down.
They say that God is still
—where? I am too stupid
to understand it like Einstein.

I made a golden disk
like a Keltic relic
that I saw in Dublin.
I do not love it,
it doesn't keep me warm,
but I hide and stare
at it and into it
flat and impenetrable.

It says, "Your eyes are going blind,
you have three teeth and cannot chew,
often you are dizzy.
Yet it is quiet here
in our neolithic cave
and you do love me
although you glimpse I am
a flat evil fetish."

I love the English language.
She has loved me.
I used to stutter, fear stuck
my voice inside my mouth
—my rebel double
fought with me she should speak.
Now I say fearlessly
what I didn't know I knew.

[Connary, Blodgett, Day, Hapgood]

Connary, Blodgett, Day, Hapgood
and Dennis are the names in the graveyard
of the abandoned church. The local French
are buried Catholic with their own.
A Jew newcomer, I have also chosen
to lie in this pretty land of my exile.
"Goodman" will look as quiet
as the rest under the maple trees.

Ballade of the Moment After

Table and chair were overturned,
bread and wine spilt on the floor,
King Macbeth stared straight in front
and still he saw what was before;
his lady's voice came from afar
over his shoulder wooingly
but not to the point anymore,
the moment after the catastrophe.

In a cloister, by a dried-up font
—di Chirico that cloister saw—
the shadow of a man was burnt
in the pavement and its length was more
than a man is high; beyond the door
a locomotive silently
puffed, and it was half past four,
the moment after the catastrophe.

So little Perseus did confront,
tricycling down the corridor,
the gorgon of his mother's cunt
before his mother could withdraw.

Nothing was said by either or
but from that day he chose to see
the world backward in a mirror,
the moment after the catastrophe.

The wonder that I waited for
suddenly has come to be.
My hands are clenched around neither/nor
the moment after the catastrophe.

[Woman eternal my muse, lean toward me]

Woman eternal my muse, lean toward me
again from heaven for these
comforters on the earth have died
or left me, and none others please.

You were Ariadne my leader
to where the monster lay,
I met him there, and you restored
me forth unscathed under the sky.

Three-person'd Fate, who draw my thread
and measure out and cut its length,
passing along from hand to hand
I rest assured in their strength.

I know you as Persephone
the queen of Hell and Flowers
who idly guide my course
to where is only guessed by me.

My limbs are shuddering
but I am not afraid
for it is I the requiem made
for those who died in the Dead of Spring.

FROM *Sentences for Matthew Ready, Series II*

104. Now only praise makes me cry,
      when David Hume praises Alfred
      I read it through a shine of tears,
      and if a poet praises loud
      —naturally loud is praise—some ancient
      hero who never lived in this world,
      then my heart breaks and I bawl
      for joy in this land of loss.

A Gravestone, August 8, 1968

19. The Sun and the Ocean
    and Death are unique,
    the limiting conditions
    within which we live.

And there is one single Night
(although De Falla sang
of nights in the gardens of Spain),
Freedom too

is indivisible,
its flag is therefore black
not like the other flags
that have armorial bearings.

Come and see, on this granite grout
gravestone is the motto cut
of all the youth of the world:
Twenty Years Unregistered.

Off Route 3 it is,
a few miles north of Groveton,
if you want to know something,
among the orange hawkweed.

[It was good when you were here,]

It was good when you were here,
    I am lonely now.
Nighttime is the worst
    when the light drops out of the sky

and the colored fields that were
    company vanish.
I dislike to go out
    into the dark open

but in my empty house
    is the presence of your not-being,
the speech we do not sound,
    the touch I cannot reach.

Surely long ago
    I wrongly set out toward
this familiar encounter
    with no one at all.

During my prime years
    my country passed me by.
I made do. (America
    alas has not made do.)

God bless you who from time to time
    have brought me peace for a day

and saved me from writing only prose
   while my hair turns gray

and may to me God give
   the grace of the poor:
to praise without a grudge
   the facts just as they are.

JORIE GRAHAM ▪ ▪ ▪ ▪ ▪ ▪ ▪ ▪ ▪ ▪ ▪ ▪ ▪ ▪ ▪

Breakdancing

(*Teresa:* Saint Teresa of Avila)

Staying alive the boy on the screen is doing it,
   the secret nobody knows like a rapture through his limbs,
the secret, *the robot-like succession of joint isolations*
   that simulate a body's reaction to
electric shock.
   This is how it tells itself: pops, ticks, waves and the

float. What
   is poverty for, Mr. Speed, Dr. Cadet, Dr. Rage,
Timex? Don't push me the limbs are whispering, don't push
   cause I'm close to the edge the footwork is whispering
down onto the sidewalk that won't give in, won't go some other
   where while the TV

hums and behind me their breathings, husband, daughter, too slow,
   go in to that other place and come back out
unstained, handfuls at a time, air, air—
   The flag of the greatest democracy on earth
waves in the wind with the sound turned off. The current

rubs through the stars and stripes
   like a muttering passing through a crowd and coming out an
anthem,
   string of words on its search
and destroy
   needing bodies, bodies. . . .
I'm listening to where she must not choke. I'm listening
   to where he must not be betrayed. I'm trying

to hear pity, the idiom. I'm trying to lean into those
   marshes and hear

what comes through clean,
    what comes through changed,
having needed us.
    Oh but you must not fail to eat and sleep Teresa murmurs to
her flock,

staying alive is the most costly gift you have to offer Him—all the while
                                watching,

    (whispering Lord, what will you have me
do?) for his corporal
    appearance
in the light of the sixteenth century, in the story that flutters
    blowzy over the body of the land
we must now somehow ram
    the radioactive waste

into. He
    showed himself to her in pieces.
First the fingertips; there in mid-air,
    clotting, floating, held up by the invisible, neither rising
nor falling nor approaching nor lingering, then hands, then a

few days later feet, torso, then arms, each part alone, each part
    free of its argument, then days, then eyes,
then face entire, then days again, then *His*
    most sacred humanity in its risen form
was represented to me

completely. "Don't try
    to hold me in yourself (the air, hissing) but try to hold yourself
in me," Nov. 18, 1570. I'm listening to where she must not choke,
    I'm listening to where he must not, must not. . . . Air,
holding a girl in a man's arms now,
    making them look like wind,
what if they can't be returned to you
    the *things* now reaching me—the three

exhalings, hum, blue light, the minutes, the massacres, the strict
                            halflife of

    radioactive isotopes, the shallow
graves, the seventeen rememberable personal
    lies? What if they go only this far, grounding
in me, staying
    alive?
Here is the secret: the end is an animal.
    Here is the secret: the end is an animal growing by

accretion, image by image, vote by
    vote. *No more pain* hums the air,
as the form of things shall have fallen
      from thee, no more pain, just the here and the now, the
                              jackpot, the
watching, minutes exploding like thousands of silver dollars all
                            over your
face your hands but tenderly, almost tenderly, turning mid-air,
                         gleaming,
so slow, as if it could last,
    frame after frame of nowhere

turning into the living past.

Underneath (1)

Painful to look up.
No. Painful to look out.

Heard the bird hit the pane hard.
Didn't see it. Heard nothing
drop.

To look out past the shimmering screen to the miles of
grasses.

—————

Wind-hurryings.
Low-lying of stoppages.
No Reason.
Always tried knew how to try.

—————

Birdcall in the farthest windsounds: atoms.
Opening to it: atoms.
Smaller birdcalls   interruptions
In the swellings   and droppings-off

of current-gush: atoms.
Always.
The sun on the miles of tall-grass seed-tips.
The screen glimmering the world into a silver grid.
Inside the grid nothing complete. Everything that was plunging
                        now runny with
organization.—Fence grass wind gate

open gate or closed.
Distance.

Near noon all the tall grasses for an instant stiff at
attention,

then a sturdy nervousness from left to right—
Deep bending of the light—
light carried across on the backs, in on the tips—
the screengrid forced so deep into the eye it's in
disappearance—or the mind—as

you   will
have   it
No   where
No   two

silvers alike although all bendings or bowings
identical
except for the fact of
difference

As in
Yes Sir

where the raven suddenly wetly and rawly
roughens the low vacillations of various windsweeping
hushings—as if he's clawed
a thing truly all the way to

atom and taken it
from here
leaving behind again only bendings
in wind—
and circlings and circlings and circlings and circlings—

the ruling class
of what was
said

grass turned

you tripped up
cried on the phone

someone told
their dream

the full moon
is awaited
this night

what's its name?

and that one does not kill

and that one does not kill

look   it is dead

there is   sun all over it
like a moneying up of it

sparkle

——

You have whispered it all to me but I
wasn't listening you were too
close for me to make
out in-

dividual words all I
heard was the wind rushing into my
opening the ear like a field splaying

all this way then
that as you took in
air to make

the next phrase which
was also atoms—sparkling—meaning—
while the whiteness of
the walls my eyes—
(the only part of me
not yet held down
by you)—my free

eyes, scanning and rescanning, watch, darkens
into corners—your
teeth and lips holding my
whole ear   of joy   also

your hand over my
mouth   in the century   of possibility

yr voice not such   the sun entering
yr saying   the hotel window
so filled with   from the street

yr exhalation   and cries on it
it drowns itself   strangely the right color for
drowns in the *mine* of   cries

itself—all desire   crossing the history
yielding to secrecy   of inwardness vs insideness
spume of syllables   the seepage of

we were hungry   this was our century

hungry for   hungry from
(century)   (century)
         yr hand now

(actually over)   my throat

Underneath (2)

ghosts   not having
lived   alive now

       it   possible
       eventually

explain   calm
explain   vision
explain   property

also   summer compromise
as   soon   as

explain   hidden life
explain   echo
also which flower is
heaviest   how it
has   any bearing
on   color

explain   energy

bear   waste

explain   place
explain   accident

    after gods

is born

(fall)
(I'll catch)
(you)

I'm asking   for weight
The Ready   flowers

Underneath (3)

explain   given to
explain   born of

explain preoccupied

asks to be followed
remains to be seen

explain preoccupied

mind large as an apple
all summer long filling with
more atoms more day
noise of the sparrows
of the   universals
have you counted the steps

have you counted your steps

is crying now

(is crying now)

(is crying now)

begin again

in a strange tree   of atoms   of

wrong afterwards again show remember freedom

(which will be mine of   the atoms?)

      go back
      need more

having lived it leaves it   possible

explain inseparable   explain common

(the phone rings at dawn) (very occasionally)

For One Must Want/To Shut the Other's Gaze

What are you thinking?
Here on the bottom?
What do you squint clear for yourself
up there through the surface?

Explain   door ajar.
Explain   hopeth all.
Explain   surface   future   subject-of.

Pierce.

Be swift.

(Let's wade again)

(Offstage: pointing-at)
(Offstage: stones placing themselves on eyes)

Here: tangle and seaweed

current   diagram   how deep?   I have

forgotten.

Don't leave me. I won't.

Of course.

Explain   saturated.
Explain   and I had no more eyes.

(Oh did they really cross the sea)

Even the least
Even the last

This is certain

(of course)   (take up the arms)   (name the place)

The real plot was invisible

What are you thinking?

Underneath (7)

Mirror. Roll away
the stone, unrip the veil. Re-
pair.

And handle me. And
see. Behold my hands my feet.
That it is I, myself.

Mirror: a thing not free
it's seeking reply
from.

Mirror. These are not questions,
these glances coming back
for more.

The repeated vacancy
of touch
begging for real work.

Door ajar.

Bone so still a guest.

Touching you in sleep
along the lips I start to wake.
Inundation.

Fear being mistaken.

A thing not free we seek
reply from.

Reach your fingers here.

Reach your hand here.

Blessed are those who have not seen
yet have
believed.

Oh look closer. . . . Kneel.
Is it as new as you thought it would be?
As faithless?

Mirror—
Crashsite—
Fear being

mistaken.

See that it is *I*, myself,
repairing the rip it's making as it goes—

the feeling behind your back—

the bough springing back into the tree.

LINDA GREGG ■ ■ ■ ■ ■ ■ ■ ■ ■ ■ ■ ■ ■ ■ ■ ■

The Clapping

Did I go there enough? Was it enough when I tried
to get there? I remember the view of the bay,
but not what was said when I got there.
Was waiting in that apartment all summer and all
winter an end in itself? Was it the secrecy
that mattered? I remember the life. You carrying
a bowl of soup you made (with oysters in it)
carefully across two rooms to give me, not spilling
any. There is the memory of me by the door. A memory
about summer darkness under a tree, and one of birds
in a bush as soon as it got light. I remember
sitting on the stairs after I gave up our place,
pressing my eyes against your stomach with your
open coat covering each side of my face. Pictures
mixed with blank pages like quiet mixed with silence,
light mixed with snow, sun on glass. And the heart
never tired, the passion never lessened. Eyes open
and mouth closed, mouth open and eyes closed.
I imagine my bicycle leaning on the outside steps
that lead to your door. You recognize it as mine
and move it while thinking about that boatload
of people all clapping as you embrace me on shore.
Which shore? Was there an earth? There was,
there was. There were streets. There was you

over me on the bed with all your clothes on,
even your winter coat and scarf. You naked another
time, sitting cross-legged on the bed happily clapping
at me. Loving everything, even the kitchen table.
Saying *now,* and *now,* and later *forever.* You and I
innocent in purity and magnificent disorder.

The Edge of Something

I have decided I will not be like John Hu anymore
taken to France in the seventeenth century
and strange to everyone. Dragging his mattress
off the bed, sleeping by the open window in winter,
standing in the garden looking at the full moon
with his arms stretched out. Now I have chosen
Po Chu-I with his three pine trees and idleness
trying for union with the everlasting things.
As Po, I will not tell of the terrible things you did,
though I do not forget and still suffer.
When Po Chu-I was unhappy, he could still write,
narcissus are blooming in my backyard. The tulips
are not open yet, but the green is turning red.
I will not go out to see them in the morning.
I sleep late to allow my dreams luxury
and go out when the sun is starting down.
Afterwards, I practice my Chinese characters,
taking pleasure in feeling my mind yield
to what the symbols mean. This is *her,*
this is *him.* This one I think means *car.*
Later, I eat tofu and rice with cold asparagus
in a sauce of sesame oil, soy and white vinegar
with a little sugar. No more seabirds screeching,
"Kiss the feet, kiss the fingers and the teeth.
Kiss the skull washed up on the beach. Kiss it,
kiss it, or you will be taken by dwarfs to the woods
where your love perches calling your name in the dark."
There is a great director in New York recovering
from a stroke who says, "Tea yes? tea no? Music
yes? music no?" Substance without outline.
When the deer on this summer mountain raise
their ears and look my way, I stop—knowing they will run
if I don't. A family of animals all of a kind.
We are the same in the same world. Same color
and stillness. Similar in our foreignness.
Foreignness married by air. This is as close
as we will come. This is the edge of not running.

What Is Kept

There is a coldness I do not want
to be close to. Something alive remains.
And what is kept, well kept inside,
needs only this silence to complete it.
Well kept and taken. So keen a care kept.
If they ate a pork-chop sandwich and fries
by the train underpass, it was with the glee
of trespassing suddenly into the ordinary
of the world. The refinement of attention
in a room on the second story of a farmhouse
for seven weeks. There is a discipline to it.
A flock of birds flying across the sky
is something more than itself.
There is a secret kept within the silence,
being left and kept, loved and left,
held whole and nurtured inside another.
Each hair on the head is numbered.
Far fonder a care kept.
The desire to know. Striving to exist.
If only they could sit again on the bench
feeding pigeons. That he could be with her
again at night in the Amish village. But no,
it is kept far fonder. She might have lost it.
Kept safe in the strongest place inside.
No swing in an Amish town clanging in the wind
against its own trappings. She might have
lost it: no one getting out of the car
by the underpass to buy two pork-chop
sandwiches and fries. It is far fonder
a care kept when a thing is held at peace
and whole. No eating soup together
in the restaurant they would go to.

Fishing in the Keep of Silence

There is a hush now while the hills rise up
and God is going to sleep. He trusts the ship
of Heaven to take over and proceed beautifully
as he lies dreaming in the lap of the world.
He knows the owls will guard the sweetness
of the soul in their massive keep of silence,
looking out with eyes open or closed over
the length of Tomales Bay that the herons
conform to, whitely broad in flight, white

and slim in standing. God, who thinks about
poetry all the time, breathes happily as He
repeats to Himself: There are fish in the net,
lots of fish this time in the net of the heart.

Past Perfect

Memory is what has died,
is all ghost,
is moonlight on the rough stones.
The viper who slept at night
under the pile of rocks
just below my house.
Lay as king on my path
in the sunlight,
stopping my heart.
The almond tree,
my only almond tree,
rough with ruin.
In perfect beauty,
the leaves tinged with
their withering.
Inside the house an oil lamp,
a book, all the dishes
washed clean. The three dishes.
Two years ago.
The dead. Field after field,
street by street.
Ten thousand suns and moons.
Ten thousand joined bodies.
Nothing anymore real.
Life is when one is alive
in the present.
Knowing and having.
Once I sat under
the giant sycamore tree,
in that summer
saw snow through a window,
and someone with me.

Official Love Story

There is a painting by Lucas Cranach
of a thing pink and white and motionless.
Nymph of the Spring. A young woman

stretched out naked against
her red robes which are bundled
behind her head and arm, casually,
to resemble an open rose.
A pair of plump quail in the foreground
echoing her breasts and belly.
A sacred pool with water spilling down
into it from a small cave darkened
like her mystery. She considers
with her young, elegant mind
the sound of the water on water.
Always smiling,
her eyes looking down.
Probably there is the sound of horns.
Everything in the best
German tradition.
The cream of her being.
The world slow with desire.
Passion announced by the shadows
everywhere in the picture.
Soon a perfect prince will come
with shining arms and black hair,
and oriental eyes. He will beg her
for the flower of her body.
She will consider it with her neat mind
which smells of lemon,
the way roses smell. Everybody will clap,
wanting the world to be made
out of passion and grace.
The voices of children will sing sweetly
of Christ in his loss and fear,
sing of the birth after,
sing of the Mystery to come.

BARBARA GUEST ■ ■ ■ ■ ■ ■ ■ ■ ■ ■ ■ ■ ■ ■ ■

The Advance of the Grizzly

go from the must-laden room
move to the interior
the remarkable bird in the case;
                    wing
(like a pillow).

bird out of cloud—dissembling of trees; locks;
icicle; out of the margin

falling from the grim margin the axle of skin;
enamoured with the fell wing.

I will move in my skin with the hollow
the neck and the brimming over the latitude
over the latitude onto the brink.

                frame of snow "within
squares of diminishing size"
ink hushed the snow; a blank sky rolled to the verge
parable heaved through drift . . .
and the moon weighted
with coil of thistle.

evoked our willing to believe in a sudden pull
of the immense frame at the heel:

                    spilled exactly
to destroy a circular return
from the ragged prose clump
clump on the cold landscape.

white grown fatter . . . place of sharpened skin;
wet feasts.

romantic fever and snow
fresh from the gorgon bed
           dendrophagous "feeding on trees"
to sustain the romantic vision route over snow
the sudden drop into pines:

                "feeding on trees"
new mouths red of Okeechobee.

(and ate the alligator and spat out the part
wedded to the green clavicle.)

loss of the sun

blight of the sun the looney forest
a gondola loops the sky;
who will walk out of the plush interior into
the excited atmosphere?

an outlet for prose the advance of the grizzly.

Red Dye

> . . . in the blood of my thoughts and writing
> cochineal was running.
> —PASTERNAK

Ether broke into the house
                    from Russia;
wild berries fell from the ceiling
the brown-eyed water was
mother-of-pearl.

do not come near the red cochineal
dried insects bury
immortal stings in the hemp.

as you scarlet Kazak
with a wave of your cut hand
enter my blood by imagining.

fires hum through the ceiling;
into the wayside jumble march
the inflammable trousers

and ether's enameled wind
destroys their rope.

You Can Discover

You can discover for yourself
attitudes and the musky codes

or pigeons
the figure against the wall
birds in a cage the frost
pagoda.

You can follow those pigeons
brushed with iodine

slave of Lilith
and read her deadly poems.

the pumpkin blooms
at the murky gate
the glass coach arrives
at the murky gate.

Motion Pictures: 4

At first he had felt the scrape of a little murmur, his own throat struggling with speech. Now seated in the car next to this Japanese film director began the dry hacking sounds. He feared they would continue each day while projections for *The Cough* were considered.

"Allergy," said Nagao with confidence, "allergy to our film." On Nagao's clear unwrinkled skin were little ribbons of smile.

At the intersection of the road in Nagasaki where in Japanese films a short dark woman usually squats, Wilhelm pointed out a break between two buildings where light creeps through like an oyster. He said he would like to do a 'take' there. "Cliché," said Nagao.

Wilhelm observed Nagao in his "work clothes" of dark blue denim, he wondered whether their film should be called *Dark Blue Denim* or *The Oyster.* He would like the noise of an oyster to get into the film. Nagao compared the oyster noise to the noise the eye makes when it blinks. "Pachi pachi in Japanese."

Wilhelm suggested the sound wood makes when it creaks for when the film begins to roll toward the climax of two people lost in the garden. "Pachi pachi better," Nagao said, "more subtle."

Wilhelm believed the action of the film had slowed and he desired a more violent crescendo as when the body fell down the cellar stairs he wanted another body to fall on top of it. "Rain, maybe," said Nagao.

Wilhelm was feeling as usual when a film got off the ground that someone was chasing him. When he directed those shots up in the sky with two planes flying parallel to each other he also was in the sky chase. In this film there were sky petals of flowers growing on the wings of the plane.

"Liquid soap on the stairs," suggested Nagao. Liquid soap sold well in Tokyo and it might be a title for one of the diary sequences. Wilhelm felt the soap go down his throat. He was ready to suggest that tomorrow he should return to his home for awhile and the scenarist could work on her own. She might put a little of her own story into the script, about how she was hired for the picture. There was probably something going on between her and Nagao that could go into the picture.

He thought of his home as a possible sequence and *Home* started to roll past with short camera views. *Home* also needed editing, especially the scene with his analyst when they discussed his cough that was like another room in the movie. His cough alone and the door opening with a creak.

Nagao said there didn't have to be explanations it slowed the movie and he agreed this one was too slow. It was old-fashioned to explain why gangsters upset the fish cart.

"Like Utamaro," said Wilhelm who believed in a capsule of real life. He thought of a new title, *Dreams of Real Life.*

"Allegory is dead as little fishes, better *Cough*," said Nagao, both eyes blinking.

Motion Pictures: 15

They were on location in the hills above a small California town and before breakfast the Assistant Director and a member of his crew were scouting out possible locations for the movie they were going to make. It was tentatively called "Preparedness" or "He is Prepared" or "Without Preparedness"; the word "Preparedness" or "Prepared" was ordered to be in the film title. This had to do with an idea of the Producer's that all bad things in the world happened because people were unprepared. "For What?" This was asked all over the set. But no one had found an answer.

The men had climbed to about three thousand feet and were surveying the gentle land that lay about them. There were wildflowers amid the eucalyptus trees and there were chestnut trees with pale rose colored blossoms at their long fingertips. An azalea or two became part of a disordered group of cultivated flowers blown there by the bay winds. All was serenly natural and even stately with the yellow iris and the browned peony buds a straggling rose and the carpet of wildflowers violet and pink, sometimes yellow. The flowers, the soft breeze laden with scent and trees changing color as the morning passed, and the light filled with yellow charmed these Hollywood men and their talk became less indignant.

They could see the water of the Bay below them with small boats anchored at its shores. A cloud rolled over from a mountain above the Bay. The light changed on their mountain to a dark grey. The sun slowly entered the cloud and the cloud was mottled with a yellow glow from the sun forcing its way through the grey cloud. On top of the far mountain there was a contest between the color of the sun forcing its way through the cloud and the dark cloud coming from behind the mountain forcing itself into the yellowed light.

The movie men noticed that the ground below them and beside them was mottled with this color coming from across the bay and the leaves on the ground began to pick up a little wind. The flowers began a slow nodding and what had been simple now began to turn into a darker more complicated color; the breeze was picking up and this caused the leaves of the tree near them to flatten and show their dull greyish green sides. The odor of the flowers began to penetrate this slow changing of the guard on the mountain. The odor began to enter the new stillness and halt there.

One of the men who was sensitive to attacks of heat and cold began to shiver. Another took out a package of cigarettes and was going to light up when a hand reached across and closed the package. He was reminded that smoking was forbidden. The land had been too dry, too crisp and eager for fire, and they began to discuss the terrible fire that had ravaged a mountain nearby.

A bird flew across the horizon. He was large and the swoop that his wing made was slightly disturbing. Yet the dipping of his wings as he sailed across the canyon created no disorder in their vision, but indicated a calmness, as always in an elegant finesse of nature, it was noted. This brought the men to a conversation about elegance and how sometimes it was needed in a film. Just enough of it might save a picture from the tawdriness it was willing to fall into. Elegance, as in the length of the swoop of the hawk's wing. One of the men looked at his watch wishing to time the swooping, if possible. The hawk obligingly flew over them again even as the first drops of rain fell. With the beginning of the rain the hawk began to fly higher like an airplane, seeking another altitude. So they were unable to time the hawk and its elegance became a memory. But memory is useful they remarked. They were talking about the memory necessary to a film, of course, because none of them had much use for anything outside their work.

The rain had by now muddied the hill path and the color of the flowers became more brilliant against the ground before their soft heads were utterly destroyed. Across the bay a streak of lightning hit a mountain peak and they watched the rain pour from a cloud and into the bay. The men had brought no umbrella or raincoats, they were unprepared for this natural seizure of land and color. They were unprepared for the sudden swirl of water around their ankles as a torrent got in their way going down. But they were laughing. Their teeth outside their mouth in the widening of the mouth for laughter getting wetter and wetter until each of them was swallowing the rain water. They had been unprepared for this torrent of water but now they knew how the scene would play out.

DONALD HALL ■ ■ ■ ■ ■ ■ ■ ■ ■ ■ ■ ■ ■ ■ ■ ■

To a Waterfowl

Women with hats like the rear ends of pink ducks
applauded you, my poems.
These are the women whose husbands I meet on airplanes,
who close their briefcases and ask, "What are *you* in?"
I look in their eyes, I tell them I am in poetry,

and their eyes fill with anxiety, and with little tears.
"Oh, yeah?" they say, developing an interest in clouds.
"My wife, she likes that sort of thing? Hah-hah?
I guess maybe I'd better watch my grammar, huh?"
I leave them in airports, watching their grammar,

and take a limousine to the Women's Goodness Club
where I drink Harvey's Bristol Cream with their wives,
and eat chicken salad with capers, with little tomato wedges,
and I read them "The Erotic Crocodile," and "Eating You."
Ah, when I have concluded the disbursement of sonorities,

crooning, "High on thy thigh I cry, Hi!"—and so forth—
they spank their wide hands, they smile like Jell-O,
and they say, "Hah-hah? My goodness, Mr. Hall,
but you certainly do have an imagination, huh?"
"Thank you, indeed," I say; "it brings in the bacon."

But now, my poems, now I have returned to the motel,
returned to *l'eternel retour* of the Holiday Inn,
naked, lying on the bed, watching *Godzilla Sucks Mt. Fuji,*
addressing my poems, feeling superior, and drinking bourbon
from a flask disguised to look like a transistor radio.

Ah, my poems, it is true,
that with the deepest gratitude and most serene pleasure,
and with hints that I am a sexual Thomas Alva Edison,
and not without collecting an exorbitant fee,
I have accepted the approbation of feathers.

And what about you? You, laughing? You, in the bluejeans,
laughing at your mother who wears hats, and at your father
who rides airplanes with a briefcase watching his grammar?
Will you ever be old and dumb, like your creepy parents?
Not you, not you, not you, not you, not you, not you.

Eating the Pig

1

Twelve people, most of us strangers, stand in a room
in Ann Arbor, drinking Cribari from jars.
Then two young men, who cooked him,
carry him to the table
on a large square of plywood: his body
striped, like a tiger cat's, from the basting,
his legs long, much longer than a cat's,
and the striped hide as shiny as vinyl.

Now I see his head, as he takes his place
at the center of the table,
his wide pig's head; and he looks like the *javelina*
that ran in front of the car, in the desert outside Tucson,
and I am drawn to him, my brother the pig,
with his large ears cocked forward,
with his tight snout, with his small ferocious teeth
in a jaw propped open
by an apple. How bizarre, this raw apple clenched,
in a cooked face! Then I see his eyes,

his eyes cramped shut, his no-eyes, his eyes like X's
in a comic strip, when the character gets knocked out.

This afternoon they read directions
from a book: *The eyeballs must be removed
or they will burst during roasting.*   So they hacked them out.
"I nearly fainted," says someone.
"I never fainted before, in my whole life."
Then they gutted the pig and stuffed him,
and roasted him five hours, basting the long body.

2

Now we examine him, exclaiming, and we marvel at him—
but no one picks up a knife.

Then a young woman cuts off his head.
It comes off so easily, like a detachable part.
With sudden enthusiasm we dismantle the pig,
we wrench his trotters off, we twist them
at shoulder and hip, and they come off so easily.
Then we cut open his belly and pull the skin back.

For myself, I scoop a portion of left thigh,
moist, tender, falling apart, fat, sweet.

❋

We forage like an army starving in winter
that crosses a pass in the hills and discovers
a valley of full barns—
cattle fat and lowing in their stalls,
bins of potatoes in root cellars under white farmhouses,
barrels of cider, onions, hens squawking over eggs—
and the people nowhere, with bread still warm in the oven.

Maybe, south of the valley, refugees pull their carts
listening for Stukas or elephants, carrying
bedding, pans, and silk dresses,
old men and women, children, deserters, young wives.

No, we are here, eating the pig together.

3

In ten minutes, the destruction is total.

His tiny ribs, delicate as birds' feet, lie crisscrossed.
Or they are like cross-hatching in a drawing,
lines doubling and redoubling on each other.

Bits of fat and muscle
mix with stuffing alien to the body,
walnuts and plums. His skin, like a parchment bag
soaked in oil, is pulled back and flattened,
with ridges and humps remaining, like a contour map,
like the map of a defeated country.

The army consumes every blade of grass in the valley,
every tree, every stream, every village,
every crossroad, every shack, every book, every graveyard.

✿

His intact head
swivels around, to view the landscape of body
as if in dismay.

"For sixteen weeks I lived. For sixteen weeks
I took into myself nothing but the milk of my mother
who rolled on her side for me,
for my brothers and sisters. Only five hours roasting,
and this body so quickly dwindles away to nothing."

4

By itself, isolated on this plywood,
among this puzzle of foregone possibilities,
his intact head seems to want affection.
Without knowing that I will do it,
I reach out and scratch his jaw,
and I stroke him behind his ears,
as if he might suddenly purr from his cooked head.

"When I stroke your pig's ears,
and scratch the striped leather of your jowls,
the furrow between the sockets of your eyes,
I take into myself, and digest,
wheat
that grew between
the Tigris and the Euphrates rivers.

"And I take into myself the flint carving tool,
and the savannah, and hairs in the tail
of Eohippus, and fingers of bamboo,
and Hannibal's elephant, and Hannibal,
and everything that lived before us, everything born,
exalted, and dead, and historians
who carved in the Old Kingdom
when the wall had not heard about China."

I speak these words
into the ear of the stone-age pig, the Abraham
pig, the ocean pig, the Achilles pig,
and into the ears
of the fire pig that will eat our bodies up.

"Fire, brother and father,
twelve of us, in our different skins, older and younger,
opened your skin together
and tore your body apart, and took it
into our bodies."

SAM HAMILL ▪ ▪ ▪ ▪ ▪ ▪ ▪ ▪ ▪ ▪ ▪ ▪ ▪ ▪ ▪ ▪

What the Water Knows

What the mouth sings, the soul must learn to forgive.
A rat's as moral as a monk in the eyes of the real world.
Still, the heart is a river
pouring from itself, a river that cannot be crossed.

It opens on a bay
and turns back upon itself as the tide comes in,
it carries the cry of the loon and the salts
of the unutterably human.

A distant eagle enters the mouth of a river
salmon no longer run and his wide wings glide
upstream until he disappears
into the nothing from which he came. Only the thought remains.

Lacking the eagle's cunning or the wisdom of the sparrow,
where shall I turn, drowning in sorrow?
Who will know what the trees know, the spidery patience
of young maple or what the willows confess?

Let me be water. The heart pours out in waves.
Listen to what the water says.
Wind, be a friend.
There's nothing I couldn't forgive.

Another Duffer

"The poem is the cry of its occasion,
Part of the *res* itself and not about it."
The poem speaks the poet.

Just as you, head steady as a rock,
let the left shoulder drop
unnaturally, arms brought

back extended, so that
what the body most becomes
is a pendulum,

and the clear smooth arc
of the ball leaves no mark
across the sky and the eye

must lift too late to see—
beginning to foregone conclusion—
what the mind already perceives

accurately, in perfect detail: poem:
like the man and the club and the turf and the ball in golf,
like your finger and the moon, like the water and the whale,

like three or four brands of Zen,
various music of singer and song,—
is,—are,—will be,—has been,—

and, finally, *am.*

Abstract

It was a dream and you were walking through a field of hosannas
and the immense sea rocked with the blue voices of the dead
when you stretched out supine to dream lotus dreams which I
could not read.

A cathedral of sky arched overhead. I wanted to know
whether your eyes were closed, I wanted your dream or song or prayer,
o I wanted, and the sun grew brighter and the breeze fairer
that immaculate day

unfolding like a poem, like a song I half-remember and ask,
Did we sing it once a long time ago, did we sing it together,
was it our hymnal, our beautiful tragic chorus, our anthem,
the day like a new white canvas.

and here I add marine blue, and there cobalt blue, and a cloud in amber,
and the light is transparent yellow, and the brush makes a sound
like wind over sand, but there are no whitecaps, no sailboats,
only canvas and paint and the body's dance.

No kite. No gull. No *things*. Everything goes.
No dream, no dreamer. No certainty, no doubt.
Only the infinitely blossoming hosannas of the emptiness within,
echoing the emptiness without.

JOY HARJO ■ ■ ■ ■ ■ ■ ■ ■ ■ ■ ■ ■ ■ ■ ■ ■ ■ ■

The Woman Who Fell from the Sky

Once a woman fell from the sky. This woman who fell from the sky was nei-
ther a murderer nor a saint. She was rather ordinary, though beautiful in her
walk like one who has experienced freedom from earth's gravity. When I see
her I think of an antelope grazing the alpine meadows in the mountains
whose names are as ancient as the sound that created the first world.

Saint Coincidence thought he recognized her as she began falling toward
him from the sky in a slow spin, like the spiral of events marking an ascen-
sion of grace. There was something in the curve of her shoulder, a familiar
slope that led him into the lightest moment of his life.

He could not bear it and turned to ask a woman in high heels for a quarter.
She was of the family of myths who would give everything if asked. She
looked like all the wives he'd lost. And he had nothing to lose anymore in
this city of terrible paradox where a woman was falling toward him from the
sky.

The strange beauty in heels disappeared from the path of Saint Coinci-
dence, with all her money held tightly in her purse, into the glass of adver-
tisements. Saint Coincidence shuffled back onto the ice to watch the
woman falling and falling.

Saint Coincidence, who was not a saint, perhaps a murderer if you count the
people he shot without knowing during the stint that took his mind in Viet-
nam or Cambodia—remembered the girl he yearned to love when they
were kids at Indian boarding school.

He could still see her on the dusty playground, off in the distance, years to
the west past the icy parking lot of the Safeway. She was a blurred vision of
the bittersweet and this memory has forced him to live through the violence
of fire.

Then they stood witness together to strange acts of cruelty by strangers, as well as the surprise of rare kindnesses.

The woman who was to fall from the sky was the girl with skinned knees whose spirit knew how to climb to the stars. Once she told him the stars spoke a language akin to the plains of her home, a language like rocks.

He watched her once make the ascent, after a severe beating. No one could touch the soul masked by name, age and tribal affiliation. Myth was as real as a scalp being scraped for lice.

Lila also dreamed of a love not disturbed by the wreck of culture she was forced to attend. It sprang up here and there like miraculous flowers in the cracks of the collision. It was there she found Johnny, who didn't have a saint's name when he showed up for school. He understood the journey and didn't make fun of her for her peculiar ways, despite the risks.

Johnny was named Johnny by the priests because his Indian name was foreign to their European tongues. He named himself Saint Coincidence many years later after he lost himself in drink in a city he'd been sent to learn a trade. Maybe you needed English to know how to pray in the city. He could speak a fractured English. His own language had become a baby language to him, made of the comforting voice of his grandmother as she taught him to be a human.

Johnny had been praying for years and had finally given up a god who appeared to give up on him. Then one night as he tossed pennies on the sidewalk with his cousin and another lost traveler, he prayed to Coincidence and won. The event demanded a new name. He gave himself the name, Saint Coincidence.

His ragged life gleamed with possibility until a ghost-priest brushed by him as he walked the sidewalk looking for a job to add to his stack of new luck. The priest appeared to look through to the boy in him. He despaired. He would always be a boy on his knees, the burden of shame rooting him.

Saint Coincidence went back to wandering without a home in the maze of asphalt. Asphalt could be a pathway toward God, he reasoned, though he'd always imagined the road he took with his brothers when they raised sheep as children. Asphalt had led him here to the Safeway where a woman was falling from the sky.

The memory of all time relative to Lila and Johnny was seen by an abandoned cat washing herself next to the aluminum-can bin of the grocery store.

These humans set off strange phenomena, she thought and made no attachment to the thought. It was what it was, this event, shimmering there between the frozen parking lot of the store and the sky, something unusual and yet quite ordinary.

Like the sun falling fast in the west, this event carried particles of light through the trees.

Some say God is a murderer for letting children and saints slip through his or her hands. Some call God a father of saints or a mother of demons. Lila had seen God and could tell you God was neither male nor female and made of absolutely everything of beauty, of wordlessness.

This unnameable thing of beauty is what shapes a flock of birds who know exactly when to turn together in flight in the winds used to make words. Everyone turns together though we may not see each other stacked in the invisible dimensions.

This is what Lila saw, she told Johnny once. The sisters called it blasphemy.

Johnny ran away from boarding school the first winter with his two brothers, who'd runaway before. His brothers wrapped Johnny Boy, as they called him, with their bodies to keep him warm. They never made it home but became part of the stars.

Johnny didn't make it home either. The school officials took him back the next day. To mourn his brothers would be to admit an unspeakable pain, so he became an athlete who ran faster than any record ever made in the history of the school, faster than the tears.

Lila never forgot about Johnny, who left school to join the army, and a few years later as she walked home from her job at Dairy Queen she made a turn in the road.

Call it destiny or coincidence—but the urge to fly was as strong as the need to push when at the precipice of any birth. It was what led her into the story told before she'd grown ears to hear, as she turned from stone to fish to human in her mother's belly.

Once, the stars made their way down stairs of ice to the earth to find mates. Some of the women were either angry at their inattentive husbands, bored, or frustrated with the cycle of living and dying. They ran off with the stars, as did a few who saw their chance for travel and enlightenment.

They weren't heard from for years, until one of the women returned. She dared to look back and fell. Fell through centuries, through the beauty of the night sky, made a hole in a rock near the place Lila's mother had been born. She took up where she had left off, with her children from the stars. She was remembered.

This story was Lila's refuge those nights she'd prayed on her knees with the other children in the school dorms. It was too painful to miss her mother.

A year after she'd graduated and worked cleaning house during the day, and evenings at the Dairy Queen, she laughed to think of herself wearing her uniform spotted with sweets and milk, as she left on the arms of one of the stars. Surely she could find love in a place that did not know the disturbance of death.

While Lila lived in the sky she gave birth to three children and they made her happy. Though she had lost conscious memory of the place before, a song climbed up her legs from far away, to the rooms of her heart.

Later she would tell Johnny it was the sound of destiny, which is similar to a prayer reaching out to claim her.

You can't ignore these things, she would tell him, and it led her to the place her husband had warned her was too sacred for women.

She carried the twins in her arms as her daughter grabbed her skirt in her small fists. She looked into the forbidden place and leaped.

She fell and was still falling when Saint Coincidence caught her in his arms in front of the Safeway as he made a turn from borrowing spare change from strangers.

The children crawled safely from their mother's arms. The cat stalked a bit of flying trash set into motion by the wave of falling—

or the converse wave of gathering together.

A Postcolonial Tale

Everyday is a reenactment of the creation story. We emerge from dense unspeakable material, through the shimmering power of dreaming stuff.

°　　　　°　　　　°

This is the first world, and the last.

°　　　　°　　　　°

Once we abandoned ourselves for television, the box that separates the dreamer from the dreaming. It was as if we were stolen, put into a bag carried on the back of a whiteman who pretends to own the earth and the sky. In the sack were all the people of the world. We fought until there was a hole in the bag.

°　　　　°　　　　°

When we fell we were not aware of falling. We were driving to work, or to the mall. The children were in school learning subtraction with guns, although they appeared to be in classes.

o   o   o

We found ourselves somewhere near the diminishing point of civilization, not far from the trickster's bag of tricks.

o   o   o

Everything was as we imagined it. The earth and stars, every creature and leaf imagined with us.

o   o   o

The imagining needs praise as does any living thing. Stories and songs are evidence of this praise.

o   o   o

The imagination conversely illumines us, speaks with us, sings with us.

o   o   o

Stories and songs are like humans who when they laugh are indestructible.

o   o   o

No story or song will translate the full impact of falling, or the inverse power of rising up.

o   o   o

Of rising up.

JIM HARRISON ▪ ▪ ▪ ▪ ▪ ▪ ▪ ▪ ▪ ▪ ▪ ▪ ▪ ▪ ▪

Letters to Yesenin

1

to D. G.

This matted and glossy photo of Yesenin
bought at a Leningrad newstand—permanently
tilted on my desk: he doesn't stare at me
he stares at nothing; the difference between
a plane crash and a noose adds up to nothing.

And what can I do with heros with my brain fixed
on so few of them? Again nothing. Regard his flat
magazine eyes with my half-cocked own, both
of us seeing nothing. In the vodka was nothing
and Isadora was nothing, the pistol waved
in New York was nothing, and that plank bridge
near your village home in Ryazan covered seven feet
of nothing, the clumsy noose that swung the tilted
body was nothing but a noose, a law of gravity
this seeking for the ground, a few feet of nothing
between shoes and the floor a light year away.
So this is a song of Yesenin's noose which came
to nothing, but did a good job as we say back home
where there's nothing but snow. But I stood under
your balcony in St. Petersburg, yes St. Petersburg!
a crazed tourist with so much nothing in my heart
it wanted to implode. And I walked down to the Neva
embankment with a fine sleet falling and there was
finally something, a great river vastly flowing, flat
as your eyes; something to marry to my nothing heart
other than the poems you hurled into nothing those
years before the articulate noose.

2

to Rose

I don't have any medals. I feel their lack
of weight on my chest. Years ago I was ambitious.
But now it is clear that nothing will happen.
All those poems that made me soar along a foot
from the ground are not so much forgotten as never
read in the first place. They rolled like moons
of light into a puddle and were drowned. Not even
the puddle can be located now. Yet I am encouraged
by the way you hung yourself, telling me that such
things don't matter. You, the fabulous poet of
Mother Russia. But still, even now, school girls
hold your dead heart, your poems, in their laps
on hot August afternoons by the river while they wait
for their boyfriends to get out of work or their
lovers to return from the army, their dead pets to
return to life again. To be called to supper. You
have a new life on their laps and can scent their
lavender scent, the cloud of hair that falls
over you, feel their feet trailing in the river,
or hidden in a purse walk the Neva again. Best of all
you are used badly like a bouquet of flowers to make

them shed their dresses in apartments. See those
steam pipes running along the ceiling. The rope.

3

I wanted to feel exalted so I picked up
Dr Zhivago again. But the newspaper was there
with the horrors of the Olympics, those dead and
perpetually martyred sons of David. I want to present
all Israelis with .357 Magnums so that they are
never to be martyred again. I wanted to be exalted
so I picked up Dr Zhivago again but the tv was on
with a movie about the sufferings of convicts in
the early history of Australia. But then the movie
was over and the level of the bourbon bottle was dropping
and I still wanted to be exalted laying there with
the book on my chest. I recalled Moscow but I could
not place dear Yuri, only you Yesenin, seeing the Kremlin
glitter and ripple like Asia. And when drunk you appeared
as some Bakst stage drawing, a slain tartar. But that is
all ballet. And what a dance you had kicking your legs from
the rope—we all change our minds Berryman said in Minnesota
halfway down to the river. Villon said of the rope that my neck
will feel the weight of my ass. But I wanted to feel exalted
again and read the poems at the end of Dr Zhivago and
just barely made it. Suicide. Beauty takes my courage
away this cold autumn evening. My year old daughter's red
robe hangs from the doorknob shouting stop.

4

I am four years older than you but scarcely an unwobbling
pivot. It was no fun sitting around being famous, was it?
I'll never have to learn that lesson. You find a page torn
out of a book and read it feeling that here you might find
the mystery of print in such phrases as "summer was on the
way" or "Gertrude regarded him somewhat quizzically." Your
Sâgane was a fraud. Love poems to girls you never met living
in a country you never visited. I've been everywhere to no
particular purpose. And am well past love but not love poems.
I wanted to fall in love on the coast of Ecuador but the girls
were itsy-bitsy and showers are not prominent in that area.
Unlike Killarney where I also didn't fall in love the girls
had good teeth. As in the movies the latin girls proved to be
spitfires with an endemic shanker problem. I didn't fall in love
in Palm Beach or Paris. Or London. Or Leningrad. I wanted to fall
in love at the ballet but my seat was too far back to see faces
clearly. At the Sadko a pretty girl was sitting with a general
and did not exchange my glance. In Normandy I fell in love but

had colitis and couldn't concentrate. She had a way of not paying
any attention to me that could not be misunderstood. That is
a year's love story. Except Key West where absolutely nothing
happened with romantic overtones. Now you might understand why
I drink and grow fat. When I reach three hundred pounds there
will be no more love problems, only fat problems. Then I will
write reams of love poems. And if she pats my back a cubic yard
of fat will jiggle. Last night I drank a hundred proof quart
and looked at a photo of my sister. Ten years dead. Show me a
single wound on earth that love has healed. I fed my dying dog
a pound of beef and buried her happy in the barnyard.

5

Lustra. Officially the cold comes from Manitoba;
yesterday at sixty knots. So that the waves mounted
the breakwater. The first snow. The farmers and carpenters
in the tavern with red, wind burned faces. I am in there
playing the pin ball machine watching all those delicious
lights flutter, the bells ring. I am halfway through
a bottle of vodka and am happy to hear Manitoba
howling outside. Home for dinner I ask my baby daughter
if she loves me but she is too young to talk. She cares
most about eating as I care most about drinking. Our wants
are simple as they say. Still when I wake from my nap
the universe is dissolved in grief again. The baby is sleeping
and I have no one to talk my language. My breath is shallow
and my temples pound. Vodka. Last October in Moscow I taught
a group of East Germans to sing "Fuck Nixon," and we were
quite happy until the bar closed. At the newstand I saw a
picture of Bella Ahkmadulina and wept. Vodka. You would have
liked her verse. The doorman drew near, alarmed. Outside
the KGB floated through the snow like arctic bats.
Maybe I belong there. They won't let me print my verses. On the
night train to Leningrad I will confess everything to someone.
All my books are remaindered and out of print. My face in
the mirror asks me who I am and says I don't know. But stop
this whining. I am alive and a hundred thousand acres of birches
around my house wave in the wind. They are women standing
on their heads. Their leaves on the ground today are small
saucers of snow from which I drink with endless thirst.

9

What if I own more paper clips than I'll ever use in this
lifetime. My other possessions are shabby: the house half
painted, the car without a muffler, one dog with bad eyes
and the other dog a horny moron. Even the baby has a rash on
her neck but then we don't own humans. My good books were

stolen at parties long ago and two of the barn windows are
broken and the furnace is unreliable and field mice daily
feed on the wiring. But the new foal appears healthy though
unmanageable, crawling under the fence and chased by my wife
who is stricken by the flu, not to speak of my own body which
has long suffered the ravages of drink and various nervous
disorders which make me laugh and weep and carress my shotguns.
But paperclips. Rich in paperclips to sort my writings which
fill so many cartons under my bed. When I attach them I say
it's your job afterall to keep this whole thing together. And
I used them once with a rubberband to fire holes into the
face of the president hanging on the office wall. We have freedom.
You couldn't do that to Breznev much less Stalin on whose
grave Mandelstam sits proudly in the form of the ultimate
crow, a peerless crow, a crow without comparison on earth.
But the paperclips are a small comfort like meeting someone
fatter than myself and we both wordlessly recognize the fact
or meeting someone my age who is more of a drunk, more savaged
and hag ridden until they are no longer human and seeing
them on the street I wonder how their heads which are only
wounds balance at the top of their bodies. A manuscript of
a novel sits in front of me held together with twenty clips.
It is the paper equivalent of a duck and a company far away
has bought this perhaps beautiful duck and my time is free again.

10

It would surely be known for years after as the day I shot
a cow. Walking out of the house before dawn with the sky an icy
blackness and not one star or cockcrow or shiver of breeze, the rifle
barrel black and icy to the touch. I walked a mile in the dark
and a flushed grouse rose louder than any thunderclap. I entered
a neck of a woodlot I'd scouted and sat on a stump waiting for
a deer I intended to kill. But then I was dressed too warmly
and had a formidable hangover with maybe three hours of sleep so
I slept again seeing a tin open fronted cafe in Anconcito down
on the coast of Ecuador and the eyes of a piglet staring at me as
I drank my mineral water dazed with the opium I had taken for
la turista. Crippled syphletic children begging, one little boy
with a tooth as long as a forefinger, an ivory tusk which would
be pulled on maturity and threaded as an amulet ending up finally
in Moscow in a diplomatic pouch. The boy would explore with his
tongue the gum hole for this Russian gift. What did he know about
Russia. Then carrying a naked girl in the water on my shoulders
and her shorthairs tickled the back of my neck with just the suggestion
of a firm grip behind them so if I had been stupid enough to turn
around I might have suffocated at eighteen and not written you
any letters. There were bristles against my neck and hot breath
in my hair. It must be a deer smelling my hair so I wheeled and shot.

But it was a cow and the muzzle blast was blue in the grey light.
She bawled horribly and ran in zig-zags. I put her away with a shot
to the head. What will I do with this cow? It's a guernsey and she
won't be milked this morning. I knelt and stared into her huge eyeball,
her iris making a mirror so I combed my hair and thought about the
whole dreary mess. Then I walked backward through a muddy orchard
so I wouldn't be trailed, got in my car and drove to New York nonstop.

ROBERT HASS ▪ ▪ ▪ ▪ ▪ ▪ ▪ ▪ ▪ ▪ ▪ ▪ ▪ ▪ ▪ ▪ ▪ ▪

A Pact

"I am he who aches with amorous love."
Well yes. But if you would settle
for two hours of talk across a table,
her hair just washed, and . . . if you would
barter all your books and your car
and one of your children, no,
none of your children, your job
and every poem in your drawer except
the one you wrote last night
to be with her for half an hour
in the coffee shop, let's say,
under the Palace of Fine Arts
where the white wine is very cold
and her hair just washed
and you allowed to touch it once . . .

Now Winter Nights

We were sitting in a small room
and we talked around our lives
by talking about skin flicks,
death, voyeurism, the definition
of 'sentimental,' performing
rituals of the mind's precision
on the desperate stuff
of twentieth century pleasures.
There was a woman there—
cornsilk hair but not, a texture
of that pale gold from which sheer cloths
are woven in ancient,
fragmentary poems,

garments tossed aside in the last line
the scholars can make out
beside a phrase suggesting wetness
and the god of dawns. The bones of her face
were clear and formal. She had been reading
Thomas Campion all that afternoon.
Though she was earnestly attentive and
though we were learning that Mohammedan angels
make love exclusively by means of delicate
and intensive masturbation while the windows
gave us back ourselves with wounds
of light, her eyes grew heavy
and she fell asleep. Her hair sprawled
in the same slow curve
as the fern above her on the desk.

Elm

What gathers in this sky
is everything the trees regret
and the trees regret nothing.
They would pray if they could
but they are dreaming of women.
Roots and a sunward quickness,
the light by which we enter
and the dark hall, this writhing
that is neither prayer nor orgy
though it burns us. It is
unforgiveable the sky should be
so clear; always they dream of them,
the woman named enough and
the woman named never.

Elegy: Residence on Earth

When my cat preens in dusty sunlight
the moth of her tongue
proves the soul does not exist.
She has never heard of Pablo Neruda
who knew more about cats than she does
and loved them better. She crouches
still as Buddha on the back lawn.
There is nothing to grieve for.
He will survive as a song
of the tension in the distance

between a sparrow and a cat.
Maybe he will be reborn an olive tree
or a lemon or a nun who lives
in a little north Brazilian convent
downwind from the stink of the poor,
a girl who is watchful and quiet, who read
Veinte poemas de amor y una cancion desperada
in high school and keeps under her pillow
a newspaper photo of Camillo Torres
beside the rosary she fingers quietly,
having examined her conscience
and omitted, with misgivings,
a prayer for the well-being of the rich
and the chiefs of state who are derringers
in the armpit holsters of the rich.
There is nothing to grieve for,
not Neruda or the girl, not the rich
who must tolerate, like the rest of us,
the elegance and indifference of cats,
their grace and shameless lechery,
and who, facing their mirrors mornings,
dream viciously of lemons
and wind in an olive tree.

To Phil Dow, in Oregon

The *Gita* says three *gunas*
trick us into craving
endless birth.
Sattva: poems,
for example, Creeley
harrowing the bones
of light, old Landor
in the mind's Italy
of English Latin.
Rajas: thighs,
labial dreams,
the heart pounding
when a pair of teal,
gone by, wheel
back at you. *Tamas:*
reading book reviews,
sleeping in the afternoon,
the habit of loving,
greed. The *gunas*
are strands. They stitch
us to unravelling in the dark.

I haven't been doing
much, Phil, but it's becoming
strange to me to wake up
every morning born.

Spring Rain

Now the rain is falling, freshly, in the intervals between sunlight,

a Pacific squall started no one knows where, drawn east
as the drifts of warm air make a channel;

it moves its own way, like water or the mind,

and spills this rain passing over. The Sierras will catch
it as last snow flurries before summer, observed only by
the wakened marmots at 10,000 feet,

and we will come across it again as larkspur and penstemon
sprouting along a creekside above Sonora Pass next August.

And the snowmelt will trickle into Dead Man's Creek and
the creek spill into the Stanislaus and the Stanislaus into
the San Joaquin and the San Joaquin into the slow salt marshes
of the day.

That's not the end of it: the gray jays of the mountains
eat larkspur seeds which cannot propagate otherwise.

To simulate the process you have to soak gathered seeds
all night in the acids of old coffee

and then score them gently with a very sharp knife before
you plant them in the garden.

You might use what was left of the coffee we drank in Lisa's
kitchen visiting.

There were orange poppies on the table in a clear glass vase,
stained near the bottom to the color of sunrise;

the unstated theme was the blessedness of gathering and the
blessing of dispersal—

it made you glad for beauty like that, casual and intense,
lasting as long as the poppies last.

An Iron Spike

So like a harrow-pin
I hear harness-creaks and the click
of stones in a ploughed-up field.
But it was the age of steam

at Eagle Pond, New Hampshire,
when this rusted spike I found there
was aimed and driven in
to fix a cog on the line.

It flakes like dead maple leaves
in the track of the old railway,
eaten at and weathered
like birch stumps dressed by beavers.

What guarantees things keeping
if a railway can be lifted
like a long briar out of ditch-growth?
I felt I had come on myself

in its still, grassed-over path
where I drew the iron like a thorn
or a dialect word of my own
warm from a stranger's mouth.

And the sledge-head that drove it
with a last opaque report
deep into the creosoted
sleeper, where is that?

And its sweat-cured, polished haft?
Ask those ones on the buggy,
inaudible and upright
and sped along without shadows.

From the Republic of Conscience

I

When I landed in the republic of conscience
it was so noiseless when the engines stopped
I could hear a curlew high above the runway.

At immigration, the clerk was an old man
who produced a wallet from his homespun coat
and showed me a photograph of my grandfather.

The woman in customs asked me to declare
the words of our traditional cures and charms
to heal dumbness and avert the evil eye.

No porters. No interpreter. No taxi.
You carried your own burden and very soon
your symptoms of creeping privilege disappeared.

II

Fog is a dreaded omen there but lightning
spells universal good and parents hang
swaddled infants in trees during thunderstorms.

Salt is their precious mineral. And seashells
are held to the ear during births and funerals.
The base of all inks and pigments is seawater.

Their sacred symbol is a stylized boat.
The sail is an ear, the mast a sloping pen,
The hull a mouth-shape, the keel an open eye.

At their inauguration, public leaders
must swear to uphold unwritten law and weep
to atone for their presumption to hold office—

and to affirm their faith that all life sprang
from salt in tears which the sky-god wept
after he dreamt his solitude was endless.

III

I came back from that frugal republic
with my two arms the one length, the customs woman
having insisted my allowance was myself.

The old man rose and gazed into my face
and said that was official recognition
that I was now a dual citizen.

He therefore desired me when I got home
to consider myself a representative
and to speak on their behalf in my own tongue.

Their embassies, he said, were everywhere
but operated independently
and no ambassador would ever be relieved.

A Shooting Script

They are riding away from whatever might have been
Towards what will never be, in a held shot:
Teachers on bicycles, saluting native speakers,
Treading the nineteen-twenties like the future.

Still pedalling out at the end of the lens,
Not getting anywhere and not getting away.
Mix to fuchsia that "follows the language."
A long soundless sequence. Pan and fade.

Then voices over, in different Irishes,
Discussing translation jobs and rates per line;
Like nineteenth century milestones in grass verges,
Occurence of names like R.M. Ballantyne.

A close-up on the cat's eye of a button
Pulling back wide to the cape of a soutane,
Biretta, Roman collar, Adam's apple.
Freeze his blank face. Let the credits run

And just when it looks as if it is all over—
Tracking shots of a long wave up a strand
That breaks towards the point of a stick writing and writing
Words in the old script in the running sand.

The Disappearing Island

Once we presumed to found ourselves for good
Between its blue hills and those sandless shores
Where we spent our desperate night in prayer and vigil,

Once we had gathered driftwood, made a hearth
And hung our cauldron like a firmament,
The island broke beneath us like a wave.

The land sustaining us seemed to hold firm
Only when we embraced it *in extremis*.
All I believe that happened there was vision.

JUAN FELIPE HERRERA ■ ■ ■ ■ ■ ■ ■ ■ ■ ■ ■

Fuselage Installation

(My loved ones drift into nothingness
—with little red gifts still
in their anxious arms. Little shirts.)

Blaze, the missile shards; your fuselage glitter, stuttered
over the wild crazed mountains; a blast at the exact interval
when coffee was being served; on the last plate,
a frayed napkin casts a claw shadow.

Lift. The hill with little people—tardy saints. Kneel.
They are your lecturers, your gloomed witnesses
with elongated hats; alarming
scarves blossom from their torsos.

The fuselage is—the child, her back mandril blue.
What stone amphitheatre sings, what peasant trumpets glare for her?
This dragon vestment is all we have, now: nameless quills,
unknown fins, burning gauze without candle wicks.

You assemble new artillery, set up a helmet monument
inevitably, you salute with pleasure. We follow
in this dome—your basilica of quiet blood. This is your kingdom,
earthquake light.

Penance? Go there,
to the waters of the glazed city. All the electric fish, whitened,
loosened from their tarnished silver boots—the ones they used
to bully you.

They too float above your hand, eerie;
their purple smoke mouths, triumphant.

The Weaning of Furniture-Nutrition

My leg stiffens. The crutch that holds me has become my aromatic rosary.
My exact duplicate sits behind me. He wears the same sickness.

The cabinet in the front is halfway open. Dali says that this is proper,
that I should find the ecstacy on this shore, in the form of a wooden box,
in Van Gogh's love for green boats sliced with bloody stripes.

The sea goes through me.
I remember my mother's death this way: the last taxi
in San Jose, the wrong street, 4th street to the abandoned
apartments of the homeless instead of the hospital. This
comes to me in times of quiet and rebelliousness.

Ten days the doctor said.
Is she ready for her sacraments the priest said.

We were in a mechanical room of hoses and meters,
tubes and needles. I was sitting with her as she looked up
for the last time. As I held her hand.

What could we say at this time? What were the words worth?
How could I apply the face cream holding itself inside the jar?

The horizon has a gospel. It sings for me far ahead
where the grayness becomes whiteness. I stretch out my right leg
and place a handkerchief over my bad knee.

My dead eye peeks through the furniture.
Chucho and Velasquez, my cell brothers wait for me.
We wear the same clothes when the sea rolls out its bread.
We pick up stones
and scratch our names on sand. We sit bowed and astute.
The replicas behind us do the same. Our dead mothers float
far from where we sit. They drink from the green bottles still
on their medicine chest. The little chest of drawers, the one
that smells of apples and duck feathers.

Hallucinogenic Bullfighter

The story comes apart near Gala's eyebrows.
This is where the plot shreds itself, where the foreign planet dissolves,
the one with the face of Jupiter and the sky plagued by half-eyes—

bacteria,
with a shorn continent; half of Africa or was it half of Chiapas?

The lines of my face match her jugular; we both go up
in an odd column, fast and folded. This language is futile,
the letters empty themselves of the ink and the ink spills
in rough circles and mythic shapes.

I want to dream into them to find the next line or the next kiss.
Alone this time.

The Obraje and the Goddess have curled back into the air,
the pulp inside the tree form, into the infinite staircase above
Cadaquez in California.

If you hold your hand upright. If
you spread the muslin mantle over the tabla. If you sit back for
a second. If you raise your voice this time there will be a series
of black dots in the mirror. Each one contains the ova for the next
universe. No one, knows how to decipher this today. No one,
except Zapata, the old Macehual sorcerer, the commoner who
lives out his days in the hidden vault below Velasquez's cave.
Velasquez told me this was his own secret. He said that he often
spoke with Zapata. I am the one who feeds him fresh cut lamb
shanks, he told me. Between my paintings, in the middle of sleep,
I go to him and lift the small iron lid over his cell. I call out to him
as candle light falls onto his face. I toss the meat to him
and to the Jaguar on the opposite chamber walled off by bars
of Carrara. Zapata says that the mystery of our lives depends
on the spatter of dots and glyphs on the Jaguar's pelt, he says
it depends on the motion of these figures as the Great Omen
paces in the wet darkness.

Zapata has the face of a woman. Velasquez said.
The lips, the tresses.

BRENDA HILLMAN   ■ ■ ■ ■ ■ ■ ■ ■ ■ ■ ■ ■ ■

Dark Existence

—You lay down in your bed
for ten years, and after ten years
you got up. The room was full of weak color

but there was an interesting little hill of rich life
from which all things streamed;

and you saw between
existence and the fringe of your
quotes non-
being on the wall
an active shadow that could not reconcile itself to earth
and was not ironical, that is, not split;

but nothing could be done without some
cooperation between this

shadow and whatever refused it in this world
so you invited it in—

dark existence that comforts and terrifies—
bright existence that could not stay—

Every Life

—And right before daybreak the little owl returned:
two small solid o's,
like napkin holders.

Then the briefer, brighter o's of another bird of prey,
not a victim,
came across the field to welcome her.

Dawn has four stages. In the third,
everything chooses how much more it will become;
until then,
the door is the same color as the hinge,

poems fit into other poems, every life
fits into every life,
bright into dark, not deciding.
After that,

the wall notices the shadow pulled out of the soul,
gray as a puritan

and the brave, dreamy hyacinth starts to be seen—

could the garden have said
to the gardener, I made you grow? They were
beside one another.

Could that which was not yet
press forward in the world? It seemed for a brief time
it could—

Little Furnace

—Once more the poem woke me up,
the dark poem. I was ready for it;
he was sleeping,

and across the cabin, the small furnace
lit and re-lit itself—the flame a yellow
    "tongue" again, the metal benignly
hard again;

and a thousand insects outside called
    and made me nothing;
moonlight streamed inside as if it had been . . .

I looked around, I thought of the lower wisdom,
spirit held by matter:
    Mary, white as a sanddollar,

and Christ, his sticky halo tilted—
    oh, to get behind it!
The world had been created to comprehend itself

as matter: table, the torn
veils of spiders. . . . Even consciousness—
missing my love—

was matter, the metal box of a furnace.
As the obligated flame, so burned my life . . .

What of the meaning of this suffering I asked
and the voice—not Christ but between us—said
you are the meaning.

No no, I replied, That
is the shape, what is the meaning.
You are the meaning, it said—

Black Series

    —Then in the scalloped leaves of the plane tree
a series of short, sharp who's:
a little owl had learned to count.

You lay in your bed as usual not existing
because of the bright edges pressing in.

All at once the black thick o's of the owl
made the very diagram you needed.
Where there had been two
kinds of infinity, now there was one!
The smudged circle around the soul
was the one the gnostics saw around the cosmos,

the mathematical
toy train, the snake eating its tail.

Relieved by the thought that the owl's o's
had changed but not you, that something
could change and not be lost in you,

you asked the voice for more
existence and the voice said
yes but you must understand
I loved you not despite your great emptiness
but because of your great emptiness—

EDWARD HIRSCH ▪ ▪ ▪ ▪ ▪ ▪ ▪ ▪ ▪ ▪ ▪ ▪ ▪ ▪ ▪

Milena Jesenská

Thank you for attending this tribute to love.
I present myself to you as a Czech journalist
and translator—and also as a modern woman
who has recognized the cruelty of our century.
Thus far it has been a calamitous century;
I haven't lost my vital optimism as a woman
or my curiosity as a practicing journalist,
but tonight's lecture is an obituary for love

because Franz Kafka—the writer—has died.
He was a master of the alienated sentence,
a Jew, a jackdaw, a cauldron of anxiety,
a crisis masquerading as a human body.
He never should have entertained a body
since it caused him overwhelming anxiety
which he transformed into a guilty sentence
that turned on itself and would never die.

Kafka saw a strange and terrifying world
filled with invisible wingbeats and demons.
He suffered for years from a lung disease
which he also encouraged by his thinking.
He had his own gruesome way of thinking
about the dark receptivity of his disease:
he viewed his lungs as a cradle for demons
who would tear apart and destroy his world.

I suspect he was too vulnerable to live,
too kind to fight. He had a frightening
delicacy, an uncompromising refinement.
Few people ever knew him as a human being
because he was such an odd, solitary being.
The books he wrote have great refinement—
I find them stark, funny, and frightening.
Is it possible he knew too much to live?

He had nothing to do with earthly business—
strangeness came through everything he said.
For him money, typewriters, foreign exchange
were mysterious secrets, mystical things.
He tended to overestimate practical things
he couldn't cope with, manage, or change.
Thus he admired his fiancée, so he said,
because she was very "good at business"

and therefore a true person of the world.
When I told him about my husband, Ernst,
who was unfaithful to me a hundred times,
his face lit up with genuine amazement.
It was the same awe—the same amazement—
he felt for conductors who know the times
of all the trains. He was completely earnest
in his respect for those who run the world.

He was a naked man trying to live alone
in a universe where everyone was dressed.
He had no refuge from the elements, exposed
to those things from which we are protected.
He was lost because he was unprotected,
a human negative who had been exposed.
I supposed his terror could be addressed,
but night was a blankness he faced alone.

No sanatorium could possibly cure him
because he never recovered from his fear
of living like an insignificant cockroach
sacrificed on the altar of the abnormal.
But what if we are sick and he was normal?
He perceived the courage of the cockroach
who crawls in the dust and encounters fear.
The darkness was a mirror reflecting him.

I admit I needed him. I tried to help,
but my love turned into one more catastrophe.
I have his letters, diaries, stories

that scrutinize an inscrutable disaster.
Maybe his character *was* a human disaster,
but he paid for it with uncanny stories
which will survive the coming catastrophe.
And now we must live without his help.

Tristan Tzara

There is no such thing as a dada lecture
a manifesto is addressed to the whole world
I am opposed to every system except one
love is irrational and you are the reason

a manifesto is addressed to the whole world
but bells ring out for no reason at all
love is irrational and you are the reason
I am a bridge harboring your darkness

but bells ring out for no reason at all
you are a fresh wind assaulted by sails
I am a bridge harboring your darkness
let's not lash ourselves to the flagpoles

you are a fresh wind assaulted by sails
I am a wound that sprays your salt
let's not lash ourselves to the flagpoles
let's not swim to the music of sailors

I am a wound that sprays your salt
ambassadors of sentiment hate our chorus
let's not swim to the music of sailors
we cast our anchors into the distance

ambassadors of sentiment hate our chorus
they can't pollute our smokiest feelings
we cast our anchors into the distance
we sail our boats for the netherworld

they can't pollute our smokiest feelings
each of us has a thousand virginities
we sail our boats for the netherworld
I'm giving you all my nothingness

each of us has a thousand virginities
we still consider ourselves charming
I'm giving you all my nothingness
I have doubted everything but this

we still consider ourselves charming
there is no such thing as a dada lecture
I have doubted everything but this
I am opposed to every system except one

JACK HIRSCHMAN ▪ ▪ ▪ ▪ ▪ ▪ ▪ ▪ ▪ ▪ ▪ ▪ ▪

The Painting

So there it is:
a painting of the late black heroic
mayor of Chicago
in woman's underwear
in the name of artistic iconoclasm
and free expression
and constitutional liberty
and individual civil rights.

And there they are at last,
the city aldermen
taking it off the walls
removing it from the exhibition
in the name of the working masses
whose constitutional liberties
and free expression
and civil rights

have been smothered, censored,
bribed, shunted, overlooked;
and now whose heroes
are made into kitsch,
pornogrified, transvesticized
to reflect the most cheapshot
degrading and racially humiliating
business-as-usual nation on earth.

Well, what do you say?
Were they wrong to remove the painting
of the progressive mayor
who'd led the working people
toward the destruction
of a rotting fascist machine
that wants to re-assert
its disgusting oppression
now that Harold Washington is dead?

Bubbubbubbut removing a painting!
Bubbubbubbut the artist's individual . . .
the artist's individu
the artist's individ
the artist's indiv
the artist's in
Whawhawhawhat about the artist?

What about the class?

Provoprovoprovoprovocation is the essence of art!

Provocation for what, Mr. Curator?
Mr. Institutional Curator,
Mr. Corporate-Funded Institutional Curator,
Mr. Elite Corporate-Funded Institutional Curator,
Mr. Deathshead Elite Corporate-Funded Institutional Curator,
Provocation for what?

Bubbubbubbut what about the empty wallspace, the violation
of the artist, the damage to culture . . . !

You are the empty wallspace, Mr. Curator,
you are the violation of the artist
and the damage to culture.
David Nelson painted *Mirth & Girth*
out of the hundred twisted fantasies
of the sleaze of politics and the politics of sleaze,
of the terror of the sex of blackness
and the blackness of sex—
fantasies used by capitalism
secretly through racist aesthetics
or openly through markets of porn
to displace imagination with a price,
to keep artists and workers alike
filthy in their purity,
paralyzed in dirty-minded liberty,
fugitives from human dignity
and political struggle,
stupefied when confronting collective life
or revolutionary action.

We are partisan, Mr. Make-It Curator,
and you, Mr. Make-It-New Artist,
we're at war
with art as privilege,
with the kitsching up of soul,
with the gooning of the truth
about those who help working people see

how beautiful the reality
of their imagination as a class
in motion actually is.

Do we acclaim the removal of the painting?
Emphatically, provocatively
Yes.

The Tremor

Two young guys
in the rear of a San Francisco bus
loudly interweaving
raucous talk about
    food food food,
      tacos smeared with hotsauce,
      pizza to make them
      "full as fuck,"

their obscenities frightening
the eyes of the children
sitting nearby, sensitive as books,
on either side of their mother.

Allover town handshakes
are turning into panhandles.

"Food, food, muthuhfuckin'
food's what it's all about!"

The dying, the lies
written in the eyes
and at the corners
of the mouths allaround.

Just below the pursed lips,
the twist,
    the truth
cursed by control, terrorized
into taut silence.

"Food, food, muthuhfuckin'
food's what it's all about!"
—brash, noisy, dashing
everything
    (books, newspapers, thoughts)
against the bus windows,

because they're hungry
and they want their lust for food
to get down and in under everybody's skin,
they want the whole bus to know
they're hungry
and their hunger
is forever being beaten down,
pommelled and spat upon
every day of their lives.

Sometimes
I can be so still,
I can feel
the trembling of my age, the earthquake
of the young demanding the justice
a decrepit generation
of hustlers and thieves
were forced to rob them of,
as their generation
and the generation before theirs had been robbed,
and I unite with the coming tremor.

The Weeping

Walking to my room from the park
where I'd been sunning
my words on a bench with a buddy,
I passed a couple of women
and it seemed to me
as they walked and talked
they were weeping.

I continued on, and another
woman passed, and she too
seemed to have come
from somewhere mournful,
her eyes at once dry and yet
inconspicuously weeping.

I looked this way and that
at the corner, hoping
to find the source
of the sudden feeling
that someone had died,
someone I knew in the neighborhood,
but I could find nothing.

Could it have been your despair,
dear woman with whom I've lived
but live no longer,
two hours before you came to visit
and tell of it? Could your wandering
mournfulness have come to me
in the glisten of those women's eyes?

O friend, see, even as we
stroke our bliss
of sadness away,
a blush subsists
under the sallow
skins of one or another
of our addictions,
like the unforgettable blush
on that woman's face

in the hotel corridor
in the small town
in Romania
in the morning,
lactic with roses,
innocent and enduring and smiling
as if she had something
profoundly to do
with the awful physical night
of smoke and poisons and violence
that we are forced every day
to lug along with our bodies
into the sunlight.

JANE HIRSHFIELD ▪ ▪ ▪ ▪ ▪ ▪ ▪ ▪ ▪ ▪ ▪ ▪ ▪ ▪ ▪

Osiris

They may tell you the god is broken
into a higher life,
but it isn't true:
the one who comes back remains,
even riveted, even pieced-
together in spring,
an always-broken god.
The knots survive in his body,
the clenched-grain scars.

And the iced, winter ponds are real—
the children, skating lightly there,
feel a secret shiver as they cross
the blue places
of darkness rising-to-meet,
where the other face of the god
is looking up.

At Night

it is best
to focus your eyes
a little off to one side;
it is better to know things
drained of their color, to fathom
the black horses cropping
at winter grass,
their white jaws that move
in steady rotation, a sweet sound.

And when they file off to shelter
under the trees
you will find the dark circles of snow
pushed aside, earth opening
its single, steadfast gaze:
towards stars ticking by, one by one, overhead,
the given world flaming precisely out of its frame.

That Falling

You turn towards meteor showers in August,
wishing yourself like that:
bright and burning wholly out.
When feeling finally comes it is
that falling, matter breaking away
from air, the sound
of crickets moving through the grass like fire—
and the strangely twisted metal
in the field that a child finds:
residue, crown.
Then there's the story of the Chinese sage,
in anger and despair, who cut his body away in pieces,
flung them into the lake.
Each one, becoming finned and whole, swims off.

Invocation

This August night, raccoons,
come to the back door
burnished all summer by salty,
human touch: enter secretly & eat.

Listen, little mask-faced ones,
unstealthy bandits whose tails
are barred with dusk:
listen gliding green-eyed ones:
I concede you gladly
all this much-handled stuff,
garbage, grain,
the cropped food and cropped heart—
may you gnaw in contentment
through the sleep-hours
on everything left out.

May you find the house
hospitable,
well-used,
stocked with sufficient goods.
I'll settle with your leavings,

as you have settled for mine,
before startling back into darkness
that marks each of us so differently.

Ars Poetica

These flat and leathery leaves
of a dry country,
dust of window ledges, grip
of roots in the dirt—
see
how the crone cups us
in parched palms,
blows a little wind into the ear:
garlic, wild rose.

Kinda Blue: Miles Davis Died Today

for Michael S. Harper

In print you told the world, the first imprint
on your ears'-eye was the tear-
shaped blue gas flame. Its organic funk
from things long dead. The burner's hiss

the sound of an after-life.

Your indulgent, Garveyite father,
a dentist who didn't shine grins,
spoiled you but saw that you grew black,
saw that you blew blueblack.
Taught you "America."
Taught you personal freedom, like love,
is a twelve-bar blues, Dunbar's blue steel cage.
Showed you the way to play in
and the cost of playing out. In the City

caged, bar-bending Bird blew you away,
your mouth agape,
your wide eyes busted grace notes; slack-jawed,
you had no chops for Diz
and you wallowed in wannabe.

You found your father's blues, found you
rang true, ROUND
MIDNIGHT, at the height of your humanity,
when The City's cops beat you for
being.
You
peeped the stacked deck of union I.D. cards
—for blacks only—pass books,
American Apartheid, pointed
to the concert hall poster of your Horn-
Of-Africa face, modulated, "My Nation
T' is Of Thee," to, This is me! This is me!!
The night stick played Langston Hughes's hard Bop
on your head.
You bled blue notes
all over your white shirt, your vines
setting yet another trend:

blood-red blues,
and titled it "Boplicity."

Suited you to fit Bubber Miley's mute
to your belled horn, a plunger for the
burnt out throat, cool ice blue artifice. You forged split notes
from metallurgy and alchemy of brass, shaped
the tear-intense gas blue flame and burned.

Burn Miles! Before the burner's turned off! Cook! You a gas!

Your trumpet's voicing focused baby-blue
spotlight on an inner intense
tenderness, propane-flame-pure, spare
phrasings from the source of our spirituals:
you gave birth to the cool.
Maybe too coolly, muting

rage in a silent way. Putting down,
beating up what you loved: you
woman-beating, Coltrane-smacking, Monk-abusing,
heart-renting-not-so-funny-valentine.
Beating up yourself, smacking your own
face with heroin, the near-death blow,
nearly out on Duke's East St. Louis
Toodle O-O-O, knocking yourself all the way down the dirty dozen
steps to heaven, self-absorbed, yet
unselfish, generous with what really matters.

*You cool! You bad!! You Miles!!! You "mother . . . . . ." you
dead but not IN A SILENT WAY.*

LINDA HOGAN ▪ ▪ ▪ ▪ ▪ ▪ ▪ ▪ ▪ ▪ ▪ ▪ ▪ ▪ ▪

Crossings

There is a place at the center of earth
where one ocean dissolves inside the other
in a black and holy love;
It's why the whales of one sea
know songs of the other,
why one thing becomes something else
and sand falls down the hourglass
into another time.

Once I saw a fetal whale
on a block of shining ice.
Not yet whale, it still wore the shadow
of a human face, and fingers
that had grown before the taking
back and turning into fin.
It was a child from the curving world
of water turned square,
cold, small.

Sometimes the longing in me
comes from when I remember
the terrain of crossed beginnings
when whales lived on land
and we stepped out of water
to enter our lives in air.

Sometimes it's from the spilled cup of a child
who passed through all the elements
into the human fold,
but when I turned him over
I saw that he did not want to live
in air. He'd barely lost
the trace of gill slits
and already he was a member of the clan of crossings.
Like tides of water,
he wanted to turn back.

I spoke across elements
as he was leaving
and told him, Go.
It was like the wild horses
that night when fog lifted.
They were swimming across the river.
Dark was that water,
darker still the horses,
and then they were gone.

Return: Buffalo

One man made a ladder
of the stacked-up yellow bones
to climb the dead
toward his own salvation.
He wanted
light and fire, wanted
to reach and be close to his god.

But his god was the one
who opened his shirt
and revealed the scar of mortal climbing

It is the scar
that lives in the house with me.
It goes to work with me.
It is the people I have loved
who fell
into the straight, unhealed
line of history.
It is a brother
who heard the bellowing cry of sacred hills
when nothing was there
but stories and rocks.

It was what ghost dancers heard
in their dream
of bringing buffalo down from the sky
as if song and prayer
were paths life would follow back
to land,

And the old women, they say,
would walk that land,
pick through bones for hide, marrow,
anything that could be used
or eaten.
Once they heard a terrible moan
and stood back,
and one was not dead
or it had come back from there,
walked out of the dark mountains
of rotted flesh and bony fur,
like a prophet
coming out from the hills
with a vision
too unholy to tell.

It must have traveled the endless journey
of fear,
returned from the far reaches
where men believed the world was flat
and they would fall over
its sharp edge
into pitiless fire,

and they must have thought
how life came together

was a casual matter,
war a righteous sin,
and betrayal
wasn't a round, naked thing
that would come back to them
one day.

Chambered Nautilus

It's from before the spin of human fire,
before the dreaming that grew out of itself,
before there were people who ate the brains
of the dead,
before wind was leaving through a hole in the sky,
before zero and powers of ten,
before nets drifting the empty miles of water,
from when moon was the only tyrant that ruled the sea
and was the god shells rose to at night,
the builder of chambers,
the geometry of light, even infinity
is shaped this way
and the curve of sea lives in it,
the unwritten laws of water,
and it still rises
to the surface of darkness,
the country of drifting,
seeking a new kind of light to live inside,
from when we were less savage than now,
when shells were barter for corn
and cloth, and mirrors,
and we built dwellings of stone.
We were strong.
We were full.
Europeans did not powder our bones
and drink them, believing their powers
would grow
and there were no torturers leaving stone prisons
at night to buy bread and sugar
for their wives.
It was before there were bearslayers
and slayers of women and land
and belief. We knew earth was a turtle
swimming between stars
and everything that was savage in us
fought to the quick
because everything that lived had radiance

like the curve of water and shell
of whatever animal
still inside
that has brought me here.

JOHN HOLLANDER ▪ ▪ ▪ ▪ ▪ ▪ ▪ ▪ ▪ ▪ ▪ ▪ ▪ ▪

Some Walks With You

1.

This is neither the time nor the place for singing of
Great persons, wide places, noble things—high times, in short;
Of knights and of days' errands to the supermarket;
Of spectres, appearances and disappearances;
Of quests for the nature of the quest, let alone for
Where or when the quest would start. You are the wrong person
To ask me for a circus of incident, to play
Old out-of-tunes on a puffing new calliope,
Or to be the unamused client of history.
But tell me of the world your word has kept between us;
I do what I am told, and tell what is done to me,
Making but one promise safely hedged in the Poets'
Paradox: *I shall say "what was never said before."*

(Refusing to Tell Tales)

2.

Lying in love and feigning far worse (we love to know
That show of pain consumed it and none was left to feel)
For so long we had made up dozens of excuses
—Excuses for making up excuses they were—out
Of the stuff of love. Ah, but even saying it makes
The heart sink: what do we make things out of—need? desire
To have, to make? Or rather out of whole cloth? or yet
Of tattier fabric of vision and oversight,
Undersong humming along with it all, Gretchen's wheel
Spinning its own disco music? This can go on and
On, but what of candor now, of truth? We must reflect
On this obscurity with a bright, open face, not
Foolish, and musingly look at the dark and light up.

(The Pretext)

3.

So we came at last to meet, after the lights were out,
At someone's house or other, in a room whose ceiling
Light was accidentally switched off—and there you were
In a corner where I had not seen you just before
When I had rushed in looking for someone else. Even
Then the shadow of an earlier time deepened the
Room—and this was before I learned that in my childhood
You lived across the alley-way, the light of your room
Crept through my window-blinds, throwing ladders of light up
My ceiling in the dark (when I was four I thought that
"Shadows" meant spills of illumination from without).
Then, years later, I stumbled upon you, standing next
To an unlit floor lamp, against a mute looking-glass.

(The Shadow)

4.

At first you used to come to me when everything else
Seemed to have gone away somewhere—even those winter
Absences which themselves will desert cold orchards in
The January thaw, before returning the land
To its definitive hardness—and where a few broad
Strokes preserved the momentary pink, scratched at by bare
Trees, of winter twilight. Hedged around by denials
Of scene, we could deem ourselves to be the place we made.
Now, speaking figures of light, we redeem the barren
Plenitudes of picture, even in postcards and views
Crammed with the illustrative, as of the dumb head of
El Capitan at the specious twilight's first gleaming,
Or of lonely Neuschwanstein on its tinhorn summit.

(Then and Now)

5.

An anecdote: I sat here in this chair last month, and—
Wow! you came up right behind me, startling me so that
I broke the last word off the line I had been working
At, abandoning the feature-story of despair
I had been fashioning, and turned back to see whether
You had deliberately crept up to rob me of
The last word, or whether simply to tell me someone
From Porlock or from Washington had telephoned me.
What ever could you have thought to do with that missing
Word? Pelt me with it, as with a berry in a broad
Field of fruited bushes we were slowly moving through?
Feed it to me, in the starlight, in some ultimate
Rebuke? I'll never know, but you've helped me mend my ways.

(The Last Word)

6.

These two tales I tell of myself and the life I led
To its destruction, one dark, one bright: one gathered from
A few gleaming moments—a slice or two of the cake
From where it was perfectly marbled—the other one
Rising from an undersong of despair. In neither
Case is the truth of the story—or the story of
The possibility that either one could be true
Of false at all—of any interest. What matters
Is what they might be good for: the story of a lost
Joy, as a sad anchor to drop below the surface
Of where we keep on going; the other version of
What was, the tale of a hell escaped, easily sounds
Like a noisy breath of wind filling my patched old sails.

(Tales of the Sea)

7.

Your bright younger sister whom so many fancy to
Be you was always getting in the way when your friends
Were about. An "altogether inconvenient child
With an alarming memory" one of them said once.
She would help you sometimes when a trick was to be played,
A pompous visitor to be derided, something
Lost, or broken, to be covered for; but for the most
Part, she was up to all her own mischief. "From her gaze
Nothing was safe." But then, what she did was all for show,
Nothing was changed, the ongoing of every day outgrew
Her goings-on. But it is your doings that have made
The difference to me; I walk down the boulevard
With you unnoticed: her red hat makes everybody stare.

(Fancy-Pants)

8.

Now: There was a tall girl once whom I mistook for you
—Or was it you I thought was she? (Just like a tall tale
From some lovely book that I had not allowed myself
To see the figurative meaning of at all) My
Heart was dim, the lady's name was light; how gently once
We sang, I now remember, in Indiana in
The summer night, and she warmed my distant winter that
December. Unchained to the letter now, your spirit
Plays hide-and-seek, now in the fair and tall, now in the
Dark and small. I am most near it sometimes when hiding
My impatient eyes, counting to fourteen, piercing your
Disguise. Here I Come, Ready Or Not. Where are you, Love?
The tall girl's long gone, it is a summer night again.

(August Recall)

9.

Here by the ruins of this fountain where water played
With stone while the light was playing with it, long sessions
Were held on pleasant afternoons, with talk of shadows
Seated on the sunny grass, of substance there along
The marble benches. There they walked together with their friends—
Laurie, Stella, Delia, Celia, Bea and the others.
But over on the hill there were those who spoiled the fun—
Dirty old Dick Dongworth, his mighty line no longer
Standing for him (when their stichs go limp even Uncle
Walt's dildo won't do for them any more), and Louise
Labia, her heart an open book—eye your body
From their past, as we pass by the places where they lurked
Jealous of the others, too early to have met you.

(The Lovers)

10.

It was not for such fragments that we wandered so far
A field, a mountain, an old city by a river.
But more and more the broken pieces we saw in our
Meanderings came to have a power to command
Devotion that the unfractured images themselves
—Venus entire, a solemn family on a grave
Stele—could never have had at their time, let alone
From us. So we see these interruptions of an arm's
Extent, these abstract structures replacing familiar
Dispositions of the body's tribe of parts, these shapes
Of breakage passing over faces like traces of
Thought, and knowing how they figure our way of being
In our bodies, we believe in them as in ourselves.

We consider this archaic maiden who has lost
Her head over time, and gained her patch of fractured stone
Here, along a newly conceived plane, more personal
Than the half-ineffability of her fixed grin.
Stone can hardly be in pain, yet this has undergone
Something beyond its original shaping, something
Beyond that origin of feeling an inner edge
Of the outside world, the end of oneself. But in the
Light of our dry brooding, figure yields its truth to form;
Form returns to marble; and to broken stone we cry
"Good! You deserved it! What flesh has always had to know
You now have learned." Yes, but when stone has been turned into
A trope, what we see fractured here will be heartbreaking.

(Breakage)

11.

To say that the show of truth goes on in our outdoor
Theatre in the round may be no more than to remark
That one is always led out of some cave or other
Into the irritating glare of what is never
More than a high, wide, sunny, open local chamber
Of our general system of caves. But that it plays,
Night after night, under lights, drawing crowds even when
It is most archly stylized, let alone when lines are
Mouthed, and crotches scratched, in flatly stylized masquerades,
Means more. Truth sank all she had into this spectacle;
What's behind the scenes is openly part of the show,
As is everything that you lean over and whisper
To me knowingly as we watch one of the tryouts.

(Long Run)

12.

The figure ahead of us on the trail, looking back
From an easy stance of pause belying the extreme
Difficulty of the country, he has gone before:
Both in that it was in the past that he trod the ground
Which now we stand on looking at him with far less ease
Than he, and that he waits before our gaze like a part
Of the high trail itself. His glance, open but clearly
Asymmetric, borrows flashes of sunlight among
Leaves of underbrush to do its winking with, winking
Of acknowledgment that he knows what we know of him,
Preposterous graybeard with a touch of the farouche,
Behind us and ahead of us at once, one eyebrow
High overarched there in his momentary bower.

Still, the trail lies all before us. Neither alone, nor
With a tour, you and I walk our own kind of *via
Media.* Even when he or she accompanies
My rambles of the afternoon, you will be walking
At my other hand, pointing out how immediate
Presences—the gray, unquestionable rock I see,
The untranslatable, loud wind I hear—yield themselves
To the scentedness, warm of blood, full of heart, of the
Living thing midway between them. Moving up the path
With you is as if mounting some trim companionway
From the ingenious turbines up to the high points
Of lookout, not rejecting where we had been before
But bearing a part of what was into what will be.

(On the Trail)

13.

Let me say first that, although in the demanding light
Of morning the discrepancies rattling our discourse
Speak of a noisier afternoon, what can be heard
Is the sound of things evening up between our two
Conditions—as if we were light and sound disputing
Claims for primacy at the morning of the world; till
The odd, evening hour, neither yours nor mine, but ours,
When our hands reach out to touch like object and image
Moving toward the mirror's surface each through the magic
Space that the other's world must needs transform in order
To comprehend; when our voices have surrounded one
Another, each like some penumbra of resonance.
So that you have the last word now I give it to you.

(At the End of the Day)

RICHARD HOWARD ▪ ▪ ▪ ▪ ▪ ▪ ▪ ▪ ▪ ▪ ▪ ▪ ▪ ▪

Vocational Guidance, with Special Reference to the Annunciation of Simone Martini

Ordinarily
when the Messenger, otherwise known
as the Angel, makes himself
known, the rest of life absorbs his arrival—
or the rust of life;
not that we tell lies,
but we shall always be in terror
of the truth. Habitual
disorders suffice to hold fast to the small
change of small changes:
the dog keeps doing
undoable harm to the Bokhara,
your mother has called, again!
and that letter from the bank is anything
but reassuring.
Events are enough—
what Baudelaire calls *la frénésie
journalière*—to mitigate
an inopportune disclosure, to muffle
Angelic demands.
For Mary herself
the moment was unmanageable;

according to old masters
the Virgin resorted to household effects,
    a dither of forms
                in a minor world
    where whatever is the case is lower
        case, a means of avoiding
the garbled message: was it Give or Give Up
    Something Capital?
                You know how it is.
Not yourself for days (we all have spells),
    you need *things* around the house
to help out—objects of *virtù* to shield you
    from the articles
                of a faith that goes
    against the grain of mere existence.
        With some degree of success
you make your way into the gradual warp,
    pleasant evasions
                in which the masters
    specialize, plastic as all get out—
        when there He is! utterly
demanding, utterly demonic, speaking
    unutterable
                truth *and* consequence
    of truth. Disaster, even triumph—
        no matter what the Angel
says, it is the Angel saying it: how can
    that be anything
                but gibberish, how
    can you bear it? Only by binding
        an extra strand of daily
confusion around your Messenger, turning
    text into texture,
                praise into no more
    than prose, a general excuse for
        reading languidly between
the lines when an Angel pronounces your fate
    in brisk iambics.
                Mary was finding
    her comfort in Deuteronomy:
        "With the smooth stones of the stream
is thy portion, there thy lot," when Gabriel
    lighted before her.
                Simone saw it,
    and not all the plausible veneers
        of Siena can rival
his unvarnished truth (though many times restored)
    in the Uffizi.
                It might be your life:

no vainglorious architecture
vaults into, no garden leads
your eye out of, the picture. Lilies, a bench,
and the two of them
up against flat gold
and cold marble—no getaway, no
domesticity, unless
you call the still-fluttering plaid stole knotted
at Gabriel's throat
a domestic touch.
Even the scarf draped behind
Mary can be misleading:
it looks more like wings, when wings are the last thing
in the world she wants:
wings are terrible,
they take up too much room, too much air,
they speak volumes. Gabriel
speaks only words, marring the gold but making
right for Mary's ear—
words are terrible.
No olive-branch he bears, no wreath
he wears can ease this meeting,
and Mary—Simone Martini's Mary,
you can see, abhors
her bright Intruder.
She was just . . . she *was.* Sulking now for
the rape of that imperfect:
"I was reading when I heard . . ." Why is he here?
Who needs an angel?
A glance at her hair
and Gabriel's (identical gold)
explains. It is Simone's
method, this auburn pun, his way of saying
we ourselves summon
Angels. Unwilling?
Unready? Giving rise to second
thoughts . . . If it had been enough
to brood over books, she never would have seen
her Visitor;
resentful, reverent,
Mary at this moment discovers
that she wills him to appear—
even the wings are part of her—no use tugging
the long blue mantle
away from the Good
Tidings into an almost abstract
or Japanese pattern of
refusal. Pay those bills, call your mother back,
and clean up after

the dog: no dodging
the moment when you meet the Angel,
when he announces what you
have known all along. No second-guessing:
"Father, let this cup
                    pass from me"—his words
must enter the porches of your ear,
      hammer strike anvil, until
the choice you have made, as Simone shows,
      comes, unfurnished, home.

SUSAN HOWE ▪ ▪ ▪ ▪ ▪ ▪ ▪ ▪ ▪ ▪ ▪ ▪ ▪ ▪ ▪ ▪ ▪ ▪ ▪

Silence Wager Stories

I know I know short conviction

have losses then let me see why

To what distance by what path

I thought you would come away

1

Battered out of Isaiah

Prophets stand gazing

Formed from earth

In sure and certain

What can be thought

Who go down to hell alive

is the theme of this work

I walk its broad shield

Every sign by itself

havoc brood from far

Letting the slip out

Glorious in faithfulness

Reason never thought saw

2

You already have brine
Reason swept all away
Disciples are fishermen
Go to them for direction
Gospel of law Gospel of shadow
in the vale of behavior
who is the transgressor
Far thought for thought
nearer one to the other
I know and do not know
Non attachment dwell on nothing
Peace be in this house
Only his name and truth

3

Having a great way to go
it struck at my life
how you conformed to dust
I have taken the library
Volumes might be written
ambiguous signs by name
Near nightfall it touches it
Nothing can forbear it
so fierce and so flaring
Sometimes by the seaside
all echoes link as air
Not I cannot tell what
so wanton and so all about

4

Fields have vanished
The Mower his hopes

Bow broke time loose
none but my Shadow
she to have lived on
with the wood-seige
nesting in this poem
Departed from the body
at home of the Story
I'm free and I'm famished
And so to the Irish
Patrol sentinel ensign
Please feel my arms open

5

The issue of legitimation
Identity of the subject
Circumcision of a heart
driven outside its secret
Elysian solitary Legitimation
by doubt but not by sight
Fear that forever forever
perfect Charity casts out
The Canticle is an allegory
unchangeable but changeable
Fluttering robes of Covetous
He is incomprehensible he
makes darkness his covert

6

Ages pre-supposed ages
the darkness of life
out of necessity night
being a defense by day
the cause and way to it

From same to the same
These joining together
and having allegiance
Words are an illusion
are vibrations of air
Fabricating senselessness
He has shattered gates
thrown open to himself

7

Though lost I love
Love unburied lies
No echo newlyfledge
Thought but thought
the moving cause
the execution of it
Only for theft's sake
even though even
perturb the peace
But for the hate of it
questionless limit
unassuaged newlyfledge
A counter-Covenant

8

Mysterious as night itself
all negligently scenery
if Nothing could be seen
Sacraments are mysterious
Ambiguous in literal meaning
the Pentateuch the Angels John
all men form a silent man
who wrote the author down

Sackcloth itself is humility
a word prerogatives array
Language a wood for thought
over the pantomime of thought
Words words night unto night

9

Drift of human mortality
what is the drift of words
Pure thoughts are coupled
Turn your face to what told me
love grazed here at least
mutinous predominant unapparent
What is unseen is eternal
Judgements are a great deep
Confession comes to nought
half to be taken half left
From communion of wrongdoing
doubleness among the nouns
I feed and feed upon names

10

Claim foreign order
dismantling mortal
Begotten possibility
plummet fetter seem
So coldly systems break
Fraught atvantaging
Two tell againstself
Theme theme heart fury
all in mutiny
Troublous or sadder
Estranged of all strange

Let my soul quell

Give my soul ease

11

Antic prelate treason

I put on haircloth

Clear unutterable

Secret but tell

What diadem bright

Theme theme heart fury

Winged knowledge hush

Billeted near presage

such themes do quell

Claim foreign order

Plummet fetter seem

wild as loveDeath

Two tell againstself

12

Strange fear of sleep

am bafflement gone

Bat winged dim dawn

herthe midmost wide

I did this and I

But for ever you say

Bafflement nether elegy

herthe otherwise I

Irreconcilable theme

keep silent then

Strange always strange

Estrange that I desire

Keep cover come cover

13

Lies are stirring storms
I listen spheres from far
Whereunder shoreward away
you walked here Protector
unassauged asunder thought
Unsettled familiar thought
you walked here Overshadow
I listen spheres of stars
I draw you close ever so
Communion come down and down
Quiet place to stop here
Who knows ever no one knows
to know unlove no forgive

———————————

Half thought thought otherwise
loveless and sleepless the sea
Where you are where I would be
half thought thought otherwise
Loveless and sleepless the sea

RICHARD HUGO ▪ ▪ ▪ ▪ ▪ ▪ ▪ ▪ ▪ ▪ ▪ ▪ ▪ ▪

Letter to Gale from Ovando

Dear Vi: You were great at the Roethke festival this summer
in Portland. I love your phrase "and birds move on" because here
that's exactly what they do. It's far far better to say
than "fly away" because that indicates they might have stayed
while "move on" says they're vagabond and starved. I'm hungry when
I'm here. It looks anytime like sunday with John Wayne in church,
leaving me helpless, waiting for the villains to ride in.
I only stop here on my way to fish, Brown's lake, or Cooper's,
to feel a part of the west, the brutal part we wave goodbye to

gladly and the honest part we hate to lose, those right days
when we helped each other and were uniformly poor.
How scattered we become. How wrong we end finally alone,
seeing each other seldom, hearing the wind in our teeth.
Roethke himself knew and hated to know the lonely roads
we take to poems. Miriam Patchen was right in her speech
in Portland: it's a one man route and sad. No help. No friend
along the way, standing beside the road with trillium.
And Dickey was right in Playboy, that part about the mind
becoming the monster and the monstrous ways we feed it
and it grows. My monster's desolate and kind. And in my
desolate home, the wind leaks in on sundays and finally
for all the gloom, I, not John Wayne, put the villains away
to rest, mark the headstones "no one" and start another poem.
Listen to yourself, Vi: "Lakes change, trees rot and birds move on."
And listen to ourselves move on, each on the road he built
one young summer while the world was having fun. Lakes change.
Trees rot. Roads harden. Whatever road, it was the blind one
and the only. Poems are birds we loved who moved on and remain.
Think of poems as arms and know from this town I am writing
whatever words might find a road across the mountains. Dick.

Letter to Hill from St. Ignatius

Dear Bobbi: God, it's cold. Unpredicted, of course, by forecast,
snow and bitter air drove in from Canada while we, some
students and I, were planning a weekend fishing trip
to Rainbow Lake where, just last week, five of us in four
hours took 44 trout. For all I know that lake is frozen tight,
the trout dormant under the ice for the next five months.
We are shut down. This is a quiet town on the Flathead
Reservation, the staggering Mission Range just beyond,
the mission itself of local historical fame. A priest
some 80 years back designed a ceremony for Good
Friday, Indian-Catholic, complete with Flathead chants
in dialect. It's lovely. This early sudden cold I think
of it, how it reminds me of simple times that no doubt
never were, the unified view of man, all that. I wept
the first time I saw it, the beleaguered Indians wailing
the priest to Stations of the Cross. The pall bearers bearing Christ
outside around fires and crying the weird tongue stark
through the night. Bobbi, I don't mind those real old days broke down.
We had (still have) too many questions. You've known embittering winds
in Green Bay and you are not bitter for all the license
they gave. I resent you once told me how I'd never know
what being Indian was like. All poets do. Including

the blacks. It is knowing whatever bond we find we find
in strange tongues. You won't believe this but after my grim years
alone, a woman who loves me has come along. And she
chants when she talks in the strangest of tongues, the human.
I take her in my arms and don't feel strange. She is tall
and she curls in bed like a cat. And so, like Indians,
I chant the old days back to life and she chants me alive.
It's snowing, Bobbi. The flakes seem heavy and they fall hard
as hail. I claim they ring like bells. And sure enough the far
cathedral complements my claim. Chant to me in your poems
of our loss and let the poem itself be our gain. You're gaining
the hurt world worth having. Friend, let me be Indian. Dick.

Letter to Blessing from Missoula

Dear Dick: You know all that pissing and moaning around I've
been doing, feeling unloved, certain I was washed up with
romance for good. That has come to an orgiastic halt.
From nowhere came this great woman. I wasn't looking
even when she was suddenly bang in my life. I mean
bang in all the best ways. Bang. Bang. Richard Blessing. And years
of loneliness faded into some silly past where I
stared moodily out my windows at the grammar school girls
passing each morning and fantasized being young again
but with circumstances better than the first time and with
an even newer than new morality current. To
say nothing of saying to myself over and over
"I am retired from romance. I am a failure at love.
Women don't like me. Lecherous, treacherous, kindless klutz.
Oh, that this too too flabby flesh should grow solid. Do not
go gentle into that defeat. Let us go then, you and I
into the deserts of vast eternity." As you can no doubt
see, things became warped, including my memory of how
certain lines go, and all for the wisest of causes:
self-pity. Do not depend on others for sympathy.
When you need sympathy, you'll find it only in yourself.
Now, I need none but I still defend self-pity. I still
say, if this woman hurts me I'll crawl back to my cave.
The snow doesn't get me down. The solid gray overcast
doesn't make me moody. I don't get irritated by
cold clerks in the markets, or barbers who take too long
trimming my hair. This woman is statuesque and soft
and she loves me; meaning she is at my mercy. Have you
noticed when women love us how vulnerable they are?
How they almost challenge us to test them, to be bastards,
to see how much outrageous shit we can fling their way?

Maybe, that's why we've been ripping them off for centuries,
I don't blame them for bitching, turning to movements, fem lib
or whatever they call it. This time, I'm not saying, prove it,
prove your love by not objecting as I steal your money,
set fire to your hair and break your toes with the boots
I took off a dead German soldier at Tobruk. I am
simply going to prove I'm worthy of her love and I feel
I am, which must mean I love her. Boy, am I becoming
tender, and am I ever certain she will not hurt me.
I'll give her no cause. I accept maybe for the first time
love and I luxuriate in it, a glutton, a trout
who had a hard time finding the spawning ground, who swam time
after time the wrong river and turned back discouraged
to the sea, though at moments the sea was fun. Those sex crazed
sharks and those undulating anemones, can't beat them
when you've had a few drinks though you wake up diseased and raw,
your gills aching and your fins stiff with remorse. That's enough
metaphor. This morning I feel as masculine as you,
and I regard you as the C. C. Rider of poetry,
criticism and trout. This woman will curve from now on
lovely in poems and streams. Look for her in the quarterlies
and pools. I mean real pools, the ones you come to
with Lisa when you take her on picnics. And take Lisa
on picnics. Give her and her cooking my love. Your friend, Dick.

Letter to Oberg from Pony

Dear Arthur: In a country where a wealthy handful
of people tear down anything you could possibly love,
break your affectionate connections with yourself by whim
for profit, would move, if they could make money moving it,
the national capitol to Dubuque, have already
torn down Walt Whitman's home, tried, damn their souls,
to wreck the Pike Place Market, and in their slimy leisure
plot to dismantle Miss Liberty and move her one piece
at a time to Las Vegas where, reassembled, she
will be a giant slot machine (pull the right arm please,
the one with the torch), you'd love to pack your things and move here.
This is lovely. This is too great for a poem. The only
way here is by dream. Call it Xanadu or Shangri-La
or Oz. Lovely old homes stand empty because somewhere
in this floundering world, the owners toil and plan to come
back here to die. I hope I die here. I want to spend my
last years on the porch of the blue house next to the charming
park the town built and no one uses, picnic tables ringed
by willows and the soft creek ringing in the grass. I hope
to sit there drinking my past alive and watching seasons

take over the park. This is only to assure you, Art,
that in a nation that is no longer one but only an
amorphous collection of failed dreams, where we had been told
too often by contractors, corporations and prudes that
our lives don't matter, there still is a place where the soul
doesn't recognize laws like gravity, where boys catch trout
and that's important, where girls come laughing down the dirt road
to the forlorn store for candy. I love Pony like I love
maybe fifty poems, the ones I return to again
and again knowing my attention can't destroy what's there.
Give my best to Barbara and take care. Dick.

Letter to Goldbarth from Big Fork

Dear Albert: This is a wholesome town, really. Cherries grow
big here and all summer a charming theatre puts on
worthy productions. It is Montana at its best, lake
next to town, lovely mountains close by, and independent
people, friendly, generous, always a discernible touch
of the amateur I like. Nothing slick. Montana is
the rest of America 50 years back. Old barber shops
you walk into and don't have to wait. Barbers who take
a long time cutting your hair to make sure they get in all
the latest gossip. Bars where the owner buys every fifth round,
and you buy one for him now and then. Albert, I love it
despite what some think here reading my poems. The forlorn towns
just hanging on take me back to the 30's where most poems
come from, the warm meaningful gestures we make, the warm ways
we search each other for help in a bewildering world,
a world so terrifyingly big we settle for small
ones here we can control. There's a bitter side, too, a mean
suspicion of anything new, of anyone different
or bright. I hate that. I hate feeling as I become well
known that I'm marked: poet, beware. He has insight.
I don't like being tagged negative because I write hurt
as if my inner life on the page is some outer truth,
when it is only my view, not the last word. When it is
not the world photoed and analysed, only one felt.
I like best of all in Montana how people who've had
nothing from the beginning, never expected a thing,
accept cruelty, weather and man, as normal and who have felt
the bitter strokes of life's gratuitous lash (oh, poets
catch that one), are cheerful, receptive and kind to the end.
So for all their suspicion and distrust of me, they are
my women, my men. And I, who came from the seacoast,
who love the salmon, the damp air of Seattle, finally
have come to call this home. That means, when I say it, I lived

here forever and I knew it first time I saw it nine
years ago. Albert, Big Fork brings out the mountain in me.
And trout help, too. Just now, a stranger drove by and waved.
And I waved back my best wave, Albert. I shouted at him
"hello," and it came back doubled by hills. At you too. Dick.

Letter to Haislip from Hot Springs

Dear John: Great to see your long coming, well crafted book
getting good reviews. I'm in a town that for no reason
I can understand, reminds me how time has passed since we
studied under Roethke, Arnold Stein, Jack Mathews and
Jim Hall at Washington. Two of them are gone already.
I think of that this morning and I get sad. This motel
I took for the night, hoping to catch the morning fishing
at Rainbow Lake, is one that survived after most others
went broke when they discovered the hot springs simply didn't
work. No therapeutic value. None of that. The old climbed
up out of the steaming water still old. The cripples still limped
after three weeks of soaking. I'm a little lame myself
these days. Bad hip from a childhood accident. Skeletal
problems show up as we enter middle age. Our bones
settle in and start to complain about some damn thing that
happened years ago and we barely noticed it then.
Who thought 25 years ago we'd both be Directors
of Creative Writing, you at Oregon, me here at
Montana, fishing alone in the Flathead wind, in lakes
turned silver by sky, my memories so firm, my notion
of what time does to men so secure I wish I'd learned to
write novels. Now I can understand the mind that lets Sam
wander off to Peru on page 29 and come back
twenty years later in the final chapter, a nazi.
I know why I always feel sad when I finish a novel.
Sometimes cry at just the idea that so much has happened.
But then, I'm simply a slob. This is no town for young men.
It sets back off the highway two miles and the streets stand bare.
When I drive in, I feel I'm an intrusion. When I leave,
I feel I'm deserting my past. I feel the same sadness
I feel at the end of a novel. A terrible lot has happened
and is done. Do you see it happening to students?
I do and say nothing, and want to say when some young poet
comes angry to my office: you too will grow calm. You too
will see your rage suffer from skeletal weakness you picked
up when young, will come to know the hot springs don't work, and love
empty roads, love being the only man casting into
a lake turned silver by sky. But then, maybe he won't,

no matter. The morning is clear. I plan to grab breakfast
at the empty cafe, then head to the lake, my Buick
purring under the hood as Stafford would say. And I plan
to enjoy life going by despite my slight limp. Best. Dick.

Letter to Birch from Deer Lodge

Dear Michele: Once, according to a native, this town
had a choice: state prison or university, and chose
the former. They didn't want whatever radical
was called in those days students and professors with ideas
messing up their town. Now guards in towers, nothing to do,
keep tabs on the streets, the teens cruising the streets in cars,
and report to parents or police anything amiss.
So the town became the pen. They even built a drive-in
across the street from the wall. Burger D and fries within
the shadow of penance. I think, when I'm here, how silly
prisons are, how, if we tore down the grotesque wall and let
all but a handful out, life would be no different, and how
we imprison people not for crimes but simply because
we don't like them, they are unrefined. Crime is our excuse.
Some poets equate themselves with criminals. That may be
because we share the same desolate loves, the same railroad
spur along the swamp ignites some old feeling of self
inside and when the sky comes gray late afternoon across
the world on sunday, we know we're friendless and the hounds bay
in the distance sniffing for our trail. We are equally cowed
by the official, by men who never clown or smile.
And we, poet and felon, know how certain times are right
for others, wrong for us. We die 4 P.M. on friday
when the fun begins for others. And we are like the teens
of Deer Lodge, always under the censorial eye
of the tower. We find secret ways to play. No one
except poets know what gains we make in isolation.
We create our prison and we earn parole each poem.
Michele, our cell door's open like the dawn. Let's run and run.
The day is windy and alive with fields. Your friend. Dick.

Letter to Libbey from St. Regis

Dear Liz: Here's where I degraded myself for the last time
in front of a clerk, in the gift shop fingering copper
and begging one warped triggering response. Since then
I've been stable, lonely as this town, the solitary river

moving north. I never stop here on my way to Coeur d'Alene.
I pass through hoping 50 years of shame will ripen
into centuries and all men understand. A feeble hope.
Even now I see their grins. I look away at mountains
and I pray all distance widens and I grow old soon. You know,
reach that age where no one wonders why I can't get women.
The worst thing is, I burn alive each day. A letter comes
from some ex lover and I burn. I tell others she
is coming back to town and they say good, then things may start
again, and I say yes, and inside I am screaming 'save me'
and she never comes. I went back to the petty compensations,
writing poems to girls like this one, hoping to imply
a soul worth having, hoping old timidities returned
are temporary and the sun will win. On good days, this
is just a town and I am just a lonely man, no worse
than the others in the bar, watching their lives thin down
to moments they remember in the mirror and those half
dozen friends you make in life who matter, none of them
after you are young. I remember being laid three times
each morning by a tiger angel and that didn't solve
a thing. I went limp to work, feeling like a man, but hell.
I was the same one. And the demons, when they came,
wore the same demonic green they wear in Ireland.
Once, I stopped in Italy, the land no longer torn
by war and wholesale poverty, some village in the south
for coffee. I wowed them joking in bad Italian
and they yelled 'ritorni' when I drove away. That's the day
I must remember as the distance widens and I grow old,
not too rapidly. I am dating a 19 year old lovely
and things slip into place, days I find worth having,
stops I find worth making, flashing some of the old charm
at the waitress and murmuring 'ritorno' as I drive away.
And you? How are you doing? Wherever in the world. Rain
has washed grass vivid where we threw up on the lawn, and bars
we hid in have improved the lighting. Next time through
to Coeur d'Alene, I'll stop here more than just to mail a letter.
I'll send you copper, a pendant or a ring. And I'll joke
the clerk to roaring. I plan more poems like this one, poems
to girls, to tiger angels better dawns provide. The dark
that matters is the last one. Autumn's spreading like the best joke
ever told. And I send this with my best laugh, as always. Dick.

In Your Dream After Falling in Love

Two cops who are really famous actors
playing cops are arrested and must go
to jail. "Not there," one cries, "We'll be killed."

They enter jail with fear. The other prisoners
gloat and yell, "Look who's here. Let's scrub them
good." They give the cops a bath. The cops protest
but seem to enjoy it. You are relieved. You know
things are all right. You are on a tall building
counting the cars way down in the street.
A man whispers, "They seem to be crawling."
"No. No," you say, "they are bright." A worm
turns on you, a giant, big teeth. He means
to eat you alive. You think quick. You
tell him a joke. He laughs himself sick.
He becomes a gull. He climbs up out
of the world of stale air. He is soaring,
a monster glider, and singing, "I am me."
The cell door opens. Fred Astaire dances
his way past the warden into the country.
The warden applauds. A headline says
prisons are abolished. You feel hurt.
You think you'd like your old cell back.
"No way," the grass murmurs, "no way."
You know you have lots of time to catch
the luxurious ship parked at the pier.

In Your Racing Dream

You hitch a ride with a cyclist. You sit in back
and hold on. He's leading in a race. With you
on the cycle he slows down and others pass.
You say to him, "Faster. You'll lose." He says
"I'm thinking of food." You drift a sleepy canal
on a barge, warm horses on the bank, sweep
of grass to trees the wind and light bend
far off in warm air. The water barely moves.
It will take months to cruise home. You snarl
at a horse, "I'm running out of time."
The cyclist goes by. He yells, "I'm winning."
You try to yell "Wait" but choke. He goes on.
You are mayor of a town. The people bring
you their problems. You give advice from
your window. You cannot remember
the canal. You ask, "How did I get here?"
Someone calls you to dinner. You try
and try to remember the cyclist's name.

DAVID IGNATOW ■ ■ ■ ■ ■ ■ ■ ■ ■ ■ ■ ■ ■ ■

Each Day

Cynthia Matz, with my finger in your cunt
and you sliding back and forth on it,
protesting at the late hour and tiredness
and me with kidneys straining to capacity
with piss I had no chance to release
all night, we got up from the park bench
and walked you home. I left you
at the door, you said something
dispiriting about taking a chance
and settling on me. I had left Janette
to chase after you running out
of the ice cream parlor where the three
of us had sat—I had felt so sorry
and so guilty to have had you find me
with her in the street. You and I
had gone to shows together,
you needed me to talk to and I was glad.
The talk always was about him
whom you still loved and he had jilted
you for someone else. I'm sorry, Cynthia,
that it had to end this way between us too.
I did not return the next day,
after leaving you at the door.
I did not return the following day either.
I went with Janette in whom I felt nothing
standing in the way, while with you
it would have been each day
to listen to your sadness
at having been betrayed by him.
I was not to be trusted either,
I too wanted love pure and simple.

The Pit

I cannot be shaken into explanations for my life;
it has its pit like any cherry
and that's its hardness. One
will land in the dirt
and I will name it for myself,
to your health.

We will do the dance of the leaves together.
How I longed to be loved was the beginning.

My writing teaches me
how to die tomorrow,
when the weather improves,
by dying with the sun,
a law unto itself
as I am.
There is this happiness.

Crystal Chandeliers

I wait for the mailman.

Why do you wait for the mailman?

He gives me something to anticipate, the opening of letters, finding bills and reminders of sales and notes from friends to say hello and what are you doing and why don't you write or come for a visit or can he come to visit me or he may have something to say about a mutual friend divorced or remarried or a success at love or publishing. Something, that is what I am waiting for.

Well, may I wait with you, then?

Is there going to be mail for you too, in my batch?

No.

Then why wait?

It will be nice watching you open your letters. It's something to anticipate, as you say, and I would like to enjoy it along with you, or if that's too personal and intrusive I could stand at a distance and just watch your face as you read each letter.

Oh, then you watching me will add a new wrinkle. It'll be something new to me too, being watched as I watch myself, a triple perspective.

Right, and then I knowing you are watching me watching you will add still another dimension.

Exactly, and knowing that both of us will be watching each other will add still another dimension.

Intensely?

Imaginatively?

Authentically?

With pleasure and pain and sorrow and joy and happiness and fear and dread, depending upon the letter.

And perhaps in satisfaction and fulfillment.

In consummation.

Hinting at the mysterious in us.

And around us.

Awe.

Worship.

Godhead.

Paradise.

Hell?

Purgatory?

In letters?

They'll be coming from humans like ourselves, filled with their own needs and joy, pleasure, identity, dread, happiness, terror and awe.

At sending us the letters.

Aren't we altogether in this?

Giving each other love, hate, bills, friendship and gossip.

Giving each other a circle, a closed circle.

A mystery?

An awesome awareness of us. We live in a circle.

As if we were living in millions of bodies and brains and always with the same image flashed back to us, the same thoughts and emotions.

Is this happiness?

Is this with dread and expectation, fear and joy, love and hate?

Is this the life in which we stand in awe?

Afraid to love, afraid to die, yearning for more of it.

Yearning for ourselves, more of ourselves, always more and more.

Always centered upon ourselves and emerging from ourselves to converge upon ourselves.

Renewed.

Refreshed.

Or hurt and sad.

Or killed outright.

By the hand of another man whom we know to be our self turning against us.

Divided within our self.

Bent on suicide.

What should we say to all this appalling commentary upon ourselves?

That it is us and we are living it and that we are the life we live and no other.

Do you have a solution?

We must think.

The letters have arrived. Here is the mailman.

Good morning, Mr. Mailman. We are very pleased to see you.

Thank you, but I get paid for doing this.

And we are grateful there is money with which to pay you.

Otherwise I would not be here.

Really.

I'd be out looking for another job.

And what about our letters?

Goodby, Mr. Mailman.

Did you see him shrug at my question?

And he did not even say goodby. Now I am sad.

And now perhaps we can make ourselves happier with the opening of these letters.

The better part of us.

We are turning ourselves around and around like a crystal chandelier, showing to ourselves all our lovely parts and unlovely parts.

Crystal chandeliers.

ROBINSON JEFFERS ▪ ▪ ▪ ▪ ▪ ▪ ▪ ▪ ▪ ▪ ▪ ▪ ▪ ▪ ▪

Home

She'd thrust the canyon out of her mind; she never thought of the whispering
    fall, the ferns, the hawk-haunted
Hills intense in the sun; no more than the child remembers uterine life: but after
    her mother
Died, and Phil Maybrick was holding her to the promised marriage; when time
    for some reason grew terrible:
"Why does it taste like ashes? Have children, begin it all over again, the anxious
    fable? Or have none,
Lie in his arms like stagnant water in the awful emptiness?" She was convinced
    that some insanity,
Obstruction in the mind, nothing in the nature of things, a wall of perverse
    thought that might be thrown down,
Threatened her away from normal happiness. "I've taught school three years and
    always hated it. I'll take
One month of perfect rest, away from the town, away from the people I
    know:"—suddenly her mind
Was like a city built with towers, full of a vision
Of the heights that she was born under, hills like humped cattle herded to the
    ocean, south of Monterey—

"I shall come back and be myself, be human like the others." She wrote it all in a
    letter to him.
Except the place; and promising love forever, her name, Rachel Devine. If he
    were too angry
It was not, perhaps, paradise . . . would crumble.

                                                She went to the place, and
    boarded at the farmer's below.
How long was it, nine years? These people had come since hers . . . departed: her
    name wasn't remembered.
The hills were undiminished, as great and sun-beaten and solitary as ever of old,
Though she'd been but a child, but twelve years old, last seeing them. Three days
    she wandered on the great heights
Over the ocean. She wanted to enter the canyon; she was afraid; the fourth, she
    entered the canyon
With the shamed fear that a child feels
Who listens in the night to terrible sighs and whispers and the bed of her parents
Straining, the shame and fear: the paths were not much overgrown; though the
    dwelling she knew was ruinous
Men still drove cows through the deep canyon to the hills at the head. The creek
    sang the old music, the cresses
Were all in white flower. A mile up the deep cleft, in sight of the remembered
    roof, the path split.
One way led over the stream by the great blocks of stone to the clump of willows
    . . . her father, when the world
Darkened about him: she remembered his body
Brought from the blood-stained willows. She never had seen the puddle of
    blood; her mind had seen it so dreadfully
On the dead earth under the willows:
The red glaze blackening in from the edges was clearer than memory. She never
    had seen the wound; for his face
Had not been torn outward, he held the muzzle in his mouth. "Dear God no
    wonder," she thought "no wonder
With such wounds in my mind! Here is the place I should have fled from: I have
    come to this place." She lingered
At the split way, tasting the sickness high in her throat. The choked path to the
    house less painful,
She followed that path: no ghost: herself was the ghost: she'd thought it might
    have stood grizzled and blood-splotched:
But nothing came along the thick leaves. The gapped doorway and the glassless
    windows. "Well: if I go in:
Because I've caught something from the lean hawks on the hillside. But really I
    feel little, why almost
Nothing, feel nothing, that's wise. The coast's heavy with stone." She entered the
    squalid rooms, the disgrace
And wreck of the house. Mice ran, and a linnet
Dodged out the far window. In the next room, one side of the cold hearth, the
    floor was all rotted,

Some tribe of burrowers had heaped earth there, through the brown hole, higher
  than the broken planks. She approaching
A rattle buzzed hard and she drew back from the planks. She thought of finding a
  stick, but turned in the doorway
Happy with her new thought: "This is my house and you're my watchdog. Meet
  strangers for me."

All night
In the farmhouse in the strain of the sea's voice, in dreams and waking she was
  not unhappy, remotely consoled
By the utter ruin of what she had visited; most by the snake at the hearth.
  Returning after two days
She heard one in the grass by the door and saw another in the house, by the
  rotted planks. In the basket
The farmer's wife had given her, a little bottle of milk was packed with the food;
  she found a cracked saucer
Back of the house, filled it with milk and crumbs of bread, she set it on the floor,
  then heedfully pushed it
With the fork of a long rod to the edge of the planks, the ridged brown opening.
  Had she read somewhere of pouring
Milk for the household spirit, the serpent? She seemed remembering . . . that
  was no matter: if the act in itself
Gave pleasure: "I love their enemies." Then she remembered gently, with distant
  loneliness, her city lover.
"I'm out of the net. Something from the hills
Comes in here, cold strength." She was feebler than flesh and her heart knew it.
  At least not afraid of death she wandered
Outside the house, the dusty squalor within was too repulsive to suffer. Old oaks,
  the sweet leaves
Of alders, the polished fragrance the mountain laurels, and standing over a notch
  in the trees the tall dark
Mountain southward, an obelisk-shaped growth of deep redwoods heavy in the
  sun climbing the chief
Fold in the furrowed flank. She breathed with pleasure. "No humanity, no
  humanity at all.
Well done destruction."

Rachel returned to the farmhouse.
A horseman at the gate of the yard talked with the farmer. He was not a cowboy;
  clean cloth, bright leather,
Ruling the restless horse. She felt his eyes touch her approaching, saw him speak,
  imagined the farmer
Answering, "Young schoolteacher from town." She looked up frankly toward the
  rider as she entered the gate,
Question for question, she went on to the house feeling his eyes. Some
  troublesome spring of perplexed . . .
Memory perhaps? . . . had spoilt her confidence. A brutal face; sunburnt and
  strong, handsome you'd call it,

Older than she'd supposed, forty, no doubt. How far from Philip's sensitive
    features, the charm
And the shy power. It came through her mind
That she was too coarse for Philip, a cattleman's daughter from the rough coast:
    Oh worse than that, or he'd not
Have gone down the red path. The farmer came in,
She asked who was that man on horseback? And pale, thinking "I should have
    known, remembered, I am calm
As the hills themselves," heard the man's name: Charlie McCandless, the man
    who'd pressed her father to the pit,
Who'd brought the charge against him. "They'd think it was strength,"
She thought, "this quietness. It's not: I feel nothing." Owned her father's house
    now, this man, the shameful
Wreck of a house, and the sweet canyon. His own was over the ridge southward;
    his hills, his ranges,
His prosperity. The one had killed himself and the other had prospered. He was
    almost her father's murderer;
He had brought the charge that had brought death.

                                 She thought in the night it
    was soft folly to expect reason,
Justice or any human rightness in life. God, if there was one: the rattlesnakes'
    God also.
The milk she poured them next day (she poured it again) was a libation. Did they
    drink? The saucer was empty
But a sour crust at the edges. Perhaps the little lives that serve them for food had
    lapped it, been caught,
Life for life, all's fair. "The thing is, to find one's meat. That's what they
    know."

      She went up stream, by the boulders
And the slip of shore. The cliff and the thick leaves enclosed the widened creek,
    clear-currented cauldron,
One stone on the edge, the sun gilded. In the heat; by the stream; chiefly in the
    clean deliverance from eyes:
She felt all thoughts dropping, all that disturbs quietness falling, peace coming
    up, clear water.
She was not tired enough for peace, through the dark surface
Like a shark's fin, like a tower of white stone: whom would she wish come up
    from the water, naked companion?
A marble boy; minion not lover . . . Antinous . . . no one with personality, no one
    known to her;
Her own creature; she needed weakness to be strong with, coolness for fever, her
    own creature;
So shy that he'd need wooing, so young and soft that he'd need nursing, between
    the rose-crested hills,
Before some life of her own should filter into his arteries, the soft whiteness grow
    stronger, the child

Petted to life sharpen its softness to go home . . . "Ah, shame, shame,"
She felt her cheeks blazing, "you that were nerved for all the unreason, the
savage energy, the snakes' God,
Hide in a cave to dream?" She thought "If I could give away my virginity, that's
what weakens me.
That caution once lost: there's not a man: to the stone hills. Fool," she whispered
to herself, and finding
A break in the cliff forced herself upward through the thicket, felt with sharp
satisfaction the branches
Breaking, the twigs like thorns; in the midst it was a nightmare of heat and
pressure; she crept beyond it,
Lay panting on the open slope; her clothes were scarred, her hands bleeding.
She'd never go back: it was this
Was needed: harsh touches, steep freedom, recklessness. Labored up hill in the
steep heat, gained the first summit,
Felt the great hills ringing like gongs in the universal sunlight, the bronze
reverberance, the beating
Hammers of light. Then having to make water she looked for shelter and she
thought, "No, here and publicly."
It gave her pleasure on the open height, she felt the shudder imagined of love,
the consecration,
And dizzy with yearning toward no person wandered down westward; the ocean,
taut blue, strung in the acute
V of the violent hills.

Phil Maybrick was at the farmhouse. "I knew you would go
to this place, Rachel.
Oh I'm glad. I was afraid I'd not find you. I've waited hours here." The thin
young face lighted with confidence,
The luminous eyes: her own hardened, her blue ones. "I asked for a month."
"Dearest . . ." "Take the apple green then.
But come away from the house." His car was in the withering grass outside the
gateway, they stood by it,
Then Rachel: "You've caught me honest. You came too soon Philip, you never
needed to have known anything.
Dupes are happy." "What do you mean, what do you mean?" "I meant to cheat
you happy. Push in
While the fire's roaring? Be burnt then. Your fault.
I would have fooled you." "You're not well, Rachel, you're pale, you've torn your
clothes too, this insane talk
Has no meaning in the world." "Well it's a wonderful relief for me too, I was
going to marry you;
Live in a coop, we'd know the smell of each other and you'd take me to shows
Once a week. That's finished." "I only know you're talking horribly, horrible
things . . ." "If you want
Everything told plainly: I've got a man here, one that I want really, I meet him
back here
At a dead house. You thought I was . . . white? He had me before I left here: I
was twelve years old then: he had me.

So I came back for a month, Philip.
You'd kept away you might have had an eight-month baby next winter. People
    will take what they get.
I never *talked* shamelessly before: not till you came pushing in unwanted: now
    take it,
Shameless and all."
"Why," he said, "you're lying; that's all. You must come back with me." She,
    trembling: "Bound to be cheated? I'll tell you more:
This was my father's enemy, the man that made him kill himself. That's
    something. Now he's got married, has children;
I'm the luxury." Philip began to tremble, but silent, and Rachel: "Probably you
    won't believe me
Until I hide you in a closet in the dead house. When you see the skirt lift."
    Mumbling, he answered
With dead lips, "I believe you. Well. No," he shouted.
"I've got my mother to think of. You thought I'd let myself be tried for murder,
    for a whore's sake?" His dead-seeming
Lips mumbled so, she thought he was gathering slime behind them to spit in her
    face. He shuddered. "I'm not
The fool you think me. But," he said, "everything's horrible.
You've that much triumph. This'll never be wiped, never be wiped, I'll never look
    at the stars
But see dirt. Are you diseased yet? When't blotches your face
I'll pay the doctor." He frowned and coughed into his hand. "It's time to go back.
    Thanks for telling me.
I'd never have guessed, you know, Rachel." He stepped into the car and started
    the engine; the tires
Dug the dead grass.

                    She stood by the gateway, watched it slide up the coast-road,
        under the tawny-carpeted
Slopes: "Carefully he drives. Me to be like him, driving carefully. Not as if it had
    been
Worth anything: worth anything. What's to come. I'll get over. Nothing hurts."
    She thought "I'm not tired:
That's strange: I could begin the day again." She thought, "My enemy
Passes this way when he goes north, it's the only road." They had dinner at six,
    long daylight afterwards,
While Rachel wandered south on the road, she gathered sweet roses from a briar,
    the thorns were the best,
A rider came up the road but not McCandless, a Spanish cowboy. But about
    sunset McCandless
Came up the road as if he'd been sent. Rachel stepped into the road, he drew
    rein. "Mr. McCandless.
I wanted to ask you something." She'd made herself look as beautiful as she
    could, and some of the briars
Pinned at her breast, he appeared pleased to look at her. "Whether I might . . .
    You own the canyon back there:"

It had been called by her father's name, her own, she'd not name it: "if I might camp up there for a week
In the ruined house." "What," he said, "all alone?" "Oh, I'd be careful of my fires." "But what for?
You're staying at Carter's, I saw you yesterday." "That's how I knew your name Mr. McCandless. You see,"
She said whitening, "I've spent most of my money, I can't stay there much longer. It's so beautiful here.
If I could stay a week longer." "Long as you like." He was so heavy, thick-necked, powerful, she thought
"The stick of dynamite that can blast the hill open." She trembled and looked down from his eyes.
The hooves were restless in the deep dust; she heard the horse mouthing its bit and the man saying
"Long as you like. I'll come up in a day or two, see how you get along." She answered trembling
"Oh thank you," and lifted her head by violence, and smiled.

                                        In the morning Rachel
        went up the creek and not pausing
At the split pathway crossed the ford to the clump of willows. There couldn't be any stain on the ground
After nine years. "It was here perhaps." "It was here perhaps, hid in this opening." "Father I seem
Not to feel anything at all. Makes three of us, for God doesn't: suppose there's one, the spirit of the serpents
And the cold stones. I've stepped over the edge to you, you cold spirits. They fooled us in school but I see
Nothing makes any difference, not really.
You wouldn't expect me to go through the world tearing, with this in my body?" She was cutting willows,
She'd brought a big knife she'd always kept because it had been her father's; it kept some edge yet; by sheaves
Cutting the long shoots with the foliage on them she carried them over the ford to the dead house,
Framed them with larger branches below and formed and wove them into a couch, like the nest of an eagle,
But low on the floor, by the mouldering boards, by the silent hearth-stones. No rattle had sounded to-day, though the saucer
Was half emptied. She formed the couch, lengthened it, narrowed it; drew a clean blanket from the farmhouse bed
Over the mound, "the snakes are all asleep," she was thinking,
"The cold bodies relaxed," it sang in her mind like an old tune, "I do the housework and the darting
Bodies relaxed in the hidden darkness." But when the room was cleaned, and the brown hole by the hearth
Stopped with sweet boughs that hid the wound, not closed it over: she dreaded quietness, she dared not linger,

Walked up and down the leafy canyon, down almost to the road, by the rustling
   water, and the sun
Stood south, she wandered back through the white patches, the flaming sunlight,
   she thought "I'll go up to the pool,
Bathe in the pool where I was yesterday." She thought that she knew nothing, "I
   know nothing. What horror
Comes up the canyon? What's it like, dying? being eaten by a worm?" She came
   to the clear pool that the leaves
And cliffs cavern with shadow. The bitter water made her tremble to see it: go in
   there naked,
The unprotected white shivering body?
She thought "They all suffer it: if the enemy's loved it's easier: means bondage
   afterwards." She looked at herself
With love and pity, shivering in the tent of dark leaves, the clear smooth arms
   and the long thighs,
Slight breasts, how could they endure the burden? Her mind was moving so
   much faster since yesterday, flooded
River streaming the strangest drift, the take of destruction, dead cattle rolling,
   dead father, in the yellow
Fall of the flayed hills: the gentle idyll of the widened brook,
The nuptial water: she hardly remembered
Entering, she lay in the pool and scoured herself with the clean sand and the
   water, and stood on the bank
Stroking the drops from the flushed skin. She dressed and hurried back to the
   house. No one was there.
He might have come and returned; he'd come on horseback; there were no hoof-
   marks.

       He came when the coolness begins,
An hour sooner than sunset. The rushing flood of her mind stopped suddenly,
   froze dead. She went to meet him,
And at the stirrup: "I thought maybe you'd come. It's beautiful here, I'm glad to
   thank you." He answered,
Moving his head on the thick neck, "See whether you needed anything.
   Everything's all right . . . Miss . . . Miss . . ."
"Rachel," she said pitiably shuddering,
Twisting her hands, "I'm on a holiday, last name's no matter." He stared down at
   her face, and dismounting
Darted quick eyes toward the house. She imagined he suspected she was not
   alone, there was someone hidden,
She said "I've seen no one all day. I haven't been lonely." "You'd rather I hadn't
   come then?" "My father's
Murderer," she thought pressing her thighs together; "ought to be charm in that
   knowledge: means nothing to me:
Why's everything without meaning?" "Well," he said sharply watching her, "I can
   go back." But he drew the reins
Over the pricked gray ears and let them trail from the bit. She answered "No . . .
   no . . ." And he: "I was thinking

Maybe I could help fix the place up. Aren't used to camping, are you?" "Oh. It
doesn't matter. Nothing

Makes any difference. I fixed myself a place to sleep on." He undid the rope
from the saddle-back. "I'll tie him,

Find some stones for the fire-place." She stood frozen watching him gather the
reins and loop the halter,

And lead the horse to a clear tree. He was always looking sidelong toward her,
and she thought "I can't bear

The preparation . . ." When the horse was tethered

She said and her mouth shuddering, "You needn't bother about a fire-place, I'll
get breakfast at the farm,

Meals . . . at Carter's. I thought maybe you came to collect rent for the camp-site
. . ." "Oh he'll understand me

Now," she thought, squeezing one hand in the other, arching her shoulders

As if to save the struck breasts. He turned a blank face of astonishment: "What
are you talking about?

Rent?" So ridiculously astonished she couldn't help laughing, he peering under
the eyebrows with lowered

Forehead saw twist like flame the slenderness under the earth-colored cloth, saw
the eyes shining with terror,

The mouth with laughter, the arms straightened down at the sides and the face
averted, flung upward, as of one defiant

Showing her desirableness, from throat to ankles, under green leaves: he said
"What will you pay me?"

She felt her throat ache with stopped cries; she thought what she must answer,
she was not able to, she murmured

"Nothing," and swayed a step into the foliage, then in trapped fear beat with her
hands and her breasts

On the heavy buckthorn, silently. He came behind her

And when she felt his hand she was quiet. It lay like heated iron on her flank and
she heard him hoarsely

Against her ear, and as if through waters: "What's wrong? Nobody's going to hurt
you." The other hand grasped

The bent round of her shoulder, turned her to face him among the branches; the
lines of her face confused him,

The under-lip held by the teeth, the half opened eyes and widened nostrils, a
mask of wantonness

That changed his conception of why the body trembled so hard. He drew her in
his arms against him; she twisted

Her face backward to avoid the kiss, and her neck

Under the ear felt the vile warmth and wetness. He lifted her out of the boughs
and she felt her body

Jerking like a caught hare's, she labored so hard to quiet the muscles, she was not
able to speak:

Though he carried her the wrong way, carried her up hill, she'd thought he'd
take her to the house: struggling against him,

Striking his throat with the weak fists: she found his mouth, striking at random,
felt the soft lip,

The hot breath on the teeth: when he groaned angrily and dropped her

She wrenched from his hand, ran down toward the dead house; he followed, not
    running; she avoided the clumps of deerweed
Thinking what spiral springs of poison might be hid in them, thinking the man,
    stiff leather to the knees,
Safe from the needles in the hard jaws: only his clutching hands and heavy-boned
    wrists were liable:
She entered the house, ran home, panting, home, home.

                            The flood of her mind
Ran faster than before he had come; the dead returned out of destruction,
    washed down from the mountain,
The beautiful chestnut horse her father had ridden, neck arched above the water
    and the withers floating,
The forehooves striking foam in the stream; the serpents in the swift water; the
    enormous cross of black cloud
She a child had seen over the canyon sunset: "Why it must be nearly sunset
    already," she thought
Standing in the midst of the room, "he's coming." She was her mother, frail and
    weary, and her father was coming;
The child's asleep: there's pleasure in being used to it, submitting willingly.

                                        Mc-
Candless stood in the doorway
Darting quick eyes about the bare room, under drawn brows. He saw her in the
    midst of the square, standing
Erect, the dark hair turbulent, the wide blue eyes meek and submissive. She
    looked straight toward him, quiet eyes,
But the lips quivered. Her throat was flushed, the cloth was torn there, her
    cheeks were chalk white. She quietly and clearly:
"Where've you been? You were so long coming: I thought you'd got lost." He
    astonished at her changes of mood:
"You wanted me to come . . . Rachel . . . why did you hit me?" "I had to go
    home." That would be dark to him: she added
"I had to go home." She crept backward he approaching, suddenly found herself
    trapped in the other corner,
No escape: "If I scream," she whispered, "someone might come and save me."
    He barred the corner with his arms, not touching her.
"Nobody'd hear you. You don't know what you want, little fool, is the trouble."
    She turning her body to the wall,
Her face over the shoulder: "I know what I want. I'm afraid: be kind to me. It's
    the first time. My father,"
She said stammering with eagerness, "hid some bottles under the floor by the
    hearth: ten years, they're still there.
I looked when I came. Get me some whiskey for the honeymoon to make me
    happy." He said, "Your father?
You used to live here, you're old Devine's girl?" "The thief's. That's why I'm
    shameless. I said I'll go for a holiday.
Get me the drink first. I broke up the boards by the hearth, they were all rotten,
    I dug for the bottles.

Push in your hand and get one: under the leaves there." "Afterwards," he said.
  "Oh" she said, "yes, yes, afterwards.
That's what I meant." "The old fellow has a beautiful daughter: dear girl, dear
  sweetheart." She unresisting
Felt his hands handle her, in the whirl of her mind
Praying to the secret serpents. She was on the couch, he was plucking anxiously
  about her clothing, her fingers
Remembered resistance, the rest of her body
Grown fatalist lay relaxed without imagination awaiting the event. The fingers
  grew tired.
She closed her eyes because his face became horrible. She watched the dead
  man walking through the dim house
Counting on his fingers . . . the calves misbranded, the stolen horses? Ah never
  turn your back to me father,
For the gap under the gory gray hair . . . the pain, tearing . . . when the bullet
  entered surely it was quiet,
The pain gorging the entrance,
Working the wound, and the earth over the grave was less heavy. Suddenly her
  spirit
Like embers to flame, like a hawk flapping up,
Shot from the bitter seed of endurance: the orgy of martyrdom shook her mind
  like a flag, no pleasure,
But the pain forgotten in the ecstasy of martyrdom: the dove of clear fire
That visited the saints on racks and gibbets, the spiritual joy, the splendor of the
  dove.

In the rigid quietness
She lay wondering and burning. What had become of the gray old man? Earthed
  again? Dig up, dig it up,
We must wash out the earth from the wound, the dirt-plug with the blood from
  among the gray hair and the dirt
In the eye-lashes in the eyes, the earth's bones
Relaxing, the mound of the grave softening and cracking make it easy to dig
  treasure, the earth relaxing,
Dig up the bottles . . . but really there were no bottles . . . he had lifted himself,
  she lay on the couch faintly
Moaning, but feeling extreme pleasure in the stone-quietness, the self-
  abandonment, the knees to the waist
Uncovered made it most clear, a new corpse is not careful. The man had taken
  her hand and was murmuring
Luke-warm love-words, his duty. Remembering a drunken girl in the night street
  in front of the theatre
She essayed laughter, lewd answers, then lifting
Her face like a spear: "Listen. Will you serve the drinks? I came here for a
  holiday, I have to teach school
At home. Under the green there." Would the watch-dogs be faithful . . .
Was too lucky to hope for. Therefore she took the knife she'd cut the willows
  with, it hid by the couch-side
Under the folded blanket-edge; the man knelt down by the gapped planks;

His coat was off it was easy to see the blade's home, on the flank over the belt,
    the fat flesh bulged there,
He stooping, between the ribs and the belt: no bone in the blade's way:
But Rachel could not move her body from the couch; it did not tremble, it had
    turned stone, and she crouched
Stone, with the knife. The man fumbled in the opening. He muttered some
    question,
His chest on the floor, his arm strained sidewise under it. The following moment
Was blinding bright in Rachel's mind and instantly forgotten. The shoulder
    humping and twisting upward
From the struck arm: she knew as clearly as if she had eyes under the floor how
    the flat triangular
Barbed head hung to the hand's edge, the thin-drawn neck straining behind, it
    had struck without warning, was faithful
Beyond hope or reason: the victim's hoarse cough
Of pain sluiced fire through her flesh, he writhing to rise she felt the hard
    abundant fire of her body
Cross him like a wave, cover him. The imagination
Of her father's wound so bright in her mind she could not strike at the mark
    chosen but struck where the wound was,
Behind the neck, where the flesh was creased in the cropped hair. The point
    turned on the neck-bones, the edge
Gritted on the guiding bone, the big muscle part severed the head swung
    sidewise. The left arm yielding
The man rolled over on his left flank, the girl recovering the knife dipped it in
    the soft belly
Twice, each time grunting like a woman in labor. He wailed in a high childlike
    voice and she felt
With exultance for thought they had changed sexes; but he caught the knife-
    wrist, she could not move it, and at the one time
Got his knees under her body and shot her off backward. He appeared not to
    think of her again, he surged up
Like a mired bull, she crouching where fallen
Saw him rise and fill the room above her, his deformed bulk, red mists about
    him, and the high unmanlike
Chirping of his pain. It seemed impossible that so great and distorted an agony
    could pass the doorway,
He contracted himself toward it, ran outward, she following
Saw him trot under the trees, the head hung sidewise, both hands covering the
    belly. She felt the white fire
Licking about the roots of her hair, she ran and screamed behind him, he
    swerved to face her and she passed
Avoiding him; she reached the horse, cut the halter, pricked the rump with the
    knife-point.

       Remained no means of remembering
Why it was when a running horse went by her
A man dropped on his knees to her and bowing forward
Showed the gashed neck; nor why she felt pain

In a protected place, and her clothing disordered. Apparently she'd served God
    with the empty body
And not the mind, not kept her mind on her prayers, but the wounded neck
Was moaning where the solemn red sundown lay among the trees, and when she
    approached it begged her get help,
It would soon die: "Oh yes you will die: you got the snake-bite for stealing
    horses," the lips answered it,
But the mind was not touching the words, the mind was thinking
Her baby was all alone in the house. It was getting dark in the house, the child
    not wakened, she remembered
The baby's cot was in the living-room by the hearthside: they had been so cold:
    but the fire had gone out:
She gathered the blanket from the bed and folded it for a child in her arms and
    the child's face
Was the dark stain. Standing in the door
She understood the vague pain that troubled her: because the child had just been
    born, the pain was quite natural,
A girl-baby named Rachel, Rachel Devine is a sweet name, "Oh hush little
    Rachel," she murmured
Swaying from the hips, folding her arms about the little delicate imagined body,
    and she watched
The rose-flowing sunset through the still trees. "Oh never run down to the ocean,
    Rachel."

            Behind her happiness
Lay like a flood of misery—so the banked flood hangs on the dyke over the
    meadows—the dim
Thought that she'd done and suffered so much violence in vain, she had
    sharpened herself to compass deliverance
From the net of the mind, here she was netted the deeper, among delusions,
    among images, now nothing
Real in the world: this misery her dream
Resolved to a threat of the darkening forest against the baby, the beasts under
    the trees were its enemies,
Wolves with lit eyes, and the young mother
Held a wide door against the hunger of the world.

                          She lay on the bed of boughs
    when the night darkened.
She brooded her more than life in her arms. She loosened the clothing from her
    throat and brought out the small breasts,
Greedily the tiny warm lips . . .

                In the night,
Wakening she knew there was no child, and that horrible things
Had been done easily. She had left him living, she must go and find him. The
    journey in the darkness
Was worse than any suffering before. He had crept perhaps a few feet and died
    in another place,

It needed many circuits among the trees by the path before she found him. The
flesh was wet-cold.
She dipped her finger into the wound in the neck: no warmth was hidden there.
After she had sat eternally
Came the gray light. After it was light
She saw that with his pocket-knife, with his left hand
He had slashed the blackening right one where the fangs had gone in: still
reaching at life, living to the end:
This dead man cutting himself for life's sake. The other dead man
Died in her mind; her father had been the wastrel, the fugitive; her lover the
brave one. She, sane and prepared,
Sat close by her chosen; she watched the dawn flower in the trees, the
intolerable beauty and the desolation.

DONALD JUSTICE ▪ ▪ ▪ ▪ ▪ ▪ ▪ ▪ ▪ ▪ ▪ ▪ ▪ ▪ ▪

In Memory of My Friend the Bassoonist John Lenox

1

One winter he was the best
Contrabassoonist south
Of Washington, D.C.—
The only one. Lonely

In eminence he sat,
Like some lost island king,
High on a second-story porch
Overlooking the bay—

His blue front lawn, his kingdom—
And presided over the Shakespearean
Feuds and passions of the eave-pigeons.
Who, during the missile crisis,

Had stocked his boat with booze,
Charts, and the silver flute
He taught himself to play,
Casually, one evening;

And taught himself to see,
Sailing thick glasses out blindly
Over a lily-choked canal—
O autodidact supreme!

2

John, where you are now can you see?
Do the pigeons there bicker like ours?
Does the deep bassoon not moan
Or the flute sigh ever?

No one could think it was you
Slumped there on the sofa, despairing,
The hideous green sofa.
No, you are off somewhere,

Off with Gaugin and Christian
Amid hibiscus'd isles,
Red-mustached, pink-bearded
Again, as in early manhood.

It is well. Shark waters
Never did faze you half so much
As the terrible radios
And booboiseries of the neighbors.

Here, if you care, the bay
Is printed with many boats now,
Thick as trash; that high porch is gone,
Gone up in the smoke of money, money;

The barbarians . . .
                            But enough.
You are missed. Across the way,
Someone is practicing sonatas,
And the sea air smells again of good gin.

—Coconut Grove

CLAUDIA KEELAN ▪ ▪ ▪ ▪ ▪ ▪ ▪ ▪ ▪ ▪ ▪ ▪ ▪ ▪ ▪

To the New World

Saturday grieves
          Puritan seeking *more weight*
Machines look unhappy in the desert
          "you can't tell <u>me</u>
<u>he</u> didn't do it"
          no one there and it's true
Her hands against the window
Her breath

The empty backs of trucks are screaming
what more do you want from me
I'll be as clear as I can
My son <u>knows</u> the puddle is an ocean
Our camera killed Her
He fell by himself
Imperfection is everywhere. I wear her star.
Africa is a long scar in my head.
Sad grass.
Lovely mud ocean.
I'm seeing a world, no, a room, or
       a space like a musical phrase
princess, sister/s'aint & tribe
       imperfect under funeral flowers
P/ity   Merc(I)(Y)   Peace
                      &
                 luve
All alone in our boats

Blue Diamond

I am virtually gone
                author or victim
I wanted   in you   to be nothing
     to be a solitude
Attached   by emptiness   to everything

Last night   one coyote
             this morning two   They were nature

Keep the children close
                author or victim
The desert looks flat, lies
     flat   what does realism save?
They were animals running across the surface
They are gone

Gravity and Grace

1.

À *fin*   all was strange   of my heart
    a landscape   of I am not
Disappearing,   things   became perfect

Once   to hear, see, touch   eat
    deprived God   something saying   I
a landscape   disappearing   in I am not

Now perfect   disappearance   appearing perfect
        see hear   *sear*   touch not
a landscape *fin*   in I   of I am not

                              2.

If my window   is red   I cannot see
        anything   but rose   accord
to rose   the window   to revolt

Mountains, rocks   fall upon us   Hide us
        far   I deserve this   wrath
the red principle   of revolt   the rose

Room the red   window   Violence
        trains view   Mountains, rocks   fall
train wrath   Tho I die   doing

                              3.

Suffer   suffering   to reduce it
        Not sacred enough   Being and others
Rock upon   the obstacle   the rock

Suffering spread   beyond reduct   -ion
        Sacred good   or beautiful thing   an insult, then
being inside rock   transformed mud   & others

Forgive   the void beautiful   in being
        a branch   to a drowning future
Sacred enough   or not   Writing

                                           forgiveness

                              4.

Good broken up into   pieces
        a host of women   or of men
I leaves marks   on the world it destroys

Broken good   never anything *new*   everything
        equivalent   a host of   /or of
I was your friend   once

Lost her   knowing good but hating good
        she broke into   equivalent pieces
I held her   lost good

In a broken   factory   a single tear
        destroys Host   and Host
                                    I destroyed

preserving her

GALWAY KINNELL ■ ■ ■ ■ ■ ■ ■ ■ ■ ■ ■ ■ ■

The Fundamental Project of Technology

A flash! A white flash sparkled!
—Tatsuichiro Akizuki, Concentric Circles of Death

Under glass: glass dishes that changed
in color; pieces of transformed beer bottles;
a household iron; bundles of wire become solid
lumps of iron; a pair of pliers; a ring of skull-
bone fused to the inside of a helmet; a pair of eyeglasses
taken off the eyes of an eyewitness, without glass,
which vanished, when a white flash sparkled.

An old man, possibly a soldier back then,
now reduced down to one who soon will die,
sucks at the cigaret dangling from his lip, peers
at the uniform, scorched, of some tiniest schoolboy,
sighs out bluish mists of his own ashes over
a pressed tin lunch box well crushed back then when
the future first learned, in a white flash, to jerk tears.

On the bridge outside, in navy black, a group
of schoolchildren line up, hold it, grin at a flash-pop,
swoop in a flock across grass, see a stranger, cry,
hello! hello! hello! and soon, goodbye! goodbye! goodbye!
having pecked up the greetings that fell half unspoken
and the going-sayings that those who went the morning
it happened a white flash sparkled did not get to say.

If all a city's faces were to shrink back all at once
from their skulls, would a new sound come into existence,
audible above moans eaves extract from wind that smoothes
the grass on graves; or raspings heart's-blood greases still;
or wails infants trill born already skillful at the grandpa's rattle;
or infra-screams bitter-knowledge's speechlessness
memorized, at that white flash, inside closed-forever mouths?

To de-animalize human mentality, to purge it of obsolete
evolutionary characteristics, in particular of death,
which foreknowledge terrorizes the contents of skulls with,
is the fundamental project of technology; however,
pseudologica fantastica's mechanisms require:
if you would establish deathlessness you must eliminate
those who die; a task attempted, when a white flash sparkled.

Unlike the trees of home, which continually evaporate
along the skyline, the trees here have been enticed down

317

to form eternity here. No one knows which gods they enshrine.
Does it matter? Awareness of ignorance is as devout
as knowledge of knowledge. Or more so. Even though not knowing,
sometimes we weep, from surplus of gratitude, even though knowing,
twice already on earth sparkled a flash, a white flash.

The children go away. By nature they do. And by memory—
in scorched uniforms, holding tiny crushed lunch tins.
All the pleasure-groans of each night call them to return, satori
their ghostliness back into the ashes, in the momentary shrines,
the thankfulness of arms, from which they will go
again and again, until the day flashes and no one lives
to look back and say, a flash, a white flash sparkled.

The Waking

What has just happened between the lovers,
who lie now in love-sleep under the memory
of owls calling and answering each other
in the dark woods, call, answer, call,
until now one lags, or now one hastens,
and suddenly the two whoo together
in a shimmering harmonic, is called "lovemaking."
But lovers who come exalted to their trysts,
from opposite directions, along a path
by the sea, among the pines, meet, embrace,
go up from the sea, lie crushed into
the other under the goldening sky already
deep-blueing its moon and stars into shining,
know they don't "make" love, but are earthlings
who fuck—here no other word will do—
one another forever if possible across the stars.
That word, perhaps formed when lovers
sat at night by the sea and tossed a stone
and out in the dark a mullet leapt and fell back,
has had its map of the way that leads back
to the beginning trampled out of it.
The may be no word now, but still a spirit,
a flame on a wick, inside the tongue,
that lights each word as it passes, reminding it
to remember; as when flamingos
change feeding places, and there is
a moment just after the first to fly puts
its head into the water in the new place,
and just before, in the old place, the last
looks up to see that the rest have flown,
when, scattered with pink bodies, the entire

sky has become one vast remembering.
They still hear, in the distance, the steady
crushing and uncrushing of bedsprings;
they imagine a sonata in which the violins'
lines draw all the writhings and shiftings.
The moment's memory of what has just happened
is their proof for life of the actual existence
of existence. They lie with heads touching,
thinking themselves back across the blackness.
On the lightening bedsheet their bodies re-form,
heaps of gold their embraces have ripple-sluiced
out of the night. The bed, caressed
threadbare, worn almost away, is more than
before the site where such light as humans can
shine with blooms up into us. The eyelids,
which love the eyes and shuts them to sleep,
open. *This is a bed. That is a fireplace.*
That is last morning's breakfast tray
which nobody has yet bothered to take away.
This face, too rich in feeling to outlive
the world in which it is said, "Ni vous sans moi,
ni moi sans vous," so openly archaic
this day might be breaking in the Middle Ages.
is the illusion randomness chooses
to beam into existence, now, on this pillow.
The lovers don't have words to know this through.
The scraps of verse they do possess mean less
in love's language, than "Want a cracker" or
"Pieces of eight," in our common parlance.
Seen through tears, motes cross, mingle,
collide, lose the way, pass, in this puff
of ecstatic dust. Now the tears overwhelm
the eyes, wet their faces, drain quickly
into their smiles. One leg hangs off
the bed. He is still inside her. His big toe
sticks into the pot of strawberry jam. "Oh migod!"
They laugh. They have to remind themselves
how to. They kiss while laughing, and hit teeth,
and remember they are bones, and laugh
naturally again. The feeling, perhaps
it's only a feeling, perhaps due
to living always in the overlapping lifetimes
of only dying things, that time starts up
again, comes over them. They get up,
put on clothes, go out. They are not
in the street yet, but for a few moments longer
stand in their elsewhere, beside a river,
their arms around each other, in the aura
the earth has when it remembers its former beauty.

Riverbirds . . . honk. Sounds arrive fully formed
into their mouths . . . *Bleecker* . . . *Carmine* . . . *Avenue*
of the Americas . . . An ambulance sirens
a shroud-whitened body toward St. Vincent's.
A police car running the red lights parodies
in high pitch the owls of paradise. The lovers enter
the ordinary day the ordinary world
providentially provides. Their pockets ring.
Good. For now askers and beggarmen
come up to them needing change for breakfast.

•

The Pen

Its work is memory.

It engraves sounds into paper and fills them with pounded nutgall.

It can transcribe most of the sounds that the child, waking early, not yet knowing
which language she will one day speak, sings.

Asleep in someone's pocket in an airplane, the pen dreams of paper, and a feeling
of pressure comes into it, and, like a boy dreaming of Grace Hamilton who sits
in front of him in the fifth grade, it could spout.

An old pen with unresilient ink sac may make many scratches before it inks.

The pen's alternation of lifts and strokes helps thoughts to keep coming in a
rhythmic flow.

When several thoughts arrive together, the pen may resort to scribbling "blah
blah," meaning, come back to this later.

Much of what pens write stands for "blah blah."

In the Roman system, the pen moves to the right, and at the margin swerves
backwards and downward—perhaps dangerous directions, but necessary for
reentering the past.

The pen is then like the person who gets out of the truck, goes around to the
rear, signals to the driver, and calls, "C'mon back."

Under increased concentration the pen spreads its nib, thickening the words that
attempt to speak the unspeakable.

These are the fallen-angel words.

Ink is their ichor.

They have a mineral glint, given by clarity of knowing, even in hell.

The pen also uses ink to obfuscate, like the cuttlefish, by inculcating the notions
that reality happens one complete sentence after another, and that if we have
words for an event, we understand it—as in:

How's your pa?
He died.
Oh.

When my father died, leaving my mother and me alone in the house, I don't
know even now what happened.

What did Rilke understand on the death of his father, who by then had become a
speck in the distance?

Did his mother suddenly become larger?

It seems that soon after she married him, Rilke's wife also began turning into a speck.

He told her in eloquent letters it was good for his artistic development for them to live apart; meanwhile women arrived from all over Europe, to spend their allotment of nights in his bed.

I called it "my work" when I would pass weeks on the road, often in the beds of others.

This Ideal pen, with vulcanite body, can't resist dredging up the waywardness of my youth.

Fortunately pens run out of ink.

Villon had to cut short the bitter bequests of *Le Lais* only when his inkwell froze and his candle blew out.

Like a camel at an oasis with stomachs completely empty, the pen thrusts itself into the ink and suctions in near-silence.

Filled, it starts again laying trudge marks across the paper.

Yesterday, when trying to write about my sister Wendy, my little mother in childhood, I couldn't find the words in the ink.

Then I had a visit from a poet a few years widowed, who talked about her husband and about how she felt thwarted in her writing and had lost her way—though in the rhythmical tumbling forth of her words she seemed to be finding it.

I wished I had collected some of the mascara-blackened fluid on her cheeks to mix into my ink.

But when I started writing about Wendy again, the ink had replenished its vocabulary, and from the street came the bleats of a truck in reverse gear and a cry, "C'mon back, c'mon back."

KAREN KIPP ▪ ▪ ▪ ▪ ▪ ▪ ▪ ▪ ▪ ▪ ▪ ▪ ▪ ▪ ▪ ▪ ▪

Ditches

for Sheila Griffin

I suggested the opera because he said he had never been
and besides the Met had loaded up their Don Giovanni on panel trucks and were taking him to
places like Cleveland
As I told him the story, he said that he thought the women were bitches
expecting me to counter with him being a bastard I suppose
but I was thinking of the dogs in the film version
huge dumb harlequin Danes, gorgeous
as alabaster, finely chiseled like delicate sculpture, and patched with a deep black soot

as if they had been digging down in a chimney corner after the fire had died
These dogs followed the master around like the glorious ghosts of his tattered
soul and turned their animal heads when he took Zerlina
during the wedding celebration

I liked those dogs as I liked that boy, skidding into my parent's drive in his pied
primered truck, so cavalier
slamming the door, setting his boots down on the asphalt. I watched him
from the front porch, where I was sitting, wearing a white muslin dress, wrinkly
    and thin
with spaghetti straps and paper rosebuds. I always hated that dress
though he said he liked it, that I looked great, and that he decided that he didn't
want to go to the opera, that it was bullshit, and besides, he wasn't
dressed. And he was charming
wearing a pair of painter pants, a leather coat, and a t-shirt
He had a bottle of cheap champagne under his arm and offered a single flower as
    an apology
He was calculated for dash and I let it ride

I rode with a tanned arm hooked over the cracked side-view mirror. At nine it
    was just dusk
After the last swallow, he hooked the bottle out the window, and it shattered
against a young birch—I wondered what he was really aiming for
but he seemed pleased with the green explosion of glass against the tree's
slim, papery waist
I braced a hand against the dash
as he braked to stop, and leaned the truck to the shoulder of a country road
I started in on the warm six-pack as he talked about smoking hash and cutting
    classes
and how he ditched the security guards in the warehouse and thought he was
    free
until the dogs cornered him. "Like Cerberus," I said
and he smiled unevenly and I liked that broken smile
I finished the last, warm Budweiser and told him to wait while I went to pee

He was waiting for me in the ditch as I was making my way back in the patchy
    dark
He had frightened me, and so let me push him down in mock anger. He stayed
    down. I stood
watched, only a moment. Then I came down to him
Of course, I never heard from him again and threw the dress away, I felt
    unburdened
but no wiser. I had only gained the proof of what I already knew, as it was no
    surprise
to the lady when the insolent Leporello unrolls the scroll beneath her nose,
    revealing
all of those names. There is no innocence
except that of the self
to itself

The ditch we go into, we stay in
Only a statue, a ghost, can come back out. Come out as something stronger,
  colder
pure

The Rat

It used to be that the rat was a cynic. It used to be that the rat had trouble
believing things. The other rats were ugly, especially his own young, who were
pied and pink and whom he wanted to eat, if only his bitch-rat wife would have
let him. . . . Then a day came when it was different. A pudgy hand reached into
his tank and stuffed the rat into its overcoat. The rat had been shoplifted. Soon
he was riding the streets on the shoulder of a two-hundred and fifty pound
punk with a sad-looking mohawk. Sometimes, in a dark bar, surrounded by
other humans, the punk would stick the rat's head into the beery cave of his
craw. The rat thought he was supposed to be hearing something, but he never
did. Eventually the rat had another idea—perhaps it was supposed to be the
other way around. . . . The rat put his pointy snout to the punk's pierced ear.
"Turn right, turn right," whispered the rat, and the punk did. Then, "we're out
of cheese, we need to go to the Quickstop." Sometimes the rat *wanted* to be
with the humans. The more humans the better. "The Deadwood," the rat
would say, "let's duck in for a beer." In the smoky darkness, overlooking the
warm mugs and the crowded ashtrays, the rat would say, "see that girl over
there, you need to fuck her." The rat was not a cynic. The rat could believe
things. He had discovered his affinity for the other animals, and God, was the
world glorious.

I'm Sending You Saint Francis Preaching to the Birds

Even before the Renaissance they realized that there was a simplicity in keeping
things in perspective at eye-level
We always practiced this
by aloofness, and a gentle balance of our affectations
so that they tended to border on realism, like the day I got out of the hospital
wearing the kicked-dog tags and the gauze badge of stupidity, and you felt no
  need
to make a comment, and when we fucked, you were no more gentle than usual
This is the kind of kindness that is sublime
It was the understanding we had when we went to see bad movies together
the un-said words completed the picture
I'm saying that I miss the simplicity of not having to spy on each other's books
Dick Francis was never embarrassed to be on my desktop, and your Nietzsche
  that peered dog-eared
from under your bed was never pretentious, the veneer of dust that covered him
  was simplistic
un-planned

Now everything is planned—even the simple is too complex
"He's humoring us," that's what the caption of the last Polaroid photo she sent
    me said
It shows you slipping
your hand into an empty 4x5 film box, the way Tom used to slip Jerry into a
    sandwich
but instead of licking your chops, you're looking up, disgusted, into the camera
How do I know what this means? With you too far beyond the fault
with Betsy, in San Francisco
It's strange that she still writes to me so much, even though I failed
my side of the triangle
but it was not an isosceles situation that kept the three of us together

Aloofness is not something that will carry over distance
but maybe cryptics can
I'm sending you a copy of a painting I've run across
they think it was done by Giotto. It's Saint Francis preaching to the birds
It shows him leaning forward with enthusiasm to a flock of pigeons
like the way a drunk
tilts toward you in a bar when he's telling you his life story. See
the trees are huge stalks of broccoli, and the Saint's halo, a gold coin
stamped around his head. And that horizon line, the way it cuts the picture plane
    neatly in
half, as if it were that simple to divide things
Michael, it was almost as if it were planned, the way those pigeons are peeling off
    the fresco
as if taking flight from under his blessing hands

ETHERIDGE KNIGHT ▪ ▪ ▪ ▪ ▪ ▪ ▪ ▪ ▪ ▪ ▪ ▪

A Poem to Galway Kinnell

Sat., Apr. 26, 1973
Jefferson City, Mo. 65101
(500 yards, as the crow flies,
from where i am writing you
this letter, lies the Missouri
State Prison—it lies, the prison,
like an overfed bear alongside
the raging missouri river—
the pale prison, out of which,
sonny liston, with clenched fist,
fought his way, out of which,
james earl ray ripped his way
into the hearts of us all . . .)

dear galway,
    it is flooding here, in missouri,
the lowlands are all under water and at night
the lights dance on the dark water,
our president, of late of watergate,
is spozed to fly above the flooded areas
and estimate how much damage has been done
to THE PEOPLES. . . .

dear galway,
    it is lonely here, and sometimes,
THE PEOPLES can be a bitch

dear galway,
    i hear poems in my head
as the wind blows in your hair
and the young brown girl
with the toothpaste smile
who flows freely because she has heard OUR SOUNDS. . . .

dear galway,
    OUR SONGS OF LOVE are still
murmurs among these melodies of madness. . . .
dear galway, and what the fuck are the irish doing/
and when the IRA sends JUST ONE, just one soldier
to fight with say the American Indians, then i'll believe them. . . .

dear galway,

    the river is rising here, and i am
scared and lonely . . . . . .

Mary and the children send their love
to you and yours

              always

        Imamu Etheridge Knight Soa

A Poem for a Certain Lady on Her 33rd Birthday

    Who are we
    to ride the curves of air
    or to worry about the waning moon?
    The mountains will not tremble
    and the sea will not give up her dead.

Time is now, said the African Poet,
unfelt as our touch
across these seasons
unending as the circle
of our dead fathers and unbornsons—
the rise and fall of our laughter—
the measure of our steps
as we move
to each other.

Years are strips of tinsel
hanging on hunky brains.
Our time is the constant blooming
of our love.

The Bones of My Father

There are no dry bones
here in this valley. The skull
of my father grins
at the Mississippi moon
from the bottom
of the Tallahatchie,
the bones of my father
are buried in the mud
of those brooks and creeks that twist
and flow their secrets to the sea.
but the wind sings to me
there the sun speaks to me
of the dry bones of my father.

There are no dry bones
in this northern valley, in the Harlem alleys
young black men with knees bent
nod on the stoops of the tenements
and dream
of the dry bones of my father . . .
(and young white longhairs flee
their homes and bend their minds
and sing their songs   of brotherhood
and no more wars are searching for
my father's bones.)

There are no dry bones
here, my brothers. We hide from the sun.
No more do we take the long straight strides.
Our steps have been shaped by the cages

that kept us. We glide sideways
like crabs across the sand.
We perch on green hills, we search
beneath white rocks . . .
THERE ARE NO DRY BONES HERE
The skull of my father
grins at the Mississippi moon
from the bottom
of the Tallahatchie.

My Uncle Is My Honor and a Guest in My House

for Jim Cozart and Ezekiel Mphalele

1

In the center of the bloodvein
       is kinkiss
       is a boiling
and a calling of your name
in the nightime.

From the corners
of the curtained rooms
thru the bone-filled alleys
where bibles and blades
       lay like lovers
the shadows flee like petty thieves
before the gold-bright
            teeth of my Uncle
who is my Honor
and a Guest in my House.

2

The fakes, the unforgivers, the fearfeeders
and the CIA
deny the kinkiss—deny the boiling
and shout their slogans
of "free world"
       and "individualism"—
like gene autry riding off/into the western sunset
alone—
and point to the stones
clinging to my tongue
as I call out your name

in the nightime
from the cave
crossed with spears, on whose
wall are written:
"all men
shit over two shoes
and put on their pants one leg at a time."

3

In the center of the circle,
stands my Uncle, legs apart,

singing poems
to the blue-eyed men

who squat
in the shadows
and shake their fists at the darkening sky.

Once on a Night in the Delta: A Report from Hell

for Sterling Brown

Gravel rattles against the fenders of the van.
The River flashes in the distance.
The wind is thick with the scent of honeysuckle.
The road from Greenville curves like the sickle
Of the new moon, now hanging over east Texas.
Moun' Bayou sleeps on a straight street.

The poor lives on both/sides/of the tracks
In this town peopled by Blacks.
Tho the bloods/now/pack pistols
And rap on two-way radios,
And the homes of a few are spacious and new,
With sunken patios;
Tho the dice are/shot/thru a leather horn and
The whiskey burns my belly in the early morning,

We still shuffle in lines, like coffles of slaves:
Stamps for food—the welfare rolls and the voting polls.
We frown. Our eyes are dark caves

Of mourning.—So I'd like to report to you, Sir Brown—
From away/down/here—
Mississippi is *still* hell, Sir Brown—
For me and of Slim Greer.

—June, 1981

a black poet leaps to his death

for mbembe milton smith

was it a blast to the balls dear brother
with the wind ringing in the ear
that great rush against the air
that great push
               into the universe

you are not now alone mbembe
of the innocent eyes   sadder
than a mondays rain   it is i
who hear your crush of bone
        your splatter of brain
        your tear of flesh
on the cold chicago stone

        and my october cry
when the yellow moon is ringed with blood
of children dead in the lebanese mud
      is as sharp as a kc switchblade
your pain is a slash across my throat
i feel a chill   can the poet belie
the poem

      old revolutionaires never die
it is said
      they just be born again
(check chuck colson and his panther from folsom)
but you are *dead*
mbembe   poetman in the home of the brave
the brown leaves whisper across you grave

but it must have been   a rush   a great gasp
      of breath
      the awesome leap to your death
o poet of the blood and bone
      of the short song
      and serious belief
i sing you release

                   —October, 1981

On the Removal of the Fascist American Right from Power

Come on, you too, whoo/do, we can do it,
You can do it, truck driver, you can,
Cab driver, you can do it, take away
Their power! you can do it,
High school student, you can, you can do it,
College student, take it, take it away,
They have no right to it anymore,
They have *betrayed* the American Revolution!
It's yours, take it back, Grandmother.
FREEDOM FOR ALL AMERICANS FIRST!
You can do it, Stop them from selling Death,
Speak, you/gay/man with streaks in your hair,
You can do it, Gay woman with sad eyes,
You can do it, Black man, take it,
In the Name of Crispus Attucks, take it,
In the Name of Frederick Douglass, take it!
FUCK THE FOREIGN THOUGHT! take it,
Take back the American Revolution
From the big daddies and the little wives,
You can do it, White man, take it,
In the Names of Lincoln, Paine, Adams,
Jefferson, you know who, White man,
Take back the Revolution from the Fascists
In the Names of John Brown and Martin King,
Take it, you can do it, take it from them:
The American Ayatollahs: Jerry Falwell,
Billy Graham, Oral Roberts, Kahane,
And the Mormon maniacs, wrap yourselves
In Betsy Ross's Flag, it was meant for
You, white man, so take it back, say NO
To your Fathers, Say NOOOOO!
Say FREEDOM! SAY FREEEEDOOOOM!
Say FREEDOM FOR ALL AMERICANS FIRST!
Say FUCK THE FOREIGN THOUGHT!
FROM THE EAST OR THE WEST, OR BOTH!
You can do it, farmer man, you can,
You can do it, Latino, Native man, you can,
GrandFather, take it, tell them:
FREEDOM FOR ALL AMERICANS FIRST
Is in "our national interest,"
Come on, you intellectual left, you can do it,
Teach us Jeffersonian Principles, teach us,
Teach us the thoughts of Adams, DuBois, and Black Elk—
FUCK THE FOREIGN THOUGHT! you can do it,
O Black woman, O white woman, O Mothers,

You can do it, take it take away their power,
In the Names of Susan Anthony, Harriet Tubman,
In the Names of Emma Goldman, Sojourner Truth,
In the Name of Betsy Ross, Take back the D.A.R.,
Overrun the League of Women's Voters, you can do it,
Be the true Daughters of the American Revolution!
Encircle the lil wives of the Big Daddies in a Dance,
A Revolutionary Dance, confront the lil wives
With Revolutionary Songs, you can do it, you can,
Say NO, say NOOOOO!
You can take their power away, you can,
You can do it, with the Good Power, the Right
Power that comes from the Left, the heart/side,
you can do it,
Say FUCK THE FOREIGN THOUGHT!
Say FREEDOM FOR ALL AMERICANS FIRST!
Say FREEDOM! say FREEEDOOOM!

Eat Helen B Happy

(a found poem)

Eat, Helen,
Be, happy.

Eat Helen—

Be happy!

"Eat it here—
Or take it home?"

Beyond this green field,
Men assault the earth, trees,
Building a prison—*damn!*

Brothers: deer, bear, trees . . .
O Blue Mountain! when bombers
Blast/slash this air,
Do your hearts tremble like mine?

O friend Madeleine!
Mother of five flowers!
Power's most men's fool . . .

Genesis II

The WORD was/is/will BE:
The Beginning, and the End, BE,
And the Word/is/Round,
And Warm and Rolling;
And the Word/be/the Verb,
And the Verb/be/a Woman . . .

BILL KNOTT ▪ ▪ ▪ ▪ ▪ ▪ ▪ ▪ ▪ ▪ ▪ ▪ ▪ ▪ ▪ ▪ ▪ ▪ ▪

Monodrama

Don't think, I said, that because I deny
Myself in your presence I do so in mine—
But whom was I talking to? The room, empty
Beyond any standpoint I could attain,

Seemed all sill to stare off before someone's
Full length nude, at halfmast their pubic flag
Mourned every loss of disguise, allegiance
More to the word perhaps than its image—

But predators always bite the nape first
To taste the flower on the spine-stem, so
I spoke again, which shows how unrehearsed
I failed to be. I went to the window:

Sky from your vantage of death, try to see.
Flesh drawn back for the first act of wound, it's me.

Save As: Salvation

Somewhere is the software to ID all
The snowflakes falling in this storm, but there
Ain't enough RAM crammed in my brain to call
Them forth by name, each crystal character
Putered and programmed, made to have a soul:
And even if I compelled the power
To inscribe them here as equals, in whole
Terms, I would not permit such an error.

But which is which, cries Ms. Ubiq-Unique.
We're not formatted for whiteout. And when

The screen of your vision freezes in flurries
And the core of this word blizzard hurries
To melt again, to find itself again,
Won't mine be the sign these syllables seek?

Mrs. Frye and the Pencilsharpener

I'll remember how in 6th-grade English class, always
bending toward the desk I would try to avert my eyes
from the mysterious ways Mrs. Frye's hair displaced
the blackboard's space with its black coils, to the paper
my penciltip raced across, certain to pass each test:
and if these gaze shifts got too switcheroo I'd retreat
(daily, it seems) to the back of the packed classroom

where, leaning forward on my toes, I could push with
my left hand the nubile tube of wood into the mouth
of the pencilsharpener which hung there like some
natural protrusion of the wall, an indigenous Deity,
the mask of a Goddess, erosion-endowed, rockformed—
then feel my righthand fingers and thumb slowly turn
the oiled wheel while knowing I would have to face

close to that sac-shaped sharpener, have to smell
(want to smell!) its earthy, odorous depths, seeing
in my mind the parings inside, the musky dark curls
whose incense was increased of course like mold-mildew
by the subtle saliva we kids might use to lick the lead's
point, though nearly none of our tongues could unblunt
the conundrums grownups posed, in my case Mrs. Frye

especially: so if I lingered back there, grinding away,
it was not to gloat, not to play the saintly A-student
snickering from behind at the others' heads bent intent
as penitents, because I too, I sinned at times, whenas,
no matter how proud I was of my proper grammar or
propounded syntax, stuffing my text thick with fetish
parsemarks, I myself went taunted, teased by the urge

to erase the very prodigy evidence my page revealed—
all the knots and quirks of those perfectly traced letters—
to restore the blankness I spoiled with each sentence,
to castrate every phrase before its errors rose by rote
to make my ethonic-greatest mistake grow and grow
erectile, inherent, that habit hateful male participle
I always was unable to shear the nib off of, the stub—

(But how could I flub and flunk such a crucial ordeal?—
Forgive me: I was lost pondering, musing about a poem
memorized from the boys' bathroom, tongued fluent
but not understood: yet how truthshod its lines ran
to my anxiety—their meaning escaped the precocious,
the goldstar me—so if I stalled—if I stayed chewed over
and left a stammering dimwit by their immallarméan

import, which paired its print alongside a syllabus
of pornocoiled stick figures whose mouths were pierced
by the sharpened ends of toonballoons—verses verse
alone can't explicate in systematic prosaic terms that
forced and torsoed my head shy—if I was stuck on
their sphinxian simplicity—unable to decipher any
of the prodigal doggeral lessons gesticulated down

our school's scribbly corridors, snicked and snatched at
across its game fields, a whole curriculum of secret lore,
a litany of my-big-brother-told-me's, my-uncle-said's,
a rumor primer which claimed complete mastery of
the only discipline inpenetrable to my inquisitive
quests never mind the autodidact airs I had to affect
during discussions of this topic, the nods and knowing

grins I wore to pass, to show my mastery of its arcana,
to prove what a pored nerd drill-diligent pupil I was
of those endless piss-walls, those scrawled rhymes and
confident lectures by croneys and guys who made sense
of the insane instructions re the sole subject I mark
zero on: all the dunno-dumb ideas I dunned then drove
core to me, carved their myths into me—and one in

particular goes to this poem, from the gendergabble
that gorged my brain: it hissed that She/the unknown
reared an inward toothly sheathdeath essence geared
to *vagina dentata* whatever pendant-pendant I'd proffer,
I, alma-matered to cram every exam with phallocratic
tits and sexist tripe pseudotype scionbabble, the entire
wisdom of my mentors' art-patriarch, old gobbledy-tropes—)

All gradeschool the fear of failing hovered in overstudy
as children riddled fears never to be learned, but could
I have continued to hone my fate, could I have stood
there for years and still the pencilsharpener wait
like a patient questioner, a warm, smiling teacher
filled with such dense scents, shavings, shorn graphite,
its soil rich with words no-one would ever have to write.

Winter Regrets

The snow on my ladder's rings
seems to be stepping upward,
returning to that cloud which hangs
framed in the faded cardboard

of an old calendar landscape
whose dust holds the days I desire
to live in, fixing to climb up
past that summer sun and hammer

the scene in whole. I didn't haul
my ladder in and now it's too late—
I turn from the window and stare

lost at a vista of August air
tacked, half-peeled from the kitchen wall.
All the undone chores must wait.

A Comic Look at Damocles

Sometimes Damocles is less afraid that the sword may drop
than that his enthusiasm for his plight might
—through the illogical process of displacement—
cause him to rise exuberantly up to it.

Once he glues a plastic bust of himself atop his pate;
once, while paring his fingernails with a pocketknife,
he sees an ant on the floor and throws it at it.
But all (both artistic and magic) remedy fails.

By old age he has quite forgot the deadly blade:
to his feeble sight, that gleaming flash above him
is himself, I mean his soul getting a headstart, already in flight.

In heaven he hears about an angel who tied a noose
to his own halo and hung himself from it, but sees
no way to apply the case, retroactively or otherwise.

KENNETH KOCH ▪ ▪ ▪ ▪ ▪ ▪ ▪ ▪ ▪ ▪ ▪ ▪ ▪ ▪

A New Guide

What is needed is a guide to all situations and places . . .
—LE VICOMTE DE CYRILLAC

Vous voyez cette ligne télégraphique au fond de la vallée
et dont le tracé rectiligne carpe lza forêt sur la montagne d'en
façe/Tous les poteaux en sont de fer . . .
—BLAISE CENDRARS, *FEUILLES DE ROUTE*

1

Look at this Champagne factory
It is in Epernay
From it comes dry white wine with innumerable bubbles
(It is made in a series of fifteen gabled white buildings—sheds)
Borges writes that mirrors and fornication are "abominable"
Because they increase the amount of reality
This champagne factory transforms reality rather than simply increasing it
Without it Epernay champagne wouldn't exist.

2

Look at this wolf.
He is lighter than a car
But heavier than a baby carriage.
He is highly effective.
Each wolf manifestation is done entirely in the classic manner of a wolf.
He stands completely still.
He is not "too busy to talk to you,"
Not "in conference" or "on the phone."
Some day there may not be any more wolves.
Civilization has not been moving in a way that is favorable to them.
Meanwhile, there is this one.

3

Look at this opera.
People are moving without plan.
They are badly directed.
But how they can sing!
One can tell from the faces of the audience how marvelously they sing.
That man there's face is like a burst of diamonds
That very slim woman has fallen in a faint.
Four nights ago at this opera house a man died.

The opera stopped four young men came with a stretcher to carry him out.
I was told that when he was in the lobby a doctor pronounced him dead.
Look at the audience now. They are full of life.

4

Look at this camel.
A man unused to camels is trying to mount it.
The camel's driver motions for the camel to kneel down
On its front knees, which it does.
The man mounts it, the camel gallops away.
To qualify for his position the man must demonstrate his ability to ride a camel.
  He has failed.
Maybe he will be given another chance—if it is decided that this was a defective
  camel.
The worst thing that can happen is he will be out of a job. He will not be shot.
The camel crouches down now in the sand,
Quiet, able, and at ease, with nothing about it defective.
If the camel were found to be defective, it would be shot.
That much of the old way still goes on.

5

The purple architecture runs all around the top of the Buddhist temple and then
  it is graduated into sculptured green, yellow, and pink strips.
Look at the young monk in a yellow and orange silk gown—he begins a prayerful
  journey up the four hundred and fifty steps.
Red blue white and purple sculptured kings and demons and Buddhas look down
  at him as he climbs and then look level at him but never look up at him
For they are near the top and their heads aren't constructed so that they are able
  to bend.

6

Look at this orange.
It was "made" by that orange tree over there.
That orange tree seems to be smiling
As it waves a little bit, just the slightest little bit, in this Andalusian wind.
If it waved much more it might start to lose its oranges.
It would.

7

Look at this arch.
It is part of a building more than seven hundred years old.
Every day from the time he was eighteen, probably, the man who made it worked
  in stone.
Sometimes he had a day off—the stone would be in his mind.
He would find in his mind ideas for patterns, lines, and angels.

Now those ideas are gone.
We have a different art.
But for what we believe most we don't have art at all.

8

The woman is covered by a sheet and the man has on a white mask.
The man takes out the woman's heart
And puts in another. He bends down to listen—
The new heart is beating! He asks for the wound to be closed.
He takes off his mask and goes into another room.
The woman stays in this room. She has a good chance of staying alive.

9

Look at this old tower in Lisbon that is now a museum for Portuguese blue tiles
    called Azulejos.
On each tile is a patterning of blue lines,
Thick ones and thin ones curving and straight but more curved ones than straight
    ones
And on most of them a picture and on some of them, actually on a good many of
    them, words.
One tells the story of Orpheus
On this one is a young woman
Holding a cane she points to an allegorical landscape—
A river, a bridge, and sheep. Underneath the image is written
WHATEVER PROSPERS, PROSPERS BEST IN ITS OWN PLACE.
This other tile (there are, it is said, eighty
Thousand of them, one cannot describe them all)
Shows a large blue-and-white-scaled fish. Underneath it, it says
In dark blue letters, in Latin, PISCIS NUNQUAM DORMET: THE FISH (or
    THIS FISH) NEVER SLEEPS.

10

You see this actor, on this stage, he is rehearsing his role in a play
Shakespeare's *A Winter's Tale*. He wears jeans and a frayed white shirt.
It is not yet dress rehearsal. He is rehearsing the part of Florizel. He is speaking
In unrhymed decasyllabic verse. Over here to his left is a young woman, Perdita.
She too is casually dressed—shirt and jeans.
Her brown hair is tied behind her head in a knot.

11

Look at this Greece.
It is hardly the same as Ancient Greece at all
Not even the old buildings:
Look at this man walking with this woman.

In a public park in Athens, in possession of happy lust.
Their faces can't have been the same in the fifth century BC.
Nothing can have been.

12

Look at this woman.
It has taken the human race millions of years for anyone to get to be the way she
   is:
An old woman in a red dress sitting looking at television.
Look at her hands.
They are a little dry but she is healthy.
She is eighty-two years old.
On the television screen is pictured a ship. There is a close-up of the deck, where
A little boy is playing with a dog. The woman laughs.

13

Look at the clouds.
They may be what I look at most of all
Without seeing anything.
It may be that many other things are the same way
But with clouds it's obvious.

The motorboat runs through the sky reflected in the river.
Look at the long trail of clouds behind.

14

Look at this celebration.
The people are festive, wearing masks.
There is a great variety of masks—dog mask, horse mask, mermaid mask, mask of
   a giant egg—
Many people are drinking despite the masks.
To get the drink to their lips they tilt the mask.
The masks, tilted upwards, look like hats.

15

Callé de los Espasmos
This is Spasms Street, named for a symptom of a fever one can get from
   mosquitoes at the very end of this street, where it becomes a path, near the
   mountain and surrounded by jungle, and leads to a waterfall and also
   sometimes to this fever.
Few people contract the disease and few know why the street is named Spasms
   Street. It is identified by signposts about every half mile: Calle de los
   Espasmos. The house this woman lives in is a kilometre from here, the zone is
   not dangerous.

16

Look at this bannister.
People put their hands on it as they went down.
Many many many many hands. Many many many many times.
It became known as the "Bannister of Ladies Hands." It was said one could feel
     the smoothness of their hands when one touched it oneself.
Actually what one felt was the smoothness of the marble
That had been worn down by so many touching hands.
Look at the sign that is on it now: The Bannister of Ladies Hands. To Preserve
     This Monument Each Person Is Requested To Touch It Only Once.
Look at the young boy there touching it twice, then a third time.
What if a guard catches him.
The fear is that if the bannister is touched too much it may completely wear
     away—the illusion of touching the soft hands of women in low-cut red dresses,
     going down to their friends and lovers, will exist no more.
The sensation will have vanished from the world.

17

Look at this beautiful road
On which horses have trodden
Centuries ago. Then it was a dirt road.
Now it is a stone road
Covered with tar.
The horses' prints are no longer visible.
Nothing is visible. Yes,
Now a motorcycle and a car go past.

18

Look at my friend.
He is saying to me Did you know that I am sixty-three?
He has a beautiful wrinkled face but in which the face has an almost complete
     mastery over the wrinkles. The wrinkling process is still held in abeyance by
     the face.
You're looking pretty good to me, I say.
He smiles.
Some day his face will be totally invaded by wrinkles like the pond in the
     Luxembourg Gardens on a windy fall day.
Even then, though, the main features of his face that I like will be visible.

19

This Egyptian temple is five thousand years old.
Look at the lion and look at the baboon. Both are in sphinx shape.
Look at the structure of the notes on this sheet of music.
Look at this well-known beauty now seventy years old. She says
It's fine up till seventy when you can still be sexually appealing. But after that—
Look at the harbingers of tempest—or of spring?—birds,

Birds are like thoughts that the sky had after it made a decision
About what to do, and today they are flying violently.
Look at this cloth
Spread out on the roof, beginning to show drops of rain.
Look at the green iris of this Peruvian flamingo's eye.
Look at the gravel on this path. Look at this old man's unevenly knitted grey
    sleeve.

20

Look at this woman.
The man she is with can't believe she has any connection to him.
She doesn't. She turns the corner.
But he walks after her.
After a few hundred feet he has the courage to say Hello.
You are very beautiful. May I walk with you a little ways.
She nods her head, smiling. She doesn't understand him because he is not
    speaking Spanish,
The only language she understands.
The man says, in English, I have just arrived in Barcelona.
She smiles, not understanding a word, except "Barcelona."
Two women and three men go by, speaking Catalan.

YUSEF KOMUNYAKAA ▪ ▪ ▪ ▪ ▪ ▪ ▪ ▪ ▪ ▪ ▪ ▪ ▪ ▪

Captain Amasa Delano's Dilemma

That day the albatross
    colored the sky with shit,
        I stumbled upon

Benito Cereno's pirate
    ship limping along the high
        seas. A Spanish sailor

locked eyes with me
    & gestured at the hot sky
        with his marlingspike.

But I wasn't a reader
    of Free-Mason signs
        or symbols of modern

oblivion. The motley lot
    sat on the quarterdeck
        dragging down the sun

to polish their hatchets,
    & it were as if God
        conspired with them

so I couldn't see
    through their percussion.
        That old sea salt

who handed me the wet
    Gordian knot to undo,
        his words were lost

because Cereno stole
    my mind with a litany
        of silent signs,

though I mastered
    satire & irony
        a lifetime ago.

I would have sat
    in the captain's chair
        & said, "Shave me,

Nigger." To me, Babo
    could've only been a body
        servant. Those sphinx

shadows posted as lookouts
    & lieutenants of the plot,
        they were only malingers

to me. The cries of babies
    leapt from my groin
        when I saw the negress

slumbering like a mermaid
    on a rock. How was I to know
        this wasn't the season myths

sang flesh & blood
    to sleep? That bastard,
        the headsman, Babo,

his skull was a hive
    we had to nail to a pole
        in the plaza as a warning

to ourselves. They say
   I didn't master the beast
      inside my own head,

but I want the naysayers
   to know I am the corpus
      of words & deeds

before my conception,
   before I kicked against
      the walls of the womb,

& my unblinking eyes
   weren't gazing toward
      a monastery on Mount Agonia.

Cante Jondo

Yes, I say, I know
   what you mean.
      Then we're off,

improvising on what
   ifs: can you imagine
      Langston & Lorca

hypnotized at a window
   in Nella Larsen's
      apartment, pointing at

bridges & searchlights
   in a summer sky, can you
      see them? Their breath

clouds the windowpanes,
   one puffed cloud
      indistinguishable from another.

They click their glasses
   of Jamaican rum. *To your*
      great King, says Lorca.

Prisoner in a janitor's suit,
   adds Langston. Their laughter
      ferries them to a sidestreet

in the Alhambra,
    & at that moment
        they see old Chorrojumo.

King of the Gypsies
    clapping his hands
        & stamping his feet

along with a woman dancing
    a rhumba to a tom-tom's
        rhythm. Is this Florence

Mills, or another face
    from the Cotton Club
        almost too handsome

to look at? To keep
    a dream of Andulusian
        cante jondo alive,

they agree to meet
    at Small's Paradise
        the next night,

where the bells of trumpets
    breathe honeysuckle & reefer,
        where women & men make love

to the air. You can see
    them now, reclining
        into the Jazz

Age. You can hear Lorca
    saying he cured his fear
        of falling from the SS *Olympic*

by dreaming he was shot
    three times in the head
        near the Fuente Grande

on the road to Alfacar.
    But the word *sex* doesn't
        flower in that heatwave

of 1929, only one man touching
    the other's sleeve, & heads
        swaying to "Beale Street Blues."

Forgive & Live

Ralph Ellison didn't
    have his right hand
        on her left breast

& they weren't kissing
    in the doorway of Blackmur's
        kitchen. But Delmore

Schwartz tried to slap
    his wife, Elizabeth,
        at the Christmas party

anyway. When he pulled
    her into a side bedroom
        the house swelled into a big

white amp for Caliban's
    blues. Maybe their fight
        began one evening about sex

years earlier, not enough
    money for food & gasoline.
        But she'd only been leaning

against Ellison's shoulder
    to let him light her cigarette,
        just a lull in a conversation

about Duke Ellington's
    "Creole Love Call"
        & the New Critics.

That night, the falling
    snow through the windows
        was a white spotlight

on his dark face,
    a perfect backdrop
        for Delmore's rehearsal

for the women
    who would pass
        through his life

like stunned llamas,
    for the drunken stars
        exploding in his head,

for the taxicabs
    taken from Cambridge
        to Greenwich Village, the fear

of death, the Dexedrine
    clouds & poison-pen letters
        floating back to earth,

for the notes in margins
    of Rilke's *Duino*
        Elegies & his love-hate

of T.S. Eliot,
    for Chumley's Bar,
        those days of grey

boxcars flickering past
    as he paced Washington
        Square Park, impulsive

bouquets stolen from gardens
    & given to lovers with dirt
        clinging to the roots,

for his fascination
    with Marilyn Monroe,
        the Dreyfus case, Kafka

quoting Flaubert, the day
    after JFK's assassination
        spent wandering the streets

in unbuckled galoshes,
    for Cavanaugh's Irish Bar
        in Chelsea & the Egyptian

Gardens on West Twenty-ninth,
    Dixie's Plantation Lounge,
        for his last night on earth,

stumbling from a forest
    of crumpled girlie magazines,
        as he takes the garbage

down to the lobby,
    singing about lovers
        in the Duchess's red shoes.

Homage to a Bellhop

. . . it startled us no more
than a blue vase or a red rug.
—*BLACK BOY*, RICHARD WRIGHT

Looks that weren't
  looks, like dazed
    swimmers gazing up

through twenty feet
  of untroubled water,
    you flexed your brimming

strength, a naked mask
  rehearsal. Because
    of unspoken treaties between

shadows & antebellum
  porticoes, between you
    & a prostitute, the third

face in the room was always
  erased from such a burlesque.
    You tipped your bright top hat

for every half dollar
  palmed into your calloused
    hands. The small secrets

multiplied till they pulled
  you toward aquamarine waves
    & hills, or down in the basement

with the shoeshine boy,
  reading *Flash Gordon*
    & dime-store novels

till the next buzzer
  summoned you up.
    Familiar with the sounds

of each slurred blue note
  & faked orgasm, you
    fixed your face before

that old soft knock
  on the door. Passionfruit
    quartered on a crystal dish

red as forbidden lips.
  You didn't see the woman
    on the bed, tied to the man

by a string of pearls.
  How many bets did they lose
    trying to make you betray

your daughter at Fisk?
  But you were a stone
    beside a river, a tiger

fashioned into a pussycat.
  Even later, in the deep nights,
    you couldn't escape

them—when you crawled
  into bed to make love
    to your wife, their hands

would rest on the darned sheet
  & their sighs would pool
    into your inner ear.

WILLIAM KULIK ▪ ▪ ▪ ▪ ▪ ▪ ▪ ▪ ▪ ▪ ▪ ▪ ▪ ▪ ▪

Flexible

It's a beautiful day: sunny, crisp, cloudless. I'm walking down the boulevard in the middle of my life, just a tiny fist of apprehension in the center of the chest as I catch a glimpse of myself in a store window, reminding me I'm out looking for an eight millimeter to tape myself dancing because someone said I'm too stiff in the middle though I figure I'm OK for a white guy. So I find a camera shop: the owner is doing his best to fix me up but I don't see anything I like til his sister appears in a short red dress, displaying an expanse of gorgeous thigh. She shows me the latest thing. "*Consumers'* gives it a ninety-two," she says, thrusting a hip at me. "You're at least a ninety-two," I say with a dry mouth, "Maybe a hundred, but you must have a flaw somewhere." Her lips are very red and wet. "If you start licking," she says, "Maybe you'll find it." "Sorry," I say shortly, "But I've got a previous engagement."

And I do. Outside, under that brilliant sky, I'm on the ground with the store detective's thirty-eight against my ear. "Shoot!" somebody hollers. He cocks and squeezes six times. Watching me shake uncontrollably, he laughs.

"You deserve this," she says, standing right above me, legs apart. My eyes trace the curve of her thigh til it disappears in the darkness. A voice whispers "Maybe if you were taller you'd get more." I think: that's it. First thing tomorrow, cowboy boots.

Old House Blues

for Alex P.

Everyone's here, and because I love old things, I've rented a grand Victorian in a part of town devoted to preservation, where even a splendid place such as this one—broad corridors and stairwells, dark, narrow arteries leading from room to room, each with its own period architectural marvels—is common. After a welcoming dinner, we walk the halls: floor polish, cedar, sachet—wonderful old odors—toward the evening's entertainment. On our way, we stop to admire each room's unique details. In the study, tales of Dionysius and his cohort molded on plaster cornices, Pan and Syrinx in a bedroom, garlanded by wreaths and berries and, on the drawing-room ceiling, the feature attraction: an oval painting of Echo and Narcissus. In each room walnut floors, cherry baseboards, carved oak mantels, all glowing with the magic of lost arts, of artisans long-gone. I order the house lights turned up to make everything clear, but am told it isn't possible: soon the show will begin. That's odd, I think, shivering as we arrive at the end of the house—doesn't the power reach this far? I open the door to the final wing: panic seizes me. Floors sag, lath shows through the fallen plaster. This'll take some work, I think, my spirits high as I recall the fortresses I'd made out of other houses that were vulnerable to roving gangs. But the jumble of wires on the floor, guitars and amps everywhere, make it clear my son and his friends have taken over. I try to persuade him to return to his room in the main body til I can get things back to normal, but he's adamant. "You're too serious, pops," he says. "Besides, the play's the thing." Seeing the empty bottles, the piles of crumpled Mickey D. and Cheese Doodle wrappers, I feel the panic again. Suddenly the lights blink three times, then go out. From a darkened corner, stage right, a woman giggles. "The metaphor's trite," she says. The audience titters. Smiling into the darkness behind her, I pat the lease in my breast pocket. "Try again, Kafka!" she shouts. This time the laughter is loud. A few hoots. Twisting the top off a bottle of beer and popping a bag of chips, I wonder if something's over. "You bet it is, Big Daddy!" she calls out for a third time. Taking my cue, I step forward, bow, then turn and walk toward the curtains. Applause is general, but there are no encores: just the old odors—floor polish, cedar, sachet—and a single rose.

Hi

in Memory of Wolfman Jack

My name's James, enlightenment's my game. Comin' at y'all with Soul Break, the two-minute hot spot on the hottest spot in town: station WSLF Millennium Radio 2000 on your dial where we know the pose of those who think the sword can cut itself and you out there usin Twoness to reach Oneness thinkin you ain't really real with a capital R til you like old Frog-in-Suchness—don't know his ass from his eyeball but give you one helluva Chugarumph! do that jump-in-pond-sound thing y'all dig on—cause you be thinkin' he got somethin you *don't* have, which is where you wrong and why I'm here tryin to get in your Original Face, tell you there ain't nothin' here to realize actualize fecundize: you can't *get it* cause you already got it, and if you *could* get it, it wouldn't be *it,* got it? Just you lookin for the Ultimate's a joke! Hell, any state *you* could find wouldn't be Ultimate if *you* could find it, ain't I right? And dig this: what you in your Twoness call the Illusion created by your Twoness which Illusion you are usin to reach the Oneness you in your Illusion think you ought to reach—all that mess is what the Man, Brah-Man, is already doin; and, like the man says: "Console thyself, thou woulds't not seek me if thou hads't not already found me." Now that's the *truth,* ain't no illusion—but it's all there is for now, brothers and sisters in the Land of Pure Delusion. Time for James to park it on his little satin pillow fold hands and stare at the dot he painted on the wall. Cause I got my own confusion. 'Night, y'all.

Fictions

In that novel you bought at the chain, a young woman looks back on her life. She's 30, a teacher married to a Harley-riding oil exec, mother of two sons. They have an apartment uptown, take exciting trips, but she's bored, frozen, galvanized into life only during rough sex or when she pictures him dying on one of his drunken, lights-off rides across the Throggs Neck Bridge. She thinks, as you do, her dad may have abused her: dreams and flashbacks tell her it's true. Meanwhile he, driven by his own demon, is made by the author to describe their life as "a simple story of seduction, rape and madness, the usual preoccupations." Now deep in the book, you wonder if they're being readied for some sinister ritual the one will create, the other acquiesce to. You wish they'd come to grips but it's hopeless: he won't give up his rage against a cold, demanding mother, she the hold on reality perfect order gives her. When their fate is revealed, you applaud silently, a witness to the truth of those struggles with the past that imitate your secret life so well you identify, are consoled. But are you liberated? Any more than if you'd watched the war that prompts those sounds of agony amplified by two huge speakers under the ring on whose sweaty canvas Killa Quadzilla meets Dr. Death in a world of faked falls, stomps and roars, the theatrical shame of the one about to be drop-kicked into the screaming crowd, the other suddenly real to you in the cocky strut and powerful hairy arms, hand on the helpless throat, you and your brother huddled in a corner of the room hugging crying Mommy daddy please stop we love you we're sorry

MAXINE KUMIN ▪ ▪ ▪ ▪ ▪ ▪ ▪ ▪ ▪ ▪ ▪ ▪ ▪ ▪ ▪ ▪

Hay

Day One: Above the river I hear
the loud fields giving up their gold,
the giant scissors-clack of Ruddy and Ned's
antique machine laying the timothy
and brome in windrows to be tedded,
this fierce anthood that persists
in taking from and giving back to the land,
defying the chrome millenium
that has contempt for smallscale backbreak.

Three emeralds, these interlocked three fields
free-leased for the tending and brushing out,
tidied up every fall like a well-swept
thrifty kitchen, blackberry and sumac
held at bay, gray birch and popple
brought down, the wild cherry lopped,
and gloriously every March
the wide white satin stretch besmirched
with dripping cartloads of manure.

Day Two: Sun bakes the long lines dry.
Late afternoon clouds pile up to stir
the teased-up mass with a southerly breeze
and since the forecast's fair, Ruddy and Ned
relax, play-punch, kidding each other,
calling each other Shirley, a name neither
owns up to, although once Scots-common
enough in New England back when
their patched rig was a modern invention.

Their dogs, four littermates,
Nutmeg, Cinnamon, Allspice and Mace,
Chessies with gums as pink as rubber
erasers and pink-rimmed eyes,
flat irises you can't look into,
their dogs, companionable roughnecks

always riding in the backs of their pickups
or panting, lying under them for shade,
look benignly on their sweating labors.

Day Three: The old baler cobbled from
other parts, repaired last winter,
cussed at in the shed in finger-
splitting cold when rusted bolts
resisted naval jelly, Coca-Cola, and
had to be drilled out in gritty bits,
now thunking like a good eggbeater
kicks the four-foot cubes off
onto the stubble for the pickups

and aggie trucks—that's our three-quarter ton
Dodge '67, slant-six engine
on its third clutch, with a new tie rod,
absent one door handle and an
intermittent taillight—
we'll carry fifty-two bales at a time
if they're pitched up and set on right.
Grunters and haulers, all of us
in these late-August heroics.

Interlude: The summer I was eleven
I boarded on a dairy farm in Pennsylvania.
Mornings we rode the ponies bareback
up through eiderdowns of ground fog,
up through the strong-armed apple orchard
that snatched at us no matter how we ducked,
up to the cows' vasty pasture, hooting and calling
until they assembled in their secret order
and we escorted them down to the milking barn
where each one gravely entered her stanchion.
There was no pushing or shoving.
All was as solemn as Quaker Meeting.

My four were: Lily, Martha, Grace and May.
May had only three tits. I learned to say *tit*
as it is written here. I learned to spend
twenty minutes per cow and five more stripping,
which you do by dipping your fingers in milk
and then flattening the aforementioned tit
again and again between forefinger and thumb
as you slide down it in a firm and soothing motion.
If they don't trust you they won't let down.
They'll get mastitis and their agony will be
forever on your conscience. To this day
I could close my eyes and strip a cow correctly.

I came to love my black and white ladies.
I loved pressing my cheek against each flank
as I milked. I almost came to love cowflops,
crisp at the edges, smelly pancakes.
I got pinkeye that summer, they say
I caught it from the cows, I almost lost the eye.
Meanwhile, we had squirt fights, cow to cow.
We squirted the waiting kittens full.
We drank milk warm from the pail,
thirsty and thoughtless of the mystery
we drank from the cow's dark body,
then filed in for breakfast.

They put up hay loose there, the old way,
forking it into the loft from the wagon rack
while the sweaty horses snorted and switched off flies
and the littlest kids were commanded to trample it flat
in between loads until the entire bay
was alight with its radiant sun-dried manna. . . .
It was paradise up there with dusty sun motes
you could write your name in as they skirled and drifted down.
There were ropes we swung on and dropped from and shinnied up
and the smell of the place was heaven, hurling me back
to some unknown plateau, tears standing up in my eyes
and an ancient hunger in my throat, a hunger. . . .

Perhaps in the last great turn of wheel
I was some sort of grazing animal.
Perhaps—trundling hay in my own barn
tonight and salivating from the sweetness—
I will be again. . . . When I read Neruda's
we are approaching a great and common tenderness
my mind startles and connects to this
all but obsolete small scene above the river
where unspectacular people secure
their bulky loads and drive away at dusk.

Allegiance to the land is tenderness.
The luck of two good cuttings in this climate.
Now clean down to the alders in the swale,
the fields begin an autumn flush of growth,
the steady work of setting roots, and then
as in a long exhale, go dormant.

The Layers

I have walked through many lives,
some of them my own,
and I am not who I was,
though some principle of being
abides, from which I struggle
not to stray.
When I look behind,
as I am compelled to look
before I can gather strength
to proceed on my journey,
I see the milestone dwindling
toward the horizon
and the slow fires trailing
from the abandoned camp-sites
over which scavenger angels
wheel on heavy wings.
Oh, I have made myself a tribe
out of my true affections,
and my tribe is scattered!
How shall the heart be reconciled
to its feast of losses?
In a rising wind
the manic dust of my friends,
those who fell along the way,
bitterly stings my face.
Yet I turn, I turn,
exulting somewhat,
with my will intact to go
wherever I need to go,
and every stone on the road
precious to me.
In my darkest night,
when the moon was covered
and I roamed through wreckage,
a nimbus-clouded voice
directed me:
"Live in the layers,
not on the litter."
Though I lack the art
to decipher it,
no doubt the next chapter
in my book of transformations
is already written.
I am not done with my changes.

Passing Through

—on my 79th birthday

Nobody in the widow's household
ever celebrated anniversaries.
In the secrecy of my room
I would not admit I cared
that my friends were given parties.
Before I left town for school
my birthday went up in smoke
in a fire at City Hall that gutted
the Department of Vital Statistics.
If it weren't for a census report
of a five-year-old White Male
sharing my mother's address
at the Green Street tenement in Worcester
I'd have no documentary proof
that I exist. You are the first,
my dear, to bully me
into these festive occasions.

Sometimes, you say, I wear
an abstracted look that drives you
up the wall, as though it signified
distress or disaffection.
Don't take it so to heart.
Maybe I enjoy not-being as much
as being who I am. Maybe
it's time for me to practice
growing old. The way I look
at it, I'm passing through a phase:
gradually I'm changing to a word.
Whatever you choose to claim
of me is always yours;
nothing is truly mine
except my name. I only
borrowed this dust.

The Round

Light splashed this morning
on the shell-pink anemones
swaying on their tall stems;
down blue-spiked veronica
light flowed in rivulets
over the humps of the honeybees;
this morning I saw light kiss

the silk of the roses
in their second flowering,
my late bloomers
flushed with their brandy.
A curious gladness shook me.

So I have shut the doors of my house,
so I have trudged downstairs to my cell,
so I am sitting in semi-dark
hunched over my desk
with nothing for a view
to tempt me
but a bloated compost heap,
steamy old stinkpile,
under my window;
and I pick my notebook up
and I start to read aloud
the still-wet words I scribbled
on the blotted page:
"Light splashed . . ."

I can scarcely wait till tomorrow
when a new life begins for me,
as it does each day,
as it does each day.

Hornworm: Summer Reverie

Here in caterpillar country
I learned how to survive
by pretending to be a dragon.
See me put on that look
of slow and fierce surprise
when I lift my bulbous head
and glare at an intruder.
Nobody seems to guess
how gentle I really am,
content most of the time
simply to disappear
by melting into the scenery.
Smooth and fatty and long,
with seven white stripes
painted on either side
and a sharp little horn for a tail,
I lie stretched out on a leaf,
pale green on my bed of green,
munching, munching.

Hornworm: Autumn Lamentation

Since that first morning when I crawled
into the world, a naked grubby thing,
and found the world unkind,
my dearest faith has been that this
is but a trial: I shall be changed.
In my imaginings I have already spent
my sightless winter underground,
unfolded silky powdered wings
and climbed into the air
to sail over the steaming fields,
alighting anywhere I pleased,
thrusting into deep tubular flowers.

It is not so: there may be nectar
in those cups, but not for me.
All day, all night, I carry on my back
embedded in my flesh, two rows
of little white cocoons,
so neatly stacked
they look like eggs in a crate.
And I am eaten half away.

If I can gather strength enough
I'll try to burrow under a stone
and spin myself a purse
in which to sleep away the cold;
though when the sun kisses the earth
again, I know I won't be there.
Instead, out of my chrysalis
will break, like robbers from a tomb,
a swarm of parasitic flies,
leaving my wasted husk behind.

Sir, you with the red snippers
in your hand, hovering over me,
casting your shadow, I greet you,
whether you come as an angel of death
or of mercy. But tell me,
before you choose to slice me in two:
Who can understand the ways
of the Great Worm in the sky?

PHILIP LARKIN · · · · · · · · · · · · · · ·

Aubade

I work all day, and get half drunk at night.
Waking at four to soundless dark, I stare.
In time the curtain-edges will grow light.
Till then I see what's really always there:
Unresting death, a whole day nearer now,
Making all thought impossible but how
And where and when I shall myself die.
Arid interrogation: yet the dread
Of dying, and being dead,
Flashes afresh to hold and horrify.

The mind blanks at the glare. Not in remorse
—The good not done, the love not given, time
Torn off unused—nor wretchedly because
An only life can take so long to climb
Clear of its wrong beginnings, and may never;
But at the total emptiness for ever,
The sure extinction that we travel to
And shall be lost in always. Not to be here,
Not to be anywhere,
And soon; nothing more terrible, nothing more true.

This is a special way of being afraid
No trick dispels. Religion used to try,
That vast moth-eaten musical brocade
Created to pretend we never die,
And specious stuff that says *No rational being
Can fear a thing it will not feel*, not seeing
That this is what we fear—no sight, no sound,
No touch or taste or smell, nothing to think with,
Nothing to love or link with,
The anaesthetic from which none come round.

And so it stays just on the edge of vision,
A small unfocused blur, a standing chill
That slows each impulse down to indecision.
Most things may never happen: this one will,
And realisation of it rages out
In furnace-fear when we are caught without
People or drink. Courage is no good:
It means not scaring others. Being brave
Lets no one off the grave.
Death is no different whined at than withstood.

Slowly light strengthens, and the room takes shape.
It stands plain as a wardrobe, what we know,
Have always known, know that we can't escape,
Yet can't accept. One side will have to go.
Meanwhile telephones crouch, getting ready to ring
In locked-up offices, and all the uncaring
Intricate rented world begins to rouse.
The sky is white as clay, with no sun.
Work has to be done.
Postmen like doctors go from house to house.

ANN LAUTERBACH ■ ■ ■ ■ ■ ■ ■ ■ ■ ■ ■ ■

Here and There

for Hector Leonardi

Some days start already swung from rafters,
naked, in London, at the ambassador's house.
What makes an exhibitionist? Baseball fever,
Fassbinder, the need to undress
after something French.
Today also will have remittance.
Here is a crowd of angels from Padua,
one all gold, one red, the rest obscured
apart from their heads which, profiled,
stare forward. Mary returns from her nuptual rite.
She is kept from the rest by blue space
and her hand grips her dress
so that a dark arch forms just below the waist.
I dress white, pull the curtains, see a child's face.

We almost escape narration
and, after the war, the noise our brothers made
we did not hear. There were remnants of a garden
where the landscape dipped, and old flowers
grew wild around stone relics of a birdbath.
Those were the days: stones, legends, fates,
slow passage of color through leaf
and fear incited by illumined walls at night.
We used to have a reputation for reality
and now these. What happened? The mist
is rising off the river; a low boat slides by.
Up ahead: the androgyny of winter
when all things seek gray, and the great star
chills us back into dreams under late and later dawns.

Revelry in Black-and-White

A shanty shade figured among the makers.
Doubt doubled its ante: left brain
Overactive, right brain dead. As ill at ease as
Any introduction, any gear might slip, anyone appear.
The honeymooners sailed away.
The honeymooners sailed away
And this made heroism possible: high seas,
Remorse, the forgotten cup, a dog
Left standing on the shore.
But in the full rain's hungover effect
There's an image of a blond woman
In a white dress wishing she had been the bride
As the groom sits in a chair in near darkness.
That night, that very night, she had scalded
The bouquet but none among them noticed.
She had flirted dangerously as stars flirt with light.
An unnatural glare sequestered such image-incited bruises,
Extra glasses were provided as sparklers flared.
The blond, a photographer, photographed
The bride as she stepped into a cherry red convertible.
This, she thought, was her merit, her redemption.
That winter, on assignment in Russia, it was unusually mild.

Untoward

Reading I spilled the wine.
Do you care? Are you wet? Do you care?
In a later epistle, hands dry, I will say
What is not so, although
Something may come of it.
The instance, allowed to speak, is not yet
Embodied, the big vacancies filled with bigness
As from beyond, or behind, an image:
A serpent hides in a tree,
A man falls into an abyss.
I spilled the wine or the wine escaped.
A gaze enhances the partial stain.
He might have drowned in the eclipsed target
Its drum first inscribed and wiped clean
Before I arrived. What day? What year?
Was it here, enduring the evening's long facade
Like a favorite monk extolling his service?
Omit distance; forbid silence.
Gain a dry incentive's leap.
The wine spilled. Eyes dry, hands wet,
Whatever new choices and limit.

He stood up as if to wander.
Cloudy again, distributed thinly, unanimous.
Are you wondering? Are you clear?
The decision omits its conclusion, obviously;
I crossed only to here, another lure
Without fruition and no need for boots, gloves, hat.
When asked if I had written about her
I said no, not exactly. She became the wild.

Procedure

Borrow me borrow my life
In the itinerant heat's final days.
Placed under the binoculars the pale wood
Preserves its veneer as if in welcome without stress.
"How long is it?" you had asked, not speaking
Of the table but of the table's address.
I cannot tell you now.
What could I tell you now?
The daily journal said it otherwise of course.
The letters also. The album also.
The hitch is how, burning, in pencil, how.
You had not asked to borrow the pencil
Because the house was cool not cold
And the vacation had been the best yet.
Only three quarrels and those about absence.
Meanwhile, the ancient triangular sail
Came down in no wind and the brute earth gave way.
Kafka, on the other hand, wrote keeping her always in mind.

Gesture and Flight

1.

She could be seen undressing
That is, in the original version
She could be seen undressing

A red jacket
Across a white chair

At first she had needed a coin
A shelter, marriage, and these
Led quickly to her doubt

"feminine" "visceral"
Quoted rudely

Which then fell rudely
Through a ring and into her chamber
Where she could be seen undressing

A gesture, a glance
So the thing stood for its instance

Folded tidily under the lamplight
With the logic of fact

In another instance, a volcano
Is hidden in the distance, a triangular hood
Under the sky's usual pan
And unusually adept clouds
But the image on the stamp is cloudless.
In yet another, masculine, version,
An arc intersects process
As ribbons of color are technically masked
So as not to bleed / her jacket
Falling off the chair as she turns, her mouth/
The gesture of the brush exploited, willfully exploited:
"volition" "deceit." And the girl's own story
Includes shoes, bottles, beds,
A jacket, hair

Then both or all sexes
Foregather under the island's moon
Without so much as an announcement from the captain
We are experiencing turbulence telling us
What we already know. Already lovers
Are rowing across the inlet
As the moon rises.
Let us hope there is no photograph of the event.

2.

A half-finished sensuality
Bloom, opiate
          No
The partial locale of things
Residence, place
          No
The ardor of the provinces
Well, how was Italy?
          No

Spun from an initial prop—
Avoid the the—
So here goes this part—
Would into what looks like—
Family romance: caprice plus longing equals—
Vessel, accoutrement, waking—

Wake up!
Is the map a puzzle or the puzzle a map?
The sun is not an earring. The moon is not its mate.
Each variant shuffles into view or is shot
Through the hole where the button was
On colder mornings, and cloth
Is pinned to the wall with neon pilings.
Hardly a story yet and yet
Plot must be the succinct
Restored to its aftermath.
Turn her slowly, her here, ere he

Eerily, sun comes through as time, and I'm
Found in its provenance: trees and such and *plish,*
Wet polish over old boards where he and she stand
Among arresting branches, their countless
One and one and one. A picture? A map? A match?
They must hear air moving among broken anomalies of air
Its chant revived in the actuality of their needing it:
Hymnal, not critique, nothing to touch, to see, to eat.

That would be flight
But this, a ripped adventure
In tandem's everlasting grip, also
Is subject to song: so go on
Up the tune's horizon, up up up
Its prohibitive curl, snarl, smile
Almost as visible as

If only air could carry such inferences,
If things could be thusly sung,
An option of partial seeing
And of plentiful response

Each iteration—
Tentative plow, wild new damage—
Moving from stranger to stranger
Tracing, as if, an intimacy.

Ice doth hang stiffly.

3.

What were those kisses made of,
And those tissue-clad children,
Their remnants laid across the hills like fog?
Had she danced in the temple where the Egyptians lay?
Had they? That was the city's ruse
To keep us moving from station to station
Hoping for chance to erupt
From the dangerous crux of endings.
There is a list and everyone is on it.
But to be turned toward a discrete, ravelled flame
Composed of the foreground, lasting only as long as passage—
Could nearness ever suffice?
In this version, she takes a screen from its window
And air is relentless,
A rhythmic presentation of toward,
As the foggy grid subtracts to its object
The object to its pile. Certainly
She could be seen undressing
As she stretches her arms overhead
As she touches her shoe.

DORIANNE LAUX ▪ ▪ ▪ ▪ ▪ ▪ ▪ ▪ ▪ ▪ ▪ ▪ ▪ ▪ ▪

What Could Happen

Noon. A stale Saturday. The hills
rise above the town, nudge houses and shops
toward the valley, kick the shallow river
into place. Here, a dog can bark for days

and no one will care enough
to toss an empty can or an unread newspaper
in his direction. No one complains.
The men stand in loose knots

outside Ace Hardware, talk a little, stare
at the blue tools. A few kids
sulk through the park, the sandbox full
of hard scrabble, the monkey bars

too hot to touch. In a town like this
a woman on the edge of forty
could drive around in her old car, the back end
all jingle and rivet, one headlight

taped in place, the hood held down with greasy rope,
and no one would notice.
She could drive up and down the same street
all day, eating persimmons,

stopping only for a moment to wonder
at the wooden Indian on the corner of 6th and B,
the shop window behind it
filled with beaten leather, bright woven goods

from Guatemala, postcards of this town
before it began to go under, began
to fade into a likeness of itself.
She could pull in at the corner store for a soda

and pause before uncapping it,
press the cold glass against her cheek,
roll it under her palm down the length of her neck
then slip it beneath the V of her blouse

and let it rest there, where she's hottest.
She could get back in her car
and turn the key, bring the engine up like a swarm
of bottle flies, feel it shake

like an empty caboose.
She could twist the radio to high
and drive like this for the rest of the day—
the same street, the same hairpin turn

that knocks the jack in the trunk from one wheel well
to the other—or she could pass the turn
and keep going, the cold soda
wedged between her legs, the bass notes

throbbing like a vein, out past the closed shops
and squat houses, the church
with its bland white arch, toward the hills,
beyond that shadowy nest of red madrones.

The Lovers

She is about to come. This time,
they are sitting up, joined below the belly,
feet cupped like sleek hands praying
at the base of each other's spines.
And when something lifts within her
toward a light she's sure, once again,

she can't bear, she opens her eyes
and sees his face is turned away,
one arm behind him, hand splayed
palm down on the mattress, to brace himself
so he can lever his hips, touch
with the bright tip the innermost spot.
And she finds she *can't* bear it—
not his beautiful neck, stretched and corded,
not his hair fallen to one side like beach grass,
not the curved wing of his ear, washed thin
with daylight, deep pink of the inner body—
what she can't bear is that she can't see his face,
not that she thinks this exactly—she is rocking
and breathing—it's more her body's thought,
opening, as it is, into its own sheer truth.
So that when her hand lifts of its own volition
and slaps him, twice on the chest,
on that pad of muscled flesh just above the nipple,
slaps him twice, fast, like a nursing child
trying to get a mother's attention,
she's startled by the sound,
though when he turns his face to hers—
which is what her body wants, his eyes
pulled open, as if she had bitten—
she does reach out and bite him, on the shoulder,
not hard, but with the power infants have
over those who have borne them, tied as they are
to the body, and so, tied to the pleasure,
the exquisite pain of this world.
And when she lifts her face he sees
where she's gone, knows she can't speak,
is traveling toward something essential,
toward the core of her need, so he simply
watches, steadily, with an animal calm
as she arches and screams, watches the face that,
if she could see it, she would never let him see.

KATHERINE LEDERER ■ ■ ■ ■ ■ ■ ■ ■ ■ ■ ■ ■

A Dream of Mimesis

It is duty and not hospitality that has diverted the ancient guest.
It is the whispered threat of sentiment and ignorance.
There is a plenitude of foresight. Before the diversion of the light.
The light is now spilling over. We now recognize him by his scar.

The feelings are being externalized. No contour is blurred, but of light
There is only the thin throat of it that hits his head. He rises—
Is seen through the curtains. Now lax   with the wind, made more solid. They
  are lying
Open. Their mouths are opening and closing, glistening slick in the yellow light.
They are speaking in syntax. He is wanting to fuck.
The thigh is clean. The scar on the thigh is newly healed.
In the episode's chaste entrée ("once . . . when a boar . . .")—here—
He must straddle her ass. We are patient. Here, his organs begin to swell—
Lest they are spiritual, his courage will fail him. His organs are swelling—we
  have, here,
Great depths—trimmed by delicate vulvic folds. Flesh dangles, cut.
A syntactical culture develops between them. They talk. Her hand, fraught,
Grabs at his clean, polished cock. Gradually, historically, the choice has befallen
  him.
Idols aged rot on the verge of legend. It runs too smoothly. The river beside her.
  Angst.
The river is blue. The river is not very wide. He is raping her. The situation is
  complicated.
His penis is very large. The scar on his thigh is newly healed. Let's not see it just
Yet—let's see both of their bodies illuminated in a uniform fashion. He slaps her.
She grabs at his ass. A suggestive influence of the unexpressed. The separation of
  styles.
Light hits her throat. The thighs of each swell—then abate. The sublime action
  dulls them.
He "persecutes" her. He is not afraid to let the realism of daily life enter into his
  sublime.
There are clearly expressible reasons for their conflict. The human problem has
  dealt with them
In this fashion. They are using two styles. The concept of his historical becoming
  has disturbed him
Into action. The episodic nature of her pain is obscured by the sublime action of
  his cock.
He is the simile of the wolf. He is seeking her nipples with his mouth.
  Disentangled from
The syntactical challenge she nips at his ear ("A god himself gave him . . .") The
  introduction of
Episodes. An eloquent foreground. A uniform present entirely foreign to the
  story
Of his scar ("The woman now touched it . . .")

Dreaming of Hair

Ivy ties the cellar door in autumn.
In summer, morning glory wraps the ribs of a mouse.
Love binds me to the one
whose hair I've found in my mouth,
whose sleeping head I kiss,
wondering is it death?
beauty? the dark star
spreading in every direction
from the crown of her head.

Donna's hair is autumn hair.
There the sun ripens.
My fingers harvest the dark vegetable
of her body.
In the morning I remove it
from my tongue and sleep again.

Hair spills through my dream,
sprouts from my stomach, thickens
my heart, and tangles the brain.
Hair ties the tongue dumb.
Hair ascends the tree of my childhood—
the willow I climbed
one bare foot and hand at a time,
feeling the knuckles of the gnarled tree,
hearing my father plead
from his window *Don't fall!*

In my dream I fly past summers and moths
to the thistle caught in my mother's hair,
the purple one I touched and bled for,
to myself at three,
sleeping beside her,
waking with her hair in my mouth.

Along a slippery twine of her black hair,
she ties *ko-tze* knots for me:
fish and lion heads,
chrysanthemum buds,
the heads of Chinamen,
black-haired and frowning.

Li-En, my brother, frowns when he sleeps.
I push back his hair, stroke his brow.

His hairline is our father's,
three peaks pointing down.

What sprouts from the body
and touches the body?
What filters sunlight
and drinks moonlight?
Where have I misplaced my heart?
What stops wheels and great machines?
What tangles in the bough
and snaps the loom?

Out of the grave my father's hair bursts.
A strand pierces my left sole,
shoots up bone, past ribs,
to the broken heart it stitches,
and down again, swirling in the stomach,
in the groin, and down again,
through the right foot.

What binds me to this earth?
What remembers the dead
and grows toward them?

I'm tired of thinking.
I long to taste the world with a kiss.
I long to fly into hair
with kisses and weeping,
remembering an afternoon,
when kissing my sleeping father,
I saw for the first time,
behind the thick swirl of his black hair,
the mole of wisdom,
a lone planet
spinning slowly.

Sometimes Donna is melancholy
and I hold her head in my hands.
Sometimes I remember
our hair grows after death.
Then, I must grab handfuls of her hair
and, I tell you, there are apples, walnuts,
ships sailing, ships docking, and men
taking off their boots, their hearts breaking,
not knowing which they love more,
the water, or their women's hair,
sprouting from the head, rushing toward the feet.

The Gift

To pull the metal splinter from my palm
my father recited a story in a low voice.
I watched his lovely face and not the blade.
Before the story ended he'd removed
the iron sliver I thought I'd die from.

I can't remember the tale,
but hear his voice still,
a well of dark water, a prayer.
And I recall his hands,
two measures of tenderness
he laid against my face,
the flames of discipline
he raised above my head.

Had you entered that afternoon
you would have thought you saw a man
planting something in a boy's palm,
a silver tear, a tiny flame.
Had you followed that boy
you would have arrived here,
where I bend over my wife's right hand.

Look how I shave her thumbnail down
so carefully she feels no pain.
Watch as I lift the splinter out.
I was seven when my father
took my hand like this,

and I did not hold that shard
between my fingers and think,
Metal that will bury me,
christen it
Little Assassin,
Ore Going Deep for My Heart,
and I did not lift up my wound and cry,
Death visited here!
I did what a child does
when he's given something to keep.
I kissed my father.

DENISE LEVERTOV ▪ ▪ ▪ ▪ ▪ ▪ ▪ ▪ ▪ ▪ ▪ ▪ ▪ ▪

The Malice of Innocence

A glimpsed world, halfway through the film,
one slow shot of a ward at night

holds me when the rest is quickly
losing illusion. Strange hold,

as of romance, of glamor: not because
even when I lived in it I had

illusions about that world: simply because
I did live there and it was

a world. Greenshaded lamp glowing
on the charge desk, clipboards
stacked on the desk for the night,

sighs and waiting, waiting-for-morning stirrings
in the dim long room, warm, orderly,
and full of breathings as a cowbarn.

Death and pain dominate this world, for though
many are cured, they leave still weak,

still tremulous, still knowing mortality
had whispered to them; have seen in the folding
of white bedspreads according to rule

the starched pleats of a shroud.
                              It's against that frozen
counterpane, and the knowledge too
how black an old mouth gaping at death can look

that the night routine has in itself—
without illusions—glamor, perhaps. It had
a rhythm, a choreographic decorum:
when all the evening chores had been done

and a multiple restless quiet listened
to the wall-clock's pulse, and turn by turn

the two of us made our rounds
on tiptoe, bed to bed,

counting by flashlight how many pairs
of open eyes were turned to us,

noting all we were trained to note,
we were gravely dancing—starched

in our caps, our trained replies,
our whispering aprons—the well-rehearsed

pavane of power. Yes, wasn't it power,
and not compassion,
                            gave our young hearts
their hard fervor? I hated

to scrub out lockers, to hand out trays of
unappetising food, and by day, or the tail-end of night

(daybreak dull on gray faces—ours and theirs)
the anxious hurry, the scolding old-maid bosses.
But I loved the power
of our ordered nights,

            gleaming surfaces I'd helped to polish
making patterns in the shipshape
halfdark—
                    loved
the knowing what to do, and doing it,
list of tasks getting shorter

hour by hour. And knowing
all the while that Emergency
might ring with a case to admit, anytime,

if a bed were empty. Poised,
ready for that.
                        The camera
never returned to the hospital ward,

the story moved on into the streets,
into the rooms where people lived.

But I got lost in the death rooms a while,
remembering being (crudely, cruelly,

just as a soldier or one of the guards
from Dachau might be) in love with order,

an angel like the *chercheuses de poux*, floating
noiseless from bed to bed,

smoothing pillows, tipping
water to parched lips, writing

details of agony carefully into the Night Report.

Woman Alone

When she cannot be sure
which of two lovers it was with whom she felt
this or that moment of pleasure, of something fiery
streaking from head to heels, the way the white
flame of a cascade streaks a mountainside
seen from a car across a valley, the car
changing gear, skirting a precipice,
climbing . . .
When she can sit or walk for hours after a movie
talking earnestly and with bursts of laughter
with friends, without worrying
that it's late, dinner at midnight, her time
spent without counting the change . . .
When half her bed is covered with books
and no one is kept awake by the reading light
and she disconnects the phone, to sleep till noon . . .
Then
selfpity dries up, a joy
untainted by guilt lifts her.
She has fears, but not about loneliness;
fears about how to deal with the aging
of her body—how to deal
with photographs and the mirror. She feels
so much younger and more beautiful
than she looks.
                  At her happiest
—or even in the midst of
some less than joyful hour, sweating
patiently through a heatwave in the city
or hearing the sparrows at daybreak, dully gray,
toneless, the sound of fatigue—
a kind of sober euphoria makes her believe
in her future as an old woman, a wanderer,
seamed and brown,
little luxuries of the middle of life all gone,
watching cities and rivers, people and mountains,
without being watched; not grim nor sad,
an old winedrinking woman, who knows
the old roads, grass-grown, and laughs to herself . . .
She knows it can't be:

that's Mrs. Doasyouwouldbedone by from *The Water Babies,*
no one can walk the world any more,
a world of fumes and decibels.
But she thinks maybe
she could get to be tough and wise, some way,
anyway. Now at least
she is past the time of mourning,
now she can say without shame or deceit,
O blessed Solitude.

The Life of Art

The borderland—that's where, if one knew how
one would establish residence. That watershed,
that spine, that looking-glass . . .   I mean the edge
between impasto surface, burnt sienna, thick,
    striate, gleaming—swathes and windrows
    of carnal paint—
    (or, canvas barely stained,
    where warp and weft peer through),

and fictive truth: a room, a vase, an open door
giving upon the clouds.

A step back, and you have
the likeness, its own world. Step to the wall again,
and you're so near the paint you could lick it,
you breathe its ghostly turpentine.
                      But there's an interface,
immeasurable, elusive—an equilibrium
just attainable, sometimes, when the attention's rightly poised,
where you are opulently received
by the bravura gestures hand and brush
proffer (as if a courtier twirled
a feathered velvet hat to bow you in)
and yet, without losing sight of one stroke,
                one scrape of the knife,
you are drawn through into that room, into
its air and temperature.

Couldn't one learn to maintain
that exquisite balance more than a second?
                    (One sees even
the pencilled understrokes, and shivers
in pleasure—and one's fingertips

touch the carpet's nubs of wool, the cold fruit in a bowl:
one almost sees
what lies beyond the window, past the frame, beyond . . .

Ikon: The Harrowing of Hell

Down through the tomb's inward arch
He has shouldered out into Limbo
to gather them, dazed, from dreamless slumber:
the merciful dead, the prophets,
the innocents just His own age and those
unnumbered others waiting here
unaware, in an endless void He is ending
now, stooping to tug at their hands,
to pull them from their sarcophagi,
dazzled, almost unwilling. Didmas,
neighbor in death, Golgotha dust
still streaked on the dried sweat of his body
no one had washed and anointed, is here,
for sequence is not known in Limbo;
the promise, given from cross to cross
at noon, arches beyond sunset and dawn.
All these He will swiftly lead
to the Paradise road: they are safe.
That done, there must take place that struggle
no human presumes to picture:
living, dying, descending to rescue the just
from shadow, were lesser travails
than this: to break
through earth and stone of the faithless world
back to the cold sepulchre, tearstained
stifling shroud; to break from *them*
back into breath and heartbeat, and walk
the world again, closed into days and weeks again,
wounds of His anguish open, and Spirit
streaming through every cell of flesh
so that if mortal sight could bear
to perceive it, it would be seen
His mortal flesh was lit from within, now,
and aching for home. He must return,
first, in Divine patience, and know
hunger again, and give
to humble friends the joy
of giving Him food—fish and a honeycomb.

Stele (I–II c. B.C.)

They part at the edge of substance.
Henceforth, he will be shadow
in a land of shadow.
And she—she too will be going
slowly down a road of cloud,
weightless, untouched, untouching.
This is the last crossroad.
Her right hand and his left
are clasped, but already,
muffled in his acceptance of fate,
his attention recedes from her.
Her left hand rises, fingertips trace
the curve of his warm face
as it cools and fades.
He has looked down his road,
he is ready to go, not willingly
yet without useless resistance.
She too accepts the truth, there is no way back,
but she has not looked, yet, at the path
accorded to her. She has not given herself,
not yet, to her shadowhood.

One December Night . . .

for Yarrow

This I had not expected:
the moon coming right into my kitchen,
the full moon, gently bumping
angles of furniture,
seeming to like the round table
but not resenting corners.

Somehow the moon
filled all the space and yet
left room for whatever
was there already, including me,
and for movement. Like a balloon,
the moon stirred at a breath
and unlike a balloon did not
rise to the ceiling, but wandered
as if sleep-walking,
no more than a foot from the floor.

Music accompanied this lunar visitation—
you would imagine harp or lute, but no,
I'd say it was steel drums,
played with an airy whispering touch.
(Those scooped concavities
might serve as moon-mirrors.)
The greenish tint of white spider-chrysanthemums
resembled the moon's color,
but that was lighter, lighter.

I have been given much, but why this also?
I was abashed. What grand gesture of welcome
was I to make? I bowed, curtsied, but the modest moon
appeared unaware of homage.
I breathed, I gazed; and slowly, mildly,
the moon hovered, touring stove and cupboards,
bookshelves and sink, glimmering
over a bowl of tangerines. And gently
withdrew, just as I thought to summon courage
to offer honey-mead or slivovitz.

The Hymn

Had I died? or was I
very old and blind? or
was the dream—
this hymn, this ecstatic paean,
this woven music
of color and form, of the sense
of airy space—
was the dream
showing forth the power
of memory *now*, today or at any
moment of need? Or the power
of the inner eye, distinct
from memory, Imagination's power,
greater than we remember,
in abeyance, the well in which
we forget to dip our cups?

At all events,
that broad hillside of trees
all in leaf, trees of all kinds,
all hues of green, gold-greens, blue-greens,
black-greens, pure and essential

green-greens, and warm and deep
maroons, too, and the almost purple
of smoketrees—all perceived
in their mass of rounded, composed forms
across a halfmile of breezy air,
yet with each leaf
rippling, gleaming,
visible almost to vein and serration:

at all events, that sight
brought with it, in dream
such gladness, I wept
tears of gratitude
(such as I've never wept, only read
that such tears sometimes
are shed) amazed to know
this power was mine, a thing given,
to see so well, though asleep,
though blind,
though gone from the earth.

For Those Whom the Gods Love Less

When you discover
your new work travels the ground you had traversed
decades ago, you wonder, panicked,
'Have I outlived my vocation? Said already
all that was mine to say?'
                              There's a remedy—
only one—for the paralysis seizing your throat to mute you,
numbing your hands: Remember the great ones, remember Cézanne
doggedly *sur le motif,* his mountain
a tireless noonday angel he grappled like Jacob,
demanding reluctant blessing. Remember James rehearsing
over and over his theme, the loss
of innocence and the attainment
(note by separate note sounding its tone
until by accretion a chord resounds) of somber
understanding. Each life in art
goes forth to meet dragons that rise from their bloody scales
in cyclic rhythm: Know and forget, know and forget.
It's not only
the passion for *getting it right* (though it's that, too)
it's the way
radiant epiphanies recur, recur,
consuming, pristine, unrecognized—

until remembrance dismays you. And then, look,
some inflection of light, some wing of shadow
is other, unvoiced. You can, you must
proceed.

PHILIP LEVINE ▪ ▪ ▪ ▪ ▪ ▪ ▪ ▪ ▪ ▪ ▪ ▪ ▪ ▪ ▪ ▪

On a Drawing by Flavio

Above my desk
the Rabbi of Auschwitz
bows his head and prays
for us all, and the earth
which long ago inhaled
his last flames turns
its face toward the light.
Outside the low trees
take the first gray shapes.
At the cost of such
death must I enter
this body again,
this body which is
itself closing on
death? Now the sun
rises above a stunning
valley, and the orchards
thrust their burning
branches into the day.
Do as you please, says
the sun without uttering
a word. But I can't.
I am this hand that
would raise itself
against the earth
and I am the earth too.
I look again and closer
at the Rabbi and at last
see he has my face
that opened its eyes
so many years ago
to death. He has these
long tapering fingers
that long ago reached
for our father's hand

long gone to dirt, these
fingers that hold
hand to forearm,
forearm to hand because
that is all that god
gave us to hold.

The Red Shirt

. . . his poems that no one reads anymore
become "dust, wind, nothing," like the
insolent colored shirt he bought to die in.
—VARGAS LLOSA

If I gave 5 birds
each 4 eyes
I would be blind
unto the 3rd
generation, if I
gave no one a word
for a day
and let the day
grow into a week
and the week sleep
until it was
half of my life
could I come home
to my father
one dark night.

On Sundays an odd light
grows on the bed
where I have lived
this half of my life,
a light that begins
with the eyes
blinding first one
and then both
until at last
even the worn candles
in the flower box
lay down their heads.

Therefore I have come
to this red shirt
with its faultless row
of dark buttons, 7

by my count, as dark
as blood that poured
over my lips
when the first word
of hope jumped
and became a cry
of birds calling
for their wings,
a cry of new birds.

This is the red shirt
Adam gave to the Angel
of Death when he asked
for a son, this
is the flag Moses
waved 5 times
above his head
as he stumbled
down the waves
of the mountainous sea
bearing the Tables of 10,
this is the small cloth
mother put in
my lunch box
with bread and water.

This is my red shirt
in which I go to meet
you, Father of the Sea,
in which I will say
the poem I learned
from the mice. A row
of faultless buttons,
each one ten years
and the eye of the bird
that beheld the first world
and the last, a field
of great rocks weeping,
and no one to see
me alone, day after
day, in my red shirt.

LARRY LEVIS ∎ ∎ ∎ ∎ ∎ ∎ ∎ ∎ ∎ ∎ ∎ ∎ ∎ ∎ ∎ ∎

1974: My Story in a Late Style of Fire

Whenever I listen to Billie Holliday, I am reminded
That I, too, was once banished from New York City.
Not because of drugs or because I was interesting enough
For any wan, overworked patrolman to worry about—
His expression usually a great, gauzy spiderweb of bewilderment
Over his face—I was banished from New York City by a woman.
Sometimes, after we had stopped laughing, I would look
At her & see a cold note of sorrow or puzzlement go
Over her face as if someone else was there, behind it,
Not laughing at all. We were, I think, 'in love.' No, I'm sure.
If my house burned down tomorrow morning, & if I & my wife
And son stood looking on at the flames, & if, then,
Someone stepped out of the crowd of bystanders
And said to me: "Didn't you once know . . .?" *No.* But if
One of the flames, rising up in the scherzo of fire, turned
All the windows blank with light, & if that flame could speak,
And if it said to me: "You loved her, didn't you?" I'd answer,
Hands in my pockets, "Yes." And then I'd let fire & misfortune
Overwhelm my life. Sometimes, remembering those days,
I watch a warm, dry wind bothering a whole line of elms
And maples along a street in this neighborhood until
They're all moving at once, until I feel just like them,
Trembling & in unison. None of this matters now,
But I never felt alone all that year, & if I had sorrows,
I also had laughter, the affliction of angels & children.
Which can set a house on fire if you'd let it. And even then
You might still laugh to see all of your belongings set you free
In one long choiring of flames that sang only to you—
Either because no one else could hear them, or because
No one else wanted to. And, mostly, because they know.
They know such music cannot last, & that it would
Tear them apart if they listened. In those days,
I was, in fact, already married, just as I am now,
Although to another woman. And that day I could have stayed
In New York. I had friends there. I could have strayed
Up Lexington Avenue, or down to Third, & caught a faint
Glistening of the sea between the buildings. But I wanted
To touch her nakedness everywhere, until her body was, again,
A bright field, or until we both reached some thicket
As if at the end of a lane, or at the end of all desire,
And where we could, therefore, be alone again, & make
Some dignity out of loneliness. As mostly, people cannot do.

Billie Holliday, whose life was shorter & more humiliating
Than my own, would have understood all this, if only
Because even in her late addiction & her bloodstreams'
Hallelujahs, she, too, sang often of some affair, of someone
Gone, &, therefore, permanent. And sometimes she sang
For nothing, even then, & it isn't anyone's business, if she did.
That morning, when *she* asked me to leave, wearing only
That apricot tinted, fraying camisole, I wanted to stay.
But I also wanted to go, to lose her suddenly, almost
For no reason, & certainly without any explanation.
I remember looking down at a pair of singular tracks
Made in a light snow the night before, at how they were
Gradually effacing themselves beneath the tires
Of the morning traffic, & thinking that my only other choice
Was fire, ashes, abandonment, solitude. All of which happened
Anyway, & soon after, & by divorce. I know this isn't much,
But I wanted to explain this life to you, even if
I had to become, over the years, someone else to do it.
You have to think of me what you think of me. I had
To live my life, even its late, florid style. Before
You judge this, think of her. Then think of fire,
Its laughter, the music of splintering beams & glass,
The flames reaching through the second story of a house
Almost as if to, mistakenly, rescue someone who
Left you years ago. It is so American, fire. So like us.
Its desolation. And its eventual, brief triumph.

There Are Two Worlds

Perhaps the ankle of a horse is holy.

Crossing the Mississippi at dusk, Clemens thought
Of a sequel in which Huck Finn, in old age, became
A hermit, & insane. And never wrote it.

And perhaps all that he left out is holy.

The river, anyway, became a sacrament when
He spoke of it, even though
The last ten chapters were a failure he devised

To please America, & make his lady
Happy: to buy her silk, furs, & jewels with

Hues no one in Hannibal had even seen.

There, above the river, if
The pattern of the stars is a blueprint for a heaven
Left unfinished,

I also believe the ankle of a horse,
In the seventh furlong, is as delicate as the fine lace
Of faith, & therefore holy.

I think it was only Twain's cynicism, the smell of a river
Lingering in his nostrils forever, that kept
His humor alive to the end.

I don't know how he managed it.

I used to make love to a woman, who,
When I left, would kiss the door she held open for me,
As if instead of me, as if she already missed me.
I would stand there in the cold air, breathing it,
Amused by her charm, which was, like the scent of a river,

Provocative, the dusk & first lights along the shore.

Should I say my soul went mad for a year, &
Could not sleep? To whom should I say so?

She was gentle, & intended no harm.

If the ankle of a horse is holy, & if it fails
In the stretch & the horse goes down, &
The jockey in the bright shout of his silks
Is pitched headlong onto
The track, & maimed, & if , later, the horse is
Destroyed, & all that is holy

Is also destroyed: hundreds of bones & muscles that
Tried their best to be pure flight, a lyric
Made flesh, then

I would like to go home, please.

Even though I betrayed it, & left, even though
I might be, at such a time as I am permitted
To go back to my wife, my son—no one, or

No more than a stone in a pasture full
Of stones, full of the indifferent grasses,

(& Huck Finn insane by then & living alone)

It will be, it might be still,
A place where what can only remain holy grazes, &
Where men might, also approach with soft halters,
And, having no alternative, lead that fast world

Home—though it is only to the closed dark of stalls,
And though the men walk ahead of the horses slightly
Afraid, & at all times in awe of their
Quickness, & how they have nothing to lose, especially

Now, when the first stars appear slowly enough
To be counted, & the breath of horses make white signatures

On the air: *Last Button, No Kidding, Careless Love—*

And the air is colder.

Family Romance

> Dressed to die . . .
> —DYLAN THOMAS

Sister once of weeds & a dark water that held still
In ditches reflecting the odd,
Abstaining clouds that passed, & kept
Their own counsel, we
Were different, we kept our own counsel.
Outside the tool shed in the noon heat, while our father
Ground some piece of metal
That would finally fit, with grease & an hour of pushing,
The needs of the mysterious Ford tractor,
We argued out, in adolescence,
Whole systems of mathematics, ethics,
And finally agreed that *altruism,*
Whose long vowel sounded like the pigeons,
Roosting stupidly & about to be shot
In the barn, was impossible
If one was born a Catholic. The Swedish
Lutherans, whom the nuns called
"statue smashers," the Japanese on
Neighboring farms, were, we guessed,
A little better off. . . .
When I was twelve, I used to stare at weeds

Along the road, at the way they kept trembling
Long after a car had passed;
Or at the gnats in families hovering over
Some rotting peaches, & wonder why it was
I had been born a human.
Why not a weed, or a gnat?
Why not a horse or a spider? And why an American?
I did not think that anything could choose me
To be a Larry Levis before there even *was*
A Larry Levis. It was strange, but not strange enough
To warrant some design.
                                        On the outside,
The barn, with flaking paint, was still off white.
Inside, it was always dark, all the way up
To the rafters where the pigeons moaned,
I later thought, as if in sexual complaint,
Or sexual abandon; I never found out which.
When I walked in with a 12 gauge & started shooting,
They fell, like gray fruit, at my feet—
Fat, thumping things that grew quieter
When their eyelids, a softer gray, closed,
Part of the way, at least,
And their friends or lovers flew out a kind of sky light
Cut for loading hay.
I don't know, exactly, what happened then.
Except my sister moved to Switzerland.
My brother got a job
With Colgate-Palmolive.
He was selling soap in Lodi, California.
Later, in his car, & dressed
To die, or live again, forever,
I drove to my first wedding.
I smelled the stale boutonniere in my lapel,
A deceased young flower.
I wondered how my brother's Buick
Could go so fast, &,
Still questioning, or catching, a last time,
An old chill from childhood,
I thought: why me, why her, & knew it wouldn't last.

Two Variations on a Theme by Kobayashi

The year I returned to my village, the papers
And the mail, uncensored, were delivered
Faithfully, each day.
They treated me with kindness
Where I worked, & the bars, softly lighted,

Opened every night with their music.
Appointed Master of Riddles,
I felt I had stepped onto the dock of the New World,
Toting the old one (a fresh book of poems!)
On my back. Even strangers
Bought me drinks, & someone assured me that
I would be able to get any drug I wanted,
Should I desire drugs.
And when I drove to Arkansas to read
My poems, & saw the Ozarks—
Hills full of shifting mists & a flower
That turned whole meadows white
Against the anxious hint of leaves—& when
Some of my audience walked out because I read a poem
With two obscene words, I was delighted!
For in the North, obscenities are quaint.
That year, I taught one child how to hear
Hexameters in English, & she
Stopped crying about things she could do
Nothing to change. That year,
Because I play no instrument, I met
Many musicians—they spoke to me, mostly,
Of poetry, & I told them
How, if one doesn't have much time, rhyme
And a strong refrain line ought to
Govern everything—especially if one finds himself
In a republic determined to stay young
At any cost. Something new,
I reminded them, would come, even from their fatigue
After closing. Twice, my son
Came to visit me.
And I showed him two caves in Missouri.
Mark Twain, as a child, had played in one of them.
The cave, our tour guide said, was
Over one hundred million years old. My son
Loved it—even though it is lighted,
Now, throughout, & I kept wishing that the cave
Were darker, or that I was younger.
There was nothing I could do
About either, & the blonde girl
Showing it to us knew all her lines
"by heart." Almost pretty, but she looked as if
Nothing in the world could make her laugh.
She & her children will, I'm sure, inherit this earth.
My son is four, & curious.
That year, I had to explain
My father's death to him, & also
The idea of heaven, & how
One got there, physically, after death. Therefore,

I had to lie for the first time
To my son, & therefore I had to give him up
A little more.
And though my wife & I spoke of reconciliation,
The snows came down with their ancient,
Cruel jokes, & each one
Was just as funny. Just as cruel.
We both felt stronger, after hearing
Them, & I went on
Living in my decaying neighborhood with the finch,
The elm, the spider, & the mouse,
And, if they could speak,
Each one spoke to me of its lowly position,
Its pathetic marriage, its doomed romance, & how
Much it hated the village—
And each one had different problems, different desires!
That year, the moon looked, each dawn,
Like a jilted suitor, a boy with an ashen face,
Sitting alone in the pool hall.
My neighbors & the townspeople avoided me,
But with the respect or courtesy
One shows for something
Misunderstood, passing, perhaps dangerous
To the education of their children—
But still a fact, like the woods sloping down
Behind an abandoned row of houses
Condemned by the new highway commissioner: bird calls,
The gray smoke of a tramp's fire,
A place where the fox we surprised, once, moved
Too quickly for human description,
And too quietly.

                              °

                                    ". . . No.
That year, I wore black,
And a headband flecked with crimson & meant
To terrify anyone in a gang of youths
I met, often, on the road. That year, because
Of the taxes required by the Shogunite, no one
Had any money, & often
I would pause, wondering how those who truly
Had something to complain of could
Bear it any longer—
Those who were poor & with sick children, whose father
Pawned heirlooms meant to last a thousand years—
The cold wind swirling through each split
Matting of rushes meant to hold
Their house together,

Their frail argument against the wind,
Their kneeling to pray in a season
Of high fever.
I do not wish to exhibit a feeling which some,
Perhaps out of political ambition
Or simple indifference,
Might consider too generous & boastful.
Many of us thought the same things,
Many of us, in our youth, had known
Such people, & have indeed wondered where
They have gone.
Towed up the river to some new town,
We would look back at them as they
Waved to us from the pier.
We thought we would live forever, then;
We did not know that we were lights dancing
On black water. Soon,
We stopped writing them long letters, although
Once, we would have said
such letters continued to be written, always,
In our hearts. But it is
No longer fashionable to say such things, the way
We once said them, before we found out
About style, & how completely
It explains us to each other.
It is as if, without knowing it, we all
Suddenly longed to be diminished: lights going out
Along a river, & a whole
Town abandoned! But sometimes,
I still think of that great dead lord,
Whom I defended, &
For whom I would slit an enemy open, from
Forehead to abdomen, when he at last
Displayed that hint of hesitation
In the body, by which
One recognizes a liar. I moved, using one stroke;
No second thoughts.
It would have been the same for him
If I had discovered, in a sudden weightlessness
In my shoulders, a laughter throughout my whole body,
The same lie in myself.

                    "I know
There are those who think we are thieves
Interested only in profit.
I prefer to believe, with my old master,
That there are men & women in this world
For whom I would willingly give my life, &
That we, who studied in such schools,

Are the last to know
How to move gracefully
In those exact measures meant to correct
Time, which knows
Nothing of itself, nothing
Of the damage it can do,
And which it is condemned to do:
My wife is dead.
My daughter is beautiful;
The first snow has just fallen & if I am older
It is because I have looked out & noticed it;
It is because
It has tricked me into this final maneuver,
This turning toward a white window,
Something my master always told me it would do, &
Against which all swords are useless!"

LISA LEWIS ■ ■ ■ ■ ■ ■ ■ ■ ■ ■ ■ ■ ■ ■ ■ ■ ■ ■ ■

February

This is the second month of the year I turn thirty-seven.
Already the weather is warming in southeast Texas, rushing
The weeks along; the trees have to work to keep up. One day
I'll look over my head and the elm will be leafed out,
And then it will be summer. Probably I'll be working
On my birthday, probably teaching a couple of classes,
And I'll say to myself, it's just as well, who needs to think about
Turning thirty-seven, and I'll go back to my regular life,
Smiling and talking to students in the hallway,
Breaking a sweat on the short walk from the door
To the parked car, rolling all the windows down
But not without glancing at the sky for stormclouds,
Because a storm will be breaking every day then after noon,
Lasting about an hour, and subsiding back to sun. You learn
Such things about the weather when you've lived in a place
For a while. Or maybe it's really what some people say,
It's like that everywhere; I haven't been anywhere near
Everywhere, and maybe I'll never make it.
But there were years when I liked to search out danger,
Late nights I learned each secret worn-out cars
Bouncing through the ruts of logging roads could take me to.
I learned about love like that; the full moon pierced
The windshield like a spike and I knew it was love
When the strong, agile boy above me sighed

And pushed deeper inside me. I knew it was love
When I didn't want to close my eyes. I learned about trouble
And I knew it was trouble when I dropped out of high school
My senior year and took to prowling the roads with boys;
We took to shooting heroin under the spring sky,
We'd lie back together in the roadside grass and all let go
Of our suffering, we were having a hard time growing up,
It felt good to do a terrible thing together.
No one could find us there. No one was looking.
We would've counted the stars, but that was work.
Instead we talked about loving one another, and I guess
You'd say it was the heroin talking, but we thought we felt it,
We were free together, we knew how we were when no one
Could know us because we were doing evil. I took myself
Far from those foothills the first chance I could.
I didn't find out what became of my friends, it looked like
Some of them were headed for prison; I loved them once
But I wouldn't love them now, and I didn't want to
Think about mixing love and trouble, the trick I learned
And never gave up; I just got older, and stopped
Getting into the trouble of the young. I discovered
The troubles of the older.
                              This is the second month
Of the year I turn thirty-seven. Already the little fists
Of leaves are forming inside the knotted ends of twigs
All over Houston. The cold weather is over. This winter
Again there was no freeze. And tonight it's very late,
And it's Sunday, and no cars pass on the big road
By the house, but out there in the night
Some kids about seventeen are doing terrible things
They'll get by with, and grow out of, and remember
The way they'll remember what love felt like at first,
Before it stopped being the surest path to ruination,
Before it had done the worst it could and passed away.
To them it's as if those who lived this life before them
Moved with the jerky speeded-up gestures of characters
In old-fashioned movies, their expressions intense
And exaggerated; they roll their eyes and loll their tongues
When the heroin hits their blood. It's as if the beauty
Of evil lives only in the present, where the drop of dope
Trembling at the tip of the stainless steel point
Catches the light like dew; and it doesn't matter
That the light falls from a streetlamp with a short in it,
And the impatient boy with the syringe in his hand
Will touch the drop back into the spoon
So as not to waste it. It's his instinct telling him
How much it means to live this now, before he knows
Better, while he still has a chance to survive it.

It's the moon over his head with its polished horns
That would slip through his skin if he touched them.
It's the trees leaping to life in his blood, greenness
Unfurling so hard it almost bursts his heart.

Responsibility

It did no good to think, or to stop thinking. It did no good
To think in a straight line, a starburst, or a circle.
It did no good to think driving down the highway,
Or walking alone in a park with live alligators.
It was no use thinking what had happened, or what
Was going to happen. If there'd been one image
She could've dreamed to make the thoughts move over,
She would've bowed to its significance: a fallen barn
Against empty sky. Sidewalks strewn with clippings
In a suburban neighborhood where the residents walk
After the sun goes down. The silhouette of a man
Straightening his tie. But it did no good to speak,
Or to stop speaking. It did no good to look, or to stop looking.
Her eyes closed when she felt sleepy, and when she woke
Nothing was different. Her eyes opened when light
Shone through the window; the light was different
From the light that stayed on in the hall at night,
But nothing else was different. If the air was cool,
That was the extent of it. If the air was close and warm,
That was the extent of it. She looked at her feet that paced
The wood floor for hours, getting nowhere. She looked
At the shape of her calves, thinner, harder, from walking.
She looked at her knees, disappointing knees under
A layer of skin that just got thicker. She saw she had
The legs of an animal; she saw she had the hands
Of an animal. She looked in the mirror and saw she had
The snout of an animal, two holes to breathe through.
That was something to think about; but the trouble
With thinking was it didn't go anywhere, there was
A shape inside her head like a loaf of bread,
Pressing so things went blurry. Then she thought
It must be time she was looking at, that's why
She couldn't see at a distance; she took out her pencil
And made a list of questions. Her animal hand
Scratched marks on paper her animal eyes couldn't read.
Her animal eyes closed in the darkness, she had worked
Hard without thinking about it, and nothing
Was different. There was nothing to do but wait
For time to catch up. It was going to be a long wait,

What with the moon passing through its phases,
People dying without saying goodbye, decisions made
Without asking permission, and the body still
Just the shell that keeps something alive inside.
If she hadn't waited so long already, she might've learned
To stop thinking about it, but she was in a hurry,
No one else holding, as she did, the hands of time.
It was as if she'd offered to sit by the sickbed of a loved one,
But the illness was long and debilitating, and the mind
Went first; and when the patient died, she wasn't free
To go, but had to remain by the decomposing body.
It was just an idea she had, to sit by the body; but no one
Was there to release her from her duty, and no one
Could've convinced her that wasn't her proper place.

LAURENCE LIEBERMAN ▪ ▪ ▪ ▪ ▪ ▪ ▪ ▪ ▪ ▪ ▪ ▪

The Organist's Black Carnation

Odd music,
cutting through horn blasts and squawks of traffic, asserts
                    its live and public wash
        of sound rolling in waves across the town square. . . . Christ Church
            Cathedral. Once in the Church rear courtyard, we find
        we can disencumber the river of organ song from percussive
            street blare—
        its source, the deep hall within tall double doors,
                unbolted. Mother
                        and I, goose-stepping
        on circular, wide ceramic tiles of the walkway, traverse
            the Church
        gardens, and pass through the side entrance. The instrument,
            itself, so near the door, we almost collide
        with the seated performer, his arms and legs all pumping
                together, the four limbs
utterly weightless, his moves between upper and lower keyboards
effortless, unwilled.

as buoyed up
by a hidden well of pure feeling as his side-to-side runs
                across any one keyboard.
        Tall. Blond. Bearded. American. Stops to turn pages. Smiles
            Hello. *Any music you prefer,* he asks? *Oh yes,*
        any Bach. Bach Preludes unfold, at once—the music open
                before him.

But he could be playing from memory. Or sightreading.
    A little of each,
                      I'd guess, never up close
to an organist expert before, I gasp at agilities
    of legwork,
the sheer quantity of wooden pedals, joined in a concave arc
    recessed below his legs, his knees spreading wide,
wider, as he reaches for the pedals at either far end—
        there are so many
moving parts, keys and pedals above and below, I can see, at last,
why organ solo

music I've heard
can sound like a whole orchestra of virtuosos. How lightly
        he taps the keys, oceans
of rich basses circulating around the whole chapel, cloister,
    and outer chambers—the tall pipes widely distributed
throughout the walls, as if the entire church is the vehicle
        and body
of the instrument, the keyboards and pedal valves
        a mere touch control
                  relay . . . Organ melody
outside the church, diffused, half-muffled by traffic,
    is carried
afar, and, for moments, rushes close to the distant listener's
    ears; but withindoors, the whole church interior
is charged with the music's amplified wave pulsings, notes
        that seem to pass beyond
all time limits, as in Bruckner's symphonies. It's all a breathing,
influx and efflux

of lungs shaped
like tall pipes, the wide oval pipe tops releasing blent voices,
        four voice octaves rolled
into the one chorale. . . . He chats with us now as he plays, simpler
    passages he *must* know from memory. Keeps turning pages,
though. No mistakes. His movements all dancelike. I look and look,
    scrutinize
his hands, the faraway pipes, for clues to the miracle
    of lightness of touch—
                so feathery his patter
of the keys. Now the church walls seem to shudder,
    the pipe mouths
recoiling upon the seeming pantomime of his performance,
    a magic dumbshow of silently flicking the keys
with velvet-soft fingertips. And there is no way I can fathom
    the hairlinefine exchanges
between his ten fingers' prowl of three keyboards and those distant
tall pipe-groanings,

pipe-wailings. . . .
We'll embark, today, on our mother-son, off-the-beaten-path
        Island treks. So we attend
    to his genial warnings. The bars are all dangerous. But back
      in the ghettoes—*we call it Over the Hill*—the risk
of muggings, or worse, is critical. In broad day light. Chamber-
    of-Commerce
    won't hear of it, but, night or day, no hill or backwoods
        sector is safe! Then,
                      why has *he* stayed on
    these six months, braced for still another six, grit
      and pluck
stamped on the cast of his jaw, his tall slender profile,
    orange-freckled face, neck and arm. Now he stands,
    for a moment, flashing his smile in the lit column of dust motes
        whirling in a pool of sun
that pours through the skylight. He signals the three black nuns
in the chapel doorway

to step back!
So doing, their twenty-odd local charges (boys and girls
        in equal numbers: ages
    five to nine, say) come racing to the organ bench. He resumes,
      playing his own transcriptions of nursery songs,
Christmas carols, a few native Island hymns—the children singing
      out of tune,
    getting the words wrong, no two in sync, but all
        finding another home
                    to inhabit in the piped
    lullabies and jingles. Two forward children squat
      on the floor
near his feet, staying just clear of those pumping knees,
    intrigued by his undulations—the split second
reflexes of his feet floating over the pedals. A round-faced
      petite girl clambers
upon the organ cabinet, and sits, cross-legged, alongside
keyboards, memorizing

taps of his keys
beneath her legs. Two boys squeeze next to him, on opposite
        ends of the bench; while many
    form a ring around his seat, arms on each other's shoulders.
      He sings with them, not to lead the tunes, but more
    to tag along. The churchwomen scowl, from time to time—threaten
      to send away
    the few least controlled kids, but he calms them all
      with his *Hush, now!* (finger
                    to his lips). The children,
asway, appear to dance from the hips, their legs bobbing

in place. . . . *I*
see two dozen blackbirds, or ravens, perched on his shoulders,
   his balding scalp, weightless, hopping on jointed-twig
legs across his redhaired curly forearms, alighting on his knees,
      his wrists. And one blackbird
lands on the tip of his nose, both perfectly still. Now it's
a black butterfly.

Those soft wings,
flapping, turn to petals of a black carnation, which fall
            to his shirt lapel. . . . I waken
   from a standup daydream, a bird romance, the blond organist
      still playing singalong tunes—the kids humming offkey,
   while they follow their holy guides, public maidservants (in God)
         to the school
      van parked in the rear, their short midday recess
            come to a close. . . . He fears
                     he's losing his touch
      at the organ knows he may well fail his instrumental
         M.A. exam
   when he sails back home to Seattle it's been such a hot summer
      can't practise when he perspires so much for weeks
   he's been soaking in his own stale body foetors. . . . No less
            absorbed in his Bach scores,
for carrying on two conversations with mother, with me—he blossoms
musical feast for us. . . .

The Architect Monk

      The whole nation, some seven hundred scattered
      dots and free form
      mobile cutouts of land, strewn over
   a six-hundred-mile
   wide arc

         of Caribbean Sea. . . . In these flat isles, we
      are impressed by low
      heights: a hillock titled *Mountain,*
      the tall white water
      tower

         of Nassau a local skyscraper. The monk,
      stricken with a mild
      rage for altitude, chose Cat Island's
      Como Hill—two hundred
      fifty feet

at the peak—for his first monastery:
himself sole architect
and builder, the job of ten years'
fitting board on board,
aided

    by primitive tools only. And basic manual
homecrafts . . . The last nail
struck, the last bucket of mortar
emptied, its contents
hardened

    between the misshapen loaves of rough stone
he'd chiseled and cut
from the sandstone steep butte flanking
the cliff's west rim. Yes,
ten years'

    disavowal of speech, no word spoken
but in chaste society
of shore birds, led him to rescind aiders—
he the lone quarry
gouger,

    he the stone mason, stained-glass-smith, steel
smelter, roof shingler.
He propped the roof's welded zinc A-frame
on a colossal sawhorse
apparatus. . . .

    His first hermitage overtops any lighthouse
or high watchtower
in the sickle-curved sweep of isles. Today
a migrant contractor
of chapels.

    tabernacles, bell towers, and mission
quarters, he lays
biennial cornerstones, and erects
a colony of two dozen
churches

    on sites rotated over five islands, the last
St. Augustine's Monastery
in Nassau, capped with a science lab
and planetarium's mosquelike
bubble dome. . . .

FRANK LIMA ■ ■ ■ ■ ■ ■ ■ ■ ■ ■ ■ ■ ■ ■ ■ ■ ■ ■

Cuauhtemoc

This knife is as long as my wife in the pool
and I am as dark as the sun
The silence from the moon is as dark when we sleep

I always bring my captives here
and let the grapevines choke them

The stars will crash and last for years
I grin at them and give them fruit
I am an expert at my job
I am their home

I spend the morning writing letters
while the machines crush the priest
I remember their flat runways
when they stripped for weddings

It was the death of all the warriors
and their enemies
When the wind screamed around their feet
I would listen to my knife

It was the time to pull their hearts out
and give them to the children

I have given them the wings to heaven
and they are my last legend
frozen like the hands of a small monkey

We call their last sounds the wind
This sound brings us childhood
as if it were life
These are the days of our calendar

Our children pray to them
and play with their hearts with sticks
We pray to the children and their sticks
and it rains for hours on the crops

Lightning makes the trees smell like my knife
As long as the heart is quiet we are waterproof

I am the king of the shade in the green jungle
The people hurry to see my accidents

The mothers among them hold their children
up to me as *ixiptlas*
Their small bones make very little noises
and their small eyes will become
beans for Texcatlipoca

They exchange gifts
Some of them have not seen
each other since the last rain.

Year's End

I

When I pause, anemones fall on the month of December.
And I am foolish enough to answer the phone, like a drop
of water sliding across a linen tablecloth, falling
on the lap of a lover. I have,
in my hand, the channel of sovereign energy, the quiet
continent that hardens into soil. A fine Minnesota rain
falls on the swans that have given their wet bread to
the enemy in the pool. What shall I bring tomorrow?

II

Nature's caricatures have left us the tender sounds
of a throat in mourning for the throbbing of the Earth.
So we ascend through our afflictions to catch a fleeing
thought, the loveliest of the airs between us. A hand is lost
in the Oblivion. How many thoughts does it take to make
a century? Life, with all its evenings,
religiously returns each morning like
a mountain opening up within the heart.

III

I suspect when I pause on the month of December anemones fall.
Dear sacred heart, each Friday I crawl away from your soft
leather orchid that shatters my soul with its dark
shudders of moonlight.

The Hand

The hand is all heart. It hops around like a toad to prove its
dexterity. It presses your pockets on cold winter days and,
in its profound state, polishes an apple for you. Silently

it waits in the subways when it rains and is more of a hand
than ever. It emerges from your humid coat, like a swollen
hyena with its rancorous juices, to offer the young lady next
to you a flat heart. Of course you get a slap and someone's
boring hand dials the police, who arrive with fat hand . . .
　　The hand requires few words. It howls, repels odors
and keeps the body of its lover from becoming slippery. A
drop of water splashes in the crater of its palm, Merlin's pure
lapis in the middle of the night. The lover's hand imagines itself a lover
in the flabbiness of a perspiring torso, rolling
in the wash of sighs. Armless, the hand spanks and slides around
the mass of the sexual object with giant fingers that
appear like rubber slugs in the moonlight.

JOHN LOGAN ▪ ▪ ▪ ▪ ▪ ▪ ▪ ▪ ▪ ▪ ▪ ▪ ▪ ▪ ▪ ▪ ▪ ▪

Poem: Tears, Spray and Steam

I

Peering stung,
　　　　　bleared,
　　　　　　　　hung-
over and lame
I feel somewhat
　　　　　panicky,
weird, about my sweat-
　　　　　　　　ing body.
For where do we and our vapors end?
Where does the bath begin?

Strange to be able to see through the steam
(but satisfying to the point of calm,
like the vision of the perfect, new born)
for the first time
the whole,
　　　　　beautiful body of a friend.
Like a god
　　　　　damned eternal thief
of heat,
　　　clouds
wreathing round
your black, bearded head,
belly, limbs and your sex
(but no piercing eagle about,
yet)

you lie flat on your back
on the rock
        ledge bench in the bath,
Promethean in your black
           wrath.

II

In our nun's or monk's
           black
rubber hoods
(lace-paper coifs
          just visible at the tops
of our heads),
as if about to pray,
and black rubber coats
           to our feet
because of the spray,
we walk the Niagara Tunnel.
You can tell
        almost for sure
which ones the kids are,
but you can't tell men from women here.
Unsexed in these catacombs we watch
for the asperges of the bath.
The damp walls bleed rice.
All dark, all si-
        lent, we all pass.
We bow, each to each,
and some,
        not only the young
give the ancient kiss of peace,
standing in the alcoves again.
We reach for rain.
The Fall's spray touches each of us.
The glass
      over our eyes
          weeps.
Cheeks are wet. Lips.
Even our teeth if our mouths gape.
We are caress-
        ed with wetness
all about our cloaks,
and we sway
        and float
broken out in a dark sweat,
complex, prodigious:
female, white, male, black, lay religious.
At last we all

peer out the stone holes
at the back of the falls
and see nothing but The Existential Wall:
water roaring out of the hidden hills.
Power passes us, detached, abstract,
except for this cold steam
that licks and teases
                    until at last
we turn our drenched, glistening backs.

III

Aging, still
          agile
poet Eric Barker,
who has been coming
(I almost said springing)
back here
          for many years.
and I and two friends
strip at the still springs
with their
          full smell of sulphur—
here where bodies and warm water
are moon- and candle-lit, wind woven,
in a shallow cavern
                    open
to the heaving iridescent sea
near Big Sur,
and we invade the great,
                    Roman bath
intimidat-
ing the Esalen teacher with his small class:
three naked girls in three corners of the big tub—
he, their leader,
                in the other.
The candles waver
as the class takes cover
                    and the mad teacher
leaves with one student to find
a night watchman, leaving behind
the others:
          one of them
already slithers
in a smaller tub with one of our friends.
The third girl now fully dressed—
and for the moment repress-
ed—stares
          at the rest of us

lolling and floating our masculine flowers
as we give a naked reading of William Butler
Yeats to each other
                              (taking care not
to get the book wet)
and then we read to her
as she begins to listen.
                              So she too strips and
slips into the fourth corner,
becomes for a moment our teacher.
Her breasts come alive in the water.
Yeats will wait,
and Keats—for Barker, with whom
we have been drinking wine
all afternoon
                    knows
                              all the Odes
by heart as well as many
                                        bawdy songs:
"My long
          delayed erection,"
he'd laughed, sighing, "rises in the wrong direction."
But he too is silent
for the while, and
                              sits stately,
buoyed by the water: its movement
makes his white,
body hair seem to sprout.
Soon,
          we begin
                    to say the poems again
and to touch each other—
                              the older
man, me,
the boys and the girls read-
ing over the sea's
sounds
          by the candles'
light and the moon bright, burgeoning,
shin-
          ing time to time
                              as
the clouds pass.
                    In this quietly flash-
ing light then
we all leave the tubs and run
dripping down the shore
together, before
                    any others come—

as hostile teacher, watchman.
But in that warm spring
water we briefly left everything
                              eventually heals:
for, by
        the sea
it flows out of these ancient, California hills,
which are the trans-
                formed,
giant body of a once
powerful bone, feather and torquoise adorned
Indian Prince,
                  and the sulphur is the changed
sharp incense
                he burned daily as he chanted
year and year over for the sick young princess—
who took her loveliness
from the many-colored, fragrant trees
and the flickering sea.
Finally, unable to help,
                    he thought,

the beautiful prince died of his grief,
and his body became this mount-
ain. And everybody here who comes together
                                    in belief
is somehow bound, bathed
                        and made
whole, e-
        ven as was she
by this gradual, glinting water,
the prince's continual tears for his sister.

So, when we return a little later
from our dance along the
                        open shore
we find the Esalen
                teacher there again,
and the watchman,
each with a woman.
They wait
        in that gentle, lunatic light for us.
They smile as they undress.
Eric Barker takes a leak,
begins reciting Keats
and, in the new waters of brother, sister,
we all bathe and sing together.

ROBERT LOWELL ■ ■ ■ ■ ■ ■ ■ ■ ■ ■ ■ ■ ■ ■ ■

Shifting Colors

I fish until the clouds turn blue,
weary of self-torture, ready to paint
lilacs or confuse a thousand leaves,
as landscapists must.

My eye returns to my double,
an ageless big white horse,
slightly discolored by dirt,
cropping the high green shelf diagonal
to the artificial troutpond—
unmoving, it shifts as I move,
and works the whole ridge in the course of a day.

Poor, measured, neurotic man,
animals are more instinctive virtuosi.

Ducks splash deceptively like fish;
fish break water with the wings of a bird to escape.

A hissing goose sways in stationary anger;
purple bluebells rise in ledges on the lake.
A single cuckoo gifted with a pregnant word
shifts like the sun from wood to wood.

All day my miscast troutfly buzzes about my ears
to empty my mind . . .

But nature is sundrunk with sex—
how could a man fail to notice, man
the only pornographer among the animals?
I seek coolness unimpassioned by my body,
I am too weak to strain to remember, or give
recollection the eye of a microscope. I see
horse, meadow, duck and pond,
universal, consolatory
description without significance,
transcribed verbatim by my eye.

This is not a directness that catches
everything on the run and then expires—
I would write only in response to the gods,
like Mallarme who had the good fortune
to find a style that made writing impossible.

The Wordsworths: William and Dorothy

The "New Sensibility" or not
the master and his servant sister
surely knew some guilt for the blot
of sex on their long history.

A bowl of milk, a mutton chop, some bread
and the blazing days at Dove Cottage.
Coleridge: "I wish, I wish I were dead,"
a slob, a slave, in fast dotage

from opium. These were ecstatics,
more on mountains than on lakes,
who walked and talked all day, frantic
for music, a life in which the stakes

were high: to make it matter more,
the song, to make it matter most.

Thrombosis Trombone

In a major vein shooting blood
to the brain a trombone goes off,
its slide hammering the arterial wall
over and over. Nobody—not the bandleader
with his pointy stick, not
a star-stricken audience—calls
for the trombonist to stand
and take his solo
but once he does
and then sits down again: organic dementia,
maybe aphasia, and you talk to God,
who talks right back,
or, you talk to somebody named Dorothy
whom you implore repeatedly
to make a cheese sandwich, please. Not much
will be the same again
after the furniture in the brain
is rearranged: the wrong doily
under the umbrella, the candelabra
in the stove. What goes on inside
the body is a wonder, Allah,
is a wonder. We who are about to live
tip our sheep to you.

The Creature Has a Purpose

The hard hook-finger clutching down to the bottom
of the belly, all
nerve-roots awash, aswirl
with *want this, want this and this*
over and over against the wharf's eaten pillars.
Tides of this . . . this fearful *need*, avalanches

of it, typhoons, tsunami followed by tsunami
dogged. What is it beats the engine,
rips with a thong the donkey's flank raw,
what lament-drenched struggle
so hard in comparison diamond is cream?
To what end, purpose, to serve

what obsession the kindergarten
teacher moonlighting as gravedigger, the heiress
taking in laundry, the priest
wearing beneath his vestments satanic tattoos?
What is it drives it? Sex? *Love me, love me*
over and over, that? Or money,

just money—*give me that, if I have
this I*. . . . Is it money,
is that why the soul reaches out with pincers
after what is outside the soul?
What is it, how to make it palpable?
Is it the old thing, the cave man thing,

maybe even the monkey thing: fear
of nothingness which even the philosophers
cannot make go away: *don't die, don't
die?* What creates the purpose,
what fuel, what fire lights the lantern
in the skull?

A Little Tooth

Your baby grows a tooth, then two,
and four, and five, then she wants some meat
directly from the bone. It's all

over: she'll learn some words, she'll fall
in love with cretins, dolts, a sweet
talker on his way to jail. And you,

your wife, get old, flyblown, and rue
nothing. You did, you loved, your feet
are sore. It's dusk. Your daughter's tall.

Commercial Leech Farming Today

for Bob Sacherman

Although it never rivaled wheat, soybean,
cattle and so on farming
there was a living
in leeches
and after a period of decline
there is again
a living to be made
from this endeavor: they're used to reduce
the blood in tissues
after plastic surgery—eyelifts, tucks,
wrinkle read, or in certain
micro-surgeries—reattaching a finger, penis.
I love the capitalist
spirit. As in most businesses
the technology has improved: instead
of driving an elderly horse
into a leech pond, letting him die
by exsanguination,
and hauling him out
to pick the bloated blossoms
from his hide, it's now done at Biopharm
(the showcase operation in Swansea,
Wales)—temp control, tanks, aerator
pumps, several species,
each for a specific job. Once, 19th century,
they were applied to the temple
as a treatment for mental
illness. Today we know
their exact chemistry: *hirudin,*
a blood thinner in their saliva,
also an anesthesia
and dilators for the wound area.
Don't you love
the image: the Dr. lays a leech along
the tiny stitches of an eyelift.
Where they go after their work is done
I don't know
but I've heard no complaints
from Animal Rights
so perhaps they're retired
to a lake or adopted
as pets, maybe the best looking
kept to breed. I don't know. I like the story,
I like the going backwards
to ignorance
to come forward to vanity. I like

the small role they can play
in beauty
or the reattachment of a part,
I like the story because it's true.

CLARENCE MAJOR ▪ ▪ ▪ ▪ ▪ ▪ ▪ ▪ ▪ ▪ ▪ ▪ ▪ ▪ ▪

Funeral

American Airlines to Chicago.
Mae is here grinning,
the same cheeks I grew up
touching. And her cool,
beautiful movements. The
moving staircase and,
"Man, whata you got
in that bag?"

And Nebraska and Missouri.

Maybe next we will go
to Topeka and down
to Mexicali and San Diego.

But my stepfather dies.
And they have his face
propped up. Powdered, he is
neatly tucked in a suit.
There is this quiet
hysterical laughter
we all share.

Later, the young folks
from everywhere, Kentucky,
Tennessee, South Carolina,
Virginia, gather
in the front
and the old folks,

from Mississippi, North
Carolina, Oklahoma, Arkansas,
sip hard liquor
in the kitchen. My mother

has fried chicken & mashed potatoes
spread out. And a dude

is talking about Wichita Falls
last summer some fifty year
old white chick who fell in
love with him. Daddy, daddy

Now the next morning here we are
in Alabama watching the dead
one go down into the earth . . .
so smoothly with artificial words
near a bright, sunlit national park.
And the same light on us
as we drive back to an address
I cannot remember.

Bruce & Nina

Nina got out
of herself while
Bruce unsnapped
the things holding her.

And himself.

But nothing really
helps for long. You
have to keep
making the world

new, and interesting.
Some go crazy over
large things. Others
simply wait a minute

and do it again. And
again. Bruce now stands
waiting for Nina
to change his life, where

there is nothing
to work with, but ideas

Little Girls Posing All Dressed Up

They saw their mamas put one foot out
like that. Twist it a little to the right.
If you stand to the right. Models too do it.

One is the spitting image of Chris. I also see
Banana face, with her lovely hair wild
everywhere. Hands on hips, Ribbons, Shoes with
buckles, straps. Way back when. Eyes so sure,
so fixed so firm the slight tilt of the grownup
head, get to these little sureshots. Blue & red
shoestrings and yellow dresses and pink dresses.
They all stand outside a dirty city building
advertising an employment agency. Saying
"Colored help." They see their dance teacher
put her foot out like this, if you wanna be
a model. Or if you want to grow up
and get a husband & a baby & a little white house
with a green fence around it.

The Jefferson Company

No need to go
there, spying on the place.
He sees it
in your face.
You two hands.

Brentwood
and Oakville.
The Black section too.
Where your best ambitious friend
from high school
days turns into a beer belly
and a TVset.

The Jefferson Company?

Walk Cass Avenue as it runs
to the Mississippi. That time
you let him beat you
across MacArthur Bridge?

Remember highway 70.
And the lady
with the shoppingbag
full of guts?

I smell ragweed now.
Near the railroad tracks?

Here, feel my muscles.
They are bigger
than yours. Hillside

and Pine Lawn. No need
to remember the names.

The feeling holds
together with no touch.

And his quick mind
makes itself up inside
your own slow fingers.

All the Same

It is not as though you come
from the Broken Hill
in Australia or
the Coral Sea or even the New
Caledonia Island.

We come from the same place:
where birds are baptized and
streetfights are common. A

bucket of blood in every block.
A big buck the rarest thing
in the world. Remember

our sand hills and our Okefenokee
and the Macon fatback & sundays
and sunlight. We fought

our love in the reddirt and
on the pavement of different streets.
But never really saw
each other.

Yet grew up crowded together,
eating, sleeping the same West
Virginia dreams. Getting turned
back the same way. Moving
ahead in different paths. Ways
all the same I stopped

at Greensboro and you continued
on to the Great Basin out West.

The luck came first to you
and caught me, bitter, on 12th Street

in Rockford anyway always meant
to thank you for that warm,
timely letter
that time from Grand Rapids.

I needed that. Need it
again now. By the way,
next time you get a minute:
stop by. I'll introduce you
to the local ordained pimp. Have
mama roast a bird. Show you
my boot collection.

S. J. MARKS ▪ ▪ ▪ ▪ ▪ ▪ ▪ ▪ ▪ ▪ ▪ ▪ ▪ ▪ ▪ ▪ ▪ ▪

Poem in Three Parts

1.

Snow sweeps through February,
lacy flakes swarm against the window,
grasses poke through the crust.
Snow blows over the whole field.
February knows so many
stories of human sadness.

2.

Parts of my childhood are like a dream.
I went around crying,
mimicking the sorrow of the grown-ups.
"Will I ever see you again?"
"To know you breathe the same air as I do."

The treetrunks and bare branches against
the darkening violet evening sky
tell me what I want to know.

Today, at lunch with Francine,
she said something about being between people—
maybe her mother and father,
after her car accident shattered her nose and skull—
something I wanted to remember but can't,
so sad,
but I can't remember what it was.

3.

Where you are worth nothing, you should want nothing.

Nothing is more real than nothing.

The trees, changing color,
seem to be changing their very nature,
a series of selves that will die and be replaced,
that reach far back in their lives
washed by time.

Not being aware of yourself is the strangeness of strangeness—
it has touched you, it has made you all its own.

Often our fears can't be told
though we can only fully digest them long afterwards.

The only basis of form,
Beckett once said, he saw in his work
was the ceaseless screaming
of a man he heard in a hospital,
dying of throat cancer.
Feeling and flesh are pain,
and so, of course, is the mind—
one withdraws into oneself in one's loneliness
echoing with guilts, memories,
regrets, fears, protests, fixations.
One perseveres despite pointlessness—
one slogs on,
you know it's there but you don't care.

Dusk is falling
on this last day of my life.

To Go Through Life Is to Walk Across a Field

How delicious to walk into the stillness—
the mist surrounds us, we sink into the tall wild grasses,
the meadows blur in the heat,
the edge of the sky's purple.

You're dozing—you're not asleep, but dreaming
you long for sleep.

Gulph Creek cuts through the valley.
I'd like to know
what will happen in the rest of my life.

I remember the people in Chekhov's plays saying goodby,
"We shall never see each other again," or
"I'll never see you again."

The wind's everywhere—
in the trees, in the rain, in the house, in this poem,
in death, everywhere.

In the evening light
the maple tree glows red.
I feel the warmth of your hands.

The birches, the street, our faces lit
by a car's headlights.

Home now,
raining, the sound of
water running down the drainpipe
heard
in this room.

I came to see you because I know
suffering warms the coldness of life.

Poem With Two Seasons Right Now

What there is of it,
this heartache continues.

I go out and play racquetball—
smashing the small blue viciously hard regulation racquetball
with fanatical cuts and drives and slams,
beating and slashing at it in hatred for the blind strength of the wall itself.
Sweating it out.

Nothing fills the spaces.

It is like this—
this autumn when the grass
has a thick silken green.
I go through life
as life seems to want me to.

When the wind stops
I don't notice the great quiet
that comes over the field.
What I hear and see is a young woman patient,

anguished and despairing over her life and the murder
of her cousin—
the number 1 ranked welterweight in the world—
say, "Nobody promises you tomorrow."

And now this—
you dream while frozen lilac twigs
clap at your storm windows.
You have been left here holding someone
when there is no one anymore to hold.

Returning in Wind and Drizzle to My Home

Sea-wind and fog hover over the river's waves,
the evening's mist,
green hills suddenly disappear, fugitive.

A universe glitters, pure as crystals of ice.
Beneath the river sky an Indian fisherman
in a short brown hunting jacket looks like a porcupine,
his boat a waterfowl. Fish
burrowing deep in winter mud escape his fishing hooks,
a few gilled in his nets. As he walks home,
branches along the trail bend and break, nothing to prop them up.
He knocks at a gate in the night, hears frogs croak.
Bridge into the reservation, boats tied up, no travelers in sight.

I want salmon roasted over a glowing fire.

Lying awake here, once again I'm a wanderer,
ashamed of myself, I look at this photograph—
"Returning in wind and drizzle to my home."

November Woods

for Masao Abe

Gray sky, mist, the trees black and wet,
branches dripping rain,
soggy ground and oak leaves squish under my feet.

A day of unknowing, of knowing I do not know,
a day of uncertainty,
the day of my life.

Somehow,
I breathe easier here—
in the cool damp air.

I move through the woods,
moving slowly through the drizzle,
stepping carefully on the spongy wet leaf mold on the forest floor,
rain spattering the trees and fallen leaves
deadens the sound of my footsteps.

We can change what yesterday did to us.
After watching my mother being operated on for adrenal cancer,
and, sitting with and talking to my just-born daughter
who I know will die in four hours,
I can hear what is. All of what is. Whatever it is.

I walk to where you're staying,
to your class,
to hear you say these kind thoughtful words,
"You do not know what water is. You might visit the Zen master
and ask him. He may pour the jar of water into a glass and say
by word or gesture, 'Please drink it,' " and, later, in another context,
"He may say, 'When you have none, I will take it away from you.' "

Two things more—
after class, you tell me how you fell on the snow and ice
in New Haven and bruised your shoulder and side; I take leave of you,
and, a few hours later, my shoulder and chest ache so much,
I have to take to bed and sleep. Then, in Washington
on the weekend at the Freer Gallery,
Zou Fulei's plum branch—
spring's like breath,
it goes but must return,
the smoky mist dies out,
the empty room's cold,
this ink branch keeps its shadow on my mind—

Losing Myself

I sit drinking wine and, for a long time, don't notice the dusk.
The delicate sweetness of pink emperor lilies fills my nostrils.
I get up and walk and see again the faces of old friends
as if they were here.
The birds are silent,
you're asleep. No one else is around.
The way through the trees seems never to end.
On the rocks along Gulph Creek
the moss is slippery, rain or no rain.

To the Ocean

I am no longer sure of anything.

Perhaps,
that's what life's about—people leaving you
and you learning how to live again.

You smell sea-weed and iodine. You breathe in the wind.

In a poem, I will explain all you have to do
in order to be happy, and all you must not do.
You must know sadness all the time.
Dreams are difficult to hold onto.

I like to penetrate deeply in new people—their spoken and unspoken meanings,
their secrets, their mysteries, their lies.
To pay with oneself. I can't find the words I want.
I look for others that mean the same thing.

They ache all over. They can't manage to tell
of their experiences. They have nothing left to give.
No words.

My outrageous appetite for living, my apparent hardness.
The sea today stings me.
It is in water that I forget those things I don't like
about myself. The water bears my body and courses off it.
The water conceals my body.

Salt cures my body. Regenerating me,
so as to be able to touch others—the people I love
and cannot do without.

I love others so much that, since I've been napping,
I fall asleep listening to music.

I have enough dead people as it is. Indeed,
even if my suffering is attributable to the living,
I have all these dead people cluttering up my mind.

I don't know how to write accurately
and I feel vulnerable faced with the world as it is.
I ache all over.
One mustn't think with words.
One must let the dead live within one.
It's the only way to help bear separation.

I return to life deprived of everything
I thought it impossible to do without.

We talk. The years sweep away. Your voice
is the same. So is your face. There is
the same understanding between us.

You are always within your own unique absence.

I want to be open—open in the sense
I believe one should say everything.
I believe in words, but I can't often find them.
I believe so much in forms of words
that I'm to suffer my flesh on account of them.

You need to be unable to make sense of things,
of people, in order to be able to discover them ultimately.

I abandon myself to those lips
that have become so welcoming.
I remember the extraordinary tenderness
that overcomes me when I feel guilty.

The taste for water—
words are no longer having an effect,
they can't get through.

I dream of you—you're passionately
touching my hands.
When I wake up, it is my own hands
that are clutched to my heart. I don't feel lonely,
but filled with a great gentleness.

How far will I have to go to understand you?

Here I am again, incapable of describing it.
When I don't know who I am, my language is clear.
It's the part of me that makes you suffer.
I become intrusive. I should leave you alone
to get on with your own sorrow, but I don't.

It's the body that is let go or dropped—a part
of your life has been wrenched away from you.
Very young, I had seen myself as a man in memory only.

The words are coming back. You don't need me any more
and I can't manage to express that pain and turn it into a poem.
I believe these little phrases gathered here and there
will lead me somewhere. It's like writing you a letter that talks of sadness
that might no longer exist when you receive it.

To bring everything back to earth,
to be loved by someone who no longer expects anything of life.

Everything is possible if one comes to terms with oneself.
At fifty, one ends up getting used to what one is.

Your skin is soft.
The agelessness of desire and love. A boy at fifty.
To make my actions more supple, to be free
from the profound timidity which is physical
as well as psychological.

A painting of the sky at twilight—
a dusky rose.
In order to make such colors, one must extrude one's suffering.

Your skin is so soft there—that skin remains
soft until the end of time.
My aim is to be lying next to you.
In your eyes I see all you've refused me at first—
tenderness, anguish.
For me, lips are the vehicle of emotion.
I'd like to tell you something.

The softness is in the manner.
You refuse to explain, to give yourself away.
You leave sentences unfinished, look away, sigh to yourself.
What are you thinking, what do you want,
what are you feeling?

You teach me about myself, you
make me understand things without trying to teach me.
You teach me how to know myself, to use my faults, not to take
myself seriously, to see things in a real way.

The more the years go by the less I know.
If you give explanations and understand everything,
nothing can happen.

What helps me go forward is that I stay receptive,
I feel anything can happen.

I like people to come to me. It's one way I feel loved.
When I go toward people, I feel insecure. I don't want to impose myself.
I don't let myself get eaten by people.

I concentrate on a futile moment, an ordinary exchange,
and let things of greater importance slide by with silence.

I need love, but it's also friendship,
and what you feel for children, and what you do.

It's so much better to desire than to have. The moment
of desire is the most extraordinary moment.
The moment of desire, when you *know* something is going to happen—
it is the time
when you've got the most patience and tenderness
and you know the waiting will be over.

WILLIAM MATTHEWS ▪ ▪ ▪ ▪ ▪ ▪ ▪ ▪ ▪ ▪ ▪ ▪

Good Company

At dinner we discuss marriage.
Three men, three women (one couple
among us), all six of us wary.
"I use it to frighten myself."
Our true subject is loneliness.
We've been divorced 1.5 times
per heart. "The trick the last half
of our lives is to get our work done."
The golfer we saw from the car
this afternoon, his angered
face in bloom with blood, lashed
his strict ball for going where he'd hit it.
We watched him turn from a worse shot
yet and give us a look like our own,
and on we dawdled through
the afternoon toward dinner,
here. Here means the married
couple's house, of course.
The rest of us use so much time
being alone we don't entertain much.
The wind loops and subsides.
"What a fine night to sleep!"
Upstairs a book falls off a shelf.
We'll be sitting here ages hence:
the scent of lawns, good company, Sancerre,
fitful breezes suddenly earnest.
"What sense does marriage make now?
Both people want jobs, the sad
pleasures of travel, and also
want homes. They don't want dark houses
or to live with cats. They have lives
waiting up for them at home.
Take me, I must read half-an-hour
of Horace before I can sleep."

The conversation luffs. The last
bottle of wine was probably too much
but God we're happy here.
"My husband stopped the papers
and flea-bathed the dog
before he left." One of us has a friend
whose analyst died in mid-session,
non-directive to the end.
Now we're drifting off to our nine lives
and more. Melodramatic wind,
bright moon, dishes to do, a last
little puddle of brandy or not,
and the cars amble home:
the door, the stairs, the sheets
aglow with reticence and moonlight,
and the bed full to its blank brim
with the violent poise of dreams.

Unrelenting Flood

Black key. White key. No,
that's wrong. It's all tactile;
it's not the information
of each struck key we love,
but how the mind and leavened
heart travel by information.
Think how blind and near-
blind pianists range along
their keyboards by clambering
over notes a sighted man
would notice to leave out,
by stringing it all on one
longing, the way bee-fingered
blind, mountainous Art
Tatum did, the way we like
joy to arrive: in such
unrelenting flood the only
way we can describe it
is by music or another
beautiful abstraction,
like the ray of sunlight
in a child's drawing
running straight to a pig's ear,
tethering us all to our star.

Descriptive Passages

Your hair is drunk again,
someone explains to me.
And it's not only my hair:
no matter how rack-natty
my clothes were, they're rum-
pled on my body, dressed up
like a child performing
for its parents' guests.
How much of childhood
is spent on tiptoe! Clean up,
wise up, speak up, wake up
and act your age. But also one
is uppity: something's gone
to his head, a bubble
in the bloodstream, a scratch
in the record, a bad habit.

No theory can explain
personality, which expands
to include, if it can, all
its contradictory urges.
It's so hard to think about
this fact that we don't:
we use crude code. The one
with the limp, with big tits,
with the drunk hair. And we love
so much to be loved—
or, failing that, remembered—
that we limp a little, and thrust
out our chests. On me it looks
good, as the hunchback said.

Use description carefully.
For example, today as I
glower out at morning fog
I can feel the fatigue
of matter, how glum a job
endurance is. The gulls
over Lake Union look heavy
and disconsolate, like office life.
Is this all there is, I could ask,
secretly excited
because if it is I've saved
myself so much response
and responsibility.

It's harder than we think
to name our children, but how

can we be accurate?
They'll find stories to live by.
I envision my children
sitting loosely in middle age.
I give them good wine to talk by,
I've lit them a fire if it's cold.
I can't leave them alone, I think
from the grave: a father's work
is never done. One son turns
to the other and says, *You know
how I always think of him?
I remember his drunk hair.*
There's a pause. It's harder
than we think to name
our emotions. *There were those
sentimental poems he wrote
about us, and his drunk hair,*
the other son says, proud
for the intimate talk and sad
for how little such talk says,
though it wasn't drunk that often.

THOMAS McGRATH ■ ■ ■ ■ ■ ■ ■ ■ ■ ■ ■ ■ ■

The Skull of the Horse

On the salt plaza
The ants hold court.
Beyond them,
Like a country of purest marble,
Stretch the lunar provinces.

In the empty eye holes,
The villages of the smallest tribesmen . . .
Their tents made of portable darkness
Their prince the prince of the dead.

Night Meeting

Through different streets that are all alike we walk down toward the docks:
Past the drunks sleeping on the subway gratings, past
The hookers like plastic flowers burnt out by the neon of bars:
Streets that are streaked with cold rain, ice, the filthy snow of cities,
Or steaming in the abyss of dead summer heat dog days stinking August:

By separate streets we descend through this pain and torment:
Past the blocks of burnt-out cars without wheels or motors—childrens'
    playgrounds—
Down past the gutted tenements where the darkness gapes
On open ground-floors clotted with rubble. Furtive movements of rats.
Junkies drunks punks broken-down whores, poor people's pushers
Their night medicine cops pay-offs casual murder
These night-black colonies lined with garbage spiced by excrement
These homes for the homeless where they sleep in peril
Men women and children starving shivering sweating pillowed by stone
Their sleep troubled by rats rape knives by screams
Like sheets ripped from a tin roof by a cyclone cries of hunger sex despair,
The laments of millions encaged in false consciousness
In cells of priestly fraud and patriotic prisons
All the grand night music of the dying culture of money.

So we descend on different streets through the guts of the great misery machine,
The spontaneous sweat-combustion engine of capitalism,
Where the neon tells us, and the poet, in sorrow, irony and anger:
"We are the greatest city, the greatest nation, nothing like us ever was!"
All of which must be changed.

So we descend, till, almost at the bottom, just up from sea level,
We enter the house of an unemployed carpenter
Across from the old waterfront longshoremen's bar *The White Horse.*
One by one we enter sit and wait
Until the last one of us comes in sweating, dripping or freezing
And the organizer says "Ok, comrades; the group is complete. Time to begin."

A Visit to the House of the Poet—Nicaragua, 1987—
Homage to Rubén Darío on His Birthday

1.

Era un aire sauve: the calm and gentle air
Of early morning in little Ciudad Darío—
Which opens the eyes of cocks, roosters (even burros)
In a general serenade to the light now opening the leaves

And the brilliant feathery fans of the Nicaraguan trees:
To carry this grand opera of the morning south: down:
The horny and plumed back of the vast flinty cordillera:
Green backbone of the continent under which Quetzalcoatl sleeps.

This arrogant and militant dawn ignites the fuses of sweet . . .
Flowers: so the whole world seems blazing in subversive colors:

And around the Poet's house the villagers rehearse your natal day.
But I don't believe La Marquesa Eulalie is on this ground:

Though Verlaine may be: lost: in the streets: with the gathering crowd.

2.

In the house of the Poet the floor is of polished earth:
Glossed by many bare feet. And here the Nicaraguan soil
Entered him: from below: and was never wholly lost—
Though his boots polished the polished pavements of the polished cities of the
    world.

Two beds: one of wood and rope: hard: where he dreamed: cold:
Of Roosevelt (Teddy) "hunter . . . invader of our native America."
And a hammock: Marquesa Eulalie: a Parnassian bed:
Verlaine . . . Banville (!) . . . dreams made for warm Parisian sleep . . .

In the northwest corner a stone and earthen stove: where beans
And rice were cooked: as on the brightening street outside:
Now: they cook their beans and rice in front of your tiny
Magnificent house, Poet: in this most powerful place in America:

Where on the beaten, loved, Nicaraguan earth
In *your* yard the children of illiterates now read your poems.

3.

What does fame mean?
                El Pájaro azul?
                        Maybe—
Or maybe not. Fame is food for the novitiate poet:
Without it, though stuffed he starves: it staves off bodily hunger,
And is his soul's caviar, his Host, his spiritual whiskey.

The blue bird does not fill the campesina's wish-pot,
Nor does *les sanglots longue des violins* assuage.
Though Verlaine sang lots of songs, the vile winds at auctions
(Sheriffs' sales) blew peasants' lands into El Jefe's banks.

But your fame belongs to all of us now. No one is thankless—
Though it puts no tiles on roof or patio nor thickens the casings
Of cast-off tires from which crafty artisans fashion our sandals.
You have enlarged us all and lightened our steps on the mountain.

And so, as the lamps come on at the end of your day,
You are part of the light in which the village is haloed:
Here: *el palacio del sol* where once you lived and labored.

Longing

In these days,
When the winds wear no wedding rings,
Everything seems to be going away:
My sweet son filling his sails at a distant college,
My springtime friends on trail to the ultimate West,
And, even in central summer,
I feel the days shortening,
The stealthy lengthening of the night.

And so, in the imperial extension of the dark,
Against which, all my life, I opposed my body,
I long to pass from this anguish of passings
Into the calm of an indifferent joy . . .

To enter October's frail canoe and drift down
Down with the bright leaves among the raucous wildfowl
On the narrowing autumn rivers where, in these longer nights,
Secretly, in the shallows or on reedy shorelines,
Ice is already forming.

Working in Darkness

I think of the ones like the poet John Haines,
During those long years in Alaska,
Working alone in a cold place,
Sitting in darkness outside the pool of light:
Ice-fisherman facing the empty hole of the page,
Patient, the spear poised, waiting for a sign.

And coal miners go out in the cold darkness
In search of fire and light.
In darkness they return to their homes.
The long years go by in the night that is under the earth
But they remember the sun.

And I think of my grandfather—how we planted potatoes
By the dark of the moon: each silvery wedge with an eye
To see on their journey and guide them quick to the sun,
And when, building the great ships, I hunted the signs
To weld the galvo or rivet the plates to the deck.

A kind of searching, translation of signs, a kind of hunting:
As when the bowman peers through the night-bound forest:
Reading the sounds of a shaken bush or a rattle of stones,
Patient and impatient, driven and hungering, following,

Through the cold day and the moon-patched colder night,
The wounded beast his calling says pursue—
Though he have nothing to eat in the hunt but its bloody droppings.

Reading by Mechanic Light

In the early evening
The dark comes in like a heavy tide . . .
The blackness empty of god—
Thank god!—that dismal bed
We used to smother in.

And now the full moon
Godless—no witches' moon—
Pitches over the houses like an empty ship:
Darkening the stars in the heaven's empty
Spider web.

The moon like a white bone . . .
Now not even a witch—
Ditched into darkness, bald as a skull.
How does it pull from pole to pole,
The careless sea?

But it has the sea in thrall:
Leashed like a small dog.
And so the tides must thole
In durance vile—as we
Endure our bankruptcy

Now neither goddess or witch—
And precious little light
To read on a page of stars
What once we dreamed was ours:
Before the light went out.

End of a Season

—song from a play

The bones of birds are full of air,
The bones of men with rank despair—
Where, where shall away
Finch and Jay
But how shall fare my darling?

We walk in crowds, but have no names,
Have many houses but no homes.
The winds will steer
Feather and fur
But who shall cheer my darling?

The snow may warm both skin and bone
But winter kills the one alone.
Warm is the lair
Of fox or bear
But who'll care for my darling?

Advertisements

All this dead wood
Just above tide line—
The sea is preparing coffins . . .

Today I will not take the Ferry!

Half Measures

Above high-tide mark on the long beach
There is one old shoe.
Someone of little faith
Has gone for a long walk on water.

The Language of the Dead

There is no grammar for the language of the dead.
The only verb is intransitive.
No punctuation except a period.
In that dictionary—
Nothing.

Or a single noun.

HEATHER McHUGH ▪ ▪ ▪ ▪ ▪ ▪ ▪ ▪ ▪ ▪ ▪ ▪

After You Left

It is better to say "I am suffering"
than to say "This landscape is ugly."
—SIMONE WEIL

From the piling's kelp I drew
the five blunt fingers of a starfish.

First I thought the creature
less than handsome, less of a hand

than I expected it to be, too rigid,
with a stumpy gray asymmetry of grasp. It hadn't

kept its grip, so maybe it was dead? It took
a while for me to look, after I claimed to see:

I turned the matter over, and beheld
its thousands of minute transparent

footlets, feelers, stems,
all waving to the quick, and then

the five large radials beginning
gradually to flail

in my slow sight
and then (in my thin air)

to drown. I'd meant
to send it, as a gift

to you who were my missing part, so far
inland. Instead

to a world the sighted have no rights to,
to the dark that's out of mind, I made

myself resign it,
flinging the hand from my hand.

JANE MEAD ··············

La Guardia, the Story

I

A man in the clot of colors—which are people—
is holding a naked iris, is watching
the long line of faces unloading.
He holds the flower up to his chest, then
down at a tilt to his side—in one hand
behind his back makes a surprise.
He runs through his posture
now and again. He uses
one shoe at a time for standing.

The long line of faces—its trickle and blurt—
hurts me. He is watching for her face.

She must have sat at the back of the plane—
a seven-forty-seven, she's been smoking.
Perhaps something has happened that matters.
Perhaps what has happened is nothing—
but the face that arrives is never
the face that left us. Remember that.

I want to rest my head on his back,
or his blue flannel shirt. I imagine
her face which must arrive. I imagine
that she must not disappoint him.
Will I know her before he sees her?
What does their story mean to me?

I used to walk through Kensington gardens
every morning on my way to school
that winter we lived at Lancaster gate.
This is a story too—does it have meaning?
Is it about something that matters—does it
tell how the branches aged the white sky?
Is its secret in the fog or the red sun rising,
in the ducks on the Serpentine as seen
through a layer of mist? Can it explain
why my mother whimpered in her sleep that year?

In the frame story she walks off last,
sees the flower—hands up for a moment
for *surprise* before she takes it.

She gives him a small kiss and they head off
arm in arm in the direction marked "Baggage"
and "Ground Transportation," down the long hall
happily, until I can no longer see them.

This is the story as I saw it happen.
The story as I told it.

In their second story he waits with the iris
long after she doesn't arrive—
but for some other reason than for
so I can save him—she has been delayed—
perhaps by something inconsequential,
we don't know yet, but in the second story
she does not arrive. This is the story
as I imagine it—the story that exists.

Is there any other possible story?

Walking home from school in the afternoons
I'd stop and sit by the Serpentine
and rub my fingers on the curbstone.
I loved the raw circles I made in their tips—
symmetrical and red as the skin
under the popped bubble of a blister.

Is there any other story possible?
Who must I be to complete it?

Make her exist.

                                    II

I am stuck in the middle of the story,
not knowing if she will arrive.
I saw her face, this makes no difference—
there is a man at La Guardia
holding an iris. When I think of it
I cannot stop fearing for him.

How do you unlock a story? How
do you recognize the image—
the one that might change you?

If I put in the part about my mother
and step-father fighting, if I describe
—perfectly—his body in action,
his shadow on the wall behind him,
or add the bit about it all boiling down

to inquisitions in the rational morning—as in
whose dark anus holds the safe-box key—
will we have a story with a moaning?

There is a way to discover a truth
about anything you want to know.

I imagine there's a way to know what's real.

Listen—I walked through an empty park
every morning on my way to school
and knew that it was good to be human.

Listen:
Some nights I make a killer pot of coffee—
I put on the music that I love,
and dance. Sometimes I dance for hours.

Go to your phonograph. Put on
Brandenburg Concerto number six.

This is about something very hard.
—This is about trying to live with that music
playing in the back of your mind.

—About trying to live in a world
with that kind of music.

Delphi, Coming Around the Corner

Delphi, coming around the corner of the house,
one shoe on foot, one shoe in hand, says
he thought the dog shit was just a shadow.

This has happened before.
He scrapes it off on my door stoop, off
to the side, we wait for rain.

Meanwhile, my idea of an afternoon
is a couple of dogs chewing cow toes
in my bed—and me, and Delphi,

whom I love. Delphi, who
cannot read or write. Sometimes
I try to teach him—goes like this:

This is my Oil of Olay, T.M., this
is my shell-pink polish, also T.M.ed,
and those are the little shrimps that are my toes.

Later I try again. *This is the other*
side of the story, I say,
picking up the book and quoting:

"Writing is that (dot dot dot) space
where all identity is lost, starting with the
(dot dot dot) identity of the body writing."

Unquote, I say, adding a footnote[1]
just in case. Delphi puts the book
on the floor. Later I try again.

This is my poem for you, I say,
this is the place where I can't,
for a song, put the song in. So I sing it.

Delphi sings harmony, the dogs stop chewing.
Delphi knows the end to every story,
his literal, illiterate eyelids fluttering shut.

PABLO MEDINA ■ ■ ■ ■ ■ ■ ■ ■ ■ ■ ■ ■ ■ ■ ■

Nocturno de Washington

for Marta Sánchez Lowery

As the XVth Century Chinese scholar Xyangyan
swept the path to his shack, a pebble hit a stalk
of bamboo and at that moment he achieved the
enlightenment he had searched for all his life.
—IN "THE FLIGHT OF THE SIXTH PATRIARCH"
BY KANO MOTONOBU

1.

They called forth the train whistle at midnight,
the end of October, the wrecking-ball month.
They called forth the snow and it came in ricochets,
singes of ancient fires.

[1]Barthes, Roland. *Image—Music—Text.* New York: Hill and Wang, 1977.

They suited up. They brought home
bacon and oranges, the twelve-month year,
the lawns of the wealthy, the shacks of the poor,
God gave his blessing and it was good.

They made the twelve tribes and the rabbit ears,
the cemeteries, tractor-trailers, parakeets,
the ivory trade, the undersea stones, pews
and pencils, commuter lines at dawn.

They stopped, looked out over the vast creation,
saw the empty fields covered with weeds,
the gutters glutted with bottles, the board
rooms with barrel-chested har, har, har.

They recycled empties, restored the ruins
of Hollywood props, they colorized Ava Gardner's
lips, Bogart's ashen skin, pulled levers,
made bridges rise and mountains disappear.

A sailing ship sailed on, *corazón, corazón,*
down to the bottom of the ocean, the darkest amplitude,
the starkest drowning. The captain wrote
"Rocks and sharks have come upon us unaware."

They called forth flamingos and the third race
at Hialeah when the two-year-old filly stumbled
and broke a leg. They called forth compassion,
a bullet through the brain.

They loved the right things right,
then went home before intolerance,
"so without all manhood, emptie of all pity . . ."
and the dirty fingernails of wisdom.

They called forth hunger, the Western wind,
a peg-legged woman sleeping on a park bench
(Walker Evans, Havana, 1933). They called forth
dust-bowls and breadlines, tenements and ideology.

They brought up children and long rains,
longer droughts, 17,000 wars to end all wars, old men
cooked in greed, the buzzard hubris pecking out
the eyes of saints, *América la grande, América en pavor.*

They called forth the left and called forth
the right, wrote down the seven moralities,
the twenty amenities, signed manifestoes,
sold condoms on credit, pantihose to patriarchs.

They joined a long line of indigents
wanting tickets to Paradise, but the show
was sold out. They called forth bilge and arbitrage,
an ignorance like prairie fire.

They called forth whimpers intertwining,
una niña azul bañada en la tristeza, Bleed
America, Inc., breach in the stone, Bleed America,
Inc., hymen broken, leaf abstracted,

and the river glass-like, silent,
slithering through travesty, and the rats
in the tenements chewing and contemplating,
blinking and defecating.

2.

At midnight the Washington Monument rises.
Here in the clouds is the cusp
of power it says to the snow whirling down,
here is the center of all matter.

Let no one mistake our intent, let no one
come here doubting the limits of our strength:
perpetuity, policy like glass, unblemished,
invariable. The monument stands behind, before all.

The president is asleep, his cabinet is asleep,
the people's representatives, every one under covers.
Only a scholar up late with his books fixes coffee,
looks out the window, wonders when the snow will end.

In the distance the train whistle bleats.
The sky is falling on government, wasting itself
on mall and monument. The scholar thinks
knowledge is nothing, knowing is all.

Night everywhere, leaving its dust under fingernails,
behind ears. Night filling up with snow,
replicating sleep. Night of tantrum
songs and howling dogs and tears.

Night the substance of solitude,
the bucket of fog, the insomnia overcoat.
Night the misanthrope, the ambidextrous,
lipless laughter, empty room.

If there is no option, let the winter out.
If there is no residue, let the haunches grow.

If the past does not billow to the future, let the ship
be shoaled, and the cold muffle the nightmare-hum.

The scholar sits in yellow light.
He remembers wife and children, the parents
he left behind. He remembers the jasmine in the garden,
the river flowing past his fishing line,

past the places of his dreams, the offices
and roads, the city and the sea: One life, one
moment out of which grows the need, the calling,
the sound of a pebble swept against a bamboo stalk.

WILLIAM MEREDITH ▪ ▪ ▪ ▪ ▪ ▪ ▪ ▪ ▪ ▪ ▪ ▪ ▪

Two Masks Unearthed in Bulgaria

for Kolyo Sevov

When God was learning to draw the human face
I think he may have made a few like these
that now look up at us through museum glass
a few miles north of where they slept
for six thousand years, a necropolis near Varna.
With golden staves and ornaments around them
they lay among human bodies but had none.
Gods themselves, or soldiers lost abroad—
we don't know who they are.

The gold buttons which are their curious eyes,
the old clay which is their wrinkled skin,
seem to have been worked by the same free hand
that drew Adam for the Jews about that time.
It is moving, that the eyes are still questioning
and no sadder than they are, time being what it is—
as though they saw nothing tragic in the faces
looking down through glass into theirs.
Only clay and gold, they seem to say,
passing through one condition on its way to the next.

John and Anne

"I would call the subject of Anne Frank's *Diary* even
more mysterious than St. Augustine's, and describe it as:
the conversion of a child into a person. . . . It took place
under very special circumstances which—let us now
conclude as she concluded—though superficially
unfavorable, were in fact highly favorable to it; she was
forced to mature, in order to survive; the hardest
challenge, let's say, that a person can face without defeat
is the best for him."
—"THE DEVELOPMENT OF ANNE FRANK," BY JOHN BERRYMAN

Are you grown up now, John, now that it's over?
Do you sit around sober and peaceful these days,
listening to the big people's palaver,
nobody interrupting, nobody famished for praise?

(We have to fable some such place of good talk
—*Nobody listens to me,* the child would shout—
because we ourselves remain shrill little folk:
there must be somewhere we'll hear each other out.)

Do you engage your friends in the ghostly scene
with decorum you could only parody as a man:
Anne Bradstreet and the Governor, St. Augustine,
Jarrell, and this other, child-woman Anne?

It was a long time coming, this quiet,
this hard adulthood, after tantrums of enquiry.
Nobody answers my questions, the child would shout.
You went from the one bottle to the other, thirsty.

"The hardest challenge, let's say, that a person can face
without defeat is the best for him." She could weep
at Auschwitz for the naked gypsy girls gassed in that place.
Dying at Belsen, she helped you to grow up.

Ideogram

I am trying to describe to you a river at first light.
The water is glassy, under a scud of mist.
It is taking the color of the new sky
but the mist has something else in mind than pink—
a force of discoloration, it would have everything white.
On the far bank are serried low hills, tree-clusters
occasionally the lights of a car.

This river I want you to see is being remembered.
I tell you this not to make us self-conscious
or conscious of words, but hoping to heighten
the peculiar vividness of a thing imagined.
I put no water-bird or craft on the surface:
the poem is absolutely quiet at about 5 a.m.
Rose-grey water slips away to left and right, silky,
upstream and downstream, just before sunrise,
just before we are called away,
you who don't know me, I who don't know you.

Soon it will be full light. We will blink this river away
and my talking to you, a stranger, as if I knew you,
as if our partaking a strange river at the edge of light
had been no impertinence—this will yield to another subject.
A river talked away, may be the new subject, or,
Mist burned off by the sun, an ancient, common figure,
a nearly dead metaphor, for enlightenment, and
it occurs to me now that someone may have already
accomplished this for you, hundreds of years ago,
someone deft with a brush, in China.

The American Living-room: A Tract

> Embruted every faculty divine:
> Heart-buried in the rubbish of the world.
> —YOUNG, *NIGHT THOUGHTS*

i

Ideally, you should be in your own
when you read this. Think of it as an oddity—
the one indoor space where living
is deliberately pursued, as in others
we transact dining, sleeping, bathing,
perhaps TV or children. Wherever there are two
one should be kitchen. For the rich,
rooms can be spun out indefinitely:
drawing-, dressing-, morning-, and special
chambers called library, pantry, nursery.
Many still house their cars.

ii

Most people inhabit shelters too small
to partition off with words, and always
some people have none. Is it better

to feel at fault for this, or not
to feel at fault? The meagerest American house
is a gross Hilton compared to where most people
take shelter on the inclement world.
To start with, feel fortunate.

iii

You have made the effort to dress yourself
in character, probably well beyond the requirement
of mere covering—you have already risked
that much misunderstanding. Then comes
this second habiliment, no matter how
reluctant or minimal a statement,
a room which gives you away: with the things
you've acquired at cost, the things you've been given
and kept, the things you choose to exhibit.
The accumulation seems to have been only partly voluntary.
Yet no one you'd want to know could stay
for a month, in a rented room in Asia, without
this tell-tale silt beginning to settle.
When people die, their children have to come dig
for them like Winckelmanns, among many false Troys.

iv

Prisons recognize the need to arrest
this form of identity. Cells
are deliberately ill-fitted uniforms
which you are issued to wear over
the deliberately ill-fitted cloth ones. You
are put there to forego living.

Military quarters may appear more permissive,
yet the space for personal effects is limited
and subject to unscheduled inspection. Nobody
is encouraged to bring along a two-volume dictionary,
a Hopi mask, a valuable paperweight, to a war
or to the interminable rehearsals of camp and shipboard.

v

The room we're in now is like something you've said,
whether off-hand or considered. It's in a dialect
that marks you for a twentieth-century person,
(enthusiastic about this? dragging your feet?)
rich or poor or—more commonly—a little of both;
belonging to a nation and an eclectic culture.
The room risks absurdity, as you risked that again

when you put your clothes on this morning,
but because it is capable of being judged
apart from you, in your absence, the risk is greater,
Why has he got and kept this, and only this?
anyone can ask. *Why so much?* To others
this room is what your scent is to a dog.
You can't know it or help it.

vi

With us in America, a person who has a printed poem
is likely to have a living-room (though not always—
there will always be some to whom poetry is not an amenity).
For reasons of its own, poetry has come to this,
with us. It has somehow gone along
with the privileges of the nation
it intends to change, to dispossess of material demons.
Admittedly, this is part of its present difficulty.

For the moment, though, you are holding this poem.
Its aim is that of any artifact: to ingratiate.
It would like nothing better
than to be added to the dear clutter here.

W. S. MERWIN ▪ ▪ ▪ ▪ ▪ ▪ ▪ ▪ ▪ ▪ ▪ ▪ ▪ ▪ ▪ ▪ ▪ ▪ ▪

A Calling

My father is telling me the story of Samuel
not for the first time and yet he is not quite repeating
nor rehearsing nor insisting he goes on telling me
in the empty green church smelling of carpet and late dust
where he calls to mind words of the prophets to mumble in a remote language
and the prophets are quoting the Lord who is someone they know
who has been talking to them my father tells what the Lord
said to them and Samuel listened and heard someone calling someone
and Samuel answered Here I am and my father is saying
that is the answer that should be given he is telling me
that someone is calling and that is the right answer
he is telling me a story he wants me to believe
telling me the right answer and the way it was spoken
in that story he wants to believe in which someone is calling

Feast Day

Almost at the end of the century
this is the time of the pain of the bears
their agony goes on at this moment
for the amusement of the wedding guests
though the bears are harder to find by now
in the mountain forests of Pakistan
they cost more than they used to which makes it
all the more lavish and once they are caught
their teeth are pulled out and their claws pulled out
and among the entertainments after
the wedding one of them is hauled in now
and chained to a post and the dogs let loose
to hang on its nose so that the guests laugh
at the way it waves and dances and those
old enough to have watched this many times
compare it with other performances
saying they can tell from the way the bear
screams something about the children to be
born of the couple sitting there smiling
you may not believe it but the bear does

The Marfa Lights

Are they there in the daytime
east of town on the way to Paisano Pass
rising unseen by anyone
climbing in long arcs over Mitchell Flat
candles at noon being carried
by hands never seen never caught on film
never believed as they go up the long stairs
of the light to glide in secret or dance
along the dazzling halls out of sight
above where the air shimmers like a sea

only when the curtain of light
is fading thin above the black Glass Mountains
and the first stars are glittering
do the claims of sightings begin that may
occur from anywhere facing
the removes of those broken horizons
though most of them nowadays
are likely to come from somewhere on route 90
looking south toward the Chinatis
a marker has been set up by the road there

and cars begin to stop before
sundown pulling over into the lay-by
designated with rimrocks folding chairs
are unlimbered while there is still light
and positioned among the piled stones in places
expecting them as niches along
sea cliffs expect the old fishermen
tripods are set up and telescopes
they all seem to know what they are waiting for

then buses with lines of faces
peering over each other at the windows
once out there was the place to take
a date it used to mean something different
if you said you had been out to see
the lights but almost everybody had
seen them whether or not they
had seen the same things and were shadowed by the same
explanations there were reports
of those lights before there were cars or ranches

they were seen over wagon trains
on their way up from the valley and shining
above the bare moving forests
of cattle horns in the pass sometimes a light
would drift and swell and suddenly
shudder and fly up bursting apart from one
color to another some say
they will turn out to be something simple
a trick of the atmosphere
and some do not think they are anything

insisting that people will believe
whatever they want to in the same way
that herdsmen and cowhands in the Chinatis
for a hundred years would whisper
that the lights were the ghost of the war chief
Alsate who had been captured
and dragged off to his death and his followers
sold into slavery of course
by now there have been investigations

inconclusive until the present
telling us in our turn what we do not know
what the evidence amounts to
perhaps and how far the theories have gone
to suggest what these bright appearances
portend in the eye of the mind where we know

from the beginning that the darkness
is beyond us there is no explaining
the dark it is only the light
that we keep feeling a need to account for

Tide Line Garden

to Stanley Kunitz

With what you know now about a garden by the sea
I wish you had seen the one I walked in
one evening at the end of summer when I was young

I did not know then that it was a season
from which I would number the years that were to come
my eyes were still full of the south
the bleached slopes and hayfields
midday shimmering over the gray stones
lichen on parched plum bark
it had been the time of finding the ruined farmhouse half buried
under brambles on the ridge
where I would be living before long
it was that year and we were travelling north
up along the coast in the early days of September

the second war was still fresh in people's minds there
less than a decade after the Normandy landings
there was the quiet couple with the farm above the dunes
its old doors and windows recently painted sky blue
who talked of the nights before the invasion
the panzers waiting out under their apple trees
the blond young men shouldering into the cellar
walking out with their calvados talking loudly calling to the orchard
and the couple thinking Drink up Drink up young men
a little sorry for them
sitting up listening after the singing was over
for the sound of the RAF
that had known where to find those young men at daybreak
before they were even awake

the coastal cities were still mostly rubble
cobbles piled in the streets
Bayeux the stones darkened with rain
water running down the broken walls still trickling mortar
and the tapestry hanging in the long hall

the colors peering through shadows
that nobody could do anything about

tho sound of feet edging beside that landing in silence
like the shuffling of a small wave
past Harold standing with the arrow in his eye
after most of a thousand years

sun along that coast and the sea wind had fallen late in the day
I can remember no other guests at the old house
its stones catching the west light off the salt meadows
which appeared to reach almost to the horizon
with the tide all the way out and flocks of sheep and white geese
drifting rimmed in light with their long shadows floating beside them

the house had become an inn some time after the war
the man in charge must have remembered those years
and he was pleased to show the place but scarcely open to questions
he said that much had been forgotten
and that often that was for the best
for a moment the smell of the occupation
seeped through the air of the meadows

beside the house a stream ran out to the salt flats
walls beyond a courtyard rose to a millpond
and a mill with a water wheel still turning
in beards of moss that dripped long strands of light

the family always kept it up he said
it was still being used even after the war

the family he said
was his wife's family
and evidently he preferred to say no more

the house must have been a place of substance for centuries
perhaps when the Sun King was building Versailles
part of an estate or the seat of a functionary
and the plain facade the stones of the windows and doorways
recalled reigns after that
inside it must all have been redone
in the years after the Revolution and Napoleon
ancient wallpaper upstairs
faded by the rays from the meadows
When you come down he said there is something
that might interest you

in front of the house he pointed along to his right
the color of the sunlight on one side of his face

the shadow of his arm draped along the hydrangeas
under the gray shutters

Down there through the garden he said
That used to be the park he said

the wall followed the small road outside
that ran above the salt meadows

he had pointed
to a broad drive that disappeared under trees
planes from the days of the armies of the Emperor
something to do with someone in the family then
the inevitable cypresses
in their dark time

stone edges from later days tumbling into shadows
under dusty ferns and piled branches
hydrangeas rusty azaleas
a few old rose bushes sinking into the shade
strap leaves of lilies darkened and drying
along one side
buried forms of forgotten gardens scarcely detectable
making the garden as it was

the drive curved under the low boughs
and I could see light at the far end through an iron gate
wide enough
as the old garden book I had just bought
recommended
for two carriages to be able to pass each other

the low light came over the wall under the trees
and along the drive near the far end
I saw a series of dark shapes
solid shadows casting solid shadow
extinction appeared to have come that far

as I approached I saw the headlights
the windshields
armored cars half-tracks gun carriers British
undamaged and looking almost new
except for the thick colorless film of nescience

I climbed into the first driver's seat
everything was there the gauges the instruments

the odometer registered fifty-three miles
before the garden

where the gates had been open
into a place long planned and never foreseen

Glassy Sea

As you see each of the stars has a voice
and at least one long syllable before
words as we know them and can recall them
later one by one with their company
around them after the sound of them has
gone from its moment even though we may
say it again and again it is gone
again far into our knowledge there are
words as we know for whatever does not
die with us but the sound of those words lasts
no longer than the others it is heard
only for part of the length of a breath
among those clear syllables never heard
from which the words were made in another
time and the syllables themselves are not
there forever some may go all the way
to the beginning but not beyond it

Migrants by Night

Weeks after the solstice
now in the winter night
the crash of surf thunders
from the foot of the sea cliffs
the heavy swells crashing
after their voyages
out of the deep north
the roar lifts from them
to roll on without them
as they break in the foam
of the ones before them
with that sound under them
carrying the mountain
into the midst of the sea

which they have always been
since the first motion

that was in no place then
out of no place began
gathering itself in turn
to become a direction
under the clear wind
from the place of origin
that now lifts the thin
swift cries of the plovers
over the dark ocean
each one calling alone
unseen to hear again
another in the wind

in a season between
journeys with no horizon
they fly in the night
as though it could be known
from season to season
as though it were their own
to hear each other in
while it turns around them
and the waves of light flow in
from the first motion
bringing it with them
all the way to the moment
when the cry comes again
again before it flies on

JANE MILLER ■ ■ ■ ■ ■ ■ ■ ■ ■ ■ ■ ■ ■ ■ ■ ■

Any Two Wheels

Firecrackers thundering day and night, and lightning silences—

a few blossoms, the lowly mountains, that pair in the tunnel of love
    —and it is a tunnel, and it is love—

it's almost like everyone is smiling on the streets of the government,
the weeds can touch us only so far up our legs
        where it will be spring, spring when we get out—

easy to live without money, without equality and power
in a bar with a lemon fizz, dancing with the two or three best lookers,
a little older than one might have picked, hippier,

—no, it wasn't a holiday!
    —I only knew one such day in my life!
        —whose fault was it, as far as art was concerned?

the flower that very night I have in my hair, I shall talk about it briefly—
the end of the war did not bring liberty, and that seems to me
more dangerous than pain, my little anacin—

my arm ached from keeping that flower intact, I have quite a head of hair,
you see, and a blue poppy is hard to find, really is
a strain on the imagination, no?
—now when the firemen put out the stars I think of it, I

—it showed me how exhausted we had been, touching language directly,
and although nothing is conceivable for us now, the borders
of language fade—film, magnetic tape, mime—if you look closely,
down on one hand if need be, you'll see the discourse there,
      incomplete, digressive,
the lovers kissing and arguing at the same time, the heat divine,
and as long as time permits, they go on smoking—
      they think it's ok sleeping alone in space—
ascending and descending the misty grapes as if there is no art of interruption
      —and they are grapes, and it is misty—
now that everyone loves the taxman and embraces the police
      whose lips are like berries too,
berries of course are now entirely terms, no amount of
gentility can conceal that fact but everyone is properly
instructed in sheer projection—listen,

a heart this big, if anyone's asking, utilizes
diamond chips, and in the poorest countries, as big as a ball of thread
which sticks to your hand and draws the boat ashore, where a hundred years
are as one day, that same woman weeping since the erection of a round tower,
      the first sign of official culture—

—was there a ridge with a lake on either side?
    —beachfront and pink sand?

the sulphur sets and the sulphur rises like a minotaur,
our bodies are straight and perfect, daylight as black as a beetle,
and white as the snow of one night, all our nights.

August Zero

Young trees the bright green of a moonless night,
lawn the red of scorpion,—

the pleasure dome drops, a drill ceases and a mower resumes.
It hides the spectacle of the mountains

and jolts us, it's been a long time
since we've had a little space to ourselves.

All the same, in spite of everything,
we are made to live in the air, which involves a certain number
of mental operations
the full force of a bow, a revision of the notion
of history,
oddly imitating the movements of animals when I think about it,
doubling back, appearing to be shot or struck—

and celestial sounds, not sound itself,
rock the bare earth, packed hard and nailed
by the language of many feet
to the tune of the unconscious,
which we regret to understand.

Don't get me wrong, there is still a knowledge of freedom,
a bath, a change of clothing,
possession of a child's heart,
a handshake, and the function of time
a detail—even in air
language is a
cross between an appetite and a mouth—

I'm not hungry when I'm lonely.
Like all the lead and neon which is forgotten
I forget
that people have died forever,
no one knows you
and the ideal place is a dome with horses' shadows
the shade of steel gin,
and what formerly acceded to a view constitutes love.

A pear—
remember now future became present—
in a kitchen and two rooms in orbit
pins the horizon with its pony body and elk head
and we enact where we first made love the camellia of our beloved—
we can't touch exactly
but attempt a profound correlation—
we grip the skeleton of a river and the sun kisses it
like one's own throat.

This is the earth, my love, all of us
have a chunk on our backs.
You are an angel
and I am an ancient
who're cast from two and a half billion cars a day
into one copter night,

and closure is that windmill
through a wall in the circle, drifting
like the once innocent

oil spills in the Pacific,
like conversation.

The Impossible

I had to give a great speech to a filled hall, beginning
with a flute sonata, and to recite from several books
only two of which I recognized,

which I accomplished, though it took everything out of me
as I tried to hold my posture erect and, failing that,
at least look good on the balls of my feet—this being
nearly impossible, I tried to give the illusion

of weightlessness, or at the very least a sense of rapprochement
with gravity, whereby my head remained light while my heart
suffered and my soul burned,

so that when asked to run, run for all I was worth,
which I tell you was not much by then, because of the pressure
to demur to those around me, cajoling and demanding,
I fled with a kind of verve even I did not foresee
since I was preoccupied with having abandoned a project
it's true only a genius or a madman might have finished
and which I had, frankly, more or less accomplished
by accident, intuition, and a sudden burst of confidence
which shocked even my dearest,

and succeeded in reaching the famous Crystal Springs
heretofore thought to be imaginary, a thing of wonder
but without substance, without substantiation, such blueness
and liquidity, it was unbelievable, but true,
that I stopped on a dime, resisting a personal moment
that surely would have overwhelmed anyone so haunted and
so driven by so many, and experienced what can only be described
as a disappointment, plain and simple, not because the waters
were any less majestic, any less transparent than rumored,
in fact, blue beyond the cerulean of sky over a south
high in the mountains of deepest earth, purpled, nearly black,
that is, if one thought of the sun ever going down
into such waters.

sad because I had never been more in love, more given over
to any one person, place, or thing, and all of existence

seemed paltry next to such feeling, if one did not count
the few stones that uncannily caught my eye, pebbles I
almost smashed out of a euphoria that overcame and nearly
destroyed me—a taste of heavenly winds swept my narrow body,
tickling my ribs with a fancy singing of spirit, tempting,
perfumed—but for the damned six or seven loosely strewn

aforementioned ugly little rocks that buckled my knees
with their gray snaky surface, pimpled, rough, impossibly
connotative, i.e., I saw a thousand lakes in the landscape
of a bird-shat mossy clump glombed to a crag, and bat faces
and bear paws and exoskeletal histories from beyond time,
and so on,

which held me face down, less recalcitrant than I had ever
been, trust me on that, and evermore eager to obey, the longer
I picked out lunar hills and valleys and the more hushed I got
between one ancient, practically moribund, megalith and another,
beamed, so to speak, from oblivion, the body of universe opened
into a gaping mouth

whose lips mercifully shined with the handiwork of creation, or
at least seemed that way to me, by now flattened to the cold
damp floor, reddened with the liveliness of movement, and of
sweat, crimson then, and moving, mouthing something, speaking
in tongues but almost immediately my language, words
I once dared to call, I grant you in a dream, the language
of love, which in this case hastened to particularize itself
in the being of a face, and then the hair and eyes and costume
of beatific figures transsexualized

by ritual and political charioteering such that I no longer
knew myself but rather a consortium of likenesses whose cocksureness
is colloquialized as immediately as the words for it are spoken—
a roaring of motorcycles and then hundreds of faceless, because
one face, hermaphroditic moderns blazed by, upstaging the mono-
chromatic past with theatric mauves and chartreuses, white-faced
and mascara-ed images, eyebrowless, and I found myself in full
color, reproduced electronically, as it were, so eroticized
as to be unreal,

a diorama o'erpowering everything else in common limelight—
dykes on bikes, fag hags, drag queens, steroidal buffs, midnight
blue black semi-nudes, boytoys, unzipped sado-masochistic
six-foot tricks, the semi-erect, the innocent, in gym shorts
and in slips, tuxedos, t-shirts and cut-offs, jeans impaled
at the crotch—godly, larger-than-life meaning assigned
to them by messages spelled out on their chests, "Silence
Equals Death," etc., until, so engorged, their numbers blur
into a mass of energy that finally disperses into the missions

and the tenderloins from whence they came, into the planetary
city named irreverently and made familiar by necessity,
"sex,"

and I passed out onto those innocuous stones, trifles
I might have missed another day, waking to stumble
between two destinations, home or on, knowing I
had forgotten—o alcatrazed face, betrayed,
abandoned!—more than any metaphor provided
because it too is ultimately betrayed and abandoned,
forgotten life because of this paper face, this alphabet
and these blanks I trusted, naturally, like a form
of breathing, life I have to return to which I made

more difficult than walking off the globe
by imagining I had to say a few tired words
into an ear, near-empty auditorium . . . beginning
with a couple of short notes, only some of which
I'd actually written . . .

CZESLAW MILOSZ ▪ ▪ ▪ ▪ ▪ ▪ ▪ ▪ ▪ ▪ ▪ ▪ ▪ ▪

Encounter

Translated by the author and Lillian Vallee.

We were riding through frozen fields in a wagon at dawn.
A red wing rose in the darkness.

And suddenly a hare ran across the road.
One of us pointed to it with his hand.

That was long ago. Today neither of them is alive
Not the hare, nor the man who made the gesture.

O my love, where are they, where are they going
The flash of a hand, streak of movement, rustle of pebbles.
I ask not out of sorrow, but in wonder.

1936

Tidings

Translated by the author and Lillian Vallee.

Of earthly civilization, what shall we say?

That it was a system of colored spheres cast in smoked glass,
Where a luminescent liquid thread kept winding and unwinding.

Or that it was an array of sunburst palaces
Shooting up from a dome with massive gates
Behind which walked a monstrosity without a face.

That every day lots were cast, and that whoever drew low
Was marched there as sacrifice: old men, children, young boys and young girls.

Or we may say otherwise: that we lived in a golden fleece,
In a rainbow net, in a cloud cocoon
Suspended from the branch of a galactic tree.
And our net was woven from the stuff of signs,
Hieroglyphs for the eye and ear, amorous rings.
A sound reverberated inward, sculpturing our time,
The flicker, flutter, twitter of our language.

For from what could we weave the boundary
Between within and without, light and abyss,
If not from ourselves, our own warm breath,
And lipstick and gauze and muslin,
From the heartbeat whose silence makes the world die?

Or perhaps we'll say nothing of earthly civilization.
For nobody really knows what it was.

Elegy for N.N.

Tell me if it is too far for you.
You could have run over the small waves of the Baltic
and past the fields of Denmark, past a beech wood
could have turned towards the ocean, and there, very soon
Labrador, white at this season.
And if you, who dreamed about a lonely island,
were frightened of cities and of lights flashing along the highway
you had a path straight through the wilderness
over blue-black, melting waters, with tracks of deer and caribou
as far as the Sierra and abandoned gold mines.
The Sacramento River could have led you
between hills overgrown with prickly oaks.
Then just a eucalyptus grove, and you had found me.

True, when the manzanita is in bloom
and the bay is clear on spring mornings
I think reluctantly of the house between the lakes
and of nets drawn in beneath the Lithuanian sky.
The bath cabin where you used to leave your dress
has changed forever into an abstract crystal.
Honey-like darkness is there, near the veranda
and funny young owls, and the scent of leather.

How could one live then, I really do not know.
Styles and dresses flicker, indistinct,
not self-sufficient, tending towards a finale.
Does it matter that we long for things as they are in themselves?
The knowledge of fiery years has scorched the horses standing at the forge,
the little columns in the market place,
the wooden stairs and the wig of Mama Fliegeltaub.

We learned so much, this you know well:
how, gradually, what could not be taken away
is taken. People, countrysides.
And the heart does not die when one thinks it should,
we smile, there is tea and bread on the table.
And only remorse that we did not love
the poor ashes in Sachsenhausen
with absolute love, beyond human power.

You got used to new, wet winters,
to a villa where the blood of the German owner
was washed from the wall, and he never returned.
I too accepted but what was possible, cities and countries.
One cannot step twice into the same lake
on rotting alder leaves,
breaking a narrow sunstreak.

Guilt, yours and mine? Not a great guilt.
Secrets, yours and mine? Not great secrets.
Not when they bind the jaw with a kerchief, put a little cross between the
    fingers,
and somewhere a dog barks, and the first star flares up.

No, not because it was too far
did you not visit me that day or night.
From year to year it grows in us until it takes hold,
I understood it as you did: indifference.

In Szetejnie

Translated by the author and Robert Hass.

I

You were my beginning and again I am with you, here, where I learned the four quarters of the globe.

Below, behind the trees, the River's quarter; to the back, behind the buildings, the quarter of the Forest; to the right, the quarter of the Holy Ford; to the left, the quarter of the Smithy and the Ferry.

Whenever I wandered, through whatever continents, my face was always turned to the River.

Feeling in my mouth the taste and the scent of the rosewhite flesh of calamus.

Hearing old pagan songs of harvesters returning from the fields, while the sun on quiet evenings was dying out behind the hills.

In the greenery gone wild I could still locate the place of an arbor where you forced me to draw my first awkward letters.

And I would try to escape to my hideouts, for I was certain that I would never learn how to write.

I did not expect, either, to learn that though bones fall into dust, and dozens of years pass, there is still the same presence.

That we could, as we do, live in the realm of eternal mirrors, working our way at the same time through unmowed grasses.

II

You held the reins and we were riding, you and me, in a one-horse britzka, for a visit to the big village by the forest.

The branches of its apple trees and pear trees were bowed down under the weight of fruits, ornate carved porches stood out above little gardens of mallow and rue.

Your former pupils, now farmers, entertained us with talks of crops, women showed their looms and deliberated with you about the colors of the warp and the woof.

On the table slices of ham and sausage, a honeycomb in a clay bowl, and I was drinking *kvas* from a tin cup.

I asked the director of the collective farm to show me that village;
he took me to fields empty up to the edge of the forest, stopping
the car before a huge boulder.

"Here was the village Peiksva" he said, not without triumph in
his voice, as is usual with those on the winning side.

I noticed that one part of the boulder was hacked away,
somebody had tried to smash the stone with a hammer, so that
not even that trace might remain.

III

I ran out in a summer dawn into the voices of the birds, and I
returned, but between the two moments I created my work.

Even though it was so difficult to pull up the stick of *n,* so it
joined the stick of *u* or to dare building a bridge between *r* and *z.*

I kept a reedlike penholder and dipped its nib in the ink, a
wandering scribe, with an ink pot at his belt.

Now I think one's work stands in the stead of happiness and
becomes twisted by horror and pity.

Yet the spirit of this place must be contained in my work, just as
it is contained in you who were led by it since childhood.

Garlands of oak leaves, the ave-bell calling for the May service, I
wanted to be good and not to walk among the sinners.

But now when I try to remember how it was, there is only a pit,
and it's so dark, I cannot understand a thing.

All we know is that sin exists and punishment exists, whatever
philosophers would like us to believe.

If only my work were of use to people and of more weight than is
my evil.

You alone, wise and just, would know how to calm me,
explaining that I did as much as I could.

That the gate of the Black Garden closes, peace, peace, what is
finished is finished.

FROM Lithuania, After Fifty-Two Years

A Goddess

Gaia, first-born daughter of Chaos,
Adorned with grasses and trees, gladdens our eyes
So that we can agree when naming what is beautiful
And share with all earthly wanderers our joy.

Let us give thanks in our own and our ancestors' name
For oaks and their rough-barked dignity,
For pines, their trunks flaming in the sun,
For clear green clouds of vernal birch groves
And for the candlesticks of the autumnal wilderness, aspens.

How many kinds of pear and apple trees in our gardens!
(Arranged as described in *The Northern Gardens* of Strumillo),
Currants, gooseberries, dogberries, barberries
For a great boiling of preserves
When the faces of our housewives are reddened by their long stay by the stove.

There was a separate corner for medicinal herbs,
Those which were grown at the advice of Gizycki's *Economical-Technological
    Herbarium.*
From them elixirs and ointments for the manor's pharmacy.

And mushroom gathering! Sturdy boletus in the oakwoods.
Strings of them, one by another, drying under the eaves.
A hunter's trumpet is heard when we search for milk cups
And our knives are stained yellow-red by their juices.

Gaia! Whatever happens, preserve at least your seasons.
Emerge from under the snows with the trickling of rivulets in springs,
Dress yourself for those who will live after us
If only in the green of mid-city parks
And the blossoming of dwarf apple trees in garden plots at the edge of cities.
I depose my petition, your lowly son.

Who?

Beyond the red traffic light, young chestnut leaves.
Who is the one seeing it,
Where does he come from, where will he disappear to,
Who is the one, instead of him,
Who will be seeing the same but not the same thing,
Because of a different pulsation of the blood?

And limbs of huge trees over a steep road,
Leaning into each other, and in that lane,

Beyond the colonnade of trunks, an open brightness.
For whom is this? And how does it vary?
Is it present every time or just imaginary?

Be yourselves, things of this earth, be yourselves!
Don't rely on us, on our breath,
On the fancies of our treacherous and avid eye.
We long for you, for your essence,
For you to last as you are in yourselves:
Pure, not looked at by anybody.

House in Krasnogruda

I

The woods reached water and there was immense silence.
A crested grebe popped up on the surface of the lake,
In deep water, very still, a flock of teals.
That's what was seen by a man on the shore
Who decided to build his house here
And to cut down the primeval oak forest.
He was thinking of timber he would float down the Niemen
And of thalers he would count by candlelight.

II

The ash trees in the park calmed down after the storm.
The young lady runs down a path to the lake.
She pulls her dress over her head
(She does not wear panties though Mademoiselle gets angry),
And there is a delight in the water's soft touch
When she swims, dog-style, self-taught,
Toward brightness, beyond the shade of the trees.

III

The company settles into a boat, ladies and gentlemen
In swimming suits. Just as they will be remembered
By a frail boy whose lifeline is short.
In the evening he learns to dance the tango. Mrs. Irena
Leads him, with that smirk of a mature woman
Who initiates a young male.
Out the door to the veranda owls are hooting.

Report

O Most High, you willed to create me a poet and now it is time for me to present a report.

My heart is full of gratitude though I got acquainted with the miseries of that profession.

By practicing it, we learn too much about the bizarre nature of man.

Who, every hour, every day and every year is possessed by self-delusion.

A self-delusion when building sandcastles, collecting postage stamps, admiring oneself in a mirror.

Assigning oneself first place in sport, power, love, and the getting of money.

All the while on the very border, on the fragile border beyond which there is a province of mumblings and wails.

For in every one of us a mad rabbit thrashes and a wolf pack howls, so that we are afraid it will be heard by others.

Out of self-delusion comes poetry and poetry confesses to its flaw.

Though only by remembering poems once written is their author able to see the whole shame of it.

And yet he cannot bear another poet nearby, if he suspects him of being better than himself and envies him every scrap of praise.

Ready not only to kill him but smash him and obliterate him from the surface of the earth.

So that he remains alone, magnanimous and kind toward his subjects, who chase after their small self-delusions.

How does it happen then that such low beginnings lead to the splendor of the word?

I gathered books of poets from various countries, now I sit reading them and am astonished.

It is sweet to think that I was a companion in an expedition that never ceases, though centuries pass away.

An expedition not in search of the golden fleece of a perfect form but as necessary as love.

Under the compulsion of the desire for the essence of the oak, of the mountain peak, of the wasp and of the flower of nasturtium.

So that they last, and confirm our hymnic song against death.

And our tender thought about all who lived, strived, and never succeeded in naming.

For to exist on the earth is beyond any power to name.

Fraternally, we help each other, forgetting our grievances, translating each other into other tongues, members, indeed, of a wandering crew.

How then could I not be grateful, if early I was called and the incomprehensible contradiction has not diminished my wonder?

At every sunrise I renounce the doubts of night and greet the new day of a most precious delusion.

HOWARD MOSS ▪ ▪ ▪ ▪ ▪ ▪ ▪ ▪ ▪ ▪ ▪ ▪ ▪ ▪ ▪

Miami Beach

Was Nature always a snob,
Distributing shorefronts only to the rich?
The poor have come to the right conclusion.

The car lots are dangerous, boutiques have closed
In the cleancut shopping mall whose potted palms
Stand helplessly guarding smashed flower boxes,

As slowly expensive logos drift away;
Subversively dreaming of the cold, signs crumble;
The place has the effect of a dead casino.

Yet the sea repeats its fire drill,
The waves coming in as they were meant to come,
All hailing light, beachcombers, tourists, one

Canadian spinster on her towelled maple,
A lifeguard selling products for the sun—
Still more arrive to take those heat waves in.

If you're high up enough to witness it,
This city's saving grace is light on water,
The bay on one side, the ocean on the other,

Collins Avenue strung out on lights—
Blue neon, the sign language of Paris—
Seen from a terrace overlooking Bal Harbour,

Though this evening's tropical aroma
Is marred by a sad old man who stands regretting
His waistline before a Men Shop's window,

Watching a coastline glassily reflected
Take its revenge, the tides undermining
The palmed investments of the big hotels,

Breaking through the breastwork of the dunes,
Thundering in to where they used to be,
To lap at the imported Louis Quinze

Already stricken with the plague of mold
Shifting on deer feet in draperied lounges
(So far no one has noticed the ugly

Patch of dry rot under the sofa,
Not even the Cuban trained in mildew,
Trained to pronounce the "doll" in "dollar,"

Otherwise it sounds too much like "dolor.")
How botched is Paradise, how gone for good
Old rock and beach, this gorgeous littoral

Of palms adoring the sun, and sea grape,
Oleander, and white jasmine blooming
Under the nursing home's blinded windows

Where the cardiacs and the sun-stroked blackouts
Wheel past the splash of a tropical fish tank
Leading a murderous life of its own.

A water hole abandoned by the young,
Either the old will take it over
Completely or South American money

Found its new capital: a kitsch Brasilia
Of pre-stressed concrete with its air-conditioned
Swiss bank branch, and a single restored

Art deco hotel for absentee landlords
Scanning the sea rehearsing endlessly
Its threatened drama never to be performed.

The New York Notebooks

1

I ran across
The blacktop of the night,

Chirico among the postal clerks,
Losing perspective . . .

2

I pour your lie
Like glass
Into the molten
Form it was.
It does not then
Become again
A vase.

3

Someone seems to be waving goodbye—
Somebody who is going
Back to a life hardly worth living.

4

I have watched
Everywhere
The unregarded
Holding out
Their empty tins of justice.

5

There have been
So many wrecks
The dead pile up
But not together—
If your nerves are bad,
Don't read on.

6

Afternoon birds! How melancholy!
They sing dry songs from beaks as dry,
Reminding me of horrors best forgot:
Halls in mental hospitals, telephone calls

Silent at the other end . . . One night
Even nature was a heavy breather.

7

I have reached that middle ground
Luck sometimes takes, I think:
Not quite to have a winning streak
Or to be able to cut my losses,
Like love, which must speak,
And to whom all words are useless.

8

The last outpost of bodily desire:
That blank place even shadows flee.

9

The alcoholic wakes at 4 A.M.
To hear the water tap let down its drop
While the moon-slicked fire escape hangs in air
And, knock-kneed, drunk, his body moves in need
Stumbling barefoot toward the Frigidaire.

10

Odd that
I should
Still
Feel
Your kiss
Long distance
And still sensuous.

11

When I turned on the path
To meet the future,
The old gang of the past
Were on the move.

12

Come on in—
Habit is ironing
Its worn-out garments,

The dead skipper
Is learning to read
The travel section.

13

As you grow older
There are more
And more desertions,
Theirs and yours,
And holes in space
Where this one
Or that one
Has fallen backwards
Into oblivion
Down a hole
Covered up quickly,
And there are deaths
That remain inconsolable,
Griefs so large
There is no cure.

14

I have been talking to you,
Or someone like you,
For years.

STANLEY MOSS ▪ ▪ ▪ ▪ ▪ ▪ ▪ ▪ ▪ ▪ ▪ ▪ ▪ ▪ ▪ ▪

An Exchange of Hats

I will my collection of hats,
straw the Yucatan, fez Algiers 1935,
Russian beaver, Irish fisherman's knit,
collapsible silk opera, a Borsalino,
to a dead man,
the Portuguese poet, my dear Fernando,
who without common loyalty,
wrote under seven different names
in seven different styles.
He was a man of many cafes,
a smoker and non-smoker.
His poets, come to live in Lisbon,
had different sexual preferences,
histories and regional accents.

Still their poems had a common smell
and loneliness that was Fernando's.

His own character
was to him like ink to a squid,
something to hide behind.
What did it matter, writing in Portuguese
after the first World War?
The center was Paris, the languages French and English.
In Lisbon, workers on the street corner were arguing
over what was elegance, the anarchist manifesto,
the trial of Captain Artur Carlos De Barros,
found guilty of "advocating circumcision"
and teaching Marranos no longer to enter church
saying "When I enter I adore neither wood nor stone
but only the Ancient of Days who rules all."
The Portuguese say
they have the "illusion" to do something,
meaning they very much want to do it.

He could not just sit in the same cafe
wearing his own last hat, drinking port
and smoking *Ideals* forever.

The Dog

I fly the flag of the menstruating black dog:
a black dog dripping blood over us all.
My flag barks, licks your face,
my flag says, "I am alive, willing,
part of the natural order of things.
You are a supernatural creature."

I walk across the road to the stream.
In a rush of water, —something surfaces,
—I hold my dog back.
A snake has caught a trout by the anus,
lifts the fish out of the water. The snake's head
cuts a line through the shaded stream
into the sunlight,
crosses the water to a ledge of gravel and jewelweed.
The trout is held into the summer air,
its brightest colors already begun to fade.
The snake uncoils and begins to devour the fish,
head first.

The trees remembering my mother
kiss me, because she told me:
be the sweet dog that licks the face and feet
of the bum passed out in the park,
—she caught a seed flying over a city street,

put it in her glove
took it home and planted it.
I sprawl with my dog on the floor
of all night restaurants
because the entire shape of time
is a greater, more ferocious beast
than anything in it.

Clouds

Working class clouds are living together
above the potato fields,—tall white beauties
humping above the trees, burying their faces
in each other, —clouds with darker thighs,
rolling across the Atlantic. West,
a foolish cumulus hides near the ocean
afraid of hurricanoes.
Zeus came to the bed
of naked Io, as a cloud,
passed over her and into her as a cloud,
all cloud but part of his face
and a heavy paw, half cloud, half cat
that held her down.
I take clouds to bed that hold me
like snow and rain, gentle ladies,
wet and ready, smelling of lilac hedges.
I swear to follow them like geese,
through factory smoke,
beyond the shipping lanes and jet routes.
They pretend nothing—opening, drifting, naked.
I pretend to be a mountain
because I think clouds like that.
A cloudy night
proclaims a condition of joy.
Perhaps I remember a certain cloud,
Perhaps I bear a certain allegiance
to a certain cloud.

CAROL MUSKE ▪ ▪ ▪ ▪ ▪ ▪ ▪ ▪ ▪ ▪ ▪ ▪ ▪ ▪ ▪

A Former Love, a Lover of Form

When they kiss,
she feels a certain revulsion,
and as they continue to kiss

she enters her own memory
carrying a wicker basket
of laundry. As the wind lifts,

the clothes wrap themselves
around her: damp sleeves
around her neck, stockings

in her hair. Gone her schoolgirl's
uniform, the pale braids and body
that went anywhere anonymously.

Her glasses fall forward on her nose,
her mouth opens: all around
are objects that desire, suddenly, her.

Not just clothes, but open doorways,
love seats, Mother's bright red
espadrilles kicked off in the damp grass.

If she puts on lipstick, she'll lie
forever. But she's too nearsighted,
you see, she doesn't spot the wind

approaching in a peach leisure suit—
or the sheer black nightie swaying
from a branch. Is she seducer or seduced?

And which is worse,
a dull lover's kiss or the embrace
of his terrible laundry?

She'd rather have the book
he wrote than him.

Stage & Screen, 1989

Disguised as a mutant,
my kid spins in the backyard.
She has the fly's compound eye
and that familiar flat robot
voice, hesitant, deflective: a human dial tone.
Her business is to rescue every person
recently changed into an insect.

Misunderstanding passion, (the old poet told me)
a poem goes wrong in two ways: first,

like an amateur tragedian milking
the best lines of emphasis,
pushing quite innocent everyday dialogue

into enormity. Then what remains to be seen
can't be. Not the broken string of red glass beads
rolling under the table, the white chair pushed away,
the child's lidded, fearful sidewise look—but look out
for the narrator's shadow falling on everything.
The images standing in for the self,

the fiery sky-divers stepping ahead of you into space,
first light on the row of talking monuments.
Outside, the mutant climbs the china-berry tree.
Inside, a nostalgia for the not-too-human rears up,
groans, goes all trembly-fingered down the proscenium arch.

Outside again, she's just a kid in green mask and socks,
back on the ground, spinning. See what I mean?
The wind keeps blowing, it's hard-edged, shining,
self-contained as a struck pendulum. So pour
some coffee, go outside, feel something enormous, stop.

Red Trousseau

> What is woman but a foe to friendship . . .
> —MALLEUS MALIFICORUM
> *WITCHES' HAMMER,* 1494

I.

Because she desired him,
and feared desire, the room
readied itself for judgment:
though they were nothing to
each other, maybe friends,
maybe a man and a woman
seated at a table
      beneath a skylight
through which light poured,
interrogatory.

II.

Because his face always appears to her
half in shadow,
      she chooses finally
to distrust him and her seared memory,

even though it was noon, when the sun
hovers in its guise of impatient tribunal,
seizing every contradiction in dismissive brilliance:

the white cloth, their separate folded hands,
a mock-crucible holding fire-veined blossoms.
No, it was a bowl of fruit, a glass of red wine,
the simplest, thoughtless vessel, that was it,
wasn't it, held up, like this, an offering?

III.

Reading the accounts of the trials,
late at night, she sees that the questions
must have begun in a friendly, almost desultory
fashion: rising slowly in pitch and intensity,
to reveal, finally, God's bright murderous gaze,
the mouth of the trap. Conviction required stigmata,
the search for the marks of Hell's love on the un-male
body, the repetitive testimony of men: that she midwifed
the stillborn, curdled milk, spied, screamed at climax,
grew wings—and worse, *Looking over her shoulder,*
I saw her laughing he said *laughing at me*

till, at the end, days later, she could feel
her way eagerly, blind, cleansed of memory,
through the maze of metal doors to the last door:
the single depthless mirror.

IV.

They were already disappearing, sitting there together
talking in a forthright way, laughing, unaware of their
faces reflected, enlarged like cult images, effigies:
dark hair, light hair. Already the ancient lens
sliding into place between them, whose purpose is not
to clarify sight, but rather to magnify, magnify till
its capacity for difference ignites.

Tell me why it was only his gaze on her,
why his right to primary regard, *her* life under scrutiny,
her life reduced to some fatal lack of irony, naïve midwife
to this monstrous *please*?

See how the lens bends the light
into what amounts now to tinder . . .
So sight can come, now, heatedly
alive, living wood, corrected

V.

I admit now that I never felt sympathy for her,
as she stood there burning in the abstract.
Though condemned by her own body
(the ridiculous tonsured hair, bare feet
and bruised cheek, as if she'd been pushed up
against a headboard in passionate love)—
I suspected her mind of collaboration,
apperceptive ecstasy, the flames wrapped
about her like a red trousseau, yes,
the dream of immolation.

But look at the way her lips move—
it is the final enlightenment. Below
the nailed sign of her craft
                    are the words published
from her lover's mouth
the mouth of the friend who betrayed her:
her naked body, his head on her breast
like a child's *heal me*—
and her answer?

God, tell me there was a moment
when she could have willed herself into language,
just once, into her own stammering, radical defense:

I am worth saving

before the flames breathed imperious at her feet
before her mouth, bewitched, would admit to anything

JACK MYERS ▪ ▪ ▪ ▪ ▪ ▪ ▪ ▪ ▪ ▪ ▪ ▪ ▪ ▪ ▪ ▪

What's Left

Today I'm going into town to give away what's left.
I drag my memory down like a black wool suit,
let the dead air disrobe from the last sad occasion,
yawn, and inhale the house. It held me as my woman
held me, while the shadows fell and filled my shape.

In the market they will ask did I ever face my life?
Yes I say, I sat inside it. Only backwards. I watched

the beginning being crushed by landscapes rushing toward it.
Now I toss that in for free, a black dot impossible to lift.

I see the few small things I've gathered in the wagon
make a quiet music. Moored on the warm river in the wood
they nod in the mild wind like grown men settling down,
then they change back into things I can't tell from myself.

At my age I should have one last child and face him
like a mountain. Blind and deaf. Tell him it's easy
to learn when there's nothing left. All this I hitch up
to a strong dumb horse. He will pull it twitching into town,
bearing high his faceful of flies like a torch.

The Instinct

A man feels humiliated
when his wife turns her private
landscape over and leaves him
falling through black space.

There is a horse kicking
in the mind that must be let out.
Men see it in each other's eyes
and hold onto their women.

Young girls who have ridden
this horse in their dreams
cross their legs, still burning,
and concentrate on small talk.

Once in a while a stray woman
who can get over anything
opens her blouse and teases
the horse into following her home.
As she unlocks the door it occurs to her
how huge he will seem in the house.

Sometimes a man will punish his wife
with abstinence. The horse shrinks
into a small dog who rolls over
the edge of sleep while his master
wanders the house eating leftovers
and shouting to himself.

The woman who hears this
decorates her house and makes breakfast

like a wife in the old days.
She averts her eyes and serves him
a future that is possible,
now that he has let her out.

The Experts

When the man in the window seat
flying next to me
asks me who I am
and I tell him I'm a poet,
he turns embarrassed toward the sun.
The woman on the other side of me
pipes up she's 4´10˝ and is going to sue
whoever made these seats.

And so it is I'm reminded how I wish I were
one of the aesthetes
floating down double-lit canals
of quiet listening, the ones
who come to know something as
mysterious and useless
as when a tree has decided to sleep.

You would think for them
pain lights up the edges of everything,
burns right through the center of every leaf,
but I've seen them strolling around,
their faces glistening with the sort of peace
only sleep can polish babies with.

And so when a waitress in San Antonio
asks me what I do, and I think
how the one small thing I've learned
seems more complex the more I think of it,
how the joys of it have overpowered me
long after I don't understand,

I tell her "Corned beef on rye, a side of salad,
hold the pickle, I'm a poet," and she stops to talk
about her little son who, she says, can hurt himself
even when he's sitting still. I tell her
there's a poem in that, and she repeats
"Hold the pickle, I'm a poet,"
then looks at me and says, "I know."

Eileen's Vision

One night I was home alone
quite late past eleven
and my dog was whining and
moaning and I went over
to stroke her & pat
her & proclaim
her beauty &
then I returned
to my art review
but Rosie wouldn't
stop. Something was
wrong. & then
I saw her.
It looked like a circle
a wooden mouth
in the upper third
of my bathtub
cover which
was standing
on its side
it is the Lady I thought
this perfect sphere
on the wooden
bathtub cover
incidentally separating
kitchen &
middle room
in my home
where I
live &
work. That is
all. I'm just
a simple
catholic girl
I had been
thinking, pondering
over my
review. That's
why it's
so hard
for me but the
Lady came &
she said, stay here

Eileen stay here
forever finding
the past
in the future
& the future
in the past
know that it's
always so
going round &
it is with
you when
you write

& she didn't
go, she
remains a stain
on the bathtub
cover, along with
many other stains,
the dog's leash &
half-scraped lesbian
invisibility stickers
and other less specific
but equally permanent
traces of paper &
holes   four of
them and they
are round too
like the Lady
& I don't have to
tell anyone.

Rotting Symbols

Soon I shall take more
I will get more light
and I'll know what I think
about that

Driving down Second Ave. in a car
the frieze of my hand
like a grandmother
captured in an institution
I know I'll never live here again etc.
many many long years ago
Millions of peeps in the scrawl
the regular trees

the regular dog snort &
dig. In the West Village
you could put on a hat
a silly hat & it's clear
whereas over here
20 years passed
that rotting hat
it's loyalty to someone or something
that's really so gone
the moment clenched
like religion or government.

Wait a minute. I prefer
umm a beatle's cap
when it's really really old
neighborhood devoted to that.

Poetry is a sentimental act
everything spring she said
being surrounded by so much rot.
Pages & pages
mounds of them that I'm in
not some library but in your
little home, like you.
Every season I know I'm leaving
I'm as loyal as the cross
to this smeltering eccentricity
down by the river with Daddio
toss your ball in the river
in the future over bridges
they say you have to imagine
the 20th century. *All these buildings were colored*
a blasted interior
scarlet curtains rattling day
cobwebs on inexplicable machinery
a theater once dwelled here
all I see is rotting ideas
the epics I imagined
the unified cast of everyone
eating turkey together
on a stage
my idea
like water towers popping up
feeling mellow
not exactly nothing all this time
but the buildings that are absolute
gone that I never
described. You can't kill
a poet. We just get erased &

written on. It aches in
my brain, my back
this beauty I'm eating my toast
everyone I knew you would
be dead tomorrow
& you were. The composing camera
infatuated with the shovel
on the lid & the pile
of rocks. He is not aging
same Alexandrian
blond in Bini-bons
the sirens are gods
when I lifted my head
from my swarming difficulty
You were so marvelous
bringing those toys to my feet
in between the invisibility of
the constant production & consumption
the network of that
& apart from the mold.
You survived.

Taxing

I hate feeling
that home
is a place
where
all I have
to do
is fix
things. Moving
money, shovelling
words from
one part
of the
country
to the
next,
resettling
livestock.
Big puffy
ones
that are
clearly
getting
fed differently

from the
days
when you
were the sole
approach.
I feel
sad about
what
my life
has grown
into:
a series
of bangs,
soup, all
of us
doing
our job in
this ancient
& lonely
way. I'm
a shepherd
that's
what I
am. Craning
my neck
so
far &
wide
the world
is empty.
There
is no
lamb.

HOWARD NEMEROV ▪ ▪ ▪ ▪ ▪ ▪ ▪ ▪ ▪ ▪ ▪ ▪ ▪ ▪

IFF

1.

Hate Hitler? No, I spared him hardly a thought.
But Corporal Irmin, first, and later on
The O.C. (Flying), Wing Commander Briggs,

And the station C.O. Group Captain Ormery—
Now there were men were objects fit to hate,
Hitler a moustache and a little curl
In the middle of his forehead, whereas these
Bastards were bastards in your daily life,
With power in their pleasure, smile or frown.

2.

Not to forget my navigator Bert,
Who shyly explained to me that the Jews
Were ruining England and Hitler might be wrong
But he had the right idea. . . . We were a crew,
And went on so, the one pair left alive
Of a dozen that chose each other flipping coins
At the OTU, but spoke no civil word
Thereafter, beyond the words that had to do
With the drill for going out and getting back.

3.

One night, with a dozen squadrons coming home
To Manston, the tower gave us orbit and height
To wait our turn in their lofty waiting-room,
And on every circuit, when we crossed the Thames,
Our gunners in the estuary below
Loosed off a couple of dozen rounds on spec,
Defending the Commonwealth as detailed to do,
Their lazy lights so slow, then whipping past.
All the above were friends. And then the foe.

IFF = Identification Friend or Foe, a signalling device carried on aircraft for that purpose.
OTU = Operational Training Unit.

Intimations

Alan Turing's Imitation Game,
Where the artifice of intelligence began,
Turned in the first place on a single theme:
How can you tell a woman from a man?

Alas, life imitates not only art,
But science, too. They can't be told apart.

Playing the Machine

You open P-K4, it thinks, or blinks,
For thirty seconds and answers with the same.
It's merciless with tactical mistakes,
Perfected at following the game's First Law,
Bother The Enemy, deploys its forces
Faster and better than you do because
It threatens you with this while you think that
And that while you think this; you sacrifice
A willing pawn to get mobility,
Before you notice it snaps up two pawns more;
It knows where the second bishop ought to go
While you're still thinking how like love that is
(where do you put the other arm?), and so
It ought to wipe up the board with you every time.

But something intervenes, maybe the maker
Complaining to the programmer: "If you won't
Allow the schlemiels to win one now and then
How will I ever sell your dumb machine?"

So unexpectedly it puts its queen *en prise*
And leaves it there, or castles into mate,
Making you wonder if you really won
Or if its circuits, trying to imitate
The true stupidity of the human mind,
Became recursive and put it into doubt.
But up at Level Seven, or so say
The instructions, it enters The Infinite Mode
Where it will think deeper and deeper still
Until you press it to stop and make its move
Whatever—or you can always turn it off,
Declare a victory and leave it there,
Somewhat the way you leave a telling dream,
Taking its faithless memory away.

The Bluejay and the Mockingbird

The mockingbird, knowing he owned the tree,
Flew close on the tail of an interloper jay.
Through and around they went one after one
With considerable skill not hitting a branch
Nor even it seemed disturbing a single leaf,
And neither left the precinct of the tree.

For all we're told of territoriality,
There was no pecking, they seemed to be having fun
Of a serious sort; at intervals agreed
Each one retired to a neutral branch,
Where the bluejay screamed and the mockingbird copied him.

In the Beginning

Thus Freud deposed about our infant state:
Omnipotent and impotent at once;
Wawl and it shall be given.

Though what is given is never what we want,
So we must wawl again. O chiefs of state,
Are you like this, like us in this?

And God, you holy terror
With the big bang for the buck,
Are you as ourselves in this also?

Like any terrorist making all things new
Including the freedom of the will and the huge
Unsuitable purple hat

Aunt Sadie wore to sister's wedding?
And this verse also, was it there
When the morning stars sang together

And the other celebrities shouted for joy?
And is that why the infant in the crib,
Bearing revenge's infancy, condemned
To suck his thumbs till able to bite his nails,
Hollered like Freud among the cattle and kings?

The Celestial Emperor

Against the invisible antagonist
Waiting across the squared-off court below,
The emperor plays chess with living men,
The pieces all convicted criminals
For economy's sake already sentenced to die,
Which happens to them as they're sacrificed,
Exchanged, or merely lost by accident,
The emperor's or his enemy's misplay.

The men go through the motions as they're moved.
Moaning or sighing as the gambit goes,
And some, that are left in play for long enough,
Become connoisseurs and critics of the game
With exclamation point or question mark
As they approve or disapprove the choice.
He hears them not nor heeds, but listens to
The music of his clockwork nightingale

Immortally singing the fashionable songs
That imitate our planetary fates
Moving against a figured ground of stars
That are fixed and firm as he, and never moved.
So many destinies are in the world
That to each of them the appointed child is born;
Though God be dead, he lived so far away
His sourceless light continues to fall on us.

FRANK O'HARA ■ ■ ■ ■ ■ ■ ■ ■ ■ ■ ■ ■ ■ ■ ■

The War

The war pleased me to know of my interest
and came and went like fog. The garden, wandered
of my true delight delectable, had changed her face
and where the gate had stood horrible teeth
opened on tribal hinges to outcast me. Yet
had I become gone for something rare, and dreaded
no punishment so much as its betrayal in flesh
I saw identical. To push always onward!
over the hill, to other homes that might be laid
in ruin, beautiful sunset of the fist! sole
amusement for the renegade who wears the colors
of some brushed-by conquistador. "A mean one"
the cops say, they can always tell us, not that there
are many. And it is so. Black souls inside black eyes.
No mirrored world. You part the curtain;
the muzzle stares into heaven of its own choosing
and recoils at the competitive vulgarity of targets.
I'm back and you and you drop plates, seeing the puffs
of dust spring from a door that's dead to my white clenches.

A Litany

Night sweet are you
as a cloud lying
between our eyes
kissing our forehead
with reverence and
I mean anyone's.

You night entertain
us like an acrobat
strutting in pink
absentmindedly in love.
The stars—yellow and
glass—figure out

problems in arithmetic
while we know not what
elephants think. They
look on dispassionately
as if we were at a
circus. It's our show.

The warmth of night
ignores our gesture—
like the boy from Moon
who sings as a woman
in love with cups of
saki—or almost nothing.

The circus sinks quickly
because we look too
hot and there's no work
tomorrow. No bearings
to be taken and the
home is every back.

Before morning we may
be equal to our forehead
bending back by logarithm
to touch dutifully the
abyss. Because it's black.
To pay a debt. To rest.

So elephants disappear
on the softest shoulders.
Inquire into our motives

o night! and put up signs.
Strut no vengeance! think
up a breeze from, say,

Siam. In your attack on
Aldebaran use our straight
shooting and be pleased
with our planet unknown
elephants and all. Oh
don't be lazy or funny

night! and dictate no
eye in the middle of our
forehead. Our brothers
did not invent fire.
We love you as you are.
Our quarry. Our corollary.

The Trout Quintet

Okay let's go swimming
I don't want to
well then don't
I want some peanut butter
I want some cream soda

last night the moon seemed to say something
it said "eat"
I said there's nothing
it mentioned plankton
but it had all drifted away

do you think the sand
kills stones
(keep rippling)
no I don't think that
I'm still rippling

well who ever said anything's
done at Radio City Music Hall
except the bolero
but who's ever seen it
who asked

you will think the light
comes from somewhere else
but it comes from the floor

otherwise you wouldn't see it
you're always looking down

after the swim I sat
and rubbed the sand into my crotch
I want to go
to Spain
where the olive trees

A Greek Girl at Riis Beach

The girl fishes up the sea.
A tube beside her holds the pole
and she tugs the ribbon, dirty
ribbon holding her and then
tumbling jet hair falls into wind
flashing with the sun's rays,
the stinging tails and arrows
of the jumping rabid ocean.

Red skirt blows up to nipples
and she lunges her pole over
the scared sea, flailing and rushing
retreating waves, terrified faces
of the little white dogs. Her eyes
in their wilderness gather fishes,
dreaming salmon leap over cheekbones
into the hot spring of her blood
and her lips, wet with the flavor
and the subtle scales, glitter
against the horizon. Birds flush
from her sweating palms. aieeeeeee!
barracuda! tarpon! ray!

Mounting the sandy mare, rearing!
throbbing legs astride she gallops
into a furious sunset whose fire
is quenched by the prodigality
of fishers who fly the seas.

To John Ashbery on Szymanowski's Birthday

Whitelight, keenair, someone
with a Polish accent: j'ai septembre,
et les milles-fois-retours d'Ashes,
like so many violins, from Paris.

The memory of seven sickening seconds
at the top of Carnegie Hall, where
the bow was pulled of its horse-hairs
and the insect suddenly started

humming, unwinding the silver cord
that binds the heart. That was
a concerto! simply-moving glacier
of northern sympathies, sliced banyans

wrapped in glistening green leaves,
lying in an enormous white freezing unit.
Did you practice the piano, John,
while you were gone? summoning thunder

as the delicate echoes of Slavic
nostalgia pretend to have defeated
Napoleon? and have, heaving into a
future of crystalline listening.

I am conducting you in his Symphonie
Concertante. Remember our successes
with the Weber Konzertstück? It is no
repetition, when the marvellous

is like taking off your earmuffs
at the North Pole. I am writing to invite
you to the Polish Embassy for cocktails,
on this superb fall day, musicien amèricain.

Windows

This space so clear and blue
does not care what we put

into it   Airplanes disappear
in its breath and towers drown

Even our hearts leap up when
we fall in love with the void

the azure smile the back of a
woman's head and takes wing

never to return   O my heart!
think of Leonardo who was born

embraced life with a total eye
and now is dead in monuments

There is no spring breeze to
soften the sky   In the street

no perfume stills the merciless
arc of the lace-edged skirt

The Ideal Bar

The jasmine blinker of your breath
opposed across the bar your whiskey eyes
and the miserable distances only stank
for thumbsucking zebras and poilus.

We were the pink chair of plush
rolling its tongue to the window, night,
and the bastards who lived below
the hall. It was in line for our scratches

and for the bellyaches of venery. The
smile, the same smile for the management
as for the Sixtine putti, sand towards
the dark corner's secret peopled incense.

The music floated from discs of
beery autumn in gardens and promenades,
the soul of the Kermesse: your pure
eyes which flared the void my heart fed.

A Military Ball

Valuably, the tune unwinds us! with, ah!
its brash formality and its melancholy echoes
of vulgarity. We are swept fast about by winds,
loving the surprise of sudden power over
each burning waltzer of the body's parade, tenting
tonight inside the bunting carrousel.

Rollicking with laughter at pretty things
and not even regretting our rompers as
naked we dance towards the silliness of our pain,
not acknowledging the boom and buzz of the band, the

endless explosion of its music, or the easy toss of
your and my heart on the baize, the ocean, the sward.

Love blooming in bombardment this is, dear,
all we know before we fall to silent wars: Violet,
not the glamor of your uniform by mine, but these
game convolutions on your voice above the dark.

The Painter's Son

Joe Rivers

The impetuous purple success
the slap of brush or blob
wander off the canvas sky
at a scowl from the fierce dark boy

and the meddling with real
lives, art as midwife and lech,
pestilential singing
beside the bed of whirling flowers

all the illuminations, warfares,
whirligigs and
troglodytic rites, don't
escape this kunst-clubbing prattler

all fragilities wreck like
bicycles when he takes over
but! his bony fists splinter
beautifully on the tough heart of art.

Forest Divers

Fellow-trees, bell so frail and brown
outroaring charm, paces,

aren't you dreaming of ruby watches?

Do you feel in your voice-box
and in its salt response
quite humble and arbitrary?
and is it a ticket to Rangoon
and are you rusty like a fox?

Elbow lifted to plunge and rend,
elephant of the Nilus waters,
elucidate always the choice of propriety,
elegantly trailing eyes.

SHARON OLDS ▪ ▪ ▪ ▪ ▪ ▪ ▪ ▪ ▪ ▪ ▪ ▪ ▪ ▪ ▪ ▪

True Love

In the middle of the night, when we get up
after making love, we look at each other
in total friendship, we know so fully
what the other has been doing. Bound to each other like
soldiers coming out of a battle,
bound with the tie of the birth-room, we
wander down the hall to the bathroom, I can
hardly walk, we weave through the dark
soft air, I know where you are
with my eyes closed, we are bound to each other with the
huge invisible threads of sex, though our
sexes themselves are muted, dark and
exhausted and delicately crushed, the whole
body is a sex—surely this
is the most blessed time of life,
the children deep asleep in their beds like a
vein of coal and a vein of gold
not discovered yet. I sit on the
toilet in the dark, you are somewhere in the room, I
open the window and the snow has fallen in a
deep drift against the pane, I
look up into it, a
world of cold crystals, silent and
glistening so I call out to you and you
come and hold my hand and I say
I cannot see beyond it! I cannot see beyond it!

The Wellspring

It is the deep spring of my life, this love for men,
I don't know if it is a sickness or a gift.
To reach around both sides of a man,
one palm to one buttock,

the other palm to the other, the way we are split,
to grasp that band of muscle like a handle on the
male haunch, and drive the stiff
giant nerve down my throat till it
stoppers the hole of the stomach that is always hungry,
then I feel complete. And the little
hard-hats of their nipples, the male breast
so hard, there are no chambers in it, it is
lifting-muscle. Ah, to be lifted
onto a man, set tight as a lock-slot down
onto a bolt, you are looking into each
other's eyes as if the matter of the iris were the
membranes deep in the body dissolving now—
it is all I want, to meet men
fully, as a twin, unborn, half-gelled,
frontal in the dark, nothing between us but our
bodies, naked, and when those melt
nothing between us—as if I want to die with them.
To be the glass of oily gold my
father lifted to his mouth. Ah, I am in him,
I slide all the way down to the beginning, the
curved chamber of the balls. I see my
brothers and sisters swimming by the silver
millions, I say to them Stay here—for the
children of this father it is the better life;
but they cannot hear me. Blind, deaf,
armless, brainless, they plunge forward,
driven, desperate to enter the other, to
die in her and wake. For a moment,
after we wake, sometimes we are without desire—
five, ten, twenty seconds of
pure calm, as if each one of us is whole.

The Request

He lay like someone fallen from a high
place, only his eyes could swivel,
he cried out, we could hardly hear him,
we bent low, over him, his
wife and I, inches from his face,
trying to drink sip up breathe in
the sounds from his mouth. He lay with unseeing
open eyes, the fluid stood
in the back of his throat, and the voice was from there,
guttural, through unmoving lips, we could
not understand one word, he was down so

deep inside himself, we went closer, as if
leaning over the side of a well
and putting our heads down inside it.
Once—his wife was across the room, at the
sink—he started to garble some of those
physical unintelligible words,
Rass-ih-AA, rass-ih-AA, I
hovered even lower, over his open
mouth, *Rassi baaa,* I sank almost
into that body where my life half-began,
Frass-ih-BAA—"Frances back!"
I said, and he closed his eyes in his last
yes of exhausted acquiescence, I
said, She's here. She came over to him,
touched him, spoke to him, and he closed his
eyes and he passed out and never
came up again, now he could move
steadily down.

April, New Hampshire

for Jane Kenyon and Donald Hall

Outside their door, a tiny narcissus
had come up through the leaf-mold. In the living room,
an old butterscotch dog let me
get my hand into the folds
of the mammal, and knead it. In their room,
Don said, *This is it, this
is where we lived and died.* To the center of the dark
painted headboard—sleigh of beauty,
sleigh of night—there was an angel affixed
as if bound to it with her wings open.
The bed spoke, as if to itself,
it sang. The whole room sang,
and the house, and the curve of the hill, like the curve
between a throat and a shoulder, sang, in praising
grief, and the earth, almost, rang,
hollowed-out bell waiting for its tongue
to be lowered in. At the grave-site—
next to the huge, smoothed, bevelled,
felled, oak home, like the bole
of a Druid *duir,* inside it what comes
not close to being like who she was—
he stood, beside, in a long silence,
minutes, like the seething, harness-creaking

when the water of a full watering is feeding
down into dirt, and he looked at us,
at each one, and he seemed not just
a person seeing people, he looked
almost like a different species, an eagle
looking at eagles, fierce, intent,
wordless, eyelidless, seeing each one,
gazing deep
into each—
miles, years—he seemed to be Jane,
looking at us for the last time
on earth.

Her List

At breakfast, my mother has a list of things
which she thought of during the night. She wants
to tell me she killed a frog, once—
put it on a radiator
and it got off, and she put it back on,
and it got off, and she put it back on
and spread it out. She wants to tell me
she did not cry at her mother's funeral,
she shows me how she peered between the
funeral-home curtain panels, at
the audience, her lips squinched up,
her eyes slitted, like a young witch.
She wasn't sorry when her mother died,
she and her sister just looked at each other,
got in her sister's car, and drove
half the night, talking and planning.
She hunches at the breakfast table, she consults
her list. Her mother threw her term paper
out the window, into the rain.
Her mother came to her classroom and told
the other fifth graders that she was a liar.
Her mother sat her on the toilet till she stuck—I knew that,
her mother took her curlers out in her sleep—I knew that,
her mother arrived two hours late
for a party in her honor, and wouldn't let her children
eat or drink anything
because the party was in her honor, not their honor.
My mother's eyes narrow at me fiercely
as if she is furious at me—when she bit
her nails, her mother tied her to the bed
and would not let her get up to pee.
How many times did she do that?

Once, I think, my mother says.
I look at her—she tied me up
once. I say, You know what this is
called now, Mom? You were a little abused—not
much, but a little abused.
She laughs without pleasure, she looks at me
without delight or sorrow, she says I never thought of that.
I put my arms around her, stroke
the hardish lump on her back—her permanented
head feels a little close to my breast,
but if she tries anything, I think wildly,
I could break her wrist. I pet her carti-
laginous hump—she was a child, she arrived
without having harmed anyone.
She had formed in darkness, inside her mother,
in liquid her mother had never touched
and had little to do with. She formed in pallor
with shapes of what would be her breasts and
womb swimming, free, through her body,
toward their place of mooring.

The Clasp

She was four, he was one, it was raining, we had colds,
we had been in the apartment two weeks straight,
I grabbed her to keep her from shoving him over on his
face, again, and when I had her wrist
in my grasp I compressed it, fiercely, for a couple
of seconds, to make an impression on her,
to hurt her, our beloved firstborn, I even almost
savored the stinging sensation of the squeezing,
the expression, into her, of my anger,
"Never, never, again," the righteous
chant accompanying the clasp. It happened very
fast—grab, crush, crush,
crush, release—and at the first extra
force, she swung her head, as if checking
who this was, and looked at me,
and saw me—yes, this was her mom,
her mom was doing this. Her dark,
deeply open eyes took me
in, she knew me, in the shock of the moment
she learned me. This was her mother, one of the
two whom she most loved, the two
who loved her most, near the source of love
was this.

[O Quadriga,]

O Quadriga,
here in the Eastern sky,
there, in winter, directly above my head
so I had to strain my neck to see you
(happy, on my hill, in the clear cold
of the best of my life) salute you,
tonight, life no longer what then I
did not know how to identify why
you, in particular, of all the night's forms
had come to be important to me, replacing the known or more stylish
exhibits, a lessoning I did not understand
yet stood certain under you, you were a window-light
of my own skull.
Now in summer in Gloucester, driven as a Christian out onto
the highways, suckered into the present as a soul
forced out of fortune, with no lead but myself,
with no love, with life solely to be lived,
with nothing, therefore, of any of it interesting, see you
ahead of me, and it is one of the seven sacred wonders
you are my instructor at last, there are no landings
you also were Pluto, you did take my girl, you are
triumph (trump before the Trump herself) I hail you, Driver,
in your place upon the sky

[As Cabeza de Vaca was]

As Cabeza de Vaca was
given the Guanches gift
and so could cure
And did, at Corazone,
New Mexico, remembered
in the name

From Fuerteventura crossing
by the Dog, Gran Canaria, Gloucester
is nearly Guanche too
And may she too have
as well-thought, and felt
a place in men's minds

The Telesphere

Gather a body to me
like a bear. Take it on
my left leg and hold it off
for love-making, man or woman
boy or girl in the enormity
of the enjoyment that it is
flesh, that it is to be loved, that
I desire it, that without it
my whole body is a hoop
empty and like steel
to be iron to grasp
someone else in myself
like those arms which hold
all the staves together
and make a man, if now as cold and hot
as a bear, out of me.

Wednesday November 15th (1967)

[The boats' lights in the dawn now going so swiftly the]

The boats' lights in the dawn now going so swiftly the
night going so swiftly the draggers'
lights shoving so sharply in what's left
clouds even like the puff
of cottons she left which, forgotten,
even with all her care   care of such an order
love itself was put down as over-
ably as, if she chose   and she had
still no choice to organize
every thing: love made as straight
as if   if you could get her womb out
if she cld that is   and it was so close
to the mouth   both my own and her
legs all the distance of her
hair to the tip of the rounded boy
behinds   I could hold both of them in
my one hand   her hair itself
even on her head more clouded
and dense than any depth at all
there was before her womb's mouth
was at the entrance: love's puff
of irritated
wetness   puffs
in the sky and the night

still dark and handsome as the
face of her legs lifted
wetly to be loved and those hurrying
silly two lights boats busily
like little hurrying nifts going too fast
and now too small even though bright
in the still dark but coming now earliest
or latest of earliest light and latest of
night as the darkness and the white puffs
on and by the bed the girl whose head
and whose love she lifts opening
and raising her legs are so
alike night still light already
too far out and the small draggers
too small and bright in the first dawn since
she left was here and
I was
covered as I am not now
alone ill of
separation I cannot
allow love having
not on my own part taken
it
part in her
face & face
hair & hair depth
to my eye and hands
one hand
so much as caught
in her
hair my member my
middle finger right on her crown
love as large and tight as her great
mouth's turning
in perfect tuned love lying
all out three parts each at
a different rate and
interchange of
time

GEORGE OPPEN ■ ■ ■ ■ ■ ■ ■ ■ ■ ■ ■ ■ ■ ■ ■

To the Poets: To Make Much of the World

of that passion *that light within*
and without   no need

of lamps in daylight writing year
after
year the poem

discovered

in the crystal
center of the rock   image
and image   the transparent

present tho we speak of the abyss
of the hungry we see their feet their tired

feet in the news and mountain and valley
and sea as universal

storm the fathers said we are old
we are shrivelled

come

        To the shining of rails in the night
the shining way the way away from home
arrow in the air
hat-brim fluttered in wind as she ran
forward and it seemed to me so beautiful
the sun lit air it was no dream all's wild
out there as we   unlikely
image of love found the way
away from home

Disasters

        of wars o western
wind and storm

of politics I am sick with a poet's
vanity legislators

of the unacknowledged

world *it is dreary*
to descend

and be a stranger how
shall we descend

who have become strangers in this wind that

rises like a gift
in the disorder the gales

of a poet's vanity it our story shall end
untold to whom and

to what are we ancestral *we wanted to know*

if we were any good

out there the song
changes the wind has blown the sand about

and we are alone the sea dawns
in the sunrise verse with its rough

beach-light crystal extreme

sands dazzling under the near
and not less brutal feet journey
in light

and wind
and fire and water and air *the five*

bright elements
the marvel

of the obvious and the marvel
of the hidden is there
in fact a distinction dance

of the wasp wings dance as
of the mother-tongues can they

with all their meanings

dance? *O*

O I see my love I see her go

over the ice alone I see

myself Sarah Sarah I see the tent
in the desert my life
narrows my life
is another I see
him in the desert I watch
him he is clumsy
and alone my young
brother he is my lost
sister her small

voice among the people the salt

and terrible hills whose armies

have marched and the caves
of the hidden
people

Fear

once once only in the deluge

of minutes a tree
a city

a stone in the road waiting

stones eagles seagulls sliding
sideways down the wind I cannot find

a way to speak

of this the source
the image the space

of the poem our

space too great
or too small where the world rides the words
speak of too little

time remaining
fearful

of sorrow in this once once only
among atoms, eagles, and alone

Gold on Oak Leaves Said Young

        Mary's poem   vision
image the pure body

of idea rang in the young

voice but for the gold
light I would drown

(in the gold
light) as many dreams

as dreamers on this salt and sleepless

seat guilts   guilts

pour in to the full song sung
among us I haunt an old

ship and leaky the sun

glints thru the ragged

caulking I would go out
past the axioms' wandering

timbers garboards keelson the keel   full

depth

of the ship in that
light into all

that never
knew me

The Whirl Wind Must

for the huge
events are the   symbols

of loneliness (a country

poem of the feminine) and children's

trinkets in the gravel
of the driveways the warm

blood flows
in her the hot

river in the drama
of things caught
in the face

of things village
things long

ago a wind destroyed

shelter   shelter more lonely
than suns

astray over earth music
in the dark music

in the bare light suddenly I saw
thru Carol's eyes the little road leading
to her house the trampled

countries of the driveways to face
the silence of the pebbles the whirl wind must

have scattered under the sun the scattered

words that we can muster where once
were the grand stairways

of sea captains   language

in the roads speech

in the gravel the worn
tongues of the villages

The City of Salt

In the sun-drenched
city of salt
where the window boxes
are little coffins
full of red geraniums,
flower
that offers up
earth's smell of death
like water
from a deep well.

In that city of salt
where my mother walks
with a basket
over one arm—
she's off to market,
she's going to buy
all those things
she forgot to give us
when she was alive.

In that city of salt
the sun never sets,
the rooms of her apartment
fill up
with vegetables:
the purple globes
of eggplant, asparagus
like the blunt bolts
a crossbow fires,
and peppers convoluted
as the heart
and sweet to taste.

Elegy for a Child

Here are consoling pieties
like a tightly-packed
warehouse
of mortuary statues

through which you
must elbow a path.

Here are sparrows
on a porch
sorting sand from seed
with their beaks.

Here's the hour
that has forgotten
the minute,
though the minnow
remembers the stream.

Here are the roots
in one world,
and the blossom
in the other.

Who'd Want to Be a Man?

With his heart
a black sack
in which a small
animal's trapped.

With his grief
like a knot
that's tied at birth,
balled up and hard.

With his rage
that would smash
the ten thousand things
without blinking.

With his mind
like a tree on a cliff—
its roots, fists
clutching stone.

With his longing
that's a dry well
and where is the rain?

A Litany

I remember him falling beside me,
the dark stain already seeping across his parka hood.
I remember screaming and running the half mile to our house.
I remember hiding in my room.
I remember that it was hard to breathe
and that I kept the door shut in terror that someone would enter.
I remember pressing my knuckles into my eyes.
I remember looking out the window once
at where an ambulance had backed up
over the lawn to the front door.
I remember someone hung from a tree near the barn
the deer we'd killed just before I shot my brother.
I remember toward evening someone came with soup.
I slurped it down, unable to look up.
In the bowl, among the vegetable chunks,
pale shapes of the alphabet bobbed at random
or they lay in the shallow spoon
like creatures washed up on a beach.

BRENDA MARIE OSBEY ■ ■ ■ ■ ■ ■ ■ ■ ■ ■ ■ ■

Geography

the geography i am learning
has me place myself
at simultaneous points
of celebration
and all you see and hear in me
is these women
walking in the middle of the road
with their hoodoo in their hands.

this map leads you to a desert place
and flowers daring brilliance
in the most cruel and merciless sun
and all you see for miles around
these women
tender past hurting
visibly bruised
only on the very edges.

this place no one chooses
is the land i tarry in.

this ritual i go through
is as old as its name
and the prophet-women who dance it:

first you place one foot
and then the other.

this map has been used before.
you have seen these travelers
all their hoodoo
walking behind them
in the dust:

first you place one foot.

this journey has been made before
in the middle of the day
your friends and your family
carrying this same hoodoo
leaving you behind:

first you place one foot
and then the other.

i said
first you place *one* foot.

this body has done
its share of the journey.

Everything Happens to (Monk and) Me

we hustle hard as the rest of the folk me and my baby
but it never seems to count.
so
we stop off nights and hear the best and worst of everybody.
my baby's down in heart but that hasn't stopped him yet.
me i'm just down.
we struggle-in.
we sit ourselves down.
we believe in everything.
we know the other life is a club called havana.
we dream in unison how it will be there
and have never had this conversation because we do not need to.
we believe in everything my baby and me.
we *know* that life on the other side is a club called havana
and sometimes we ache for it
but not out loud.

the music in this city is not heard in clubs.
this is not a thing we recite
we know this
by heart.
no.
it's in the thrumming of the empty streetcar tracks
the thrumming of the old wooden banquettes beneath the newer cement
it's in the bricks the slaves are cursing over eternally
the way the poorest of the crazies look up from rheumy eyes
the way a workingman hauls his haunches home to his woman
a little low on one side his walk
a little bit too hurried or too slow
for him for her one
the way she doesn't wait but puts his plate over water
pretending to watch the news
washing her hands
or else not stirring
pretending not to daydream
over porkchops and brown gravy

the thrumming is in the way it hangs
the whole city hanging
at the edge of a water no one will wade
the whole city hanging
the way the not-so-young-anymore men used to say
"can you *hang* with that?" and mean it
mean it.
that's the problem with this city
we *all* mean it so hard.
and this is a soft city
a city of softness
turning turning ever on the edge of its own meaning
and hanging on to *us* for dear life.
we really
really
mean
to get it right soon some glorious day some soft thrumming night
and "oh" cry out the pretty little street-stepping-boys sometimes
"ain't we righteous, y'all!"
yes sweetness we mouth in their direction when we hear or see or care
we really truly are

and that's what started the whole damn thing to begin with:

me and my baby just want to hear some music from time to time.
well i do.
my baby he loves me and sometimes just says okay.
and sometimes he just fakes it like he doesn't *have* this longing.
my baby thinks he's stoic—

that old negro stoicism sterling loved so.
but no
he wouldn't be so sad around the eyes late evening into night
after supper and before cigarettes
   —we still have supper here
   and late-night breakfast
   and say "good evening" after twelve noon—
he wouldn't have those *eyes*
not from being old-fashioned sterling/negro-stoic
oh-but-no we say here (first syllable stressing)
truth is he's old-fashioned negro-martyr heroic.
i get him.
then i get him out.
we get out into or behind the crowd
we do not need to look at one another
we nod
we hang our hands about as if we've known it all along.
we thrum
we thrum
we thrum
inside the city

at least that's how it is
when we condescend to our hipper selves

"oh baby" we say together later on
"oh
oh, baby"

but ain't we righteous y'all?

and out of nowhere in the night
solo
standards
the funny-sad
the halved
the tired
witty
unlovely chords
and everything within us that ever hoped for hipness stirs.
not following that sound
we laugh into the night
because we were young once
and very very hip.
we were young once
and very very wise.
we were young once
these streets were always ours
we paved them with the flats of our heels

we danced
and never bothered to tire
or if we did it hardly mattered
our hippest coolest livest selves

out late and full up with heart
valiant as the very streets
we wind we wind me and my baby
we reach the other side the place called havana
we reach our own unlovely selves
—bitter chords—
reach for each other
and are wise
enough to know better
our tender places older than before.

it never ends.
we follow the sweep of the river downtown and up.
somewhere is music we can hear
havana and unlovely chords
and right here with us
the city and the indigo night
its tuneless keyboard silent altogether for the moment
we play upon the night
each key a treasure we have close-*tight* between us
unrighteous
and unlovely
full up with longing
in the streets.

MICHAEL PALMER ▪ ▪ ▪ ▪ ▪ ▪ ▪ ▪ ▪ ▪ ▪ ▪ ▪

Twenty-four Logics in Memory of Lee Hickman

The bend in the river followed us for days
and above us the sun
doubled and redoubled its claims

Now we are in a house
with forty-four walls
and nothing but doors

Outside the trees, chokecherries, mulberries and oaks
are cracking like limbs
We can do nothing but listen

or so someone claims,
the Ice Man perhaps, all enclosed in ice
though the light has been shortening our days

and coloring nights the yellow of hay,
scarlet of trillium, blue of block ice
Words appear, the texture of ice,

with messages etched on their shells:
Minna 1892, Big Max and Little Sarah,
This hour ago

everyone watched as the statues fell
Enough of such phrases and we'll have a book
Enough of such books

and we'll have mountains of ice
enough to balance our days with nights
enough at last to close our eyes

Wheel

You can say the broken word but cannot speak
for it, can name a precise and particular shade
of blue if you can remember its name
(Woman of the South, New Lilac, Second Sky?)

As the light, close to blinding, fell—falls
in bars across a particular page, this
then another, some other
followed far too closely by night

Or as the sleeping
pages recall themselves, one by one,
in dream-riddled, guarded tones,
recall themselves from path

to sloped meadow, meadow
to burnt shore, shore
to poised wave, dismay
to present, any present

of the bewildered and the buried alive
(we've been told they were buried alive)
Is there a door he hasn't noticed
and beyond it a letter which created the door

or claims it created a door
which would open either way

"or anything resembling it"

The hills like burnt pages
Where does this door lead

Like burnt pages
Then we fall into something still called the sea

A mirrored door
And the hills covered with burnt pages

With words burned into the pages
The trees like musical instruments attempt to read

Here between idea and object
Otherwise a clear even completely clear winter day

Sometimes the least memorable lines will ring in your ears
The disappearing pages

Our bodies twisted into unnatural shapes
To exact maximum pleasure

From the view of what is in any case long gone and never was
A war might be playing itself out beyond the horizon

An argument over the future-past enacted in the present
Which is an invisible present

Neva streaming by outside the casement
Piazza resculpted with bricolage

Which way will the tanks turn their guns
You ask a woman with whom you hope to make love

In this very apartment
Should time allow

What I would describe as a dark blue dress with silver threads
And an overturned lamp in the form of a swan

A cluster of birches represents negativity
Flakes of ash continue to descend

We offer a city with its name crossed out
To those who say we are burning the pages

H

We sat on the cliff-head
before twin suns.

For all I know we were singing
"Dancing on the Ceiling."

Descending I became lost
but this is nothing new.

From the screen poured
images toward me.

The images effected a hole
in the approximate center of my body.

I experienced no discomfort
to my somewhat surprise.

This was many weeks ago
many times of days ago.

Yet as far as history goes
it was no time at all.

Many kinds of days ago
I should have said above.

The body has altered
many times since.

Has bent a little over on its stem
and shed a layer of film.

Winter has come and gone
should be remembered.

White occasions like clouds
she may once have whispered.

To that I would add, fields
unplanted, some still burning.

Wonderless things
days at a time.

As a storm begins as a night storm
to end as an ice storm.

Some by now certainly have left
to seek shelter in the mountains.

Only to be met there
by the force of spring rains.

Paths turned to mud
boulders torn loose from above.

The difficulties with burying the dead
she may then have said.

But this letter is something like a door
even if a false door.

Unvoiced as breath
voiced as ash.

To that I would add
there is a song opposite itself.

To that I would add, we have drawn
necessary figures from the sack of runes or tunes.

Echo and wormwood
conspire at the base of the throat.

Snail climbing acanthus
measures our pace.

On the plate by the mark of difference
a mark is made we call the first mark.

Weathering so
the wheel of days.

Gaia the bag lady
in sadness below.

Untitled (April '91)

La narrativa says you must paint a flower
paint a flower with a death's head

flower with a death's head at its center
center with a desert at its center

clock with ochre hands
its face a sun the sun

a multiple sun at 3 a.m.
sun of limbs and sun of the lens

flower as if it were a limb
anemone, rose, yellow marigold

gravity a word from the narrative
word that bends in the narrative

as if suns would flower as sparks of paint
then fall before the retinal net

fall into actual space
space of minarets and streets

Says, Here is a word you must erase
a word made of particles of paint

Here is a word with no points in space
The Higgins black ink has dried in its bottles

so it's true, as angels have said
that there are things of glass

light-gatherers, cat's-eyes, keys and bells
and that glass is a state of sand

It's impossible to hold such a key in your hand
and it's light you see traveling through angels of glass—

through knells—
causing the il- lis- les- the li- lil- lit-

forming the l's you're never to understand
like the tongues of syllables wreathed in the wells,

like tongue-tied and transparent angels
The painting wall still stands

Studio at night
Everything in place

to P.G.

Construction of the Museum

In the hole we found beside the road
something would eventually go

Names we saw spelled backward there

In the sand we found a tablet

In the hole caused by bombs
which are smart we might find a hand

It is the writing hand
hand which dreams a hole

to the left and the right of each hand

The hand is called day-inside-night
because of the colored fragments which it holds

We never say the word desert
nor does the sand pass through the fingers

of this hand we forget
is ours

We might say, Memory has made its selection,
and think of the body now as an altered body

framed by flaming wells or walls

What a noise the words make
writing themselves

to E.H.
11 apr 91

I Do Not

Je ne sais pas l'anglais.
—GEORGES HUGNET

I do not know English.

I do not know English, and therefore I can have nothing to say about this latest
war, flowering through a night-scope in the evening sky.

I do not know English and therefore, when hungry, can do no more than point
repeatedly to my mouth.

Yet such a gesture might be taken to mean any number of things.

I do not know English and therefore cannot seek the requisite permissions, as
outlined in the recent protocol.

Such as: May I utter a term of endearment; may I now proceed to put my arm or arms around you and apply gentle pressure; may I now kiss you directly on the lips; now on the left tendon of the neck; now on the nipple of each breast? And so on.

Would not in any case be able to decipher her response.

I do not know English. Therefore I have no way of communicating that I prefer this painting of nothing to that one of something.

No way to speak of my past or hopes for the future, of my glasses mysteriously shattered in Rotterdam, the statue of Eros and Psyche in the Summer Garden, the sudden, shrill cries in the streets of São Paulo, a watch abruptly stopping in Paris.

No way to tell the joke about the rabbi and the parrot, the bartender and the duck, the Pope and the porte-cochère.

You will understand why you have received no letters from me and why yours have gone unread.

Those, that is, where you write so precisely of the confluence of the visible universe with the invisible, and of the lens of dark matter.

No way to differentiate the hall of mirrors from the meadow of mullein, the beetlebung from the pinkeltink, the kettlehole from the ventifact.

Nor can I utter the words science, seance, silence, language and languish.

Nor can I tell of the arboreal shadows elongated and shifting along the wall as the sun's angle approaches maximum hibernal declination.

Cannot tell of the almond-eyed face that peered from the well, the ship of stone whose sail was a tongue.

And I cannot report that this rose has twenty-four petals, one slightly cancred.

Cannot tell how I dismantled it myself at this desk.

Cannot ask the name of this rose.

I cannot repeat the words of the Recording Angel or those of the Angel of Erasure.

Can speak neither of things abounding nor of things disappearing.

Still the games continue. A muscular man waves a stick at a ball. A woman in white, arms outstretched, carves a true circle in space. A village turns to dust in the chalk hills.

Because I do not know English I have been variously called Mr. Twisted, The
One Undone, The Nonrespondent, The Truly Lost Boy, and Laughed-At-By-
Horses.

The war is declared ended, almost before it has begun.

They have named it The Ultimate Combat between Nearness and Distance.

I do not know English.

AMANDA PECOR ▪ ▪ ▪ ▪ ▪ ▪ ▪ ▪ ▪ ▪ ▪ ▪ ▪ ▪ ▪ ▪

A Product of Evolution, I Invest in a Mutual Fund

Sometimes I feel like my money's gone to Heaven.
I do not feel this way because of the interest it earns,
for I know, of course, that I have earned nothing,
and thus whatever I've gained must have been taken
from someone else by force, and, if not
by force, through deceit, coercion, and abuse,
and even if that's not the case, Jesus clearly stated
that I should give everything away.
Therefore I am not feeling particularly angelic about interest,
though, pathetically, I prefer it to losing money.
I do, however, feel like my money's gone to Heaven,
in the sense that it is no longer tangible, like my purse.
When my purse disappears I feel acute distress.
I search for it like God in pursuit of a lost soul.
My money can't be lost, in that sense.
My money now exists in a different realm than I,
therefore I cannot leave it in a cafeteria or on a bus.
Things happen to it, as a result of the Invisible Hand of the Market,
which I, of course, have never seen, though experts assure me
it determines my fate. Have the experts seen it?
No. But then I've only seen Jesus in a single vision (dubious),
and Heaven not even once.

Furthermore, I've read several books that suggest
that evolution is thinking and we are its thoughts.
If anything's thinking in this universe,
I don't think it's likely to be us.
Evolution's thought doesn't seem to have a goal or purpose,
but I ramble a lot myself, as you can see,
and other people still seem to think of me as a thinking entity,
not that their opinions would count for much, in light of this theory.
A hummingbird plunges its head into a deep-throated flower
and comes out crowned with golden dust.
Who thought of this?

Not the hummingbird, not the flower, not us.
That doesn't leave too many candidates.
Plato thought everything essential existed somewhere else,
and it's easy to see why, if you think about this example.

It's hard to think clearly if you're right up close.
Just look at the way we manage our lives.
Evolution doesn't care about the hummingbird, the flower, or us.
On this, expert opinion is virtually unanimous.
As for God, that's more of a heated debate;
let's call it a toss up:
God either cares or He doesn't.
As for us, we care, and when we don't,
it's because we're distracted, caring so much about something else.
This last condition hardly seems possible with God or evolution,
just as my money, wherever it is, can there be neither forgotten nor loved.

SAM PEREIRA ▪ ▪ ▪ ▪ ▪ ▪ ▪ ▪ ▪ ▪ ▪ ▪ ▪ ▪ ▪

An Entity of Its Word

This morning in a car off Sunset   The sky
Carried its tune to my barrio and said
Get In   There is no explaining the mind
Of a true Californian in the morning   Sometimes

You do as you are told   I got in and the sky
Said buckle asshole and watch out for the mud
Of what you often call heaven   The mean
Are on the doorstep and you want us to believe

That you can sit there stroking a woman   Stroking
A woman's thigh in the daylight while
Boys drill someone's sister and blame it on the moon
And the smog   I'd take you to meet someone

Says the sky   But he isn't one of the mean
Folks of the world   Seems he's the breakfast
Of the mean and apparently likes it that way

From here on the sky didn't say a word   It just drove
Past all of it because the sky was an entity of its word
Past the hills that this town was famous for   Past
A woman sitting alone and listening to air and calling

It the sweetest sound since *Hotel California* drove
All the surfers into the city for cocktails because
Everyone had to grow up sometime   The air might just be
The only thing left of quality for her   The mean

Had dropped stilettos behind each of her charming ears
And had told her in their inimitable way that the Johnny
Of her glorious life had taken off with the sky
In the sky's own car   That she could rest her head

On the legs of the air during rush hour   That
As the sky at this very moment screams   It
Is almost like being in love   That song ago

SYLVIA PLATH   ■ ■ ■ ■ ■ ■ ■ ■ ■ ■ ■ ■ ■ ■

Incommunicado

The groundhog on the mountain did not run
But fatly scuttled into the splayed fern
And faced me, back to a ledge of dirt, to rattle
Her sallow rodent teeth like castanets
Against my leaning down, would not exchange
For that wary clatter sound or gesture
Of love: claws braced, at bay, my currency not hers.

Such meetings never occur in märchen
Where love-met groundhogs love one in return,
Where straight talk is the rule, whether warm or hostile,
Which no gruff animal misinterprets.
From what grace am I fallen. Tongues are strange,
Signs say nothing. The falcon who spoke clear
To Canacee cries gibberish to coarsened ears.

Morning in the Hospital Solarium

Sunlight strikes a glass of grapefruit juice,
flaring green through philodendron leaves
in this surrealistic house
of pink and beige, impeccable bamboo,
patronized by convalescent wives;
heat shadows waver noiseless in
bright window squares until the women seem
to float like dream-fish in the languid limbo
of an undulant aquarium.

Morning: another day, and talk
taxis indolent on whispered wheels;

the starched white coat, the cat's paw walk,
herald distraction: a flock of pastel pills,
turquoise, rose, sierra mauve; needles
that sting no more than love; a room where time
ticks tempo to the casual climb
of mercury in graded tubes, where ills
slowly concede to sun and serum.

Like petulant parakeets corked up in cages
of intricate spunglass routine,
the women wait, fluttering, turning pages
of magazines in elegant ennui,
hoping for some incredible dark man
to assault the scene and make some
gaudy miracle occur, to come
and like a burglar steal their fancy:
at noon, anemic husbands visit them.

Black Pine Tree in an Orange Light

Tell me what you see in it:
      the pine tree like a rorschach-blot
black against the orange light:

Plant an orange pumpkin patch
      which at twelve will quaintly hatch
nine black mice with ebon coach,

or walk into the orange and make
      a devil's cataract of black
obscure god's eye with corkscrew fleck;

put orange mistress half in sun,
      half in shade, until her skin
tattoos black leaves on tangerine.

Read black magic or holy book
      or lyric of love in the orange and black
till dark is conquered by orange cock,

but more pragmatic than all of this,
      say how crafty the painter was
to make orange and black ambiguous.

Rhyme

I've got a stubborn goose whose gut's
Honeycombed with golden eggs,
Yet won't lay one.
She, addled in her goose-wit, struts
The barnyard like those talonned hags
Who ogle men

And crimp their wrinkles in a grin,
Jangling their great money bags.
While I eat grits
She fattens on the finest grain.
Now, as I hone my knife, she begs
Pardon, and that's

So humbly done, I'd turn this keen
Steel on myself before profit
By such a rogue's
Act, but—how those feathers shine!

Exit from a smoking slit
Her ruby dregs.

STANLEY PLUMLY ■ ■ ■ ■ ■ ■ ■ ■ ■ ■ ■ ■ ■ ■ ■ ■

Nobody Sleeps

One theory is that acid wastes in the blood
accumulate and depress the brain so much
it wants to lie down at the mouth of a cave
on a high hard ledge shelving over nothing.
It wants to think of nothing, be nothing,
and wake up empty with sleep in its eyes.
Another is that during waking the brain
uses up its oxygen faster than the body
can replace and is so starved by the end
of the day it seeks a bed of branching
in order to lay its head on laurel green.
And a third says that because the afferent
impulses of the neurons are contractile
with the dendritic process of the cells
any interruption over time isolates
the cortex from external stimuli and
as interruptions peak in sync with dark

the brain wants to lie all night by fire.
The theory of anaemia, involving the loss
of tone in the vascular heart of the medulla,
is too particular, especially since,
except in fits and starts, nobody sleeps—
though there are children who sleep through
anything, even memory and waking, and adults
who work the nightshift or the street
who only pretend by closing their eyes,
even in daylight. But the vertical brain
wants to lie down, beside water if it can
or under wind topping the tall pale grasses.
It wants to alter its relation to the bed
to give up gravity to the ground, to let
the mind float out in spirit-buoyant air,
to feel, at the foliate edge, the mind
relieved. And because it cannot sleep
it wants to dream the sexual narrative
of longing and connection, the journey
of the body in light continually dying,
the cold wet morning air silvering down
on the night earth warming toward the sun,
and then to hear the first bell-clarity of song,
which, if you were dreaming, would wake you.

Alms

The woman in my building who skips
each perpendicular is a water-bug,
weightless in her ability to lift
and fall lightly, ever afraid
she'll break her mother's back,
though if the reading of faces
has any value she has. Her friend
is thirty and touches every line
she crosses in her step-and-a-half
steps since her stroke, as if
she'd been struck on her whole
left side by lightning: she fades
in and out of talking and lets
the man she lives with—twice
her size and boiled at birth
in anger—speak for her. Then
there are those at the elevator
less obvious, bent internally
as by some soulful choice, sworn,
like most of us, to keep it secret.

But the woman with her head
confessionally down, who dances
over lines, and her friend
with the long gray scar, who has
half a body, have no choice—
one the leaper, the other a kind
of leper—moving in their theater
across the lobby. In a strange
city by a stranger river once,
balanced above the Isola Tiberina,
two gypsy women tried to rob me—
they were girls and one of them
was pregnant: they came straight
at me singing in their language,
pointing all their fingers at
their mouths, pouring their hands
through my poor tourist's pockets.
It happened in a moment that took
hours. Then they ran.

Constable's Clouds for Keats

They come in off the sea peaceable masters
and hold the sea in the sky as long as they can.
And you write them down in oils because of their
brilliance, and to remember, in its turn, each one.

It's eighteen twenty-two after the Regency,
and it would be right in the year after his death
to think of these—domed above the Heath
in their isolated chronicle—as elegies

of the spirit; right to see these forms
as melancholy hosts, even at this distance.
Yet dead Keats is amorphous, a shapelessness
reforming in the ground, and no one you know enough

to remember. He lies in the artist's paradise
in Rome, among the pagan souls of sheep at pasture.
You'll lie in Hampstead where he should have stayed
to meet you on your walks up Lower Terrace

or along the crowning High Street heading home.
Your clouds grow whiter, darker, more abstract
from one elaborate study to the next,
correlatives, or close, to the real sentiment

that lives, you say, in clouds . . . subjects to counter-
weigh the airy gravity of trees and leaping horses.
Keats could have met you—you must have seen him once
against the light, at least. He could be

crossing on Christchurch Hill Road now, then
over to the Elm Row and down Old Admiral's Walk.
He could be looking at the clouds blooming between
buildings, watching the phantoms levitating stone.

He was there your first Heath summer writing odes,
feeling the weather change from warm to chill,
focused, no less than you, on daylight's last detail,
wondering what our feelings are without us.

Cardinals in a Shower at Union Square

At first they look like any other birds
on gun line from the underbrush, so someone
calls them sparrows and someone who thinks
he knows, scarlet tanagers or something else
exotic, as if they've slipped captivity—
one of those white sky August days the hammer
of the heat picks out the old one or the child
locked in a car, while gathered above the blank
grave of the pavement, at the altitude of snow,
enough rain to almost forgive it all.
Only two are really red, the rest a buoyant
rust blood brown, young or female, all of them
with masks and crests that make them what
they are, explosions from the other side
or blown in, with the paper, with the storm.
Whoever starts the clapping is answered
by a show of hands to meet baptismal waters
and a couple, who are high, bird-dancing.
Whoever starts the shouting is quieted
by the lady who hears silences,
cupping her clownish ears. . . .
For a moment the ringing air is clean, then
for a moment nothing happens, nothing moves
except the cardinals, in and out of trees.
And in that moment ends. The cloudburst
passes, the air turns into fire again,
the sirens sing their distances, the walls
of light burn down. And in no time,
in the time it takes the runoff to drain
back underground, there's no one left

but lifers and the dealers and rain birds
swallowed upward by the sun, and rain, new rain,
in the rivers and the reservoir uptown,
ready to rise and to pour its heart out all over

CARL RAKOSI ▪ ▪ ▪ ▪ ▪ ▪ ▪ ▪ ▪ ▪ ▪ ▪ ▪ ▪ ▪ ▪ ▪ ▪

Song

There never was
a simple world

since Adam,
nor a kind one

with a fanfare
to the common man

yet there's music
in the lot
of the Adamite.

History, blow, blow.
Fiddle this:

who spits
in the glass

eye of Moloch?
nobody, nobody

To the Man Inside

A woman's heart is like an inn.
—Russian saying

Get up, you old dog.
You've been lying in front
of the fire too long.

Out! Out! The inn
is temporarily closed
for remodelling.

The ladies are inside
cleaning house and laughing
at the inn idea.

"Say boss," minces
one, "who's
the innkeeper here?"

The new tenant
is indistinct.

Will there be larks
and metaphors
at the inn, sweet ladies?

The Old Country

The other day
I was stricken
non compos mentis

by an inscription
over a urinal:

'The tree is older
than its principle'

That pulled me
into a deep zone
older than Dante's

and played the way
the clarinet, true
to its principle

plays to the goats
in the old country
an ambiguous *tristesse.*

Ode on Arrival

A maquette

Here I am
in the house
of aesthetics,

in its great silence
where the air
is an abstraction.

I am in
the presence
of purity

and a great mass
as of a sphinx behind me.

Sphinx,
are you there?

Best not look
too closely
lest I lose my way,

my courage,
my self,
my everything.

This could be
The Great One.

Silly me, here I am
talking to
a figure of speech.

I'll be bold.
Sphinx, open up,
speak!

JOANNA RAWSON ■ ■ ■ ■ ■ ■ ■ ■ ■ ■ ■ ■ ■ ■ ■

The Border

(Moshav Neot Hakikar, Negev Desert)

Sliding from half-up the eucalyptus trees, the wild desert pigs practice flight,
While the salt mines flaunt their electric necklaces, a city of runways

For the suicide squads in their bedevilled outdated two-wingers,
Those sporadic Arab pilots gliding noiselessly
Off the serrated dark bluffs across the valley,

Blown to smithereens by the cockeyed
Jew gunners secreted away in folds of sandstone and night chill.

The moon was a gaping beckoning
Eye, a charm on the desert that caused men
To sail the air, silver, wicked, toward the flat saltplain,
Though no one admitted the sea had sunk back into the planet,
Leaving behind a white crescent scar long as a myth.

What water was left
They could not crash or drown in, so empty and saline its remains.
They floated those black motorless birds
Toward the appointed border, as if already underwater.

In the day, we worked the fields—eggplants, dates, the intricate
Machine-sprinkled tomatoes unfolding under veils of plastic.
Beside us, their dark-eyed clobbered women
Imported from across the border on ramshackle buses at dawn,
With spines like roaming slopes and toddlers flocking
Their skirthems, dirt labor
Who counted and mumbled in a tongue odd to me,
Suffered the barren
Clay-hot late afternoon hours like soldiers themselves.

We did not dream their dreams, fuselage, petrol, that clutch of fury
That propels the antics of heroism.
I guess I knew even then that by night

They swaddled the bodies of their sons and lovers in black cotton and hoods
And oiled up the wheels of some discarded creaking glider.
I guess their shins and leathered faces
Aroused suspicion on my part,
Like beetles on a rose they were, like spiders on a fresh white wall.

I knew by the proud conspiring way they assailed the air
With betel-juice spit, and struck with precision the nail
On the outhouse door, or the top lacehole
Of the crewhead's boot, though no one spoke of it.

Self-portraits by Frida Kahlo

Blood was her dress and her embassy,
No one suffered with such grace.
She attended her only live exhibit in bed,
They rolled her in with three monkeys
Riding the thin canopy. Above
Her eyebrow where the third eye
Opens and slams like a loose shutter,

Her husband the magnificent slob Diego Rivera
And a white medallion skull
Trade watch over the crawl-space. Imagine
The stamina of standing for years
With that crushed spine aligned in wire,
With vines oozing from the trapdoor
In her chest, onto the seething ground,
Imagine capturing your own excruciating pose
In oil, fashioning it, flattening it, fastening it
By a hook to your deathbed frame.
Which of these agonizing entrances to the interior body
Did she find most glamorous?
No one suffered from such eagerness.
She lay all afternoon giving birth
In the gallery, to arrows, scars, to garlands
Severed from her stillborn generation.
No one left her altar unharmed.
No one took more pleasure
In the shattered mirror on the ceiling than she.

LIAM RECTOR ▪ ▪ ▪ ▪ ▪ ▪ ▪ ▪ ▪ ▪ ▪ ▪ ▪ ▪ ▪ ▪

Him, His Place

for Donald Hall

My grandfather died one morning in dampness,
tamping, watering the roses for the coming season. . . .
On his knees then, he must have bowed

to the worn harness snapping in his chest and sending him
finally into memory for us, into the waters of spirit
submerged and remembered. . . . He must have known before—

he said nothing about it—that he would soon be going
from us. People look back and say that the dead, days
before they die, have their ways of saying goodbye

to us, if we only knew what to look for. . . . He did visit
relatives he had long ignored and went
to sing his agnostic prayer in their church,

the week before he died. And he went so far
as to ask my grandmother, a woman he had not slept with
for twenty years, to fix his favorite meal for him,

the evening before he left us. And she went ahead
and fixed it. . . . Part of what you got as a tenant farmer
in those days was the morning milk, two pigs a year,

a cinderblock house and a plot where you planted
what your family needed, but I think what kept him alive,
aside from the habit of living, was the evening

and the hills he watched each evening after eating,
as some people watch water. Those were the staring hours
in which I came to know him, sitting with him, watching

the fields move and all but live our lives for us. . . .
As the cows shifted and the cars moved by below at the bottom
of the hill, I felt the motion of fields the man carried

so quietly with him. And when I asked him
about women, as I did often that last summer
I came, he usually said nothing, though as a sparrow

mounted a sparrow one evening he did mention
a woman from a time long before mine, remembering outloud
"the stiff cock I gave her in the back of a buckboard,"

a wagon pulled by horses and driven out to drive-in movies
just before the horses went back to the field, just as the farms
were giving themselves over to the cars, the tractors. . . .

I howled in complicity, thinking I was getting, at last,
some real man-talk from him. . . . It was the cars
eventually took all his children from him, the ones

after the war which the children jumped in
and used to drive towards the money, the cities,
the places where I grew up on the movies. . . .

I lived in the suburbs and was eighteen and heart-blown
when told over a phone he would no longer
be there to sit with. I had been the only one

he finally ever talked to, and I thought of him, his place,
as the only home I ever had. Fourteen years later,
after my generation's war and the stalling we did

having children, my second wife and I had our first child,
Virginia, and filled our rowhouse near the water of Baltimore
with the sound of two oars placed in the boat and drifting. . . .

And tonight, as I was filling my wife with a stiff cock
ruddered towards our second child, we went down to those fields
moving between us, and heard the sleep of children as they move

in the wet darkness of their first home before it perishes
and they dry-dock into the body of boat and the fate
of water, the great collapsible moment of motion we are.

DONALD REVELL ▪ ▪ ▪ ▪ ▪ ▪ ▪ ▪ ▪ ▪ ▪ ▪ ▪ ▪ ▪

At the Exhibition of Parables

I have the address exactly. I know her name.
Right now, the espaliered wood-rose, a lampwork
of flowers and trained birds, is falling
out of her yard and into traffic. I am too late
to see it torn apart by three cars.
The flattened petals and displaced birds;
Balkanized, unlucky address by Anne's name.

The new polity is a collective of small
hearts biding out of reach among hybrid flowers.
It has relocated the past to suburbs
I cannot bear. Anne used to wake early,
would go down quietly into the yard to shape
the trees into candelabra. On the worst night,
she set them ablaze. The fires spread to the house.

The new polity enjoyed the change. Anne
moved far away into a smaller house
in a warm climate that did not use fires.
I remember she had freckled hands year round
and in the hot months the fingers darkened
like rose twigs so heavy with roses
they snap into pieces in a hard rain.

Everything must be set ablaze to be seen.
And then a hard rain comes and the maps
are redrawn to explain the ashes, the old borders
buried under heaps of roses.
They are poor Anne's fingers. The new maps
show not even a single country with her name,
no border of flowers that resembles her.

Anne is elsewhere. I have the exact
address and know how she lives. At first light,
she tends to the wood-rose, teaching it to grow
into a lamp that burns flowers and beautiful
trained birds one night in its lifetime. Right now
she is safe indoors. There is a new polity.
It is a murderous traffic of small hearts.

Fauviste

for Bin Ramke

Five minutes with his paintings and I remember.
This is life on the boats, and anyplace
to stand is a dead wife bobbing under daubs
of wet lanterns, not a thought of home,
no imagining how the three beds
of iris will burst and stand beside the house.
Five minutes, and I cannot picture my own life.

I don't think there is any use looking backward.
The boats were lowered by other hands than mine
as I slept. When I awoke, we were already
far from the sinking and had new names.
My wife was dead or in love with someone else
in another boat. At night, we strung up lanterns
and we had five minutes of a beautiful painting.

We were never rescued. And I am sure
that rescue only happens to the faithful,
that seeing five minutes of the world with no wife
and all the lanterns hanging close to the water
changed my eyes into other things that see
but cannot see rescue when it comes.
I see my wife and flowers in everyone's hands.

I don't think there is any use painting irises.
The three beds that I know my wife tended
were lost at sea. Their petals washed towards land
and into the mouths of rivers painted by Frenchmen.
I cannot picture them. I only know that they fell to pieces
as I slept and that someone in France made something
out of them that is my life on the boats.

The World

Where is India or even one body
rising out of flowers like a mountain?
I am always trying to read landscapes,
the signal glass beneath the leaves,
the bodies of men and women escaping
in the curve of hills and the cataract of shadows between hills.
Not absence. Not even silence, that cloud
anyone can fill with his own mind.
Only the earth itself, and maybe the figure
of a man martyred to change on a high mountain
or woman in a dress I can feel between my fingers,
she was that victimized.
I want to read and to begin by reading India.

Their gods were too much in love with games.
It was too much like suffering, spilling
out of temples, multiplying
into the less admirable bodies of laughter,
little flowers the size of your thumbnail
dividing hillsides and the air into so many
loving fragments that the temples died
of increase. I knew a man who died in the rioting.
I know a woman who mistook those flowers
for the government of heaven.
She was there with her arms open, in her best dress,
and the camera saw gods capering round her feet and nothing
inside of her or rushing into her arms. Only
the whole landscape, a game too much like suffering,
and she could not feel that.
The more I think of the man and the sad woman,
the harder it is to see India.

The whole landscape of the world keeps widening.
In the increasing absences between things, storms
kill people outright or starve them of the just
government of nature they will not see.
I must give up trying to read.
And then I will have lost my friend forever
to the nearly straightened curve of the hills.
I will lose a woman I love in the same moment.
A cataract of shadows will fill her arms
and she will think it is India, not knowing
that little flowers like suffering have made nonsense of India
and of every place she could possibly stand in her best dress.
When I was a boy, my father drove me once

very fast along a road deep in a woodland.
The leaves on the trees turned into mirrors
signalling with bright lights frantically.
They said it was the end of the world and to go faster.

1919

All that year, the fronts of houses
wore the faces of rebel angels
and eyes draped with the figures of human bodies
in the attitudes of a dance,
the dancers' limbs curved like lemon flowers.

The palace was a keyboard instrument.
The cafés floated on early snow
and the boulevardiers eddied like yellow petals
in the whorls of snow between the tables.
In that year, each mouth kissed your neck

with a damp flutter, almost too softly.
I need to go backwards that far to see
the faces of the last actors
aware of no difference between aspiration
and silliness, hope and kitsch.

People end up with one another.
The sex is terrible, or the sex is nothing.
Late, with a metropolitan lateness,
couples lower the eyes of their freedom,
and a brief, annihilating music

reminds them in narrowing whorls, so many
useless futures and a passion
nearly to bite through handcuffs.
I like earliness and the feel of the provinces.
I love the wonderful year 1919

and daring housefronts newly scrubbed
postered with slogans announcing
no need to be ashamed of hope,
no limit to aspiration which is to be shared
with the actor on your right hand

and a dazzling sequence of actors—
sky, drapery, and the human figure—on your left.
But people end up with one another in great cities.

I get up late, and as she is still sleeping
I go out. The buildings say only

that they have seen over the stelo of the future
and stand guard against the emptiness there
because I could not bear it.
In 1919, men and women stood at the height of buildings.
They played upon each other as upon keyboard instruments.

KENNETH REXROTH ■ ■ ■ ■ ■ ■ ■ ■ ■ ■ ■ ■

On Flower Wreath Hill

I

An aging pilgrim on a
Darkening path walks through the
Fallen and falling leaves, through
A forest grown over the
Hilltop tumulus of a
Long dead princess, as the
Moonlight grows and the daylight
Fades and the Western Hills turn
Dim in the distance and the
Lights come on, pale green
In the streets of the hazy city.

II

Who was this princess under
This mound overgrown with trees
Now almost bare of leaves?
Only the pine and cypress
Are still green. Scattered through the
Dusk are orange wild kaki on
Bare branches. Darkness, an owl
Answers the temple bell. The
Sun has passed the crossroads of
Heaven.
          There are more leaves on
The ground than grew on the trees.
I can no longer see the
Path; I find my way without
Stumbling; my heavy heart has

Gone this way before. Until
Life goes out memory will
Not vanish, but grow stronger
Night by night.
                    Aching nostalgia—
In the darkness every moment
Grows longer and longer, and
I feel as timeless as the
Two thousand year old cypress.

III

The full moon rises over
Blue Mount Hiei as the orange
Twilight gives way to dusk.
Kamo River is full with
The first rains of Autumn, the
Water crowded with colored
Leaves, red maple, yellow gingko
On dark water, like Chinese
Old brocade. The Autumn haze
Deepens until only the
Lights of the city remain.
Autumn haze, or the smoke of
Osaka mills? Still, it was
Hazy in Murasaki's time.

IV

No leaf stirs. I am alone
In the midst of a hundred
Empty mountains. Cicadas,
Locusts, katydids, crickets,
Have fallen still, one after
Another. Even the wind
Bells hang motionless. In the
Blue dusk, widely spaced snowflakes
Fall in perfect verticals.
Yet, under my cabin porch,
The thin, clear autumn water
Rustless softly like fine silk.

V

This world of ours, before we
Can know its fleeting sorrows,
We enter it through tears.
Do the reverberations
Of the evening bell of

The mountain temple ever
Totally die away?
Memory echoes and reechoes
Always reinforcing itself.
No wave motion ever dies.
The white waves of the wake of
The boat that rows away into
The dawn, spread and lap on the
Sands of the shores of all the world.

VI

Clustered in the forest around
The royal tumulus are
Tumbled and shattered gravestones
Of people no one left in
The world remembers. For the
New Year the newer ones have all been cleaned
And straightened and each has
Flowers or at least a spray
Of bamboo and pine.
It is a great pleasure to
Walk through fallen leaves, but
Remember, you are alive,
As they were two months ago.

VII

Night shuts down the misty mountains
With fine rain. The seventh day
Of my seventieth year,
Seven-Seven-Ten, my own
Tanabata, and my own
Great Purification. Who
Crosses in midwinter from
Altair to Vega, from the
Eagle to the Swan?
Intelligent interstellar
Jellyfish, ten light years wide.
Pterodactyls link wings and
Form a bridge across the River
Of Heaven, under the earth,
Against the sun. Orion,
My guardian king, stands on
Kegonkyoyama.
So many of these ancient
Tombs are the graves of heroes
Who died young. The combinations
Of the world are unstable

By nature. Take it easy.
Nehan.
Change rules the world forever,
And man but a little while.

VIII

Oborozuki
Drowned Moon

The half moon is drowned in mist
Its hazy light gleams on leaves
Drenched with warm mist. The world
Is alive tonight. I am
Immersed in living protoplasm,
That stretches away over
Continents and seas. I float
Like a child in the womb. Each
Cell of my body is
Penetrated by a
Strange electric life. I glow
In the dark with the moon drenched
Leaves, myself a globe
Of St. Elmo's fire.
I move silently on the
West forest path that circles
The shattered tumulus.
The path is invisible.
I am only a dim glow
Like the tumbled and broken
Gravestones of forgotten men
And women that mark the way.
I sit for a while on one
Tumbled stupa and listen
To the conversations of
Owls and nightjars and tree frogs.
As my eyes adjust to the
Denser darkness I can see
That my seat is a cube and
All around me are scattered
Earth, water, air, fire, ether.
Of these five elements
The moon, the mist, the world, man
Are only fleeting compounds
Varying in power, and
Power is only insight
Into the void—the single
Thought that illuminates the heart.
The heart's mirror hangs in the void.

Do there still rest in the broken
Tumulus ashes and charred
Bones thrown in a corner by
Grave robbers, now just as dead?
She was once a shining flower
With eyebrows like the first night's moon,
Her white face, her brocaded
Robes perfumed with cypress and
Sandalwood; she sang in the Court
Before the Emperor, songs
Of China and Turkestan.
She served him wine in a cup
Of silver and pearls, that gleamed
Like the moonlight on her sleeves.
A young girl with black hair
Longer than her white body—
Who never grew old. Now owls
And nightjars sing in a mist
Of silver and pearls.

The wheel
Swings and turns counter clockwise.
The old graspings live again
In the new consequences.
Yet, still, I walk this same path
Above my cabin in warm
Moonlit mist, in rain, in
Autumn wind and rain of maple
Leaves, in Spring rain of cherry
Blossoms, in new snow deeper
Than my clogs. And tonight in
Midsummer, a night enclosed
In an infinite pearl.
Ninety nine nights over
Yamashina Pass, and the
Hundredth night and the first night
Are the same night. The night
Known prior to consciousness,
Night of ecstasy, night of
Illumination so complete
It cannot be called perceptible.

Winter, the flowers sleep on
The branches. Spring, they awake
And open to probing bees.
Summer, unborn flowers sleep
In the young seeds ripening
In the fruit. The mountain pool
Is invisible in the

Glowing mist. But the mist-drowned
Moon overhead is visible
Drowned in the invisible water.
Mist drenched, moonlit, the sculpture
Of an orb spider glitters
Across the path. I walk around
Through the bamboo grass. The mist
Dissolves everything else, the
Living and the dead, except
This occult mathematics of light.
Nothing moves. The wind that blows
Down the mountain slope from
The pass and scatters the Spring
Blossoms and the autumn leaves
Is still tonight. Even the
Spider's net of jewels has ceased
To tremble. I look back at
An architecture of pearls
And silver wire. Each minute
Droplet reflects a moon, as
Once did the waterpails of
Matsukaze and Murasame.
And I realize that this
Transcendent architecture
Lost in the forest where no one passes
Is itself the net of Indra,
The compound infinities of infinities
The Flower Wreath,
Each universe reflecting
Every other, reflecting
Itself from every other,
And the moon the single thought
That populates the Void.
The night grows still more still. No
Sound at all, only a flute
Playing soundlessly in the
Circle of dancing gopis.

Floating

Our canoe idles in the idling current
Of the tree and vine and rush enclosed
Backwater of a torpid midwestern stream;
Revolves slowly, and lodges in the glutted
Waterlilies. We are tired of paddling.
All afternoon we have climbed the weak current,
Up dim meanders, through woods and pastures,
Past muddy fords where the strong smell of cattle

Lay thick across the water; singing the songs
Of perfect, habitual motion; ski songs,
Nightherding songs, songs of the capstan walk,
The levee, and the roll of the voyageurs.
Tired of motion, of the rhythms of motion,
Tired of the sweet play of our interwoven strength,
We lie in each other's arms and let the palps
Of waterlily leaf and petal hold back
All motion in the heat thickened, drowsing air.
Sing to me softly, Westron Wynde, Ah the Syghes,
Mon coeur se recommend à vous, Phoebi Claro;
Sing the wandering erotic melodies
Of men and women gone seven hundred years,
Softly, your mouth close to my cheek.
Let our thighs lie entangled on the cushions,
Let your breasts in their thin cover
Hang pendant against my naked arms and throat;
Let your odorous hair fall across our eyes;
Kiss me with those subtle, melodic lips.
As I undress you, your pupils are black, wet,
Immense, and your skin ivory and humid.
Move softly, move hardly at all, part your thighs,
Take me slowly while our gnawing lips
Fumble against the humming blood in our throats.
Move softly, do not move at all, but hold me,
Deep, still, deep within you, while time slides away,
As this river slides beyond this lily bed,
And the thieving moments fuse and disappear
In our mortal, timeless flesh.

ADRIENNE RICH ▪ ▪ ▪ ▪ ▪ ▪ ▪ ▪ ▪ ▪ ▪ ▪ ▪ ▪ ▪

Burning Oneself Out

for E. K.

We can look into the stove tonight
as into a mirror, yes,

the serrated log, the yellow-blue
gaseous core

the crimson-flittered grey ash, yes,
I know inside my eyelids
and underneath my skin

Time takes hold of us like a draft
upward, drawing at the heats
in the belly, in the brain

You told me of setting your hand
into the print of a long-dead Indian
and for a moment, I knew that hand,

that print, that cave,
that sun producing powerful dreams
A word can do this

or, as tonight, the mirror of the fire
of my mind, burning as if it could go on
burning itself, burning down

feeding on everything
till there is nothing in life
that has not fed that fire

Burning Oneself In

In a bookstore on the East Side
I read a veteran's testimony:

the running-down, for no reason
of an old woman in South Viet Nam
by a U.S. Army truck

The heat-wave is over
Lifeless, sunny, the East Side
rests under its awnings

Another summer
The flames go on feeding

and a dull heat permeates the ground
of the mind, the burn has settled in
as if it had no further question

of its right to go on devouring
the rest of a lifetime,
the rest of history

Pieces of information, like this one
blow onto the heap

they keep it fed, whether we will it or not,
another summer, and another
of suffering quietly

in bookstores, in the parks
however we may scream we are
suffering quietly

August 1972

Two horses stand in a yellow light
eating windfall apples under a tree

as summer tears apart and the milkweeds stagger
and grasses grow more ragged

They say there are ions in the sun
neutralizing magnetic fields on earth

Some way to explain
what this week has been, and the one before it!

If I am flesh sunning on rock
if I am brain burning in fluorescent light

if I am dream like a wire with fire
throbbing along it

if I am death to man
I have to know it

His mind is too simple, I cannot go on
sharing his nightmares

My own are becoming clearer, they open
into prehistory

which looks like a village lit with blood
where all the fathers are crying: *My son is mine!*

Harpers Ferry

Where do I get this landscape? Two river-roads
glittering at each other's throats, the Virginia mountains fading
across the gorge, the October-shortened sun, the wooden town,

rebellion sprouting encampments in the hills
and a white girl running away from home
who will have to see it all. But where do I get this, how
do I know how the light quails from the trembling
waters, autumn goes to ash from ridge to ridge
how behind the gunmetal pines the guns
are piled, the sun drops, and the watchfires burn?

I know the men's faces tremble like smoky
crevices in a cave where candle-stumps have been stuck
on ledges by fugitives. The men are dark and sometimes pale
like her, their eyes pouched or blank or squinting, all by now
are queer, outside, and out of bounds and have no membership
in any brotherhood but this: where power is handed from
the ones who can get it to the ones
who have been refused. It's a simple act,
to steal guns and hand them to the slaves. Who would have thought it.

Running away from home is slower than her quick feet thought
and this is not the vague and lowering North, ghostland of deeper snows
than she has ever pictured
but this is one exact and definite place,
a wooden village at the junction of two rivers
two trestle bridges hinged and splayed,
low houses crawling up the mountains.
Suppose she slashes her leg on a slashed pine's tooth, ties the leg in a kerchief
knocks on the door of a house, the first on the edge of town
has to beg water, won't tell her family name, afraid someone will know her family
    face
lies with her throbbing leg on the vined verandah where the woman of the house
wanted her out of there, that was clear
yet with a stern and courteous patience leaned above her
with cold tea, water from the sweetest spring, mint from the same source
later with rags wrung from a boiling kettle
and studying, staring eyes. Eyes ringed with watching. A peachtree shedding
    yellowy leaves
and a houseful of men who keep off. So great a family of men, and then this
    woman
who wanted her gone yet stayed by her, watched over her.
But this girl is expert in overhearing
and one word leaps off the windowpanes like the crack of dawn,
the translation of the babble of two rivers. What does this girl
with her little family quarrel, know about arsenals?
Everything she knows is wrapped up in her leg
without which she won't get past Virginia, though she's running north.

Whatever gave the girl the idea you could run away
from a family quarrel? Displace yourself, when nothing else
would change? It wasn't books:

it was half-overheard, a wisp of talk:
escape   flight   free soil
softing past her shoulder

She has never dreamed of arsenals, although
she's a good rifle-shot, taken at ten
by her brothers, hunting

and though they've climbed her over and over
leaving their wet clots in her sheets
on her new-started maidenhair

she has never reached for a gun to hold them off
for guns are the language of the strong to the weak
How many squirrels have crashed between her sights

what vertebrae cracked at her finger's signal
what wings staggered through the boughs
whose eyes, ringed and treed, has she eyed as prey?

There is a strategy of mass flight
a strategy of arming
questions of how, of when, of where:

the arguments soak through the walls
of the houseful of men where running from home
the white girl lies in her trouble.

There are things overheard and things unworded, never sung
or pictured, things that happen silently
as the peachtree's galactic blossoms open in mist, the frost-star
hangs in the stubble, the decanter of moonlight pours her mournless liquid down
steadily on the solstice fields
the cotton swells in its boll and you feel yourself engorged, unnamable
you yourself feel encased and picked-open, you yourself feel unenvisaged
There is no quarrel possible in this silence
You yourself stop listening for a word that will not be spoken; listening instead to
    the overheard
fragments, phrases on the air: *No more   Many thousand go*
And you know they are leaving as fast as they can, you whose child's eye followed
    each face wondering
not how could they leave but when: you knew they would leave
and that so could you but not with them, you were not their child, they had their
    own children
you could leave the house where you were daughter, sister, prey
picked open and left to silence, you could leave alone.

This would be my scenario of course: that the white girl understands
what I understand and more, that the leg torn in flight

had not betrayed her, had brought her to another point of struggle
that when she takes her place she is clear in mind and her anger
true with the training of her hand and eye, her leg cured on the porch of history
ready for more than solitary defiance. That when the General passes through
in her blazing headrag, this girl knows her for Moses, pleads to stand with the
    others in the shortened light
accepts the scrutiny, the steel-black gaze; but Moses passes and is gone to her
    business elsewhere
leaving the men to theirs, the girl to her own.
But who would she take as leader?
would she fade into the woods
will she die in an *indefensible position,* a *miscarried raid*
does she lose the family face at last
pressed into a gully above two rivers, does Shenandoah or Potomac carry her
north or south, will she wake in the mining camps to stoke the stoves
and sleep at night with her rifle blue and loyal under her hand
does she ever forget how they left, how they taught her leaving?

The Art of Translation

1

To have seen you exactly, once:
red hair over cold cheeks fresh from the freeway
your lingo, your daunting and dauntless
eyes. But then to lift toward home, mile upon mile
back where they'd barely heard your name
—neither as terrorist nor as genius would they detain
                     you—

to wing it back to my country bearing
your war-flecked protocols—

that was a mission, surely: my art's pouch
crammed with your bristling juices
sweet dark drops of your spirit
that streaked the pouch, the shirt I wore
and the bench on which I leaned.

2

It's only a branch like any other
green with the flare of life in it
and if I hold this end, you the other
that means it's broken

broken between us, broken despite us
broken and therefore dying

broken by force, broken by lying
green, with the flare of life in it

3

But say we're crouching on the ground like children
over a mess of marbles, soda-caps, foil, old foreign
                                                    coins
—the first truly precious objects. Rusty hooks,
                                        glass.

Say I saw the earring first but you wanted it.
Then you wanted the words I'd found. I'd give you
the earring, crushed lapis if it were,

I would look long at the beachglass and the sharded self
of the lightbulb. Long I'd look into your hand
at the obsolete copper profile, the cat's eye, the
                                        lapis.

Like a thief I would deny the words, deny they ever
existed, were spoken, or could be spoken,
like a thief I'd bury them and remember where.

4

The trade names follow trade
the translators stopped at passport control:
Occupation: no such designation—
Journalist, maybe spy?

That the books are for personal use
only—could I swear it?
That not a word of them
is contraband—how could I prove it?

Camino Real

~

Hot stink of skunk
crushed at the vineyards' edge

hawk-skied, carrion-clean
clouds ranging themselves
over enormous autumn

that scribble   edged and skunky
as the great road winds on
toward my son's house seven hours south

~

Walls of the underpass
smudged and blistered eyes gazing from armpits
THE WANTER WANTED   ARMED IN LOVE AND DANGEROUS
WANTED FOR WANTING

~

To become the scholar of : :
: : to list compare contrast events to footnote lesser
    evils
calmly to note *bedsprings*

describe how they were wired
to which parts of the body
to make clear-eyed assessments of the burnt-out eye: :
    investigate
the mouth-bit and the mouth
the half-swole slippery flesh the enforced throat
the whip they played you with the backroad games the
    beatings by the river
O to list collate commensurate to quantify:

I was the one, I suffered, I was there

never
to trust to memory only

to go back   notebook in hand
dressed as no-one there was dressed

over and over to quantify
on a gridded notebook page

The difficulty of proving
such things were done for no reason
that every night
"in those years"
people invented reasons for torture

Asleep now,   head in hands
hands over ears   O you

Who do this work
every one of you
every night

~

Driving south: santabarbara's barbarous
landscaped mind: lest it be forgotten
in the long sweep downcoast

let it not be exonerated

but O the light
on the raw Pacific silks

~

Charles Olson: *Can you afford not to make
the magical study
which happiness is?*

I take him to mean
that happiness is in itself a magical study
a glimpse of the *unhandicapped life*
as it might be for anyone, somewhere

a kind of alchemy, a study of transformation
else it withers, wilts

—that happiness is not to be
mistrusted or wasted

though it ferments in grief

George Oppen to June Degnan: *I don't know how
to measure happiness*

—Why measure? in itself it's the measure—

~

at the end of a day
        of great happiness if there be such a day

drawn by love's unprovable pull

I write this

LEN ROBERTS ■ ■ ■ ■ ■ ■ ■ ■ ■ ■ ■ ■ ■ ■ ■ ■

Acupuncture and Cleansing at 48

No longer eating meat or dairy products or refined sugar,
I lie on the acupuncturist's mat stuck with twenty
needles and know a little how
Saint Sebastian felt with those arrows
piercing him all over, his poster
tacked to the wall before my fourth-grade desk
as I bent over the addition and loss,
tried to find and name the five oceans, seven continents,
drops of blood with small windows of light strung
from each of his wounds, blood like
the blood on my mother's pad the day she hung
it before my face and said I was making her bleed to death,
blood like my brother's that day
he hung from the spiked barb
at the top of the fence,
a railroad track of stitches gleaming
for years on the soft inside of his arm,
blood like today when Dr. Ming extracts a needle and dabs
a speck of red away, one from my eyelid, one from my cheek,
the needles trying to open my channels of *chi,*
so I can sleep at night without choking,
so I don't have to fear waking my wife hawking the hardened mucus out,
so I don't have to lie there thinking
of those I hate, of those who have died, the needles
tapped into the kidney point, where memories reside,
tapped into the liver point, where poisons collect,
into the feet and hands, the three *chakra* of the chest
that split the body in half, my right healthy, my left in pain,
my old friend's betrayal lumped in my neck,
my old love walking away thirty years ago
stuck in my lower back, father's death mother's
lovelessness lodged in so many parts
it may take years, Dr. Ming whispers, to wash them out,
telling me to breathe deep, to breathe hard,
the body is nothing but a map of the heart.

And Where Were You

*for my father, R.R.R., French-Mohawk,
long dead in Cohoes, New York*

with your teepee and Lucky Strike
signals of smoke, when she cornered
me in the hallway, cold as a rat
she smashed with the broom handle
till it broke and began
with her small fists?
And when I disappeared under the bed,
behind the long black dress of the closet,
when I turned into words at the kitchen
table, *bologna, mischievous, fluorescent,*
when I grew faster than the parti-
colored flash cards, a quotient, a divider,
a remainder, then a continent, yellow
Asia, brown Australia, mysterious blue
South America and castanets clicked in my fingers
and my heart grew claws that scratched to get out,
where were you, wooden Indian deader than
the Chief who stood outside Bernie's Cigar Shop
all nicked and carved and scuffed
with just one good eye left to look out
on Ontario Street and the swirling ice-floed Mohawk River?
Where were you, dream catcher who floated
above my black bed with the red coal living
at the far end of your every breath,
my dark man, my ten crooked fingers with five rings
and five diamond chips, five gold initials
that told everyone but me you were just another drunk,
dirty hands on her white, white breasts,
dirty cock in her silk-satin cunt,
stupid half-breed thinking you could fuck
her white gloves and polka-dot dress and rows
of neat teeth and still be free to peddle bread
in your Golden Eagle truck's
eighty-miles-an-hour snowdrifted roads throughout the Adirondacks
where your grandfathers ate bark.
Dumb, long-dicked, alcoholic, pock-marked,
malarial-ridden, purple-hearted Indian, where
are you now I've grown big and strong
and am ready to bloody my hands with the bitch?

Sister Ann Zita Shows Us the Foolishness of the Forbidden Books

The Plague of God, the Rod of God
Sister Ann Zita wrote on that clouded blackboard
while Donald Wilcox whispered
the Cock of God, the Cock of God
into Karen Awlen's red ear, making her lean forward,
her breasts shifting under the starched white blouse,
the silver dog on the silver chain dangling in that seventh-grade sunlight
as we all watched the Serpent of the Bottomless Pit
coil through the 9 planets beneath which
Richie Freeman dunked strands of Donna's long gold hair into the inkwell,
Ann Harding and Ronny Michaels passing back and forth a note folded
at least ten times with *I love you* written in red at the crinkled center,
Al Aldon's fart so loud when he grabbed it mid-aisle
that Sister looked up from her Book of Devils and Stars to ask what was going on,
pointing to the demon with 7 serpent heads, 14 faces and 12 wings,
telling us St. Paul said it would have been better if we had not been born
since we were all sinners, Donald whispering
Yes, Yes, in the alley behind the Union Diner,
as he flapped his wings back there by the clothes closet till he fell
out of his seat, Sister reminding us it took Satan 9 days, not a split-second,
to drop from Heaven to Hell, the hands of the big clock above the door
clicking toward twelve making me bend to tie my laces and see Barbara McGill
scratching her thigh, skirt hitched up to the mound of her ass,
the four lines her fingernails had raked a wavery blood red
through the short, yellow-white hairs, the bluish tint of her white, white skin.

God's Blessing

When Sister sent Joe to the nurse's office,
we could hear his leg braces clatter
down the long green corridor, the heavy
door squeaked open, clicked shut,
Sister's voice reminding us
that God gave Joe polio to test
him, and to bless him, and I thought
of my father's jungle-rotted face,
my older brother's crossed eyes,
wondered what God had in store for
me now that we were all driven out of *Paradise,*
word Sister flung at us as she held
up the picture of Adam and Eve, a big
green snake coiled in an apple tree just
like the one by Big John's fence I planned

to climb that very dusk, when the shadows
darkened and no one would see me run, bent,
from tree to tree with my stick, knocking down
the apples that were not mine,
delicious, juicy apples I'd eat in the backyard's
garbage shed; knowing it was a sin,
cracking open the thick core with my teeth
so I could get to the black shiny seeds.

JANE ROHRER ▪ ▪ ▪ ▪ ▪ ▪ ▪ ▪ ▪ ▪ ▪ ▪ ▪ ▪ ▪ ▪ ▪ ▪

In the Kitchen Before Dinner

The winter sky past the feeder,
Beyond the wood of straight trees
And the field rising to the ridge,
Is unnervingly delicate.
But you are acquainted with the country
And you know poems. You've heard this.

Years, years and years, I've looked out
From this window, stirring—
    Straight out of the sun
    a cardinal swoops to the feeder,
    his sweep, not his shape,
    the unstrokable wing of art.
Seeing that,
I want to tell you:
    The sun of poems is on the snow
    on the slope past the wood
    to the pond. What I see at 5:00.
    It marries the music from my living room.
    It is not that simple.
    I cannot explain it.
Saying that,
I think I cannot ever leave.
I'm grounded by attachment, I'm rapacious
For facts: That bowl.
      His gloves on the chair
      holding each other.
These I can explain.

Orchard in the Spring

I am shaking life a leaf in the orchard.
Green parachutes are caught in the trees,
A lace drapes the crabapple.
On the ground thick pruned branches
Lie in disarray, waiting.
I am not waiting.
If you are calling me,
I am over here, staring at the ground
Where fallen cuttings meet and pass
And a short-lived face appears,
An augury on blowing grass.

I am sad in the white drizzle of blossoms.
Elmer, in the lower field,
Bobs along atop the plow
Drawn by a six-mule team
Opening a furrow, closing it,
Opening, closing.

I lie down in the grass and look up.
Now I am waiting.
Someone I know is that dried apple
Holding on since last fall.
Soon a green shoot will push it from the limb
To the ground.

Bad Truth

If I had no memory
I would say this is perfect,
This June late afternoon
And early evening.
Cat is walking the rim of the pond below
And here on the porch
We drink some wine while dinner cooks.

Let me go on: Behind us
            Through the blue screen door
              (We're eased in green and purple canvas chairs)
Hard rock rolls rumors
Which turn explicit as I write.
He is reading *North of Jamaica* (excuse me
                        but a bird of classical proportion
                        just flew to the walnut tree)
And I am holding a book by Pinsky

When this day tilts.　The Rickenbacker rips
　　　　　　　　a drum-thump
　　　　　　　　and a bass full of moans
For a bad truth.

The garden hose lies coiled and reminds me
Yesterday I saw a snake in the gully
Turn its dry white underbelly up.

RICHARD RONAN ■ ■ ■ ■ ■ ■ ■ ■ ■ ■ ■ ■ ■

Love Among Lepers

First, for kindness, we must assume the dark;
it is not right to see this. Not outright, perhaps not even inwardly.
Things often wound the eye & remain like picks of glass, wounding again,
tearing again through the recent scabbing of the thing seen & seen again,
a red dream recurring.
Darkness then. And in it wordlessness.
Let us be strict in this, for we can never know our partner's
latest turn of unhealth, if he has, since last loved, lost a lip
& is now imperfect of any answer, even to our softest, sweet word.
No, kinder not to speak at all, even if we still can.
Besides, what is there to say? What framing, what bodying
forth in speech can you or I give this slow process,
the gradual cessation of systems. Pieces & pieces, feelings
in the loving arm forgetting themselves by bits,
losing the long-assumed narration that has kept it in its shape
& in its kind of sentence so long.
The corrosion of vessels, of living nerve confused
as if with ash, ash of a forest burnt black upstream,
one that leapt carbonized & howling into the cooling blood?
How could we ask with any tenderness after the damage upriver,
the cellular losses, the soldiery in the blackened slough,
the muck driving down from the minute frontiers of wilderness,
from the high stairway, from the pith of the heart,
flowing from trickles to lava runs, a nutrient stew,
poison now, alpha gone all omega, the horror
we must watch even in darkness & await.

No, the etiquette, though broken so often with sobbing,
must be silence: at least we must not speak.
Any word can run mad with itself, and with evisceration of itself
& there is no word for living through this, there is no word for witnessing

our beloved fail piecemeal, no word to speak the itch
inside the fingers to be off, candle wax thinning to the bone-wick,
no word conveying the centering toward a more & more
essential which is itself essential to nothing & no one
but ourselves, in useless love, in unsupporting darkness, tongues
 numb and as slow as sick dogs.

Darkness in the room. Darkness in the mind, the heart & spirit
the clean table, the finger like a glass pen drawing us in contours of light.
Eyes. Yours. Skin. Your skin,
misted as if by the spray of luminous surf,
salty & damp as sweat, your abrupt vigor, the shudders
& jolts from where you sat once upon me & reeled dizzy into
selflessness—I see it with the darkened eye
& touch you, still whole enough to read you,
to have always read you & beyond you & through you into you
& into that which was divine, that to which you gave flesh,
this radiance that cannot still our pain.
Is there still this, in the life-worn husks we've weathered into?
remnants of it embering of our deep and volatile love,
some fossil of a phoenix to redeem what has come to be,
with what had once been? Oh, what a wet planet we were,
made half of great fire and how we descend the stairs,
mountains melting into slag-laden flumes, iron poured
on the hot sea, the sea boiled off into a brief power
of thunderheads, spewing a molten rain onto nothing remaining,
but this: remembered passion, the distant passion.
We are the things of such things that see nothing in our pain.

Here, we've forgotten again our meagre impulse toward love,
we fall onto softened shoulders. You sob.
I am too tired to weep. We lose the thought of what we meant
to do together.

Beloved, I love you & there is no god.
Oh, I love you and there is no hope.
Look how we are still so hungry for each other
& still we will not live.
The linens clenched in your white fists as you sit up, dark,
a felt shape that I cannot see & you are sounding
a long sharpened EEEEEEEE in the throat, far off,
as if far off, the knife cutting another pound,
another god-hating, faith-rotten day of gristle & ash.
And then it is me—EEEEEEE—again and I see the bloodless,
open-mouthed loss of you. Again.
And again I close your imperfect eyes because again
they are left half open & no one to stare through them,
again the autumn sunlight outside & your face no longer yours.
Oh what was it I was? Where is he I loved?

The wind, the sun
The wind EEEEEEEE
and tell me again,
why it is we live to see such as this again?

MURIEL RUKEYSER ■ ■ ▪ ▪ ■ ▪ ■ ■ ▪ ■ ▪ ■ ▪ ■

The Gates

1.

Waiting to leave all day I hear the words;
That poet in prison, that poet newly-died
whose words we wear, reading, all of us. I and my son.

All day we read the words:
friends, lovers, daughters, grandson,
and all night the distant loves
and I who had never seen him am drawn to him

Through acts, through poems;
through our closenesses—
whatever links us in our variousness;
across worlds, love and poems and justices
wishing to be born.

2.

Walking the world to find the poet of these cries.
But this walking is flying the streets of all the air.

Walking the world, through the people at airports,
this city of hills, this island ocean fire-blue and now this city.

Walking this world is driving the roads of houses
endless tiled houses, fast streams, now this child's house.

Walking under the sharp mountains through the sharp city
circled in time by rulers, their grip; the marvelous

hard-gripped people silent among their rulers, looking at me.

3. New Friends

The new friend comes into my hotel room
smiling. He does a curious thing.

He walks around the room, touching
all the pictures hanging on the wall.
One picture does not move.

A new friend assures me : Foreigners are safe,
You speak for writers, you are safe, he says.
There will be no car
driving up behind you, there will be
no accident, he says. I know these accidents.
Nothing will follow you, he says.
O the Mafia at home, I know, Black Hand
of childhood, the death of Tresca whom I mourn,
the building of New York. Many I know.
This morning I go early to see the Cardinal.
When I return, the new friend is waiting. His face
wax-candle-pool-color, he saying
"I thought you were kidnapped."

A missionary comes to visit me.
Looks into my eyes. Says,
"Turn on the music so we can talk."

4.

The cabinet minister speaks of liberation.
"Do you know how the Communists use this word?"
We all use the word. Liberation.

No, but look—these are his diaries,
says the cabinet minister.
These were found in the house of the poet.
Look, Liberation, Liberation, he is speaking in praise.

He says, this poet, It is not wrong
to take from the rich and give to the poor.

Yes. He says it in prose speech, he says it in his plays,
he says it in his poems that bind me to him,
that bind his people and mine in these new ways
for the first time past strangeness and despisal.

It also means that you broke into his house and stole his papers.

5.

Among the days,
among the nights of the poet in solitary,
a strong infant is just beginning to run.
I go up the stepping-stones

to where the young wife of the poet
stands holding the infant in her arms.
She weeps, she weeps.
But the poet's son looks at me
and the wife's mother looks at me with a keen look
across her grief. Lights in the house, books making every wall
a wall of speech.
                    The clasp of the woman's hand
around my wrist, a keen band
more steel than the words
Save his life.

I feel that clasp on my bones.

A strong infant is beginning to run.

6. The Church of Galilee

As we climb to the church of Galilee
Three harsh men on the corner.
As we go to the worship-meeting of the dismissed,
three state police on the street.
As we all join at the place of the dispossessed,
three dark men asking their rote questions.
As we go ahead to stand with our new friends
that will be our friends our lifetime.
Introduced as dismissed from this faculty, this college,
this faculty, this university.
'Dismissed' is now an honorary degree.
The harsh police are everywhere,
they have hunted this fellowship away before
and they are everywhere, at the street-corner,
listening to all hymns,
standing before all doors,
hearing over all wires.
We go up to Galilee.
Let them listen to the dispossessed
and to all women and men who stand firm and sing
wanting a shared and honest lifetime.
Let them listen to Galilee.

7. The Dream of Galilee

That night, a flute
across the dark, the sound
opening times to me, a time
when I stood on the green hillside
before the great white stone.
Grave of my ancestor

Akiba at rest over Kinneret.
The holy poem, he said to me,
the Song of Songs always,
and know what I know, to love
your belief with all your life,
and resist the Romans, as I did,
even to the torture and beyond.
Over Kinneret, with all of them,
Jesus, all the Judeans,
that other Galilee
in dream across war I see.

8. Mother as Pitchfork

Woman seen as a slender instrument,
woman at vigil in the prison-yard,
woman seen as the fine tines of a pitchfork
that works hard, that is worn down, rusted down
to a fine sculpture standing in a yard
where her son's body is confined.
Woman as fine tines blazing against sunset,
wavering lines against yellow brightness
where her fine body becomes transparent in bravery,
where she will live and die as the tines of a pitchfork
that stands to us as her son's voice does stand
across the world speaking

The rumor comes that if this son is killed
this mother will kill herself

But she is here, she lives,
the slender tines of this pitchfork standing in flames of light,

9.

You grief woman   you gave me a scarlet coverlet
thick-sown with all the flowers
and all the while your poet sleeps in stone

Grief woman, the waves of this coverlet,
roses of Asia,
they flicker soft and bright over my sleep

all night while the poet waits in solitary

All you vigil women, I start up in the night,
fling back this cover of red;
in long despair we work write speak pray call to others
Free our night   free our lives   free our poet

10.

Air fills with fear and the kinds of fear:

The fear of the child among the tyrannical
unanswerable men and women, they dominate day and night.

Fear of the young lover in the huge rejection
ambush of sex and of imagination;
fear that the world will not allow your work.

Fear of the overarching wars and poverties,
the terrible exiles,
all bound by corruption until at last! we speak!

And those at home in jail who protest the frightful war
and the beginning : The women-guard says to me, Spread your cheeks,
the search begins and I begin to know.

And also at home the nameless multitude
of fears : fear in childbirth for the living child,
fear for the child deformed and loved, fear
among the surgeries that can cure her, fear
for the child's father, and for oneself, fear.
Fear of the cunt and cock in their terrible powers
and here a world away fear of the jailers' tortures
for we invent our fear and act it out
in ripping, in burning, in blood, in the terrible scream
and in tearing away every mouth that screams.

Giant fears : massacres, the butchered that across the fields of the world
lie screaming, and their screams are heard as silence.
O love, knowing your love across a world of fear,
I lie in a strange country, in pale yellow, swamp-green, woods
and a night of music while a poet lies in solitary
somewhere in a concrete cell. Glare-lit, I hear,
without books, without pen and paper.
Does he draw a pencil out of his throat,
out of his veins, out of his sex?
There are cells all around him, emptied.
He can signal on these walls till he runs mad.
He is signalling to me across the night.

He is signalling. Many of us speak,
we do teach each other, we do act through our fears.

Where is the world that will touch life to this prison?

We run through the night. We are given his gifts.

11.

Long ago, soon after my son's birth
—this scene comes in arousal with the sight of a strong child
just beginning to run—
when all life seemed prisoned off, because the father's other son
born three weeks before my child
had opened the world
that other son and his father closed the world—
in my fierce loneliness and fine well-being
torn apart but with my amazing child
I celebrated and grieved.
And before that baby
had ever started to begin to run
then Mary said,
smiling and looking out of her Irish eyes,
"Never mind, Muriel.
Life will come will come again
knocking and coughing and farting at your door."

12.

For that I cannot name the names,
my child's own father, the flashing, the horseman,
the son of the poet—
for that he never told me another child was started,
to come to birth three weeks before my own.
Tragic timing that sets the hands of time.
O wind from our own coast, turning
around the turning world.

Wind from the continents, this other child,
child of this moment and this moment's poet.
Again I am struck nameless, unable to name,
and the axe-blows fall heavy heavy and sharp
and the moon strikes his white light down over the continents
on this strong infant and the heroic friends
silent in this terrifying moment under all moonlight,
all sunlight turning in all our unfree lands.
Name them, name them all, light of our own time.

13.

Crucified child—is he crucified? he is tortured,
kept away from his father, spiked on time,
crucified we say, cut off from the man
they want to kill—
he runs toward me in Asia, crying.
Flash gives me my own son strong and those years ago
cut off from his own father and running toward me
holding a strong flower.

Child of this moment, you are your father's child
wherever your father in prisoned, by what tyrannies
or jailed as my child's father
by his own fantasies—
child of the age running among the world,
standing among us who carry our own time.

14.

So I became very dark very large
a silent woman this time given to speech
a woman of the river   of that song
and on the beach of the world in storm given
in long lightning seeing the rhyming of those scenes
that make our lives.
Anne Sexton the poet saying
ten days ago to that receptive friend,
the friend of the hand-held camera:
"Muriel is serene."
Am I that in their sight?
Word comes today of Anne's
of Anne's long-approaching
of Anne's over-riding over-falling
suicide. Speak for   sing for   pray   for
everyone in solitary
every living life.

15.

All day the rain
all day waiting within the prison gate
before another prison gate
The house of the poet
He is in there somewhere
among the muscular wardens
I have arrived at the house of the poet
in the mud in the interior music of all poems
and the grey rain of the world
whose gates do not open.
I stand, and for this religion and that religion
do not eat but remember all the things I know
and a strong infant beginning to run.
Nothing is happening. Mud, silence, rain.

Near the end of the day
with the rain and the knowledge pulling at my legs
a movement behind me makes me move aside.
A bus full of people turns in the mud, drives to the gate.
The gate that never opens
opens at last. Beyond it, slender

Chinese-red posts of the inner gates.
The gates of the house of the poet.

The bus is crowded, a rush-hour bus that waits.
Nobody moves.

"Who are these people?" I say.
How can these gates open?

My new friend has run up beside me.
He has been standing guard in the far corner.
"They are prisoners," he says, "brought here from trial.
Don't you see? They are all tied together."

Fool that I am! I had not seen the ropes,
down at their wrists in the crowded rush-hour bus.

The gates are open. The prisoners go in.
The house of the poet who stays in solitary,
not allowed reading   not allowed writing
not allowed   his woman   his friends   his unknown friends
and the strong infant beginning to run.

We go down the prison hill. On our right, sheds
full of people all leaning forward, blown on some ferry.
"They are the families of the prisoners. Some can visit.
They are waiting for their numbers to be called."

How shall we venture home?
How shall we tell each other of the poet?
How can we meet the judgment on the poet,
or his execution? How shall we free him?
How shall we speak to the infant beginning to run?
All those beginning to run?

MICHAEL RYAN ▪ ▪ ▪ ▪ ▪ ▪ ▪ ▪ ▪ ▪ ▪ ▪ ▪ ▪ ▪

The Pure Loneliness

Late at night, when you're so lonely
your shoulders lean to the center of your body,
you call no one and you don't call out.

This is dignity. This is the pure loneliness
that made Christ think he was God.
This is why lunatics smile at their thoughts.

Even the best moment, as you slip
half-a-foot deep into someone you like,
deepens to the loneliness in it

and loneliness that's not. If you believe in
Christ hanging on the cross, his arms spread
as if to embrace the Father he calls

who is somewhere else, you still might hear
your own voice at your next great embrace
thinking *Loneliness in another can't be touched,*

like Christ's voice at death answering himself.

Passion

Chilly early Saturday, my study
its usual chaos: a cluster of half-digested paperbacks
around the stuffed chair and floorlamp
thinning to the rug's periphery
like a molecule's probability graph;
stacks of drafts for this or that poem
or essay, flashes temporarily shaped
into one of a trillion possible embodiments,
encrusted now before a wicker wastebasket
erupting months of slamdunked crumpled
legal sheets and looseleaf; and me—
happy after waking next to you—
diffused through this minuscule universe,
a larger but less cohesive bit of matter
than the poster of the pre-Columbian
fertility goddess staring at no one
from above the desk. I'm writing this,
for instance, because Maria Rodriguez
beams from the pile of old Sunday *Times*
I twist into knots for kindling
to get my woodstove going in the morning.
She's hugging the man she married
at San Quentin the moment the photo
was taken, where marriages are performed
in the hospitality room the first Tuesday
every month, where this month (June, 1982)
there were eleven. For a few minutes
I sit crosslegged before the stove's mouth
and try to ride with her on the free bus
for convicts' families from Los Angeles—
squabbling toddlers, rap music pumping
from a boom box, her heels and dress tucked

in an overnight case on the overhead rack
with the pearl eyeshadow she'll redo one last time
in the video-scanned hospitality room
before her man appears behind the glass partition
and floats like that, ghostly, in her mind
as she changes back afterwards into her everyday clothes
for the night ride home. Maria Rodriguez
says her friends tell her she's crazy,
and her family, forget it, none of them
would come. Statistics prove these marriages
collapse after the prisoner's released,
but it's not for then she's marrying.
It's for this passion
she had only dreamed, that she thought
happened only in movies and never believed
could be real. I believe it's real.
I remember us trying to talk about it
the day the article was published.
Passio, "suffering; Christ's scourging
and crucifixion," the Latin
from the Indo-European root for *harm*
from which also comes Greek for *destruction.*
As you read me the etymology, it melted
easily into the sacred music of Scarlatti
and aroma of coffee and bacon
that swell our home on Sunday mornings
when love seems uncomplicated and kind.
I don't remember what I said or did
the rest of that day—worked in here probably,
read the paper, watched baseball on TV—
but this morning, knotting this page for the fire,
I thought of keeping it, I thought
of clipping the photo of Maria Rodriguez
and tacking it in here so she would tell me
if I forget what passion means,
I thought of it, then jammed it
into the stove and gave it to the flames.

Moonlight

It silvers the lawn,
its off-white wash tingeing
these hours alone,
frozen dewdropped grassblades
an army of sparklers
I would love like Walt Whitman
to insinuate myself among,
drawing them out about home

before I write their letters for them
and dress the gangrenous wounds
they will soon die from,
petting the feverish ones,
kissing one or two of them
open-mouthed, long, and lingering,
my gift-satchel emptied,
my heart broken.
If you were beside me, you'd say,
"It looks like snow, only invisible,"
and the world moonlight makes,
in which even roof-tin
glints like platinum, could seem
a distillation of joyous thought,
all clarity and outline,
the great winter-stripped maple
you married me under in summer
flaring its black skeleton against the sky
as I walk straight for it
praying for no more words between us
that are killing everything.

God Hunger

When the immutable accidents of birth—
parentage, hometown, all the rest—
no longer anchor this fiction of the self
and its incessant *I me mine,*

then words won't be like nerves in a stump
crackling with messages that end up nowhere,
and I'll put on the wind like a gown of light linen
and go be a king in a field of weeds.

Complete Semen Study

morphology: "pinheads": two per cent

Laborious, stumpy, droopy, askew,
blundering into the microscopic equivalent of paths of busses
as the healthiest sperm zips by like the varsity water polo team
on their way to a party with the best-looking cheerleaders—
unbeautiful losers, unfittest and unmourned,
o my five-hundred-thousand-or-so pinheads

floundering in this plastic cup's murky bottom,
what would *you* do to be half of someone?
Wank it sitting on the toilet in a fluorescent
pea-green hospital bathroom while learning to juggle one-handed
one cup and three brown-bagged *Penthouses*
offered by the deadpan female lab attendant?
You'd wank it anyplace, I think.
They'd tie your wrists if you had wrists
to stop your rubbing off on fireplugs and brick buildings,
much less on a hand's elastic flesh
you're too dim to recognize is your own.
You're the ones who can't be taken to church
because you hump the scarlet pew cushions
while the rest of us are praying,
and try to straddle the priest's leg like a puppy
while he exchanges an inspirational personal word or two
with each of his congregation as they file from the service.
I, on the other hand, am too mature for this.
The Pet-of-the-Month could almost be my granddaughter.
My metabolism has decelerated
to that of an elderly Galapagos Tortoise.
I could do very well all day sunning myself
under a thick, warm shell, and could easily take the next century
to burn the calories in a slice of pizza.
In the world for which my body was designed
I would have checked out long ago,
immolated at the ritual bonfire by my two hundred great grandchildren
roasting a whole mammoth in my honor,
dancing for days stoned on sacred leaf-juice,
and intermarrying like howler monkeys in the bushes.
It's no doubt due to nights like this
that you weakened and malformed
and chase your own watery tails until you decompose
into what the complete semen study classifies as "debris."
The doctors say it's age or car exhaust or groundwater toxins
or they-don't-know-what, but there must have been a boy
waiting for the dopey old patriarch to die
so he could do his sister when she was stoned out of her cheesewhiz,
sweaty and writhing in the firelight. If their child, slow-witted
and guileless, showed the endearing but useless gift
to greet everyone's spirit no matter their status,
they might have thrown him the bones the dogs had finished with,
which is how they fed the shunned and the shamed,
unbeautiful losers, unfittest and unmourned,
o my five-hundred-thousand-or-so pinheads
floundering in this plastic cup's murky bottom
I hereby hand over for removal and disposal
to the now-surgically-gloved
deadpan female lab attendant.

The Use of Poetry

On the day a fourteen year old disappeared in Ojai, California,
having left a Christmas Eve slumber party barefoot
to "go with a guy" in a green truck,
and all Christmas day volunteers searched for her body within a fifteen-mile
        radius,
and her father and grandfather searched
and spoke to reporters because TV coverage
might help them find her if she were still alive,
and her mother stayed home with the telephone,
not appearing in public, and I could imagine
this family deciding together this division of labor
and what little else they could do to *do something,*
and the kitchen they sat in, the tones they spoke in,
who cried and who didn't, and how they comforted one another
with words of hope and strokings of backs and necks,
but couldn't imagine their fear their daughter
had been murdered in the woods, raped no doubt,
tied up, chopped up, God knows what else,
or them picturing her terror as it was happening to her
or their own terror of her absence ever after
cut off from them before she had a chance to grow through adolescence,
her room ever the same with its stupid posters of rockstars
until they can bear to take them down
because they can't bear to leave them up anymore—
on this day, which happened to be Christmas,
at the kind of holiday gathering with a whole turkey and a spiral-cut ham
and beautiful dishes our hosts spent their money and time making
to cheer their friends and enjoy the pleasure of giving,
in a living room sparkling with scented candles and bunting
and a ten-foot tree adorned with antique ornaments,
the disappearance of the girl kept surfacing
across the room in conversations
while I was being cornered by a man who seemed too impressed by money
whose wife is leaving him after twenty-one years of marriage
but who had to impress me-as-anyone-or-no one
with who he is in his business world;
and it did again after I excused myself to refill my punch glass
when someone dipping the dipper into the punch bowl
said what she had heard about it from someone else
who had played tennis that morning with the girl's mother's doubles partner,
before I filled a punch glass for somebody's dad
who had been brought along not to leave him home alone on Christmas,
a man in his eighties with a face like a raven's,
his body stooped, ravaged by age and diseases,
whose wife this year died a prolonged death from cancer
and his son suddenly one night in a car crash,

who told me he was amazed to still be alive himself,
but to my amazement then said the same sort of thing
as the man whose wife is leaving I had just gotten away from,
had to tell me who he was in international steel
and—ludicrously—that he was still involved
in some important projects for the navy,
and I was selfish enough to be selfless enough
to draw him out a little, and the younger man, too
(who appeared at my elbow again and started talking again),
but not enough to be able to imagine what they each were going through
since my own blinding self-importance
clouds how I see other people
including even in my imagination the family of the missing girl,
and the girl herself, and especially her murderer
although I know what it is to hate yourself completely
and believe all human community is lies and bullshit
and what happens to other people doesn't matter.

DAVID ST. JOHN ▪ ▪ ▪ ▪ ▪ ▪ ▪ ▪ ▪ ▪ ▪ ▪ ▪ ▪ ▪

A Temporary Situation

Once I was in love with a woman
& though it was a temporary situation
By that I mean an affair of only
A few weeks   still it's true
I was so in love I was really quite
Out of my mind I mean truly mad

& this woman had led   well
A very difficult & complicated life
On several continents with what seemed
To have been countless lovers
Though once in fact I did try counting
& lost track almost immediately

Once in a while at dinner
Suddenly whole years would shift away
& she'd be talking to people
Who simply weren't there
People I knew she'd once loved & spent
Hours with daily but who without question
Were no longer there

So I found my madness was nothing
Held up next to hers though I'd wanted
To make our madness one

& the entire time we were together
I swear to you it was every night
Sometimes at 2 or 3 A.M.
Though most often just before sunrise
She'd sit bolt upright in bed   staring

Off into the distance somewhere beyond the wall

At some figure or horizon she could never quite
Speak of

Though her eyes were enormous with her terror
& still she just sat there trembling
As the sweat
Rolled off her shoulders & along her breasts
Which rocked slightly as she shook

I'd put my arms around her as she awakened
Slowly into the morning
Telling her over & over again first the name
Of the city in which she was living

& then my own name

Several times   I'd have to tell her my own name
Because you see at those times she'd have
Forgotten everything & I was part
Of that   I mean everything

She could no longer recognize
When she awoke on the other side of the world

Where   I believe   nothing is taken for granted

Black Poppy
(At the Temple)

Perhaps it's a question of what
The ruins will accept   a simple flower
Or a few casual hymns by the side
Of this narrow mountain road
Where the dusty cones of sunlight are falling
Through the afternoon air

& the marble ribs of the temple are starting to blur
As the tourists come back across the fields

He slid down off the dented hood of the car
To open the door for them & acknowledge
Their praise of the view

Yet as he glanced out of habit into the side mirror
The hammered whiteness of his own face
Startled him & on
The drive back down the steep cobbled road
To the hotel in the valley   he knew that it was

Time he left his closet not a room at the rear
Of the hotel filled it seemed
With nothing but dull paintings & moldering books
& maps no one unfolded
                    time to walk away
From all of the habits that owned him especially
The habit of dreams

& that evening as he drove back up the road
Toward the crest of stars above the temple
Those ruins where he could walk & pray
To nothing

He knew that in every one of those dreams
He'd always be a dead man   just a suicide of
Elegant but precise intent
Dressed in a white summer suit & wearing
On his lapel an exquisite & dramatic black poppy

A hand-stitched blossom of glazed silk
Black as the shadow of a real poppy   black as
That moist bud of opium

Pinned to no memory of a living man

My Friend

My friend, a man I love as wholly,
    As deeply as the brother neither of us
        Ever had, my friend, who once
Greeted me at the door of his carriage house—
        Having not seen each other in seven years—
      Saying only, as he turned to place
The needle into the grooves of Mahler's unfinished 10th,

"*Listen* to this! It's just like the *Four Quartets!*"
      His head, tilted slightly back
As we listened in silence, his black scarf looped loosely
      Around his neck, not an affectation, simply
Because of the cold in the carriage house he'd redone
      With everything but heat,
The wind slicing off the East River, the mansion
In front of us lit up brilliantly that night
      By chandelier and firelight—my friend,
Whom I love as deeply as any friend, called
This morning to report the sleet blanketing the East,
      To ask about the color of the sunlight
Sweeping the beaches of California; I tell him, "A lot
      Like the green of ice at night,
Or the orange of the hair of that girl who once
Lived downstairs from you, in Cleveland. . . ."
      My friend, who said nothing for a moment,
      My friend, who had always lived the pure, whole
Solitude of Rilke, though he fell in love
      As often and as desperately as Rilke,
      Began to talk about his recent engagement, now
Past, though still not quite a memory, simply a subject
      Yet too mystifying to be ignored,
To a debutante, half-British, that is, an American deb
      With an overlay of aristocratic parquet—
Albeit with an Italian given name—a stunning woman
      He had loved desperately, silently,
      The way Rilke loved
The sky at evening as the cloud-laced sunset
Dusted the high ragged peaks of Switzerland . . .
      Yet, after a pause, he began
Again to talk, about some new acquaintances, two
      Young ladies, both painters (of course),
Who seemed to enjoy his company as a pair; that is,
      The two of them, both of the young
Ladies, preferred him as a garnish
      To their own extravagances—for example,
      They'd welcomed him into their bath one
Evening when he came to visit, only to find them lathering
      Each other tenderly. And though quite
Clearly desiring the company of each other to his alone,
      They were tolerant, he said, even welcoming,
      As the one reached up her hand
And invited him into the froth of the square black tub.
      And now this had, he reported, been
      Going on for several weeks this way, perhaps longer,
He couldn't quite be clear about those kinds
      Of details, though about other, more
Intriguing things, his memory was exact. The very night before,

He recalled, as the two young women painted
      His naked torso slowly into a tuxedo of pastel
Watercolors, they'd both wisely proposed the following:
    A joint—triadic—marriage for one month
As they travelled, all three, through Italy and France,
      A journey to visit all of the Holy Places
        Of Art, as well as
The grandparents of the one, Delphine—about whom Constance,
    The younger, had heard so many stories—at their home
      In the hills overlooking the beaches of Nice.
My friend, a quiet man, a man who remains as
Precise, in his reckonings, as a jewel cutter, a man whose
      Charm could seduce the Medusa, was,
    He confessed, totally at a loss, bewildered, delighted,
Terrified, exhausted—mainly, he said, exhausted
      From the constellations of couplings
      He'd been exercising, recognizing in the process
He was, as they say, as he said, really not quite so young
      As he'd once been, though certainly still
        As eager for invention
As any artist who takes his life work, well, seriously . . .
    And as we talked about old times, old friends, our
Old lives being somehow perpetually rearranged, at last
      He stopped me, saying, "Christ, you know—
    I can't *believe* how much the world has changed. . . ."

IRA SADOFF ▪ ▪ ▪ ▪ ▪ ▪ ▪ ▪ ▪ ▪ ▪ ▪ ▪ ▪ ▪ ▪ ▪ ▪

Standard Time

Winter was a vestibule, storing brooms
in closets, every sequence white with snow, hauling wood
in that embraceable wind. I'd like the world to be a room
in a poem, for obvious reasons. The ice was thin,
the stripped-down flesh oblivious. I had one thin coat
for protection. Could the snow drift still higher,
blocking my view? There was my marriage to look at, the war,
a friend dead of AIDS, a healthy baby for another,
all scars and snapshots (*Had I seen these before?*).

The door slammed our voices shut. But that was early.
We bombed a milk factory, that much I remember. Or was it later,
in summer? Mostly I remember holding Sascha's hand,
watching chained-up elephants—an intact family—

swaying in three-four time, making the best of it. Rodin
told Rilke, Flee from yourself. Go to the zoo. Just pay attention,
for Christ's sake. It could have been my wife. But all
the scraps and remnants splintered, everything so briefly shattered:
before I knew it I'd picked up a new pair of glasses,
the snow had stopped, and what I held in my hand,
a few snapped twigs and canvas sling of logs, was useless now.

Izzy

The prettiest shadows were impalpable, so I stored them
in this sentence, where nothing's more than a sequence of words,
thereby degrading them, the scale of gray they cast on the wall,
say, of his parent's bedroom, reduced to a silhouette,
the kind they sold on the Lower East Side to old Jewish families
who could not afford family portraits. Do you feel the pity of it, the boy
making animal shapes on the wall with his fingers, because they had nothing,
making the figures dreamy and incandescent, ancient and mythological,
half-man and half-horse, neighing and bucking, mimicking
the boarders' voices in the kitchen? They were building a subway
and wore their mining hats to breakfast, and like him, lived in a tunnel,
inside a narrow field of vision, meaning all nuances of pain and pleasure,
—unless you felt them like a steam iron on your forearm—were abstractions,
so as he told me the story, extracting bits of cloth from a moment in 1909,
one from the year preceding, a few after he began working at the cinema,
projecting shadows: Chaplin outwitting a bully,
Keaton escaping a speeding train as his house collapses at his feet—
Izzy's broom shadow to the celluloid swept up and startled into nothing—
I tried to hold everything in place, to draw a picture, since he was half-blind by
     then,
and he had nothing but a string of words to raise us up from—should I say
the tenement?—no, from his wing chair where I felt like the horse
"shaded" from peripheral view, one who carted him all over the park
so he could sharpen knives, but that was another story, and his face
was no longer draped in lamplight, his face had never been
"draped" in lamplight, but his mouth was shadow, and the tunnel of his voice,
as he brought the veil of his hand over his eyes, gave no sign
the curtain was closing, no sign that I could carry on.

There's No Rigor Like the Old Rigor II

Was it something uncleaved, clean-cut you wanted?
Something cheerleader, vacuumed, clean-shaven?
Before the truck stop marred stands of cedar. Before father
succumbed to the secretary, scribbled a note or two on his tie?

It says something about us
that we no longer read Ovid. Of course,

some don't like to be shunned, stepped on,
spurned, excluded, don't like to be shuttled back and forth
between the barge and the mansion, serving him
hot milk while he reads Stendhal by the fire.
They like to be admired, chauffeured, they like silver,
fellatio, they like to be stirred, to stray from the herd,
called not just when they're needed but missed.

You wanted something whole. One God.
What's wrong with that? In the paintings, the Gods
are happy. Why shouldn't they be? Beauty
had a certain volume. The cracked foot of the statue David.
When windows were still church windows,
before stained-glass would disintegrate into slag and gravel
if you brought back the blitzkrieg, those shiny pornographic photos. . . .

Lingerie shred in the hall. A party
you hardly remember.
It was like this. You had a few ideas about women.
A few women gave you ideas.
But why indulge in the shattered lampshade,
the painting askew on the inner wall?
What matters is what always mattered.
Standards. The station of the cross. Grace. The good
shucked from the bad with a good sharp knife.
The time before the the. The first time. The first wife.

The Depression

A critical mass came over me.
All those little things we do for ourselves—
chocolate bars, a clean shirt, good books, my favorite pew
at church—were suddenly unavailable.

Coming home was opening the vault.
Someone was sitting on me. The welt
was inside my forehead. Motion was a concept,
like algebra. In other words I was adjacent

to the maelstrom: I won't take it away
by effacing it: it was no cloudy day in November.
It was raucous, with all my pliable desires
going nowhere: I was modeling clay.

You can't figure it out, she said.
Should I thank psychoanalysis for that?
The current lingo's all immersion, self-sufficiency,
dredging up the dark and staring into it. Later,

maybe decades later, we'll laugh at the gall of it.
Since for no good reason, the she I wanted came to me.
I thought of the shiny ebony of a Steinway.
Pedals. Then petals, peeling back. Then the prattling stopped.

All the familiar figures abandoned me. You see, I was all along
unprepared for the stillness that accompanies happiness.

Grazing

Sometimes the rapid-fire channel switching is like eye music.
Or when you kill an image, another, hydra-like,
appears in its place. Sometimes there's nothing enticing at the malls,
or what we crave is ghostly, far away, long gone.

We have a slim attention span, torn fingernail thin.

They scanned the hillside for the body,
the split-wood fence with barbed wire
where the thrust of my desire was so diffuse
I could almost point to swamp grass, and say, yes,

that's what I wanted. One instant bleeding into the next.

You have to imagine the music as random,
dissonant, schizophrenic, playing and not playing,
as if synapses had been cut and sutured back together again.

Where I grew up "getting to know someone"
was alluring, provocative, arresting:
the sheer inventory of body parts, in what they indicate,
how they mark a person, dissemble or embolden them.

I can make this personal
and lyrical, if they point the camera
above and behind the ruined individuals, where I can call
the rain-slicked grass emerald green, and beyond that
call out from the granite cliffs, the twisted paths to the sea.

How white her face was, how she disdained
the out-of-doors for all its randomness and contagion.
Her flesh, if we call it flesh, was spongy and doughy, more flexible
than fungible, smudged like newly printed money.

I'm trying to bring you closer.

In the privacy of the hotel room there's a piano
on the radio, the shallow
breathing of someone whose name I won't give you.
My wrist grazing her cheek. Tracing her shoulders, her hips.

What does it mean to be inside
someone else, to feel their arm as a glove your arm wears,
to think her thoughts with and for her. . . .

where the body's incited in enactment as well as in metaphor?

For most of an hour we watched them fucking,
in the mirror hotel with the windows open, where happiness
seemed precise, itemized, silent, condensed.
The air they were breathing, we were breathing.

A certain thickness of line becomes them,
where "windows to the soul" cannot be seen.

I have the nagging suspicion that "to be saved"
is all about money, is to save up,
to put on the shelf and savor until maximum value
is accrued. But sometimes the music's

cherubic, the kind of baroque hope
Bach's preludes breed in a practicing child:
a fat little angel espousing the cloud,
as if a kettle were steaming.

To be watched, inspected, pored over, opened up,
but still receive the adjacent body
without turning away, glazing over, closing the blinds.

The valve of the door opening and closing,
canting and retracting, as the blood rushes in.

The Soul

for John Mizner

The shaft of narrative peers down.
The soul's a petrified fleck of partridge this October.
Mud-spattered, it thinks it's brush, it thinks
it's one with the brush when God aims

just below its feathers. It's too late to raise the soul,
some ossified conceit we use to talk about deer

as if we were deer, to talk about the sun, as if the cold
autumn light mirrored our lover asleep in the tub.

Nevertheless, I want to talk about it. Those scarred bodies
on the hospital table, they're white chalk children use
to deface the sidewalk. The deer fed in the gazebo,
where the salt lick was barely safe from the fox.

And when the wind didn't drag my scent to her,
I sat listless, half-awake, and watched her hunger
surpass her timidity. I should have been changed.
I should have been startled into submission

by a very white light, I should have shed my misgivings
as her tongue made that sticky sound on the lick
and two startled animals stared into what St. Francis
called a mystery. I should bring her back, the woman too,

the woman who what why words fail me here.
I should sanctify the hospital gown as it slides down
the tunnel of the cat scan, to see where
the nodules have spread into the thin, pliable tissues

we call the innards in animals, because they dwell
in scenery, they're setting for the poem, they provide
a respite from the subject who's been probed and lacerated,
who's been skinned and eaten away by the story

when I'm beguiled by the music the hooves made
on the pine floor. I can bring her back, can't I,
I'm bringing him back, the hero who was close enough
so I could watch what was inside his face hover and scatter.

LESLIE SCALAPINO ▪ ▪ ▪ ▪ ▪ ▪ ▪ ▪ ▪ ▪ ▪ ▪ ▪

FROM *that they were at the beach—aeolotropic series*

Playing ball—so it's like paradise, not because it's in the past, we're on a
field; we are creamed by the girls who get together on the other team.
They're nubile, but in age they're thirteen or so—so they're strong.

(No one knows each other, aligning according to race as it happens, the
color of the girls, and our being creamed in the foreground—as part of
it's being that—the net is behind us).

"that they were at the beach—aeolotropic series" is excerpted from the book of the same name,
by Leslie Scalapino. This sequence is one of the book's four poetic sections.

A microcosm, but it's of girls—who were far down on the field, in another situation of playing ball—so it was an instance of the main world though they're nubile but are in age thirteen or so.

My being creamed in the foreground—so it's outside of that—by a girl who runs into me, I returned to the gym.

It's in the past—yet is repressed in terms of the situation itself, poor people who're working, the division is by color. We're not allowed to leave the airport on arriving—others not permitted to stop over—we're immature in age, so it's inverted.

(Therefore receded—we get on the bus going to the city and look around, seeing people dressed shabbily).

A man—I was immature in age—was a stowaway so not having been active, taken from the ship we're on in a row boat.

(A sailor had fallen out of the row boat then, was embarrassed. So it's like paradise—the embarrassment, therefore it's depressed—seen by his waving at us as the other sailors are coming to him).

The class period ending—it's evanescence not because it's in the past, they'd stamped their feet while seated since the teacher hadn't been able to discipline them. She's old—the red hair coloring had been mocked—they're inactive.

(So it's evanescent because they're inactive. Though I am as well. She'd asked me to pull on her hair to indicate it was her real hair, which I do—them being unaware of this—as the class is disbanding, composed of girls and boys).

It is also an instance in the past, so it's depressed—yet the people on the bus aren't nubile, rather are mature.

We're girls—have to urinate which is unrelated to immaturity—refusing to do so in front of others; we require the bus to leave us. Therefore there aren't other people, we urinate, and then look around.

(So it's inactive—is depressed).

Tall, though they are nubile—playing leap frog is out of place; we're required to do so. It's contemporary in time so it's not depressed—I was immature, thirteen in age or so; responding to the other girls kicking as they jumped over some of us.

(So it's not depressed—but not as being active. I'm creamed, until the crowd of girls is pulled off by an instructor who's in the gym).

Attending a funeral—it's contemporary in time, not being in itself depressed; taking a ridiculous aspect—birds that sing loudly in the chapel where the funeral service is being held. The birds are mechanical—so it's being creamed.

(Like in the earlier episode of playing ball. Our being creamed in the foreground of the field by the other girls).

A microcosm, but it's of sailors—though I'm given attention standing in pictures with one or two of the men. They've come into a port at one time—I'm immature in age—it doesn't occur for that reason but is inverted, the sailors flirted with girls.

(Which is contemporary in time therefore. And being mechanical since I'm interested in the sailors, then merely interest).

A boy who was actually at the funeral—so it's inverted—was later playing ball, really occurring.

(Inverted also because of being at the funeral, mechanical birds part of it; so it isn't creamed in the future—not because of that).

The boy who was actually at the funeral—corresponds to work as a chimney sweep which I had for a short time—is inverted

(I didn't take the job seriously since it was in the past—I was supposed to do it awhile, was contemporary. So it's related to the boy; I got sick from the soot—so my leaving after working only two days stemmed from that).

Someone else driving—the funeral having taken place—is getting speeding tickets, with us in the car—we're older than he

So we don't say anything because we're older. Not about the police stopping him, the drive is several hundred miles at night—which is like him later going below the border

•

Him not being sentient

A man whoring—it's from the standpoint of a girl, is a situation of trying to finance going below the border to whore and staying down there as long as he can before having to return to get some job.

(It's a microcosm, is also inverted—not retroactive).

———————

We're thirteen in age or so—they're nubile—so I wouldn't say that ever in describing myself

We're bicycling as are they. Other girls who come on us from a side road. There are fields around, they race us—almost sarcastic seen while bicycling (so it's retroactive; isn't just in relation to their being nubile—contemporary in time)

—so it's the mechanical birds though it's in the past

———————

Not really being ill, but thinking he is, (it's also the mechanical birds), the man's deeply embarrassed—he's not old—at it turning out to be viewed this way after having others take him to hospitals.

(So it's the mechanical birds because he isn't old. Nor is there a funeral—but not related to one he's taken from a swimming pool, goes in an ambulance).

———————

Not really being ill—corresponds to the man who mugged me, not the one I mistook for him—it's depressed.

The real thief running away from the telephone booth is in my side vision, I don't realize it while blaming a boy standing in front of me. They're boys really—so it's inverted—though the one who'd stayed behind for a minute while I curse him flirted with me.

———————

A man mugging me—therefore inverted, not just in relation to maturity—seeing I'm frightened is almost considerate by not hitting me when I struggle with him, though finally giving him the purse.

The naiveté—on my part—he's depressed

———————

He's depressed—by mugging me—corresponds to my having a job

Having an employer, I'd made jokes seen by him to be inappropriate, had offended him—I made jokes because it's in the past (is therefore sentient—I'm fairly immature in age and my offending him is unintentional).

Winos were lying on the sidewalk, it's a warehouse district; I happen to be wearing a silk blouse, so it's jealousy, not that they're jealous of me necessarily.

They're not receded, and are inert—as it happens are bums—so it's being creamed; because it's contemporary in time—jealousy because of that.

The bums happen to be lying in the street, it really occurs that I wear a silk blouse.

So it's mechanical—because of the winos being there—not from the blouse which I'd happened to wear though going into the warehouse district.

Stevedores—I'm immature in age—who are now made to live away from their families to work, the division is by color; they're allowed to form unions but not act—so it's evanescent.

(Because it's inactive—not just in the situation itself. Or in their later not coming to the docks—so they were striking, regardless of them being fired which occurs then).

The man having been in government—it's evanescent because it's inactive, our being immature in age—he's assassinated at an airport where we happen to come in that morning. We get on a bus which goes to the ocean—it's also beefcake but not because of the man already having died, is mature.

(We haven't seen him—as with the sailors it's contemporary in time).

A microcosm, but it's of sailors—so it's in the foreground, is beefcake—is in the past

(Therefore is contemporary in time while being seen then—so beefcake is in the past—similar to the situation of the other girls also refusing as I had to walk out onto the field, my then being immediately required to— not just in relation to them cooperating then).

It's the mechanical birds because of my having gone out on the field then—is the men

So it's sexual coming—anyone—but corresponds to the floating world, seeing men on the street

---

not in relation to there being too many of them standing around on a job

•

It's hot weather—so it's recent—corresponds to them

(though the floating world was in the past). To others as well—is in the setting of me being on a boardwalk seeing crowds of people walking or rollerskating. Some happening to be immature in age—it's not retroactive

•

Being in the past—is jealousy on my part—in general

Not in relation to the people I happened to see who were immature in age—on the boardwalk—necessarily

•

Their not being sentient

The reserves—they weren't using the police, so it's inverted—were wearing battle-gear, it's beautiful weather—they were old—is crowded

not occurring now—and their being frightened of the crowd, so it's inverted because of that—I'm there but jealousy on my part, in general—stemming from that

---

I'm not retroactive—corresponds to making jokes because it's in the past

(Not retroactive because of the beautiful weather. And taking the car to be repaired; the mechanic coming out to test drive, its tires have gone flat in the short time I was in the shop. The man and I get out of the car, laugh, I walk somewhere else to have its tires filled, drive away. Buying a dip stick then, I'd done what was necessary to it myself apparently).

Beginning to honk, because a man in a car behind me looked as if he were going to take my parking place, it's near shops, is crowded—I honked before seeing that he's old. And it appearing he hadn't wanted the parking place.

(His being old not mattering because it's crowded—which is transparent, regardless of there being the one parking place—so it isn't sentient)

The background had been in the selling of the car—almost giving it away

though it's not that, but seeing it again sitting by the highway—I'm weeping because of something, am driving back from the city—so it's transparent, crowded but my being miserable; which had occurred anyway. The man who'd bought the car cheating me though saying it was worthless—it is—having occurred earlier

Corresponding to having a job—and going below the border

On the vacation—I'm fired after I returned though the employer had consented to the vacation—we get to a small town in the desert. There are mines. It's at night. We've driven very fast. A crowd of men are in the store buying liquor who are poor—so it's evanescent (it's evanescent though we're buying liquor as well)

Someone else, who's middle aged—so it's not the man with the boy, getting gasoline

—being miserable, had put his head on the steering wheel, corresponds to there being the one parking place, though he's not going then. So isn't in that one. And weeping unrestrainedly because of his life—isn't necessarily related to his age

Other people not being retroactive—because of the beautiful weather— so it's recent

people said to be working for subsistence complimented for being willing to—in a naive way by the plant owner—is then inactive

•

The construction workers whistling or catcalling at women who go by the construction site, at each woman going by—they're not sentient

(We're not—neither are they)

It's hot weather—so it's reversed, is contemporary as with the sailors

(beefcake is in the foreground)

is naive—corresponds to the floating world

_____

isn't knowledgeable of myself therefore—is the boys—who happen to be standing on a street corner, they're unemployed though it's Sunday anyway. It's necessary that they not have jobs. We're downtown driving—so there's no one else there

(is not sentient—but which is the mechanical birds, because of the weather)

_____

so it would be transparent in the past, crowded but my being miserable

—as it happens—and have it not occur now

•

Their not being sentient

Seeing a crowd of people—we'd gone to a gallery as it happened—so they're not at their jobs

_____

that they were at the beach—aren't retroactive

_____

The floating world was courtesans though

It was in a man's divorce, (he's the father of a man who'd earlier gone below the border)—and him just taking off to the south one day to be near the border for good, not wanting his job anyway—not clarifying

(it's therefore sentient—isn't for him)

isn't for me

taking a cab, the driver seems frightened, seen by him not speaking to me—stemming from his job—unfamiliar because of the streets

_____

A crazy, recognized by people around because he is always on the street—staying outside is it being crowded, though the man isn't old.

I'm going by when fraternity boys are shouting at him, making fun—didn't realize he could've shouted first, occurring to me when I saw him shouting by himself one time

Alcohol not enabling someone to be in paradise, being what he was saying therefore inverted. A man getting out of a car, another transient coming by who begins to shout for some reason, addressed the man by the car (though it's not necessarily to him)—who also shouted, but not making fun of him

---

It having to be some time ago—was related to the bus driver, we're in school. The driver is surly, in general—turning a corner driving he hits a girl because she's not out of the way, thinking she should run

he hasn't drunk anything—so it isn't dislike

•

and isn't dislike for him—so afterwards we'd always make the sound in the bus of it hitting her at that corner

---

which is their wanting to take the money I might have on me

two muggers—though they were not together—who both followed me for a time aware of each other and that I see them. I was walking quickly with my suitcase which would mean to them that I'd just arrived in the city, it's crowded with passers-by (so not enabling someone to be in paradise—is regardless of the money I might have on me).

A transient—so it's not necessary to be it—the other men in the restaurant throw him out

because he's noisy, being drunk—but having no arms so removing him is inverted, another transient comes in who has arms, is also drunk—and therefore thrown out as well (that man had reentered carrying a cat before being thrown out again).

The floating world was courtesans though

•

A girl at the time—the insects which is inverted, in a situation in which she's on the deck of a boat on the Nile, there was a swarm of locusts, coming on her suddenly—she's a friend

really the friend of a relative

•

It'd have to be some time ago—I got cake on me, handed to me by my mother, we're in a taxi. Men in another car—beside me, I'm somewhat immature in age—whistled and called to me customary stemming from seeing me eating the cake

(so I'm embarrassed)

———————

Climbing a mountain—it's Fuji—there are marines having to climb it for exercise; easily able to get far ahead of us, which we don't realize, we're girls, they wait when we have to rest—

it isn't creamed for us—though dissolution not occurring. And not occurring in the situation with the marines.

———————

it's regardless—I was immature in age, so that is mechanical

Holding one end of a jump rope, the other end is tied to a tree—a boy who was a bully riding his bicycle is going to ride across the jump rope; I pull the rope slightly as it's lying on the sidewalk before he gets to it so he sees that and knows I can do it—so it isn't mechanical in that sense

———————

is so our being fairly immature in age, we're students—the man who's discovered in the crowd—he's there to observe it, is in the F.B.I., had been in it in my childhood living nearby since he was a neighbor

Though the people in the crowd don't call to him saying they know who he is because of that—but it's mechanical because of that

———————

it being reversed

•

It's obvious—occurring recently

The checkers falling behind—after chasing a man out shouting that he has stolen, he ran far away from the supermarket—a woman I know rode after him on a bicycle (for the reason given by the checkers)

•

I went on up the street, seeing a transient who had his things with him sitting near-by—there are men pouring cement in a site, he's watching them—so isn't sentient

because of occurring recently

stemming from that—

I take her to the hospital—meaning the landlady who's in her nineties—
to visit a tenant who's fallen down having been drunk

We walk a block, the street flooding since it's raining. It isn't creamed—in
the sense of her age

as it is being caught in the rain with bags of groceries—no one's around

It's pouring, I'm on the street corner unable to carry them further—it's
funny because I should have known better. But though taxis are never in
this neighborhood, one goes by and I go home in it

So it's the bicyclist, cursing—which occurs when I almost hit a bicyclist,
he says so following my car for a block afterwards—

So I'm sentient—he is not

I'm in a packed courtroom, a crowd is outside; the man sitting there—
having been informed on as communist in a ridiculous situation—the
other members of the cell had been F.B.I. So there not having been
understanding on his part, he was embarrassed—in expression—

Therefore dissolution not occurring—my being fairly immature in age.
Not creamed for me afterwards.

I'd gotten into the hearing—of the man—because of the crowd's pushing
and the police admitting me into the courtroom

though my friends had been left outside, were more aware than I—so it's
the landlady because of them being amidst the crowd

as it is working for a lawyer only slightly older than I, I'm fairly immature
in age—I offend him unintentionally by making a joke when he says he'd
like to get into working for trusts

It's dumb work, temporary for me—so that is the landlady

it's temporary work—he's the lawyer who's slightly older than I, I was
fairly immature in age

He doesn't speak to me for a week once, we're in the car mostly—
because I'd made jokes; I hadn't meant to offend him—so it's the
landlady in that sense

•

which is like selling my car—having an ad

I have the feeling I wouldn't have luck without the car, though it won't
run—but nevertheless sell it to a man who puts the money on the grass.
I'd bent down to get it giving him the chance to grab me—picking me up
in his arms isn't the reason he buys the car—it's to repair it

———————

Seeing my old car parked on the street—I'm driving by and had

already been unhappy—regardless of the feeling that I wouldn't have
luck without the car; so that is then the landlady

•

The lawyer and I, he's only slightly older than I—working have to have
dinners; though I've unintentionally offended him—

which is the landlady for that reason. We're in expensive restaurants, he
and I fairly immature in age

———————

my being fairly immature in age—we dock, there are lines of stevedores,
men coming onto the ship—we can't get off in that port, it's the port's
authority, because a few people on the ship had become sick

but the stevedores can

———————

—making jokes

was making fun of the lawyer, our both being fairly immature in age—
though I didn't realize it

•

We're—the lawyer and I—in the car, I had made the jokes before this,
he's gotten beer

but we hadn't opened it yet; he backed into a tree, driving away from the
grocery

•

The thought that there is no riot—isn't going to be any

is connected to the stevedores

There is no riot—associated with the stevedores—the man to whom I
sold my car, he'd taken me for a drive in the hills deciding on it, had
driven it recklessly

he's trying to frighten me so I'll give him the car—which I do, though I
realize it

JAMES SCHUYLER ▪ ▪ ▪ ▪ ▪ ▪ ▪ ▪ ▪ ▪ ▪ ▪ ▪ ▪

August First, 1974

was yesterday. I went out in the yard
in back today. I didn't stay: too hot
for comfort even under the apple trees
hung—smothered in fact—by Concord
grape vines, unpruned, run rampant. But
then, my step-father, the gardner is
dead. The garden that he took such pride
in isn't much really anymore. I don't
mind it this way. It's dry (rain predicted)
and from this desk it used to be, say,
more than thirty years ago, you could look
right down the valley that leads to Olean.
Now, in August, the leaves of young trees
across the street hide all that view of
uncultivated fields where sometimes
a horse would unexpectedly appear: Jim
Westland's. Jim's dead too, and Katharine,
his wife. So kind to me when I was
in my teens. A hot breath of wind stirs
a white voile curtain: or are they
organdy or net? It couldn't matter less.
Below the window a taxus hedge: Japanese
yew, so popular for foundation plantings
in suburbs and small towns. *Qualunque:*
commonplace. I like a house to rise up
naked from the ground it stands on. Oh,
honestly I don't much care one way or the
other. And what's that small purple
flowered weed or wild flower that grows
in grass, making something like an herb
lawn? Typing this makes me sweat. No
more today. You see, I'm waiting.

Red Brick and Brown Stone

for Darragh Park

He arises. Oriane
the lurcher wants
her walk. Out into
the freeze. Oriane
pees and shits. The
shit is scooped up
in a doggy bag, ac-
cording to law: $100
fine and is disposed
of somewhere.
The sun peers down
and sees them. Ov-
altine, a fag, WNCH:
unspeakable Teleman.
The dinner table is
mahogany and silver
gleams. A carriage
clock chimes eight,
sweetly. The front
room north facing
studio, its two long
windows divided by
a pier glass. Canvas,
eight by six, cars
charge down Ninth
Avenue straight at
you. Parked, a yellow
cab. A bending tree.
London Terrace, an
eighteenth century
house now a shop,
work in progress.
Brush in pigment:
scrub stroke scour.
Hours pass. Hunger
strikes: Empire Diner
silver metal art deco.
A pork burger, salad,
tea (iced). Home. Oriane
wants out. So they do
as before. Oriane goes
home. Off by cab to
Florentine palasso
racquet club: naked,
the pool, plunge, how

many laps? Home. (Through
out the day, numerous
cigarettes. I forget
which brand. Tareytons.)
A pencil drawing of
a vase of parrot tulips.
Records: Richter:
Scriabin: Tosca: "Mario!
Mario! Mario!" "I
lived for art, I
lived for love." Sup-
per: a can of baked
beans, a cup of raspberry
yogurt. Perrier. Out?
A flick? An A.A.
meeting? Walk Oriane.
Nine p.m. Bed. A
book, V. Woolf's let-
ters. Lights out, sleep
not quite right away.
No valium. The night
passes in black chiffon.

Self-Pity Is a Kind of Lying, Too

It's
snowing defective
vision days and
X—
mas is coming, like
a plow. And in the
meat the snow. Strange.
It all reminds me
of an old lady I
once saw shivering
naked beside a black
polluted stream. You
felt terrible—but
the train didn't
stop—so. And the
white which is
some other color or
its absence—it
spins on itself
and so do the *Who
at Leeds* I'm playing
to drown the carols
blatting from the

Presbyterian church
steeple which is
the same as fight
ing fire with oil.
Naked people—old,
cold—one day we'll
just have snow
to wear too.

A View

How come a thickish tree
casts so thin a shadow
and that sign-supporting pipe
none at all? (here comes Tom)

The road dries off, lighter
and lighter (there goes
Tom, in the red car, after
flour). In the further

distance, a baby blue camper,
after reeds and dead tree trunks,
peeled and weathered,
and the creosoted phone poles

Closer, on grass, the sunlight
breathes: fades and brightens,
brightens and fades, sparkles
yellow-green on green

Out of nowhere, a breeze
tosses the junk (soon
to be leaves) on twig ends.
Here comes Charlie, the cat.

Closer, window screen and
a six light window sash
pushed part way up another
makes a fifteen light window

framed by thick white net.
Closer, a bag says, The Cellar.
Closer, a pair of slippers, and
(khaki canvas) a Maine hiking shoe

invites my foot to go
out there, into the view

of May 10th, 1988
                    Here
comes Tom (he
got the flour) and there
sits Charlie, a white
cat on a green hummock.

Noon Office

A snowy curtain
slides up the sky.
Across the road,
dead trees whose
tops a hurricane
snapped off, rise
straight and pallid
out of green honey-suckle nests. That
big tree, nearest
the house, goes
leathery, elephantine,
stands
on one leg.
The blessing—
the bliss—
of one afternoon:
an infestation
of silence. May God
forgive us. To no
one's memory we
erect dead trees.

Reserved Sacrament

This soft October
                    mid-morning
the light, what light
                        there is
that is, comes
from the east
                under the sky
not from it
            more a pulsation
than a glow
                the glow
that on Sunday

<pre>
                        (only
            yesterday? was
                        it only yesterday?
            It was
                it was) shone
            from the west
                        from
            Manhattan
                    the train throbbed
            on toward
                    light tasting
            of Chateau Yquem or
                            less grand
            more glorious
                        the fortified wine
            used as the
                        Sacrament
            in Holy Communion
                            this is the cup
            of life
                the blood
            of salvation
                    light lighting up
            the scrub
                    in red
            and purple
                    and gold
</pre>

ARMAND SCHWERNER ▪ ▪ ▪ ▪ ▪ ▪ ▪ ▪ ▪ ▪ ▪

The Next Two Tablets

Presented by the scholar-translator, transmitted through Armand Schwerner

Tablet XVI

++++++++++++ space-vase . . . . the past is lioness to swallow
this Now this Now this Now this . . . . . . ++++++++++++ grid nothing . . . . . .
   strangle or not strangle is strangle . . . .
   . . . . that it ask nothing for itself, that it is not,
   that its waves +++++++++++++++++++ grid emptiness . . . .
o beautiful no-field field I wait for you, when I wait for you
is none of your coming to me, or not wait, the same,
I'm sitting like a drunk unable to sit, attached . . . . lioness
I want to miss it all, want none in my arrivals* to this Now
                                    *presence?/craftsmanship?

not the rich black percolating loam, not
even the thick enemy clayey loam, not the mazy
sunlit dust-motes suggesting earth. If they came
I'd want to change them, to ask something of them, repeats
of yesterday's tasty stew of stomach-ache, beloved . . . . . . lioness
to fill the future with stony shit°, I'd beg them

°lentil-soup?

in spite of my refusals, me yellow-jacket self-stung to acknowledge my own
   lightning
refusal of my refusals. See saw Oualbpaga, no, not even the green teal,
or its spring shadow, or its name, or dream of it flying; see-saw
is all.
What do I fill with, or why want filling?
O Oualbpaga I would suck you off longer . . . . longer
than anyone thinks possible, your red sperm was/will-be/is/is-just-about-almost°
      Time

°tense unclear

to give myself [placenta-coming] in green rain + + + + + + + + + + expire into this
   Now
if I will/would-have/might-had-played with your balls do my fingers move
in the present, danced conjoinings in the moment, cause
without cause? Time is glue in my arms wanting to want nothing, my gut
a void, space-vase + and forty-five years to
   learn this?
To withstand the impress of flashing
is not the way, nor to not withstand, not
lust for loss of being, lust . . . .
+ + + + + + + + + + + + + + + + sitting still sitting still sitting still sitting still
   sitting . . . .
shit-god Damalo penis-hole/vagina° . . . . quiet . . . . +

°whirlpool?

we should always live in the dark empty sky, the sky
is always the sky . . . . if the lightning +
the sky is not disturbed +
   + + emptiness
into the same . . . . that the original question drove me
into the sink or swamp regularly. When will or might night
perhaps repair all the damage° not damage of not done of not arrived

°commonly 'power'

at all? clarity clear light clarity clear light toothgnash + + + + + + + + + + + + + +
   lioness

Tablet XVII

'Ahanarshi's trip': this tablet seems to belong to the familiar anecdotal homiletic
genre, though the personal presence, in combination with an almost surreal
texture, makes me suspect the intrusion of a relatively recent hand. An archetype
of spiritual friendship does pervade the text, some of whose quality arrives at
later refinement in Judeo-Christianity.

Ahanarshi . . . . in the Teacher's room . . . . . Ahanarshi
+ + + + + + + + + + + + + + + + for the Teacher . . . . interview
Ahanarshi +
　+ + + + + + + + + + + + + + + + +
and the vibrations of Ahanarshi's water body were tempest
Ahanarshi did a headstand to [homogenize] his fluids, he used
the [meditation-pillow] to prop himself up on, he sat
in the lotus flower,° Ahanarshi, at the feet of the Teacher
　　　　　　　　°etymology unclear: may signify a growth, perhaps a position
for the space of a meal,° the straggles of his hair [set ablaze],
　　　　　　　　　　　　°commonly taken as ½ hour
Ahanarshi, by the Teacher, gently by the Teacher.
Buzz of a fly buzz of a fly, random visits to the wine cask
Ahanarshi wanted to talk, wanted . . . .
wanted + + + + + + + + + + + + + + + + + + + but settled; he slid
into [himself], turquoise vase,
dust pieces strike him, Ahanarshi, his crystal body
gong . . . . sea-wind of the double flutes
Ahanarshi sees his heart is a frost-cake, he sees his heart, the smell
of low-tide decay invades his rust nostrils, he inhales
aroma of singed hair he shudders with pleasure in his throat
. . . . + + + + + + + + + + + + + + + + + + he stiff as a penis,
　prone on the river belly
sees inside to the shoal of sea-robins and flounder and porgies
which never bump, Ahanarshi sees them never touch,
cold under the chocolate river; his head turns warm, he tells
well among the [species] he tells well a while and telling
bewilders . . . . . . rage . . . . . blows of phlegm into his fat throat
. . . . rest +
　+ + + + + +
is it clear is it clear are you enveloping, Ahanarshi, are you,
or riding at the quiet of an envelopment?
the arced right foot cramps, drive of ice-pins
in the cave behind the left knee. He says 'pain, pain'
Ahanarshi says 'pain, pain' he re-enters his activity
he is present Ahanarshi no longer concentrating now he hears
air circulating in and out of the Teacher he splinters into a mine
of blue-green flints it is clear thousands of painful wisps
ride him, tiny throats, the Teacher says:
　　　　　　'we will work together'
The Teacher says 'we will work together'
the single mind . . . . to discover° the Teacher

　　　　　　　　　　　　　　　　°invent?

Key to the Tablets:
　. . . . . *untranslatable*
　+ + + + + + + *missing*
　(?) *variant reading*
　[ ] *supplied by the scholar-translator*

the work

for Phill Niblock

it is not that there is beginning is there
   no beginning
                the fluid text becomes its very river, rapids, it is not
that the text is not or that beginninglessness itself be in the heart
           of the text,
                    that search *there* is the beginning
of the mistake   of
   considering   of
     lust for a beginning hold me lover but no it is not possible
to contract for stay
       it is not possible not to *voice,* to voice
         poem must be possible there is no walking
            in this room no sitting no one listens no prone alert
there is only this endless speaking to *voice;* the head the thighs the red work
only
    this endless speaking overheard semiheard it is impossible
      to not overhear the endless speaking in all the bodies
sending sending themselves to themselves there is no
    rolling no eating there is no
      rolling in the fucking-room for no one is it possible not to overhear
the beginningless speaking lizard movement in the mind-body
    gnawing   and a great coil endless there is only the goddess
      of the endless speaking upsurging
        through the asphalt why
is there this no-beginning
      says the weary attention to rest to rest after the capture one
          moment capture of silence the unconscious gossip damped once there
can be no beginning the cut sharp
     cry of the crowbar need to connect but the endless speaking
upsurging there is no
walking no one ever eats there is no running only this speaking no one
is drawing circles or the circle is being drawn
      into the mind loop upon bright loop of the speaking
        forming endless menorah branches of the speaking guttering candles
                  of the mind's speaking   random is it
random random animalcules of the wax of the
    wax of the mind's speaking the
      clambering lizard of the mind playing as it's the moaning
        of the endless speaking or
          bright gutterings
giving the dark an Egyptian relief what's going on under or
     undercutting beyond or transshaping through the speaking
master, there is no walking no master no one is sitting here no one squeezing
    her thighs together for the lips' pleasure there is no
      listening no listening! only

the endless speaking the vast cabin of branches
   forking out in constantly unexpected emptinesses
     the raw cabin woodworld the sap of such
           joyousness! no
rest, is it awakening? could it be the attentiveness
   implicit in the red work the stems intent like old Leaky
     inside their patience their unstopping patience the watchfulness
of the stems
   branches observing branches, is this
     an awakening or a dying?
                        green-ochre lizard-color stems,
     uranium stillness
          is the action a phenomenal
            joke not patience but slavery attentive it is not
            possible
              to contract for a stay

FREDERICK SEIDEL ▪ ▪ ▪ ▪ ▪ ▪ ▪ ▪ ▪ ▪ ▪ ▪ ▪ ▪

Fucking

I wake because the phone is really ringing.
A singsong West Indian voice
In the dark, possibly a man's,
Blandly says, "Good morning, Mr. Seidel;
How are you feeling, God?"
And hangs up after my silence.

This is New York—
Some mornings five women call within a half hour.

In a restaurant, a woman I had just met, a Swede,
Three inches taller
Than I was among other things, and immensely
Impassive, cold,
Started to groan, very softly and husky voiced.
She said,
"You have utter control over me, and you know it.
I can't do anything about it."
I had been asking her about her job.

One can spend a lifetime trying to believe
These things.

I think of A.,
Before she became Lady Q.,

Of her lovely voice, and her lovely name.
What an extraordinary new one she took
With her marriage vows,
Even as titles go, extra fictitious. And ah—
And years later, at her request, paying a call on the husband
To ask if I could take her out
Once more, once, m'lord, for auld lang syne. She still wanted
To run away;
And had,
Our snowed-in week in the Chelsea
Years before.
How had her plane managed to land?

How will my plane manage to land?

How wilt thy plane manage to land?

Our room went out sledding for hours
And only returned when we slept,
Finally, with it still snowing, near dawn.

I can remember her sex,
And how the clitoris was set.

Now on to London where the play resumes—
The scene when I call on the husband. But first,

In Francis Bacon's queer after-hours club,
Which one went to after
An Old Compton Street Wheeler's lunch,
A gentleman at the bar, while Francis was off pissing,
Looking straight at me, shouted
"Champagne for the Norm'!"
Meaning normal, heterosexual.

The place where I stayed,
The genteel crowded gloom of Jimmy's place,
Was England—coiled in the bars of an electric fire
In Edith Grove.
Piece by piece Jimmy sold off the Georgian silver.
Three pretty working girls were his lodgers.

Walking out in one direction, you were in
Brick and brown oppidan Fulham.

Walking a few steps the other way, you heard
Augustus John's many mistresses
Twittering in the local Finch's,

And a few steps further on, in the smart restaurants,
The young grandees who still said "gels."

There was a man named Pericles Belleville,
There is a man named Pericles Belleville,
Half American.

At a very formal dinner party,
At which I met the woman I have loved the most
In my life, Belleville
Pulled out a sterling silver-plated revolver
And waved it around, pointing it at people, who smiled.
One didn't know if the thing could be fired.

That is the poem.

To Robert Lowell and Osip Mandelstam

I look out the window: spring is coming.
I look out the window: spring is here.
The shuffle and click of the slide projector
Changing slides takes longer.

I like the dandelion—
How it sticks to the business of briefly being.
Shuffle and click, shuffle and click—
Life, more life, more life.

The train that carried the sparkling crystal saxophone
Osip Mandelstam into exile clicketyclicked
Through suds of spring flowers,
Cool furrowed-earth smells, sunshine like freshly baked bread.

The earth was so black it looked wet,
So rich it had produced Mandelstam.
He was last seen alive
In 1938 at a transit camp near Vladivostok

Eating from a garbage pile,
When I was two, and Robert Lowell was twenty-one,
Who much later would translate Mandelstam,
And now has been dead two years himself.

I sometimes feel I hurry to them both,
Stand staring at the careworn spines

Of their books in my bookshelf,
Only in order to walk away.

The wish to live is as unintentional as love.
Of course the future always is,
Like someone just back from England
Stepping off a curb, I'll look the wrong way and be nothing.

Heartbeat, heartbeat, the heart stops—
But shuffle and click, it's spring!
The arterial branches disappearing in the leaves,
Swallowed like a tailor's chalk marks in the finished suit.

We are born.
We grow old until we're all the same age.
They are as young as Homer whom they loved.
They are writing a letter, not in a language I know.

I read: "It is one of those spring days with a sky
That makes it worthwhile being here.
The mailbox in which we'll mail this
Is slightly lighter than the sky."

Scotland

A stag lifts his nostrils to the morning
In the crosshairs of the scope of love,
And smells what the gun calls Scotland and falls.
The meat of geology raw is Scotland: Stone
Age hours of stalking, passionate aim for the heart,
Bleak dazzling weather of the bare and green.
Old men in kilts, their beards are lobster-red.
Red pubic hair of virgins white as cows.
Omega under Alpha, rock hymen, fog penis—
The unshaved glow of her underarms is the sky
Of prehistory or after the sun expands.

The sun will expand a billion years from now
And burn away the mist of Caithness—till then,
There in the Thurso phone book is Robin Thurso.
But he is leaving for his other castle.
"Yes, I'm just leaving—what a pity! I can't
Remember, do you shoot?" Dukes hunt stags,
While Scotsmen hunt for jobs and emigrate,
Or else start seeing red spots on a moor
That flows to the horizon like a migraine.
Sheep dot the moor, bubblebaths of unshorn
Curls somehow red, unshepherded, unshorn.

Gone are the student mobs chanting the *Little Red*
Book of Mao at their Marxist dons.
The universities in the south woke,
Now they are going back to the land of dreams—
Tour buses clog the roads that take them there.
Gone, the rebel psychoanalysts.
Scotland trained more than its share of brilliant ones.
Pocked faces, lean as wolves, they really ran
To untrain and be famous in London, doing wild
Analysis, vegetarians brewing
Herbal tea for anorexic girls.

Let them eat haggis. The heart, lungs and liver
Of a sheep minced with cereal and suet,
Seasoned with onions, and boiled in the sheep's stomach.
That's what the gillie eats, not venison,
Or salmon, or grouse served rare, not for the gillie
That privilege, or the other one which is
Mushed vegetables molded to resemble a steak.
Let them come to Scotland and eat blood
Pud from a food stall out in the open air,
In the square in Portree. Though there is nothing
Better in the world than a grouse cooked right.

They make a malt in Wick that tastes as smooth
As Mounton when you drink enough of it.
McEwen adored both, suffered a partial stroke,
Switched to champagne and died. A single piper
Drones a file of mourners through a moor,
The sweet prodigal being piped to his early grave.
A friend of his arriving by helicopter
Spies the procession from a mile away,
The black speck of the coffin trailing a thread,
Lost in the savage green, an ocean of thawed
Endlessness and a spermatozoon.

A vehement bullet comes from the gun of love.
On the island of Raasay across from Skye,
The dead walk with the living hand in hand
Over to Hallaig in the evening light.
Girls and boys of every generation,
MacLeans and MacLeods, as they were before they were
Mothers and clansmen, still in their innocence,
Walk beside the islanders, their descendants.
They hold their small hands up to be held by the living.
Their love is too much, the freezing shock-alive
Of rubbing alcohol that leads to sleep.

Bleecker Street

Interest points for
birthplace tourist.

Youth races blameless.
Age passes past blame.

Conundrum: should
shrink reveal patient?

No rest from the famous?
from Oz?

Some sense the ticker.
Nothing realer.

Bird-store toucan, antique
six-foot wood horse.

Tanned, graying, coifed
ladies, escorts.

One-name models,
drunk boyfriends.

The spike-heeled,
endless, inevitable.

So beautiful,
it stops the breath.

We sleep a long time.
Great ledgers of sleep.

Dazed shepherds on
silver under cobalt.

Stars beyond words.
The poet wants to help.

But exploits others' pain?
O contradiction!

Regular or decaf?
800 feigning sterling.

Stroke

Writhing,
IV in.

Wrists
buckled

to the bed.
Pleading:

free me.
It was late.

I had
to get back

to my house
to sleep.

How was it?
Sons: men.

Fathers:
sons.

In intensive
care, alone.

Composition

ANGLING

Since there are depths. Though
flesh stink, hooked jaws
cut the careless.

●

4 A.M.

War just readers win.
Each draws out his/
her own arrow.

●

HOW

Keep nothing, nothing
left, but a faint
breath of nothing.

●

DISNEY LAND

Poets, heroines
are mad. Heroes:
pure poetry.

●

MOON

Bright rim, shadow. First
draft to measure,
fill to margins.

Poem

War and greed stop food.
Tyrant and army stand.

Buy the paper.
How many words?

Never to be erased.
Many will fall.

This has been said before.
Why repeat terror?

Hope, until hope enters
the kingdom of survival.

The binary forever.
Is there no way?

Sudden tears, not words.
Like love, hunger.

The fish martyred up
through the molecular.

Photos

CHINAMAN: 1905

Hacked, naked, roped to a pole.
Chest gone, passed out—penis glows.
Red-hot dot means bought/sold.
Pray crime fits punishment.

●

KURDS

Transcendent, horrible.
Transcendent since resigned,
horrible since beautiful.
Corpse borne miles for burial.

●

SOMALI

Years ago the skeletal Biafran.
Now, its double wails on a flier.
Water poured to a child's cup.
Four dollars per well.

Dirt to Dirt

A few days to turn the pages.
Eyes worse by a half dioptor.

News furrowed on land or forehead.
It is spring; none is returning.

Flesh pierced, unabated.
Doubled over yet straightened.

Stroke

He would get the gold,
swore his "Oracle,"
no more struggle.

The ward was locked,
but they would not hold him.
Haldol stopped, delusions back.

Once he fell as if dead:
face down, nose bleeding.
Finally, in a diner.

Beaten gold is thin,
almost non-existent—
layered on the bell.

The end is the end.
"Ten more years," had he said?
Labor, now over.

End

Far but near.
At what CD rate?

Father gone.
Mother just passed.

We are children,
but dumb to be one.

Outside: mountains,
holding the sun.

Mastodon, as long
as ice lasts.

Moral?
Yield if asked.

Laureate

Ignored what needed to be ignored—though can one?
Prose: soap opera; poetry: prose.

Theories of theory, granite temples, silken lace.
Metaphor's turbines rumbling under earth.

What a bore; what an uplift.
Joined how to bones under flesh?

Table=table, chair=chair, said a master.
Citizen confessing a citizen's state.

Crowds applauding the bemedaled texts:
victorious; heroic; humble, even, out of context.

ANNE SEXTON ▪ ▪ ▪ ▪ ▪ ▪ ▪ ▪ ▪ ▪ ▪ ▪ ▪ ▪ ▪ ▪

The Furies

The Fury of Beautiful Bones

Sing me a thrush, bone.
Sing me a nest of cup and pestle.
Sing me a sweet bread for an old grandfather.
Sing me a foot and a doorknob, for you are my love.
Oh sing, bone bag man, sing.
Your head is what I remember that August,
you were in love with another woman but
that didn't matter. I was the fury of your
bones, your fingers long and nubby, your
forehead a beacon, bare as marble and I worried
you like an odor because you had not quite forgotten,
bone bag man, garlic in the North End,
the book you dedicated, naked as a fish,
naked as someone drowning into his own mouth.
I wonder, Mr. Bone man, what you're thinking
of your fury now, gone sour as a sinking whale,
crawling up the alphabet on her own bones.
Am I in your ear still singing songs in the rain,
me of the death rattle, me of the magnolias,
me of the sawdust tavern at the city's edge.
Women have lovely bones, arms, neck, thigh
and I admire them also, but your bones
supersede loveliness. They are the tough
ones that get broken and reset. I just can't
answer for you, only for your bones,
round rulers, round nudgers, round poles,
numb nubkins, the sword of sugar.
I feel the skull, Mr. Skeleton, living its
own life in its own skin.

The Fury of Earth

The day of fire is coming, the thrush
will fly ablaze like a little sky rocket,

the beetle will sink like a giant bulldozer,
and at the breaking of the morning the houses
will turn into little rocks, the waters
will turn into oil and will in their tides
of fire be a becoming and an ending, a red fan.
What then, man in your easy chair,
of the anointment of the sick,
of the New Jerusalem?
You will have to polish up the stars
with Babo and find a new God
as the earth empties out
into the gnarled hands of the old redeemer.

The Fury of Jewels and Coal

Many a miner has gone
into the deep pit
to receive the dust of a kiss,
an ore-cell.
He has gone with his lamp
full of mole eyes
deep deep and has brought forth
Jesus at Gethsemane.
Body of moss, body of glass,
body of peat, how sharp
you lie, emerald as heavy
as a golf course, ruby as dark
as an afterbirth,
diamond as white as sun
on the sea, coal, dark mother,
brood mother, let the sea birds
bring you into our lives
as from a distant island,
heavy as death.

The Fury of Guitars and Sopranos

This singing
is a kind of dying,
a kind of birth,
a votive candle.
I have a dream-mother
who sings with her guitar,
nursing the bedroom
with moonlight and beautiful olives.
A flute came too,
joining the five strings,
a God finger over the holes.
I knew a beautiful woman once
who sang with her fingertips

and her eyes were brown
like small birds.
At the cup of her breasts
I drew wine.
At the mound of her legs
I drew figs.
She sang for my thirst,
mysterious songs of God
that would have laid an army down.
It was as if a morning glory
had bloomed in her throat
and all that blue
and small pollen
ate into my heart
violent and religious.

The Fury of Sunrises

Darkness
as black as your eyelid,
poketricks of stars,
the yellow mouth,
the smell of a stranger,
dawn coming up,
dark blue,
no stars,
the smell of a lover,
warmer now
as authentic as soap,
wave after wave
of lightness
and the birds in their chains
going mad with throat noises,
the birds in their tracks
yelling into their cheeks like clowns,
lighter, lighter,
the stars gone,
the trees appearing in their green hoods,
the house appearing across the way,
the road and its sad macadam,
the rock walls losing their cotton,
lighter, lighter,
letting the dog out and seeing
fog lift by her legs,
a gauze dance,
lighter, lighter,
yellow, blue at the tops of trees,
more God, more God everywhere,
lighter, lighter,

more world everywhere,
sheets bent back for people,
the strange heads of love
and breakfast,
that sacrament,
lighter, yellower,
like the yoke of eggs,
the flies gathering at the windowpane,
the dog inside whining for food
and the day commencing,
not to die, not to die,
as in the last day breaking,
a final day digesting itself,
lighter, lighter,
the endless colors,
the same old trees stepping toward me,
the rock unpacking its crevices,
breakfast like a dream
and the whole day to live through,
stedfast, deep, interior.
After the death,
after the black of black,
this lightness—
not to die, not to die—
that God begot.

The Fury of Cocks

There they are
drooping over the breakfast plates,
angel like,
folding in their sad wing,
animal sad,
and only the night before
there they were
playing the banjo.
Once more the day's light comes
with its immense sun,
its mother trucks,
its engines of amputation.
Whereas last night
the cock knew its way home,
as stiff as a hammer,
battering in with all
its awful power.
That theatre.
Today it is tender,
a small bird,

as soft as a baby's hand.
She is the house.
he is the steeple.
When they fuck they are God.
When they break away they are God.
When they snore they are God.
In the morning they butter the toast.
They don't say much.
They are still God.
All the cocks of the world are God,
blooming, blooming, blooming
into the sweet blood of woman.

The Fury of Hating Eyes

I would like to bury
all the hating eyes
under the sand somewhere off
the North Atlantic and suffocate
them with the awful sand
and put all their colors to sleep
in that soft smother.
Take the brown eyes of my father,
those gun shots, those mean muds.
Bury them.
Take the blue eyes of my mother,
naked as the sea,
waiting to pull you down
where there is no air, no God.
Bury them.
Take the black eyes of my lover,
coal eyes like a cruel hog,
wanting to whip you and laugh.
Bury them.
Take the hating eyes of martyrs,
presidents, bus collectors,
bank managers, soldiers.
Bury them.
Take my eyes, half blind
and falling into the air.
Bury them.
Take your eyes.
I come to the center,
where a shark looks up at death
and thinks of my death.
They'd like to take my heart
and squeeze it like a doughnut.
They'd like to take my eyes

and poke a hatpin through
their pupils. Not just to bury
but to stab. As for your eyes,
I fold up in front of them
in a baby ball and you send
them to the State Asylum.
Look! Look! Both those
mice are watching you
from behind the kind bars.

The Fury of Sunsets

Something
cold is in the air,
an aura of ice
and phlegm.
All day I've built
a lifetime and now
the sun sinks to
undo it.
The horizon bleeds
and sucks its thumb.
The little red thumb
goes out of sight.
And I wonder about
this lifetime with myself,
this dream I'm living.
I could eat the sky
like an apple
but I'd rather
ask the first star:
why am I here?
why do I live in this house?
who's responsible?
eh?

The Fury of Rain Storms

The rain drums down like red ants,
each bouncing off my window.
These ants are in great pain
and they cry out as they hit,
as if their little legs were only
stitched on and their heads pasted.
And oh they bring to mind the grave,
so humble, so willing to be beat upon
with its awful lettering and
the body lying underneath
without an umbrella.

Depression is boring, I think,
and I would do better to make
some soup and light up the cave.

The Fury of God's Goodbye

One day He
tipped His top hat
and walked
out of the room,
ending the argument.
He stomped off
saying:
I don't give guarantees.
I was left
quite alone
using up the darkness.
I rolled up
my sweater,
up into a ball,
and took it
to bed with me,
a kind of stand-in
for God,
that washerwoman
who walks out
when you're clean
but not ironed.

When I woke up
the sweater
had turned to
bricks of gold.
I'd won the world
but like a
forsaken explorer,
I'd lost
my map.

The Fury of Cooks

Herbs, garlic,
cheese, please let me in!
Souffles, salads,
Parker House rolls,
please let me in!
Cook Helen,
why are you so cross,
why is your kitchen verboten?

Couldn't you just teach me
to bake a potato,
that charm,
that young prince?
No! No!
This is my country!
You shout silently.
Couldn't you just show me
the gravy. How you drill it out
of the stomach of that bird?
Helen, Helen,
let me in,
let me feel the flour,
is it blind and frightening,
this stuff that makes cakes?
Helen, Helen,
the kitchen is your dog
and you pat it
and love it
and keep it clean.
But all these things,
all these dishes of things
come through the swinging door
and I don't know from where?
Give me some tomato aspic, Helen!
I don't want to be alone.

The Fury of Sundays

Moist, moist,
the heat leaking through the hinges,
sun baking the roof like a pie
and I and thou and she
eating, working, sweating,
droned up on the heat.
The sun as red as the cop car siren.
The sun as red as the algebra marks.
The sun as red as two electric eyeballs.
She wanting to take a bath in jello.
You and me sipping vodka and soda,
ice cubes melting like the Virgin Mary.
You cutting the lawn, fixing the machines,
all this leprous day and then more vodka,
more soda and the pond forgiving our bodies,
the pond sucking out the throb.
Our bodies were trash.
We leave them on the shore.
I and thou and she
swim like minnows,

losing all our queens and king,
losing our heels and our tongues,
cool, cool, all day that Sunday in July
when we were young and did not look
into the abyss,
that God spot.

The Fury of Flowers and Worms

Let the flowers make a journey
on Monday so that I can see
ten daisies in a blue vase
with perhaps one red ant
crawling to the gold center.
A bit of the field on my table,
close to the worms
who struggle blindly,
moving deep into their slime,
moving deep into God's abdomen,
moving like oil through water,
sliding through the good brown.

The daisies grow wild
like popcorn.
They are God's promise to the field.
How happy I am, daisies, to love you.
How happy you are to be loved
and found magical, like a secret
from the sluggish field.
If all the world picked daisies
wars would end, the common cold would stop,
unemployment would end, the monetary market
would hold steady and no money would float.

Listen world,
if you'd just take the time to pick
the white fingers, the penny heart,
all would be well.
They are so unexpected.
They are as good as salt.
If someone had brought them
to Van Gogh's room daily
his ear would have stayed on.
I would like to think that no one would die anymore
if we all believed in daisies
but the worms know better, don't they?
They slide into the ear of a corpse
and listen to his great sigh.

The Fury of Abandonment

Someone lives in a cave
eating his toes,
I know that much.
Someone little lives under a bush
pressing an empty Coca-Cola can against
his starving bloated stomach,
I know that much.
A monkey had his hands cut off
for a medical experiment
and his claws wept.
I know that much.

I know that it is all
a matter of hands.
Out of the mournful sweetness of touching
comes love
like breakfast.
Out of the many houses come the hands
before the abandonment of the city,
out of the bars and shops,
a thin file of ants.

I've been abandoned out here
under the dry stars
with no shoes, no belt
and I've called Rescue Inc.—
that old fashioned hot line—
no voice.
Left to my own lips, touch them,
my own dumb eyes, touch them,
the progression of my parts, touch them,
my own nostrils, shoulders, breasts,
navel, stomach, mound, kneebone, ankle,
touch them.

It makes me laugh
to see a woman in this condition.
It makes me laugh for America and New York City
when your hands are cut off
and no one answers the phone.

DAVID SHAPIRO ▪ ▪ ▪ ▪ ▪ ▪ ▪ ▪ ▪ ▪ ▪ ▪ ▪ ▪ ▪

House (Blown Apart)

I can see the traces of old work
Embedded in this page, like your bed
Within a bed. My old desire to live!
My new desire to understand material, raw
Material as if you were a house without windows
A red stain. Gold becomes cardboard.
The earth grows rare and cheap as a street.
Higher up a bird of prey affectionate in bright grey
       travels without purpose.
I beg you to speak with a recognizable accent
As the roof bashed in for acoustics
Already moans. What is not a model
Is blown to bits in this mature breeze.
If students visit for signs
Or signatures we would discuss traces.
       We would examine each other for doubts.
Old work we might parody as an homage
Losing after all the very idea of parody.
Traces of this morning's work are embedded in this page.

Traumerei

One fine day,
open as cut lips,
more than alive—asleep and beaten powerless
you and I
like students evacuating
a burning high school
then lying flat like a drunken one next to the old boiler
in a T-shirt consumed by snow
when us the janitor awakens
we shall be
heated like dead languages after school
safe still, exempt on the illegal floor
in the high observatory
we will pardon the imbeciles
as clear, as intelligible
hardly have time for the brain that kills, bravo
then walking back to school, resolved
under the branches flinging marks
the snow is more than alive, it is asleep

in the little nut-brown street
infamous as sleet as the day repeats
Look at yourself! Look at yourself! That's why
          I'm driving you away
With my infra-red powerful ray
In the absence of a sphere of Lucky Socrates!
Lucky Socrates!
Almost too seriously, and frighteningly, oh sleep.

Archaic Torsos

after a dream

You must change your life fourteen times.
Change your way of living like writing.
You must change your method and your mind. You
Have to transform life fourteen times. Change life.
It has become necessary to change your life.
You need this change. We need to change your life.
And now you'd better change it: you, yourself.
It's up to you to exchange your life. Change, change!
Alter your life, patch and re-shape your life.
"A change come o'er the spirit of your change."
You might shuffle the cards spin wheels change wheels.
You must convert resolve revolutionize your dissolves.
You might change life itself. And you might change.
You must change. You must not outlive your life.

A Pin's Fee, or Painting with Star

The frame of the world is suddenly rotated
and the change flows through you like a mosaic of diseases
you are sealed off in a room at the bottom, fixed with stars
your earth and your magnet and your little red life

like the desire to cast the image of a woman
on a wall distant as a lamp
a dead body travelling north like an empty house, burning
High above the acanthus
stands the Siren, mourning the outlines
of a spiral

The dead are exceptionally rapt
The hair falls, freely rendered

A work well-delineated if cold
Artemis, headless

Recollection sustains a sound
like a music with thorns
You were always softer, always later
in the oblique
like the uncalled for summer's end

It is as if a clamp had been placed
over the bridge
preventing your voice
not just a sourdine, but the variations of your voice your brisk commands

It is a very ancient instrument
the smothered harp
you and I could scarcely sustain that first attack
quickly to war but all love studies liberty
and we have hated to hate
like the blue lieutenants and pastel constraints
dwarf mirrors and mirrors for clothes and time poured on mirrors of flesh

There is only one secret: the old stylelessness
freedom to visit the fugitives
("You are not a stove. Well, do you mean to insinuate
a person might be a stove")
And in winter we put up storm windows and felt around the doors

If there is only one bed
no matter how thick
There is only one air
Two window sashes, one air,
two walls, two shirts, some hollow birds
Black wax: those birds look like houses made of hollow bricks

You already a half ghost
and anyone speaking to you or drawing you even half a ghost
and then you become a whole and drop out of the game
and anyone who is half a ghost and speaks to you
becomes whole and drops out of the game

I am drawing your outline now
by memory
a quiet game which is always a way
and I am trying to place the lakes, rivers
and life's dust within a few miles of where they belong

The Weak Poet

for Michael Govrin

When a poet is weak,
like a broken microphone,
he still has some power,
indicated by a red light.

The weak poet
is fixed to the wall
like an ordinary light.

Dependent and dismal by turns,
he is a nominalist
and a razor blade
and a light.

And the demons cry,
Cast him from the kingdom
for a copy of a copy!

Remove him
like the women who supported the temple—
slaves too free and alive.
His similes are ingenious, like science among lovers.

My friend, however early
you called, you had come
too late, again.

The weak poet
has not gone grey
but his sacrificed similes
lead nowhere.

And his I is like any other word
in the newspaper and he is cut up
like fashion.

Each window was seductive,
but even his diseases could be cured.
Your low voice alone
is major like a skepticism.

We had forgotten
the place and the stories,
and the fiery method, too familiar, too distant.

We had memorized the poems,
but only for prison.
With the first new year celebrated in chaos
above the red waters of Paradise

Where a clayey groom
hears the bride's voice
like a stronger world—

Sound is all
a snake can do—
and charming sense
and strangeness.

Now the old poet
loses his voice like a garden.
But finds it again, like a street in a garden.

In the injured house
made of local sun and stone—
In the city of numbers
which everyone counts and hates and wants—

We could read together in a dark city garden,
scribbling with language over
screens like lips, scribbling the first mistranslations.

Song of the Eiffel Tower

for Lillian and Meyer Schapiro

Before the Eiffel was complete
Seurat painted it like a street
The top was a cloud, the skin was a dot
And like a nude the whole was in doubt.

The sky had no electric bulb.
But the sky was an electric bulb
For those who saw it clearly with a frame
And rented a window, but without a name.

And Meyer Schapiro
saw it all
In conte crayons in the
caricatural fall.
The woman who posed was
a tower too.

Long before the
drawing drew.

And Daniel Shapiro
went to the de Young
When he too
could hardly be called young.
He saw the Eiffel
in red and blue
In a deep case
without a postcard
view.

Drew my attention
to the small nude
of the Eiffel Tower
in its mad wood.
Like a bird in
the froth,
like a fish
in the flood.
Like a medieval
song transposed
by the mind.

We've lost it
again, like
Greek monody.
All we have is
a somber xerox copy.

Oh Eiffel Tower
Oh Sonia Delaunay
with elephantiasis
unto our day.
Let the stet stand,
let the series be
as lengthy as the
speckled tower
And all the rest
is money.
In that century,
we will be
happily blind.
Standing in such an iridescent wind.

The Eiffel
was nothing but numbers
like a lecture

by Plato
Now you may misspell
misspelling
Now you may hold your
organ like the
hero Balzac
Now you may be accused
of renting only
a house that opens
opens onto the Eiffel
and a dog on a
leash that explodes
into a light bulb

Crack open
the street,
break the
concrete.
It is distance,
it is near.
Only the junk
of the day remains,
only the top of the
peak, the poetics
of engineering
you will never reach
in everyday life:
our school.
In the picnic
on the peak,
a bridge away from
the disappearing mystique.
Oh and the lower
corner bears water
like Brooklyn,
the blue sky's name.

And a dark Lethe no doubt a copy
Ran like an academic stream filled with candy.
His father was the one-armed bailiff.
But the Tower was as strong as a shellfish.

KARL SHAPIRO · · · · · · · · · · · · · · · · ·

FROM *The Bourgeois Poet*

1

The world is my dream, says the wise child, ever so wise, not stepping on lines. I am the world, says the wise-eyed child. I made you, mother. I made you, sky. Take care or I'll put you back in my dream.

If I look at the sun the sun will explode, says the wicked boy. If I look at the moon I'll drain away. Where I stay I hold them in their places. Don't ask me what I'm doing.

The simple son was sent to science college. There he learned how everything worked.

The one who says nothing is told everything (not that he cares). The one who dreamed me hasn't put me back. The sun and the moon, they rise on time. I still don't know how the engine works; I can splice a wire. That's about it.

The dream is my world, says the sick child. I am pure as these bed sheets. (He writes fatigue on the vast expanses.) I'm in your dream, says the wicked boy. The simple son has been decorated for objectivity. He who says nothing is still being told.

DeSade looks down through the bars of the Bastille. They have stepped up the slaughter of nobles.

2

The look of shock on an old friend's face after years of not meeting, as if perhaps we were in a play, dressed for one of the final acts. The make-up of the years (infant, schoolboy, lover, soldier, judge of others, patriarch and ultimate old child) is on us. Those who remain the same and those who change their jaws. One has milky moons around the eyes or knotty knuckles. Many and varied are the studies in gray. The spectrum of whites amazes.

A generation moves in stateliness. It arrives like a pageant and passes down the street. The children sit on the curbs and watch. There are dignitaries and clowns, the men with medals and the cross-carriers. The owners walk abreast for the afternoon: they carry the banner which reads: the business of the world is—business. Manacled dictators walk alone through the crowded silence: four swordsmen guard them like points of the compass. The poets arrive on burros, bumping each other. Theologians packed in a hearse peer out like sickly popes. A phalanx of technologists singing the latest love songs in marching rhythms. Movie stars escorting diplomats (it's hard to tell them apart).

Nine of the greatest novelists, of ridiculous difference in height and girth. Two modern saints on litters. The generation proceeds to the cenotaph, the only common meeting place. In side streets the coming generation, not even looking, waits its turn and practices a new and secret language. (They think it's secret: that's what's so depressing.) Their hero is also gray and still in high school. He drives a hundred miles an hour into a tree.

3

Oriental, you give and give. No Christian ever gave like you. What is it you are giving morning and night, asking nothing in return? Pearls, silk cloths, books and scrolls, mother-of-pearl chopsticks, bronze cowbells, hand-painted poetry, tributes of every description. Flowers around my neck, morning, noon, and night: I am ready to vomit. You lay all Asia at my feet—where is your modern sense of values? You're not like a Frenchman, who gives as an investment. Not like an American whose gifts fall out of his pocket. Your gifts are permanent, an end in themselves. We'll cure you yet.

A rope of jasmine flowers round my neck at the airport, the embarrassing bow, the immaculate dark men come with their cargo. The frenzied Westerner grabs it all, the powder barrel stowed under the high altar, in case. The wise men continue to give: a sack of spices for the rotten meat of English queens; antimacassars; Zen.

It's as if you said, that's all I have to give, namely, the works. You never say, leave us alone. That's Western talk. You say, come for a swim in the old sky: my eyes are upside down. You say, the turtle can draw in its legs; the seer can draw in his senses; I call him illumined. In India eyes are never wide open. I throw a bucket of cold water over your continent. Get up from your bed of nails, you wise men of the East. I'm giving you a power plant for Christmas.

4

The rice around the lingam stone will be distributed in the dying sun to the unblessed poor. I bring neither rice nor overpowering jasmine but only my full gaze of love and loathing. With the beautiful Hindu woman I drink in the phallus. On her face the trace of a sneer. (She may be Christian.) Under the nine domes of the Kali temple we make our way to the Divine Mother, Savior of the Universe, Kali in basalt, in gold and precious stones. She stands on Siva. A garland of skulls hangs from her neck. In one of her four hands a severed human head; with another she gives the sign of peace. Her triple eyes bring peace or terror. This was Ramakrishna's darling, standing on Siva, who lies supine on the thousand-petaled silver-lotus.

He drank her smile till all was blue, that saint. He joined the hands of all the gods. In his room a picture of Christ as well. He reached the seventh plane at will.

5

Of love and death in the Garrison State I sing. From uniformed populations rises the High Art, *Oedipus King*, the Nō, the ballerina bleeding in her slippers. At the

Officer's Club adultery is rationed (their children are not allowed to play with guns; this helps whet their appetite). The ladies are discussing the chemical control of behavior by radio waves: that will solve the problem of neighbors. Symposia on causes of desertion draw record-breaking crowds. The handsomer pacifists are invited to the most sought-after cocktail parties. The women try their hand at them in the rumpus room; some progress reported. Waves of asceticism sweep the automobile industry. The mere sight of a Sam Browne belt, which used to inspire contempt, brings tears to the eyes of high-school boys. All flabby citizens are automatically put under surveillance. Chess problems supersede crap in the noncoms' barracks. The sacred number is Two: two parties, two powers sworn to mutual death, two poles of everything from ethics to magnetics. It's a balanced society.

Today the order goes out: all distant places are to be abolished: beachcombers are shot like looters. Established poets are forced to wear beards and bluejeans; they are treated kindly in bohemian zoos; mysterious stipends drift their way. They can trade soap for peyote at specified libraries. Children's prizes are given for essays on the pleasures of crisis. Historians are awarded all the key posts in the foreign office. Sculptors who use old shrapnel are made the heads of schools of design. Highways move underground like veins of ore. The Anti-Sky Association (volunteer contributions only) meets naked at high noon and prays for color blindness.

"Color is a biological luxury."

6

Quintana lay in the shallow grave of coral. The guns boomed stupidly fifty yards away. The plasma trickled into his arm. Naked and filthy, covered with mosquitoes, he looked at me as I read his white cloth tag. How do you feel, Quintana? He looks away from my gaze. I lie: we'll get you out of here sometime today.

I never saw him again, dead or alive. Skin and bones, with eyes as soft as soot, neck long as a thigh, a cross on his breastbone not far from the dog tags. El Greco was all I could think of. Quintana lying in his shallow foxhole waiting to be evacuated. A dying man with a Spanish name equals El Greco. A truck driver from Dallas probably.

When the Japs were making the banzai charge, to add insult to death, they came at us screaming the supreme insult: *Babe Ruth, go to hell!* The Americans, on the other hand, when the Japs flew over dropping sticks of explosives, shouted into the air, as if they could hear: *Tojo eat shit!*

Soldiers fall in love with the enemy all too easily. It's the allies they hate. Every war is its own excuse. That's why they're all surrounded with ideals. That's why they're all crusades.

7

The bourgeois poet closes the door of his study and lights his pipe. Why am I in this box, he says to himself (although it is exactly as he planned). The bourgeois poet sits down at his inoffensive desk—a door with legs, a door turned table—and almost approves the careful disarray of books, papers, magazines and such artifacts as thumbtacks. The bourgeois poet is already out of matches and gets up. It is too early in the morning for any definite emotion and the B.P. smokes. It is beautiful in the midlands: green fields and tawny fields, sorghum the color of red morocco bindings, distant new neighborhoods, cleanly and treeless, and the Veterans Hospital fronted with a shimmering Indian Summer tree. The Beep feels seasonal, placid as a melon, neat as a child's football lying under the tree, waiting for whose hands to pick it up.

•

71

The teachers of culture hate science but the teachers of science do not hate culture. The teachers of poetry hate machines but the builders of machines give money to poets. As priests live in two worlds, the actual world and the dim-lit world of their psychosis, so do the teachers of arts. The teachers of arts live in the church of the masterpiece and condemn all else. They despise the farmer, the mechanic, the bacteriologist. All this must be unlearned. The worshipers must be cured to live in the world outside their arts. Only then will the arts flow freely from all men to all men, as the things of science flow in every direction over the earth. For the arts carry the sickness of mind past. The enslaved paintings repeat the feudal error. Pride of nation leaps from pathological music, enshrining murder, sanctifying death. We kill the living in the child by our strong teaching. We kill with discipline and commands. Till the child is freed in the world of the school, the teaching of the things of man will continue to kill.

72

To make the child in your own image is a capital crime, for your image is not worth repeating. The child knows this and you know it. Consequently you hate each other. When the child hates the parent or the parent hates the child, both produce soldiers, quiet, beautifully dressed for the kill of "barbarians." The mother caresses the medals of her darling. The father salutes at Arlington Cemetery. The child is always lost in antique frustrations. On the child is poured the blood of churches. Babies are taught to salute the flag and to hate their sex. The suffix "hood" is made untouchable: motherhood, fatherhood, brotherhood, manhood, statehood.

A child is for love, for biologic power. A child is for play and admiration, laughter and terror. A child is for total concentration and absolute giving and absolute taking. A child demands and merits the collective affection of the universe. The child is lying in the egg of the rattlesnake or in the womb of Mozart's mother or the hating-house of Arthur Rimbaud or in the baby-green leaf of the rubber plant of the living room, but really in the child of love. The love of the child is pure destruction. Then let us be destroyed by this new beauty, who live in a time when we fight fire with fire and war with war and kill the little with the big—as if that were a solution even for the Department of Sanitation.

73

Each in her well-lighted picture window, reading a book or magazine, the Amsterdam whores look quite domestic. The canals, as picturesque as expected, add their serenity. The customers stroll from window to window, back and forth, comparing merchandise. Where a curtain is drawn, business is being transacted. These are big, fine, strapping whores, heavy in the leg, blond, as is the preference. They don't display their wares, no more than crossing a leg. It's like a picture gallery, Flemish School, silent through varnish and glaze. What detail, what realism of texture, what narrative! And look at this masterpiece:

A solid blond sits in her window at an angle. She appears to be looking out, expressionless. Just back of her stands an African king in round white hat and lengthy white embroidered robe of satin, it may be. Behind him stands his servant, very straight. The king's face is a thin and noble ebony. And without looking at either African the whore holds one hand back of her shoulder, feeling the robe of the African king with eloquent fingers, weighing the heft of the silk in her thoughtful hand.

74

The prophets say to Know Thyself: I say it can't be done. It takes many to know the one self and you are only one of the many who know yourself. Man is mostly involuntary. Consciousness is only a tiny part of us. As dreams protect the sleeper, so does the waking memory keep your pain. A man who knows himself too well falls ill. Self-knowledge is a dangerous thing, tending to make man shallow or insane. Those poets who study their own consciousness are their own monsters. Each look in the mirror shows a different self. You are not one but many yous. These many yous the feudalists of thought call soul. They would make you a slave to your dead selves; they will not let you walk away into the freedom of yourself becoming. The coral animal turns to jagged stone after it dies; the dead selves build into an underwater cathedral, housing for brilliant and deadly jaws. Know not Thyself. No two days are ever the same in the world; and no two days of the self are ever the same. All spirals outward, large or microscopic. Creation renewing itself forever does not look back. Look back and turn to rock. The shell-shocked man is sleeping peacefully. I pray that when he wakes he will be himself again. But he wakes only into his shock. Somewhere in battle he saw himself and died. The lost ones return to some old self and sit there in the corner, laughing or crying.

75

I drove three thousand miles to ask a question. No answer, naturally. It served me right; I'm not the pilgrim type. I wanted a first-hand account of *him*: when he was alive, before they murdered him. When you worked with him, before they drove him insane, I laughed like the others. I said: My friend, you swim among the blues of the lunatic fringe as always. This is only another of your voyages. But did you leave him before he died or after? Did you go to the trial? Were you there when the police smashed the equipment? Did you visit him in the sunset of his mind?

In the soft San Diego sunset you turned your back. I don't want to talk about that, you said. Your little dogs leaped up at me with teeth. Our children ran wild together. Your wife sang beautifully. In the morning you cashed me a check, arriving at the bank in a foreign car.

Did you really recover from the death of your father? I must hear about the other from someone I know as well as you. You are the only one. We didn't get along was all you said. I don't want to discuss him. The disciples are scattered. They are all in hiding. It's against the law to post his books. Everyone seems ashamed for a different reason. Is his wife living, his child? Where is truth's underground? How long does love stay murdered? Did he have to sentence himself? The lab experiment of his life is proved—there must have been another way. Pictures that he took when the bulbs popped, each brighter than a thousand suns; the spiral poems he wrote under the electronic microscope—mad scientist, good German—fixed in my mind and locked in yours.

CHARLES SIMIC ▪ ▪ ▪ ▪ ▪ ▪ ▪ ▪ ▪ ▪ ▪ ▪ ▪ ▪ ▪ ▪

Club Midnight

Are you the sole owner of a seedy night club?

Are you its sole customer, sole bartender,
Sole waiter prowling around the empty tables?

Do you put on wee-hour girlie shows
With dead stars of black and white films?

Is your office upstairs over the neon lights,
Or down deep in the dank rat cellar?

Are bearded Russian thinkers your silent partners?
Do you have a doorman by the name of Dostoyevsky?

Is Fu Manchu coming tonight?
Is Miss Emily Dickinson?

Do you happen to have an immortal soul?
Do you have a sneaky suspicion that you have none?

Is that why you throw a white pair of dice,
In the dark, long after the joint closes?

Live at Club Mozambique

Our nation's future is coming into view
With a muffled drum-roll
In a slow, absent-minded striptease.
Her shoulders are already bare
And so is one of her sagging breasts.
The kisses she blows to us
Are as cold as prison walls.

Once, it seems, we were a large wedding party.
It was always summer.
Women wore wild flowers in their straw hats
And white gloves over their hands.
Now we run dodging cars on the highway.
The groom, someone points out, looks like
President Lincoln on a death notice.

It's time to burn witches again,
The minister announces to the congregation
Using the Bible as a shade.
Are those our Cassandra's red panties
We see flying through the dark winter trees,
Or merely a lone crow taking home
A bit of fresh roadkill in his beak?

Pain

I was doing nothing in particular,
Spring was coming,
When out of the blue
I grabbed my side,
Surprised by this most awful of rewards
From which at first I wanted to
Run away and couldn't.

The pain stayed until I knew its child-like
Cruelty and innocence,
Its pettiness too.

Fear came to keep it company:
A theater director
Wearing a black cape
And offering a series of boring melodramas.

I wanted Reason to defend me.
Instead, it sought causes
Of my depravity,
Smaller reasons like piano keys
I could play to my heart's content,
While the pain continued.

Impervious to argument,
The pain came closer,
Throbbing with impatience
As if to ingratiate itself.
Mean old Fate, I complained
All you've ever given me
Is the satisfaction of moaning
And keeping my love awake!

"When all of reality hurts
You'll understand."
But it was too early for understanding.
There were just my eyes burning
With fever and curiosity
In the dark windowpane
I sometimes used as a mirror.

Watching the Hearse

Your hearse pulled by deep summer twilight,
Pulled by a street lamp,
Pulled by Venus and her retinue,
Pulled by a lone sleepwalking child,
Pulled by six white mice.

The glass hearse full of old shoes and boots,
Head of a pig roasting on a spit,
The butcher's cat sleeping in it with one eye open,
The hearse with a rooming house telephone,
With shirt-tails sticking out of its rear gate.

The hearse and you in it
Like a long siesta on the pool table,
Or like getting a close shave

In a dark and padlocked barbershop.
You're a passenger on a ghost ship,
Saying, of course, the whole thing is a joke.

LOUIS SIMPSON ▪ ▪ ▪ ▪ ▪ ▪ ▪ ▪ ▪ ▪ ▪ ▪ ▪ ▪ ▪ ▪ ▪

The Middleaged Man

There is a middleaged man, Tim Flanagan,
whom everyone calls "Fireball."
Every night he does the rocket-match trick.
"Ten, nine, eight . . ." On zero
pfft! It flies through the air.

Walking to the subway with Flanagan . . .
He tells me that he lives out in Queens
on Avenue Street, the end of the line.
That he "makes his home" with his sister
who has recently lost her husband.

What is it to me?
Yet I can't help imagining what it would be like
to be Flanagan. Climbing the stairs
and letting himself in . . .
I can see him eating in the kitchen.

He stays up late watching television.
From time to time he comes to the window.
At this late hour the streets are deserted.
He looks up and down. He looks right at me,
then he steps back out of sight.

•

Sometimes I wake in the middle of the night
and I have a vision of Flanagan.
He is wearing an old pair of glasses
with a wire bent around the ear
and fastened to the frame with tape.

He is reading a novel by Morley Callahan.
Whenever I wake he is still there . . .
with his glasses. I wish he would get them fixed.
I cannot sleep as long as there is wire
running from his eye to his ear.

Boots and Saddles

Mad Murray Kadish,
Nick D'Amato and Murray Chubinsky
were waiting on line outside the Paramount Theater

when an old guy came out of the alley
and said, "You fellers want to hear somethin?"
He was in the Seventh Cavalry.

You wouldn't believe it, he
had served in the U.S. Cavalry
in Mexico, under "Black Jack" Pershing.

At the time he was living with a Mex,
half-Indian girl.

Finally he was wise to her.
"Baby," he said, "you're a two-timer,
I'm wise to yez and the lieutenant."

Now all he wanted was bus fare.
"What the hell," said Murray Chubinsky
and gave him fifty cents.

He looked at it, started walking,
then running down the alley,
and joined his friends in the Seventh Cavalry.

They sounded "Boots and saddles"
and they all went riding off.

The Long Afternoon

Behind the glass door
stands a *babushka,*
a grandmother doll.
It unscrews. There's another
inside, a size smaller,
that unscrews, and so on.

A pipe called a *hookah*
with a malachite bowl . . .

The gramophone wheezes,
scratches, and speaks:
"Avalon. Fox trot."

White flannels and knees
intently two-stepping
step onto the floor.

At four there's a breeze.
The bamboo trunks creak
and talk in the lane.
A house lizard hops
from the vine to the rail . . .
cocks his head at me.

"Remember?" he croaks.
Dear brother, I do!

Variations on a Poem by Reznikoff

He applies for a job
in textiles. The firm
is in an old loft building.
He has to go to the sixth floor.
The elevator operator
gives him an "unpleasant" look.

The elevator is just a platform.
The shaft slides by. When it stops
he is facing a large open window
He could step right out of the window!
The elevator operator
smiles. He sees his fear.

He is being interviewed.
The job requires Yiddish,
which he knows. And he can type
with two fingers. The boss nods.
The man he would be replacing
can do neither. He is sweeping the floor
close by them, trying to hear.

The interview was successful . . .
the job is his, if he wants.
He keeps thinking about the open window,
and the other open windows
he would have to pass every day.

On the morning he's expected
to start, he puts it off . . .
then sends a telegram saying
that he can't come, he's ill.

There are things you have seen or done . . .
They don't amount to anything,
but there seems to be no way
to get rid of them, except
to write and pass them on.

The Appointment

Genaro was standing
halfway down the car.
He turned his head slowly,
the side of his head
with the hole, oozing blood.

"Thou canst not say I did it,"
Peter whispered.

                    The man next to him
gave him a look and rustled his *News*
nervously. At 14th Street he got off
with a backward glance.

                    Genaro
must have got off too. He was nowhere
to be seen.

                    •

There were three ahead of him.

Sports Month had an article,
"What fight would you have liked to see?"
Peter Jackson and Jim Corbett,
though you probably never heard of it,
he said to the sports writer.

Dark, dark, they all go into the dark,
the captains, merchant bankers, eminent men of letters,
even the silver star.
I'd rather be a peasant, said Achilles,
on a farm, feeding pigs,
than this damned plain, in a fog.

His number was being called.
He put the magazine down.
"Can't you hear?" the man at the desk
said irritably, drest
in a little brief authority.
"You coulda missed your appointment."

So he went in. The doctor
was looking at a sheet of paper.
He glanced up and looked down again.
The doctor had gray hair,
glasses with black frames,
and hair growing out of his nose.

They like to keep you waiting.
It's a test. Still, he wasn't prepared
when Nosehair said, "Why were you talking
to yourself in the waiting room?"

He saw a shadow
sliding around the ropes
to get at him. The referee
moved it back, and then
went over and picked up the count.
"One!" The fog was clearing.

He rose to a knee,
and at "nine," to his feet.
"Was I?" he said.
"My lips may have moved a little.
I was reading a magazine."

The doctor said, "All this
about Jesus,
are you still thinking about it?"

"No," Peter said. "I was sick."

•

He got on at Chambers Street.
At Times Square he looked
and saw Genaro. Sitting
and pretending to read
the advertisements.

I don't give a damn, he told him.
You can all go to Hell.

The Listeners

I walked down the street
to the harbor, by gardens
with tattered leaves and weeds,
and through an open gate.

The red roof of the house
had lost its tiles in patches,
and the windows had no glass.
A woman stood in a window

looking down. "I used to live here,"
I shouted. "Is it all right
if I just look around?"

•

A man with dreadlocks sat
on his heels, doing something
to a pot. A child stood by him.
I walked down to the shore.

A man was coming toward me.
His name was Rohan Moore.
Was I the owner, he asked.
No, I said, and heard

the appreciative murmur
of those who were listening
to my life as to a play.

•

Rohan Moore led the way
into the house. It was dark.
The wall was unpainted,
the railing rough to the hand.

A family lived in the room . . .
it seemed, in every corner,
and still there was a space
where a bed once stood, by the wall,

with a table, glass and spoon.
My father, looking small,
spoke again the last few words.

•

People were gathering
from every part of the house,
a dozen where four used to be.
They stood and stared silently.

I shook the hand of my guide,
now my friend. And another's.

"You can come and live here,
if you want," Rohan said.

There were sounds of laughter,
chairs pushed back, and voices
in the distance, going away.

A Letter from Brazil

An old friend from schooldays
wrote that he was working
in Brazil, air-shipping freight.
I was in a bad patch in my life
and of no mind to answer letters.
When I did, finally, it came back
scrawled, "Address unknown."

What is it like, air-shipping freight?
If you're successful, I suppose
you can have a fine social life.
But not with "Address unknown."
I visualized a dingy room
in a street where drumming and yelling
kept you awake. You turned on the light,
and read a magazine. Opportunities
in rapidly expanding . . . Caracas.

You strapped on your money,
put your things in a suitcase,
and took the first plane out.

•

We used to walk up and down
on the barbecue, discussing
"If Dempsey had fought Tunney again."
Or if the "Flying Scotsman" raced
"The Royal Scot," which would have won?

His letter came when I had my hands full,
simultaneously being divorced
and trying to fix up the house.

And the workmen after a while
just sat down and did nothing.
This went on for days.

I had given the contractor,
like a fool, three thousand dollars
in advance. I liked the man . . .
we had intelligent conversations.
He used the money to pay his debts,
and the workmen weren't paid,
and they packed up their tools,
leaving me with a house that looked
like an egg with the shell smashed.

I had to borrow from the bank.
This time I hired a contractor
who belonged to an old established firm.
He came, he looked at the mess,
and said nothing, just shook his head
gently, from side to side,
called in a crew, and finished the job.

•

At the beginning of vacations
those of us who lived in Kingston
would share a car going home.
You drove over the mountains
to Mandeville, then over the hills,
and out on the Spanish Town road,
doing sixty. There's the clock
at Halfway Tree. And the town,
where you drop off, one by one,
promising to get in touch.

But this isn't true. The friends
you see during the vacation
are different from your friends at school.

The first day at home
you go for a ride on your bicycle
in the lanes. Then for a swim,
the palms dipping, the harbor
glittering, with lines of foam.

It comes back to me now
with the sound of saws and hammers.
Some beams beneath our house
have been damaged and have to be replaced.

DAVE SMITH ▪ ▪ ▪ ▪ ▪ ▪ ▪ ▪ ▪ ▪ ▪ ▪ ▪ ▪ ▪ ▪

Between the Moon and the Sun

What has happened to the stars? What thief, thin-soled
with rocks hard as seeds at flesh, has stolen them?
Surely something darker than the night,

the river shuffling aimlessly through the yawning toybox
of the universe, the cocked and stunned
right arm of the mechanical soldier,

has come red-eyed and drooling. It has happened before.

I don't mean to harp on the infinite paradoxes
there is no untangling, but why

have the stars come to rest on our feet,
on our soles bloody and crusted, those little
mouths that never quite speak
what they meant to?

Perhaps it is only a cramp in our sleepless bellies,
the green apples we ate one hot afternoon.
The books have always warned us.

Lying awake in this moonless room
I think of stars like a crowd of pinched seeds
falling into the apples, sending little brass hooks
shooting through the white pulp.

By the time the apple's brown bruise comes who will know
the stars have been stolen who always rose
like fathers, in dignity, over the globes in the grass?

If I slide my heavy foot onto the floor, what
will fall from my chest? What will fall into my hands

heavy with all the curving clarity of everything that is
not imagination and the filaments
of words charred beyond hope?

Something has happened in the black room while we were
flat on our backs trying to give birth
to the stars

and the books, in their shrouds, have slept through it.
Come to the window and I will show the world without dreams,
starless, mouthing itself, and the apples as they are

growing black with nothing to tell us. Nothing.

Morning Light at Wanship, Utah

Trails of it like trout-streaks skid
the Weber River under the scald
of the interstate where swallows
roar past like trucks to build
what winter never remembers.

It has come suddenly, from the mountain,
to glow on the small girl whose hair
flies like feathers from the nest
of her gaze. She is dreaming
what moves inside that flow,

the line in her hand connecting her
to what laps at her hung foot. She
blinks at each dark zooming
of bird, as at a scar still pink
and unbelievable, and I hunch

in my shadow behind her, in slow burning
light that is pure fear, for I
know how greased with quick green
the rocks are, how cold spray
is like a handful of water dropped

from a lover's hand where a girl lies
sunning only for the first deep gaze
up into the dizzying sun, yes, and
the dead-face roll on the back
when memory can resolve nothing,

cannot even give back the face of a man
that somewhere, far upstream, waits.
What is joy but that first squint
of love through hardest light,
and the dreams roaring in futility?

Hours it seems I watch each split twig
fester toward a knot of steel-flaring

water where swallows swoop and take
what they need until at last
I lift my face and know I am

inside the dream no one ever wakes from.
In the terrible light of morning
each bird, each child is a dream
lodged until it slides out
of itself, becoming the vast pouring

dream the world is everywhere. It leans down
from the mountain to bruise the skin
of a small girl like a first peach.
Swallows scream in the air
for the grief of it, and the joy,

and I, seeing her turn upshoulder to look
into my face, want to warn her.
But what is there to say except
that she must remember this dream
brilliant as a dot of light

in a dark room? Far off on the mountainside
light spears twice and is only a man
on a battered tractor whose
dark face is unimaginable to me
but I squint as if I could see everything.

W. D. SNODGRASS ▪ ▪ ▪ ▪ ▪ ▪ ▪ ▪ ▪ ▪ ▪ ▪ ▪ ▪

FROM *The Führer Bunker*

Adolf Hitler

—1 April, 1945.

*(Easter Sunday and April Fool's Day.
Hitler sits alone in his conference room
looking at the large map of Europe on
the wall.)*

Down—I got it all. Almost.
Brat; fed sick on sugartits.
Shreds, chunks, chewed-over
Races.   It rises up again.
Say I spoiled my appetite.

(turns to the situation reports on his table)

Heidelberg, Danzig, practically undamaged;
Cone over; surrendered.   Half a million
Squirm out of our glory.   Our best troops
Sacked up in the Ruhr.   Too gutless
Even to get killed.

(takes a report from the table)

And Speer
Still lies.   Will not raze his factories,
The bridges, mines.   He'd let these ditch-worms
Go on spawning, spawning.   So yesterday
I gave Speer back his offices. Truly, truly,
You regret how kind you've been.

> Always this soft side mounting up;
> My mother's cake-and-candy-boy.
> She and I, we let him off—Alois,
> My own half-brother—let him
> Clear out of the house to England;
> Let him back here in Berlin
> Where just to shut that mouth
> Made rumors.

(another report)

Our enemies at Easter Mass. Sick, snivelling,
Forgiving Jesus of these Christians.

> With her, it was all my way.
> Talk; talk to her.   Her thoughts lay
> Open.   My voice soaked into her,
> All sides, like a showerspray.   She
> Rammed it down the old man's throat.

Sniff them; track them; let them slither out.
Strasser, my brother in the party. His brother.
Schleicher, Von Papen.   My own worst enemy.
Each triumph filled the dark with whispering:
My mercies gathering against me; a defeat; death.

> The day they buried her, I thought
> Time now; time.   I cannot live
> The mercies I mean to.   No choice:
> When did *I* choose I should die?

Ernst Roehm, finally. By then I knew
Better. Still this vile kindheartedness let him

Weasel out to South America.   Once come back
Here to Berlin, though, he dared stand against me,
My brother-in-arms, my old comrade Ernst,

> I feel already this ground
> Swallow me.   I so shall
> Swallow all this ground
> Till we two are one flesh.

We hacked them down like sewer rats—
Traitors, unreliables, all who learned
Too much, who thwarted us; dropped them
Into ditches, rivers, drop and rot there.

> That first time I could believe
> I move among the Powers once more.
> Our President's praised my gallantry.
> Faced by my firing squads, men raise
> Proud arms to heil me.   The crime
> I choose is God's law.   My lie, Truth.

> (background sounds: the Nuremberg Rallies)

> From ten million speakers, my voice
> Falls like the farmers' rain; sing, sing
> My name.   Past evil, time or consequence
> My nerves clang with the iron worlds.

> (sits down at the table)

> Too late.   The Powers move on.
> After our first putsch failed,
> This left arm shaking, pinned down
> By the right.   Since Stalingrad, this
> Shivering I can't control.

Who else is sold out?   Bremen?   Magdeburg?
They would go on in this pisswallow, in
Disgrace, shame.   Who could we send to make
Their lives worth less to them?   In our camps,
You gas them, shoot, club, strangle them,
Tramp them down into trenches, thick as leaves.
Out of the ground, at night, they squirm up
Through the tangled bodies, crawl off in the woods.
Every side now, traitors, our deserters, native
Populations, they rise up like vomit, flies
Out of bad meat, sewers backing up.   Up
There, now, in the bombed-out gardens,
That sickly, faint film coming over

The trees again, along the shattered branches
Buds festering.   In shell-holes, trash heaps,
Some few green leaves, grass spikes thrust
Up through the ashes, through the cracked cement,
Shove up into the light again.

(returns to the table and begins drawing up directives)

Well,
We may dream them up an Easter
Fool's gift yet.   Decorate a few
More street lamps.   Something
To look up to.   Then order out
Those few troops still up North.
Stalin: count on him to clean house.
Boots, bones, buckles—nothing
Sticks in that man's craw.

(rises)

So; we must go out now.   Suppose
My diet cook could be awake yet?   Suppose
We could still find a little chocolate cake?
A little schlag, perhaps?

Adolf Hitler

—20 April, 1945; 1900 hours

*(After his birthday ceremony, Hitler
has withdrawn to his sitting room
where he sits with one of Blondi's
puppies on his knee. Earlier in the
day he had gone up into the garden
for the last time.)*

Better stuffed in a bag; drowned.
My best bitch pregnant once she can't
Survive.

The man will lie down on his back; his partner crouches over his head or
chest as he prefers.

My Effie's little sister
Knocked up by Fegelein.   My luck
Lets me off one humiliation:
I breed no child.

He, of course, is completely naked.

This mockery:
Pisspot generals whining for surrender;
Party maggots bringing presents;
Careful not to wish me a long life—
Their one failure I can share.
Pulling at me, whimpering for
Their cities, populations, lives.

Sometimes, she may remove only her underthings. The private parts, suddenly exposed, can provide an exquisite shock and pleasure.

Cub, in Landsberg Prison, after
Our first putsch failed, my flowers
Filled three prison rooms.   The faithful
Sang beside me in my cell.
I unwrapped presents, cut my cake. We
laughed: where was the file inside?

The cake my mother made me . . . No . . .

Usually she will turn her back.

No. that's Edmund's cake.   My brother's.
But I ate Edmund's cake.   I spit on
What was left.

The prison Governor brought his family's
Kind regards.   His little daughter curled up,
Like this, on my lap asleep.

She must not start at once; he must ask, even beg her, to begin.

Whimpering at me; whining.   Oh,
We hear their song:

Only live. Live longer.   Lead us
To the mountain fastnesses.   Keep us
From the guns, the Russians . . .

Oh stay! don't leave us here forsaken;
Our men are waiting for their Führer.

In the mountains, could these shitheads be
Worthwhile?   Over and over, we've said
They could survive: overcome facts.

Today I climbed two flights to the garden:
Sour smoke.   Shelling.   Schoolboys lined up
Lines of graves. Hands I have to touch.

He will grovel on the floor, declaring himself unworthy to touch her shoes, even to live.

> Even the zoo animals, my good old
> Neighbors, pacing their stalls till
> Their keeper brings the right gift—
> One lead pellet.   A man who would accept
> What is, is criminal, too vile to live.

It is not the mere fact of the urine or the faeces that is significant.   The crux is that he be able to watch these emerge into existence.

> Suffer that again?   The elevator
> Locked, lurching up through dead rock
> In the mountain side?   Come out
> Freezing, over the receding plains,
> Traitorous cities, nauseous dens
> And hovels, lecherous faces with insane
> Beliefs, Czechs, Jews with blonde hair,
> Blue eyes, who would steal our birthright,
> Pull us down into putrescence, slime?

> > Edmund died though, my brother,
> > When I was eleven.   His birthday
> > Would have been some days ago.

She must now show disgust; may revile him, even kick at him.

> > She lost three others.   She, only
> > She, was glad I had survived.

Only when he is fully excited by his own demands, may she release her urine, open her bowels.   The danger of taking this matter in his mouth heightens the excitement.

> > Only live; live longer. Don't
> > Leave us to the loneliness,
> > The spoiling of affections.

> > He kept me in.   But she,
> > She made a special cake for me—
> > Only the two of us together.

Now he will probably achieve his climax, alone and without assistance.

> Namesake, cub, you've done your month
> In this filth.   My cake; I'll eat it, too.

> The First War soldiers; our old fighters—
> That was comradeship.   You have Blondi's

Underside; my diet cook, the drivers,
Secretaries—they know how to listen.

"I stay too long; the Grail has sent for me."

I can eat nothing now—only cake.
Pills and Morrell's injections.
My cake, chairs, rugs—without them,
There's the bare concrete. Like any
Jew degenerate at Auschwitz.

When he was washed and begged forgiveness, she may embrace and
comfort him.

My birthday present, my file: my
Cartridge of pure cyanide.   Crawl back
In the cave, work down in dry leaves,
An old dog deciding to lie down.

Or she may curl up by his side.

Eva Braun

—22 April, 1945.

*(Hitler's mistress received no public
recognition and often felt badly
neglected. Her small revenges included
singing American songs, her favorite
being "Tea for Two." Having chosen to
die with him in the bunker, she appeared
quite serene during the last days.)*

*Tea for two
And two for tea*

I ought to feel ashamed
Feeling such joy.   Behaving like a spoiled child!
So fulfilled.   This is a very serious matter.
All of them have come here to die.   And they grieve.
I have come here to die.   If this is dying,
Why else did I ever live?

*Me for you
And you for me*

We ought never to flaunt our good luck
In the face of anyone less fortunate—
These live fools mourning already

For their own deaths; these dead fools
Who believe they can go on living . . .

And you for me
Alone.

Who out of all of them, officers, ministers,
These liars that despise me, these empty
Women that envy me—so they hate me—
Who else of them dares to disobey Him
As I dared?   I have defied Him to His face
And He has honored me.

We will raise
A family

They sneer at me—at my worrying about
Frau Goebbels' children, that I make fairytales
For them, that we play at war. Is our war
More lost if I console these poor trapped rabbits?
These children He would not give me . . .

A boy for you
A girl for me

They sneer that I should bring
Fine furniture down this dank hole.   Speer
Built this bed for me.   Where I have slept
Beside our Chief.   Who else should have it?
My furs, my best dress to my little sister—
They would sneer even at this; yet
What else can I give her?

Can't you see
How happy we could be?

Or to the baby
She will bear Fegelein.   Lechering dolt!
Well, I have given her her wedding
As if it was my own.   And she will have
My diamonds, my watch.   The little things you
Count on, things that see you through your
Missing life, the life that stood you up.

Nobody near us
To see us or hear us

I have it all.   They are all gone, the others—
The Valkyrie; and the old rich bitch Bechstein;

Geli above all. No, the screaming mobs above all.
They are all gone now; He has left them all.
No one but me and the love-struck secretaries—
Traudl, Daran—who gave up years ago.

No friends or relations
On weekend vacations

That I, I above all, am chosen—even I
Must find that strange.   I who was always
Disobedient, rebellious—smoked in the dining car,
Wore rouge whenever he said I shouldn't.
When he ordered that poor Chancellor Schussnig
Was to starve, I sent in food.

We won't have it known, dear,
That we own a telephone, dear.

I who joined the party, I who took Him
For my lover just to spite my old stiff father—
Den Alten Fritz!—and those stupid nuns.
I ran my teachers crazy, and my mother—I
Held out even when she stuck my head in water.
He shall have none but me.

Day will break
And you will wake

We cannot make it through another month;
We follow the battles now on a subway map.
Even if the Russians pulled back—
His hand trembles, the whole left side
Staggers. His marvelous eyes are failing.
We go out to the sunlight less each day.   We live
Like flies sucked up in a sweeper bag.

And start to bake
A sugar cake

He forbade me to leave Berchtesgaden;
Forbade me to come here.   I tricked
My keepers, stole my own car, my driver Jung.
He tried to scold me; He was too
Proud of me.   Today He ordered me to leave,
To go back to the mountain. I refused.
I have refused to save my own life and He,
In public, He kissed me on the mouth.

For me to take
For all the boys to see.

Once more I have won, won out over Him
Who spoke one word and whole populations vanished.
Until today, in public, we were good friends.
He is mine.   No doubt
I did only what He wanted; no doubt
I should resent that.   In the face
Of such fulfillment?   In the face
Of so much joy?

Picture you
Upon my knee;
Tea for two
And two for tea . . .

Hermann Fegelein

—29 April, 1945; 0200 hours.

(Gretl Braun's husband was noted for
lechery.   On April 28, about to flee
Berlin with an actress, he was arrested,
demoted and jailed.   When it was learned
that Himmler had tried to contact the
enemy, Fegelein—his adjutant to the
bunker—was questioned, then led out
and shot.)

[sweet jesus bleeding asshole no they cant
just shoot me   and three days ago I had
this sick world by the short hair   can they
my own men]
             in the guards station
singing   against regulations
whats more smoking
                  [and with no trial
my own brother-in-law   shit then
my wifes sisters husband   shit then
lover   an ss general   at only 37
blue eyes   blonde   superior physique
besides he told us we could leave   so
we all swore to stay and die while
we worked out ways]
                  common soldiers
puking in the passage where the chief
takes meals
             [first run on all the snatch
down here   my stupid wife to put a
good word to the chief   besides
an ss general   shit then former
rates the ss court   which takes months

they all made their plans   shit
our golden pheasants   theyre who ought
to be here getting shot]
                              the bad phonograph
broke into the medical supplies or else
the officers good wine
                              [now this was down
the hole I had carlotta   damn well good
as anything of goebbels   and enough
swiss coin pinched out so we could buy in
on the best lake there   shit once hes
good and dead shit whod know me   37
retired and respectable]

                              screwing her
while theyre dancing in the same room
that isnt done
                              [by now evas heard
about carlotta but she ought to care
about her little sister   say she put
a good word to   no   he as good as said
pump all we could   the best stock
blue eyed   blonde]
                              spreadeagled in
the hall with her pants off   radio girl
I could have had her anytime I wanted
shit
         [three days ago when I said shit
they squat   say this was a test
at the last minute the reprieve
no]
      another gun squad off of whore patrol
thats no bad piece between them   altman
and schuler
                              [say I ordered them to
save me   no]
                              theyre leading me out
the other way   shit better ankles
on a cart horse
                              [say martin   reichsleiter
bormann   my best drinking buddy   say
he put in   no]
                              staring at me like
some numbskull serb
                              [martin came in
to finger me   said I was with himmler
in some sellout to the west   I wish
to sweet shit Id of known]
                              but I screwed them

every one   shit not that blackhaired slut
on the sofa   margaret   cocktease
turned me down
                    [theyll leave me   where
and come back in to bang these cunts
it will be all the same   who even keeps
the names]
                now shes getting hers   no
and not that fat one in the dentist chair
I never screwed one even once   not
in a dentist chair
                    [leave it to himmler
hed weasel out   after I sold him
my own boss to martin   martin   his word
fixed my ass]

                    ivan will burn you out
like pissants   shed have been rotten
anyway   its only hours   woman come
                                        [after
my loyal service to the chief   the jews
the slovak gangs   the july assassins
I sent them to the meat hooks]
                            which is
gods mercy to what ivans got saved up
for you   coming up now in the garden
youll bleed like virgins
                        [at least
I get mine from an ss squad   say Ive got
this pregnant wife   no]
                        so warm it up
for ivan
            [but it isnt fair   Im almost
his brother   shit almost   I as good
as crucified whole regiments   for him
him]
        oh youll just pray for vaseline
[sweet jesus no   they cant just
can they
        shit   shit   shit

GARY SNYDER ■ ■ ■ ■ ■ ■ ■ ■ ■ ■ ■ ■ ■ ■ ■ ■ ■ ■

[Out of the soil and rock,]

Out of the soil and rock,
the growing season and spring, death
and winter,
out of the cold and rain, dust and sunshine,
came the music of cities and streets.
The people who take that music
                    into themselves,
creatures of salt, carbon, nitrogen, water,
may sometimes hang on the point of it,
hunger, an instant,
the world round the edge.

This city smoke and building steel
already is no more;
The music and cities of the future wait beyond the edge.

New York City

Message from Outside

I am the one who gnawed the blanket through
Peeped in the hole and saw with my left eye
The one-leg sliver man put out the fire.

I dug like mice below the cabin's floor
Crawling through oil and rotted hides, I broke
Into that curious handsewn box. Pursued by birds,
Threw my comb, my magic marbles to the wind,
Caught the last bus, and made it here on time.

Stop chewing gum, I show you what I stole—
Pine-marten furs, and box within each box,
The final box in swallow tendons tied,
Inside, an eye! It screws into
The center of your head.

But there they call me urine-boy,
And this deserted newsstand is quite safe.
Peer through this and watch the people spawn:
It makes me laugh, but Raven only croaks.

I saw Coyote! And I'll buy a gun,
Go back and build a monstrous general fire.
Watch the forests move into this town

You stand cracking sunflower seeds and stare.

The Feathered Robe

for Yaeko Nakamura

On a clear spring windless day
Sea calm, the mountains
      sharp against the sky,
An old man stopped in a sandy
      seashore pine grove,
Lost in the still clear beauty.
Tracing a delicate scent
      he found a splendid robe
Of feathers hanging on a bough.

      Robe over his arm
      He heard   alarm
      Stop, and there he saw
      A shining Lady,
           naked from her swim.

      Without my feathered robe
      that useless-to-you a human,
      Robe, I cannot,
      Home, I
      Cannot fly,
          she cried

And for a dance
      he gave it back.
A dance,
      she wore it glinting in the sun
Pine shadow breeze
Fluttering light sleeves—

      old man watching saw
      all he dreamed in youth
      the endless springtime
      morning beauty
      of the world
      as

She, dancing, rose
Slow floating over pines
High beyond the hills
                 a golden speck
In blue sky haze.

Nō play "Hagoromo"

JENNIFER SNYDER ·············

Train

When I was born I was hardened and human.
I moved and rose and became a residence.
The trains went by on rusty wheels gently
Burning into the ground and I gently
Burned into the world. When I gazed at the cars
Up close I felt the layers of cold
And sleep. It was still and the mist clung
To the floors. I think I can remember smoke
Hissing into the sky. The train remarked
On men from the old days: time was a steamy
Pocket where they lived and smoked and when

The cold crept in the cabins and the party
Was over and the man with a hump was
Crying he couldn't remember his name . . .
I know how far one must go, smoke and steel
And engine poking through wasted snow,
Into the drained world only to return in tears.
The train grinds through waste and is sick and filled
With the instants of flies. There is nothing
As nude as a train reflecting November snow
Or stopping in heat. All through the desert
It sees the needy towns, the sober economy
Of dust. It is not giving and its sayings

Press into the heart. The train is old
And bitter, its wisdom is born from pain,
And when the man in Arkansas begins
To scream and shake, and the bones of flies are
Scattered in gardens, and the hills wake up
In their skins under the light and they're covered
With jingling verbena, and I'm hurt

By the size of things: out of the fog
The train comes, beautiful and shamed,
And it is an orchestra of hard light and I know
It will be light. I love the train.
When I was born I was furnished with a body

And a mind, clothes, rooms and doors.
The train burned by, radiant and haunting,
In waves and I recognized how I could
Want, how the first motion is of breaking
And changing until one wants only love
And peace and one is tired. Look out into
What we were given which is a moment
Which is almost proof: the jaws of the train
Are filled with the fumes of misery
And when at night it blazes by I feel
A great joy that runs through the field and is gone.

The Roses

I can barely imagine my mother
naked in the cramped
sobriety of water.

Because of this
she doesn't disappear
in the garden among

the movie star faces of roses.
Because of this
she is not shredded space,

although she is beautiful
as a rose's crooked tundra.
I can barely imagine my mother

on her honeymoon
when the details of her body
were a flower's siren—

her first time—
and that darkness unraveled her.

She didn't marry for love
and now her face is
a venus fly trap

tasting lost kisses.
I can barely imagine my mother
swimming naked

under the stars' stupid confetti,
her body underestimating the mathematics
of roses.

She always smells like roses
because she wants to be loved
straightforwardly

the way flowers are loved.
She shoves her hands in the dirt
and each bulb she plants

is the symbol
of a mistake she's made.
She is putting them

in muscles of space
among planets and stars.
Look out there

at the foggy tongue of her dress.
Look at how she bends over
like a question mark's artificial flower.

She is burying
the promiscuous roses
of her disappointment.

JACK SPICER ▪ ▪ ▪ ▪ ▪ ▪ ▪ ▪ ▪ ▪ ▪ ▪ ▪ ▪ ▪ ▪

A Poem Without a Single Bird in It

What can I say to you, darling,
When you ask me for help?
I do not know the future
Or even what poetry
We are going to write.
Commit suicide. Go mad. Better people
Than either of us have tried it.
I loved you once but
I do not know the future.

I only know that I love strength in my friends
And greatness
And hate the way their bodies crack when they die
And are eaten by images.
The fun's over. The picnic's over.
Go mad. Commit suicide. There will be nothing left
After you die or go mad,
But the calmness of poetry.

sent to Robin Blaser in Boston 12/13/56

WILLIAM STAFFORD ▪ ▪ ▪ ▪ ▪ ▪ ▪ ▪ ▪ ▪ ▪ ▪

Glimpses

One time when the wind blows it is years
from now. I am talking with others and
we are telling all the stories except
the one we are in; then someone starts ours:
the wind stops, we look back and then forward.
The voice carries us on, and we try to be what it says.

There is an embrace on a street corner;
two people greet, and make obsolete all the past.
They research those years for the key
event that separated them, but they can't
find it. They part again, and they never
find what it is they have missed.

Walking along, any time,
I find clues to tomorrow—how hard
a poppy is orange, how alert the leaves
are where the streetlight finds them.
My debt to the world begins again,
that I am part of this permanent dream.

At someone's pretension a thought comes—Saint Augustine:
a morning cloud throws a shadow but the sun
says light. Our time goes on, a spider
spins, the wind examines the ground
for clues—just being is a big enough job,
no time for anything else.

For the Barn at Bread Loaf

Caught in a cloud this morning, this barn
hid for awhile, coasting through August
light. The part of space these walls
explore is often so disguised.
And in winter you can stand here saved
from cold, hidden from snow that piles
its relentless softness against the door.

Someone talked, leaning back in one of these
chairs, about how the shape or size
or maybe the past of a place, or what
it is going to be, can influence us.
We looked up. The oddness of being ourselves
filled this barn, and we all breathed far.

August

It comes up out of the ocean
warm days. It reaches
for inland meadows and sighs
across grass in its cape of rain.

People come to their doors.
They look where the trees turn
gray, where hills have stepped back
of each other. Whatever it was,

It passed carefully, touching
farms, leaning over ponds,
bending down the wheat.
People stand long at their doors.

"You were good this time, August
Old Friend. So long. So long."

The Chair in the Meadow

This time of year The North goes by, bird
by bird, all day. By night a woodchuck sits
and hums at stars. The stars hum back. Rain
taps. Grass gathers close. An owl arrives.

But they don't come any more, the pair I'd have:
the white mushroom, the silent philosopher.

Priorities at Friday Ranch

1

All that juniper west of
Lava Lake will yield fenceposts
if you can get there before the crew
has to clean up for summer.

2.

The best tumbleweed you can find
would look good, hung up for shadows
about where Dave always put
his hat by the barn light.

3.

If you ever see that gray antelope
again find out if it has a white
foot—I think it had a white foot
on the back left side.

Textures

1.

The dwell of a sound for a while
will sometimes diminish all else
and a whole forest lie down at night
for hearing the moon, where the first
tick and its tock are still waiting
for what time it is.

2.

Morning color opens its eyes
where it slept in the mountains.
Oh, it's afraid! This might be
the day when white comes all the way
back from the sky where it went
when color first came.

3.

And fur—of all presence it is
the most, a million touches

at once, to assure, reassure,
instruct our lives, like this:—
Be here so well that even
one time is often.

MAURA STANTON ▪ ▪ ▪ ▪ ▪ ▪ ▪ ▪ ▪ ▪ ▪ ▪ ▪ ▪

Short Story

Last night I flew a helicopter
over the flooded lowlands.
When the engine caught fire, I swam the fields
knocking submerged tractors with my silver
fin-like feet while the farm women
drowned around me, holding their children
over their heads for rescue.

I took two children on my back, but soon
they chanted, "You aren't our mother!"
& slipped under holding hands.
Later, when I saw their hair on the water,
salt lapped in my mouth: the story
was too sad for the protagonist
in the first person, who survives too late.

Below me I saw farmers
dancing against their pitchforks in a current,
eels twined in their beards.
Surely their dissolving eyes revealed catastrophe
in all its moral delight—
but my arms wheeled on; I remembered rumors
about mermaids, how they grow heartless, heartless.

Visibility

I have no illusions.
When I roll towards you at dawn,
I can't see you in the fog.
We've simply memorized each other.
I read a story about a giant
who couldn't see his tiny wife
for all the clouds
drifting around his huge, sad head.

He'd stroke the tops of fir trees
thinking he'd found her hair.
In another version, his wife
turned into an egret,
her strong wings
brushing her husband's face;
then she fell into the sea
weighted down by his immense tear.
Let me tell you this:
I miss your shadow, too,
but I know it waits above the fog
black as the shadow of the oak
you saw in your dream
when you woke up, almost happy.
I know our town's invisible.
The pilots on the way to Alaska
think they're over the sea.
Even if they glimpsed a light
through a rift in the clouds
they'd call it a ship
loaded with timber for the south.
Still, I hear those planes.
Last night on the satellite map
I saw a land without clouds.
Remember, I groped for your hand.
Suppose the men go barefoot?
Suppose the women own fans?

The Veiled Lady

In the 19th Century, clever mediums
Would rap a table, making the dead speak.
Ghostly hands would hover in the air,
Heads would appear, Caeser, Napoleon.
Sometimes the whole immaterial body
Of someone's beloved, dead daughter or sister
Glided through a room allowing swords
To pass through it. Once a husband rose
And tried to caress what was never there,
A Veiled lady he thought was his wife,
While others in the room almost fainted
To see him step right through her crinoline.
D.D. Home could levitate out windows
And float above a busy London street.
Imagine sitting on the horsehair sofa
Almost hysterical, watching that miracle . . .
But it was done with thick plate glass and lights,

A conjuror's trick, just like the accordian
Played by a ghost in front of Robert Browning
Who shuddered when a spirit hand reached out
And put a wreath of flowers on Elizabeth
Though afterwards he called it sham, imposture.
But that's what I am, that's what we all are
To one another, a trick of light and glass
Projected before an audience of dupes.
Don't you see I'm only an illusion?
You look aghast. You think I'm cynical
But when you touch me in the dark at night
You touch biology, twitchings and snores,
Wetness, jerking muscles. Wild images
Flicker across my convoluted brain
As it constructs a person out of dreams.
That woman you say you love doesn't exist.
Look at the way our faces have appeared
On the black glass of the picture window
Now that it's evening, and the lights are on.
There she is, standing beside you, smiling.
Go to her. Embrace her if you can.

Posthuman

the trope of the posthuman is usually
associated with changing representations
of embodiment and especially the idea
that we are entering a "post-body age."

I used to peer inside
your windows while you slept,
and give you jolts of dreams.
Sometimes you glimpsed my eye
pressed against the pane
just as you woke, and screamed,
horrified by my lashes
blinking over the sun,
so I had to turn invisible.
But I kept my files on you,
recording your baby prattle,
and your first tottering steps,
proud of what I'd made,
amazed by how the linear
brain I'd invented
kept surprising me. You sang
as you fashioned slingshots,
amphoras, grand pianos,

even tiny telescopes. You began
counting the stars I'd sprinkled
across your night sky,
experiencing emotions
under the trees in fall,
naming the colors of the leaves
visionary shades of red—
crimson, plum, claret . . .
I admired you, hoping
that in a few more centuries
you'd learn to resemble
what I most desired,
a reflection of myself
conjured out of the slime
of my immense matter,
unlike my angels, failures
shaped from my thoughts,
who waste heavenly time
crowding together,
dancing on the heads of pins.

Why did I start to think
you were eternal like me?
I got excited, day dreaming
of all you'd achieve
when you perfected yourselves.
But you've begun to wear out.
Tear ducts plugged, hearts
exercised on a treadmill,
some of you insist
your familiar human faces
are only romantic delusions,
that you're just fleshy
versions of your own Stiquito,
the android mosquito,
you invented by yourselves
to fetch ping pong balls
all day in a laboratory,
triggered by radio waves
it obeys but cannot feel.
Here in my void, far above
the universe I made
by rubbing together some stars
off my enormous robe
until they exploded in a bang,
I'm frowning and pacing,
deciding what I should do.
Shall I wipe you all out
or just leave you alone?

It's hard to think up here,
surrounded by noisy angels
standing inside one another,
debating the size of nothing.

GERALD STERN ■ · · · · · · · · · · · · · · · · ·

The Sounds

After it rains you should sigh a little for the spongy world.
You should listen to the fish gasping in the underbrush
and the duck's heart beating twenty yards away.
When the music arrives you should let it take you back across the river
into the kitchens where the clean hands are linked.
You should lie on the stones underneath the cold waterfall
and let your fingers drift hopelessly through the foam.
You should float slowly past the row of barking dogs
and visit the silent opossum in his grotto.
You should go to sleep between the sobs of the 9 o'clock local on the Jersey side
and the whines of Sea-Land and Roadway on the Pennsylvania.

Behaving Like a Jew

When I got there the dead opossum looked like
an enormous baby sleeping on the road.
It took me only a few seconds—just
seeing him there—with the hole in his back
and the wind blowing through his hair
to get back again into my animal sorrow.
I am sick of the country, the bloodstained
bumpers, the stiff hairs sticking out of the grills,
the slimy highways, the heavy birds
refusing to move;
I am sick of the spirit of Lindberg over everything,
that joy in death, that philosophical
understanding of carnage, that
concentration on the species.
—I am going to be unappeased at the opossum's death.
I am going to behave like a Jew
and touch his face, and stare into his eyes,
and pull him off the road.
I am not going to stand in a wet ditch
with the Toyotas and the Chevvies passing over me

at sixty miles an hour
and praise the beauty and the balance
and lose myself in the immortal lifestream
when my hands are still a little shaky
from his stiffness and his bulk
and my eyes are still weak and misty
from his round belly and his curved fingers
and his black whiskers and his little dancing feet.

Blue Skies, White Breasts, Green Trees

What I took to be a man in a white beard
turned out to be a woman in a silk babushka
weeping in the front seat of her car;
and what I took to be a seven-branched candelabrum
with the wax dripping over the edges
turned out to be a horse's skull
with its teeth sticking out of the sockets.
It was my brain fooling me,
sending me false images,
turning crows into leaves
and corpses into bottles,
and it was my brain that betrayed me completely,
sending me entirely uncoded material,
for what I thought was a soggy newspaper
turned out to be the first Book of Concealment, written in English,
and what I thought was a grasshopper on the windshield
turned out to be the Faithful Shepherd chewing blood,
and what I thought was, finally, the real hand of God
turned out to be only a guy wire and a
pair of broken sunglasses.
I used to believe the brain did its work
through faithful charges and I lived in sweet surroundings for the brain.
I thought it needed blue skies, white breasts, green trees,
to excite and absorb it,
and I wandered through the golf courses dreaming of pleasure
and struggled through the pool dreaming of happiness.
Now if I close my eyes I can see the uncontrolled waves
closing and opening of their own accord
and I can see the pins sticking out in unbelievable places,
and I can see the two lobes floating like two old barrels on the Hudson.
I am ready to reverse everything now
for the sake of the brain.
I am ready to take the woman with the white scarf
in my arms and stop her moaning,
and I am ready to light the horse's teeth,
and I am ready to stroke the dry leaves.

For it was kisses, and only kisses,
and not a stone knife in the neck that ruined me,
and it was my right arm, full of power and judgment,
and not my left arm twisted backwards to express vagrancy,
and it was the separation that *I* made,
and not the rain on the window
or the pubic hairs sticking out of my mouth,
and it was not really New York falling into the sea,
and it was not Nietzsche choking on an ice-cream cone,
and it was not the president lying dead again on the floor,
and it was not the sand covering me up to my chin,
and it was not my thick arms ripping apart an old floor,
and it was not my charm, breaking up an entire room.
It was my delicacy, my stupid delicacy,
and my sorrow.
It was my ghost, my old exhausted ghost,
that I dressed in white, and sent across the river,
weeping and weeping and weeping
inside his torn sheet.

Lucky Life

Lucky life isn't one long string of horrors
and there are moments of peace, and pleasure, as I lie in between the blows.
Lucky I don't have to wake up in Phillipsburg, New Jersey
on the hill overlooking Union Square or the hill overlooking
Kuebler Brewery or the hill overlooking SS. Philip and James
but have my own hills and my own vistas to come back to.

Each year I go down to the island I add
one more year to the darkness;
and though I sit up with my dear friends
trying to separate the one year from the other,
this one from the last, that one from the former,
another from another,
after a while they all get lumped together,
the year we walked to Holgate,
the year our shoes got washed away,
the year it rained,
the year my tooth brought misery to us all.

This year was a crisis. I knew it when we pulled
the car onto the sand and looked for the key.
I knew it when we walked up the outside steps
and opened the hot ice box and began the struggle
with swollen drawers and I knew it when we laid out
the sheets and separated the clothes into piles
and I knew it when we made our first rush onto

the beach and I knew it when we finally sat
on the porch with coffee cups shaking in our hands.

My dream is I'm walking through Phillipsburg, New Jersey
and I'm lost on South Main Street. I am trying to tell,
by memory, which statue of Christopher Columbus
I have to look for, the one with him slumped over
and lost in weariness or the one with him
vaguely guiding the way with a cross and globe in
one hand and a compass in the other.
My dream is I'm in the Eagle Hotel on Chamber Street
sitting at the oak bar, listening to two
obese veterans discussing Hawaii in 1942,
and reading the funny signs over the bottles.
My dream is I sleep upstairs over the honey locust
and sit on the side porch overlooking the stone culvert
with a whole new set of friends, mostly old and humorless.

Dear waves, what will you do for me this year?
Will you drown out my scream?
Will you let me rise through the fog?
Will you fill me with that old salt feeling?
Will you let me take my long steps in the cold sand?
Will you let me lie on the white bedspread and study
the black clouds with the blue holes in them?
Will you let me see the rusty trees and the old monoplanes one more year?
Will you still let me draw my sacred figures
and move the kites and the birds around with my dark mind?

Lucky life is like this. Lucky there is an ocean to come to.
Lucky you can judge yourself in this water.
Lucky the waves are cold enough to wash out the meanness.
Lucky you can be purified over and over again.
Lucky there is the same cleanliness for everyone.
Lucky life is like that. Lucky life. Oh lucky life.
Oh lucky lucky life. Lucky life.

Modern Love

In a month all these frozen waterfalls
will be replaced by Dutchman's-breeches
and I will drive down the road
trying to remember what it was like
in late February and early March.
It will be 72 degrees on March 24th
and I will see my first robin
on the roof of the Indian Rock Inn.
My wife and I will go in to stare at the chandelier
and eat, like starved birds, in front of the fireplace.

I know now that what I'll do
all through supper is plan my walk
from Bristol, PA to the canal museum.
I will exhaust her with questions about old hotels
and how much water I should carry
and what shoes I should wear,
and she will meet me with sweetness and logic
before we break up over money and grammar and lost love.
Later the full moon will shine through our windshield
as we zig-zag up the river
dragging our tired brains, and our hearts, after us.
I will go to bed thinking of George Meredith
lying beside a red sword
and I will try to remember how his brain smoked
as he talked to his wife in her sleep and twisted her words.
—Where I will go in the six hours before I wake up freezing
I don't know, but I do know
I will finally lie there with my twelve organs in place
wishing I were in a tea palace, wishing
I were in a museum in France, wishing
I were in a Moorish movie house in Los Angeles.
I will walk downstairs singing because it is March 25th
and I will walk outside to drink my coffee on the stone wall.
There will still be drops of snow on the side of the hill
as we plant our peas and sweep away the bird seed.
Watch me dig and you will see me
dream about justice, and you will see me
dream about small animals, and you will see me
dream about warm strawberries.
From time to time I will look over
and watch her dragging sticks and broken branches
across the road. We are getting ready
for summer. We are working in the cold
getting ready. Only thirty more days and the moon
will shine on us again as we drive to Hellertown
to see Jane Fonda grimace and drive back
after midnight through the white fields
looking for foxes in the stubble,
looking for their wild eyes, burning with fear and shyness,
in the stunted remains of last summer's silk forest.

Bela

This version of the starving artist
has him composing his last concerto
while dying of leukemia. Serge Koussevitsky
visits him in his hospital room

with flowers in his hand, the two of them
talk in tones of reverence, the last
long piece could be the best, the rain somewhere
makes daring noises, somewhere clouds are bursting.
I have the record in front of me. I drop
the needle again on the famous ending, five
long notes, then all is still, I have to imagine
two great seconds of silence and then applause
and shouting, he is in tears, Koussevitsky
leads him onto the stage. Or he is distant,
remembering the mountains, there in Boston
facing the wild Americans, he closes
his eyes so he can hear another note,
something from Turkey, or Romania, his mother
holding his left hand, straightening out the fingers,
he bows from the waist, he holds his right hand up.
I love the picture with Benny Goodman, Szigetti
is on the left, Goodman's cheeks are puffed
and his legs are crossed. Bartok is at the piano.
They are rehearsing Bartok's *Contrasts.* I lift
my own right hand, naturally I do that;
I listen to my blood, I touch my wrist.
If he could have only lived for three more years
he could have heard about our Mussolini
and seen the violent turn to the right and the end
of one America and the beginning of another.
That would have given him time enough to brood
on Hungary; that would have given him time
also to go among the Indians
and learn their music, and listen to their chants,
those tribes from Michigan and Minnesota,
just like the tribes of the Finns and the Urgo-Slavics,
moaning and shuffling in front of their wooden tents.
There is a note at the end of the second movement
I love to think about; it parodies
Shostakovitch; it is a kind of flutter
of the lips. And there is a note—I hear it—
of odd regret for a life not lived enough,
everyone knows that sound, for me it's remorse,
and there is a note of crazy satisfaction,
this I love, of the life he would not change
no matter what—no other animal
could have such pleasure. I think of this as I turn
the music off, and I think of his poor eyes
as they turned to ice—his son was in the room
and saw the change—I call it a change. Bartok
himself lectured his friends on death, it was
his woods and mountain lecture, fresh green shoots
pushing up through the old, the common home

that waits us all, the cycles, the laws of nature,
wonderfully European, all life and death
at war—peacefully—one thing replacing another,
although he grieved over cows and pitied dogs
and listened to pine cones as if they came from the sea
and fretted over the smallest of life. He died
September 28, 1945,
just a month after the war was over.
It took him sixty days to finish the piece
from the time he lay there talking to Koussevitsky
to the time he put a final dot on the paper,
a little pool of ink to mark the ending.
There are the five loud notes, I walk upstairs
to hear them, I put a silk shawl over my head
and rock on the wooden floor, the shawl is from France
and you can see between the threads; I feel
the darkness, I was born with a veil over
my eyes, it took me forty years to rub
the gum away, it was a blessing, I sit
for twenty minutes in silence, daylight is coming,
the moon is probably near, probably lifting
its satin nightgown, one hand over the knee
to hold the cloth up so the feet can walk
through the wet clouds; I love that bent-over motion,
that grace at the end of a long and furious night.
I go to sleep on the floor, there is a pillow
somewhere for my heavy head, my hand
is resting on the jacket, Maazel is leading
the Munich orchestra, a nurse is pulling
the sheet up, Bartok is dead, his wife is walking
past the sun room, her face is white, her mind
is on the apartment they lost, where she would put
the rugs, how she would carry in his breakfast,
where they would read, her mind is on Budapest,
she plays the piano for him, she is eighteen
and he is thirty-seven, he is gone
to break the news, she waits in agony,
she goes to the telephone; I turn to the window,
I stare at my palm, I draw a heart in the dust,
I put the arrow through it, I place the letters
one inside the other. I sleep, I sleep.

Hinglish

Sacré Dieu, I said for the very first time
in my adult life and leaned on a tuft of grass
in the neighborhood of one green daffodil
and one half-drooping, and one light violet blue-bell.

I did a stomp around my willow driving
the cold indoors and letting the first true heat
go through my skin and burn my frozen liver.

I placed the tip of my tongue against my teeth
and listened to a cardinal; I needed at least
one more month to stretch my neck and one
for delayed heartbeats and one for delayed sorrows.

"Speak French," she said, and dove
into the redbud. "Embrassez-moi," I said.
"Love me a little," "I am waiting for the hollyhock
and the summer lily," she said. "I am waiting
to match our reds. Baissez-moi," she said,
and raced for the alley. "Here is a lily, my darling,
oranger than your heart, with stripes to match
and darker inside than you." "Parle Français,
mon cher; pick me a rose; gather roses
while ye may; lorsque tu peux." "Have you
read Tristan Tzara?" I said. "Suivez-moi,
there is a bee," she said. "Forget your mother,
Oubliez vos fils vos meres." Her voice
is like a whistle; we used to say, "what cheer,"
and "birdy, birdy, birdy." There is a look
of fierceness to her. She flies into the redbud
without hesitation. It's easier that way. She settles,
the way a bird does on a branch; I think
they rock a little. "Nettles are nettles," she says,
"fate is full of them." "Speaka English," I say

and wait for summer,
a man nothing left of him but dust
beside his redbud
a bird nothing left of her but rage
waiting for her sunflower seed
at the glass feeder.

"A single tear," I say.
"My tear is the sky you see it," she says. She has
the last word. Halways. A bird is like that. She drops
into the hemlocks. Her nest is there. It is
a thicket at the side of the house. "I hate
the bluejay," she says. In Hinglish. She flies to the alley
and back to the street without much effort though my yard
is long as yards go now. How hot it will be
all summer. "Have you read Eluard?" she says.
"He avoided open spaces; his poems
were like my bushes and hedges; there in the middle
of all that green a splash of red; do you like

'splash of red'? His instrument was the wind.
So is someone's else." She has a flutelike
descending song; when she speaks French the sky
turns blue. "On sand and on sorrow," he said. "He talks
just like you. He had a small desert too;
he had an early regret. There is a piece
of willow. I am building something. I'll speak
Hinglish now. I love simplicity.
I hate rank." "Little wing of the morning," I say.
"In the warm isles of the heart," says she.
"I hold the tenderness of the night," say I.
"Too late for a kiss between the breasts," say she.

sitting on my porch,
counting uprights, including the ones on my left
beside the hammock, including the ones on my right
beside the hemlock,
reading Max Jacob,
speakin' a Hinglish.

Night

If only the bell keeps him alive though that is
an odd way of looking at his new life, then
missing an hour because of sleep or guessing the
time and being off sometimes for two hours
won't be his undoing, not that alone, though it is
hard to attach yourself to a new lover
and learn how she smooths her dress down or listens
to some kind of voice there or to her own silence
which he also listens to hour after hour,
sometimes lying there so long he thinks the cat
has got her tongue or that the electricity
has stopped, as in a flood, though he says to
himself there has to be another system a
backup generator slow to crank up, he can even
hear the bell slurring, or dragging, a different sound
but reassuring nonetheless, oh more than
that, a gift in his six hour crisis, a melodic
stroking, it is new to him, and hearing it when
it is dark and he is freezing, though pleasantly,
but lying awake, and guessing, he sometimes gets it
right on the hour, but sometimes night has just started,
the drunks are only coming home and he has
four or five more hours, the sound is brief,
forbidding, harsh, indifferent, and he is surprised that
he has guessed wrong, a voice has wounded him, wind
has slammed his window shut or his door but he
just lies on his back and even opens his eyes

in the dark, for that is a life too, and he turns
to one side or the other and hangs onto something,
a chair, a window-sill, and waits for the next
shocking stroke and sometimes he changes pillows.

SUSAN STEWART ▪ ▪ ▪ ▪ ▪ ▪ ▪ ▪ ▪ ▪ ▪ ▪ ▪ ▪ ▪ ▪

Slaughter

1

Remembering the shot that seemed to burst with no
rebound (early November, a time when the light
had waxed, but verged on turning back),
I asked what had happened and how it was done,
for I had been reading the same story over
and over of the breakdown in the fullness of the world.
I finally realized that what I had hidden from
in those early years was exactly the knowledge
that had disappeared behind the given-
ness of all things to us now. I had thought
that the very sound of the shot had created the silence,
the denying silence, around it. And that the lack
of an aftermath had come to stand for the loss,
the loss of anything I might have known then.

They began with the tools, the good set
of knives, the curved one for skinning and the straight one
for cuts, and the whetstones, the steels, the cleavers
and bell scrapers, the saws and the hooks, the stunning
ax and the windlass. They told how God had wanted
meat and so Abraham went forth—resigned
to duty's technology; how some things must
be done when the season is upon us and
once begun, cannot be left uncompleted.
The animal should sleep, they said, and be given
only water—for three days before
the killing time. The stunning must be short,
exact—a blow or shot to the forehead at
the cross of an X between the horns and eyes.

2

Then the sticker stepped forward, "If you want my job, you must face
in the same direction as the animal and stretch its neck
as far as possible, then press with your foot against the jaw

and forelegs while you cut through the skin from the breastbone
to the throat—you'll see at last the wind-
pipe is exposed. Push with your shoe on the animal's
flank; the bleeding will flow most freely."
(In the wilderness a voice was burning
out of the thorn-struck bush and the stones.
God had in mind a supplement, turning
the scene against itself, and would make
what seemed at first beyond measure
something trivial, undone—a kind of swerve
like mercy, shielding us from closure.)

They explained the skinning must start with the head,
and that, very slowly, the knife should be traced
from the back of the poll to the nostril on the left,
just along the line of the eye. They said to skin
the side and a short distance down the neck
until the head would be up on its base at last and,
grasping the head by the lower jaw, they'd unjoint
it at the atlas, then cut, and twist, and pull until
it fell away, for good, on the ground.
Some of this had to be said with gestures,
but none interrupted or argued the order.
With the straight knife one would sever
the tendons at the hock joint. The hind
legs would hang then, dangling free.

3

The dewclaws have no purpose, but are taken
as a marker for splitting to the hock,
across the taut back of the thigh, and within
a few inches of the cod. Then the hide
must be split from the middle of the belly
without disturbing the abdomen's shell
or the delicate thin fell membrane.
Each name was given by Adam in the garden
during the sultry, buzzing afternoons
after the world was whole. They warned me
that the blood spots must be wiped, and
wiped away, then wiped again with water and
a warm soft cloth. The person who does this task
must have a tender kind of attention

And must make sure no leaves or dust fall
into the tin tub where the water swirls.
The caul fat must be taken out with care.
Next someone strong should loosen the pelvis
and the windpipe, then saw and split them each,
leaving them exposed. What meaning crucifixion

has depends on display and disappearance,
for when is the material ever more resistant
than when it is contradicted? The animal had lolled,
and slept, and grazed in its given hours, then gone
to the killing floor where time was rent by pain.
"Look to the heavens," they said, "count the stars,"
and so allayed the terror of the cry.
Behind the stone, the tomb yawned, empty.

4

Later the old ones told me how
to build the tripod from timbers and
how to stretch a gas pipe between the tendons
and the shank bones. Broom-handle sticks
are tied to the rope ends, then worked, lodged
as levers, to raise and spread the legs.
One explained how the skinning must proceed
with the hoisting, another told how to sever
and withdraw the stiffening tail. Taking turns,
they went into the beating of the hide,
the working loose of the rectum, the severing,
in the final stages, of the glossy violet liver.
"Wash the liver and hang it to cool slowly;
wash the heart—hang it by the small end, too.

Keep the fat clustered against the tongue
and hang it up to drain, and cool, and dry.
Save the rest of the fat for soap and tallow.
Wash the stomach until it's perfect clean and
the inner surface webbed with white. When the carcass
has been split down the center of the backbone,
the two halves should be pinned with a smooth
muslin shroud. They must stay this way
until morning so that the living heat
will disperse and the fresh cuts can be
cold, and cleanly made." Out of one
being a vastness; out of one task
the division of labor; out of one shot
the myriad silence: winter's gory fruit.

5

Now let us go back to the stunning,
to the meeting of a human and animal mind, let us
go back and begin again where the function
overwhelms all hesitation and seems like
an act of nature. But they were tired and had no time
for me; the immense weight of memory dragged up
and brought back into the present was, too, like a great

beast, beached and spoiled. I finally grasped
what had happened, how the real could not
be evoked except in a spell of longing for
the past or the mime that would be, after all,
another occasion for suffering.
There would be no more instruction,
no more, in the end, hand guiding the hand.

RUTH STONE ▪ ▪ ▪ ▪ ▪ ▪ ▪ ▪ ▪ ▪ ▪ ▪ ▪ ▪ ▪ ▪ ▪

It Follows

If you had a lot of money,
(by some coincidence
you're at the Nassau Inn in Princeton
getting a whiff of class)
and you just noticed two days ago
that your face has fallen,
but you don't believe it,
so every time you look in the glass
it's still hanging there where it wasn't.
Would you take the money you needed
for a new roof on your old house,
(the house you're paying for
over and over in property taxes)
because it's been leaking for years
and you're tired of emptying buckets
and spraying for mold,
would you take that money
and get your face lifted?
Face lift. They cut a slit
under your ears and pull up the slack
and they tack it with plastic.
Then they pull up the outer
skin and trim it because it's too long
and fasten that. (Your skin
pulls loose from the fat like chicken skin.)
Because once you were almost
as beautiful as Jane Wyman . . .
your friends all said that.
Of course at the time she was
married to Ronnie and you were
involved with the ASU—
a McCarthy suspect.
Forget about your neck.

They can't do that yet.
A face lift lasts five years.
So you could go on being a member
of new speak and re-entry—
with the unsung benefits
of radiation and by then
your roof would have rotted anyway.
Or been re-cycled by some corporate kid.
But think how you'd rather
be stripped and streaked
and while you're about it
get some implants of baby teeth buds
that they've taken from dead babies' gums
and frozen for this sort of thing.
You could still die young.

Resonance

The universe is sad.
I heard it when Artur Rubinstein played the piano.
He was a little man with small hands.
We were bombing Germany by then.
I went to see him in a dark warehouse
where a piano had been placed for his practice—
or whatever he did before a recital.
He signed the book I had with me—
it was called *Warsaw Ghetto*.
I later heard about about him—
his affairs with young women—
if only I had known—but I was
in love with you.
Artur is dead;
and you, my darling,
the imprint of your face, alert like a deer—
oh god, it is eaten away—
the earth has taken it back
but I listen to Artur—
he springs out of the grave—
his genius wired to this tape—
a sad trick of the neural pathways, resonating flesh
and my old body remembers the way you touched me.

CHRIS STROFFOLINO ▪ ▪ ▪ ▪ ▪ ▪ ▪ ▪ ▪ ▪ ▪ ▪

Lingua Franca

for C. K. and S. K.

If only now you were to emerge from
the shelter of the bell whose clapper
has been using you as a punching bag,
the hurt which merges with the headlines
as long as we're content to listen
in every form but speech
would be the leaves that wouldn't
have fallen had you not gotten
such a kick out of shaking the tree.

Emerge for faith's ready with cameras
to shoot commodities of comfort
as long as love is valued
before forgetfulness is accepted
as an ocean that holds its own
as well as a bumpersticker
which keeps togetherness content
enough to sleep beneath the clouds
that cover the stars like reporters.

Emerge and let them fall from
the isolation which is not solitude
and which haunts all but the
naughtiest of the hungry on
the ship of life we watch go down
from the rafts that would be a shore
if you could be an island without
harbouring lush vegetation
which is only fruitful to spill
over the sides, unmuzzle and multiply
to bring them to the knowledge
that loaves and fish would not nourish
were they not also pain and poison.

But don't expect them to
pardon our French in a land
where the English they make us speak
sees swearing as obscene and forgets
the tightrope walker needs no net
for the same reason a net doesn't.

LUCIEN STRYK ▪ ▪ ▪ ▪ ▪ ▪ ▪ ▪ ▪ ▪ ▪ ▪ ▪ ▪ ▪

Awakening

(Homage to Hakuin, Zen master, 1685–1768)

I

Shoichi brushed the black
on thick.
His circle held a poem
like buds
above a flowering bowl.

Since the moment of my
pointing,
this bowl, an "earth device,"
holds
nothing but the dawn.

II

A freeze last night, the window's
laced ice flowers, a meadow drifting
from the glacier's side. I think of Hakuin:

"Freezing in an icefield, stretched
thousands of miles in all directions,
I was alone, transparent, and could not move."

Legs cramped, mind pointing
like a torch, I cannot see beyond
the frost, out nor in. And do not move.

III

I balance the round stone
in my palm,
turn it full circle,

slowly, in the late sun,
spring to now.
Severe compression,

like a troubled head,
stings my hand.
It falls. A small dust rises.

IV

Beyond the sycamore
dark air moves
westward—

smoke, cloud, something
wanting a name.
Across the window,

my gathered breath,
I trace
a simple word.

V

My daughter gathers shells
where thirty years before
I'd turned them over, marveling.

I take them from her,
make, at her command,
the universe. Hands clasped,

marking the limits of
a world, we watch till sundown
planets whirling in the sand.

VI

Softness everywhere,
snow a smear,
air a gray sack.

Time. Place. Thing.
Felt between
skin and bone, flesh.

VII

I write in the dark again,
rather by dusk-light,
and what I love about

this hour is the way the trees
are taken, one by one,
into the great wash of darkness.

At this hour I am always happy,
ready to be taken myself,
fully aware.

Black Bean Soup

I shadow the pond
patient as stone, catch
the sadness of wind
carving seashells

in traces of snow
in the park. Last
night, found my wife
sobbing at words in

her crossword puzzle.
There it was—
Black Bean Soup. And
there was my father,

months before dying,
asking in, out of
shadows for black
bean soup. My sister

and I watched him
leaving us slowly. My
thoughts back in time,
nearly seventy years,

tramping through snow,
hands clasped, off
to the park. "Snow,"
he said. "Snow," I said.

Laughing together, sliding
back home. Stamping
feet on the doormat,
eager for mother's good

soup, rich and thick.
Light and dark are memories,
like mountain junipers
snared by the kudzu,

ghosts for all time.
A tabby, half cocked
on a garden wall, shakes
off snowflakes, springs

down, rubs against me
like an old friend

as I pass. In spite of
death the winter cherry

blooms. A bird flies sharp
against the chill gray sky.

Blood

1

Pen filled with ink dark
as the rowanberry,
curious rambler on paper

white as the moon. I've
weathered three hundred
seasons, sun, storm and snow.

Spare in pocket, rich in
the winding of time.
Poemed war, peace, love,

hunger, good bread of this
earth. Why then ache
for a small barefoot boy,

blond hair roughed by
the wind, traipsing
the road to that bridge?

2

Barefoot children sing
out of joy as they scoot
to the bank, whomp stones

from cobbles into the brimming
river, move on to spot freight-
cars creaking up over the hill.

The smallest bloodies his
foot on the bridge. Leaves
friends and cousins, limps

back, skirting houses with fine
carved doors, wild flowers
linking hedges and gardens.

Stops by a wagon bursting
with millet, barley, potatoes,
cabbage, brown eggs, sweetest

blueberries, now to be bartered
for cloth, candles, tools,
holy pictures and tea at his

grandfather's store. The farmer
tends to his foot, shoulders
him onto the thick-necked horse.

Nearby soldiers chat up his mother,
her sisters, jaunty in caps
like the one his father, star

of the Jesuit school, soldier,
lumberjack, dizzy with dreams,
left behind on the way to his

family in the New World. Where
he would prosper, send for
his wife, then with child. Year

by year, on tick, linens,
silverware bearing their name,
lace-collared frocks filled

the room he slept in with
his mother. Soon they would
leave for the port in the farmer's

great wagon. Staring back
at the grandfather, aunts,
uncle, cousins, friends that

he loved. It was good he
was too young to know he was
leaving them all, forever.

3

Blackbird on an eave trough
sings to a boy no longer
barefoot, taking on the language,

landscape of his new place.
Hopping through crisp copper
leaves along the gutters to

the third-floor flat they lodged
in with his father's kin,
who scorned the country girl,

his mother, homesick, wearied
after long hours in a sweatshop
to pay back for linens, silver,

lace stowed in an ocean trunk.
Times, out with his father
at the park, watched him stride off

on his secret missions, silence
meriting a box of Cracker Jacks
on the way home. Soon they had

a lodging of their own, in-a-door bed
for them, sofa for him. Squinting
in the dark he tried to see the

grandfather who'd died in the old country.
Made up stories from vague yesterdays.
Running with his gang, climbing

forbidden structures, aiming
stones from slingshots at back-
alley doors. Doing errands

for the neighbors, taking every
penny home. He had a sister now
and times were hard. They packed up,

wandering state to state, finding
odd jobs. After the market crash
they went back to the city,

and were well set. He had his
own room now, mastered sports,
read his first poem, scribbled

lines exalting the new rug,
sang art songs, arias at school,
for ladies' meetings, Easter Service

in the local church. News sent
his mother to implore her in-laws,
friends to sponsor those she loved,

to help them to the safety of
this shore. They turned away.
Sun fired the lake, fierce colors

of autumn fretworking leaves of
trees he'd shinned up when a boy.
Now Germany was on the march,

rumor echoed beyond winter's strip-
down, bones of branches left
with empty nests. Then Pearl Harbor,

and the struggle had begun. One night
his father woke him with another
secret: word had come his mother's

family had perished. He must never
mention that cursed land again.
As his father spoke he saw them,

cousins, uncle, aunts, friends,
force-marched by the houses with
carved doors, wild flowers joining

hedges, gardens, to the bridge. Shoved
in the freight cars he had waved on
with his chums, hauled a few stops

down the line to death. All night
he heard his mother's agonizing cries.
Next day he signed up, packed his

Leaves of Grass, and went to war.

MAY SWENSON ▪ ▪ ▪ ▪ ▪ ▪ ▪ ▪ ▪ ▪ ▪ ▪ ▪ ▪ ▪ ▪

Something Goes By

What are you doing?
I'm watching myself watch myself.

And what are you doing?
Pushing a stick, with a wooden wheel at the end.
I have on a white dress.

First I push the wheel, then I pull the wheel.
My dad made it, with the lathe and a bandsaw.

And where are you watching from?
From my seat on the train.
My back is to myself, back there. But with the back
of my head I'm watching myself:
on a strip of cement, by a square of grass,
pushing the wheel that isn't quite round,
so it wobbles and clacks.

I'm crossing a trestle over a river on the train . . .
the water's gray and level there below,
with stroke-marks on it, in arm-length arcs,
like wet cement that's just been planed.
My dad built our house, poured concrete for the basement,
sawed timber for the frame, laid the brick,
put on the roof, shingle by shingle,
lying along the ladder with nails in his mouth,
plastered the inside, laid the floorboards,
made our furniture out of wood:
of wave-grained oak our dining table . . .
my round, high stool he scooped in the center just like a saucer . . .

There's a hat on my lap that I mustn't leave on the train,
new shoes on my feet, that fuse my toes to flatiron shape.
I'm watching myself being carried away.

And where are you watching from?
From *here.* From out of a slit of almost sleep . . .
lying on my side,
hands between my knees.
I hear myself breathe.
My bed is a dais in the hollow room;
in the window frame a section of sky:
slow clouds puff by, over the city, on a track from the west—
like an endless—is it an endless?—train.
I hear an airplane being driven into heaven.
its drone the saw-sound, the sound
of the lathe—or is it the rasp of my own/ breath in my ear?
When I look to the window, will it be gone—
or moved to another wall? Will it be dawn
in another room?—Or in this same
room in another year?—Already I hear
November horns on the river.

Where is here?/ And what are you doing?
I'm running,/ and pushing something.
I have on a white dress.

I'm sitting,/ and something carries me.
There's a hat on my lap.
I'm lying naked, almost asleep . . .
Some/ thing/ goes/ by.

JAMES TATE ▪ ▪ ▪ ▪ ▪ ▪ ▪ ▪ ▪ ▪ ▪ ▪ ▪ ▪ ▪ ▪

Land of Little Sticks, 1945

Where the wife is scouring the frying pan
and the husband is leaning up against the barn.
Where the boychild is pumping water into a bucket
and the girl is chasing a spotted dog.

And the sky churns on the horizon.
A town by the name of Pleasantville has disappeared.
And now the horses begin to shift and whinny,
and the chickens roost, keep looking this way and that.
At this moment something is not quite right.

The boy trundles through the kitchen, spilling water.
His mother removes several pies from the oven, shouts at him.
The girlchild sits down by the fence to stare at the horses.
And the man is just as he was, eyes closed, forehead
against his forearm, leaning up against the barn.

Head of a White Woman Winking

She has one good bumblebee
which she leads about town
on a leash of clover.
It's as big as a Saint Bernard
but also extremely fragile.
People want to pet its long, shaggy coat.
These would be mostly whirling dervishes
out shopping for accessories.
When Lily winks, they understand everything,
right down to the particle
of a butterfly's wing lodged
in her last good eye,
so the situation is avoided,
the potential for a cataclysm
is narrowly averted,

and the bumblebee lugs
its little bundle of shaved nerves
forward, on a mission
from some sick, young godhead.

Inspiration

The two men sat roasting in their blue suits
on the edge of a mustard field.
Lucien Cardin, a local painter,
had suggested a portrait.
President and Vice President of the bank branch,
maybe it would hang in the lobby
inspiring confidence. It might even
cast a little grace and dignity
on the citizens of their hamlet.
They were serious men with sober thoughts
about an unstable world.
The elder, Gilbert, smoked his pipe
and gazed through his wire-rims beyond the painter.
The sky was eggshell blue,
and Lucien knew what he was doing
when he begged their pardon
and went to fetch the two straw hats.
They were farmer's hats, for working in the sun.
Gilbert and Tom agreed to wear them
to staunch their perspiration,
but they knew too the incongruity
their appearance now suggested.
And, as for the lobby of their bank,
solidarity with the farmers, their customers.
The world might go to war—Louis flattened
Schmeling the night before—but a portrait
was painted that day in a field of mustard
outside of Alexandria, Ontario,
of two men, even-tempered and level-headed,
and of what they did next there is no record.

Dream On

Some people go their whole lives
without ever writing a single poem.
Extraordinary people who don't hesitate
to cut somebody's heart or skull open.

They go to baseball games with the greatest of ease
and play a few rounds of golf as if it were nothing.
These same people stroll into a church
as if that were a natural part of life.
Investing money is second nature to them.
They contribute to political campaigns
that have absolutely no poetry in them
and promise none for the future.
They sit around the dinner table at night
and pretend as though nothing is missing.
Their children get caught shoplifting at the mall
and no one admits that it is poetry they are missing.
The family dog howls all night,
lonely and starving for more poetry in his life.
Why is it so difficult for them to see
that, without poetry, their lives are effluvial.
Sure, they have their banquets, their celebrations,
croquet, fox hunts, their sea shores and sunsets,
their cocktails on the balcony, dog races,
and all that kissing and hugging, and don't
forget the good deeds, the charity work,
nursing the baby squirrels all through the night,
filling the birdfeeders all winter,
helping the stranger change her tire.
Still, there's that disagreeable exhalation
from decaying matter, subtle but everpresent.
They walk around erect like champions.
They are smooth-spoken, urbane and witty.
When alone, rare occasion, they stare
into the mirror for hours, bewildered.
There was something they meant to say, but didn't:
"And if we put the statue of the rhinoceros
next to the tweezers, and walk around the room three times,
learn to yodel, shave our heads, call
our ancestors back from the dead—"
poetrywise it's still a bust, bankrupt.
You haven't scribbled a syllable of it.
You're a nowhere man misfiring
the very essence of your life, flustering
nothing from nothing and back again.
The hereafter may not last all that long.
Radiant childhood sweetheart,
secret code of everlasting joy and sorrow,
fanciful pen strokes beneath the eyelids:
all day, all night meditation, knot of hope,
kernel of desire, pure ordinariness of life
seeking, through poetry, a benediction
or a bed to lie down on, to connect, reveal,

explore, to imbue meaning on the day's extravagant labor.
And yet it's cruel to expect too much.
It's a rare species of bird
that refuses to be categorized.
Its song is barely audible.
It is like a dragonfly in a dream—
here, then there, then here again,
Low-flying Amber-wing darting upward
and then out of sight.
And the dream has a pain in its heart
the wonders of which are manifold,
or so the story is told.

Never Again the Same

Speaking of sunsets,
last night's was shocking.
I mean, sunsets aren't supposed to frighten you, are they?
Well, this one was terrifying.
People were screaming in the streets.
Sure, it was beautiful, but far too beautiful.
It wasn't natural.
One climax followed another and then another
until your knees went weak
and you couldn't breathe.
The colors were definitely not of this world,
peaches dripping opium,
pandemonium of tangerines,
inferno of irises,
Plutonian emeralds,
all swirling and churning, swabbing,
like it was playing with us,
like we were nothing,
as if our whole lives were a preparation for this,
this for which nothing could have prepared us
and for which we could not have been less prepared.
The mockery of it all stung us bitterly.
And when it was finally over
we whimpered and cried and howled.
And then the streetlights came on as always
and we looked into one another's eyes—
ancient caves with still pools
and those little transparent fish
who have never seen even one ray of light.
And the calm that returned to us
was not even our own.

Non-Stop

It seemed as if the enormous journey
was finally approaching its conclusion.
From the window of the train
the last trees were dissipating,
a child-like sailor waved once,
a seal-like dog barked and died.
The conductor entered the lavatory
and was not seen again, although
his harmonica-playing was appreciated.
He was not without talent, some said.
A botanist with whom I had become acquainted
actually suggested we form a group or something.
I was looking for a familiar signpost
in his face, or a landmark that would
indicate the true colors of his tribe.
But, alas, there was not a glass of water
anywhere or even the remains of a trail.
I got a bewildered expression of my own
and slinked to the back of the car
where a nun started to tickle me.
She confided to me that it was her
cowboy pride that got her through . . .
Through what? I thought, but drew my hand
close to my imaginary vest.
"That's a beautiful vest," she said,
as I began crawling down the aisle.
At last, I pressed my face against
the window: A little fog was licking
its chop, as was the stationmaster
licking something. We didn't stop.
We didn't appear to be arriving,
and yet we were almost out of landscape.
No creeks or rivers. Nothing
even remotely reminding one of a mound.
O mound! thou ain't around no more.
A heap of abstract geometrical symbols,
that's what it's coming to, I thought.
A nothing you could sink your teeth into.
"Relief's on the way," a little
know-nothing boy said to me.
"Imagine my surprise," I said
and reached out to muss his hair.
But he had no hair and it felt unlucky
touching his skull like that.
"Forget what I said," he said.
"What did you say?" I asked

in automatic compliance.
And then it got very dark and quiet.
I closed my eyes and dreamed of an emu I once loved.

The Figure in the Carpet

Even the abandoned husk of a person can sometimes
perform useful tasks and enjoy mildly good times,
light opera, dusting for cobwebs with long brooms, etc.
We walk a little, pause, look down, walk.
It's not a big effort to do any of this.
It's not as though we were crossing the forbidden
territory of Lop against icy gales,
but we would like to know what is on our minds—
a maze?—when we organize these shadows—
a slumber party?—so seductively, and yet incomprehensibly,
until we can't find ourselves anymore,
those selves that have been following us
and pestering us all these years,
which is not necessarily a bad thing.
Oh you talk a good game Binky. I can see
that you have a nervous system shaped like Florida.
A lot of good that will do you when it's time
to trace your steps back into the egg.
Did I say egg? I meant dog.
If there are no secrets to be revealed
then I shall resume darning my other sock.
And if there are they best be espied
over at Binky's place, his rotunda has a view of some.
And then when we walk back it won't follow us.
We won't even remember its name
but our next big tag sale will be ablaze with bargain incubators.
And that's all I asked for was a clue.

Nirvana

At the retreat, Lee wasn't allowed
to speak or read for ten days, just
meditate. It was bliss at first
letting go of the chattering world.
The silence was like living inside
a rose. She felt strong and clean.
Up before dawn to contemplate, and
then the simple meal with others
she didn't know, but, now, with all this

love flowing through her she knew
she must love them too. They were all
part of the same Divine Being.
In a pond of red lotuses,
in a pond of blue lotuses,
in a pond of white lotuses,
is the utter purity of mindfulness
that is indifference, rightly
penetrated by wisdom. As the days
wore on she missed chocolate,
she missed coffee and cigarettes.
She missed the office and its
endless phone calls, she missed
her secretary and her delicious
gossip. Martinis! And her husband
who was chopping his way through
the rain forest in search of
a tiny, yellow frog. Meditation
was great, but ten days of it
would be enough to make one combust.
At lunch she looked around the room:
without speech, without emotion,
her fellow campers were like ghosts,
or maybe more like mental patients
dulled by too much medication and
electro-shock, sad and empty husks
of their former selves. The Teacher
sat by himself eating his bowl of rice.
Lee stood up and began to walk
down the long path to the parking lot.
She wasn't angry. She was excited
and started skipping and singing
at the sight of her getaway car.

JEAN VALENTINE ▪ ▪ ▪ ▪ ▪ ▪ ▪ ▪ ▪ ▪ ▪ ▪ ▪ ▪ ▪

The One You Wanted to Be Is the One You Are

She saying, You don't have to do anything,
you don't even have to be, you Only who are,
you nobody from nowhere,
without one sin or one good quality,
without one book, without one word,
without even a comb, you!

The one you wanted to be
is the one you are. Come play . . .

And he saying,
Look at me!
I don't know how . . .

Their breath like a tree's breath. Their silence
like a deer's silence. Tolstoy
wrote about this: all misunderstanding.

The Free Abandonment Blues

Now I don't have to leave this place not for anybody
No I don't have to go out of this wooden house not to oblige anybody
Once I would have lifted clean out of my own place to please somebody

The blue-robed man who said You want to be loved, love me
The man in the blue robe who said I give, in order that you will give to me
I remember you my old blue-robed man, but you know this just can not be

Now if I want to warm myself I look up at the blue sky
Now I look to a number of people here and also to the round blue sky
To feel the sun, your free mouth on my mouth, not the fire that is gone by

I don't wear any clothes nowadays or say that I am me
I don't wear the right clothes in the closet or explain how I am me
I come as I go translucent oh what you get is what you see

The woman said:
They held her in their arms and knew that she would save them
They brought her into their houses and into their hands to save them
But secretly they knew so certainly that no one would ever have them

And she said,
Listen, it's only a little time longer to wait
When you have taken this path you need just a little more time to wait
Maybe not today the amazing loveliness but it won't be long for us to wait

The Under Voice

I saw streaming up out of the sidewalk the homeless women and men
the East side of Broadway fruit and flowers and bourbon
the homeless men like dull knives gray-lipped the homeless women
connected to no one streaming no one to no one

more like light than like people, blue neon,
"blue the most fugitive of all the colors"

Then I looked and saw our bodies
not near but not far out,
lying together, our whiteness

And the under voice said, Stars you are mine,
you have always been mine; I remember the minute on the birth table
when you were born, I riding with my feet up in the wide silver blue stirrups,
I came and came and came, little baby and woman, where were you taking me?
Everyone else may leave you, I will never leave you, fugitive.

American River Sky Alcohol Father

What is pornography? What is dream?
American River Sky Alcohol Father,
forty years ago, four lifetimes ago,
brown as bourbon, warm, you said to me,
"Sorry sorry sorry sorry sorry."
Then: "You're killing your mother."
And she: "You're killing your father."
What do men want? What do fathers want?
Why won't they go to the mothers?
(What do the mothers want.)
American River Sky Alcohol Father,
your warm hand. Your glass. Your bedside table gun.
The dock, the water, the fragile, tough beach grass.
Your hand. I wouldn't swim. I wouldn't fly.

The Pen

The sandy road, the bright green two-inch lizard
little light on the road

the pen that writes by itself
the mist that blows by, through itself

the gourd I drink from in my sleep
that also drinks from me

—Who taught me to know instead of not
        to know?
And this pen   its thought

lying on the thought of the table
a bow lying across the strings

not moving
held

Truth

Sharing bread
is sharing life
but truth—
you ought to go to bed at night
to hear the truth
strike
on the childhood clock
in your arms: the
cold house
a turned-over boat,
the walls
wet canvases . . .

DEREK WALCOTT ▪ ▪ ▪ ▪ ▪ ▪ ▪ ▪ ▪ ▪ ▪ ▪ ▪ ▪ ▪

Sour Grapes

That sail in cloudless light
which tires of islands,
a schooner beating up the Caribbean

for home, could be Odysseus
home-bound through the Aegean,
just as that husband's

sorrow under the sea-grapes, repeats
the adulterer's hearing Nausicaa's name
in every gull's outcry.

But whom does this bring peace? The classic war
between a passion and responsibility
is never finished, and has been the same

to the sea-wanderer and the one on shore,
now wriggling on his sandals to walk home,
since Troy sighed its last flame,

and the blind giant's boulder heaved the trough
from which The Odyssey's hexameters come
to finish up as Caribbean surf.

The classics can console. But not enough.

Sabbaths

Those villages stricken with the melancholia of
Sunday, in all of whose ochre streets one dog is
sleeping

Those volcanoes like lurid roses, or the incurable
sore of poverty, around whose puckered lip thin
boys are selling yellow sulphur stone

the burnt banana leaves that used to dance
the river whose bed was made of broken crystals
the cocoa grove where a bird whose cry sounds green
and yellow and crested with orange has forgotten
its flute

gommiers with their bark like sunburn still wrest-
ling to escape from the memory of the sea

the dead lizard turning blue as a stone

those rivers, more streams, that rewrote the same
music

that dry, brief esplanade under the drier sea-almonds
where the old men sat

their eyes playing chess with the movements of frigate-
birds

those hillsides that looked like broken pots
those ferns that left their dust imprinted on the
skin

and those roads that begin reciting their names at
vespers

mention them and they will vanish
those crabs that waited for an epoch to pass
those herons that doubted their own reflections,
enquiring, enquiring,

those nettles that waited
those Sundays, those Sundays

those Sundays when the lights at the end of the road
were an occasion

those Sundays when my mother lay on her back
those Sundays when the sisters gathered around the street
lantern

and lights passed on the horizons

The Saddhu of Couva

Sometimes I see my spirit, swiftly unsheathed,
like a white cattle-bird growing more and more small
arrowing across the ocean of cane behind Couva,
then the bird does quiver, frighten, on a salt branch
by the shallows of Manzanilla,
and my body, all day, does wait for it to come back,
like a hog-cattle armoured in mud,
because, for my spirit, India is too far.
Sometimes I see bald saffron clouds assemble
high over Couva, sacred in the evening.
Sacred even to Ramlochan
singing in his jute-hammock
under his upstairs house,
the light reflected on the sacred flanks
and silver horns of his maroon taxi,
sacred to the closed shopfronts
and the cinema posters,
as the mosquitoes whine their evening mantras,
my friend, Anopheles, on the sitar,
sacred to the fireflies for whom every dusk is Divalli.

My head is knotted in a white cloud,
my white moustaches bristle like horns,
my hands are brittle as the brown leaves on which
the Ramayana was written: once
the sacred monkeys multiplied like branches in the old-time temples,
I didn't miss them, these fields sang like Bengal,
behind Couva there was Uttar Pradesh.
I think of time as a conflagration
fiercer than the bonfires of croptime,
I will pass out of these people's memory like a cloud.
They will see a white cattle-bird over the afternoon sea
of the canes behind Couva,
and which will remember it is my soul unsheathed?

Neither the bridegroom in beads,
nor the bride, veiled,
their sacred language on the cinema hoardings.

I talked too much on The Couva Village Council.
I talked too softly, I was always drowned
by the loudspeakers in front of the stores
or the loudspeakers with the greatest picture.
I am best suited to stalk like a white cattle-bird
on legs like sticks, with sticking to The Path
between the canes on a district road at dusk.
Playing The Elder. There are no more elders.
Is only old people.

My friends spit on the government.
I do not think is just the government.
Just as is not only chills I have,
is the white bird, fear.
Suppose the gods are all elders,
suppose all the gods too old,
suppose they dead and they burning them,
and these are their bonfires and their drifting ash.
Black Kali with your arms like the snakes
that wriggling away from those canefires,
supposing when some cane-cutter
start chopping up snakes with a cutlass
he is severing the snake-armed god,
and suppose some hunter has caught
Hanuman in his mischief in a monkey cage,
that with every crop-over we keep burning the gods
not by the Ganges but by the River Carori.

Everything is either mortal or immortal.
I see the dark. The fireflies do not last.
Suppose even the minarets will blow out like candles?
Suppose all the gods were killed by electric light.
Terror is wisdom. I have grown wise at last.
Every day ends in fire, then is past.
The sparks are blowing through the smoke of night.

The Man Who Loved Islands

(A Two-Page Outline)

A man is leaning on a cold iron rail
watching an islet from an island and so on,
say Charlotte Amalie facing St. John,

which begins the concept of infinity
uninterrupted by any mortal sail,
only the thin ghost of a tanker drawing the horizon
behind it with the silvery slick of a snail,
and that's the first shot of this forthcoming film
starring James Coburn and his tanned, leathery, frail
resilience and his now whitening hair,
and his white, vicious grin. Now, we were where?
On this island, one of the Virgins, the prota-
gonist established. Now comes the second shot,
and chaos of artifice still called the plot,
which has to get the hero off somewhere
else, 'cause there's no kick in contemplation
of silvery light upon wind-worried water
between here and the islet of Saint John,
and how they are linked like any silver chain
glinting against the hero's leather chest,
sold in the free gift ports, like noon-bright water.
The hero's momentary rest on the high rail
can be a good beginning. To start with rest
is good. The tanker can come later,
but we can't call it 'The Man Who Loved Islands'
any more than some Zen-Karate film
would draw them with 'The Hero Who Loves Water'.
No soap. There must be something with diamonds,
emeralds, emeralds the colour of the shallows there,
or sapphires, like blue, unambiguous air,
sapphires for Sophia, but we'll come to that,
Coburn looks great with or without a hat,
and there must be some minimum of slaughter,
that brings in rubies, but you cannot hover
over that first shot like a painting. Action
is all of art, the thoughtless pace
of lying with style, so that when it's over,
that first great shot of Coburn's leathery face,
crinkled like the water which he contemplates,
could be superfluous, in the first place,
since that tired artifice called history,
which in its motion is as false as fiction,
requires an outline, a summary. I can think of none,
quite honestly. I'm no photographer; this
could be a movie. I mean things are moving,
the water for example, the light on the man's hair
that has gone white, even those crescent sands
are just as moving as his love of islands;
the tanker that seems still is moving, even
the clouds like galleons anchored in heaven,
and what is moving most of all of course
is the violent man lulled into this inaction
by the wide sea. Let's hold it on the sea

as we establish their ancient inter-action,
a hint of the Homeric, a little poetry
before the whole mess hits the bloody fan.
All these islands that you love, I guaran-
tee we'll work them in as background, with
generous establishing shots from Jim's car and
even a few harbours and villages, IF
we blow the tanker up and get the flames
blazing with oil, and Sophia, if she's free,
daintly smudged with her slip daintily torn,
is climbing down this rope ladder, and we shoot up
from Coburn's P.O.V., he's got the gems;
that's where we throw in Charlotte Amalie
and the waterfront bars, and this Danish alley
with the heavies chasing, and we can keep all the
business of Jim on the rail, that lyric stuff
goes with the credits if you insist on keeping it tend-
er; I can see it, but things must get rough
pretty damn fast, or else you lose them, pally,
or, tell you what, let's save it for THE END.

ANNE WALDMAN ▪ ▪ ▪ ▪ ▪ ▪ ▪ ▪ ▪ ▪ ▪ ▪ ▪ ▪

Under My Breath

Of memory there was also a song of
poems where people were bargaining
Forget these lootings that seem to sob
Forget there would be a way out
Where I am I say I repeat I am solidly about
not to go under
I need this one chance I need this to begin
This was one's friends, ungovernable,
thorny, tyrannical
They are all disloyal tonight!
This was one's friends, a lifespan
This was one's friends, to freely exhale
This was one's friends, you're duped,
quick apprehension, I see the game now
This was one's friends, a soft spot
This was one's friends, a tone, a loud consequence
stiff, delicate, fierce, so odd a case over so-called "religion"
This was one's friends, no adequate forecast
This was it, this was one's friends, a calling
This was one's friends, I told you so
This was one's friends, 17 years ago,

you met his boat at the dock
This was one's friends, a wedding, kindness & ease,
operative charm
This was it, it was like this: friends in one's heart
It was like this—friends arriving
Travelled far since that evening,
since an afternoon in April
This was called waiting for one's friends
This was one's friends, supposing everything,
fatigue not in my line, believing all you hear,
a perceptible change in one of them,
wanting an excuse for not getting along,
susceptible, a big part was talking talking,
This was one's friends in the booth by the winds,
This was one's friends rarely a sad story
(A friend jumped off a building and died)
This was one's friends, we were out on a limb
This was one's friends living in the city
One had friends in a town near the mountains
Impute to negligence, alterations, Time?
This was the way it was with one's friends
borrowing money from one's friends
eating dinner with one's friends:
stopped in, an excursion to friends, working hard,
unmistakably one's friends
dazzling for one's friends, youth, powerplays,
a little sphere of misguided concern, control,
stammer, learn something about me!
This was not significant but this was one's friends
My friends can't be bought
This was one's friends, the world became more interesting,
extemporaneous, I see them repeatedly: my friends
My friends this is how they were: busy, funny, obscure
Behaviour is a mystery to me, o friends
This was one's friends in an airplane
This was one's friends—formidable, reassuring,
suffering, peculiar
All the friends writing in luminosity: ogres & angels
How intensely I see them, how shiny they are!
What was the intent were they shy & wonderful?
Were they greatly in command of their language?
For amusement, for amusement was part of the song
of my friends
See them in the great desert of years
Friends melt away
No, stay stay
An enemy keeps close, an enemy full of vivacity
Enemy just darkened the path
(One might imagine it: emptied shade).

Fait Accompli

Look down. Heavier now. Onus of observable spectrums. A
body resounds. It waxes. It hoards ammunition. O alas. My
lights are not what they are monitored to bide in. They are
mercantile and elegant prey. Subsist on the inward motion of
laborious practices. A stricter practice. And the Arab inside
is a kind of knight in armour or old Protestant crawling to
get into secondary light. Rides a secret channel not unlike a
flashlight beams its arrogant ray upon you. Hide, hide from
your own face. Then consider what it is you recoil from.
Politics, if such a hinge exists in a random universe. Alive &
still. Not to depress my native eyeballs but understand how
such a game exists called back to roost already warmed over
nihilism. Get up & out or spake as the Messiah doth. Back
again to bid time trumpet you are already born and dead
Hosa'na! ("save us"). Compassion hath a note in here.
What's wrong to take a hand, shake a hand & kiss the lady
when she's down. On the other hand: morbid, oblique, tired of
waiting for missiles to fire off (please never go off). Writing
you from a foxhole way down under under a moonless desert.
Would-be scholar get your cerebrum out here. Respond, or
something to that effect what means are required what
tableau vivants. What are the taboos around here? Do not
swear at the higher powers & keep your suffering to yourself.
Seasonal displays are mounted. I heard Frankie Boy
warbling in a lobby in Detroit decked with pine & pink satin
bows. I heard high soprano Noël notes careening down an
even longer corridor like a scream. Neighbors light a
menorah. The newspaper says Moslems are on the move and
we do not care as a populace, "to discuss religion." I meant
to tell you about the weaponry, the scorn, the flag-waving.
How it's a threat it's a fret but confusion is like the metabolic
street. Been out there lately?

Nerves

Nerves, blind attraction to,
scholar says
the margins are safe,
but deeper inside the book
we'll go, where nerves retreat and
study balances the mind
It was night. He was right.
A mind came down on me
the one I met in a book
My nerves sang off,

sounded down, and
out way back on a later burner
Come down upon me, nerves,
and have your argument
Alive & await the tide for another siesta
that brings drinks with literature
as in "Smoke & News"
So you go out on the Mall again
lifted up from the bed of sex & news
Okay his dream, her sleep patter,
his restlessness, her trance
or old patterns repeat,
and the dream of exacto knives
in books inside libraries returns
Pages of great ones being excised
for a greater purpose because they are
severe or salient manifestos
to be put up on all the lampposts
Here's one we missed . . .
The original manuscripts
were understandably fragile
But in the dream you are in the
Library of Congress or Yale's Beineke
& you are younger, bearded, hooded
a terrorist for language,
beautiful thief of rare text
How do you get the transmission
in paper a tide across time,
how do you pass muster
in your aggression versus
erudition's good will
Did you simply *breeze by* a librarian?
Homo homini lupus is a strange motto
How true is it? How brutal?
I—do you?—wonder how a neighbor could rape a neighbor,
or sue a friend, steal the
good stuff, envy a lawn
How atrocity twists under atrocity
How many times the gospel sings
a beautiful edge to get redeemed
or demystified, and someone official
glorifies war again
To get saved no matter your sin your skin
an ethnic closure & it goes like this:
different, different, territory, fixation
they are out to get us
& there is little to go around
Climatic karmic opposites?
Will intellectual rigor respond &
save all our miserable days

Pass the word around?
What sense of opulence did
a friendlier human score under,
An earlier benign time was it?

ROBERT PENN WARREN ▪ ▪ ▪ ▪ ▪ ▪ ▪ ▪ ▪ ▪ ▪

Night Walking

Bear my first thought, as waking, I hear
First bear off the mountain ripping apples
From trees near my window—but no,
It's the creak of the door of the shop my son stays in,
Who booted and breeched but bare
From waist, now stands
Motionless, silent, face up
To the moon, tonight full, now late zenithward high
Over forests as black as old blood and the crags bone-white.
My *levis* now on, and boots, I wait.
For what? As I creep behind a parked car and guiltily crouch.

Face brown, but now talc-white in moonlight,
Lifts moonward, and I think how once,
Footloose in Greece, in the mountains, alone, asleep,
At a distant howl he had waked and
Stood up in a land where all was true.

I crouch as he slowly walks up the track
Where from blackness of spruces great birches
Stand white and monitory—
Moving on upward, face upward as though
By stars in an old sea he steered.

In silence and shadow, in my
Undefinable impulse to steal what knowledge I, in love, may,
With laggard cunning I trail to the first ridge-crest.
He stops. His gaze
Turns slow, and slower,
From quarter to quarter, over
The light-laved land, over all
Thence visible, river and mowings,
Ruined orchards, ledges and rock-slides,
The clambering forest that would claim all:
Last, the next range to westward.

High there the moon rides calm.
He lifts up his light-bleached arms.
He stands.

He goes on.

I do not guess
How far he will go, but in my
Mixture of shame, guilt, and joy, do know
All else is his, and alone. In shadow
I huddle till, in solitude, I
Can start back to bed and the proper darkness of night.

But alone now in moonlight, I stop
As one paralyzed at a sudden black brink opened up,
For a recollection, sudden, has come from long back—
Moon-walking on sea-cliffs, I
Had once dreamed to a wisdom I could not name.
I heard no voice in the heart, just the hum of the wires.

But that is my luck. Not yours.

At any rate, you must swear never,
Not even in secret, the utmost, to be ashamed
To have lifted arms up to that icy
Blaze and transforming light of the world.

The Only Poem

The only poem to write I now have in mind
Will not be written because in memory, or eyes,
The scene is too vivid, so tears, not words, I find.
If, perhaps, I forget, it might catch me then by surprise.

But the facts lie long back, and are certainly trivial,
Though I've waked in the night, as though at a voice at my ear,
Till a flash of the dying dream comes back, and I haul
Up a sheet to angrily wipe at an angry tear.

My mother was middle-aged, and only retained
A sweetness of face, not the beauty my father, years later,
Near death, would try speaking of, could not, then refrained.
But the facts: that day she took me to see the new daughter

Of my friends left with Grandma while they went East for careers;
So, for friendship, I warily handled the sweet-smelling squaw-fruit,
All golden and pink, kissed the fingers, blew in the ears.
Then suddenly was at a loss. So my mother seized it,

And I knew, all at once, that she would have waited all day,
Sitting there on the floor, with her feet drawn up like a girl,
So half-laughing, half-crying, arms stretched, she swung up her prey,
And the prey shrieked with joy at the giddy swoop and swirl.

Yes, that was all, except for the formal farewell,
And wordless we wandered the snow-dabbled street, and day,
With her hands both clutching my arm till I thought it would swell,
Then home, fumbling key, she said: "Shucks! Time gets away!"

We entered. She laid out my supper. My train left at eight
To go back to the world where all is always the same.
Success nor failure—neither can alleviate
The pang of unworthiness that is built into Time's name.

Lessons in History

How little does history manage to tell?
Did lips of Judas go dry and cold on our Lord's cheek?

Or did tears spring, unwitting, to
His eyes as lips found torch-lit flesh?

What song, in his screechy voice, and joy, did Boone,
At sunset, sing, alone in Kaintuck's Eden wilderness?

Who would not envy Cambron as he uttered his famous word,
At last—at last—fulfilled in identity of pride?

Is it true that your friend was secretly happy when the
Diagnostician admitted, in fact, the growth was malignant?

After the mad Charlotte Corday had done her work
Did she dip her hands in the water now staining the tub?

And what did Hendrik Hudson see
That last night, alone, as he stared at the Arctic sky?

Or what, at night, is the strange joy with your pain intertwined
As you wander the dark house, your wife not long dead?

What thought had Ann Boleyn as, at last, the axe rose?
Did her parts go moist just before it fell?

And who will ever know how you, at night waking,
See a corner of moonlit meadow, willows, sheen of the whispering stream?

And who know, or guess, what, long ago, happened there?

Vermont Thaw

A soft wind southwesterly, something like
The wind in the Far West they call the *chinook*,
About three o'clock, we yet high on the mountain,
Began. Snow softened to burden our snowshoes.

And if you stood perfectly still, so still
You could hear your own heart, stroke by stroke,
You could hear the forest of spruces—*drip*,
Drip, drip—and you felt that all Time, and your life,

Was like that in motionless silence, and held you
Your breath to be sure you could hear your own heart
Maintain, with no falter, that rhythm that drops
Now defined. Were you sure you remembered your name?

But there was the A-frame, the camp, snow sliding
Down the steep roof-pitch with channels of black
Where all winter your eye had loved whiteness, and now
Roof-edge dripped in the rhythm that redefined

Life. And the sun, in pink pillows of mist,
Sank, and you felt it gasping for breath.
You felt it might suffocate, not rise
Again. Inside the A-frame you found

Yourself sweating, though only one eye of a coal
Yet winked. You built up only enough
To cook by, racked up the snowshoes—all this
With no word. What word is to say when the world

Has lost heart, is dripping, is flowing, is counting
Itself away? Cooking is but
An irritation. The pre-dinner whiskey
Is tongue-hot but tangless, like rot-gut—not what

It is. When you turn on the hi-fi, your friend
Says: "None of that ordure tonight." In silence
You eat—silence except for the eaves-drip.
No banking the fire on a night like this.

You wake in the dark to the rhythm of eaves.
Try to comfort yourself by thinking of spring.
Of summer's fecundity and the plunge
Into silvery splash-spray. Of gold and flame

In benediction of autumn. Of snow's first
Night-whisper and dawn light on peak-top. But eaves,
To your heart, say one thing. Say: *drip.* Say: *drip.*
You must try to think of some answer, by dawn.

Dead Horse in Field

In the last, far field, half-buried in barberry bushes, red-fruited,
The thoroughbred lies dead, left foreleg shattered below knee,
A 30.06 in heart. In distance,
I see the gorged crows rise ragged in wind. The day after death
I went for farewell, and the eyes were already gone—
That the work of beneficent crows. Eyes gone,
The two-year-old could, of course, more readily see
Down the track of pure and eternal darkness.

A week later I didn't get close. The sweet stink
Had begun. That damned wagon-mudhole, hidden
By leaves as we galloped—I found it.
Spat on it. Just as a child would.
Next day the buzzards. How beautiful in air,
Carving the slow and concentric downward pattern of vortex, glint
On wings. From the house, now with glasses, I see
The squabbles and pushing, the waggle of wattle-red heads.

At evening I watch the buzzards, the crows,
Arise. They swing black in Nature's flow and perfection
Against the sad carmine of sunset.
Forgiveness is not indicated. They are
What they are.

How long before I go back to find
An intricate piece of fake modern sculpture,
White now by weather and sun, assuming in stasis
New beauty. Then,
Say two years after that, the green twine of vine,
Each leaf heart-shaped, soft as velvet,
Or a baby's kiss, beginning
Its benediction.

It thinks it is God.

Afterward

After the promise has been kept, or
Broken. After the sun

Has touched the western peak and you suddenly
Realize that Time has cut another notch

In the stick with your name on it, and you wonder
How long before you will feel the need

For prayer. After you have stumbled on
The obituary of a once-girl, photograph now unrecognizable,

Who used to come at night to your apartment and do everything but
It. Would fight like a tiger. Then weep.

Never married, but made, as the paper says,
A brilliant career, also prominent in good works. After

You have, in shame, lain awake trying to account for
Certain deeds of vanity, weakness, folly, or

Neurosis, and have shuddered in disbelief. After
You have heard the unhearable lonely wolf-howl of grief

In your heart, and walked a dark house, feet bare. After
You have looked down on the unimaginable expanse of polar

Ice-cap stretching forever in light of gray-green ambiguousness,
And lulled by jet-hum, wondered if this

Is the only image of eternity.—Oh, menhirs, monoliths! and all
Such thrusts of stone, arms in anguished fantasy towering, images

By creatures, hairy and humped, on heath, on hill, in holt
Raised. Oh, see

How a nameless skull, by weather uncovered or
The dateless winds,

In the moonlit desert smiles, having been
So long alone. After all, are you ready

To return the smile? Try. Sit down by a great cactus,
While other cacti, near and as far as distance, lift up

Their arms, thorny and black, in unresting ritual above
Tangles of black shadow on white sand, to that great orb

Of glowing light, queenly for good or evil, in
The absolute sky. After you have sat

In company a while, perhaps trust will grow.
Perhaps you can start a conversation of mutual comfort.

There must be so much to exchange.

Death of Time

Over meadows of Brittany, the lark
Flames sunward, divulging, in tinselled fragments from
That height, song. Song is lost
In the blue depth of sky, but
We know it is there at an altitude where only
God's ear may hear.

Dividing fields, the hedges, in white
Bloom powdered, gently slope to
Blue of sea that glitters in joy of its being.

Yes—who was the man who on the midnight street-corner,
Alone, once stood, while sea fog
Put out last lights, electric or heavenly?
Who knows that history is the other name for death?
Who, from the sweated pillow, wakes to know
How truth can lie? Who knows the jealousy,
Like a cinch-bug, under the greenest turf, thrives?
Who learned that kindness can be the last cruelty?

I have shut my eyes and seen the lark flame upward.
All was as real as when my eyes were open.
I have felt earth breathe beneath my shoulder blades.
I have strained to hear, sun-high, that Platonic song.

It may be that some men, dying, have heard it.

Dawn

Dawnward I wake. In darkness wait.
Wait for first light to seep in as sluggish and gray
As tide-water fingering timbers in a long-abandoned hulk.
In darkness I try to make out accustomed objects.

But cannot. It is as though
Their constituent atoms had gone sleep and forgotten
Their duty of identity. But at first
Inward leakage of light they will stir

To the mathematical dance of existence. Bookcase,
Chest, chairs, they will dimly loom, yearn
Toward reality. Are you
Real when asleep? Or only when,

Feet walking, lips talking, or
Your member making its penetration, you

Enact, in a well-designed set, that ectoplasmic
Drama of laughter and tears, the climax of which always

Strikes with surprise—though the script is tattered and torn?
I think how the ground mist is thinning, think
How, distantly eastward, the line of dark woods can now
Be distinguished from sky. Many

Distinctions will grow, and some
Will, the heart knows, be found
Painful. On the far highway,
A diesel grinds, groans on the grade.

Can the driver, I wonder, see color above the far woods yet?
Or will dawn come today only as gray light through
Clouds downward soaking, as from a dirty dish-rag?
I think of a single tree in a wide field.

I wonder if, in this grayness, the tree will cast a shadow.
I hold up my hand. I can vaguely see it. The hand.
Far, far, a crow calls. In gray light
I see my hand against the white ceiling. I move

Fingers. I want to be real. Dear God,
To Whom, in my triviality,
I have given only trivial thought,
Will I find it worthwhile to pray that you let

The crow, at least once more, call?

Nameless Thing

I have no name for the nameless thing
That after midnight walls the house, usually
Soundless, but sometimes a creak on a tiptoed stair,
Or something like breath to a minimum shuttered.

But sometimes in silence the effluvium
Of its being is enough, perhaps in a pale,
Not quite sickening sweetness seemingly left
By funeral flowers, sometimes like sweat

Under gross armpits. It is the odor of
A real existence lost in the unreality
Of dead objects of day that now painfully try to stir
In darkness. Every stone has its life, we know.

Barefoot, in darkness, I walk the house, a heavy
Poker seized from the hearth, I stand
Just by a door that seems ready to open.
I wait for the first minute motion, first whisper of hinges.

I hold my breath. I am ready. I think of blood.
I fling the door open. Only a square
Of moonlight lies on the floor inside. All is in order.
I go back to bed. I hear the blessed breath there.

But once, on a very dark night, it was almost different.
That night I was certain. Trapped in a bathroom!
I snatched the door open, weapon up, and yes, by God!—
But there I stood staring into a mirror. Recognition

Came almost too late. But how could I
Have been expected to recognize what I am?
In any case, that was what happened. I now lie
Rigid abed, and hear namelessness stalk the dark house.

I wonder why it cannot rest.

If

If this is the way it is, we must live through it.
Even though the spiked harrow of nightmare until dawn
Rips the humus of experience, and suggests
Your own exit therefrom. Even through bliss,
Which can seem more absolute than a clock's
Last tick in a dark-shrouded room. But

If this is the way it is, let us clamber
Crag-upward from the white-slashed beach and stare
Over tangled tumult until the soul is absorbed
In the blue perfection of unnamable distance.
The horizon is our only dream of Truth.

If this is the way it is—and I have stood
Alone, alone, past midnight long, heart empty,
In the middle of the dark and unpopulated
Piazza Navona—what is the use
Of remembering a dream from childhood? Particularly,
Since that was the future all dreams had led to.
I shut eyes now, but still see
The discarded newspaper blown
Over stones wise with suffering. The paper
Carries yesterday with it. I hear

It scrape the stones. It carries yesterday
To tomorrow.

If this is the way it is, we need, perhaps,
A new definition of Self, who have long thought
Courage enough to live by. What
Can the sea tell us of a drop we cup in the hand?
What, as tide slinks away, can a drop,
Caught on the landward side of a pebble,
Tell us of the blind depth of groan out yonder?

You Sort Old Letters

Some are pure business, land deals, receipts, a contract,
Bank statements, dead policies, demand for some payment.
But a beach-party invite!—yes, yes, that tease
Of a hostess and you, withdrawn beyond dunes, lay,
The laughter far off, and for contact
Of tongue and teeth, she let you first loosen a breast.
You left town soon after—and now wonder what
Might that day have meant.

Suppose you hadn't left town—well, she's dead anyway.
Three divorces, three children, all born for the sludge of the pit.
It was Number One, nice fellow, when she took you to the dunes,
And gasped: "Harder, bite harder!" And you did
In the glare of day. When she scrambled up,
She cried: "Oh, don't you hate me!" And wept
Like a child. You patted, caressed her.
Cuddled and kissed her. She said: "I'm a shit."

Do you seem to remember that, for a moment,
Your heart stirred? But you shrug now, remembering
How, in the end, she shacked up
With a likker-head plumber, who, now and then,
Would give her a jolt to the jaw, or with heel of a palm
Would flatten lips to the teeth, then slam
Her the works, blood
On her swollen lips—as was common gossip.

You married a little late—and now in this mess
Of old papers the words at your stare:
You were smart to blow town. Keep your pecker up!
Signed only: *Yours, maybe.*

Of course, she had everything—money, looks,
Wit, breeding, a charm

Of defenseless appeal—the last what trapped, no doubt,
The three near middle-aged fall guys, who got only
Horns for their pains. Yes, she threw all away.
And as you've guessed, by struggling
Sank deeper and deeper into
A slough of self-hate. However, you

Are no psychiatrist, and couldn't say
What or why, as you, far away, lay

By the warm and delicious body you loved
So well, in the dark ashamed of
Recurring speculations, as though this
Betrayed your love. Years passed. The end, you heard,
Was sleeping pills. You felt some confusion, or guilt—
But how could you be blamed?—Even if
Knees once were grinding sand as sun once smote
Your bare back, or, in a dream, lips,
Bloody, lifted for your kiss.

The Whole Question

You'll have to rethink the whole question. This
Getting born business is not as simple as it seemed,
Or the midwife thought, or doctor deemed. It is,
Time shows, more complicated than either—or you—ever dreamed.

If it can be said that you dreamed anything
Before what's called a hand slapped blazing breath
Into you, snatched your dream's lulling nothing-
ness into what—was it Calvin?—called the body of this death.

You had not, for instance, previsioned the terrible thing called love,
Which began with a strange, sweet taste and bulbed softness while
Two orbs of tender light leaned there above.
Sometimes your face got twisted. They called it a smile.

You noticed how faces from outer vastness might twist, too.
But sometimes different twists, with names unknown,
And there were noises with no names you knew,
Or times of dark silence when you seemed nothing—or gone.

Years passed, but sometimes seemed nothing except the same.
You knew more words, but they were words only, only—
Metaphysical midges that plunged at the single flame
That centered the inward dark of your skull, or lonely, lonely

You woke in the dark of real night to hear the breath
That seemed to promise reality in the vacuum
Of the sleepless dream beginning when underneath
The curtain dawn seeps, and on wet asphalt first tires hum.

Yes, you must try to rethink what is real. Perhaps
It is only a matter of language that traps you. You
May find a new way in which experience overlaps
Words. Or find some words that make the Truth come true.

LEWIS WARSH ■ ■ ■ ■ ■ ■ ■ ■ ■ ■ ■ ■ ■ ■ ■ ■ ■

Travelogue

To merely uncover the depths of love
By sitting here same spot establishes dignity
No more submissive than he was to his mother
A love forgotten but the lover's body remains
A ring of pure light circles the earth every hour
The point from which you begin to distort what you're trying to say
My imaginary brother follows me like a shadow
The woman upstairs says she thinks her dog found something that resembles a
    gerbil & ate it
Neitszche was fun to read in prison
You can't love something that doesn't exist
The church, family, a tree whose branches fell off in the storm
No one will punish you if you feel too much pleasure
It's not cold outside but inside—it's like winter
What I saw when I looked down at the woman & her lover was a reflection of the
    shadow of the heart broken into shards
The agency of the letter moves through the fabric of fate
I had a crush on my neighbor but she moved out of town
The dress is made of cotton—it's really a jumper
How to hold a stranger at arm's length & comfort him?
The strangest part was when there was no place to go, no home, & I had to sit on
    stoops, out-doors, or loiter in shops, linger in restaurants over glasses of iced
    coffee & mint tea
Unable to speak the language of the Cantonese waitress whose job was "off the
    books" & whose livelihood depended on the amount of money I tipped her
Everything derives from a lack of attention, broken span into which something
    drops
Depending on the day of the week or your mother I love you, hate you more
    some days
I stand on the edge of town, light burning in the window
I drive through hopeless Canada, aching with dignity

I walk into the bodega & buy a lightbulb & a loose cigarette
A transparency of hair catches the flame of his first desire
They met in 1965 & lived together 4 years
Dark hallway filled with guys I don't know, smoking
I've saved some dinner, all I have to do is heat it up
When she returns from her job she neither kisses me nor says hello
The people who cut through the fog with scythes went on strike
Desire overcomes inertia, but the stones survive.

A Man Escaped

Words escape through gaps:
meaning converts them into conduits.
Stained leaves. Dyed parchment
on which nothing is crossed out.
The words begin to swagger through the
whiteness of a last refrain,
then draw back, seductive, as if no
longer responsible, compromising
themselves like a series of defective vehicles
that have to be shipped back to the factory
from the dealership window.
Invective in a starling's mouth,
refracting pleasure down to the last decibel.

Mistaken Identity

There's a little fear piercing
the air at the boundary of the self

it's the same self I saw under the awning
back in '63

Yesterday we saw the mushroom with
the orange flecks that grew up
out of the earth after last week's big
rain

It seems like anyone could shoot an arrow
& pierce my heart

Of love, bursting into flame, I inhale
the sweet smoke, hidden under the pale
refrain of all the old leaves

& now some leaves are falling
around the steps of the porch

& the wizened fish under the dock
are suffering
in our absence

Elegy

The leaves have a sense of
where they fall when they
return to earth

but as they dangle in the wind
like corpses swaying
from a branch

they replace the pure
space of their being
with an act of attention

which passes like
a lullaby through
the eye of a storm.

Good Omen

We study other languages, the signs and mirrors,
so that we can inhabit the conversations of people
we've never met. Lava comes down from the side of the
mountain: we say *lava,* in our original tongue, and
no one knows what we mean. The fire brigade is
waiting for the flames to die out at the end of
the tunnel. I see you, cornered at the edge of a
sentence, like a German verb, immune to criticism,
open to judgement, a blue shadow igniting a wall
of flame. In the empty restaurant you say: "My
tongue is on fire," but the only lights are the
flickering candles on every table. The contortionist
brought the audience to its feet, but we weren't
watching. We decided we could only do one thing
at a time without becoming an object of concern for
those who were observing us from a distance. Nights
without sleep, endless stamina, a hundred laps,
the long days ahead filled with words like "opposite
attract" spelled out in billboard letters across

the horizon. This is the correct spelling, the
proper verb ending, the appropriate declension.
We can tutor each other at odd hours while nervously
fingering the buttons and zippers of our shirts and
blouses. This flame is for safekeeping, the tail
of a comet as it crosses the sky.

BRUCE WEIGL ▪ ▪ ▪ ▪ ▪ ▪ ▪ ▪ ▪ ▪ ▪ ▪ ▪ ▪ ▪ ▪ ▪ ▪

The Impossible

Winter's last rain and a light I don't recognize
through the trees and I come back in my mind
to the man who made me suck his cock
when I was seven, in sunlight between boxcars.
I thought I could leave him standing there
in the years, half smile on his lips,
small hands curled into small fists,
but after he finished, he held my hand in his
as if astonished until the houses were visible
just beyond the railyard. He held my hand
but before that he slapped me hard on the face
when I would not open my mouth for him.
I do not want to say his whole hips
slammed into me, but they did, and a black wave
washed over my brain, changing me
so I could not move among my people in the old way.
On my way home I stopped in the churchyard
to try and find a way to stay alive.
In the branches a red-wing flitted, warning me.
In the rectory Father prepared
the body and the blood for mass
but God could not save me from a mouthful of cum.
That afternoon some lives turned away from the light.
He taught me how to move my tongue around.
In his hands he held my head like a lover.
Say it clearly and you make it beautiful, no matter what.

Why We Are Forgiven

Men still make steel in the hellish mill
though thousands are laid off and dazed
they do the shopping
for their working wives and dream

the blast furnace rumble.
Mill dust and red slag grit
is blood for some people.
Around hot steel these men twisted bands
until their fingers would not open in the morning,
and in my hungry brain
a spirit recalls my father
home from the mill in his white t-shirt
like a god
and the smell of hot steel
all over his body
and the taste of his delicious sweat.
Those evenings when he touched me,
those lingering hours after work and beer
when he reached down
into the nowhere my fear invented
I would come alive.
I would be drunk with joy
and in my small bed I heard the ore boats
call from the river
and the rail cars
couple in the roundhouse
and the ringing hammer voices
of the night shift workers
sing us free.

Red Squirrel

I think it's good the squirrel lives with us,
in secret in our fifties style ranch
beneath the pale, unsheltered sky.
From the world she is a gift of sorts,
a strange and awkward blessing
who wakes us from our cold dawn sleep

to watch the sun come up through trees.
I think it means the air in here must be alive;
the stale basement walls a womb,
a nest inside a womb beyond
the muted rise and fall, our voices
as we move from room to room.

And she must know the odd forgiven
terrors of a family life, the love that has to fight
to stay alive. So from this man at my front door
I turn away, his traps and poison
held before him like a gift, a gilded
reckless sin I know for once not to embrace.

Our 17th Street Years

Just the luck of the draw

my father would say

slouched in his white t-shirt

long neck bottle of beer

dangling from his terrible hand

He'd meant to tell me what the world was

so I imagined

a life of my hand held out

the good spirits   waiting somehow

in the misty bamboo groves   yet

no words came as I had hoped

no webs of light connecting me

no paths that said to follow

no dove against the sky   no sky

THEODORE WEISS ▪ ▪ ▪ ▪ ▪ ▪ ▪ ▪ ▪ ▪ ▪ ▪ ▪ ▪ ▪

Flypaper

(after a drawing by Hokusai)

What's going on here?
It must be a wind we see,
gusty ghost clutching papers
and a body to make out.

Who else but a poet,
ragged gaffer on a spree,
chasing after some fantastic
image of pure ecstasy:

leaped to this sheet,
he's so inspired by what
he draws it sweeps the pages
off.
    Higher and higher
those papers flap, a few
at the top fast disappearing,
while specks—are they

letters, rancorous
at being stuck, fly-like
taking off?—every which way
fling themselves about.

Their loftiest,
tethered as to a string,
must be the star he, dangled
from, dare not let go.

He flailing out
such skyscraping caper
that sails him like a kite,
we can appreciate the mighty

transport he's set free
by way of this, his flypaper.

Shorthand

> The great draughtsman
> is bound to reveal the
> utmost . . . in him . . . in
> any scrawl whatsoever. . . .
>   —BERNARD BERENSON

With a scribble like yours
its chief delight must be
the scribbling itself, as one
walks out for walking's sake,

then pauses at the prospect
of a thought that insists
on having its own landscape
to the least detail explored.

So the wind, steady here
as if held by what it's doing,

by its voice's resonance,
in our sycamore.
                    Enough
time passed, even you make
out your scribbles haltingly,
opaque
            like hieroglyphs,
till one, engrossed in them
for their own stance, divines
their meaning,
            as if you'd
found the signature decisive
for the moment, belonging
to it alone.
                    Yet looking
back, as ever you are amazed
by unmapped routes you've
had to travel, filthy

alleys, tedious detours,
deadends also. Meant to pay
the costly toll of the truth
your thought was after?

But finally a shorthand
highway led to your pleasure:
that thought, you realize, and
what it did, the treasure,

exciting precisely because
it cannot, past its curlicues
and the sure way it wiggles
down the page, be read.

RENÉE AND THEODORE WEISS ▪ ▪ ▪ ▪ ▪ ▪ ▪ ▪

A Conference

"Everyone in this room
knows at least two languages."

The same languages
being known become different?

Twenty-two everyones
knowing forty-four languages?

Forty-four ways of
arguing about the same thing?

Forty-four ways of
making the same thing strange?

A new language flowers:
the forty-fifth? the sixtieth?

But a new language
as every poem is meant to be?

Everyone in the room
knows at least two languages.

Everyone in the room
longs to be free of language.

Everyone in the room
longs to be free of the room.

For Gil and Other Incurables

Matter? More than anything else,
getting yourself down on the page
as on a blank check that yields
whatever riches you declare.
                         No need
to consider the wild fluctuations
in the currency, the wilfulness
of the traders,
                 imponderables
like the weather, crops.
                         You
assumed everything depended on you:
your words would easily catch all
the world's hungry fishermen.
                              Now,
though you finally had to let go,
your pride, ever defiant of reality,
still blazons forth,
                     a reality
all your own that only the impossible
can make possible.

Outside the Hospital

He says
when they made this place
they sure knew what they were doing.
He carries the dead woman
everyday from her grave
in the shining sky down
into a small garden,
where a light snow
is falling.
He is her lover, and he brings her here,
knowing he is not allowed
to bring her here.
She sees the flowers he's planted
and thanks him
and tells him what their names are.
He says he will never forget them.
The two lie on the ground
beside snow-dusted flowers.
She's in love with the ground
and the flowers,
but not with their names,
and not with him, who is saying them.
She hears him, feels his face
next to her face.
Disappearing forever is the only solution.

My Life

after Henri Michaux

Somehow it got into my room.
I found it, and it was, naturally, trapped.
It was nothing more than a frightened animal.
Since then I raised it up.
I kept it for myself, kept it in my room,
kept it for its own good.
I named the animal, My Life.
I found food for it and fed it with my bare hands.
I let it into my bed, let it breathe in my sleep.
And the animal, in my love, my constant care,
grew up to be strong, and capable of many clever tricks.

One day, quite recently,
I was running my hand over the animal's side
and I came to understand
that it could very easily kill me.
I realized, further, that it *would* kill me.
This is why it exists, why I raised it.
Since then I have not known what to do.
I stopped feeding it,
only to find that its growth
has nothing to do with food.
I stopped cleaning it
and found that it cleans itself.
I stopped singing it to sleep
and found that it falls asleep faster without my song.
I don't know what to do.

I no longer make My Life do tricks.
I leave the animal alone and, for now,
it leaves me alone, too.
I have nothing to say, nothing to do.
Between My Life and me,
a silence is coming.
Together, we will not get through this.

All That Really Happens

My whole family has died.
There is a song about it.
I can't remember the sun on my skin.
Not remembering is a house.
There are no rooms in this house.
There are so many animals.
I would like to gather up one by one
the animals into my bed.
I would like to sleep with them
in the sleep that comes after the house.
My whole family is dead.
There is a song about it.
The animals would sing the song.
Each animal thinks
about singing
and then sleeps
upon a tiny word-
colored plot of sun.
Each owes on its plot,
owes more than it could possibly pay.
This owing is all that really happens.

Promise

I will turn on nothing.
I will take my walk in the fire.
I will sing the song I hear
coming from the fire where I walk.
I will not look into the fire.
I will stay in my room,
singing a song I can barely remember.
I will turn into the fire.
I will sing a song I can barely remember.
I will bury my room in my bed
and carry my bed into the fire.
I will not hear the song at all.
There will be my voice,
just my voice,
and words that couldn't possibly have been in the song.

Send New Beasts

These beasts will not do.

1 Their bleeding is decidedly inadequate—from a distance they appear not to bleed at all. Considering the likelihood of distance in today's spectator, this is not a small problem.

2 While they are exotic enough in appearance—and I assume this is why they were selected—they have a tendency, and an ability, to hide themselves in plain view. I don't claim to understand this ability—I only know that it is widely felt that, even at close range, they are difficult to get a good look at, and this is especially true when a blow is being struck upon them. It's almost as if they're immune to isolation—as if they are able to always appear, no matter how alone they are, in the noise and confusion of a herd.

3 They are far too obedient and willing to receive blows. Indeed, they seem to sense when a blow is coming and to move intuitively into it. If this movement was desperate—graceful or graceless—it might generate some interest, but it seems to fall, tragically, somewhere in between. That is, they seem able, at every point in their torture, to collapse in a reasonable fashion, as if the collapse was being dictated by their own will. No one enjoys—I don't think I even need to tell you—a reasoned collapse. It is this aspect of the beasts that most deeply defeats us, our simple want of a show.

4 Their attacks—and I hesitate to even call them attacks—are largely indistinguishable from the active reasoning of their own collapse. It is as though they seek above all to expose us to this activity of theirs—to infect us with their will to reason, and in so doing, reduce us to the unvarying rhythm of their irreducible

herd. I would like to say that we are immune to this reduction, but I am not sure. In any case, I see no good reason for continuing to subject ourselves to these attacks. It would be better to have no beasts at all—to live altogether outside of shows—than to sink numbly into tolerance of a spectacle which fails to clarify what it is that distinguishes us from beasts.

We Were a Whole Army Underground

We were a whole army underground;
we did not move.
We were replicas, at first,
but the army above,
the men we were shaped to resemble,
moved, spoke, faded, and came
to rot in shallow graves above us.
We were never them;
even as the workers painted our eyes
the colors of their eyes,
even as they hauled us by torch-light
into the vast royal burial chamber
and made us to stand the way they stood, once,
above, we were never them.
When our faces were finally finished
and our ranks were formed,
we stood guard over the absence
of the one who required us.
No one was allowed to look.
The chambers were sealed
and the last few torches burned down.
We stood suddenly alone in silent darkness.
We knew, though, that someone above
could imagine us, and we could sleep
standing up in that image.
The workers, who painted our eyes
and carved our horses' manes,
could imagine us—the priests,
who looked into our faces and blessed us
before and for this dark, could imagine,
and knew that we were there.
But then they moved, faded, and came to rot.
We were still spoken of, as time passed,
but only as an *idea,* as though
we did not actually stand here
inside the earth, in these colors,
these unseeing eyes, this dark.
No one any longer imagined us as real;
we had to imagine ourselves,

the way we looked, the way we stood,
from the inside,
from the stillness of our own hearts.
And we did learn to see ourselves in this way:
blind, colorful, standing guard over nothing.
And we came to accept, in the stillness of the years,
that we would not be found.
Our guard would not be relieved,
our faces would never be hauled up
into the sharp light that forged us.

You, then, came as a surprise.
Your small force overwhelmed us so easily—
it seems impossible to imagine
that we were, all the while, that vulnerable.
And we could not even say from whence you came.
Had you come from afar, intent on plundering our stillness,
should we not have seen you coming?
It seems more likely you came from within,
from nothing,
escaping it perhaps,
but if so, what kept you back for so long?
We surely never intended to confine you.
If you have come, after all, to relieve us of our guard—
and this is our hope, of course—
we are grateful,
we forgive you for having taken so long,
and we surrender to you all we know,
which is just the patience to withstand
the nothing you came from.

Museum

The pattern is only ever of animal success,
the cry of a real gathering
misheard and losing itself
toward the idea of a sound
which was not a blade.

We are unique only insofar as we have learned to sleep
in this sound, or in the idea of this sound,
only in so far as we imagine the pattern could be faded.
Our uniqueness, however, is all that really fades,
as certain cries cannot be tolerated, missing.

Writer

A person, for you, is a book.
Impossible to categorize,
it veers from non-sense verse
to the most tedious of novels
and back
in just a breath.
And the book ends, the book ends.
And what makes the person more real,
then,
than a book,
is just that you cannot re-read
one chapter, one sentence, one word.
You must re-write him,
her,
and you cannot.
You cannot.
This inability is the source
of everything you have to say.

Each Sentence Is Into the Fast

When none of this interests me I distort my jaw
so that the teeth in my mouth
touch one another in a new way.
The newness of the way is nothing
but the impossibly mild seizure of a stall
I cannot hope to understand or complete.
Nevertheless, I muster at the stall
until the newness of the way is old.
Until all that is new is the muster itself,
as though the devouring force could be turned
once and for all
into the fast
that even its simplest tools
cannot stop promising.

The Only Fortunate Thing

You have an idea of yourself.
It is a kind of building.

This building stands on the sound
of your heart-beat,
the imaginary width
of rhythm.

All night
it stands there.
On a sound,
an imaginary width.

It is fortunate, really—
really, the only fortunate thing—
that there is no one in the building.

REED WHITTEMORE ▪ ▪ ▪ ▪ ▪ ▪ ▪ ▪ ▪ ▪ ▪ ▪ ▪

Smiling Through

Who are these figures in the street?
They are my friends.
They are wearing armbands.
They are marching along with my coffin, and smiling,
Pleased to be taking me to the boneyard,
Wishing me well and dreaming of all the brave toasts to me
That they will make when they have disposed of me.

And who are these figures in dozens of windows upon the street?
They are my strangers.
They are happy too.

Yes, everyone is happy, even I,
Smiling in my box in the new world that is mine and theirs,
Wearing my old tuxedo.
It had a dull time when I was living.
It was always hanging in closets dreaming of ballrooms.
At last it has found its niche.
Its lapels shine. *It* is happy.

And now they have lowered and left me.
Alone at last.
I have infinite riches in a little room.
I travel much here.
And other quotations.
Also I have my smile, I have my body, I have my body fluid.
I look at my ceiling,
Which is very low and pasted with my past.
There is my mother in a yellowing snapshot,
Wearing her blue travelling suit and beret
And standing smiling into the sun beside a lifeboat
On *The Duchess of Richmond.*
And there is my father beside the very same lifeboat.

He is wearing a wrinkled white suit, shading his eyes,
Smiling.
But where am I? Oh yes I am there too, by the lifeboat.
I am busy being sixteen,
With my hair slicked back and my sullenness showing,
Asking, Why are these people broadening me with travel?
But I am smiling also, thinly. It is *de rigeur.*

Yes, and my old dog Totty is there, the samoyede,
But not by the lifeboat.
He is sitting beside me, a child, in a gravel driveway,
And he is grinning, ear unto ear, down the long years.

So here we are, happy. But quiet. For it is quiet.
If I were to breathe, the sound of breathing would be like the sound of
    waterfalls.

If I were to move, the rustling would frighten the cemetery caretaker in his ugly
    stone house.
If I were to speak—ah, but I am speaking.
It is a trick of mine, to speak as I speak without speaking,
Almost as good as to die as I die without dying.
So I am lying here. Why am I lying here? What is my state?

So hard to know sometimes. And so I am smiling.

Mother's Past

Mother's past is full of old cars with very large fenders,
Against which the young are leaning in knickers and caps
And very large skirts and fixed smiles,
As the photographer, who is mother, puts the end of her finger
On the edge of the lens, says Please Don't Move,
And then moves, pushing the button.
In a moment they will be gone down the driveway waving,
Chugging into the future with dust rising
And kerchiefs floating out wildly over the fenders,
All gone except mother who now clambers
Up the rickety steps to the porch where she sits in her rocker
With her Kodak.
But the snapshots have none of that, only the fenders
And fixed smiles, only the moments
Very far back when everyone stood
As still as they could and tried not to blink,
So that those who came later could look and say, Yes it was
Like that then, just like that, including Ma's finger.

So it was like that. A book full of fenders.
But was there not more?
Ask yourself as you flip through the pages, the Martians,
Where are they? And the funny crepuscular organs of dream sheep?
It was on the first of July in aught-seven,
As Ronald was walking home from the office at even,
That he saw at the end of the street, partly hidden by bushes,
What appeared at first to be Jesus but was not Jesus,
But Charles Darwin!
And then there was Aunt Mathilda who departed her mind
In the sweets shop and no one had film. And so many
So many others boiling and stewing
In time's pot, they were missed by the Kodak
Too. How many were missed?
Ask.
Ask how many were missed that it takes to make a good
Past for a life or a book.
The answer is always more pictures than poor mother took.

The Crow and the Fox

there was an old status quo
who lived in a rotten borough
he played auld lang syne
every morning at nine
on a Wurlitzer once owned by Nero

sang a little pink crow morosely
the little pink crow was not entirely twenty
he had beautiful long pink tail feathers with streaks of academic epiphany
glimmering at the bright edges underneath which was visible
a union label
he was tired he was cross he had been at a weeklong meeting
of liberals bleating
and wanted to break something
but had nothing handy to break so kept singing

there was a platform that died
of principles putrefied
they buried it far out at sea
lest it pollute the grand old partee
but it floated ashore on a red tide

yes he was a pitiful case
the little pink crow
he was tired he was cross he was thinking of blowing up Westchester
or maybe the Alamo

to remind himself that he was still a young crow
and he assured himself that whatever he blew up he would blow
with a clean bomb
a bomb that killed only neoconservatives
        and foxes
           and especially neoconservative foxes
so he sang
        there was an old fox in Kildare
        who lied more than anyone else there
        and did so each day
        in such a wise way
        that Kildare made him the mayor there

of course the little pink crow wished he had something better to do than sing
    sour songs
and wished too that he had something better to drown his sour in
than the glass of red wine that he held in his right claw
having picked it up at a neoconservative store
and having carried it up to his bough in his right claw
only to find it sour
which was also why he sang sour

now by a strange quirk of fortune a neoconservative fox
with a nefarious nose for grapes and the grape
was at this moment meandering in the little pink crow's arbor looking smug
he was unlike the crow
in being yellow mostly
and unlike the crow
in being tory wholly
and in singing tory
with such infelicity
as would make any pink crow sickly

        there was an industrious beaver
        who decided to make the sea over
        by trading the sea and the sand
        he did so and found it not grand
        so traded them back and felt liberaller

what clever half rhymes he thought smugly
and proceeded smugly

        there was a young swindler from Sweden
        who conspired to do the old king in
        but his anarchist friend was in France
        doing over their *ambiance*
        so he settled for socialism

alas suddenly the smug yellow neoconservative fox did not feel at all smug
he felt the smugness drain right out of him
he stood in the arbor empty as an abandoned oil drum and needing a pickmeup

panting for a pickmeup
a bit of the grape
        chilled or unchilled
            with or without soda
thinking that perhaps if he prayed for one
or genuflected gracefully for one
it would arrive
        it would suddenly be there
so that he began to think no longer of clever half rhymes or
            quarter rhymes
but of the suitable words for a suitable prayer
beginning perhaps with I thank thee fair fox on high
for the favor I trust you will now supply
        when he saw
a little pink crow
clutching a glass of the grape
        in his right claw
and he said to himself the high one
        is certainly teasing me with that one

well the little pink crow
had been watching the yellow fox for a bit
and disliking him for a bit
and thinking that with such a nose
he must be a neoconservative
who lived for the grape
a craving the little pink crow had found socially meretricious
and made fun of at meetings
by holding up a glass of red vinegaw
        such as that he now held in his right claw
and inviting topers to tope
and then watching them grimace and caw
at which time he'd sing
        as he now sang

        there was an old stew in a zoo
        whose breath was so strong it made glue
        by gad said the apes
        if those are bad grapes
        just think what the good ones could do

noble pink crow
        said the yellow fox brightly
was it your voice I just heard singing so sprightly
and is that delicate red glass that you hold in your right claw
a glass of the nectaw
often celebrated in poetry song and light operaw?

yes my dear vulpes yes
        the pink crow cawed sweetly

it is a glass of the very best burgundy
ever trampled out in napa county
it has a soft bouquet
it has won prizes in paraguay
you would find it enchanting if you could have a sip
but unfortunately it happens to be my last nip
until after the corvinal fast days
so please excuse me
           as I sit down to my burgundy

wait wait cried the yellow fox quickly
I'll have an idea quickly
and in the meantime I would remind you
           that you are too smart a crow
too musical
           too full of the essentially lyrical
to be sitting up there alone drinking alone
what you need is intelligent cameraderie
in a festive atmosphere conducive to creativity
           and for intelligent *cameraderie*
you can't beat sharing the red-eye
with a fox like me
           you simply
pour a bit of the nectaw down from the bough
while I stand below
and try to keep it from spilling

           so that is sharing
said the little pink crow
           and went to pouring
and poured the whole glass of red vinegaw
into the mouth of the fox awaiting the nectaw
           meanwhile thinking
what a lesson he was giving the fox
and how fine it would be to see him choke a bit
and maybe die a bit

so the little pink crow did not think it fine
           not at all
when the yellow fox looked up at him smiling
and thanked him grandly with a sweep of his grand tail
for the grand nectaw
often celebrated in poetry song and light operaw
and walked smugly out of the arbaw
singing

           there once was a neoconservaty
           who imbibed whate'er had liquidity
           he e'en drank a blind beggar's cash flow
           to make himself magnifico
           to true connoisseurs of cupidity

RICHARD WILBUR ▪ ▪ ▪ ▪ ▪ ▪ ▪ ▪ ▪ ▪ ▪ ▪ ▪ ▪

Cottage Street, 1953

Framed in her phoenix fire-screen, Edna Ward
Bends to the tray of Canton, pouring tea
For frightened Mrs. Plath; then, turning toward
The pale, slumped daughter, and my wife, and me,

Asks if we would prefer it weak or strong.
Will we have milk or lemon, she enquires?
The visit seems already strained and long.
Each in his turn, we tell her our desires.

It is my office to exemplify
The published poet in his happiness,
Thus cheering Sylvia, who has wished to die;
But half-ashamed, and impotent to bless,

I am a stupid life-guard who has found,
Swept to his shallows by the tide, a girl
Who, far from shore, has been immensely drowned,
And stares through water now with eyes of pearl.

How deep is her refusal; and how slight
The *genteel* chat whereby we recommend
Life, of a summer afternoon, despite
The brewing dusk which hints that it may end.

And Edna Ward shall die in fifteen years,
After her eight-and-eighty summers of
Such grace and courage as permit no tears,
The thin hand reaching out, the last word *love,*

Outliving Sylvia who, condemned to live,
Shall study for a decade, as she must,
To state at last her brilliant negative
In poems free and helpless and unjust.

C. K. WILLIAMS ■ ■ ■ ■ ■ ■ ■ ■ ■ ■ ■ ■ ■ ■ ■ ■ ■

Poem

I think I came close to being insane a few months ago.
It didn't happen the way I thought it would at all—it wasn't from love
or from some unsuspected perversity suddenly rising in me, or from politics.
It was just in a butcher shop I was waiting in line in.
One of the butchers was trimming a piece of lamb
and I was leaning on top of the counter, not thinking about anything in particular,
keeping one eye on my daughter who was playing around with a shopping-cart,
watching how the butcher was carefully paring slices of gristle off
when all of a sudden I felt frightened. It's hard to explain,
but it was as though the light that was in the room we were in
didn't quite fit right, as though the space was going to tilt
and the light was going to pour out of it into the street like water.
Whatever it was I looked away fast at Jessie
bumping her cart into the sides of the meat-cases
and it stopped, but when I looked at the butcher again it happened again even
    more strongly.
Everything was slipping, as though we were all balanced
on the very tip of a mountain and something had moved
and we were going to all fall! I looked at the meat: if I could have thought
of some way that it represented pain or death to me
I'd have felt better, but it was just meat. Then the butcher: he was old,
heavy, with a big head that came out of his chest at a peculiar angle,
like a horse's. He was very methodical. I held Jessie's hand, closed my eyes,
opened them again and looked back at him again and this time I was really
    afraid.
It was still going on, even worse. I tried to do something with my mind.
I tried to remember what'd happened to me today that could have caused this.
I tried to make believe I was in love with the butcher
or that he was my father, that he was going to turn
and come at us with his knife to cut my eyes out, but nothing worked.
All there was was the feeling that the whole reality we were in
was going to wink out of existence, as though somehow the limits
of this dimension had been reached, and it was going to switch off
like a channel changing. I left and went home. I've been back,
but it's funny, that butcher never was there again and all this
never happened to me again. I've thought about it: was I sick?
No, I felt fine otherwise. Something to do with God? I don't think so.
What about that butcher—what if everybody who looked at him felt the same
    thing?
Here's a story that doesn't have anything to do with this: it's by Isaac Babel.
There's a young soldier, a farmer. He can't go on anymore, he's too afraid.
He gets into a trench and starts masturbating, and even when his captain
screams at him to get up, he sits there saying, I can't help it, I can't help it.

Finally the captain pisses into his face, and he jumps up and bolts crying
for the front, killed before he gets half-way.
Things like that happen too. Things like putting a sign on your door,
GO AWAY! Things like standing in the middle of the street screaming
at nothing. Isaac Babel also said: No steel can pierce the human heart
so chillingly as a period at the right moment. Things like screams
that have no sound, and no ending, that you just stumble through, like an odor.

The Sanctity

for Nick and Arlene De Credico

The men working on the building going up near here have got these great,
little motorized wheelbarrows that're supposed to be for lugging bricks and
    mortar
but that they seem to spend most of their time barrel-assing up the street in,
racing each other or trying to con the local secretaries into taking rides in the
    bucket.
I used to work on jobs like that and now when I pass by there I remember the
    guys I was with then
and how hard they were to know. Some of them would be good to be with at
    work,
slamming things around, playing practical jokes, laughing all the time, but they
    could be just miserable,
touchy and sullen, always ready to get into trouble, anywhere else.
If something went wrong, if a compressor blew or a truck backed over somebody,
they'd be the first ones to risk their lives dragging you out
but later you'd see them and they'd be drunk, looking for a fight, almost
    murderous
and it would be terrifying trying to figure out which person they really were.
Once I went home to dinner with a carpenter who'd taken me under his wing
and was keeping everybody off my back while he helped me—he was beautiful
but at home he was a sulker. After dinner he and the kids and I were watching
    television
while his wife washed the dishes and his mother, who lived with them,
sat at the table holding a big cantaloupe in her lap, fondling it and staring at it
with the kind of intensity people usually only look into fires with.
The wife kept trying to take it away from her but the old lady squawked
and my friend said, "Leave her alone, will you?"
"But she's doing it on purpose," the wife said. "Just leave her alone," he said.
I was watching. The mother put both of her hands on it then, with her thumbs
    spread
as though the melon was a head and her thumbs were covering the eyes
and she was aiming it like a gun or a camera.
Suddenly the wife muttered, "You bitch!" ran over to the bookcase, took a book
    down—

"A History of Revolutions"—rattled through the pages and triumphantly handed
   it to her husband.
A photograph: someone who's been garroted and the executioner, standing
   behind him in a business hat,
has his thumbs just like that over the person's eyes, straightening the head
so that you thought the thumbs were going to move away because they were only
   pointing
the person at something far away they wanted him to see
and the one with the hands was going to say, "Look! Right there!"
"I told you," the wife said. "I swear to God she's trying to drive me crazy."
I didn't know what it all meant but my friend went wild, started breaking things,
   I went home,
and when I saw him the next morning at breakfast he acted as though nothing
   had happened.
We used to have breakfast at the Westfield truck stop, but I remember Fritz's,
   The Victory, The Eagle,
and I think I've never had as much contentment as I did then, before work, the
   light just up,
everyone sipping their coffee out of the heavy white cups and teasing the middle-
   aged waitresses
who always acted vaguely in love with whoever was on jobs around there right
   then
besides the regular farmers stopping on their way back from the markets and the
   long-haul truckers.
Listen: sometimes when you go to speak about life it's as though your mouth's full
   of nails
but other times it's so easy that it's ridiculous to even bother.
The eggs and the toast could fly out of the plates and scream and it wouldn't
   matter
and the bubbles in the level could blow sky high and it still wouldn't.
Listen to the back-hoes gearing up and the shouts and somebody cracking his
   sledge into the mortar pan.
Listen again. He'll do it all day for you if you want him to. Listen again.

The Gas Station

This is before I'd read Nietzsche. Before Kant or Kierkegaard, even before
   Whitman and Yeats.
I don't think there were three words in my head yet. I knew, perhaps, that I
   should suffer,
I can remember I almost cried for this or for that, nothing special, nothing to
   speak of.
Probably I was mad with grief for the loss of my childhood, but I wouldn't have
   known that.
It's dawn. A gas station. Route twenty-two. I remember exactly: route twenty-two
   curved there,
there was a squat, striped concrete divider they'd put in after a plague of
   collisions.

The gas station? Texaco, Esso—I don't know. They were just words anyway, then,
  just what their signs said:
I wouldn't have understood the first thing about monopoly or imperialist or
  oppression.
It's dawn. It's so late. Even then, when I was never tired, I'm just holding on.
Slumped on my friend's shoulder, I watch the relentless, wordless misery of the
  route twenty-two sky
that seems to be filming my face with a grainy oil I keep trying to rub off or in.
Why are we here? Because one of my friends, in the men's room over there, has
  blue-balls.
He has to jerk off. I don't know what that means, "blue-balls," or why he has to
  do that:
it must be important to have to stop here after this long night but I don't ask.
I'm just trying, I think, to keep my head as empty as I can for as long as I can.
One of my other friends is asleep. He's so ugly, his mouth hanging, slack and wet.
Another—I'll never see this one again—stares from the window as though he
  were frightened.
Here's what we've done. We were in Times Square, a pimp found us, corralled
  us, led us somewhere,
down a dark street, another dark street, up dark stairs, dark hall, dark apartment,
where his whore, his girl or his wife or his mother for all I know dragged herself
  from her sleep,
propped herself on an elbow, gazed into the dark hall and agreed, for two dollars
  each, to take care of us.
Take care of us. There are words that start to come into me now, they stay there,
  I think.
My friend in the bathroom is taking so long. The filthy sky must be starting to
  lighten.
It took me a long time, too, with the woman, I mean. Did I mention that she, the
  woman, the whore or the mother,
was having her time and all she would deign do was to blow us? Did I say that?
  Deign? Blow?
What a joy, though, the idea was in those days. Blown! What a thing to tell the
  next day.
She only deigned, though, no more. She was like a machine. When I lift her back
  to me now,
there's nothing there but that dark, curly head bobbing, a machine, up and down,
  and now,
tell me Freud, Marx, Fathers, tell me, what am I, doing this, telling this, on her,
  on myself,
hammering it down, cementing it, sealing it in, but a machine, too? *Why am I
  doing this?*
I still haven't read Augustine. I don't understand Chomsky that well. Should I?
My friend, at last, comes back. Maybe the words, the right words, were there all
  along. *Complicity. Wonder.*
How pure we were then, before Rimbaud, before Blake. *Take care of us. Love.
  Grace.*

The Dog

Except for the dog, that she wouldn't have him put away, wouldn't let him die, I'd
  have liked her.
She was handsome, busty, chunky, early middle-aged, very black, with a stiff,
  exotic dignity
that flurried up in me a mix of warmth and sexual apprehension neither of which,
  to tell the truth,
I tried very hard to nail down: she was that much older and in those days there
  was still the race thing.
This was just at the time of civil rights: the neighborhood I was living in was
  mixed.
In the narrow streets, the tiny three-floored houses they called father-son-holy-
  ghosts
which had been servants' quarters first, workers' tenements, then slums, still
  were, but enclaves of us,
beatniks and young artists, squatted there and commerce between everyone was
  fairly easy.
Her dog, a grinning mongrel, rib and knob, gristle and grizzle, wasn't terribly
  offensive.
The trouble was that he was ill, or the trouble more exactly was that I had to
  know about it.
She used to walk him on a lot I overlooked, he must have had a tumor or a
  blockage of some sort
because every time he moved his bowels, he shrieked, a chilling, almost human
  scream of anguish.
It nearly always caught me unawares, but even when I'd see them first, it wasn't
  better.
The limp leash coiled in her hand, the woman would be profiled to the dog,
  staring into the distance,
apparently oblivious, those breasts of hers like stone, while he, not a step away,
  laboring,
trying to eject the feeble, mucus-coated, blood-flecked chains that finally spurted
  from him,
would set himself on tip-toe and hump into a question mark, one quivering back
  leg grotesquely lifted.
Every other moment he'd turn his head, as though he wanted her, to no avail, to
  look at him,
then his eyes would dim and he'd drive his wounded anus in the dirt, keening
  uncontrollably,
lurching forward in a hideous, electric dance as though someone were at him
  with a club.
When at last he'd finish, she'd wipe him with a tissue like a child, he'd lick her
  hand.
It was horrifying; I was always going to call the police; once I actually went out to
  chastise her—
didn't she know how selfish she was, how the animal was suffering?—she scared
  me off, though.
She was older than I'd thought for one thing, her flesh was loosening, pouches of
  fat beneath the eyes,

and poorer, too, shabby, tarnished: I imagined smelling something faintly acrid as
    I passed.
Had I ever really mooned for such a creature? I slunk around the block,
    chagrined, abashed.
I don't recall them too long after that. Maybe the dog died, maybe I was just less
    sensitive.
Maybe one year when the cold came and I closed my windows, I forgot them . . .
    then I moved.
Everything was complicated now, so many tensions, so much bothersome self-
    consciousness.
Anyway, those back streets, especially in bad weather when the Ginkgos lost their
    leaves, were bleak.
It's restored there now, ivy, pointed brick, garden walls with broken bottles
    mortared on them,
but you'd get sick and tired then: the rubbish in the gutter, the general sense of
    dereliction.
Also, I'd found a girl to be in love with: all we wanted was to live together, so we
    did.

CHARLES WRIGHT ▪ ▪ ▪ ▪ ▪ ▪ ▪ ▪ ▪ ▪ ▪ ▪ ▪

Tattoos

1.

Necklace of flame, little dropped hearts,
Camellias: I crunch you under my foot.
And here comes the wind again, bad breath
Of thirty-odd years, and catching up. Still,
I crunch you under my foot.

Your white stalks sequester me,
Their roots a remembered solitude.
Their mouths of snow keep forming my name.
Programmed incendiaries,
Fused flesh, so light your flowering,

So light the light that fires you
—Petals of horn, scales of blood—,
Where would you have me return?
What songs would I sing,
And the hymns . . . What garden of wax statues . . .

1973

2.

The pin oak has found new meat,
The linkworm a bone to pick.
Lolling its head, slicking its blue tongue,
The nightflower blooms on its one stem;
The crabgrass hones down its knives:

Between us again there is nothing. And since
The darkness is only light
That has not yet reached us,
You slip it on like a glove.
Duck soup, you say. *This is duck soup*.

And so it is.
              Along the far bank
Of Blood Creek, I watch you turn
In that light, and turn, and turn,
Feeling it change on your changing hands,
Feeling it take. Feeling it.

                                        1972

3.

Body fat as my forearm, blunt-arrowed head
And motionless, eyes
Sequin and hammer and nail
In the torchlight, he hangs there,
Color of dead leaves, color of dust,

Dumbbell and hourglass—copperhead.
Color of bread dough, color of pain, the hand
That takes it, that handles it
—The snake now limp as a cat—
Is halfway to heaven, and in time.

Then Yellow Shirt, twitching and dancing,
Gathers it home, handclap and heartstring,
His habit in ecstasy.
Current and godhead, hot coil,
Grains through the hourglass glint and spring.

                                        1951

4.

Silt fingers, silt stump and bone.
And twice now, in the drugged sky,
White moons, black moons.

And twice now, in the gardens,
The great seed of affection.

Liplap of Zuan's canal, blear
Footfalls of Tintoretto; the rest
Is brilliance: Turner at 3 A.M.; moth lamps
Along the casements. O blue
Feathers, this clear cathedral . . .

And now these stanchions of joy,
Radiant underpinning:
Old scaffolding, old arrangements,
All fall in a rain of light.
I have seen what I have seen.

1968

5.

Hungering acolyte, pale body,
The sunlight—through St. Paul of the 12 Sorrows—
Falls like Damascus on me:
I feel the gold hair of Paradise rise through my skin
Needle and thread, needle and thread;

I feel the worm in the rose root.
I hear the river of heaven
Fall from the air. I hear it enter the wafer
And sink me, the whirlpool stars
Spinning me down, and down. O . . .

Now I am something else, smooth,
Unrooted, with no veins and no hair, washed
In the waters of nothingness;
Anticoronal, released . . .
And then I am risen, the cup, new sun, at my lips.

1946

6.

Skyhooked above the floor, sucked
And mummied by salt towels, my left arm
Hangs in the darkness, bloodwood, black gauze,
The slow circle of poison
Coming and going through the same hole . . .

Sprinkle of rain through the pine needles,
Shoosh pump shoosh pump of the heart;

Bad blood, bad blood . . .
                Chalk skin like a light,
Eyes thin dimes, whose face
Comes and goes at the window?

Whose face . . .
              For I would join it,
And climb through the nine-and-a-half foot-holds of fever
Into the high air,
And shed these clothes and renounce,
Burned over, repurified.

                                    1941

7.

This one's not like the other, pale, gingerly—
Like nothing, in fact, to rise, as he does,
In three days, his blood clotted,
His deathsheet a feather across his chest,
His eyes twin lenses, and ready to unroll.

Arm and a leg, nail hole and knucklebone,
He stands up. In his right hand,
The flagstaff of victory;
In his left, the folds of what altered him.
And the hills spell V, and the trees V . . .

Nameless, invisible, what spins out
From this wall comes breath by breath,
And pulls the vine, and the ringing tide,
The scorched syllable from the moon's mouth.
And what pulls them pulls me.

                                    1963

8.

A tongue hangs in the dawn wind, a wind
That trails the tongue's voice like a banner, star
And whitewash, the voice
Sailing across the 14 mountains, snap and drift,
To settle, a last sigh, here.

That tongue is his tongue, the voice his voice:
Lifting out of the sea
Where the tongue licks, the voice starts,
Monotonous, out of synch,
Yamulka, tfillim, tallis,

His nude body waist-deep in the waves,
The book a fire in his hands, his movements
Reedflow and counter flow, the chant light
From his lips, the prayer rising to heaven,
And everything brilliance, brilliance, brilliance.

1959

9.

In the fixed cross-hairs of evening,
In the dust-wallow of certitude,
Where the drop drops and the scalding starts,
Where the train pulls out and the light winks,
The tracks go on, and go on:

The flesh pulls back and snaps,
The fingers are ground and scraped clean,
Reed whistles in a green fire.
The bones blow on, singing their bald song.
It stops. And it starts again.

Theologians, Interpreters:
Song, the tracks, cross-hairs, the light;
The drop that is always falling.
Over again I feel the palm print,
The map that will take me there.

1952

10.

It starts here, in a chair, sunflowers
Inclined from an iron pot, a soiled dish cloth
Draped on the backrest. A throat with a red choker
Throbs in the mirror. High on the wall,
Flower-like, disembodied,

A wren-colored evil eye stares out
At the white blooms of the oleander, at the white
Gobbets of shadow and shade,
At the white lady and white parasol, at this
Dichogamous landscape, this found chord

(And in the hibiscus and moonflowers,
In the smoke trees and spider ferns,
The unicorn crosses his thin legs,
The leopard sips at her dish of blood,
And the vines strike and the vines recoil).

1973

11.

So that was it, the rush and the take-off,
The oily glide of the cells
Bringing it up—ripsurge, refraction,
The inner spin
Trailing into the cracked lights of oblivion . . .

Re-entry is something else, blank, hard:
Black stretcher straps; the peck, peck
And click of a scalpel; glass shards
Eased one by one from the flesh;
Recisions; the long bite of the veins . . .

And what do we do with this,
Rechuted, reworked into our same lives, no one
To answer to, no one to glimpse and sing,
The cracked lights flashing our names?
We stand fast, friend, we stand fast.

1958

12.

Oval oval oval oval push pull push pull . . .
Words unroll from our fingers.
A splash of leaves through the windowpanes,
A smell of tar from the streets:
Apple, arrival, the railroad, shoe.

The words, like bees in a sweet ink, cluster and drone,
Indifferent, indelible,
A hum and a hum:
Back stairsteps to God, ropes to the glass eye:
Vineyard, informer, the chair, the throne.

Mojo and motionless, breaths
From the wet mountains and green mouths; rustlings,
Sure sleights of hand,
The news that arrives from nowhere:
Angel, omega, silence, silence . . .

1945

13.

What I remember is fire, orange fire,
And his huge cock in his hand,
Touching my tiny one; the smell

Of coal dust, the smell of heat,
Banked flames through the furnace door.

Of him I remember little, if anything:
Black, overalls splotched with soot,
His voice, *honey, O, honey* . . .
And then he came, his left hand
On my back, holding me close.

Nothing was said, of course—one
Terrible admonition, and that was all . . .
And if that hand, like loosed lumber, fell
From grace, and stayed there? We give,
And we take it back. We give again . . .

1940

14.

Now there is one, and still masked;
White death's face, sheeted and shoeless, eyes shut
Behind the skull holes.
She stands in a field, her shadow no shadow,
The clouds no clouds. Call her Untitled.

•

And now there are four, white shoes, white socks;
They stand in the same field, the same clouds
Vanishing down the sky. Cat masks and mop hair
Cover their faces. Advancing, they hold hands.

•

Nine. Now there are nine, their true shadows
The judgments beneath their feet.
Black masks, white nightgowns. A wind
Is what calls them, that field, those same clouds
Lisping one syllable *I,I,I.*

1970

15.

And the saw keeps cutting,
Its flashy teeth shredding the mattress, the bedclothes,
The pillow and pillow case.
Plugged in to a socket in your bones,
It coughs, and keeps on cutting.

It eats the lamp and the bedpost.
It licks the clock with its oiled tongue,
And keeps on cutting.
It leaves the bedroom, and keeps on cutting.
It leaves the house, and keeps on cutting . . .

—Dogwood, old feathery petals,
Your black notches burn in my blood;
You flutter like bandages across my childhood.
Your sound is a sound of good-bye.
Your poem is a poem of pain.

1964

16.

All gloss, gothic and garrulous, staked
To her own tree, she takes it off,
Half-dollar an article. With each
Hike of the price, the gawkers
Diminish, spitting, rubbing their necks.

Fifteen, and staked to *my* tree,
Sap-handled, hand in my pocket, head
Hot as the carnival tent, I see it out—as does
The sheriff of Cherokee County,
Who fondles the pay-off, finger and shaft.

Outside, in the gathering dark, all
Is fly buzz and gnat hum and whine of the wires;
Quick scratch of the match, cicadas,
Jackhammer insects; drone, drone
Of the blood suckers, sweet dust, last sounds . . .

1950

17.

I dream that I dream I wake
The room is throat-deep and brown with dead moths
I throw them back like a quilt
I peel them down from the wall
I kick them like leaves I shake them I kick them again

The bride on the couch and the bridegroom
Under their gauze dust-sheet
And cover up turn to each other
Top hat and tails white veil and say as I pass
It's mother again just mother the window open

On the 10th floor going up
Is Faceless and under steam his mask
Hot-wired my breath at his heels in sharp clumps
Darkness and light darkness and light
Faceless come back O come back

1955

18.

Flash click tick, flash click tick, light
Through the wavefall—electrodes, intolerable curlicues;
Splinters along the skin, eyes
Flicked by the sealash, spun, pricked;
Terrible vowels from the sun.

And everything dry, wrung, the land flaked
By the wind, bone dust and shale;
And hills without names or numbers,
Bald coves where the sky harbors.
The dead grass whistles a tune, strangely familiar.

And all in a row, seated, their mouths biting the empty air,
Their front legs straight, and their backs straight,
Their bodies pitted, eyes wide,
The rubble quick glint beneath their feet,
The lions stare, explaining it one more time.

1959

19.

The hemlocks wedge in the wind.
Their webs are forming something—questions:
Which shoe is the alter ego?
Which glove inures the fallible hand?
Why are the apple trees in draped black?

And I answer them. In words
They will understand, I answer them:
The left shoe.
The left glove.
Someone is dead; someone who loved them is dead.

Regret is what anchors me;
I wash in a water of odd names.
White flakes from next year sift down, sift down.
I lie still, and dig in,
Snow-rooted, ooze-rooted, cold blossom.

1972

20.

You stand in your shoes, two shiny graves
Dogging your footsteps;
You spread your fingers, ten stalks
Enclosing your right of way;
You yip with pain in your little mouth.

And this is where the ash falls.
And this is the time it took to get here—
And yours, too, is the stall, the wet wings
Arriving, and the beak.
And yours the thump, and the soft voice:

The octopus on the reef's edge, who slides
His fat fingers among the cracks,
Can use you. You've prayed to him,
In fact, and don't know it.
You *are* him, and think yourself yourself.

1973

Notes

1. *Camellias; Mother's Day, St. Paul's Episcopal Church, Kingsport, Tennessee.*
2. *Death of my father.*
3. *Snake handling religious service, East Tennessee.*
4. *Venice, Italy; walking the streets.*
5. *Acolyte; fainting at the altar; Kingsport, Tennessee.*
6. *Blood poisoning, hallucination; Hiwassee, North Carolina.*
7. *The Resurrection, Piero Della Francesca, Borgo San Sepolcro, Italy.*
8. *Harold Schimmel's morning prayers, Positano, Italy.*
9. *Christ School, Arden, North Carolina; temporary evangelical certitude.*
10. *Visions of heaven.*
11. *Automobile wreck; hospital; Baltimore, Maryland.*
12. *Handwriting class, Palmer Method; words as "things"; Kingsport, Tennessee.*
13. *Kindergarten, Corinth, Mississippi; the janitor.*
14. *Dream.*
15. *Rome, Italy, day of my mother's funeral (in Tennessee); a dogwood tree is planted by the gravestone.*
16. *Sideshow stripper, Cherokee County Fair, Cherokee, North Carolina.*
17. *Recurrent dream.*
18. *Naxian lions, Delos, Greece.*
19. *Death of my father.*
20. *The last stanza is an adaptation of lines in "Serenata Indiana" by Eugenio Montale.*

JAMES WRIGHT ■ ■ ■ ■ ■ ■ ■ ■ ■ ■ ■ ■ ■ ■ ■

Sirmione

Looming and almost molten and slowly moving its gold down hill just behind my back is the summer villa of the poet, the Grotte di Catullo.

But I care more now for the poetry of the present moment. An easy thousand of silver, almost transparent piccoline are skimming the surface of the long slab of volcanic stone. They swim through a very tiny channel at the very rim of the lake. They tickle the skin of my ankles, smaller than Latin diminutives.

Catullus, grieving over his Lesbia's sparrow, turned *misere* from harsh *wretched* into *miselle,* poor and little and lovely and gone, all in one word.

But those tiny fish that tickle the skin of my ankles are already so diminutive that they would have dissolved altogether into droplets of mist at a mere touch of Catullus's fingertip. I reckon that is why he never wrote of them by name, but left them tiny and happy in their lives in the waters, where they still have their lives and seem to enjoy tickling the skin of my ankles.

The Silent Angel

As I sat down by the bus window in the gate of Verona, I looked over my left shoulder. A man was standing in one of the pink marble arches at the base of the great Roman Arena. He smiled at me, a gesture of the utmost sweetness, such as a human face can rarely manage to shine with, even a beloved face that loves you in return.

He seemed dressed like a musician, as well he might have been, emerging for a moment into the sunlight from one of the secluded and cool rehearsal chambers of the upper tiers of the Arena.

As the bus driver powered his motor and drew us slowly around the great public square, the Piazza Bra, the man in the half-golden rose shadow of the Arena kept his gaze on my face. He waved goodbye to me, his knowing eyes never leaving me as long as he could still see any of me at all, though how long that was I don't precisely know.

He raised his hand at the last moment to wave me out of Verona as kindly as he could. He held in his right hand what seemed to be a baton, and it hung suspended for a long instant in the vast petals of rose shadows cast down by the marble walls. Even after he had vanished back into the archway I could still see his baton.

Oh, I know it was not a baton. I was far away now, and all I could see behind me were the diminishing cicadas, lindens, and slim cedars rising, one feather folding upwards into another, into the spaces of evergreen and gold beyond the Roman Arena, beyond the river and the hills beyond the river, the beginning of everlasting change, Saint Martin's summer. All those trees, the durable and the momentary confused with one another into the eternity of Saint Augustine's despair of time. They will still be rising there long after even the Giusti Gardens, where Goethe walked, have run back to weeds, a few of my beloved lizards left to make company with them perhaps, a spider or two still designing for days and then patiently building the most delicate of ruins.

I could not afford to let myself think of the River Adige any longer, because I loved it too much. The wings of the smiling musician are folded. His baton, grown cool again by this time, rests on his knees. I can imagine that all the other musicians have risen into the riverside hills for the night, and my musician, who meant me no harm and only wanted to wave me away as gently as possible out of the beautiful space he guarded, is himself asleep with the late crickets along the river.

I turned at last away from the city, gritted my teeth, two of which are broken and snaggled, fingered the shred of pink marble in my jacket pocket, and forced my face toward Milano with its factories, London with its fear and hopelessness, and, beyond that, the final place, New York, America, hell on earth.

I felt fallen. But not very happy. Nor lucky either.

The musician had not played me a single tune, he had not sung me a single song. He just waved me as gently as he could on the way out, the way that is my own, the lost way.

I suppose I asked for it. And he did his best, I suppose. He owns that heavenly city no more than I do. He may be fallen, as I am. But from a greater height, unless I miss my guess.

Romeo, Grown Old

I know at least some of my upper teeth could have been saved if they hadn't been ripped out of my head when I was a child by a sadist in Bridgeport, Ohio, who had a mail-order degree in dentistry. I know I was lucky that his pliers weren't rusty, at least.

Somebody I still love is young and dead.

I know what a brutal and indifferent and cruel and disastrous hole this world can be, whether to be dragged out of at the price of a hard smack on the bare ass, or be eased back into on the greased rails of a coffin at sixteen thousand dollars a throw. I have been close to dying at least twice, and more than twice I have wished to God I had.

And there you are, alone in the south barrens, working in a restaurant, running from table to counter to cash register to kitchen to cash register to counter to table to counter to cash register to kitchen cash register table counter table all day long, hemmed in so you can hardly move, crowded in and alone. Your feet hurt. You have a corn on your big toe. You can hardly taste your own cigarette smoke in the ladies room when they let you go there.

We finish the day, all worn out.

And so, what is this radiance flowing behind our eyes? Whether my eyelids are open or closed, I need only look inward, and listen, and I can see the radiance.

Magnificence

They tell me that the Arena in Verona is the most beautifully preserved Roman amphitheatre in Italy, and I believe them. Twenty thousand people could sit in it comfortably. On a sunlit day its pink and white marble glow from within, and they glow from within when it is raining.

The Arena is magnificent. It means that it is greatly made. It must be twenty-five hundred years old. The Romans, like Octavius and Cicero, were sometimes as noble as Ortega in his intelligent anguish could hope for; and even his hopes were harsh and critically severe.

In this setting, whose grandeur consists in its uncluttered purity and simplicity of design, Verdi's Requiem emerged with exquisite gentleness, tenderness, and sadness. Of course, the trumpets were played high at the rim of the Arena. No human Director could have resisted that opportunity. But the great Veronese musicians were so masterful in their understanding of the music, its shapeliness as fully as its clear depth of stillness all the more passionate for its revelations of silence, that during one brief passage while orchestra, chorus, and solists were all singing lucidly and quietly together, we heard a cricket singing in the darkness at the farthest rim of the Arena.

His song was not extraordinarily melodious. He was evening. He was not trying to compete with Verdi. I think he was just trying to sing himself to sleep among the warm darkened stones.

It was characteristic of the Veronese company that the Director of the chorus had concealed himself head and shoulders behind a discreetly colored screen behind the soloists.

Only occasionally, at some moment of absolute necessity for the evocation of the chorus, we could see his beautiful hands fluttering with perfect precision above the screen, like the wings of a happy yet teetolling cabbage-white butterfly.

For some reason known possibly to God in His more responsive moments of attentiveness, one of the softest passages of the Requiem was joined from the rear end of the Arena by an extremely coarse whistle of the sort that New York delicatessen managers make when they catch small children in the act of snitching candy placed by an oversight near the entrance to the store. I do pray our cousins from Jersey go elsewhere for their vacations.

The musicians paid no attention whatever, and softly though they sang, their music rose above his cacophony, as Verdi himself, a human artist whose soul had the shape and sound of something greatly made, was present among us at once in time and beyond time, almost beyond sound, at the same moment and in the same space on one of the earth's loveliest places, both diminutive and vast, very like the city of Verona itself.

Very, very like.

And Yet I Know

Just across the street from the Instituto Dante Allighieri, Riv. Tito Livio, 21, Padova, where you can take courses in languages, there is a stone casket tomb so old its lettering is illegible.

Beside the tomb in the shade of a head of a man, a living man is lying down under a pine shrub, dead drunk. It is exactly two minutes after one o'clock in the afternoon.

Then I found later that the monument is the Funeral Kiosk of the Antinore, and beside it the tomb of the poet Lovato de' Lovati.

I have never read Lovati's poems. His name is so lovely.

I have been drunk and asleep beneath a pine shrub myself.

I wonder who this sleeper is.

Handsome Is As Handsome Does

In this moment I am sitting contented and alone in a perfect charming little park near the Palazzo Scaligeri in Verona, pondering the state of my soul and glimpsing the mists of early autumn as they shift and fade among the pines and city battlements on the hills to my left above the river Adige.

The river has recovered from this morning's rainfall. It is now restoring to its shapely body its own secret light, a color of faintly cloudy green and pearl.

Directly in front of my bench, perhaps thirty yards away from me, there is a startling woman. She is as black as the inmost secret of light in a perfectly cut diamond, a perilous black, a secret that must have been studied for many years before the anxious and disciplined craftsman could achieve the necessary balance between courage and skill to stroke the strange stone and take the one chance he would ever have to bring that black secret to light.

While I was trying to compose the preceding sentence, the woman rose from her park bench and walked away. I am afraid her black secret will never come to light in my lifetime.

And I'll be a son of a bitch if I don't have a case of stone-ache.

Wait! Wait a moment. Seize the day.

She just came into the park again and sat down.

Four Dead Sons

for Sister Bernetta

The last I heard of Paul Hanson he was dead. He was roasted in a tank in France. The last evening I spent with him it was raining very hard, and nobody seemed to recognize Paul except me. He certainly looked hangdog and forlorn. He was water-logged in one of those old World War II olive drab uniforms that never fit the occupant in the sunniest of weather. Paul Hanson in the rain looked as if he were just emerging from a fashionable bathing beach in drag circa 1895 or thereabouts. And who wouldn't?

He had a fine speaking voice and thought he would like to be a minister. He was getting ready to go overseas the next day. He looked peaked to me.

I don't know what ditch he got flung in. I doubt if he even got buried at all.

Franklin Miller had too splendid a physique to do worth a damn on the highschool track team. Just before a trackmeet with a fine team from Follensbee, West Virginia, Frank announced in the locker room that 'y God for once in his life he was going to run in the lead of the mile. The miler from Follensbee was a patient and intelligent athlete who knew perfectly well how to save his lungs for the final kick toward the finish. He also was blessed with the physique of an undernourished willow tree. His chest was flatter than Twiggy's, and naturally the wind eased him over the finish line a good fifty yards before all the others.

But for almost exactly one-half of that long mile (a mile is very long when you're eighteen years old and muscle-bound and all you can think about is love), Frank Miller led the race by some ten yards, give or take a thigh or two. Then, still in the lead, he abruptly threw his body full length on the fresh grass that grew thick and unmown inside the track. As all the other runners passed him by, Frank slowly regained his breath, rose to his good height, smiled benevolently into the brilliant April sky, bowed slightly as though in salute to the passing race of young men already gone, and puked on the cinders still fresh with the spike-marks of the track-shoes.

Frank got killed in the war, too. I don't know where.

Johann Wolfgang von Goethe possessed, I should think, as great a strength and noble serenity of character as any human being I have ever heard of. But after the death of his son, born by Christiane Vulpius, Goethe absolutely forbade the very mention of his son's name in the Goethe household until the poet's own death. It is none of my business to say why, but I suspect that Goethe was afraid he might weep and discover that not even he could stop weeping. The notion of a hysterical Goethe is enough to give anybody pause.

Far from denying the death of his own beautiful and good-humored son, Frank Miller's father on a Sunday morning about half-way through the war stood up to face the entire church congregation. He told us that Frank was dead in the war, and there was no mistake about it, Frank was dead all right. Mr. Miller was an easy-going fellow of great physical strength who sometimes took turns with my father in singing the old hymns I loved when I was a boy. On the Sunday morning I remember, Mr. Miller was not having coffee and oranges in a sunny chair. He spoke very slowly through his gritted teeth, and the muscles of his bull neck bulged, and he told us out loud, "My boy Frank is dead in this here war they got. No mistake about it. The War Department says it's the truth in a telegram, and what else I got to believe in?"

He sat down beside my father. He looked neither to the left nor to the right. He did not weep. Anyway, I didn't see him weep in public, and nobody else did either.

No, he wasn't Goethe, for Christ's sake. He was a doubler at the steel mill.

Well, this is a prayer.

I want to know something.

You heard your own beautiful son suffering and crying out.

You heard him.

And what I want to know is, did you weep?
I want to know. Did you weep?
I don't hear anything yet. This kind of silence is making me uneasy.
Maybe I better shut up while the shutting up is good.
But a son is human. At least that much.
Can't a man ask a simple question?
With God's own blood running into his eyes?

Nocturne, Aubade, and Vesper

To call it a wet dream would be too barren. I say what I can say afterwards, but nobody spoke in the dream itself. The whole room lay deep under water. I am still glad it was impossible to speak any word at all: no apology, no embarrassment, no words these that used to kill me before I got a chance to come alive.

There were sounds in the dream, and I will tell what they were. They came as you came and we came together.

You had no clothes on at all. You swam into the room all light and nakedness. You came to meet me, and we had all the preliminary loves I had ever heard of or done or thought of when I was all alone. And you were so delighted you brought some kinds of lovings I don't believe either of us had ever even heard of. Or if we had heard, then we must not have been listening. It has always been too hard for me to listen when I am only awake.

You were not a mermaid. I made the discovery as I searched and explored the beautiful darkness inside your own body with my own language, and I spoke into your darkness, I was the tongue of the whole sea.

The first sound of the dream was your cry when you came, so alive with your own delight that your cry floated upwards silently out of your lips. It was a laughter, and we heard your voice opening in the air far above our heads.

Go on. Go on singing. Don't stop now. I say to myself.

I call the dream funny not only because it was strange but also because you stirred little circles of laughter in the water.

When I started to waken I still felt damp with two bodies. It must have been four o'clock in the morning. Because just around the corner outside my window I could still hear the black Africans, the blackest I have ever seen, singing Swahili songs in the restaurant that is named The Tree Where Life Begins. One of the men was playing a guitar and singing in French. Even I could understand his French. It must have been because he and I were both strangers singing and listening in a tongue that we had not been born to sing and listen in, and our two broken accents met in some space in the air where broken voices meet in a harmony that those who can easily take their own songs and listenings for granted can never understand. When the native Parisians heard me ask for a package of cigarettes or when they hear the black African sing French songs in a Swahili accent, we must sound funny to them, strange visitors from dark trees. No wonder we do. We are.

I was smiling in the moments before the dawn twilight. I must have lain there alone and awake for two hours, feeling the sea cooling and drying all over my mouth, moving only a little as the dream rose and fell and then faded. You are not going to believe this anyway, so I may as well write the truth. I scarcely believe it myself it is so strange. In two whole hours I did not say a single word. I did not even think a single word. I smiled and, very slowly, went to sleep. I was very happy. That was the way I dreamed, and the way I woke, and the way I slept again.

Ah! (That sounds charming and romantic. I think I'll repeat it. Ah!) There it was. It was, I suppose, as beautiful a dream of loving as I have ever had, and lovelier than most. And I lived a long time on dreams. I don't care what anyone says against America now. Long ago it was my country of dreams. I used to go to the weekday matinees at a movie theatre (I love the spelling of "theatre"). It was back in Ohio at a time of day when most other people were either working or else too busy trying to keep their snotty children from wriggling all over the genuine simulated plush, the small-town elegance of the white-sheeted plush of the benches reserved for us Caucasians (do you spell it with a large "C"?). I doubt if any people would have cared even if they had seen me feeling myself when Hedy Lamarr appeared. Anybody except maybe Leroy the peanut-pusher, whom I once saw kick a stray dog out of the theatre. That God damned rat-hole smelled like the inside of Roy Campanella's catcher's mit. And perenniel drunk's puke. When Hedy appeared, high and far off and luminous and lonely for my little rosy pecker to soothe her to sleep, Leroy the usher must have hidden in the men's room on the pretext of sweeping up a little and keeping the joint sweet and fresh and clean. He wasn't afraid of dogs, but I think he was afraid of women, even the phantoms of women on the picture screen. Anyway, he was never around when Hedy Lamarr appeared. I loved her. The trouble was, she never saw me either.

Not the real me, itching with idealistic lust.

Yes, I loved my daydreams in Ohio, and I loved my wet dream in Paris.

But I don't want it. I don't care how beautiful it was. I don't want it. What the hell good is it to me? It is not going to come true. I want the truth from you. I love you.

I would rather have entered that crummy room in Paris at the same moment you entered it.

We are both trying to get through the door at the same time, and it is impossible, so we keep trying to push each other out of the way.

"Who the hell do you think you're pushing, for Christ's sake?"

"It's you I'm pushing, who the hell did you think I was pushing, Hedy Lamarr?"

"Look, neither one of us is going to get in this hole if we keep this up. Why don't you let me be the gentleman just this once, you chauvinist son of a bitch?"

And you step back with a great display of extravagant politeness and make an almost obscenely elaborate bow. It is one of the most finely conceived and executed gestures of sarcasm I have ever seen. Your hair is twisted with sweat, and you couldn't comb the tiny knots out of it if you tried. I love you. I walk straight into the room without looking back to see if you're going to follow. You follow.

We stand still for an instant. We have been traipsing all over the city for some long hours, looking for *objets d'art*.

Yes, I said *objets d'art.* In the name of sweet leaping Jesus H. Christ the Third.

You look at me, exhausted. I start to say something. I don't know what.

"Well, shut up and love me."

"Who do you think you're ordering around?"

"You."

"Well, okay."

So I love you. What the hell do you expect me to do. I'm damned if you know, I don't.

We said that sometimes down home on the river. It's a—it's a kind of— it's slang on the river, the Ohio river, and below the river. They talk that way down there.

You talk to me.

"Talk to me."

"I can't. I'm busy."

"Love me, oh come on."

"Oh, all right. There. Can you hear me?"

"Oh, I can hear you, I can hear you, I can hear you, I can hear you, I can hear you, oh, don't be so hard on me so much, you know I've been running around this whole city all day, oh, I feel lousy."

And you start to cry.

You say to yourself, "God damn it, stop it." Half-aloud, a bitter hiss through your gritted teeth. I can see the muscles in your jaws knotting up, exquisite little charley-horses of fury.

I have never expected to see you weep, never once in my life. And I know as well as you do that I never will.

And yet you weep.

And don't you lie to me either.

You weep somewhere.

In the tree where life begins, the black Africans sweep softly over their French guitars, and the Swahili accent leaves me a stranger in my own mind. I wrote down for you here the dream I had of you under water at night and the day dream of rudeness and anguish. But a dream is only a dream, day or night, airy and filmy or flaming like a twisted muscle across my shoulder where a wing should be or bulging and rotting like a tooth, one of the bones in my skull crumbling.

I have had my visions of you by night and day. Neither of them is going to come true. And do I weep? You're God damned right I weep. I am not going to come true.

Young Don't Want to Be Born

I know just how you feel. There was a time when your feet touched bottom. Then the sea polyps tangle themselves around one ankle, and a wave deep under the surface, that looks so smooth to all the idle strollers a mile behind you on the sunlit sands, knocks both feet out from under you, and you cling, desperate and terrified, to the tail of a giant sting-ray.

He is not swimming toward shore. The men who kill him for a living are waiting for him there, and one evening just after dark they damned near got him.

And now it is evening, just after supper. Your father thinks he catches a hint of what might be a perfect moon hanging just through the spidery laces of the paw-paw trees. Something or other, God alone knows what, gives him the notion that the late evening light of September is a perfect beginning.

His full stomach it is, maybe, that makes him think idly that the moon is only a reflection of your mother's face. And you are dead. It's all over. God is alone again. You are supposed to be some kind of a perfect beginning, for once. And just look at you. Well, just look at God and His own children. Just look at them.

For Christ's sake.

Miles and miles down in the darkness of the waters you grip with extravagant ferocity to the slime of the sting-ray's tail. He is going somewhere. But where? How in hell should you know? All you know is he is not going back to that shore ever again.

Lord, it is daylight sometimes. Thinking himself free and alone, the magnificent giant sting-ray allows himself some strange joy that you can't even begin to understand. He relaxes in his flight and allows himself to be lifted slowly up on a long swell that rises from some depth God alone knows how far down. The splendid giant thrashes and dances for miles on miles near the surface, from what seems one sea to another. The glory of his great fans become golden again, their scales half-blind you with their mirrors that catch and tangle the green arrows of green sunlight. He deflects them easily from those inexhaustible wings.

One afternoon he feels himself growing hungry. It is getting on toward evening. Your hands can't hold on any longer. He lets himself float idly on the surface. His eyes quicken to find something simple and not too much trouble to eat. You try to drift off a few yards in the deepening and thickening sea dusk joining the fog. The giant sting-ray hasn't seen you yet.

Hurry.

Has he seen you yet?

Oh my poor brother, gather your strength if you have any.

Hurry off.

JOHN YAU ▪

Angel Atrapado VII

The one who says: I was almost alive or nearly dead or somewhere in between, a dirty flask full of second hand tears. I thought I was inside this room inside myself, but I was walking past the window. I saw you listening to what was being said, examining the syllables, their cold sibilants, and then holding them up and asking what they were that you too could use them. But we hadn't yet spoken, nor (as it turned out) would we ever.

The one who says: They want to be friends but they cannot help themselves, and think it is business. Or they think they are moving towards business when they want to be friends. The one who licks his or her golden lips when you expose your neck, raise your head above the words you have been trained to follow all along.

The one who says: I grow inside you growing inside me, feel your voice inside the voice used to speak, the voice falling back into itself, the voice barely able to listen to itself listening, the voice full of borrowed words sent forth in borrowed clothes, the voice of that one over there lying under the bed, asking for something other than money but metallic nevertheless.

The one who says: An imbecile and his rabbit huddle under a decrepit family tree. A coolie and a taxi dancer run past the underworld. A robot and its patient argue over chess.

Or is it the one who says: I am watching bullet riddled bodies tumble beneath the final layers of evening's gift, their pastel colors describing a wall beyond the horizon, and what is taking place in front of me has started burning through all the pages held up to the light.

Or is it finally the voice cursing itself for having spoken at all, that one and that one and that one, and all of them pushing toward the mouth or empty sky they once thought was theirs and theirs alone.

Chinese Landscape Above Caracas

The heavy gray and white clouds surrounding the dark green mountaintops reminded him of his grandfather. All the stories he had ever been told about him were lies. The hand that dipped the brush into the ink was not the one that guided its colors into stylized shapes and lines, each of which told a story about the window he was looking through when he decided to see the mountains, trees, and river. All the stories he listened to, as a child. The story he read the two children sitting on the trunk was make-believe. One made it to believe it. Who believes the stories that are being told is a child. Each story believes in itself.

766

The Painter Asks

for Brice Marden

Why go toward the palaces of description
Why climb a ladder and pray to colors

as if their names are impenetrable
vaults of latin snow

Why listen to witnesses
who have swiped quartz vertices

and their piped coughs
Why go toward the stages of sky

glowing through their amber bracelet
or sentence words to sentences

Why feed wingless instruments
gathering along bottom of last dream

to touch daylight's rim
Why leaving thinking for thought.

Avila

You learn to accommodate yourself to others, to fit into the space left by their shadow. This is one way of disappearing into the smile meant for the body you have left on the carpet, where every rose is a perfect instrument of writing.

I saw myself swimming there, hidden behind the curtain some call a face.

You can put it on hold, you tell yourself. You can lie until the sun lifts itself out of your mouth. You can walk into the water and not get wet.

We were in bed talking about lives lived, our lies and lovers. The who how and where of what we had done during the years we explored the outlying districts of a landscape almost reaching the surface of our adopted skin. The breaths taken and not taken, the words used to circle off a story, select its gold plated dome, the dune it would ride into the sea.

I remember not wanting to get the couch dirty, it was brand new, you said. Smiling. The rope of my desire reached a balcony that could not be pictured except in the garage or drive-in I drove past, blue top down all the way under the sky. Black tray, newly mown stars. The buckled snug I laughed at.

I looked down into her green shoes. It was dawn, and I was hoping she had
written her name there, in the gaps that held her feet when she walked around
my twin, the one I carried with me whenever I wanted to see what I was doing.
He was the dummy and I was the flutter passing through, on my way to a parking
lot of iridescent kin.

Picadilly or Paradise

When I leap through the flung open windows of your dance
and reach toward my shadow, its drifting silk and nylon net,
everyone looks at the wind growing a new set of teeth around the moon.
Once, they were among the sweetest of the town's prize apples,
evocative names and histories a waiter would point to on the menu,
his mouth forging the budding pink and yellow clouds
that would soon swell and open above the visitor's table.
I remember praying for a dazzling array of snow and clay
to descend the stairs to the cellar where I was kept.
But she was afraid to reveal her latest desire:
blue face powder kept in the bronzed shoe of a former lover,
and velvet gloves for every bird.
                As for him,
the man with silver breath, words were like a toupee—
something he could not share with anyone.
An ink storm swept across this emblazoned map
where pompous couples prided themselves on their choice
of emerging crowd pleasers and corncob furniture.
A train full of inscribed pavement stones rattled through
the tunnels, its polished bronze instruments
swaying gently in the lower layers of the united dark.
Each of us ends up a piece of luggage carried by others.
When I am on my belly, I am glad that I am not a turtle
carrying my tiled igloo toward the advancing sea.
You flicked off your wings, but I left them in the sand.
Remember, satisfaction isn't necessarily a guarantee.
I am neither Delilah's niece nor her nephew,
because I keep a pair of scissors beneath my mattress.
A hotel would probably provide the best pillows
for our next little excursion, but I don't like numbered doors.
I like my rooms to have a name: Passionate Chitchat,
Nervous Bells of the Fragile Dawn, Delicate Smothering
Amidst Chrome Snooze Lots, Impersonal Convenience
Of A Kind You Might Not Have Known About Until Now.
I want the reception to remind you of a clean river.
No more metal shutters or rusted fences. I am positive
there are other acceptable forms of rehabilitation
that will entice me to remove my customized fingernails
from your smile, the one you have never worn

when you glide above the bolts of our mortgaged axle.
Why do some screams attract more sightseers than others?
Why do you grip your lips? Why do I grab my sagging slab?
Some questions beg the answer, others annoint their fingers.
Either I am waiting for a sign of permanent eruption
or you are dousing candles in the last yawns of our jury.

PAUL ZWEIG ▪ ▪ ▪ ▪ ▪ ▪ ▪ ▪ ▪ ▪ ▪ ▪ ▪ ▪ ▪ ▪ ▪ ▪

Eternity's Woods

The land up here hasn't been worked in years.
It's all thorns and red clay, a brittle reedy grass.
Up here the farmers don't bother.
Why should they, when the valley shrugs up corn,
Large-leafed tobacco, and the stream,
Between its double hedge of poplars,
Never runs dry.

I climb this way to reach my house.
Even when the hill sang with vines,
And dark dusty grapes sagged to the ground,
Only a poor man would have chosen it.
The Foret Barade gloomed over his land,
Its wild boars, deep-tangled shade.
But he held out, his children held out,
And their children let go.

His grandson, Jean, lives down the hill,
In a stuccoed pillbox of a house.
Jean comes up here when he can
To breathe freely, and talk about the forest
His grandfather knew, rustling poison-dark.
About witches who cooked souls in cast-iron pots,
Charcoal-burners prancing, black as devils,
Beside their acrid mounds. He talks about
The quilted silence of the old chestnut woods,
Where even thorn-vines couldn't grow,
But mushrooms came and went like odorous ghosts.

Now the woods are coming back.
Slender chestnuts pouring up visibly
From year to year; pine-shoots daring
Further from the wood-edge each time you look.
I bought the house a dozen years ago,

For its calcareous stones, its wood-burnt tiles,
Oak-beams so tough a nail bent
When you tried to hammer it in.

A hard red road scrapes the bones of the hill.
Where the woods end, silver melts
Across it, and my eyes wince shut.
I come this way to meet the postman.
The parched field boils with cicadas,
And a delirium of white scraps
Wobbling a foot or two in the air:
Butterflies doing their dance of life.
All my running has somehow ended here.
Those times when I wanted space, and wild grass;
Daylight wrestling in the moss-furred
Limbs of an old walnut tree.

The baked fragrant summer air,
The postman's yellow van teetering to a halt,
The envelopes with their white chill of distance.

A shimmer of heat distorts eternity's woods,
And the butterflies, nudging and winking
Over the field, half-wild, half-cruel,
Like the laughter of a perfectly solitary man,
Are the scraps and flutterings of eternity.

Father

I

I want to be near this mild unforgiving man,
Who comes from my hands and voice,
And is the nervous laughter
I hear before my throat expells it.

For years he slept days, worked nights,
Rode a bicycle when only boys did.
I remember his nightlong walks on the beach,
His angry quiet, which to me seemed saintly,
When it may only have been shy.

I think of him hugging some gift
Along the Brooklyn streets
When he was a boy, in the rooms
Over his Father's laundry.
He preserved it in his mind's space,
A timeless falling world where he still lives.

The gift was for me:
An amazed distance only acrobats could leap.

II

Father, there are things I never asked you,
Now the answers seem trivial.
Yet, for all your cold serenity,
Your obsessed muscular body,
What did you save by living less?
Except maybe on those long night walks,
Hearing the whisper of your beloved ocean
Which never cried for an answer,
Or beat at you with insatiate fists.

III

I think of that hard man jogging on a beach,
With his swallowed angers,
The pain on his face when I murdered grammar.
He wrestled all his life with fears
That would not become angels;
Inside his crabbed masculinity, kept
A motherly sweetness he could let out
Only when he was alone, with the packed sand
Under his feet, the curling waves beside him.
With an artistry I still marvel at,
He remade himself in that lonely space,
As he has remade himself in me.

Aunt Lil

I

They brought her to the hospital
On one of those April days
That remind us we will never live enough.
That the greeny smell of leaves, budding breeze,
Polished light glancing from windows,
Will always be too much for us.

Now she kicks the covers back, not caring
Who sees her enormous thighs,
Her birthmark crowned with inch-long silken hairs
Only lovers had seen. Ashamed when
Her mouth won't fit around some thought,
She cries out in her girlish voice,

I don't know, I don't know.
Her glancing looks seem to make out
Someone in the room who will pry
Her from her failing flesh.

II

In my fright I walked all day, remembering
The beach I played on as a child:
Scalloped sand, cold rasping waves;
My parents searching frantically to see
If I had drowned or if, like the fish
In the tale, I could breathe their furious
Guilt, and make a life of it.
With a small boy's genius, I imitated childhood,
Taking you, my large-eyed beautiful aunt,
To love passionately and simply.

Once, cruel and soaring,
You battered those you loved,
As if ecstasy and cruelty were the same.
Yet at times you were happier than anyone;
So drunk on yourself, you could hardly
Walk down stairs for the faltering heavens in your heels.

III

I remember sitting with you in the subway,
Feverish, you were taking me home,
When your voice, your enormous flesh,
Seemed to fill the subway car.
Your newspaper had a picture of smoke
Flowing upward like the hood of a snake.
Amid the screeching of subway metal,
Headlines drooping on front pages,
It was you, the singed air,
The lives melted in their footsockets,
The cloud like a boiling teat
Offering itself to heaven.

You were sick of too much:
Hope fucking laughter.
Too much power jammed into your jelly of a body.
Too much sadness too,
When you dived into your gloom,
With your gentle helpless smile.

IV

Let this be a love poem, Lil,
To your obsessed life,
To the husbands who couldn't love you
When you became gluttonous, and gobbled hearts.

Yet to me you were beautiful as time,
The brown moon of flesh.
The boy who lived as in a cold sleep,
Came strangely forth into your larger louder life.

Life Story

I

I speak, and I don't want to lie.
How my past gives off a lean light;
Everywhere strangers inviting me, frightening me,
As if they were mysteries from God,
And I the only human being on earth.

I speak of sunlight on the roof-edge,
Listening to Mozart, a Vedic chant:
Sticks crackling in a fire;
While my wife shines in her mysterious rage.

I learned that growing up took time.
That my face, like an old snap-shot,
Needed time for living to rub off on it;
For my nose and lips, the retreat of my eyes,
To become a language I whispered to anyone at all.

II

If there is an Eden, I'm sure it isn't past,
But coming: a beach in autumn;
A man trekking silently over the sand,
While the sunlight rains down.
The stages of life pass by; the beach
Is a seed swelling its pale sprout
Until it bursts in a shower of pain and light:
The fright of death, of growing old.

III

For weeks I've been thinking of a boy
With splayed ears, an empty look on his face.
When I wake up anxiously at night,
A wall touches my eyelids,
And I know he's on the other side,
Near a basement furnace,
A coal-pile sparkling in the fire-glimmer.

Each night I see him push the cellar door
And feel his way downstairs,
The sweet summer air mingling
With musty coal, dark with dark.

His father and mother wheel among the galaxies.
He is the night's child. Not the dark's,
The child of space, of the low rumble
Shaking the air, like the god in the story
Slumbering fitfully under everything.

IV

As we separate and become bitter,
I see again that basement where I stood
In a child's trance; wondering if
It is my own death in a swarming space;
If this longing is simply my quarrel

With life's partial joys:
The creak of an old floor;
A battered velvet couch, with your shape
Still hollowed in it;
A punch-drunk swaying
In the middle of the room,
Where our voices swerve and fall
Against a far wall.

Talking to you now,
Hearing you wake to a life you do not love;
Reading my life in your changed body,
While our daughter peers over the side of her crib,
Frighteningly curious,
As if it all fit from beginning to end:
That's how the story begins.

Contributors' Notes

Ai's books include *Cruelty; Killing Floor; Sin,* which won an American Book Award from the Before Columbus Foundation; *Fate; Greed;* and most recently, *Vice* (W. W. Norton). She is a native of the American Southwest and currently lives in Tempe, Arizona.

Julia Alvarez was born in the Dominican Republic and immigrated to the United States in 1960. Her books of poetry include *The Other Side/El Otro Lado* and *Homecoming: New and Collected Poems.* She is also the author of the novels *How the Garcia Girls Lost Their Accents* and *In the Time of the Butterflies.*

A. R. Ammons' book *Glare* was chosen by the London *Daily Telegraph* as the best book of 1997. His other books include *Brink Road; Sphere: The Form of a Motion;* and *Tape for the Turn of the Year.* He is Goldwin Smith Professor of Poetry at Cornell University.

Ralph Angel's books are *Anxious Latitudes* (Wesleyan) and *Neither World* (Miami University Press), which received the James Laughlin Award from the Academy of American Poets. He teaches at the University of Redlands.

L. S. Asekoff, coordinator of the MFA poetry program and faculty associate of the Wolfe Institute for the Humanities, was the Donald I. Fine Professor of Creative Writing at Brooklyn College for 1998–99. His two books of poetry are *Dreams of a Work* (1994) and *North Star* (1997), both published by Orchises Press.

John Ashbery has written nineteen books of poetry including his latest, *Girls on the Run* (Farrar, Straus & Giroux, 1999). His awards include the Pulitzer Prize, the National Book Critics Circle Award, and the National Book Award. He is Charles P. Stevenson, Jr., Professor of Language and Literature at Bard College.

Robin Becker is the author of four collections of poems including *All-American Girl* (Pittsburgh, 1996), which won the 1996 Lambda Literary Award in Lesbian Poetry. She is an associate professor of English at Pennsylvania State University and serves as poetry editor for *The Women's Review of Books.*

Marvin Bell is Flannery O'Connor Professor of Letters at the University of Iowa Writers' Workshop. His books include *A Marvin Bell Reader* (University Press of New England) and *Nightworks: Poems 1962–2000* (Copper Canyon).

Charles Bernstein's newest collections are *My Way: Speeches and Poems* (University of Chicago) and *Republics of Reality: 1975–1995* (Sun & Moon). He is editor of *Close Listening: Poetry and the Performed Word* (Oxford) and David Gray Professor of Poetry and Letters at SUNY–Buffalo, where he teaches in the Poetics Program.

Ted Berrigan (1934–1983) is the author of many collections of poetry and book-length works of both prose and poetry, and was a frequent collaborator with poets and artists. His poetry books include *The Sonnets* (reprinted by Penguin-Putnam, 2000); *Selected Poems* (Penguin, 1994); and *A Certain Slant of Sunlight* (O Books, 1988).

John Berryman (1914–1972) is the author of many collections of poetry, including the epic, *Dream Songs,* which earned him the Pulitzer Prize in 1965, a Bollingen Award, and the National Book Award. His book of criticism, *Berryman's Shakespeare,* edited by John Haffenden, was published by Farrar, Straus & Giroux in 1999.

Robert Bly is the author of the bestseller *Iron John,* which helped launch the men's movement. *The Light Around the Body* won the National Book Award for poetry in 1968. His latest collection of poetry is *Eating the Honey of Words: New and Selected Poems* (HarperCollins, 1999). He lives in Minneapolis, Minnesota.

Eavan Boland was born in Dublin. She is professor of English and director of the creative writing program at Stanford University. Her most recent book is *The Lost Land* (W. W. Norton, 1998). Other books include *Outside History: Selected Poems 1980–1990* and a book of prose, *Object Lessons: The Life of the Woman and the Poet in Our Time.*

Philip Booth has published ten books of poetry including, most recently, *Selves* and *Pairs* (both Viking Penguin). In 1996, *Trying to Say It* was published in the University of Michigan Press's Poets on Poetry Series. For twenty-five years he taught at Syracuse University. He now lives in Maine.

Henry Braun was born in Olean, New York. His book of poems, *The Vergil Woods,* was published by Atheneum. For over twenty years he taught in the English department at Temple University. He now lives in Weld, Maine.

Olga Broumas was born and raised in Greece and came to the United States in 1967. She has published seven collections of poetry and four books of translations. Her collected translations of Odysseas Elytis, *Eros, Eros, Eros: Selected and Last Poems* and her latest collection, *Rave: Poems 1975–1998,* were both recently published by Copper Canyon Press.

Stephanie Brown has published over twenty-five poems in *The American Poetry Review.* Three of these were selected for the 1993, 1995, and 1997 *Best American Poetry* anthology (Scribner's). Her book, *Allegory of the Supermarket,* was published in 1999 by the University of Georgia Press as part of its Contemporary Poetry Series.

Christopher Buckley's collection of creative nonfiction, *Cruising State: Growing Up in Southern California,* was published by the University of Nevada Press in 1994. His eighth book of poetry, *Camino Cielo,* appeared from Orchises Press in 1997.

Charles Bukowski (1920–1994) was born in Germany and brought to the United States at the age of three. He was raised in Los Angeles and lived there for fifty years. He began writing poetry at the age of thirty-five. During his lifetime he published more than forty-five books of poetry and prose.

Michael Burkard is the author of seven books of poetry including his latest, *Entire Dilemma* (Sarabande Books, 1998). His awards include the Poetry Society of America's Alice Fay di Castagnola Award, and two grants from the National Endowment for the Arts. He teaches at Syracuse University.

Hayden Carruth lived in northern Vermont for many years. He now lives in upstate New York. He has published forty-one books, chiefly of poetry but including also a novel, four books of criticism, and two anthologies. His awards include the Ruth Lilly Prize and the National Book Award for poetry.

Anne Carson's books include *Plainwater: Essays and Poetry; Glass, Irony, and God; Eros the Bittersweet: An Essay; Economy of the Unlost;* and, recently, *Autobiography of Red: A Novel in Verse.* She teaches classics at McGill University in Montreal, Canada, and at the University of California, Berkeley.

Richard Cecil is the author of three collections of poetry: *Einstein's Brain* (University of Utah Press), *Alcatraz* (Purdue University Press), and *In Search of the Great Dead* (Southern Illinois University Press). He teaches in the English Department and the Honors Division of Indiana University.

Joseph Ceravolo (1934–1988), the first winner of the Frank O'Hara Award for Poetry, wrote poetry while earning his living as a hydraulics engineer. *The Green Lake Is Awake: Selected Poems by Joseph Ceravolo,* edited by Larry Fagin, Kenneth Koch, Charles North, Ron Padgett, David Shapiro, and Paul Violi, was published by Coffee House Press in 1994.

Tom Clark's numerous collections of poetry include *Stones* and *Air* from Harper & Row. Among several biographies and novels are *Charles Olson: The Allegory of a*

Poet's Life, from North Atlantic, and *The Exile of Celine,* from Random House. His reviews appear frequently in the *London Review of Books,* the *Los Angeles Times,* and the *San Francisco Chronicle.*

Lucille Clifton's books include *Next, The Book of Light,* and *The Terrible Light.* In 1999 she received a writer's award from the Lila Wallace–Reader's Digest Fund and was elected to the Board of Chancellors of the Academy of American Poets. She is Distinguished Professor of Humanities at St. Mary's College of Maryland.

Gillian Conoley's fifth collection of poetry, *Lovers in the Used World,* is forthcoming from Carnegie Mellon University Press in 2001. Her other books include *Tall Stranger,* nominated for the National Book Critics' Circle Award. Poet-in-residence at Sonoma State University, she is the founder and editor of *Volt.*

Gregory Corso's recent collection of poems, *Mindfield: New and Selected Poems* (Thunder Mouth's Press, 1998), includes sections from six previous collections, such as *The Vestal Lady on Brattle* (1955) and *Herald of the Autochthonic Spirit* (1981), as well as previously uncollected work.

Douglas Crase is the author of *The Revisionist* (Little Brown, 1981). He was a visiting lecturer in English at the University of Rochester, and lives in New York City.

Carolyn Creedon's work was published recently in Scribner's *Best of the Best American Poetry.* She lives in San Francisco.

Robert Creeley taught at Black Mountain College in the fifties, a crucial gathering place for alternative senses of writing at that time. His most recent poetry collections include *Life & Death* and *So There.* He is the Samuel P. Capen Professor of Poetry and the Humanities at SUNY–Buffalo and a former New York State Poet (1989–91).

Sylvia Curbelo was born in Matanzas, Cuba, and immigrated to the United States as a child. She is the author of two collections of poems, *The Secret History of Water* and *The Geography of Leaving,* and has received a National Endowment for the Arts Fellowship, two Florida Arts Council Individual Artist Fellowships, and two Cintas Foundation Fellowships, all for poetry.

James Dickey (1923–1997) was poet-in-residence and first Carolina Professor at the University of South Carolina. His books of poetry include *Into the Stone and Other Poems* (1960), *Buckdancer's Choice* (1965), and *The Eye-Beaters, Blood, Victory, Madness, Buckhead and Mercy* (1970), besides his novel, *Deliverance.*

Stephen Dobyns has published ten volumes of poetry, twenty novels, a book of essays on poetry and literature—*Best Words, Best Order* (St. Martins Press, 1996)—and a book of short stories, *Eating Naked* (Holt/Metropolitan, 2000). His latest book of poems is *Pallbearers Envying the One Who Rides* (Penguin, 1999).

Rita Dove served as Poet Laureate of the United States from 1993 to 1995. She received the 1987 Pulitzer Prize in Poetry. Her latest collection, *On the Bus with Rosa Parks,* was published by W. W. Norton in 1999. Dove is Commonwealth Professor of English at the University of Virginia.

Norman Dubie's twentieth collection of poems, *The Mercy Seat: Poems 1969–1999,* is forthcoming. He teaches at the University of Arizona, Tempe.

Joseph Duemer is the author of *The Light of Common Day* (Winhover, 1985), *Customs* (Georgia, 1987), and *Static* (Owl Creek, 1996). He has held fellowships from the National Endowment for the Arts and the National Endowment for the Humanities, and is currently editing a book on collaborations between musicians and writers, *Making Musics.*

Alan Dugan won the Yale Younger Poets Prize in 1961 with *Poems,* which was awarded the National Book Award and the Pulitzer Prize in 1962. Since 1969 he has been associated with the Fine Arts Work Center in Provincetown, Massachusetts. *New and Collected Poems: 1961–1983* was published by Ecco Press in 1983 and *Poems 6* in 1989.

Stephen Dunn's most recent book is *Riffs and Reciprocities: Prose Pairs* (W. W.

Norton, 1999). His other collections include *Between Angels; Loosestrife: Poems;* and *Walking Light: Essays and Memoirs.*

Gerald Early is the Merle Kling Professor of Modern Letters at Washington University in St. Louis. He is the author or editor of several books including *The Muhammad Ali Reader* and *One Nation Under a Groove: Motown and American Culture,* both published by the Ecco Press.

Richard Eberhart was born in 1904. *The Long Reach: New and Uncollected Poems, 1948–1984* was published by New Directions in 1994. Other books include *Collected Poems, 1930–1986; Selected Poems;* and *Ventriloquist: New and Selected Poems.* He is a fellow of the Academy of American Poets.

Lynn Emanuel holds an MFA from the University of Iowa and is author of three books of poetry, *Hotel Fiesta; The Dig;* and *Then, Suddenly—.* Currently, she is professor of English at the University of Pittsburgh and director of the writing program.

Edward Field's latest books are *A Frieze for a Temple of Love* and a book of poems from the Inuit, *Magic Words.* Forthcoming is a novel, *The Villagers,* written with Neil Derrick. He is currently working on his memoirs. He divides his time between New York, London, and Paris.

Carolyn Forché's latest book is *The Angel of History* (HarperCollins, 1999). In addition to her two earlier collections of poetry, *Gathering the Tribes* and *The Country Between Us,* she has published most recently the anthology she edited entitled *Against Forgetting: Twentieth-Century Poetry of Witness.*

Tess Gallagher is a poet and short story writer, living in Port Angeles, Washington. She has published essays, *Soul Barnacles: Ten More Years with Ray* (University of Michigan Press, 2000); a short story collection, *At the Owl Woman Saloon* (Simon & Schuster, 1999); and *My Black Horse: New and Selected Poems* (Bloodaxe Books, Great Britain, available in America through Dufour Editions, Inc.), among other books.

Amy Gerstler is a writer living in Los Angeles. Her recent book of poems is *Crown of Weeds.* Penguin Putnam will publish *Medicine,* a book of poetry, in 2000. She teaches at Art Center College of Design and the graduate writing program at Antioch West.

Reginald Gibbons' sixth book of poems, *Homage to Longshot O'Leary,* was published by Holy Cow! Press in 1999. He has also published a novel, *Sweetbitter* (Penguin, 1996). From 1981 to 1998 he was the editor of *TriQuarterly* magazine. A professor of English at Northwestern University, he also teaches in the MFA program at Warren Wilson College.

Jack Gilbert's *Views of Jeopardy* won the Yale Younger Poets Prize in 1962. Recently *The Great Fires* appeared from Knopf. He currently is the Hazard Conkling writer-in-residence at Smith College.

Allen Ginsberg (1926–1997) was born in Newark, New Jersey. In 1956 he published *Howl and Other Poems.* Ginsberg continued to publish more than twenty-five books of poetry, prose, and plays, remaining a social and literary figure of world renown throughout his life. With poet Anne Waldman, he founded the Jack Kerouac School of Disembodied Poetics at Zen master Chogyam Trungpa Rinpoche's Naropa Institute in Boulder, Colorado.

Louise Glück won the Pulitzer Prize for *The Wild Iris* in 1993. The author of eight books of poetry and one collection of essays, *Proofs and Theories: Essays on Poetry,* she has received the National Book Critics Circle Award for Poetry, the William Carlos Williams Award, and the PEN/Martha Albrand Award for Nonfiction. Glück teaches at Williams College.

Paul Goodman (1911–1972) is the author of *Growing Up Absurd; Utopian Essays, and Practical Proposals;* and *Mis-Education & The Community of the Scholar.* His *Collected Poems,* edited by Taylor Stoehr, was published by Random House. He taught at many schools, including New York University and Black Mountain College.

Jorie Graham has received numerous awards for her work, including the 1996 Pulitzer Prize for poetry for *The Dream of the Unified Field: Selected Poems 1974–1994*. She was recently appointed Boylston Professor at Harvard University and currently divides her time between Iowa City and Massachusetts.

Linda Gregg's life has been split between northern California and the East Coast. Her fifth book, *Things and Flesh*, was published in 1999 by Graywolf Press. She has been awarded a Guggenheim Fellowship, a Whiting Award, and a National Endowment for the Arts grant, among other honors.

Barbara Guest spent her childhood in Florida and California, graduated from the University of California at Berkeley, and settled in New York City. Among her numerous books of poetry are *Moscow Mansions; Fair Realism; Defensive Rapture;* and her latest, *The Confetti Trees*. In 1999 Guest received the Robert Frost Medal for poetry from the Poetry Society of America.

Donald Hall has published twelve books of poetry, of which the most recent is *Without* (1998). He works as a freelance writer, publishing children's books, magazine pieces later collected into books, short stories, and poems.

Sam Hamill's poetry is collected in *Destination Zero: Poems 1970–1995* and *Gratitude*. Among his translations are *The Essential Basho, The Spring of My Life and Selected Poems* by Kobayashi Issa, *The Essential Chuang Tzu*, Lu Chi's *Art of Writing*, and *Crossing the Yellow River: Three Hundred Poems from the Chinese*. He is editor at Copper Canyon Press.

Joy Harjo, an enrolled member of the Muscogee Nation, has published many books including *She Had Some Horses, In Mad Love and War,* and *The Woman Who Fell from the Sky*. She plays saxophone and performs her poetry with her band Joy Harjo & Poetic Justice.

Jim Harrison is the author of twenty books including collections of poetry, novels, novellas, nonfiction, and screenplays. *The Shape of the Journey: New & Collected Poems* was recently published by Copper Canyon Press. His awards include a National Endowment for the Arts grant and a Guggenheim Fellowship.

Robert Hass is the author of *Field Guide; Praise; Human Wishes;* and *Sun Under Wood,* as well as a book of essays, *Twentieth Century Pleasures*. He served as Poet Laureate of the United States from 1995 to 1997. He is professor of English at the University of California at Berkeley.

Seamus Heaney was born in 1939 near Belfast, Northern Ireland. In 1995 he received the Nobel Prize in Literature. His *Beowulf: A New Verse Translation* was recently published by Farrar, Straus & Giroux. Among his books of poetry is *Opened Ground: Selected Poems 1966–1996*. A resident of Dublin since 1976, he teaches regularly at Harvard University.

Juan Felipe Herrera's recent books include *Mayan Drifter: Chicano Poet in the Lowlands of the Americas; Border-Crosser with a Lamborghini Dream; Loteria Cards & Fortune Poems: The Book of Lives;* and *Crashboomlove*. He lives in Fresno, California.

Brenda Hillman teaches writing at St. Mary's College in Moraga, California. She is the author of five collections of poetry: *Loose Sugar* (1997), *Death Tractates* (1992), *Bright Existence* (1992), *Fortress* (1989), and *White Dress* (1985), all published by Wesleyan.

Edward Hirsch has published five books of poems, most recently *Earthly Measures* (1994) and *On Love* (1998). He has also published two books of prose: *How to Read a Poem and Fall in Love with Poetry* (1999) and *Responsive Reading* (1999). He is a 1998 MacArthur Fellow and teaches in the Creative Writing Program at the University of Houston.

Jack Hirschman had a collection of his *Arcanes/Arcani* published in a bilingual edition in Italy by Multimedia Edizioni in 1999. His more than fifty books and chapbooks also includes *The Bottom Line* (Curbstone Press, 1988).

Jane Hirshfield is the author of four books of poetry: *The Lives of the Heart; The Oc-*

tober Palace; Of Gravity and Angels; and *Alaya,* as well as a volume of essays, *Nine Gates: Entering the Mind of Poetry.* Her honors include fellowships from the Guggenheim and Rockefeller Foundations. She currently teaches in the MFA Writing Seminars at Bennington College.

Everett Hoagland was born in Philadelphia. From 1994–1998 he was the mayorally designated Poet Laureate of New Bedford, Massachusetts, where he has lived since 1973. Hoagland's most recent book of poems is *This City and Other Poems,* published by Spinner Publications. His *Selected Poems: 1969–1999* is forthcoming from Pennywhistle Press.

Linda Hogan is a member of the Chickasaw tribe. Her latest book is a novel, *Power* (W. W. Norton, 1998). Her other books include *The Book of Medicines: Poems; Columbus and Beyond: Views from Native Americans;* and *Mean Spirits.*

John Hollander has published eighteen books of poetry in the United States and abroad, the most recent being *Figurehead and Other Poems* (Knopf, 1999). He is the recipient of the Bollingen Prize, the Levinson Prize, and a MacArthur Fellowship. He is Sterling Professor of English at Yale University.

Richard Howard was the recipient of a Pulitzer Prize in 1970 for his collection *Untitled Subjects.* His latest collection of poetry is *Trappings* (Turtle Point Press, 1999). His translation of Charles Baudelaire's *Les Fleurs du Mal* won an American Book Award in 1984.

Susan Howe lives in Guilford, Connecticut, when she isn't teaching at the State University of New York at Buffalo. Her recent books are *Pierce-Arrow* (New Directions, 1999) and *Frame Structures: Early Poems 1974–1979* (New Directions, 1996).

Richard Hugo (1923–1982) was born and died in Seattle, Washington. His books include *The Lady in Kicking Horse Reservoir* (1973), *Making Certain It Goes On: The Collected Poems of Richard Hugo,* and *The Triggering Town: Lectures and Essays on Poetry and Writing* (W. W. Norton, 1992).

David Ignatow (1914–1997) spent most of his life in New York City. His books include *At My Ease: Uncollected Poems of the Fifties and Sixties* (BOA Editions), *I Have a Name* (1996), *Against the Evidence: Selected Poems, 1934–1994,* and *Whisper the Earth* (1981). From 1980 to 1984 he was president of the Poetry Society of America.

Robinson Jeffers (1887–1962) lived near Carmel, California, from 1914 until his death. His poetry books include *Roan Stallion* and *The Double Axe.* He also adapted Greek tragedy for the stage, notably *Medea.*

Donald Justice was born in Miami. His most recent American collection is *New and Selected Poems* (Knopf, 1995). *Oblivion* (Story Line Press), a collection of critical writings, appeared in 1998. Among his awards are the Pulitizer and the Bollingen prizes. He lives in Iowa City, after a long teaching career there.

Claudia Keelan was born in Anaheim, California, and is a graduate of the Iowa Writers' Workshop. Her two collections of poetry are *Refinery* (Cleveland State University Poetry Center, 1994) and *The Secularist* (University of Georgia Press, 1997). She is an associate professor of English and Creative Writing at the University of Nevada–Las Vegas.

Galway Kinnell won the Pulitzer Prize in 1983. *Imperfect Thirst,* his latest collection of poems, was published by Houghton Mifflin in 1994. *The Essential Rilke,* translated by Kinnell and Hannah Liebmann, was recently published by the Ecco Press. He lives in New York City and Vermont.

Karen Kipp has an MFA from the University of Iowa's Writers' Workshops and lives and works in southern Illinois. Her poetry has appeared in *Grand Street, The Iowa Review,* and *Crazyhorse.*

Etheridge Knight (1931–1991) began writing poetry while an inmate at the Indiana State Prison and published his first collection, *Poems from Prison,* in 1968. In 1987 he won the American Book Award. His books include *Born of a Woman: New and Selected Poems* and *The Essential Etheridge Knight* (University of Pittsburgh Press, 1986).

Bill Knott teaches at Emerson College. His poetry books include *Poems 1963–1988* (University of Pittsburgh Press) and *Outremer* (University of Iowa Press). He has written a novel with James Tate, *Lucky Daryll* (Release Press, 1977).

Kenneth Koch lives in New York City and teaches at Columbia University. His most recent volume of poetry is *Straits* (Knopf, 1998). Other recent volumes include *One Train* and *On the Great Atlantic Rainway, Selected Poems 1950–1988* (both in 1994). Together they earned him the Bollingen Prize in Poetry in 1995.

Yusef Komunyakaa's *Neon Vernacular,* published by Wesleyan University Press, was awarded the 1994 Pulitzer Prize and the Kingsley Tufts Award. His other books include *Magic City; Dien Cai Dau; I Apologize for the Eyes in My Head;* and most recently, *Thieves of Paradise.* He is professor of Creative Writing at Princeton University.

William Kulik was born in Newark, New Jersey, and educated at Temple University and Columbia University. His published works include *The Selected Poems of Max Jacob* (Field, 1999). He recently retired after teaching English composition to undergraduates for thirty-nine years.

Maxine Kumin's *Selected Poems 1960–1990* was published by W. W. Norton in 1997, which also published *Connecting the Dots* in 1996. Kumin won the Pulitzer Prize in 1973, the Aiken Taylor Poetry Prize in 1995, and the Ruth Lilly Prize in 1999. She lives in New Hampshire.

Stanley Kunitz is a chancellor of the Academy of American Poets, the founding president of Poets House, and a recipient of the Pulitzer and the Bollingen prizes. His ninth collection of poetry is *Passing Through: The Later Poems, New and Selected* (W. W. Norton, 1997).

Phillip Larkin (1922–1985) is the author of *The Whitsun Weddings* (1964), *High Windows* (1974), and *Aubade* (1980). His *Collected Poems* was published in 1989 and his *Selected Letters 1940–1985* in 1992.

Ann Lauterbach is the author of five collections of poetry including *And For Example; Clamor;* and *On A Stair,* all published by Penguin. A 1993 MacArthur fellow, she is David and Ruth Schwab Professor at Bard College where she codirects the writing division of the MFA Program.

Dorianne Laux is the author of two collections of poetry from BOA Editions, *Awake* (1990) and *What We Carry* (1994). She is coauthor, with Kim Addonizio, of *The Poet's Companion: A Guide to the Pleasures of Writing Poetry* (W. W. Norton, 1997), and is associate professor and director of the University of Oregon's program in creative writing.

Katherine Lederer has published poems in *Verse: The Younger American Poets Issue,* the Web magazine *Jacket,* and elsewhere. She lives in Brooklyn, New York.

Li-Young Lee was born in Jakarta, Indonesia, and now lives in Chicago. His most recent book is *The Winged Seed: A Remembrance* (Hungry Mind Press, 1999). He has received grants from the Guggenheim Foundation, the National Endowment for the Arts, and the Whiting Foundation.

Denise Levertov (1923–1997) published more than thirty volumes of poetry including *The Jacob's Ladder; Relearning the Alphabet; Breathing the Water;* and *A Door in the Hive. This Great Unknowing: Last Poems* was published by New Directions in 1999.

Philip Levine's recent books include *The Return* (1999), *The Simple Truth* (1994), and *What Work Is* (1991), all from Knopf, and *Unselected Poems* (Greenhouse Review Press, 1997). He teaches at New York University and divides his time between New York and Fresno, California.

Larry Levis (1946–1996) published five collections of poetry during his lifetime, including *The Widening Spell of the Leaves.* A posthumous collection, *Elegy,* was published by the University of Pittsburgh Press in 1997. He was professor of English at Virginia Commonwealth University in Richmond, Virginia.

Lisa Lewis holds an MFA from the University of Iowa and a doctorate from the University of Houston. Her second book, *The Silent Treatment,* was published in 1998 by Penguin Books as part of the National Poetry Series. Her first collection of poetry, *The Unbeliever,* won the 1994 Brittingham Prize.

Laurence Lieberman is a professor of English at the University of Illinois at Urbana-Champaign. He is the author of eleven volumes of poetry including *Dark Songs: Slave House and Synagogue* (1996), *Compass of the Dying* (1998), and *Regatta in the Skies: Selected Long Poems* (University of Georgia Press, 1999).

Frank Lima lives in Flushing, New York. He received his MFA from Columbia University. He has published four books of poems, including, most recently, *Inventory/New and Selected Poems* (Hard Press, 1997) and the forthcoming *IdoBelieveIDoBelieve* (Hard Press, 2000).

John Logan (1923–1987) wrote more than thirteen volumes of poetry and received numerous awards including the William Carlos Williams Award from the Poetry Society of America in 1981 for his books *Bridge of Change: Poems 1974–1980* and *Only the Dreamer Can Change the Dream: Selected Poems.*

Robert Lowell (1917–1977) won the Pulitzer Prize in poetry in 1946 for *Lord Weary's Castle.* His other collections include *For the Union Dead; Land of Unlikeness;* and *Life Studies.* He was a chancellor of the Academy of American Poets.

Thomas Lux teaches at Sarah Lawrence College. His recent book is *New & Selected Poems 1975–1995* (Houghton Mifflin). *The Street of Clocks* will appear in 2000. He has received three National Endowment for the Arts awards and a Guggenheim fellowship.

Clarence Major, professor of English at the University of California at Davis, is the author of nine volumes of poetry and seven novels including *Configurations: New and Selected Poems 1958–1998* (Copper Canyon Press). He is also the editor of *The Garden Thrives: Twentieth Century African-American Poetry.*

S. J. Marks (1935–1991) was born in Chicago. For the latter part of his life he lived in Philadelphia, where he worked as a psychotherapist at the Family Institute. His book of poems is *Something Grazes Our Hair* (University of Illinois Press).

William Matthews (1942–1997) taught at the City College of New York beginning in 1983. His book, *Time and Money* (Houghton Mifflin, 1995), received the National Book Critics Circle Award in poetry. A book of translations, *The Mortal City: 100 Epigrams of Martial* appeared from Ohio Review Books in 1995. *After All,* his last book, was published posthumously in 1998.

Thomas McGrath (1916–1990) composed his narrative epic poem, *Letter to an Imaginary Friend,* over a thirty-year period, and published it in four parts from 1963 to 1985. It is now available as one volume from Copper Canyon Press.

Heather McHugh is a chancellor of the Academy of American Poets. Among her collections of poetry is *Hinge & Sign: Poems 1968–1993* (Wesleyan, 1994). She is Milliman Writer-in Residence at the University of Washington in Seattle and is a core faculty member of the MFA program at Warren Wilson College.

Jane Mead was educated at Vassar College, Syracuse University, and the University of Iowa. Philip Levine chose her book *The Lord and the General Din of the World* for publication by Sarabande Books in 1996. She is poet-in-residence at Wake Forest University in Winston-Salem, North Carolina.

Pablo Medina is the author of three collections of poetry, *Pork Rind and Cuban Songs, Arching into the Afterlife,* and *The Floating Island.* His awards include a Woodrow Wilson–Lila Wallace Fellowship and a Cintas Fellowship. He teaches in the MFA program at Warren Wilson College and at the New School, where he also serves as director of Eugene Lang College's Writing Program.

William Meredith was a Consultant in Poetry to the Library of Congress and is a Chancellor Emeritus of the Academy of American Poets. Among his books are

Love Letter from an Impossible Land (1944), which was chosen by Archibald MacLeish for the Yale Series of Younger Poets, and *Effort at Speech* (Triquarterly Books, 1997), which won the National Book Award in poetry.

W. S. Merwin is the author of fifteen books of poetry and four books of prose, and has translated extensively from Latin and various Romance languages. His awards include the Pulitzer Prize, the Bollingen Prize, and the first Dorothea Tanning Prize from the Academy of American Poets. He lives on the island of Maui, in Hawaii.

Jane Miller's newest collection of poetry is *Wherever You Lay Your Head* (Copper Canyon Press). Among her earlier collections are *Memory at These Speeds: New and Selected Poems* and *The Greater Leisures,* a National Poetry Series selection. She has also written *Working Time: Essays on Poetry, Culture, and Travel,* part of the University of Michigan's Poets on Poetry Series.

Czeslaw Milosz was born in Szetejnie, Lithuania, in 1911. Since 1961 he has been professor of Slavic languages and literature at the University of California at Berkeley. He received the Nobel Prize in literature in 1980. His books of poetry include *Collected Poems* (Ecco, 1988) and *Provinces* (1991). *Road-Side Dog,* prose poems, essays, and parables, appeared in 1998 (Farrar, Straus & Giroux).

Howard Moss (1922–1987) was the poetry editor of the *The New Yorker* for many years. Among his books is *Rules for Sleep* (Knopf). He won the National Book Award for poetry in 1972.

Stanley Moss's poetry collections include *The Intelligence of Clouds* (Harcourt), *The Wrong Angel* (Macmillan), *The Skull of Adam* (Horizon), and *Asleep in the Garden: New and Selected Poems* (Seven Stories Press). He is publisher of Sheep Meadow Press.

Carol Muske has published six books of poems, most recently, *An Octave Above Thunder: New & Selected Poems,* which was a *New York Times* Most Notable Book. A professor of English and creative writing at USC, her awards include a Guggenheim, a National Endowment for the Arts Fellowship, the Ingram-Merrill Award, and the Witter Bynner Award.

Jack Myers is the author of seven volumes of poetry. His *As Long As You're Happy* was a National Poetry Series selection for 1985. He has received awards from the National Endowment for the Arts and the Texas Institute of Letters. He teaches creative writing at Southern Methodist University and in the Vermont College MFA program.

Eileen Myles lives in New York and Provincetown, Massachusetts. Her recent book of poems from Black Sparrow Press is *School of Fish,* winner of a Lambda Literary Award.

Howard Nemerov (1920–1991) is the author of many collections of poetry including *The Winter Lightning: Selected Poems, 1968; The Image and the Law;* and *Guide to the Ruins.* He was Consultant in Poetry to the Library of Congress 1963–64.

Frank O'Hara (1926–1966) was posthumously awarded the National Book Award for his *Collected Poems* (Knopf) in 1971. Later collections include *Early Writing* and *Poems Retrieved* from Grey Fox Press. He was assistant curator at the Museum of Modern Art.

Sharon Olds teaches at New York University and helps run a writing workshop in a state hospital for the severely physically challenged. Her recent books are *A Wellspring* (1996) and *Blood, Tin, Straw* (1999), both published by Knopf. She was appointed New York State Poet in 1998.

Charles Olson (1910–1970) served as director of the Black Mountain School. His books include *In Cold Hell, in Thicket; The Maximus Poems; Call Me Ishmael: A Study of Melville; Projective Verse;* and *Selected Writings.*

George Oppen (1908–1984) is the author of eight books of poetry including *Discrete Series* (1932), *The Materials* (1962), *Of Being Numerous* (1968), and *Primitive*

(1978). He was awarded the Pulitzer Prize for his poetry in 1969. *The Collected Poems of George Oppen 1929–1975* was published by New Directions in 1975.

Gregory Orr has published six collections of poetry including, most recently, *City of Salt* (University of Pittsburgh Press). He is poetry editor of the *Virginia Quarterly Review* and professor of English at the University of Virginia, where he teaches in the MFA program.

Brenda M. Osbey lives in New Orleans. She has published four collections of poetry including *All Saints* (Louisiana State University Press, 1997). She was the recipient of the Academy of American Poets Loring-Williams Prize.

Michael Palmer was born in New York City and currently lives in San Francisco. He has published nine collections of poetry, numerous translations, and a prose work, *The Danish Notebook. The Lion Bridge (Selected Poetry 1972–1995)* was published by New Directions in 1998. The same press will publish his new collection, *The Promises of Glass,* in the spring of 2000.

Amanda Pecor's poems have appeared or are forthcoming in *Passages North, The Journal, Western Humanities Review, Mississippi Review, Paris Review,* and other magazines.

Sam Pereira was born in Los Banos, California, in 1949. His two collections of poetry are *The Marriage of the Portuguese* (L'Epervier Press, 1978) and *Brittle Water* (Penumbra Press/Abattoir Editions, The University of Nebraska at Omaha, 1987).

Sylvia Plath (1932–1963) began publishing poems and stories as a teenager. After attending Smith College, she was a Fulbright Scholar in Cambridge, England. HarperCollins recently reprinted her book *Ariel* as a Perennial Classics Edition.

Stanley Plumly is a professor of English at the University of Maryland, College Park. His collections of poetry include *The Marriage in the Trees* (Ecco Press, 1999) and *Out-of-the-Body Travel,* which won the William Carlos Williams Award in 1977.

Carl Rakosi's *Collected Poems* was published in 1986 by the National Poetry Foundation and his *Collected Prose* appeared in 1983 from the same publisher. *Poems 1923–1941* won the PEN Award in 1995. *Carl Rakosi, Man and Poet* (edited by Michael Heller), a critical overview of his work, appeared in 1993.

Joanna Rawson's collection *Quarry* won the Associated Writing Programs Award in Poetry and was published by the University of Pittsburgh Press in 1998. She lives in Minneapolis, where she is an editor of the weekly *City Pages* and teaches at the University of Minnesota.

Liam Rector's books of poems are *The Sorrow of Architecture* and *American Prodigal,* and he edited *The Day I Was Older: The Poetry of Donald Hall.* He lives in the Boston area and founded and teaches in the graduate writing seminars at Bennington College, in Vermont.

Donald Revell is the author of six collections of poetry: *These Are Three* (1998), *Beautiful Shirt* (1994), *Erasures* (1992), *New Dark Ages* (1990), *The Gaza of Winter* (1988), and *From the Abandoned Cities* (1983). In 1995 his translation of Guillaume Appolinaire's *Alcools* appeared from Wesleyan. He lives in Utah and Nevada.

Kenneth Rexroth (1905–1982) lived in San Francisco where he was active in the San Francisco Renaissance in the fifties. His books of essays include *Bird in the Bush* and *Assays. Sacramental Acts: The Love Poems of Kenneth Rexroth,* edited by San Hamill and Elaine Laura Kleiner, was recently published by Copper Canyon Press.

Adrienne Rich has published more than sixteen volumes of poetry, including her latest, *Midnight Salvage: Poems 1995–1998* (W. W. Norton), as well as four nonfiction prose books. Her awards include a National Book Award, a MacArthur Fellowship, and the Dorothea Tanning Prize.

Len Roberts's two recent books of poetry, *The Trouble Making Finch* (1998) and *Counting the Black Angels* (1994) were both published by the University of Illinois Press. He received a National Endowment for the Humanities Translation Award in 1999 to translate the poems of Sandor Csoori, the Hungarian poet.

Jane Rohrer was born in Virginia's Shenandoah Valley and has lived in Lancaster County and Philadelphia since 1901. She has published poems in *The American Poetry Review, Jeopardy,* and *Grain* (Canada).

Richard Ronan (1946–1989) wrote six collections of poetry: *Buddha's Kisses; Flowers; Kindred; A Lamp of Small Sorrow; Narratives from America;* and *A Radiance Like Wind or Water.*

Muriel Rukeyser (1913–1980) published fifteen collections of poetry. In 1975–1976 she served as president of PEN American Center. Several of her books have recently been reprinted by Paris Books: *The Life of Poetry, A Muriel Rukeyser Reader,* and *The Orgy.*

Michael Ryan has published three books of poetry and the autobiography *Secret Life. A Difficult Grace,* a collection of his essays, will be published in fall 2000. He is professor of English and creative writing at the University of California at Irvine and also teaches in the MFA writing program at Warren Wilson College.

David St. John is the author of seven collections of poetry including *Study for the World's Body: New and Selected Poems* (HarperCollins, 1994); and two volumes that appeared in 1999: *In the Pines: Lost Poems, 1972–1997* (White Pine Press) and *The Red Leaves of Night* (HarperCollins). He is professor of English and director of Creative Writing at USC.

Ira Sadoff has published six collections of poetry, most recently *Grazing* (University of Illinois, 1998), which received the George Bogin Memorial Award from the Poetry Society of America. His *Ira Sadoff Reader* (stories, poems, and essays) was published as part of Bread Loaf Writers Series by the University Press of New England. He is the Dana Professor of Poetry at Colby College.

Leslie Scalapino has published many books of poetry, fiction, plays, and essays. Among these, *The Front Matter, Dead Souls; New Time;* and *The Public World/Syntactically Impermanence* are from Wesleyan University Press. Her poetry includes *way* and *that they were at the beach* (North Point). Among her fiction titles are *Defoe* (Sun and Moon) and *The Return of Painting, The Pearl, and Orion/A Trilogy* (Talisman).

James Schuyler (1923–1991) is the author of eleven books of poetry including *Freely Espousing* (1969), *The Crystal Lithium* (1972), *The Morning of the Poem* (1980), and *Collected Poems* (1993). He published three novels including *A Nest of Ninnies* (with John Ashbery, 1969).

Armand Schwerner (1927–1999) was professor of English and world literature at the College of Staten Island, CUNY. His books include *The Tablets I–XXVI* (National Poetry Foundation, 1998) and *Seaweed.*

Frederick Seidel has written *The Cosmos Poems,* his sixth book, commissioned by the American Museum of Natural History to inaugurate and celebrate their new planetarium, which will open in 2000.

Hugh Seidman was born in Brooklyn. He has won New York State and National Endowment for the Arts grants, and the Yale Younger Poets prize. In 1995 his *Selected Poems: 1965–1995* was cited by the *Village Voice* and by *The Critics' Choice* as one of the best books of the year.

Anne Sexton (1928–1974) won the Pulitzer Prize for poetry in 1966 for her collection *Live or Die.* Her other collections include *All My Pretty Ones* (1962), *The Book of Folly* (1973), *The Awful Rowing Toward God* (1975), and *Complete Poems.*

David Shapiro's books of poetry and criticism include *January; Poems from Deal; A Man Holding an Acoustic Panel; The Page-turner; Lateness; To an Idea; House (Blown Apart); After a Lost Original;* and *Mondrian: Flowers.* For twenty years he has been art historian at William Paterson University and professor at the Cooper Union School of Architecture.

Karl Shapiro's numerous awards for poetry are the Pulitzer Prize, the Shelley Memorial Award, and the Bollingen Prize. He has taught at Johns Hopkins University, the University of Nebraska, and the University of California at Davis. From 1950–1956 he was editor of *Poetry*.

Charles Simic was born in Belgrade and immigrated to the United States in 1954. His latest poetry collections include *Walking the Black Cat; A Wedding in Hell;* and *Hotel Insomnia,* all from Harcourt Brace. He won the Pulitzer Prize in 1990 for his book of prose poems *The World Doesn't End*. His latest book of poems is *Jackstraws* (1999).

Louis Simpson was born in Jamaica, West Indies, in 1923, and immigrated to the United States at the age of seventeen. In 1964 he received the Pulitzer Prize in poetry for *At the End of the Open Road* (Wesleyan University Press). His other books of poems include *A Dream of Governors* (Wesleyan), *Collected Poems* (Paragon House, 1990), and *There You Are* (Story Line Press).

Dave Smith's books include *The Wick of Memory: New and Selected Poems 1970–2000; Floating on Solitude: Three Books of Poems;* and *Fate's Kite: Poems 1991–1995,* all published by the Louisiana State University Press. He is coeditor of *The Southern Review* and Boyd Professor of English at Louisiana State University.

W. D. Snodgrass is retired from the University of Delaware and lives in upstate New York. A book of his autobiographical sketches, *After-Images,* was recently published by BOA, and *Selected Translations* (1998) recently received the Academy of American Poets' Harold Morton Landon Award.

Gary Snyder is a poet, essayist, mountaineer, and Buddhist ecologist. He lives in the Sierra just north of the South Yuba River. He teaches part-time at the University of California, Davis. His most recent book is *The Gary Snyder Reader* (Counterpoint).

Jennifer Snyder's poems have appeared in many journals including *Black Warrior Review, Indiana Review,* and *Passages North*. She lives in Alabama.

Jack Spicer (1925–1965) lived in California. His work includes collected serial poems, *The Collected Books of Jack Spicer* (1975); selected early poems, *One Night Stand & Other Poems* (1980); and collected lectures, *The House that Jack Built* (1998). A biography was written by Lewis Ellingham and Kevin Killian. A collected letters is in progress.

William Stafford (1914–1993) received the National Book Award for *Traveling through the Dark* (1962). *The Way It Is,* a volume of his selected poems, was published recently by Graywolf Press. He taught at Lewis and Clark College in Portland, Oregon, for thirty years.

Maura Stanton is the author of four collections of poetry: *Life Among the Trolls* (Carnegie Mellon, 1998); *Snow on Snow* (Yale, 1975; reprinted Carnegie Mellon, 1993); *Cries of the Swimmers* (Utah, 1984, reprinted Carnegie Mellon, 1991); and *Tales of the Supernatural* (Godine, 1988). She teaches in the MFA program at Indiana University in Bloomington.

Gerald Stern is the author of nine collections of poetry including *Lucky Life; Rejoicings; The Red Coal;* and *Odd Mercy*. *This Time: New & Selected Poems* won the 1998 National Book Award for poetry. He has received the Ruth Lilly Poetry Prize.

Susan Stewart's recent book of poems is *The Forest* (University of Chicago Press). She teaches poetry at the University of Pennsylvania and is currently working with Wesley Smith on a translation of Euripides' *Andromache* for Oxford University Press.

Ruth Stone's eleventh book, *Ordinary Words,* was recently published by Paris Press. Her awards include two Guggenheim fellowships, the Shelley Memorial Award, and the Whiting Award. She is currently professor of English at SUNY Binghamton.

Chris Stroffolino is the author of several chapbooks and two books, most recently *Stealer's Wheel* (Hard Press, 1999). He is looking for a publisher for his Ph.D. dissertation on Shakespeare, *Making Fun of Tragedy*. He lives in Brooklyn, New York.

Lucien Stryk lives in DeKalb, Illinois. His latest book is *And Still Birds Sing: New and Collected Poems*. Other recent books include *Zen Poetry: Let the Spring Breeze Enter; The Awakened Self: Encounters with Zen;* and *Where We Are: Selected Poems and Zen Translations.*

May Swenson (1913–1989) published eleven books of poetry. She was a member of the American Academy and Institute of Arts and Letters and a chancellor of the Academy of American Poets.

James Tate received the Pulitzer Prize and the William Carlos Williams Award for *Selected Poems* in 1991. *Worshipful Company of Fletchers* (1994) was awarded the National Book Award. In 1995, the Academy of American Poets presented him with the Tanning Prize. His latest book is *Shroud of the Gnome* (Ecco Press, 1997).

Jean Valentine is the author of eight books of poetry including the forthcoming *The Cradle of the Real Life* (Wesleyan University Press). She lives and works in New York City.

Derek Walcott was born in Saint Lucia, West Indies. He received the Nobel Prize for Literature in 1992. His books include *In a Green Night; The Star-Apple Kingdom;* and *Omeros.*

Anne Waldman is the author of over thirty books and pamphlets of poetry including the forthcoming *Marriage: A Sentence* (Penguin Poets). A former founder and director of the Poetry Project at St. Mark's Church in New York City, she also cofounded the Jack Kerouac School of Disembodied Poetics with Allen Ginsberg at Naropa University in Boulder, Colorado, where she is currently a Distinguished Professor of Poetics.

Robert Penn Warren (1905–1989) won the Pulitzer Prize for fiction for his novel *All the King's Men. Promises: Poems 1954–1965* won the National Book Award and the Pulitzer Prize. Other collections include *Now and Then: Poems 1976–1978.*

Lewis Warsh is the author of two novels, a volume of stories, and many books of poems including *Avenue of Escape* (1995) and *Private Agenda* (1996). He is visiting professor at SUNY Albany for the year 1999–2000 and editor and publisher of *United Artists Books.*

Bruce Weigl's recent books include *Archeology of the Circle: New and Selected Poems* (Grove/Atlantic Press, 1999); *After the Others* (TriQuarterly Books/Northwestern University Press, 1999); and *The Circle of Hanh: A Memoir* (forthcoming from Grove/Atlantic Press).

Theodore Weiss is the author of twelve books of poetry and two of criticism. He recently received the Williams/Derwood Award for poetry.

Renee and Theodore Weiss have edited the *Quarterly Review of Literature* for over fifty years. They recently won a PEN Club Lifetime Achievement Award for editing, and have completed a collaborative volume of poems and letters.

Joe Wenderoth grew up near Baltimore. His first book of poems, *Disfortune*, was published by Wesleyan University Press in 1995. His next book, *It Is If I Speak,* is forthcoming from Wesleyan in the spring of 2000. He lives in Mt. Horeb, Wisconsin, and Marshall, Minnesota, where he is assistant professor of English at Southwest State University.

Reed Whittemore is professor emeritus at the University of Maryland. His poetry books include *The Past, the Future, and Present: Poems Selected and New* (University of Arkansas Press, 1990).

Richard Wilbur served as the second official Poet Laureate of the United States in 1987–88. In 1989 he received a second Pulitzer Prize for *New and Collected*

Poems. A new book of poems, *A Wall in the Woods,* is forthcoming, and he is at work on a translation of Moliere's first full-length verse comedy, *L'Edtourdi.*

C. K. Williams teaches at Princeton University one semester a year, and lives the rest of the time in Paris. His recent books include *Flesh and Blood* (1987), *Poems 1963–1983* (1988), *A Dream of Mind* (1992), *The Vigil* (1996), and *Repair* (1999), all from Farrar, Straus & Giroux. In 2000 *Love Poems and Poems about Love* will be published, as will a prose memoir, *Mourning.*

Charles Wright lives and teaches in Charlottesville, Virginia. His recent books are *Chickamauga,* winner of the Lenore Marshall poetry prize; *Black Zodiac,* winner of the *Los Angeles Times* Book Prize, the National Book Critics Circle Award in poetry, and the Pulitzer Prize. *Appalachia* will be published in 2000 by Farrar, Straus & Giroux, with a seven-poem coda, under the title *Negative Blue.*

James Wright (1927–1980) was born in Ohio, and taught at the University of Minnesota, Macalester, and elsewhere. His books include *This Branch Will Not Break* and *Collected Poems,* which won the Pulitzer Prize in 1972. He was a fellow of the Academy of American Poets.

John Yau's latest book is *My Symptoms* (Black Sparrow, 1998). He contributed essays to the catalogue *In Company: Robert Creeley's Collaborations* (Castellani Museum of Niagara University and the Weatherspoon Art Gallery, 1999), which accompanied an exhibition on national tour in 1999. He lives in New York City.

Paul Zweig (1935–1984) published poetry, criticism, and autobiography, including *Walt Whitman: The Making of the Poet* (Basic Books), *Eternity's Woods* (poetry, Wesleyan University Press), and *Three Journeys* (autobiography).

Credits

permission of Alfred A. Knopf, a Division of Random House Inc. "Prospero Listens to the Night" by Jack Gilbert. Reprinted by permission of the author. "To See if Something Comes Next," "The White Heart of God" from *The Great Fires* by Jack Gilbert. Copyright © 1994 by Jack Gilbert. Reprinted by permission of Alfred A. Knopf, a Division of Random House Inc.

Allen Ginsberg: "The Charnel Ground," "Who Eats Who?," "Not Dead Yet," "Yiddishe Kopf," "A Thief Stole This Poem" from *Cosmopolitan Greetings: Poems 1986–1992* by Allen Ginsberg. Copyright © 1994 by Allen Ginsberg. Reprinted by permission of HarperCollins Publishers, Inc. "No Way Back" by Allen Ginsberg. Reprinted by permission of the Allen Ginsberg Trust. "The Grim Skeleton" from *Collected Poems: 1947–1980* by Allen Ginsberg. Copyright © 1984 by Allen Ginsberg. Reprinted by permission of HarperCollins Publishers, Inc. "Homeless Compleynt" from *Death & Fame: Poems 1993–1997* by Allen Ginsberg. Copyright © 1999 by the Allen Ginsberg Trust. Reprinted by permission of HarperCollins Publishers, Inc.

Louise Glück: "Aubade," "The New Life," "Unwritten Law," "Roman Study," "Condo," "The Winged Horse," "Mutable Earth," "Eurydice" from *Vita Nova* by Louise Glück. Copyright © 1999 by Louise Glück. Reprinted by permission of HarperCollins Publishers, Inc.

Paul Goodman: "In the Jury Room, in Pain," "Birthday Cake," "Sentences After *Defence of Poetry*," "(Connary, Blodgett, Day Hapgood)," "Ballade of the Moment After," "(Woman eternal my muse, lean toward me)," "From *Sentences for Matthew Ready, Series II*," "A Gravestone, August 8, 1968," "(It was good when you were here,)" by Paul Goodman from *Collected Poems*. Copyright © 1972, 1973 by The Estate of Paul Goodman. Reprinted by permission of Sally Goodman for The Estate of Paul Goodman.

Jorie Graham: "Breakdancing" from *The End of Beauty* by Jorie Graham. Copyright © 1987 by Jorie Graham. Reprinted by permission of HarperCollins Publishers, Inc. "Underneath (1)," "Underneath (2)," "Underneath (3)," "For One Must Want/To Shut the Other's Gaze," "Underneath (7)" from *Swarm* by Jorie Graham. Copyright © 2000 by Jorie Graham. Reprinted by permission of HarperColllins Publishers, Inc.

Linda Gregg: "The Clapping," "The Edge of Something," "What Is Kept," "Fishing in the Keep of Silence," "Official Love Story" copyright © 1994 by Linda Gregg. Reprinted from *Chosen by the Lion* with the permission of Graywolf Press, Saint Paul, Minnesota. "Past Perfect" by Linda Gregg. Reprinted by permission of the author.

Barbara Guest: "The Advance of the Grizzly," by Barbara Guest from *Defensive Rapture* (Sun & Moon Press). Copyright © 1993 by Barbara Guest. "Motion Pictures 4" and "Motion Pictures 15" by Barbara Guest appeared in slightly different form in *Confetti Trees* (Sun & Moon Press). Copyright © 1999 by Barbara Guest. "Red Dye" and "You Can Discover" by Barbara Guest. Reprinted by permission of the author.

Donald Hall: "To a Waterfowl," "Eating the Pig" from *Old and New Poems* by Donald Hall. Copyright © 1990 by Donald Hall. Reprinted by permission of Houghton Mifflin Co. All rights reserved.

Sam Hamill: "What the Water Knows," "Another Duffer," "Abstract" from *Destination Zero: Poems 1970–1995* by Sam Hamill. Copyright © 1996 by Sam Hamill. Reprinted by permission of the author and White Pine Press.

Joy Harjo: "The Woman Who Fell from the Sky," "A Postcolonial Tale" from *The Woman Who Fell from the Sky* by Joy Harjo. Copyright © 1994 by Joy Harjo. Reprinted by permission of W. W. Norton & Company, Inc.

Jim Harrison: "Letters to Yesenin" from *The Shape of the Journey: New and Collected Poems* © 1998 by Jim Harrison. Reprinted by permission of the author and Copper Canyon Press, Post Office Box 271, Port Townsend, WA 98368.

Index